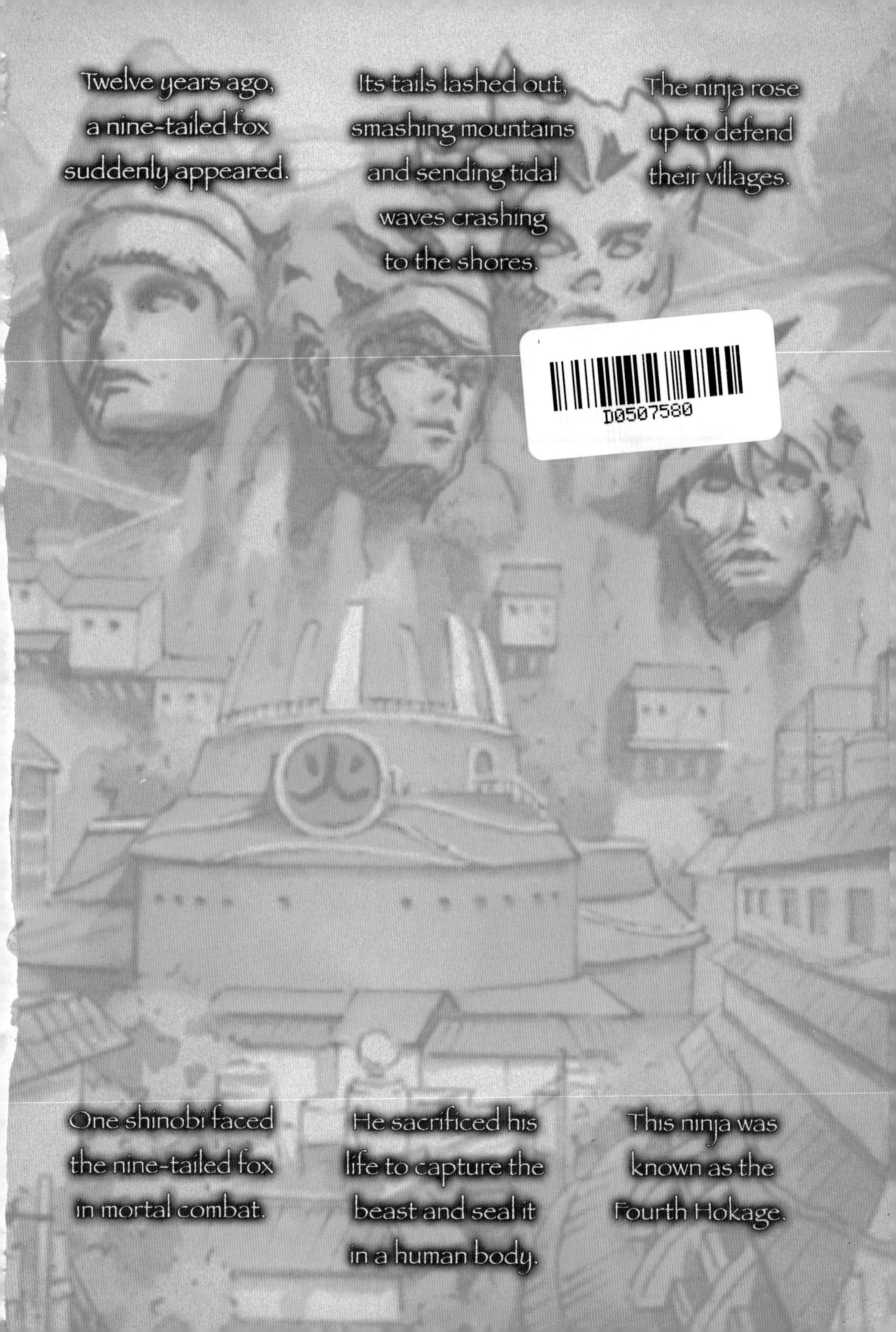
Twelve years ago, a nine-tailed fox suddenly appeared.
Its tails lashed out, smashing mountains and sending tidal waves crashing to the shores.
The ninja rose up to defend their villages.
One shinobi faced the nine-tailed fox in mortal combat.
He sacrificed his life to capture the beast and seal it in a human body.
This ninja was known as the Fourth Hokage.

RUTO ANIME PROFILES

Special supplement! When you spread it out, Naruto's world arrives like a cyclone!!

Anime Profiles

The scenes you remember… plus ones you only dreamed of, recreated through dazzling illustrations created just for this book!!

The Ninja Way: Tales of Bravery

Tales of valor as Naruto and the others develop into true shinobi!! Faithful accounts of the thrilling stories!

Ninja Profiles

Countless shinobi appear in this book…but 28 major characters are featured with a profile! Which ninja stand out from the rest?

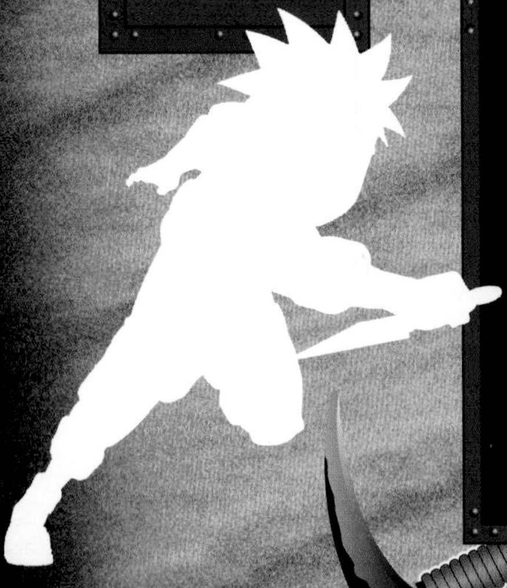

Contents

Secret Shinobi Picture Album

Iruka, Kakashi and others carefully explain, through valuable design illustrations, subjects such as the Ninja Academy, Naruto's house, and shinobi weapons!!

Anbu Special Report

The special anbu (black ops) squad, which reports directly to the Hokage, has performed a top-secret investigation on Naruto, Sasuke and Sakura. What does their report reveal?

Refresh your knowledge and learn something new!

Voice Actor Interviews

Go behind the scenes of the anime production with the voice actors and the creator of Naruto!

Chock full of detailed information!

Must-see bonus pages and puzzles that are sure to satisfy!

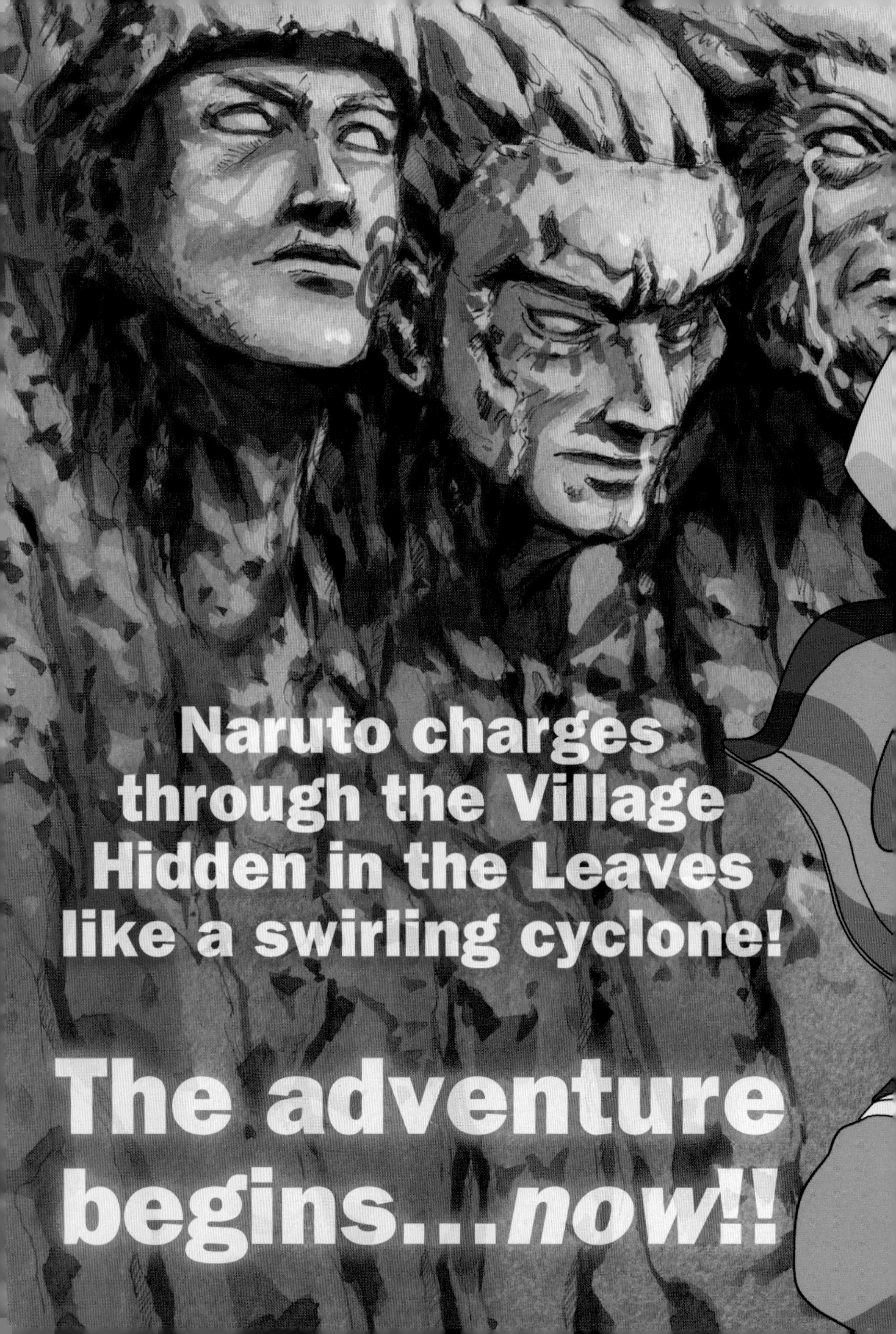
Naruto charges through the Village Hidden in the Leaves like a swirling cyclone!
The adventure begins...now!!

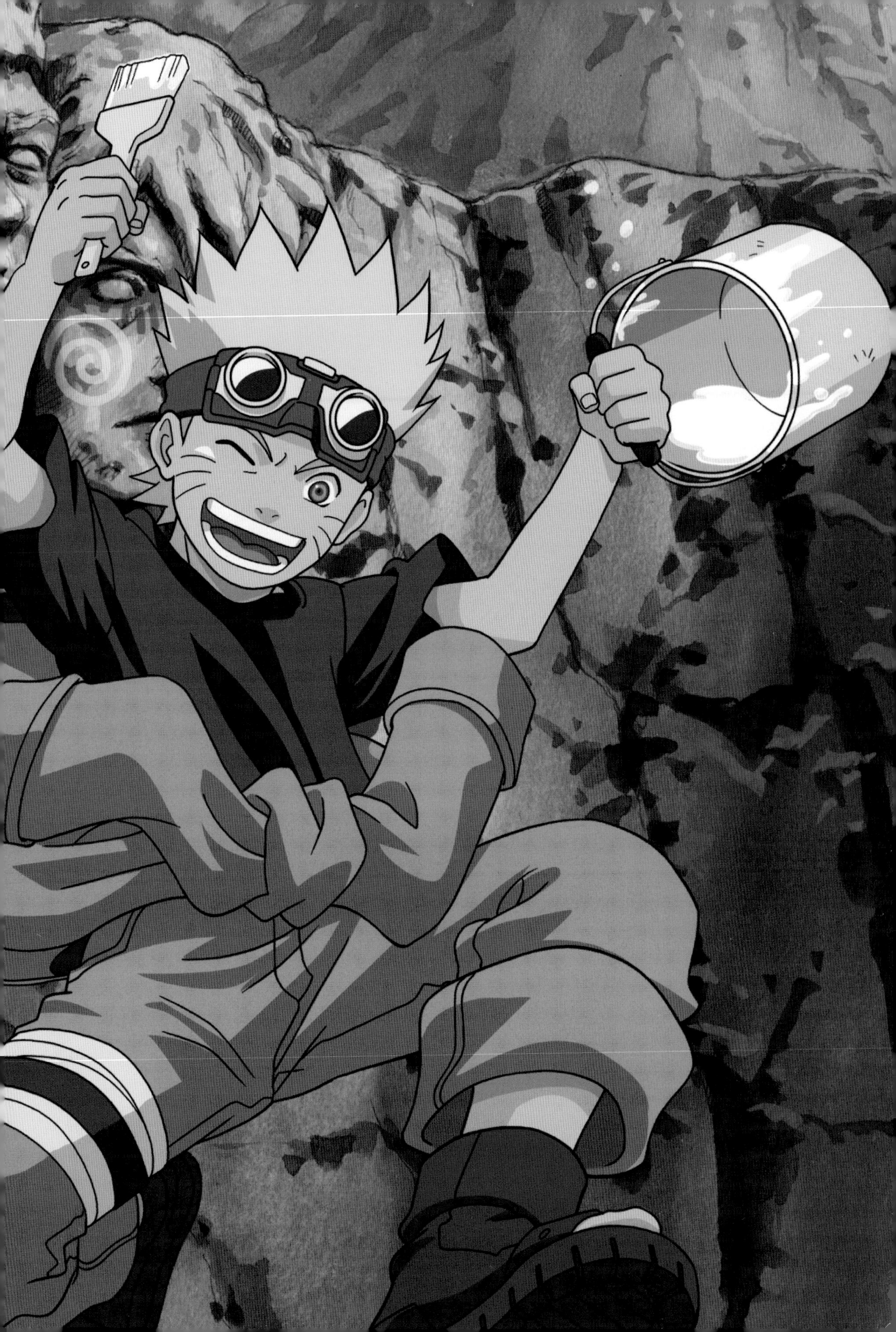

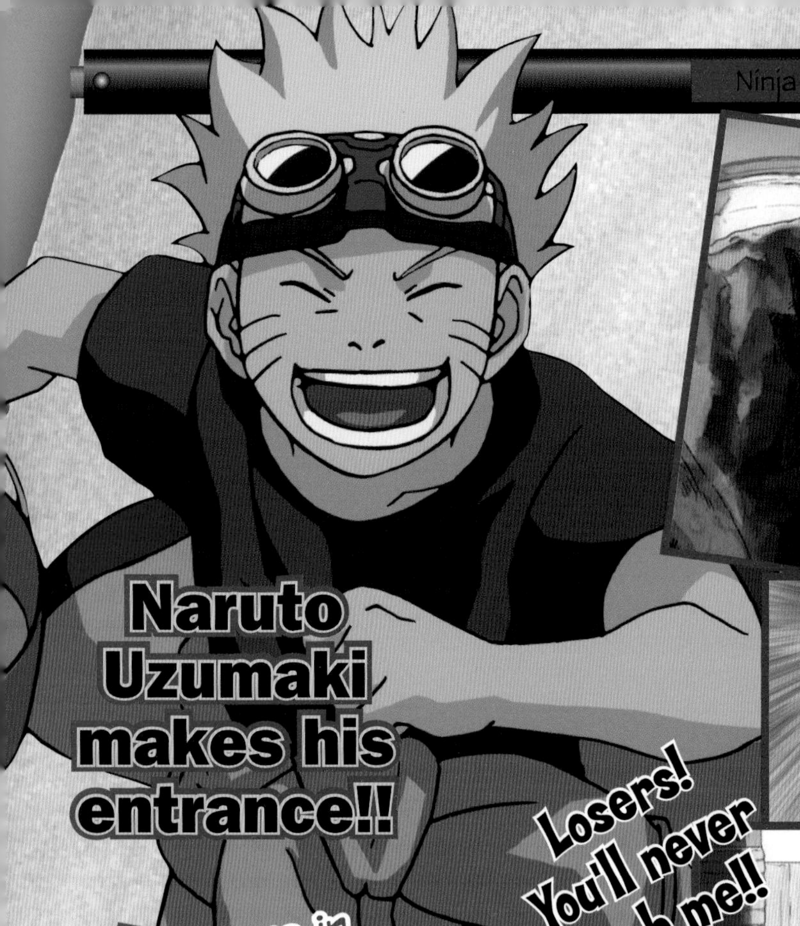

Naruto Uzumaki makes his entrance!!

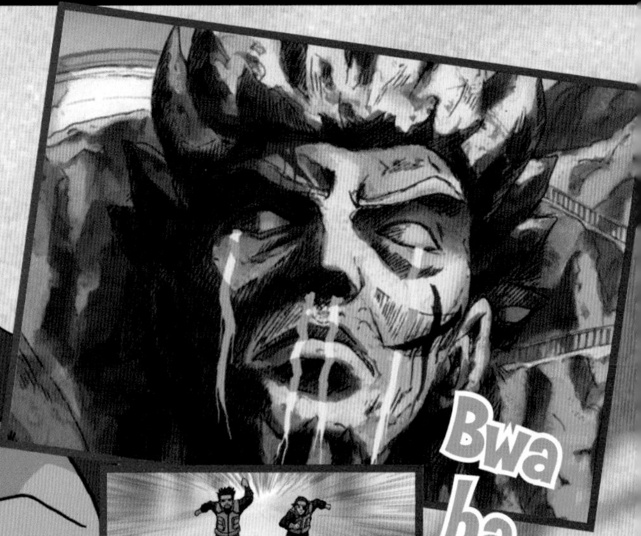
Bwa ha ha ha ha ha!

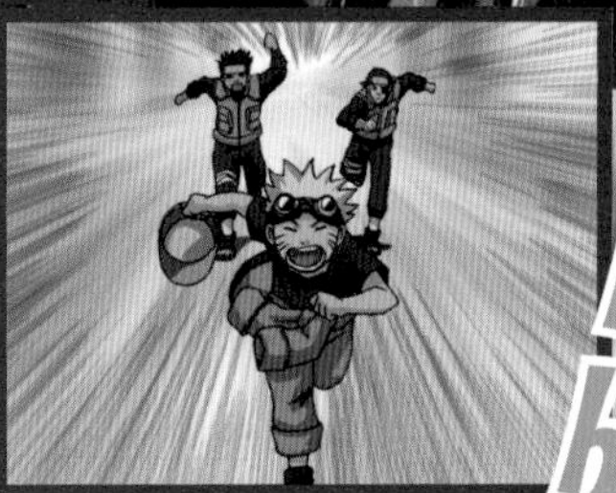
Losers! You'll never catch me!!

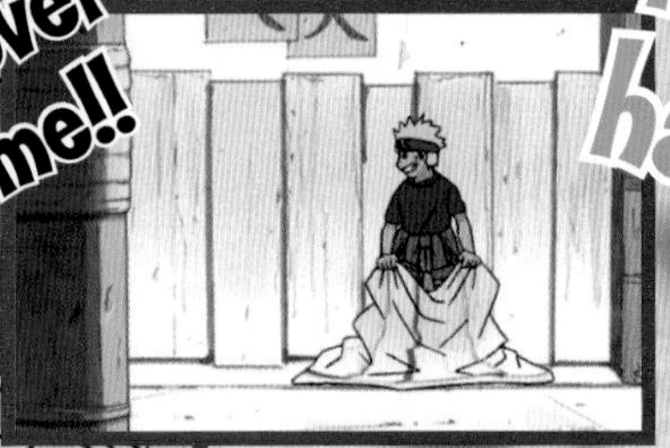

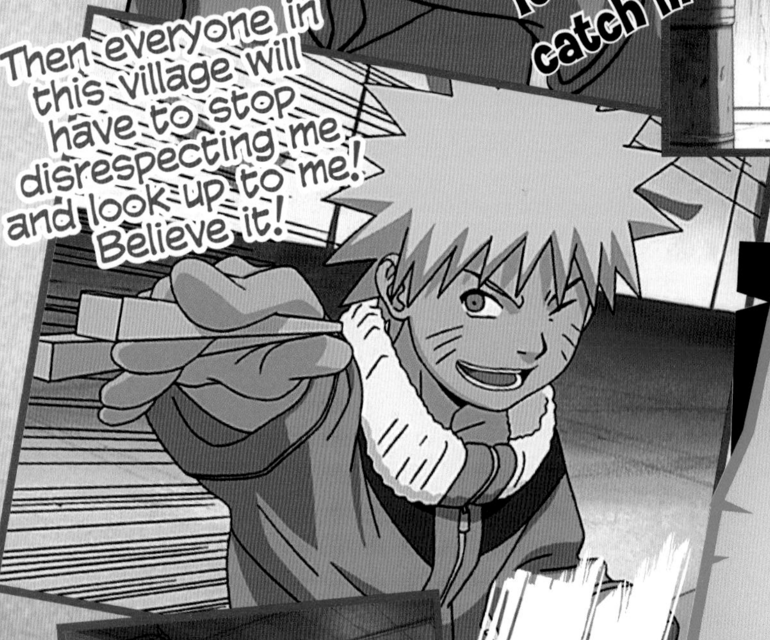
Then everyone in this village will have to stop disrespecting me and look up to me! Believe it!

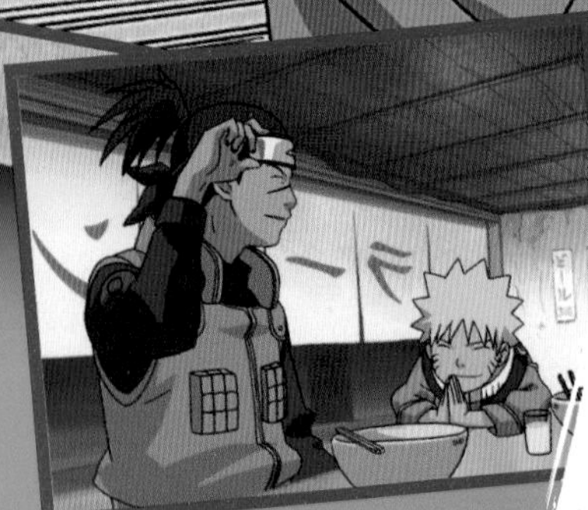
I... wanna try on your headband. Pretty please?♥

He's a first-class jokester who causes trouble for everyone!

Naruto's outrageous pranks drive everybody in the Hidden Leaf Village crazy. But Naruto's dream is to become a ninja so all the villagers will acknowledge his existence. Every day, the sounds of Naruto's laughter echo throughout the town!

Will Naruto ever graduate from the Ninja Academy?!

The graduation exam is finally here! Naruto is more determined than ever, but it turns out that the exam is on the Clone Jutsu. Even though it's his worst technique, Naruto refuses to abandon his dream of becoming a Ninja. He concentrates as hard as he can…and attempts the Clone Jutsu!!

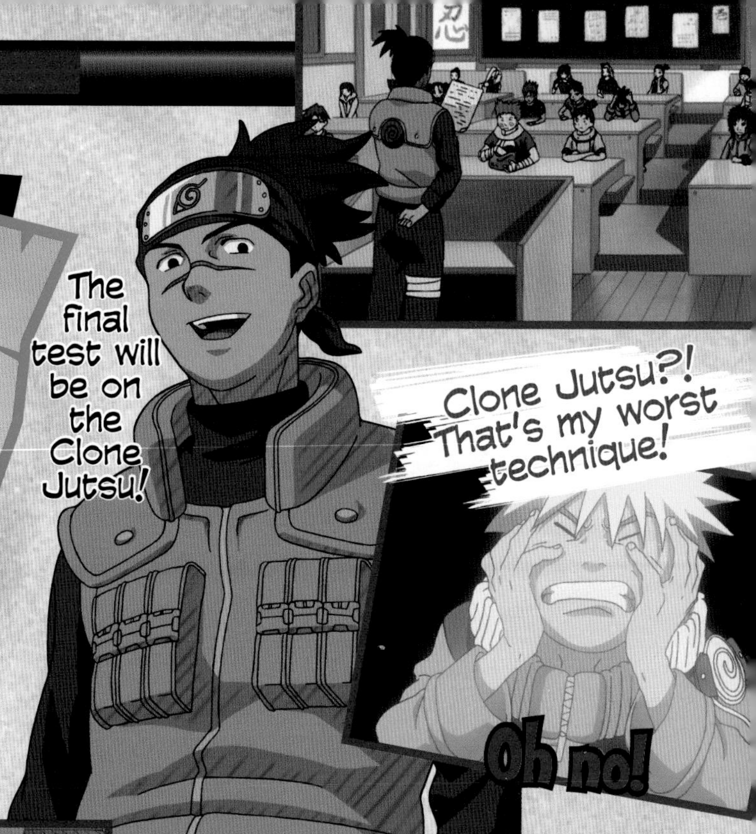
The final test will be on the Clone Jutsu!
Clone Jutsu?! That's my worst technique!
Oh no!

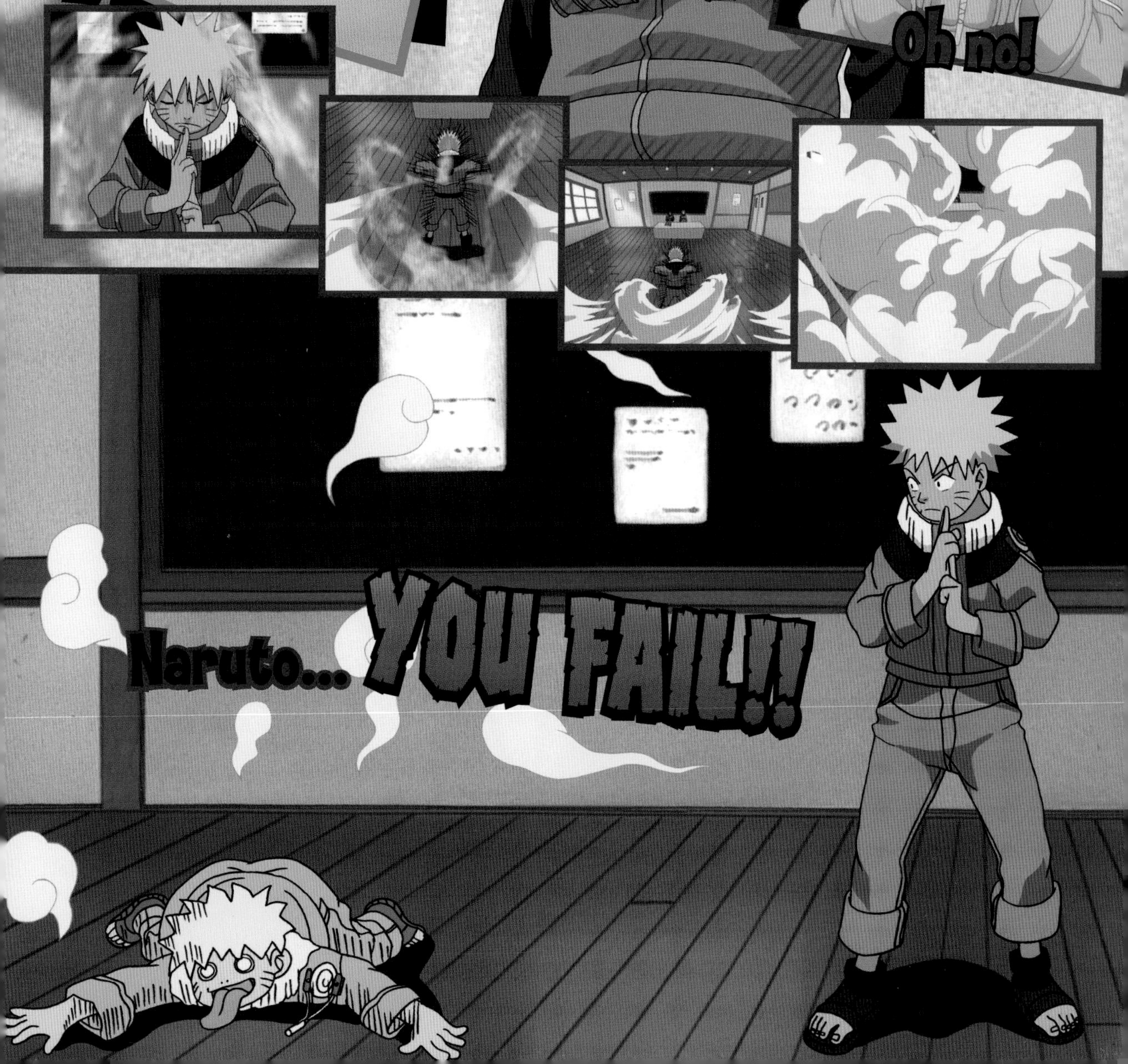
Naruto… YOU FAIL!!

A treacherous trap!!

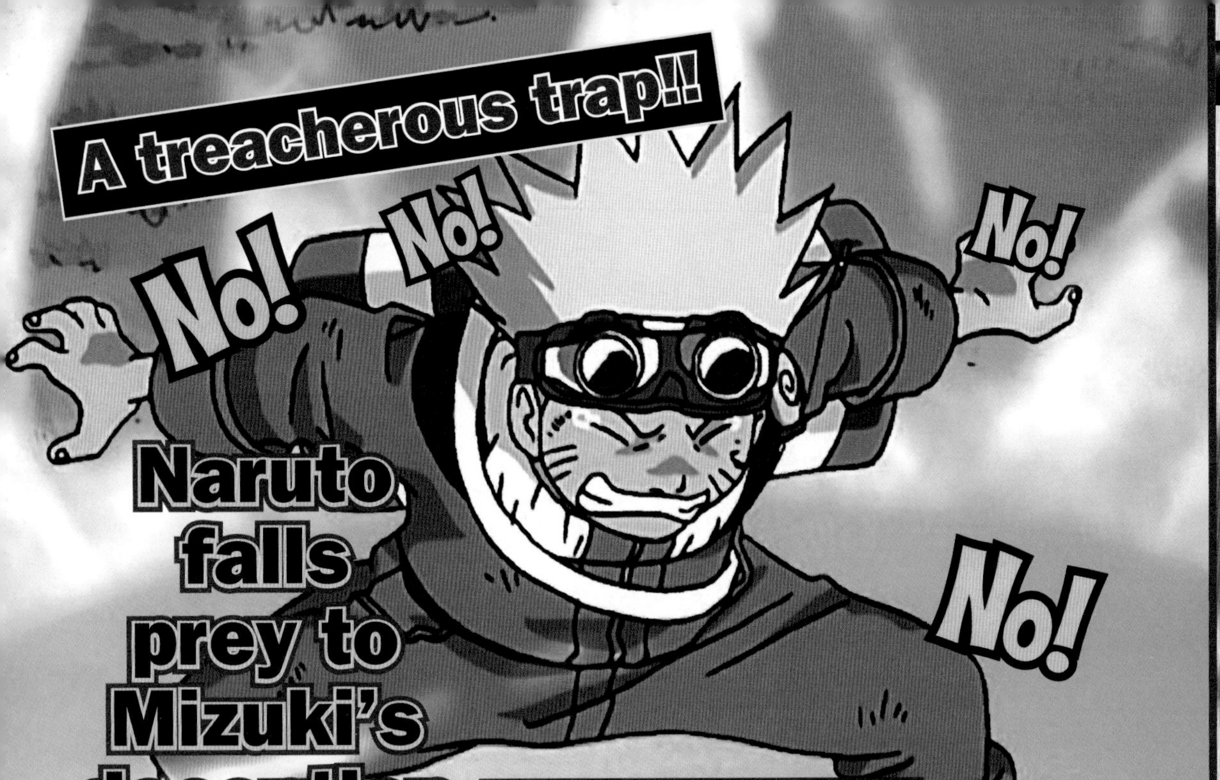
No!
No!
No!
No!

Naruto falls prey to Mizuki's deception...

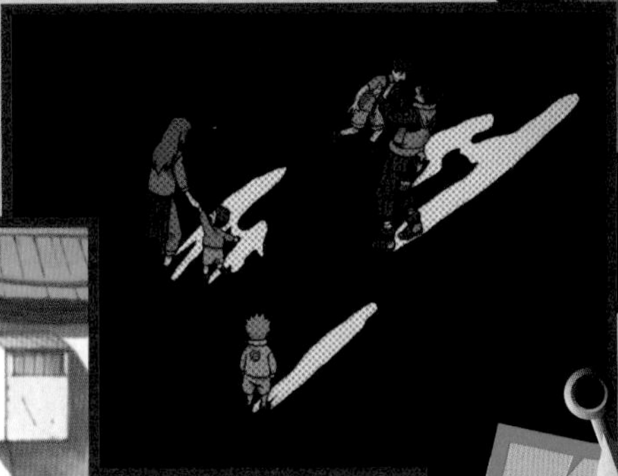

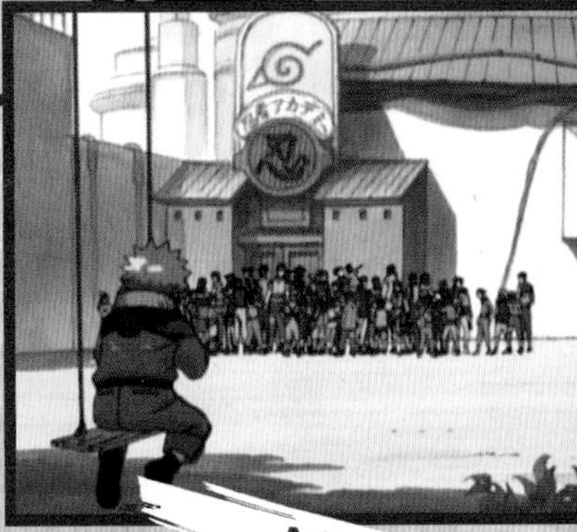

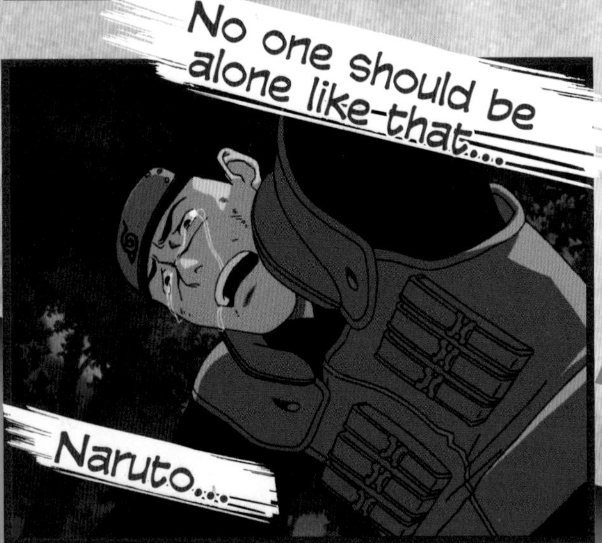
No one should be alone like-that...
Naruto...

Shunned by the villagers because of the long-held secret hidden within him...

Naruto is stunned to learn the real reason that the other villagers despise and ignore him when Mizuki reveals the decree that had been kept from Naruto all his life. With no outlet for his rage and frustration, angry tears begin to fall from Naruto's eyes...

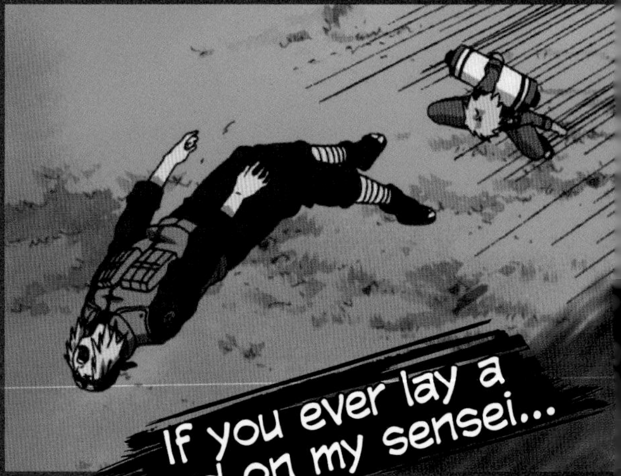

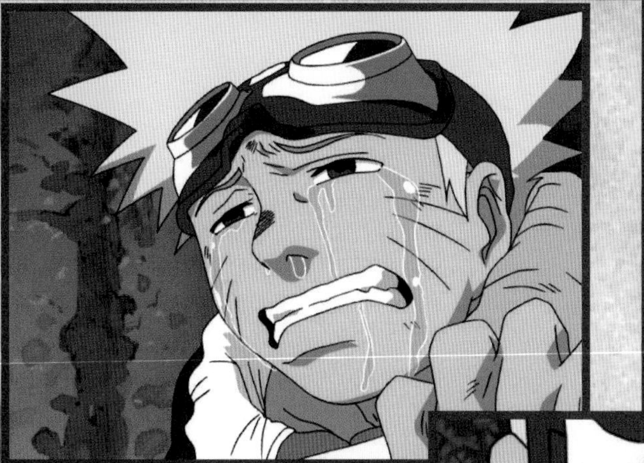

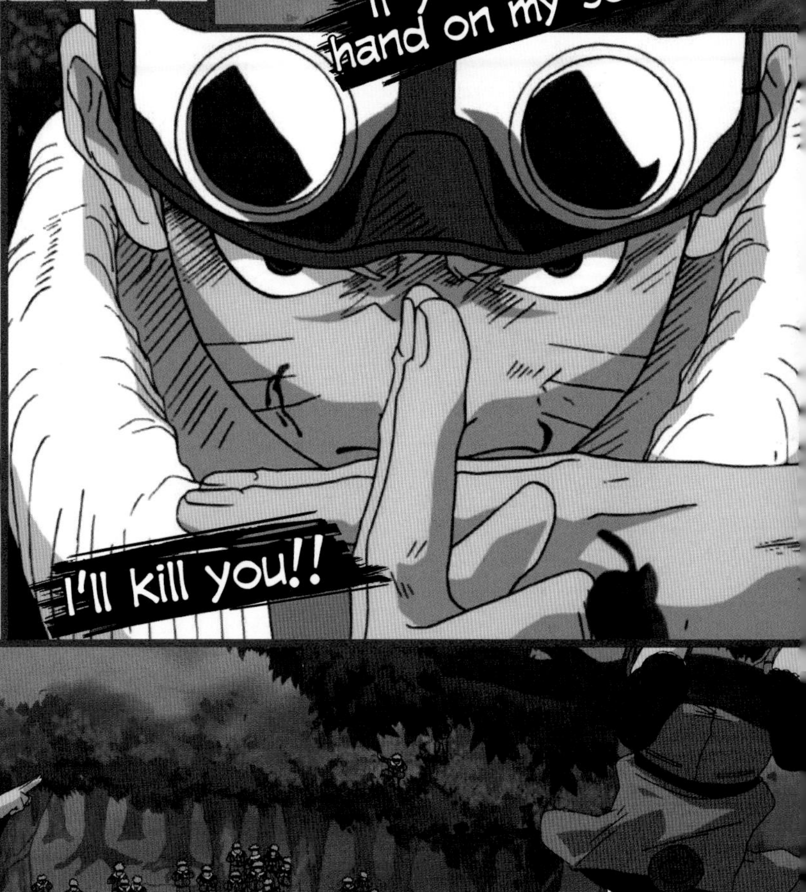
If you ever lay a hand on my sensei...
I'll kill you!!

Naruto's awakening as a Leaf-style ninja!

Iruka is badly injured, and now Mizuki wants to finish him off! When Naruto sees that Iruka's life is in danger, he feels driven to protect the only person who has ever shown him any tenderness or respect… and an unknown power awakens inside him!

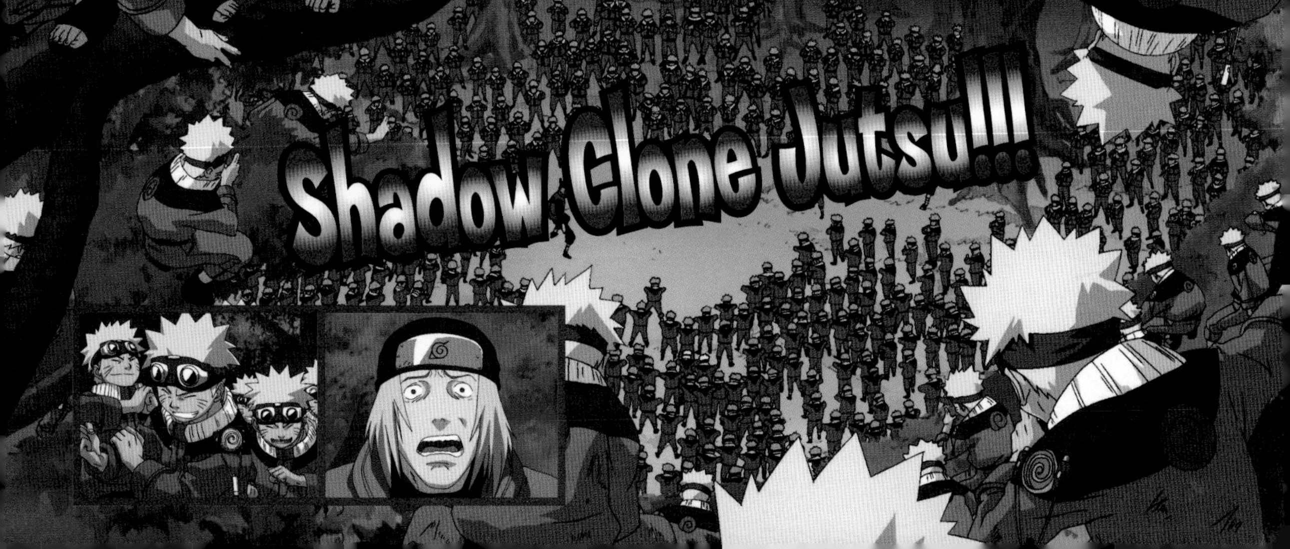
Shadow Clone Jutsu!!!

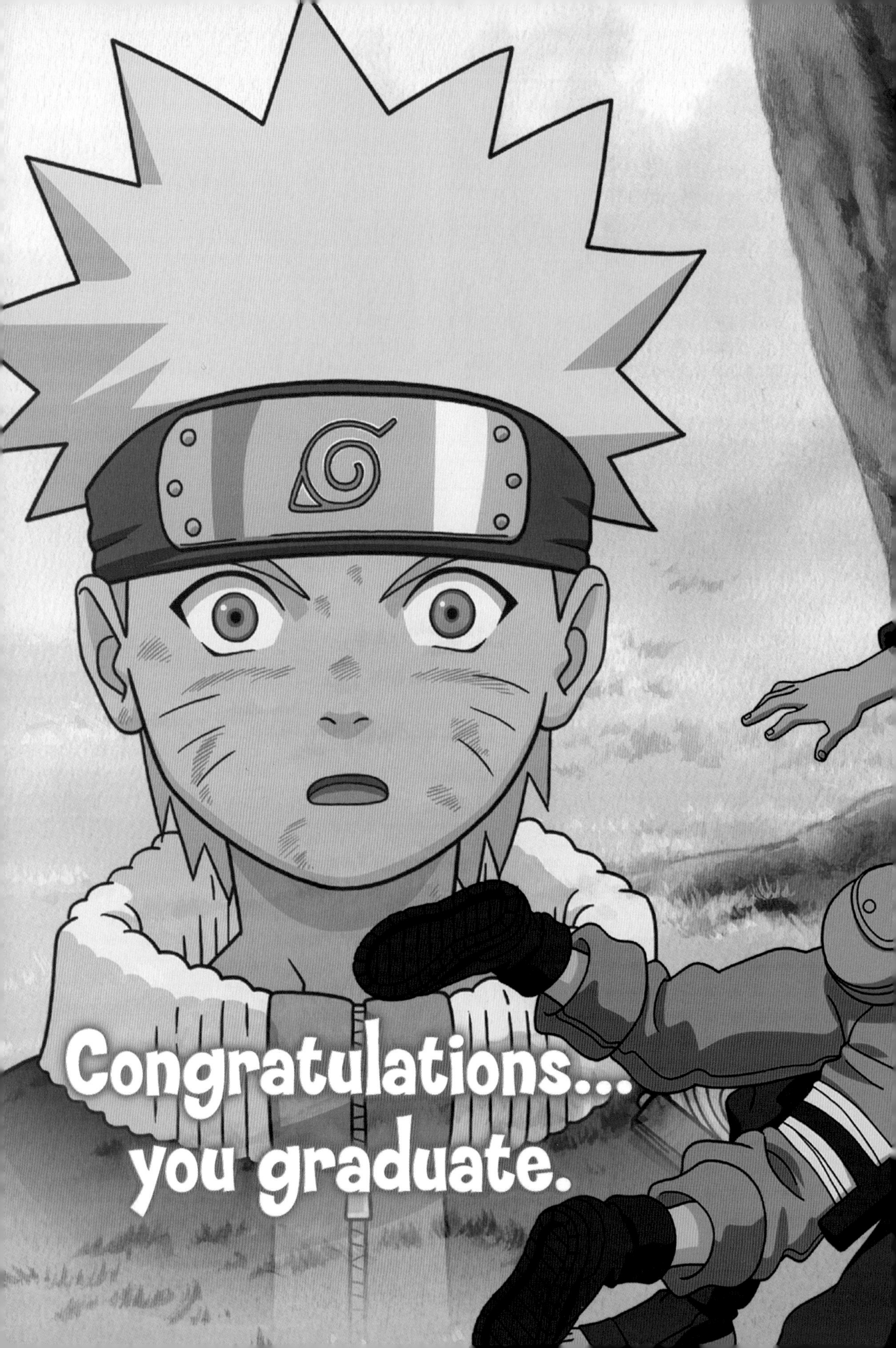
Congratulations...
you graduate.

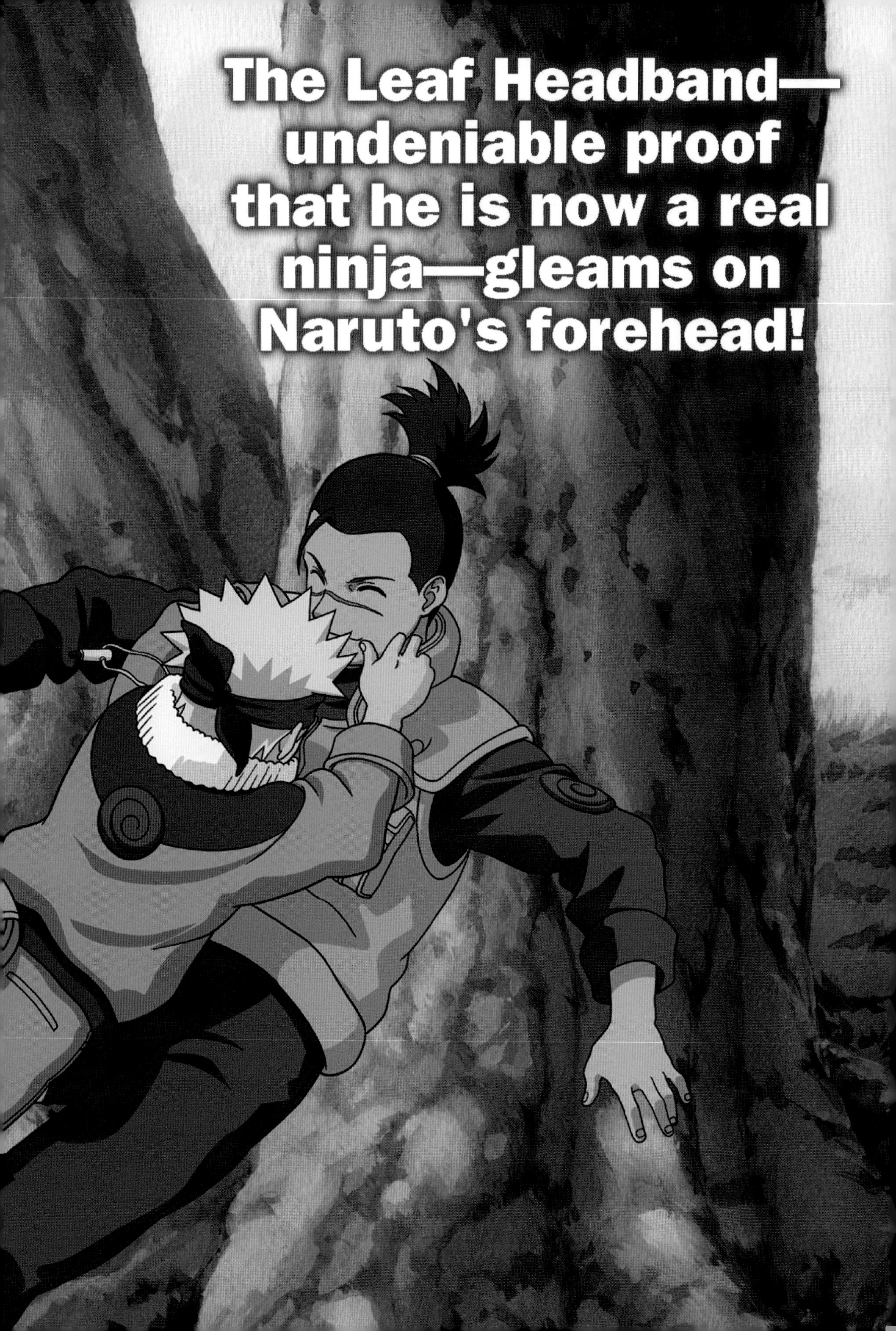
The Leaf Headband—undeniable proof that he is now a real ninja—gleams on Naruto's forehead!

Failure rate: at least 66%!

Jonin Kakashi's survival exercise!!

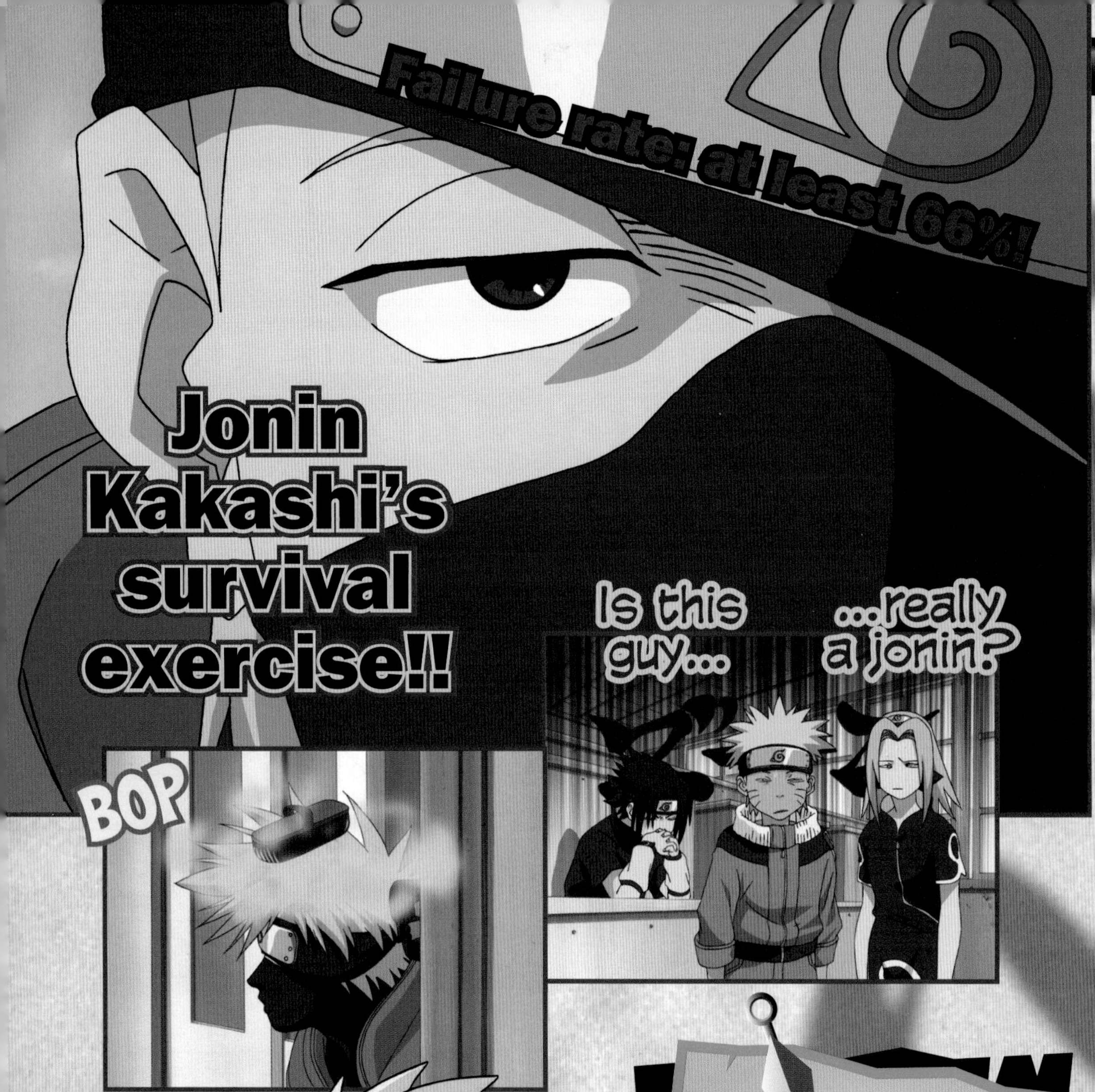
Is this guy...
...really a jonin?
BOP

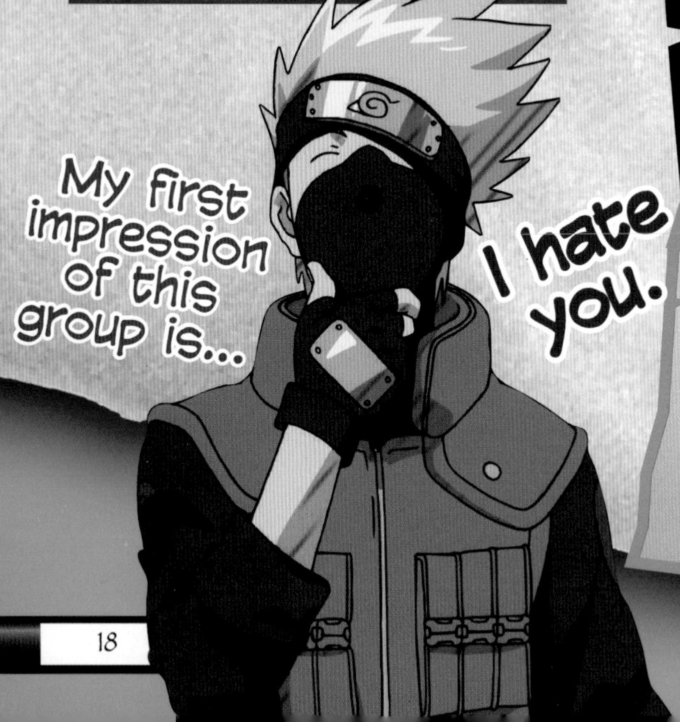
My first impression of this group is...
I hate you.

After nervously waiting to meet their instructor, their initial impressions are...horrible?!

Naruto, Sakura and Sasuke are supposed to meet Kakashi, the jonin (elite ninja) assigned to lead their squad, for the first time. But Kakashi is extremely late, so Naruto quickly loses patience with waiting and decides to play a practical joke. Sasuke rebukes Naruto for his foolishness, saying that a jonin would never fall for that kind of trick, but...

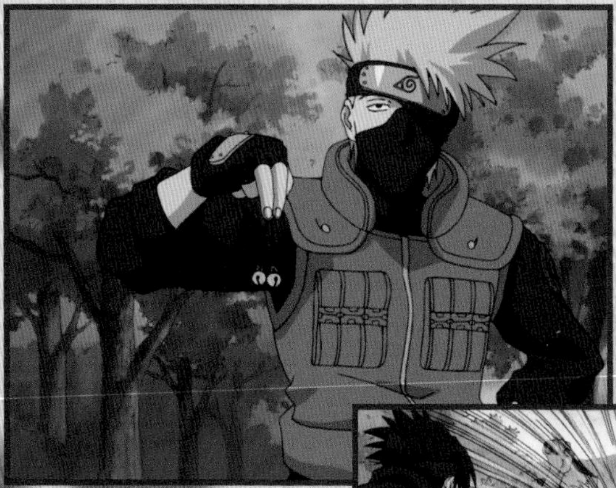

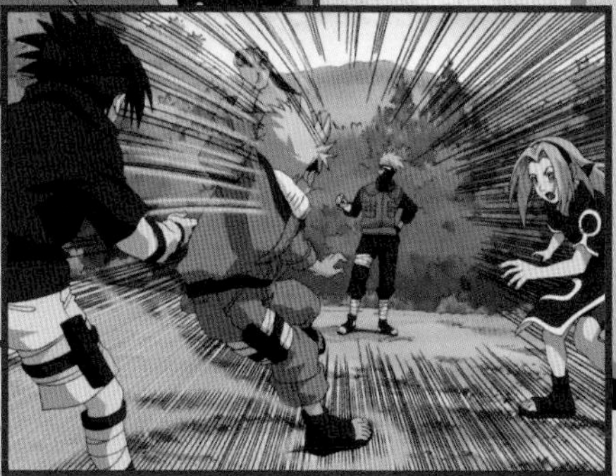

The impossibly difficult test finally begins!

All three squad members begin Kakashi's survival exercise, but everything goes wrong for Naruto before he can even get started! Naruto brashly challenges Kakashi to a head-to-head match…but Kakashi instantly goes behind Naruto's back and unleashes his secret hidden maneuver!

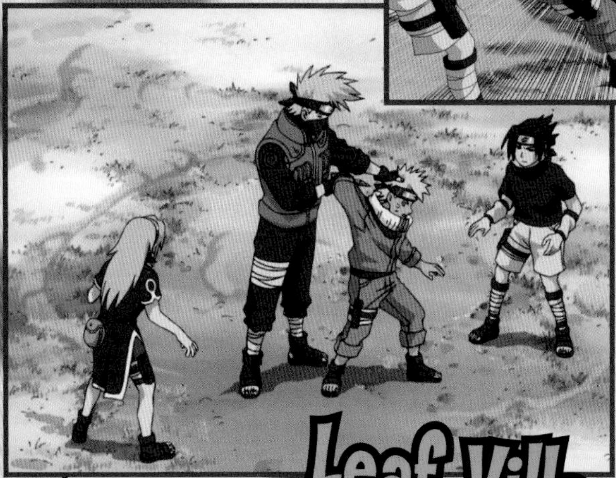

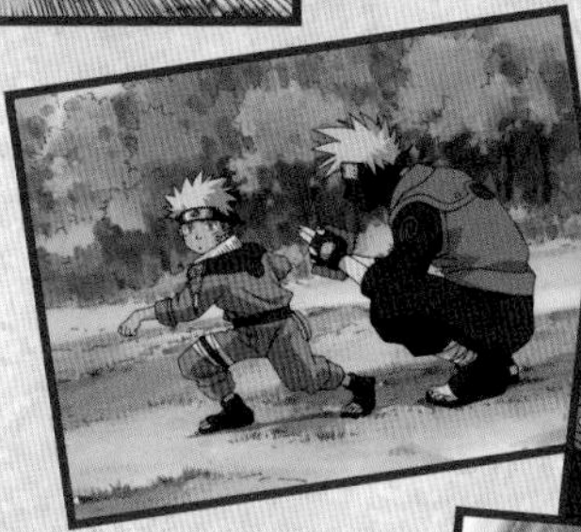

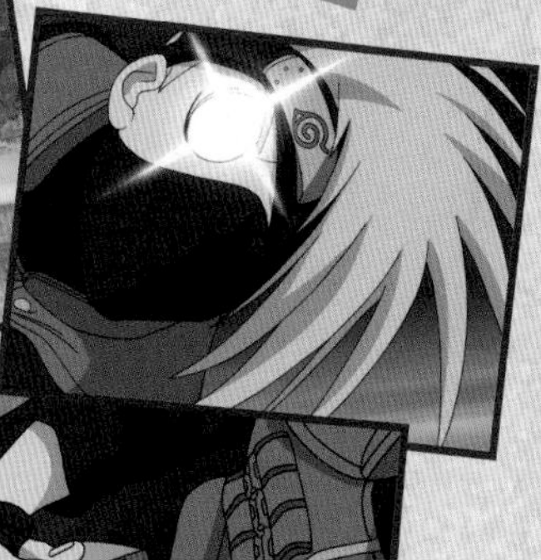

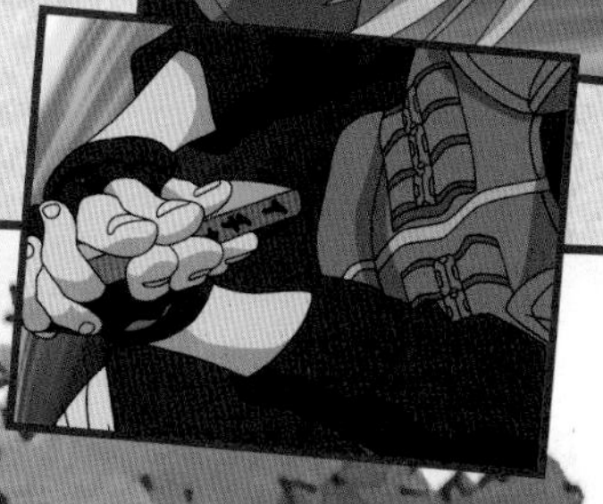

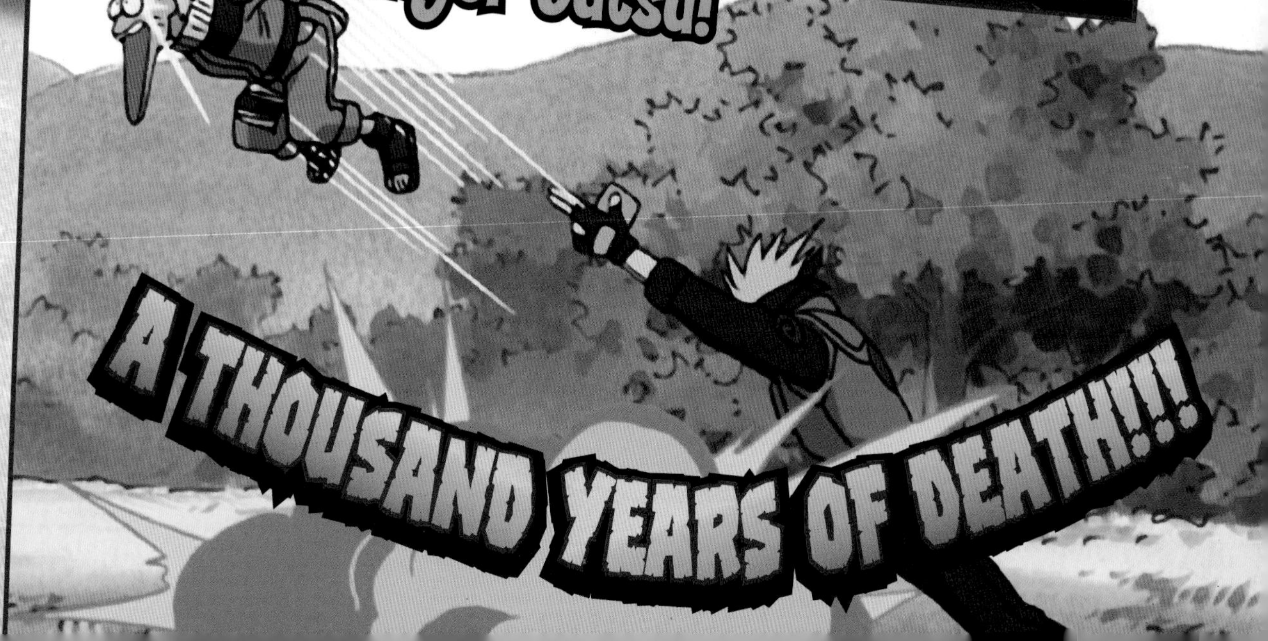
Leaf Village Secret Finger Jutsu!
A THOUSAND YEARS OF DEATH!!!

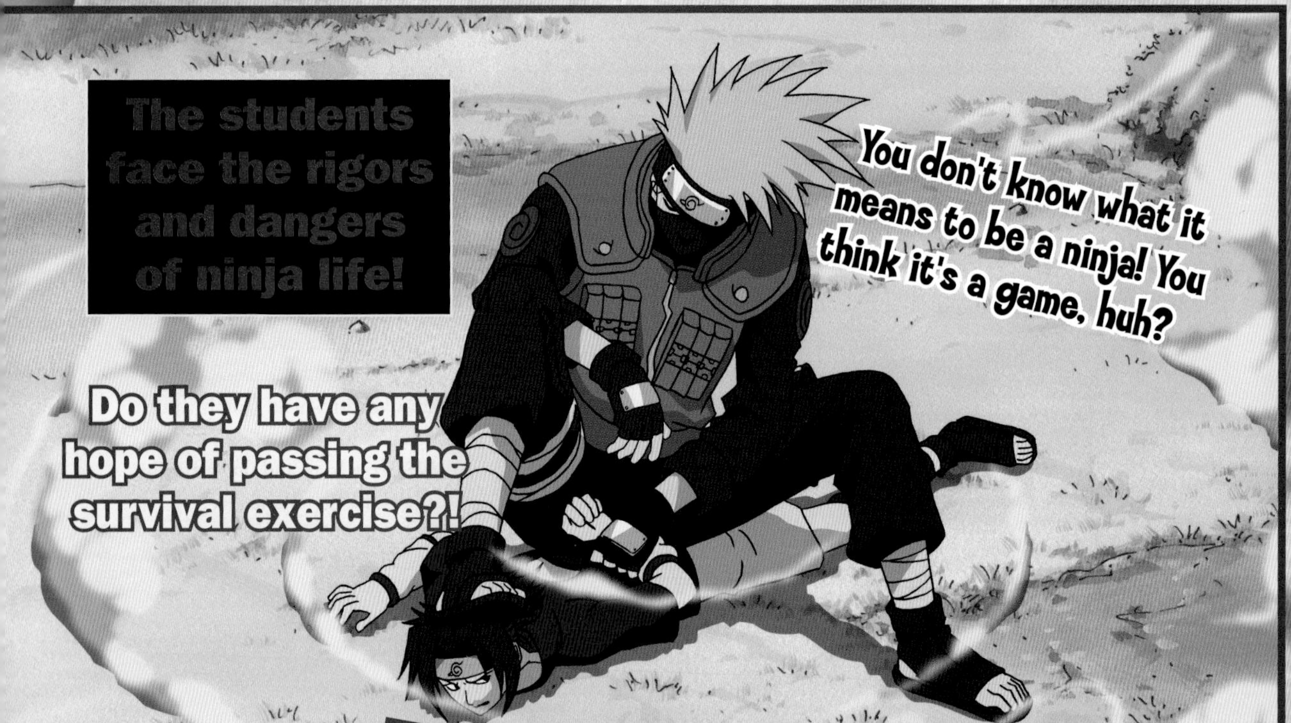
The students face the rigors and dangers of ninja life!
You don't know what it means to be a ninja! You think it's a game, huh?
Do they have any hope of passing the survival exercise?!

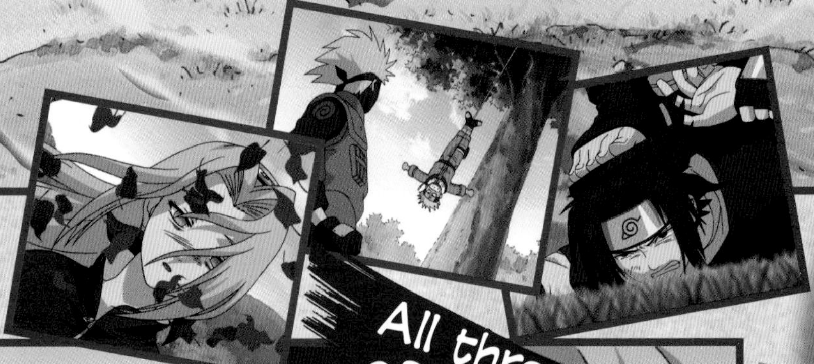

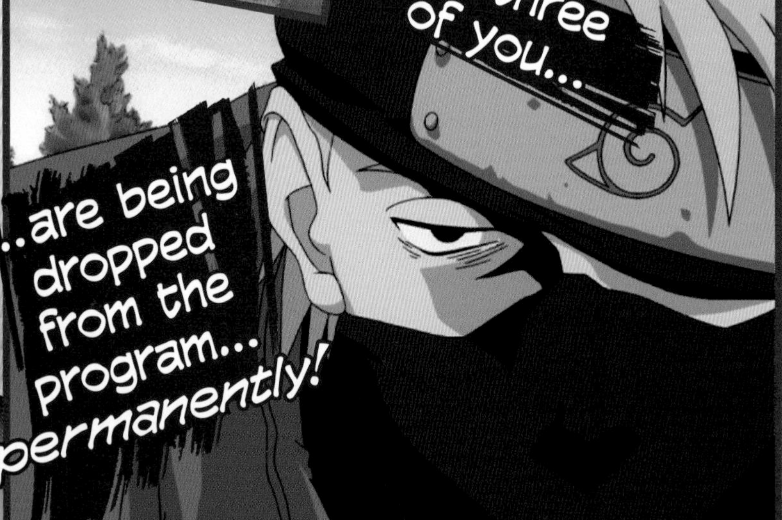
All three of you...
...are being dropped from the program... permanently!

Kakashi's true strength is overwhelming!
Naruto, Sakura and even Sasuke, who boasts the top grades at the Ninja Academy, are no match for Kakashi's power. The way things are going, will they be forced to return to the academy?

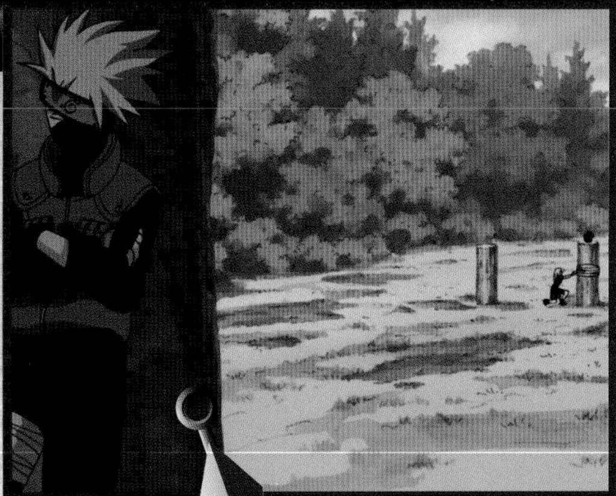

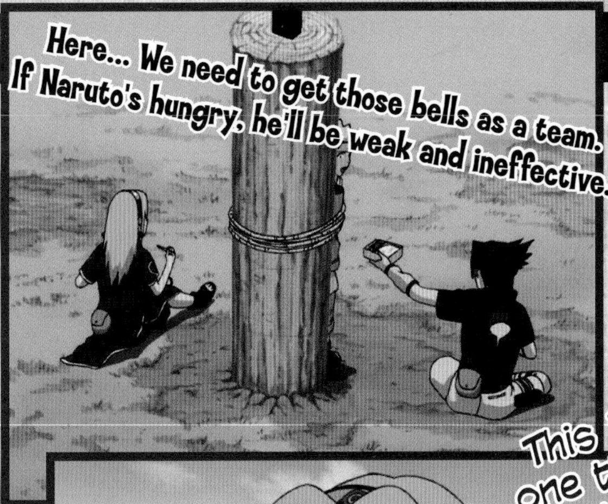
Here... We need to get those bells as a team. If Naruto's hungry, he'll be weak and ineffective.

The ultimate decision! What will be the students' fate?!

While they wait for their last chance in the survival test, Sasuke and Sakura go against Kakashi's orders and share their lunch with Naruto. But their transgression does not escape Kakashi's watchful eye…and he charges out from where he was hiding in the trees with a fierce expression on his face!

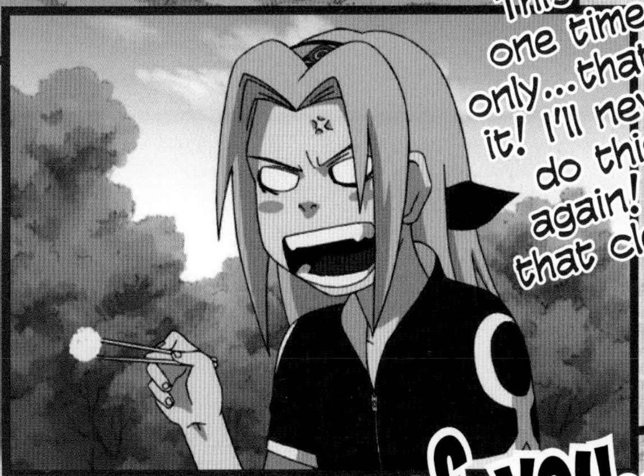
This is one time only...that's it! I'll never do this again! Is that clear?

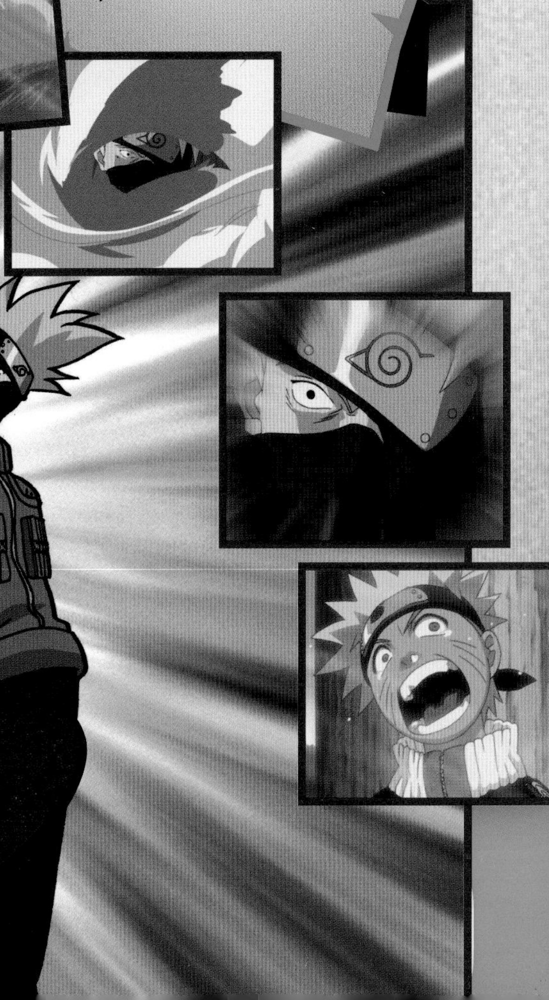

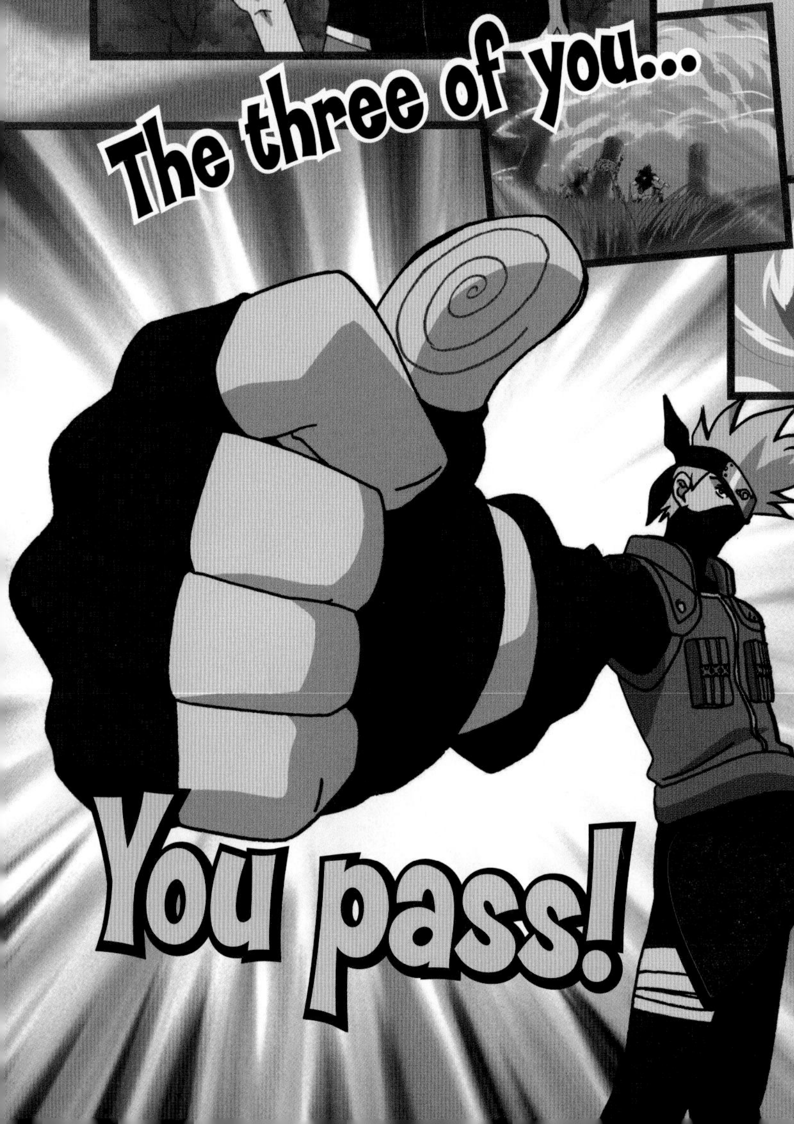
The three of you...
You pass!

Naruto Uzumaki

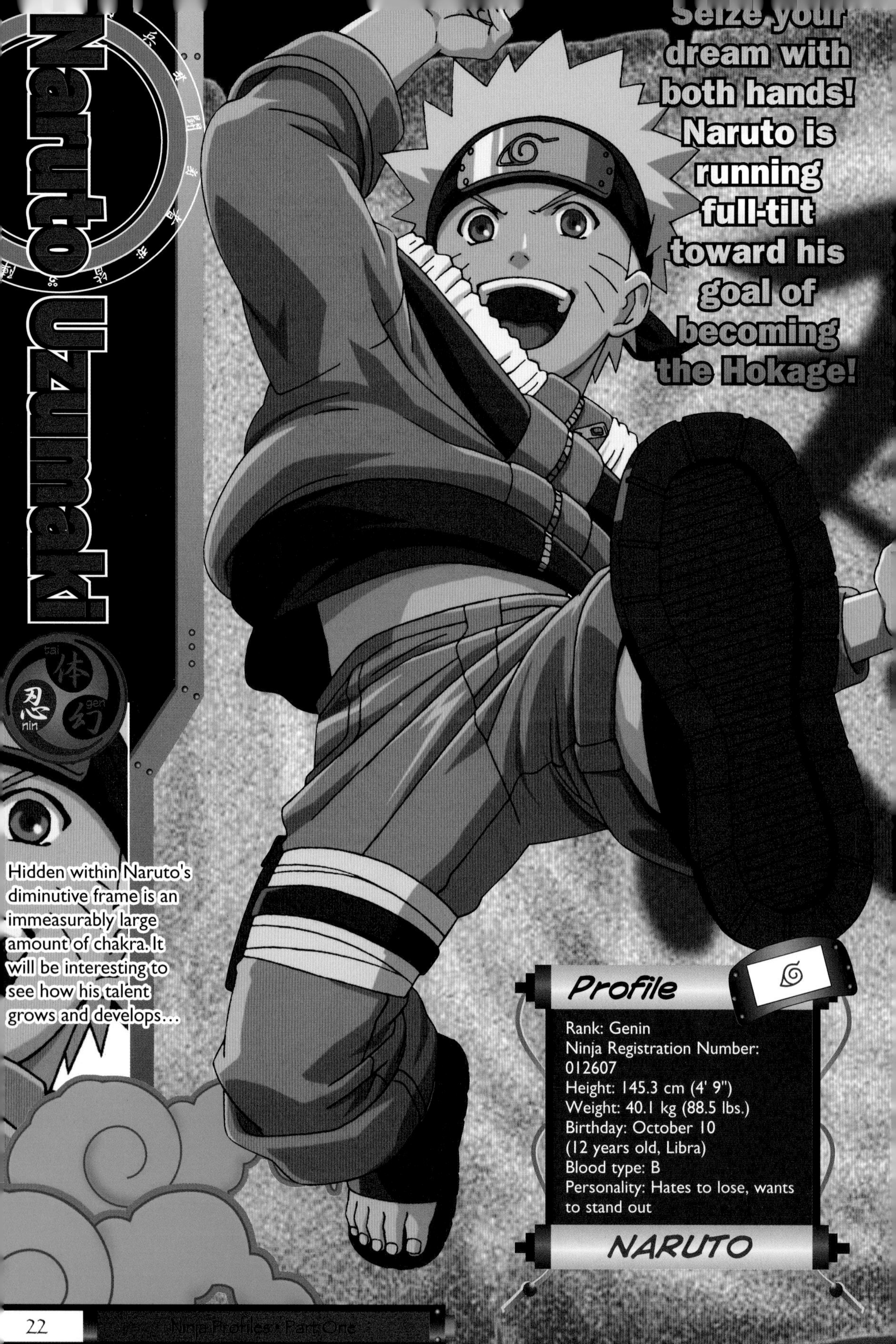
tai 体
nin 忍
gen 幻

Seize your dream with both hands! Naruto is running full-tilt toward his goal of becoming the Hokage!

Hidden within Naruto's diminutive frame is an immeasurably large amount of chakra. It will be interesting to see how his talent grows and develops...

Profile

Rank: Genin
Ninja Registration Number: 012607
Height: 145.3 cm (4' 9")
Weight: 40.1 kg (88.5 lbs.)
Birthday: October 10 (12 years old, Libra)
Blood type: B
Personality: Hates to lose, wants to stand out

NARUTO

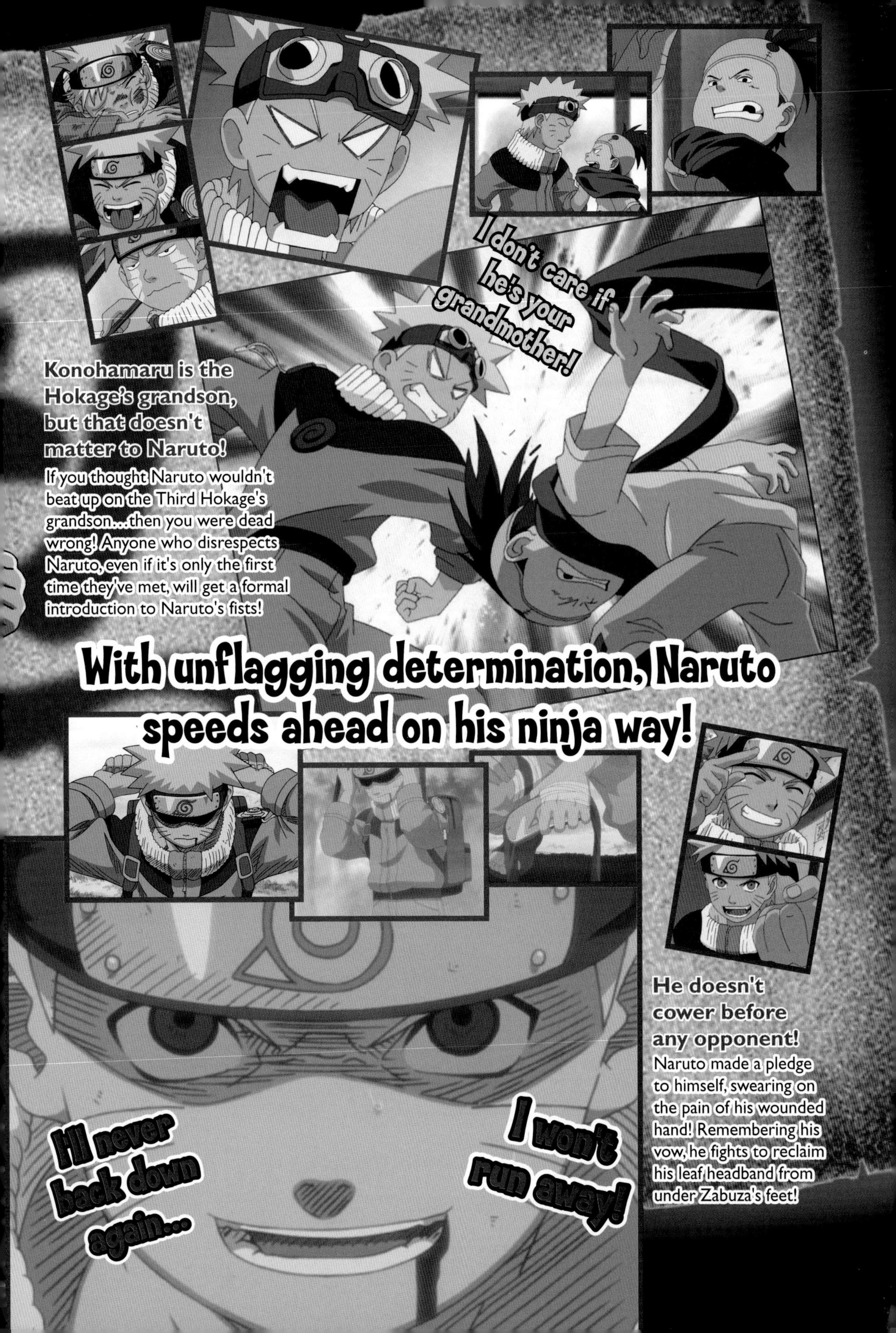
I don't care if he's your grandmother!
I won't run away!
I'll never back down again...

Konohamaru is the Hokage's grandson, but that doesn't matter to Naruto!

If you thought Naruto wouldn't beat up on the Third Hokage's grandson...then you were dead wrong! Anyone who disrespects Naruto, even if it's only the first time they've met, will get a formal introduction to Naruto's fists!

With unflagging determination, Naruto speeds ahead on his ninja way!

He doesn't cower before any opponent!

Naruto made a pledge to himself, swearing on the pain of his wounded hand! Remembering his vow, he fights to reclaim his leaf headband from under Zabuza's feet!

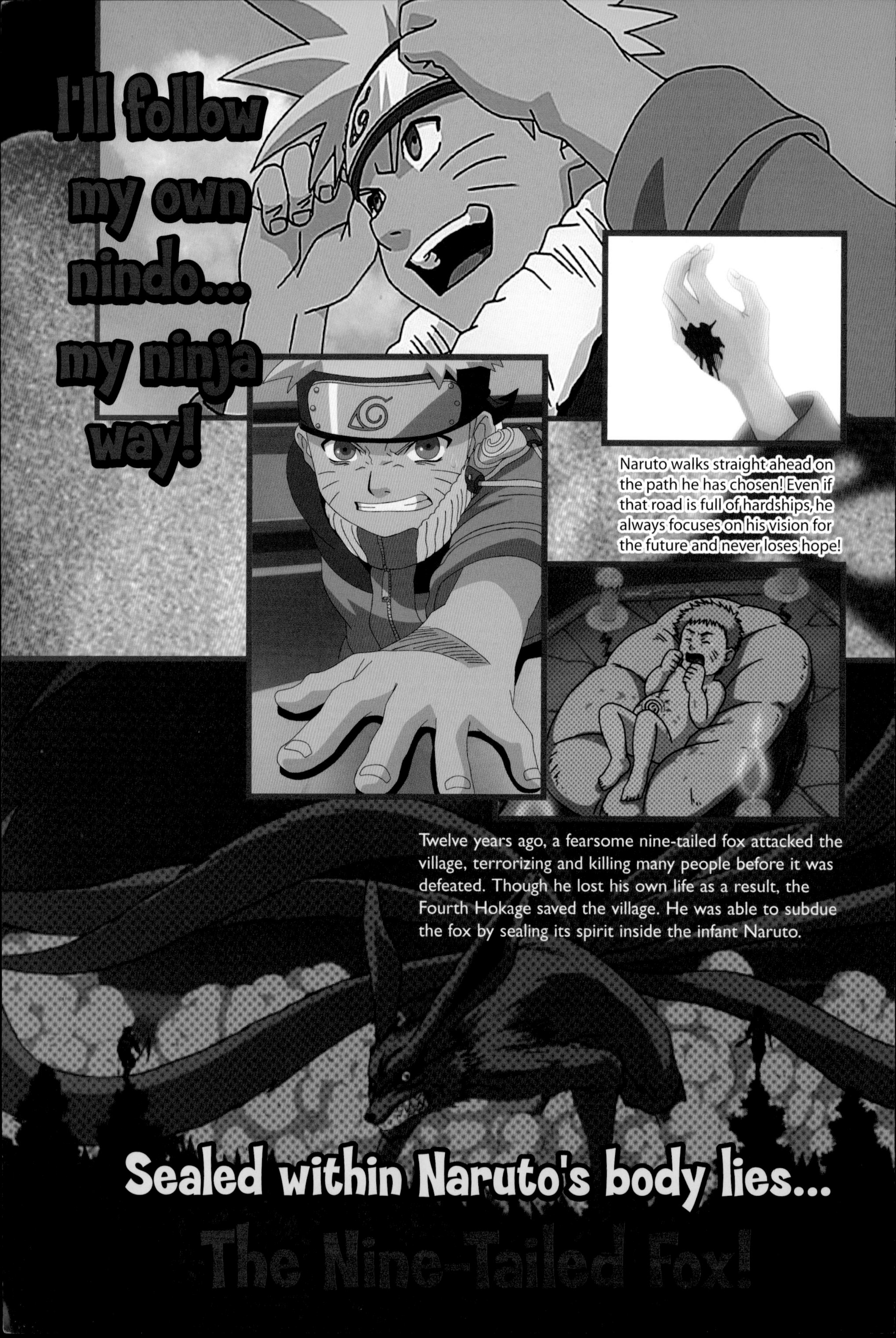
I'll follow my own nindo... my ninja way!
Naruto walks straight ahead on the path he has chosen! Even if that road is full of hardships, he always focuses on his vision for the future and never loses hope!
Twelve years ago, a fearsome nine-tailed fox attacked the village, terrorizing and killing many people before it was defeated. Though he lost his own life as a result, the Fourth Hokage saved the village. He was able to subdue the fox by sealing its spirit inside the infant Naruto.
Sealed within Naruto's body lies...
The Nine-Tailed Fox!

Transform!!

Sexy Jutsu

The number one problem child of the Hidden Leaf Village runs wild at the Ninja Academy! During an in-class review, his brilliant mischief knocks out Iruka with one blow! Even Iruka has difficulty handling Naruto…!

Naruto views Sasuke – who has the top grades at Ninja Academy – as his main competition! Naruto's rapid progress can largely be attributed to his burning desire to beat Sasuke!

Naruto Edition

Leaf Genin Squad 7

Rival

Jonin Leader

Big Crush

Respected Mentor

NARUTO UZUMAKI

NARUTO UZUMAKI

Sasuke Uchiha

The blood of the legendary Uchiha Clan runs through his veins!

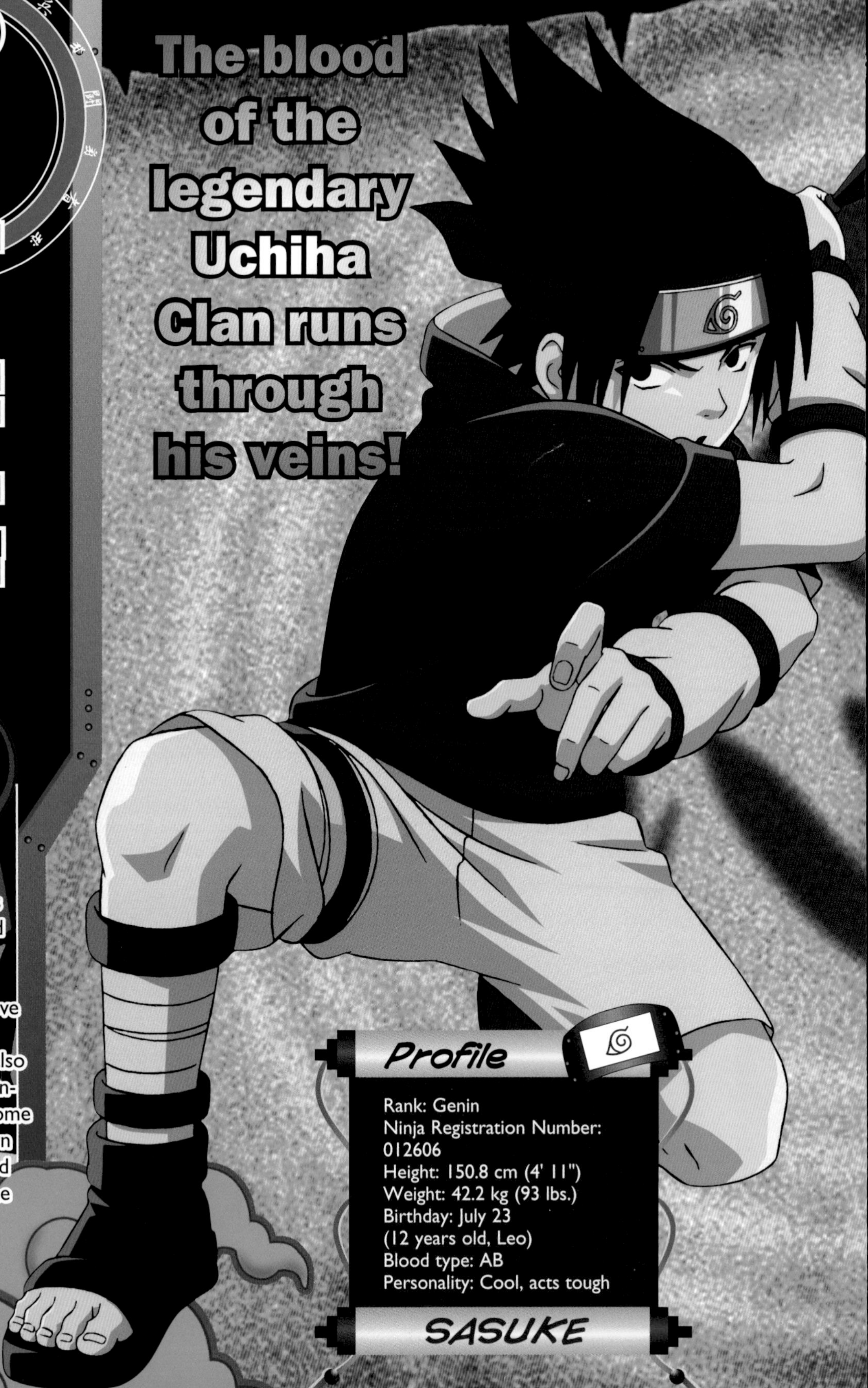

In addition to having abilities in ninjutsu and taijutsu that are head and shoulders above the other students', he also uses the Sharingan. His awesome talent is known and recognized throughout the Hidden Leaf Village...and beyond.

Profile

Rank: Genin
Ninja Registration Number: 012606
Height: 150.8 cm (4' 11")
Weight: 42.2 kg (93 lbs.)
Birthday: July 23
(12 years old, Leo)
Blood type: AB
Personality: Cool, acts tough

SASUKE

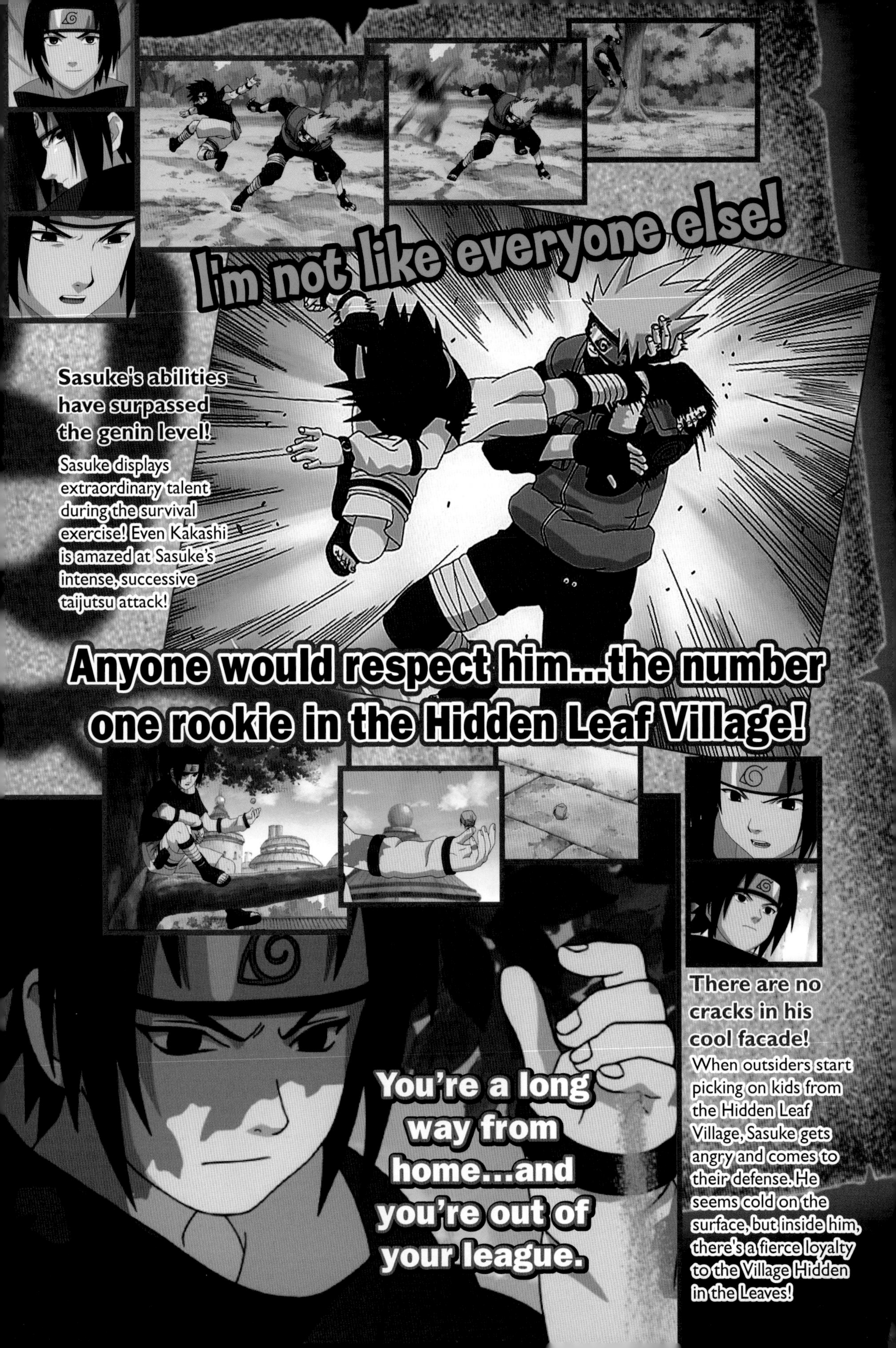
I'm not like everyone else!
Sasuke's abilities have surpassed the genin level!
Sasuke displays extraordinary talent during the survival exercise! Even Kakashi is amazed at Sasuke's intense, successive taijutsu attack!
Anyone would respect him...the number one rookie in the Hidden Leaf Village!
There are no cracks in his cool facade!
When outsiders start picking on kids from the Hidden Leaf Village, Sasuke gets angry and comes to their defense. He seems cold on the surface, but inside him, there's a fierce loyalty to the Village Hidden in the Leaves!
You're a long way from home...and you're out of your league.

Sasuke's Uchiha blood awakens the power sleeping inside him!

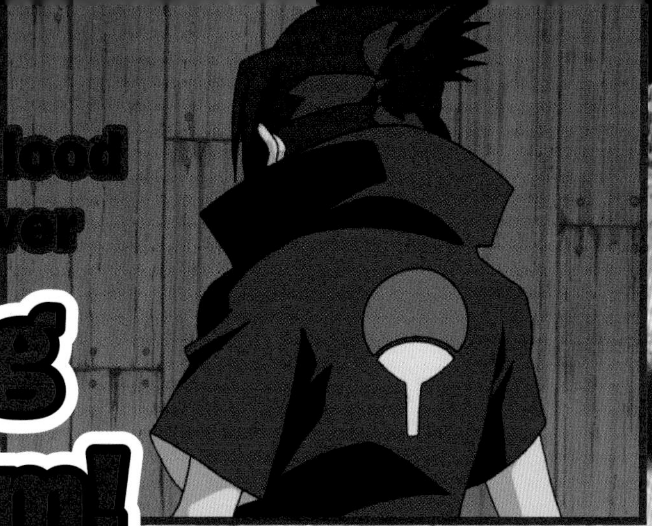

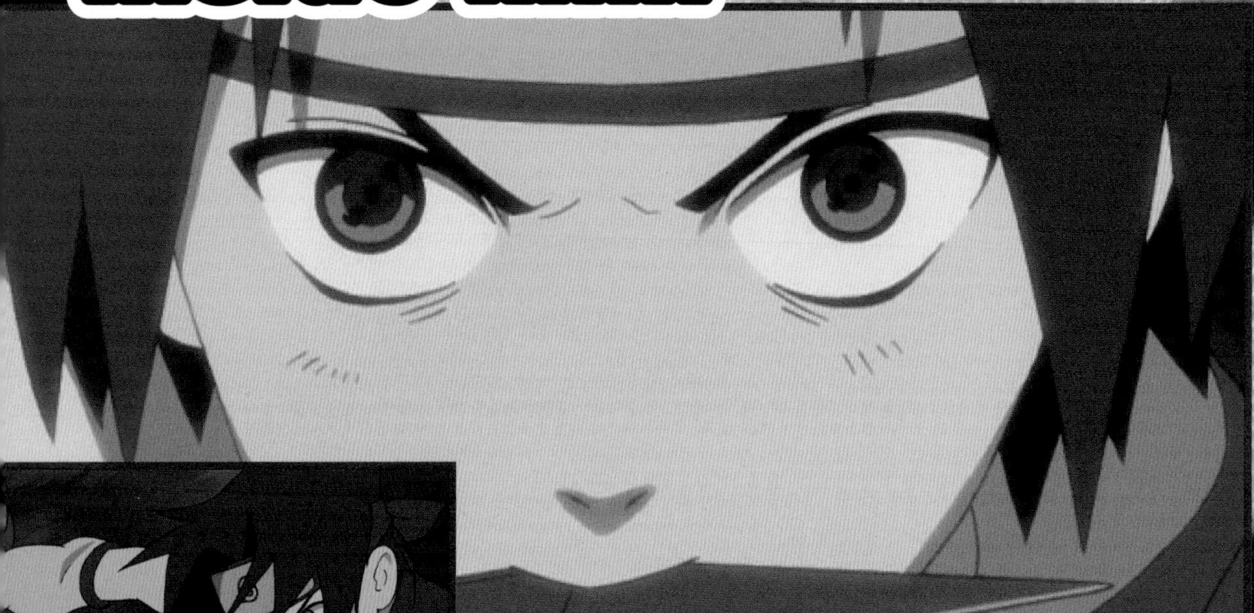

In the midst of battle, the Sharingan suddenly appears! With the awakening of his Kekkei Genkai (bloodline trait) power, which combines the abilities of insight vision, hypnosis vision, and jutsu duplication, Sasuke finally inherits the true power of the Uchiha!

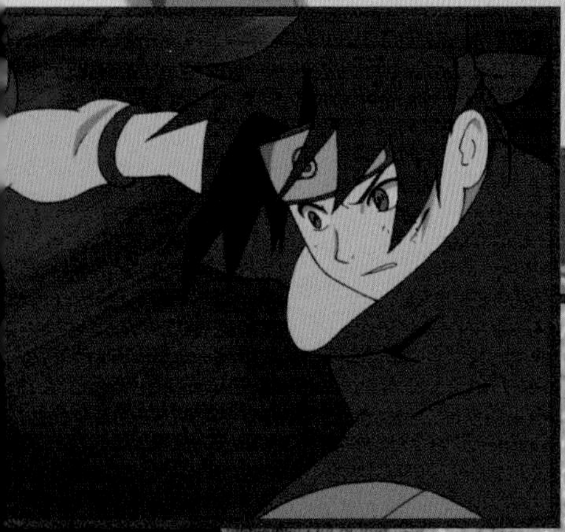

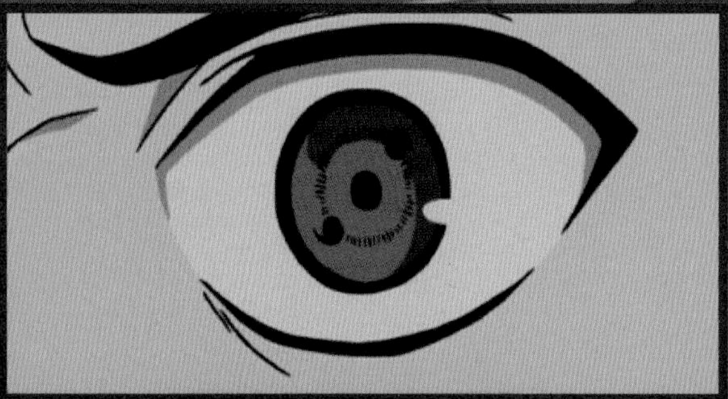

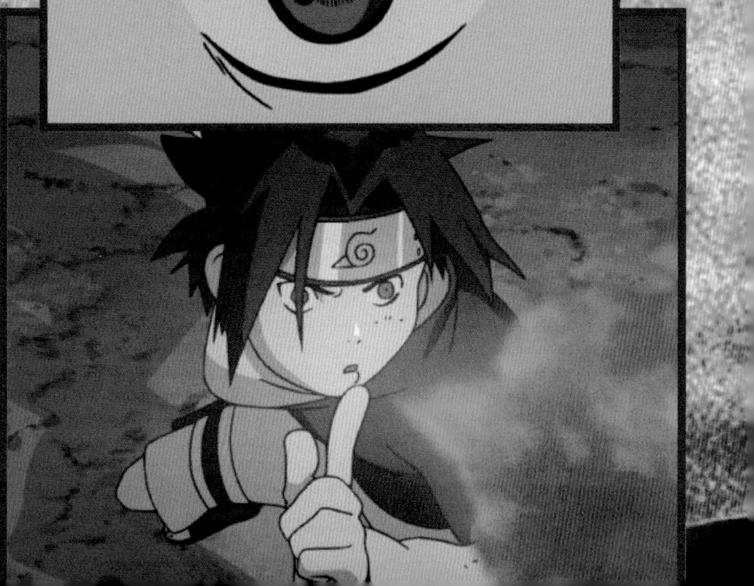

I am an avenger...

The Uchiha clan was destroyed, with Sasuke and his older brother Itachi the only survivors. Sasuke's fervent ambition to kill his brother and revive the clan indicates that Itachi was intimately involved with the destruction of their family.

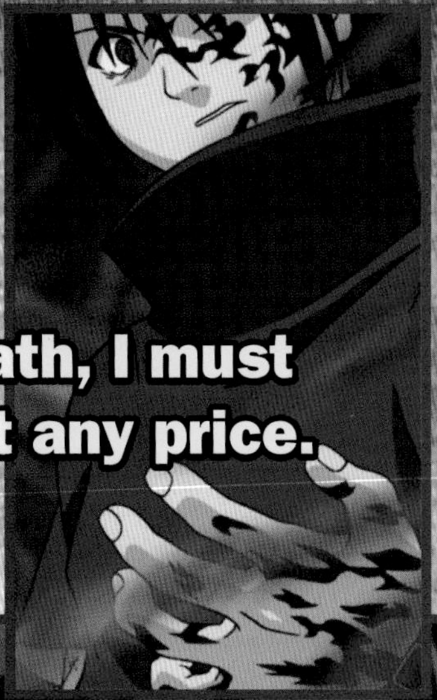

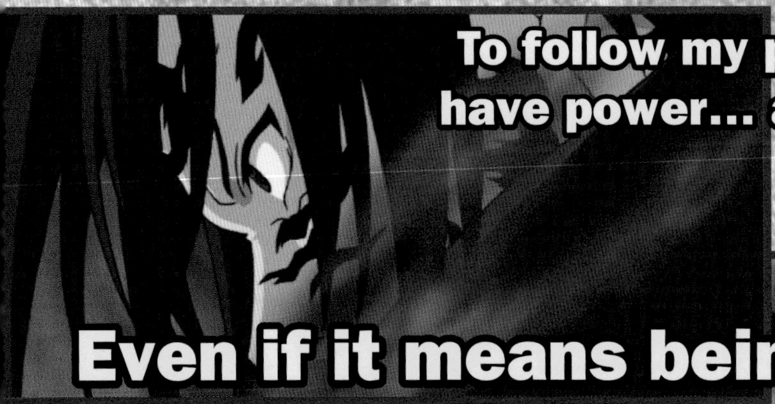

To follow my path, I must have power... at any price.

Even if it means being consumed by evil!

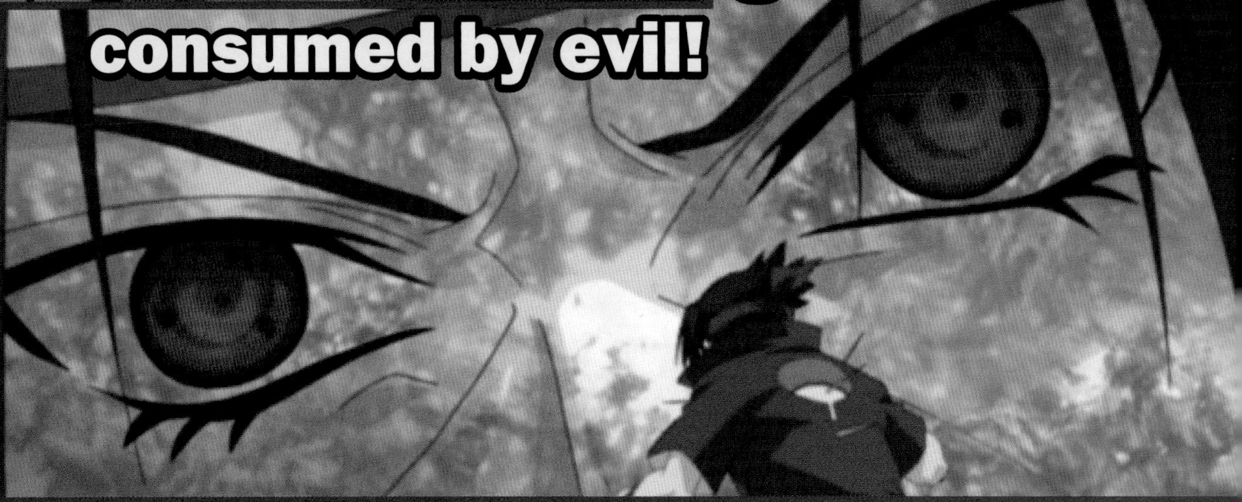

SASUKE UCHIHA

Ninja Relationships
Sasuke Edition

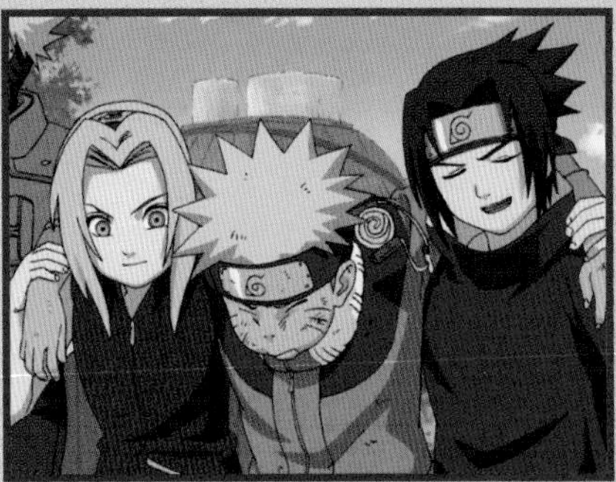

Sasuke used to show no interest in friendship or love, but since joining the same squad as Naruto and Sakura, he has gradually begun to care for his teammates.

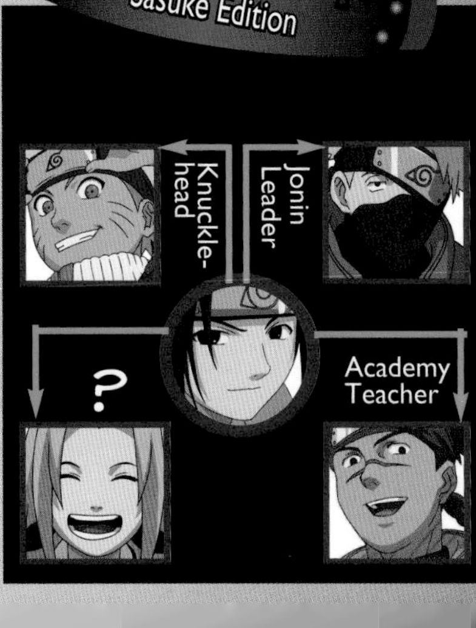
Knuckle-head
Jonin Leader
?
Academy Teacher

SASUKE UCHIHA

Sakura Haruno

A pure-minded, pretty kunoichi (female ninja) who keeps her true feelings inside!

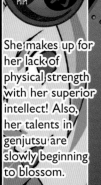

She makes up for her lack of physical strength with her superior intellect! Also, her talents in genjutsu are slowly beginning to blossom.

Profile

Rank: Genin
Ninja Registration Number: 012601
Height: 148.5 cm (4' 10")
Weight: 35.4 (78 lbs.)
Birthday: March 28
(12 years old, Aries)
Blood type: O
Personality: Top student, selfish

SAKURA

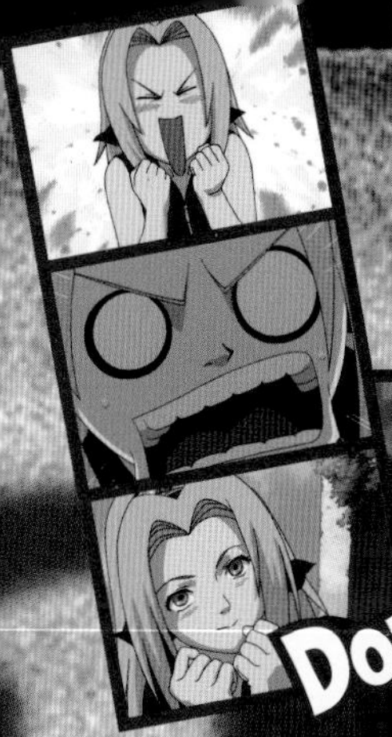

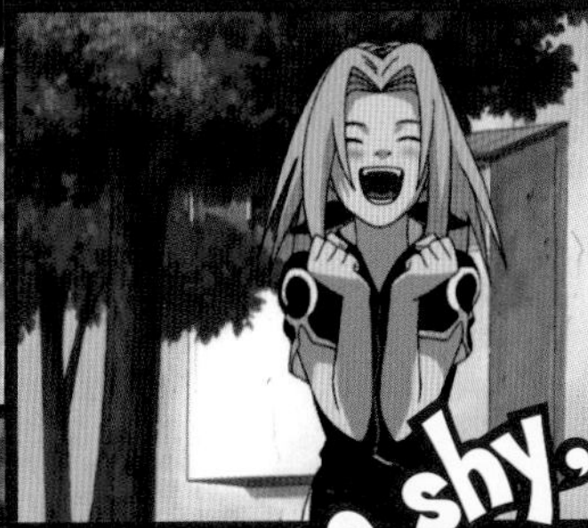

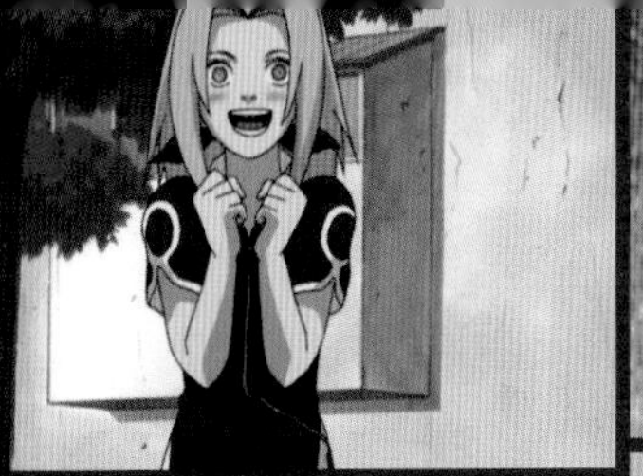

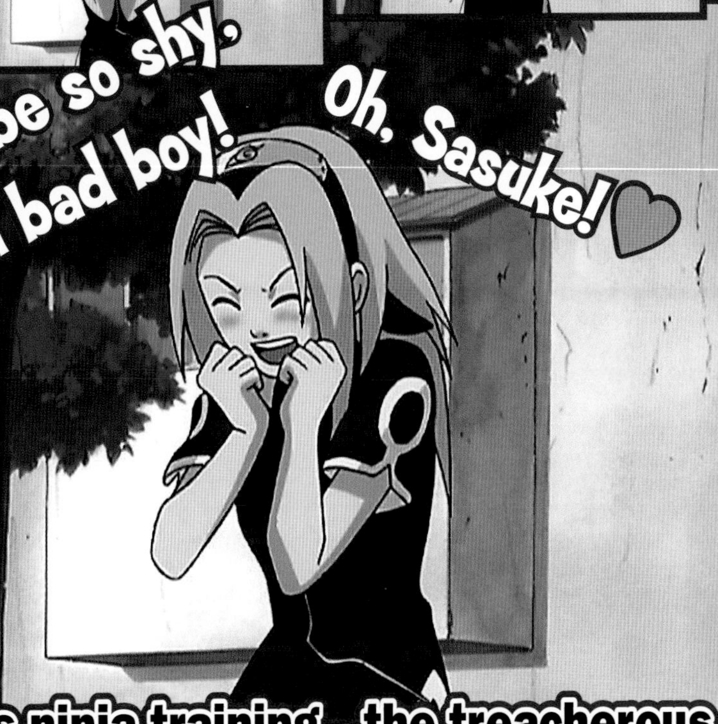
Oh, Sasuke!♥
Don't be so shy, you bad boy!

True love conquers all!

When Sakura is assigned to the same squad as Sasuke, she jumps one step ahead of Ino, her rival for his affections! Hoping to immediately start taking advantage of this opportunity, she decides to make the first move and approaches Sasuke with her most alluring smile!

Love versus ninja training...the treacherous conflict that troubles Sakura along her ninja way!

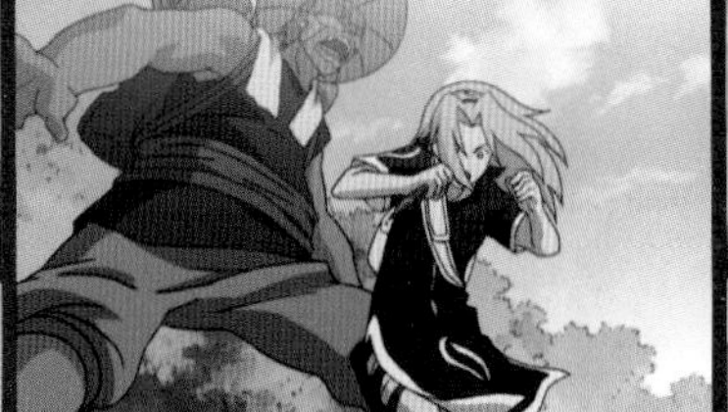

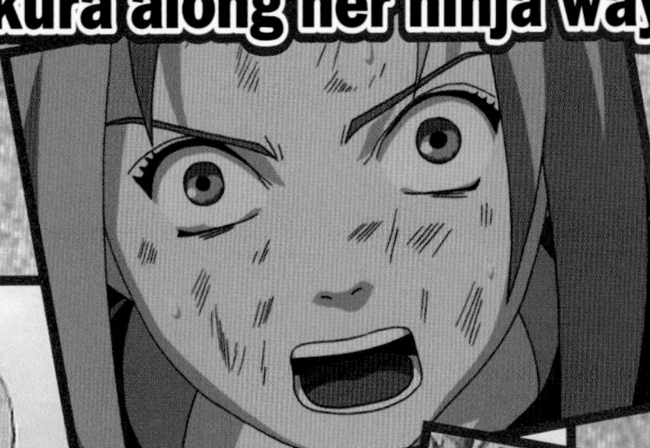

This kunoichi blossoms under pressure, showing her true mettle!

Sakura is always preoccupied with thoughts of love, but she never loses sight of her responsibilities as a shinobi! With her courage and pluck, she charges headlong into any kind of mission! She displays her true strength as a kunoichi by using herself as a shield to protect her client!

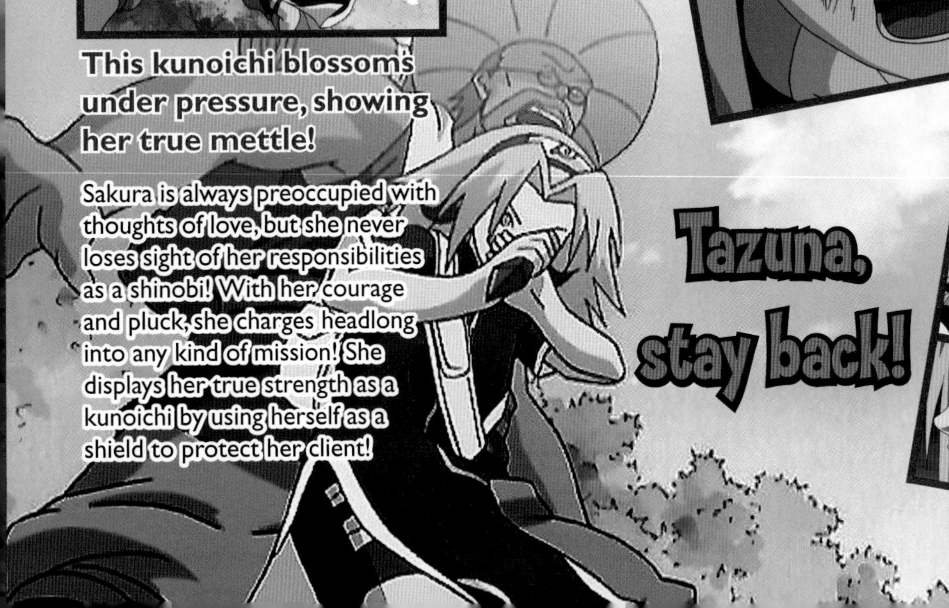
Tazuna, stay back!

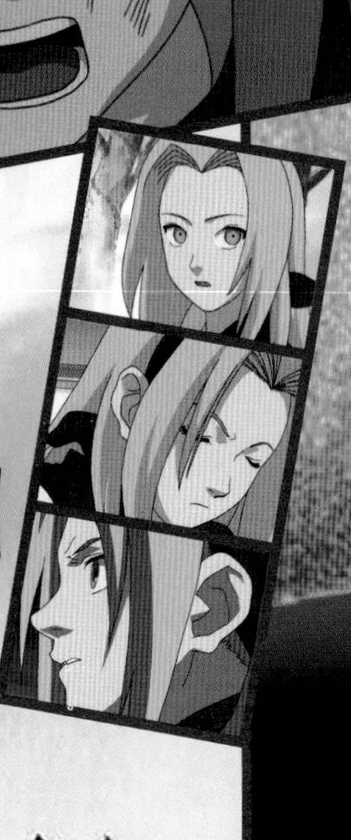

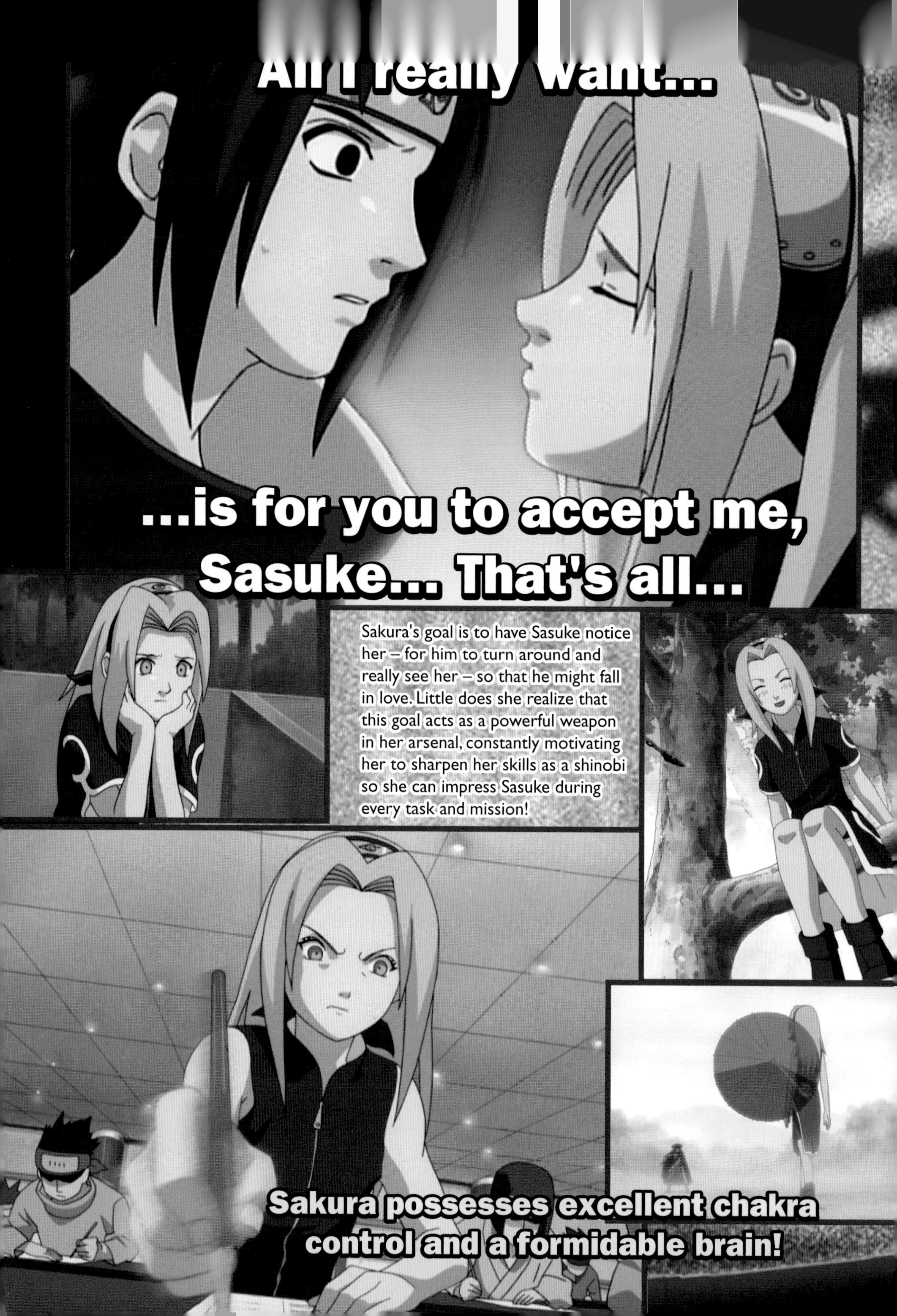
All I really want...
...is for you to accept me, Sasuke... That's all...
Sakura possesses excellent chakra control and a formidable brain!

Sakura's goal is to have Sasuke notice her – for him to turn around and really see her – so that he might fall in love. Little does she realize that this goal acts as a powerful weapon in her arsenal, constantly motivating her to sharpen her skills as a shinobi so she can impress Sasuke during every task and mission!

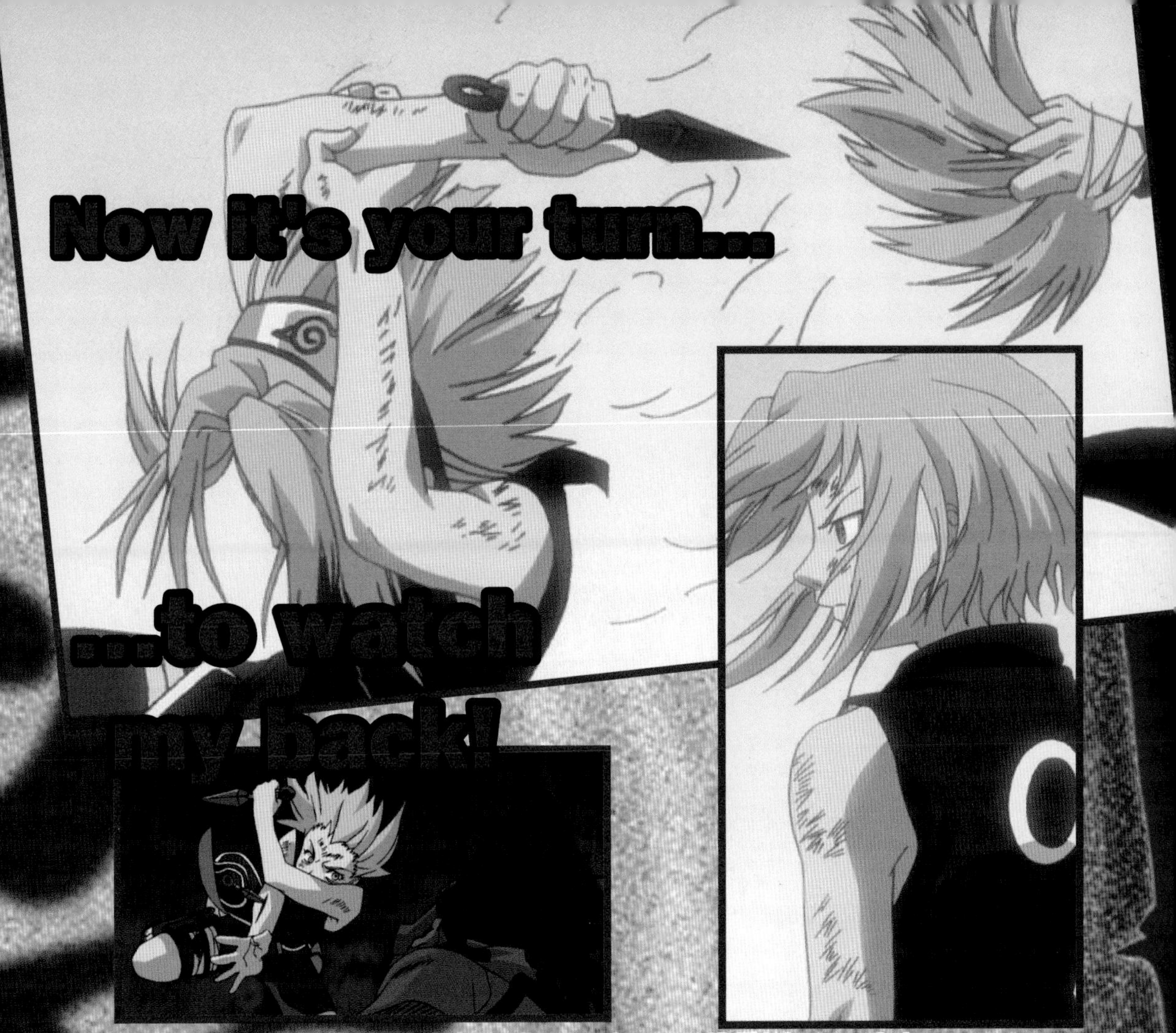
Now it's your turn...
...to watch my back!

As she slices off her hair, Sakura bids farewell to her former self! "I'd always trailed after my teammates… watching them safely from the background…" Faced with a desperate situation, will Sakura's determination lead her to a miraculous victory?!

Ninja Relationships
Sakura Edition

SAKURA HARUNO

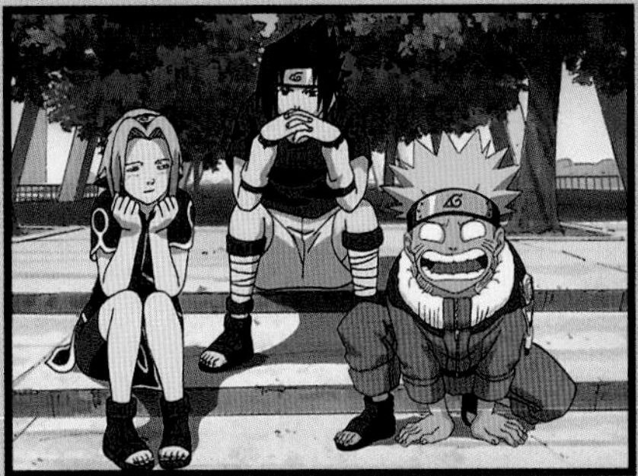

Sakura is completely focused on Sasuke, so Naruto isn't even on her radar! But now she acts as sort of a big sister figure in the squad, mediating conflicts between Naruto and Sasuke.

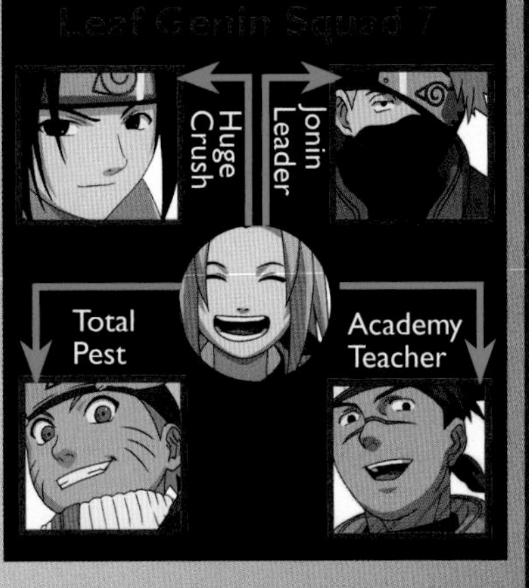
Leaf Genin Squad 7
Huge Crush
Jonin Leader
Total Pest
Academy Teacher

Kakashi Hatake

tai 体 gen 幻 nin 忍

Although Kakashi has advanced-level skills in ninjutsu, taijutsu and genjutsu, he still has the potential to develop his powers even further.

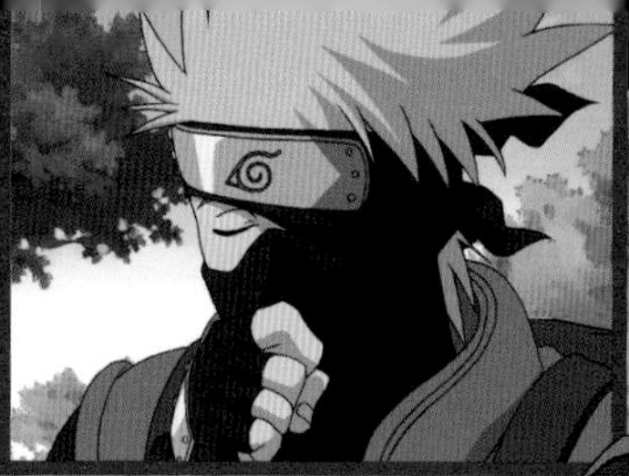

The number one ninja artisan of the Hidden Leaf Village, his name is famous across nations!!

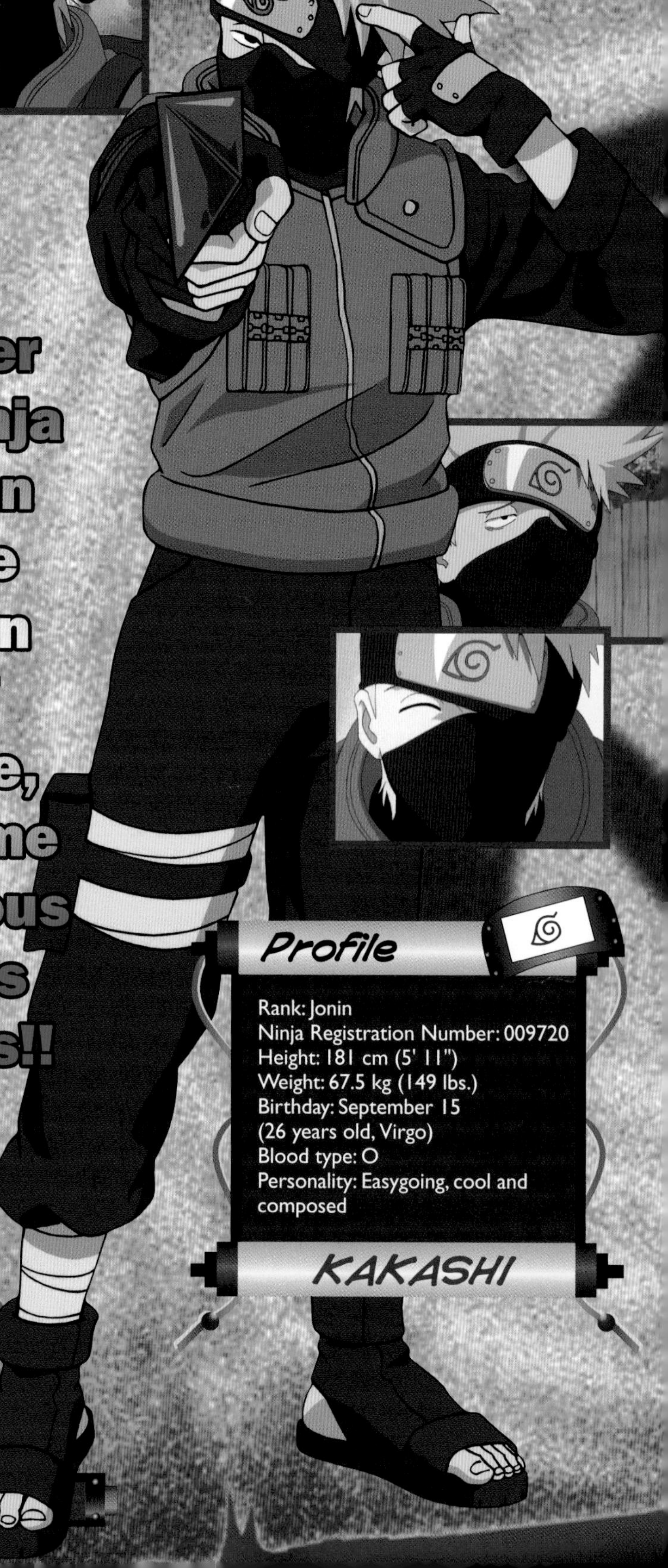

Profile

Rank: Jonin
Ninja Registration Number: 009720
Height: 181 cm (5' 11")
Weight: 67.5 kg (149 lbs.)
Birthday: September 15
(26 years old, Virgo)
Blood type: O
Personality: Easygoing, cool and composed

KAKASHI

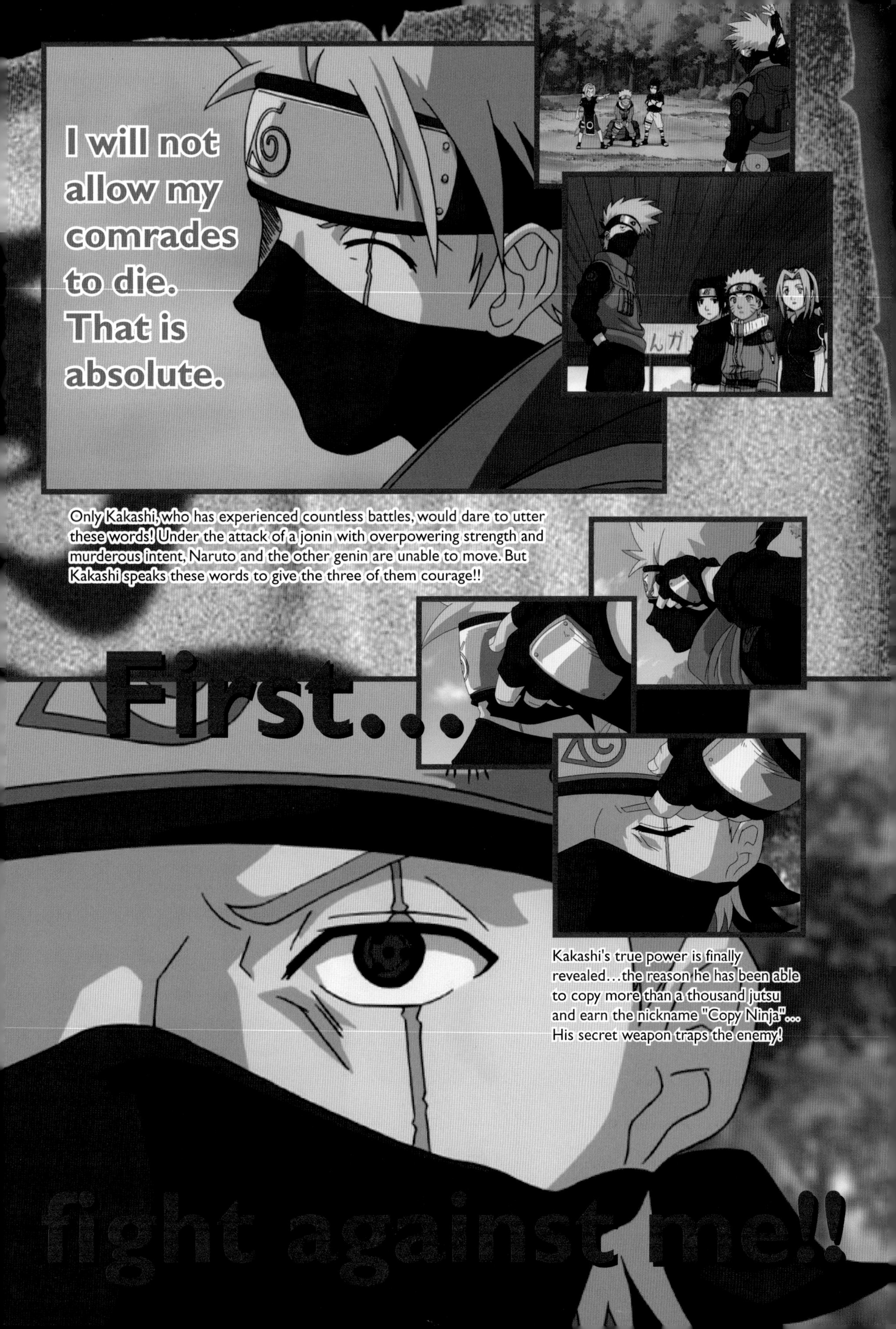
I will not allow my comrades to die. That is absolute.
Only Kakashi, who has experienced countless battles, would dare to utter these words! Under the attack of a jonin with overpowering strength and murderous intent, Naruto and the other genin are unable to move. But Kakashi speaks these words to give the three of them courage!!
First...
Kakashi's true power is finally revealed...the reason he has been able to copy more than a thousand jutsu and earn the nickname "Copy Ninja"... His secret weapon traps the enemy!
fight against me!!

Iruka

Iruka, full of integrity, looks on with a strict but caring gaze!

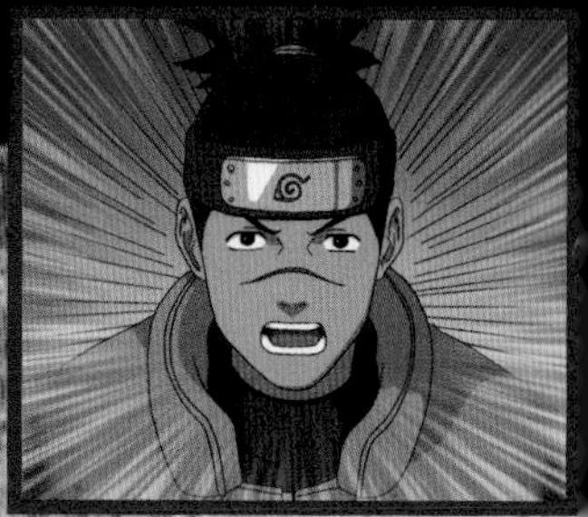

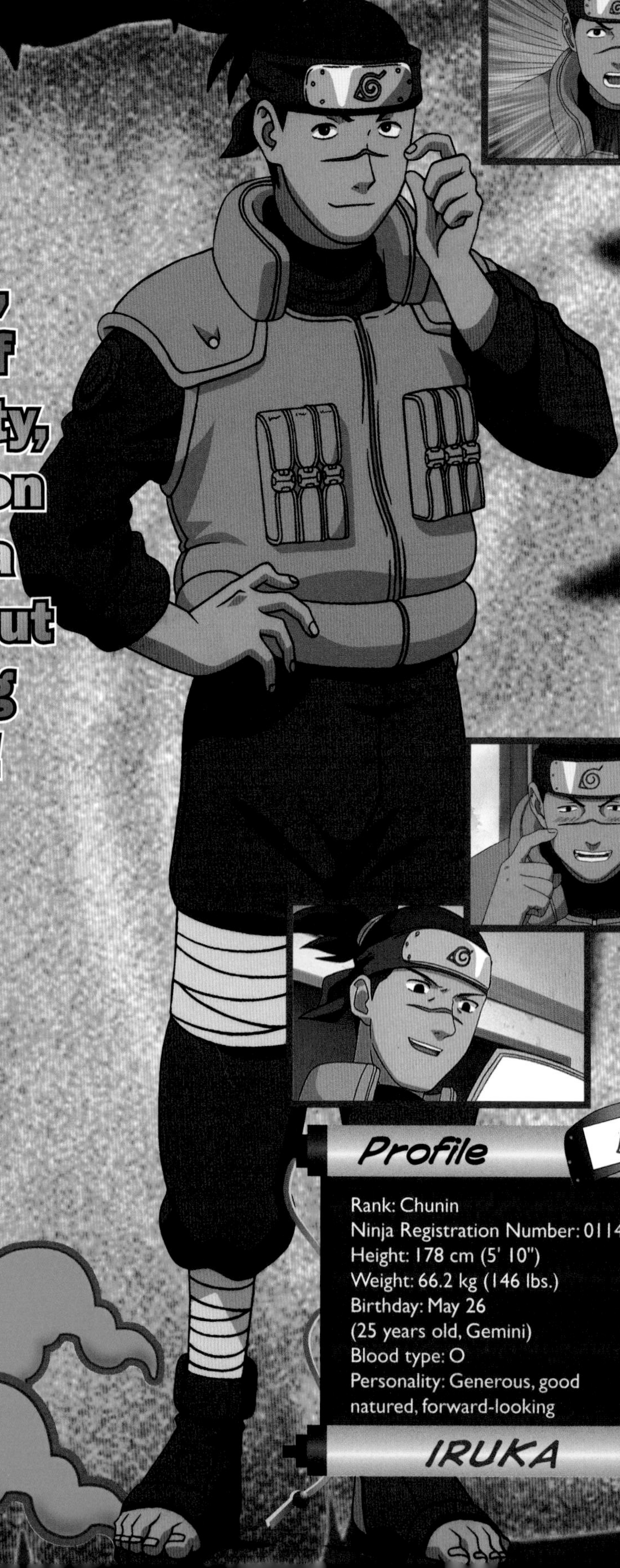

Iruka is very clear-headed, and as a chunin, possesses a good balance of ninjutsu, taijutsu and genjutsu.

Profile

Rank: Chunin
Ninja Registration Number: 011450
Height: 178 cm (5' 10")
Weight: 66.2 kg (146 lbs.)
Birthday: May 26
(25 years old, Gemini)
Blood type: O
Personality: Generous, good natured, forward-looking

IRUKA

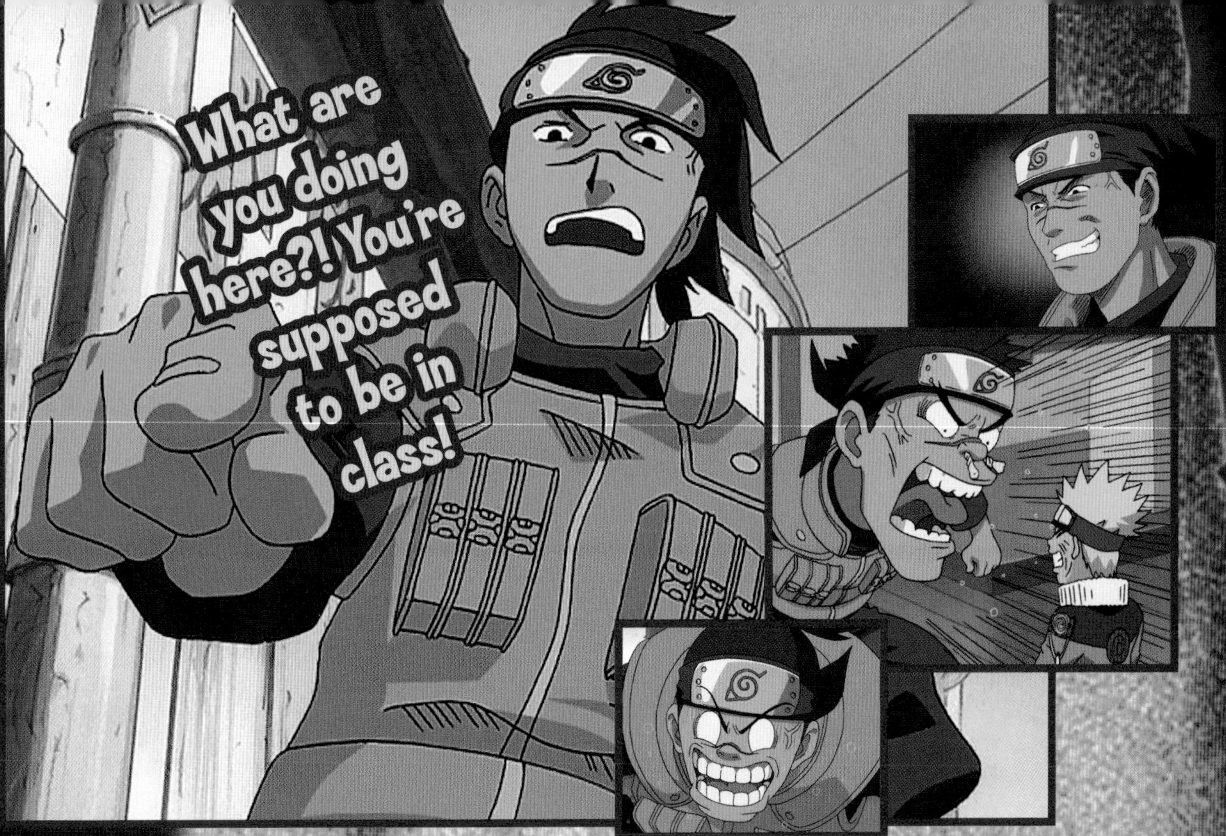
What are you doing here?! You're supposed to be in class!

As a teacher at the Ninja Academy, Iruka is responsible to both the students and the Hokage. But his hands are always full dealing with Naruto's mischief!! Again today, you can hear Iruka's angry voice resounding through the village...

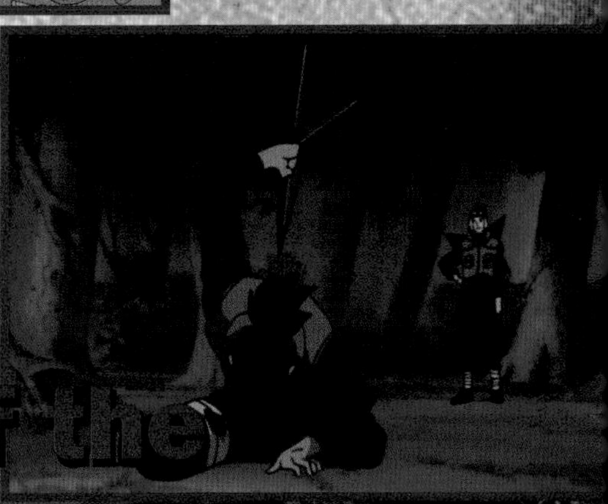

He's Naruto Uzumaki... of the Village Hidden in the Leaves!

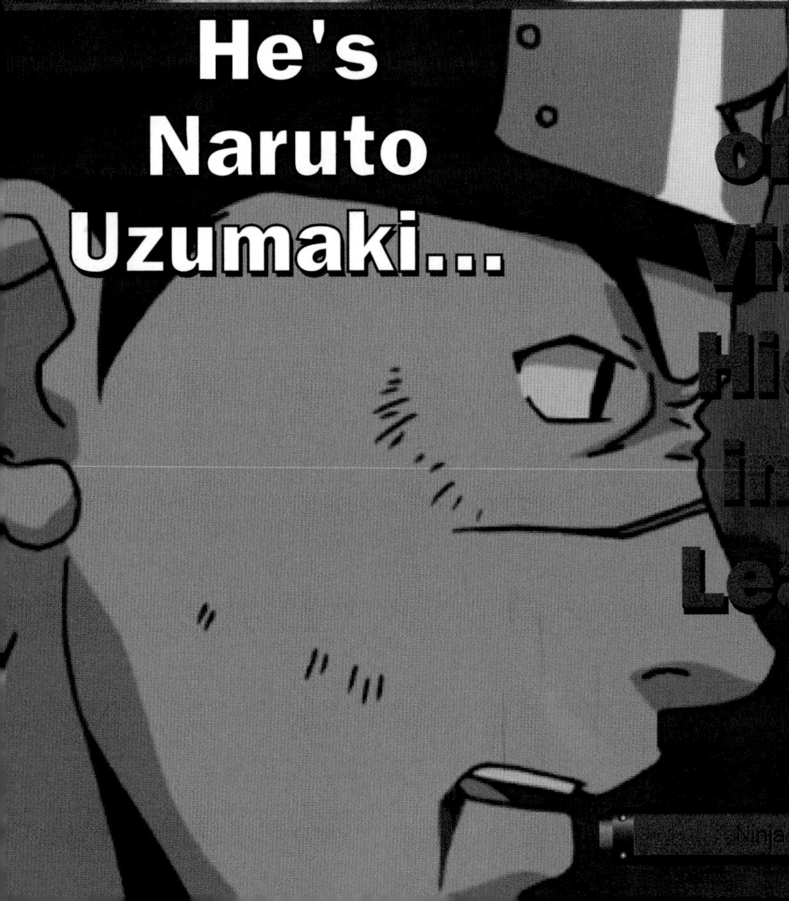

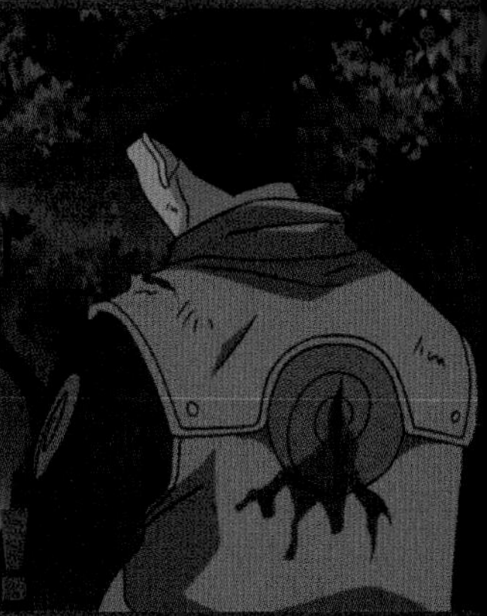

Iruka is one of the few people who understand Naruto and respect him for working hard to achieve his dream. Since he had a lonely childhood himself, he feels Naruto's pain as if it were his own.

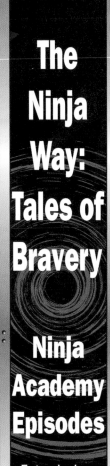

The Ninja Way: Tales of Bravery

Ninja Academy Episodes

Episode 1 to Episode 5: Naruto and his friends' long, treacherous road to become the best ninja they can be starts here!!

Episode 1

Enter: Naruto Uzumaki!

You don't have the guts to do what I do, do ya?! Losers!

Hey! Naruto!!

Naruto is the number one problem child of the Hidden Leaf Village, and mischief is sure to ensue wherever he goes! Even though his grades at the Academy are rock bottom, he dreams of one day becoming the Hokage and forges ahead with the aid of the unlimited power within him. This time, he has dared to put graffiti on the most revered monument in the village, the Great Stone Faces of the Hokage…!

The village is always in an uproar over Naruto!

↑ Iruka has his hands full with Naruto, who loves to make trouble! This kind of scene is a daily occurrence.

First Hokage

Second Hokage

Third Hokage

Fourth Hokage

The Great Stone Faces
This cliff is carved with the images of each generation of Hokage, who stood proudly and led the Village Hidden in the Leaves. This monument is the pride of the village and embodies its history.

This respected symbol of the Hidden Leaf Village displays carvings of the successive generations of Hokage!!

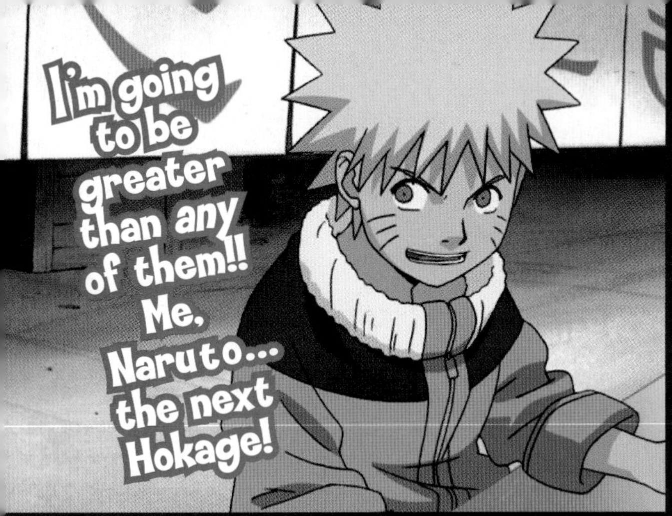
I'm going to be greater than any of them!! Me, Naruto... the next Hokage!

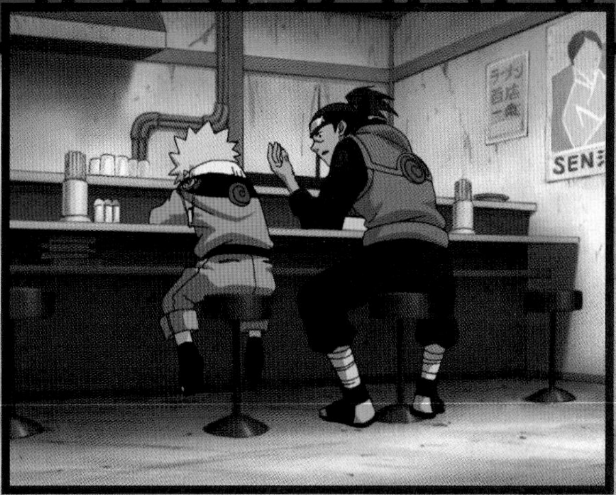

The night before the graduation exam, Naruto makes a bold statement at the Ichiraku Ramen shop, where Iruka is treating him to dinner. Does this mean he's confident that he'll pass the exam?

The first step on the path to a grand dream! What will be the result...?!

His third try at the gradua-tion exam... surely this time he'll succeed!

No matter how much he gets called a good-for-nothing, Naruto refuses to give up his dream of becoming a Ninja. As the exam begins, he's bursting with confidence and energy! Is the third time the charm?

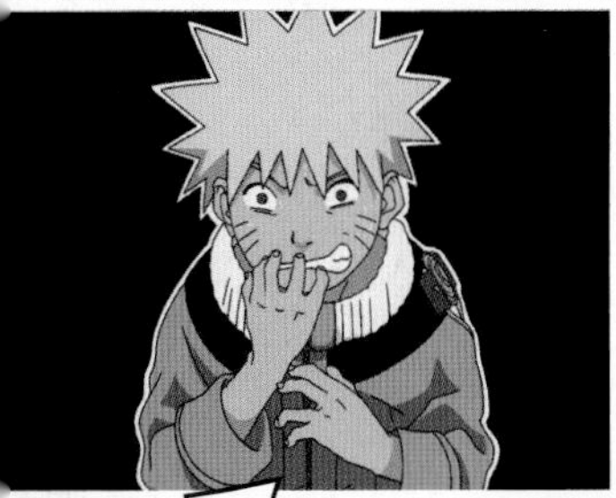

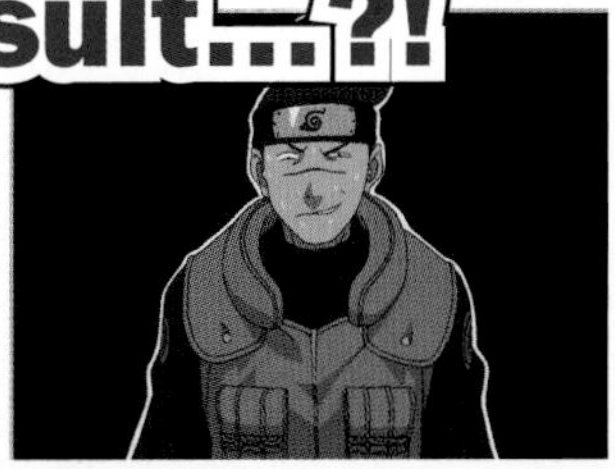

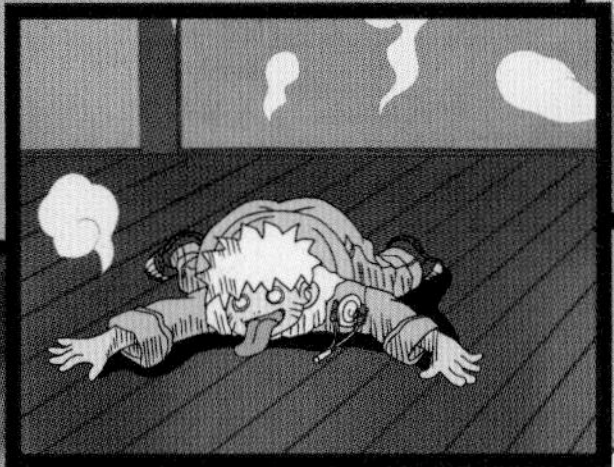

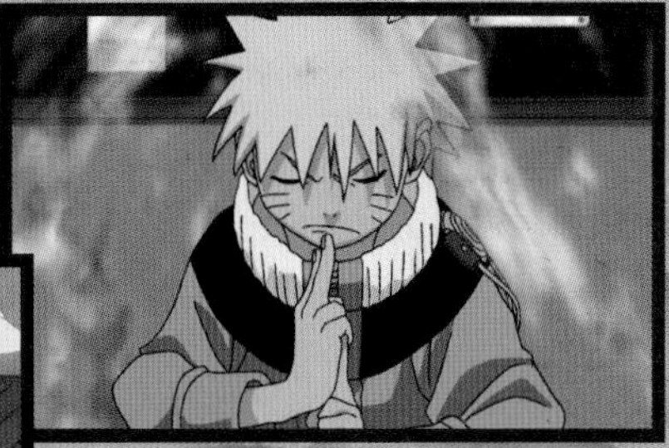

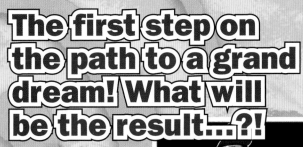

The exam is on the Clone Jutsu, Naruto's worst ninjutsu. He is able to create one pitiful clone, but...

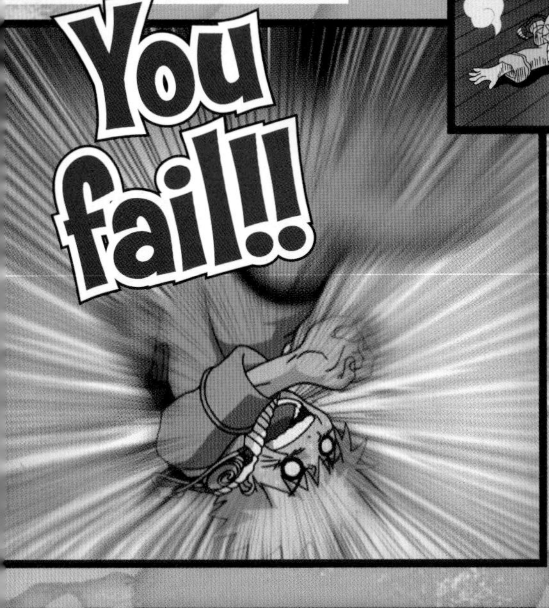
You fail!!

Naruto's favorite restaurant!

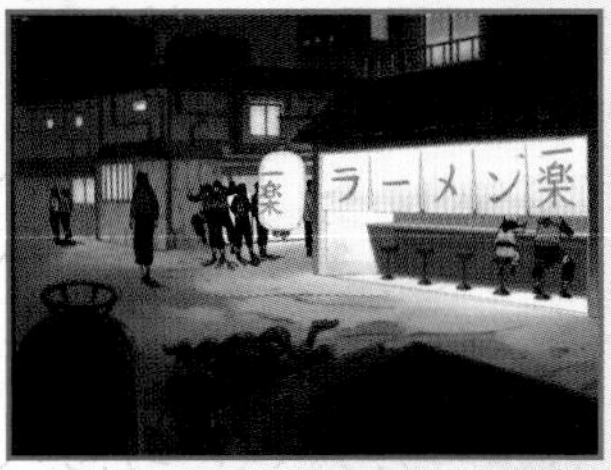
ラーメン

Ichiraku Ramen

This famous restaurant is operated by Teuchi, who has dedicated 30 years of his life to ramen, and his beloved daughter Ayame. The flavor of Teuchi's ramen, which lingers long after the meal is done, has resulted in many regulars over the years.

Mizuki's dark ambition bares its fangs!!

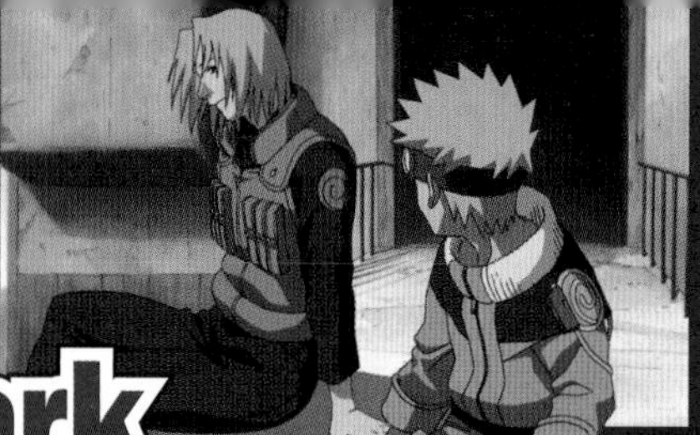

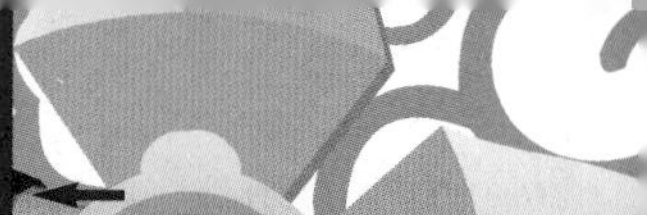

After Naruto fails the exam, Mizuki tells him of the existence of the Scroll of Sealing…

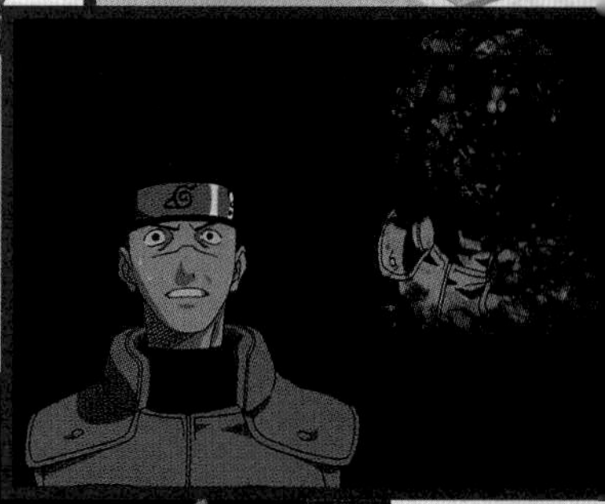

Iruka is shocked after learning of Mizuki's plan to take advantage of Naruto!

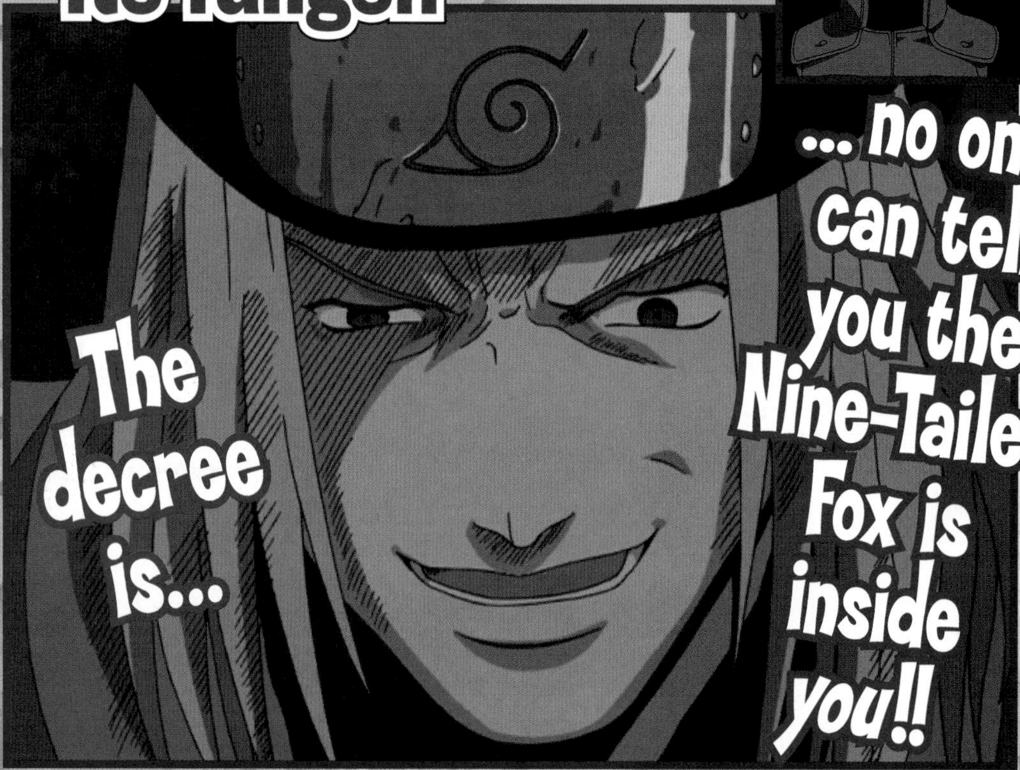
The decree is…
… no one can tell you the Nine-Tailed Fox is inside you!!

After revealing his true, sinister character, Mizuki tells Naruto the whole story of the loathsome secret…

Iruka's pained protests are futile, and Naruto finally learns that the Nine-Tailed Fox is sealed within his body!!

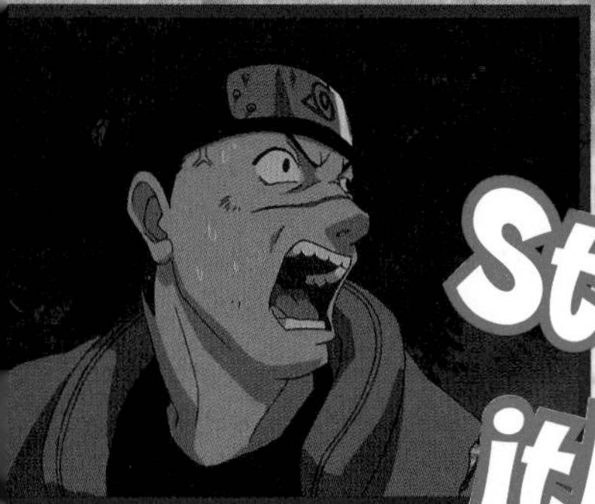
Stop it!!

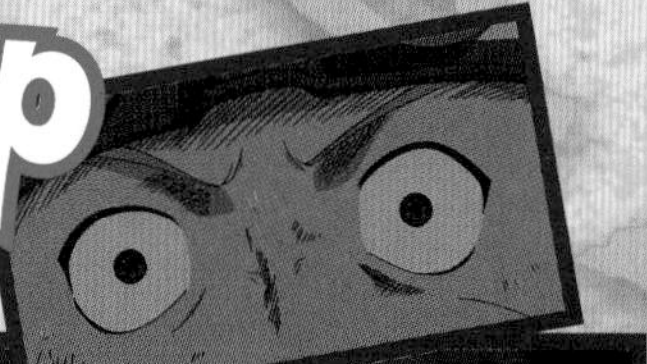

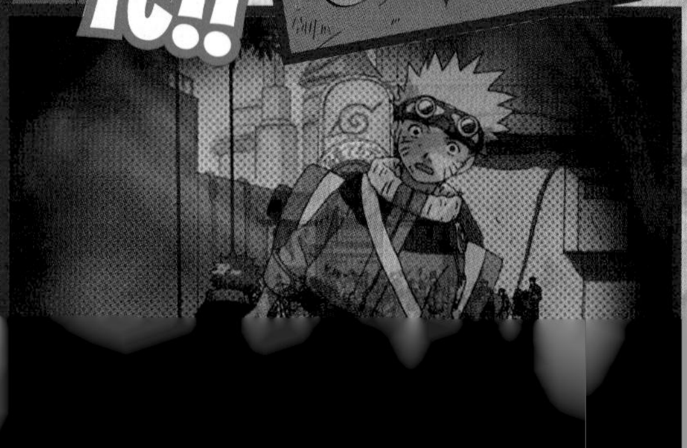

The shocking truth is revealed to Naruto!

Mizuki plans to take advantage of Naruto's depression after failing the exam by persuading him to steal the Scroll of Sealing. When Mizuki's plot is close to fruition, he breaks the decree of the village and tells Naruto the hidden secret…!

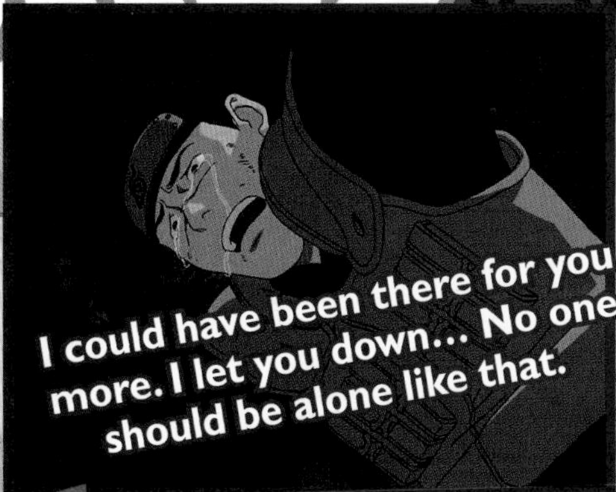
I could have been there for you more. I let you down... No one should be alone like that.

…Iruka sacrifices his own body to protect his student!

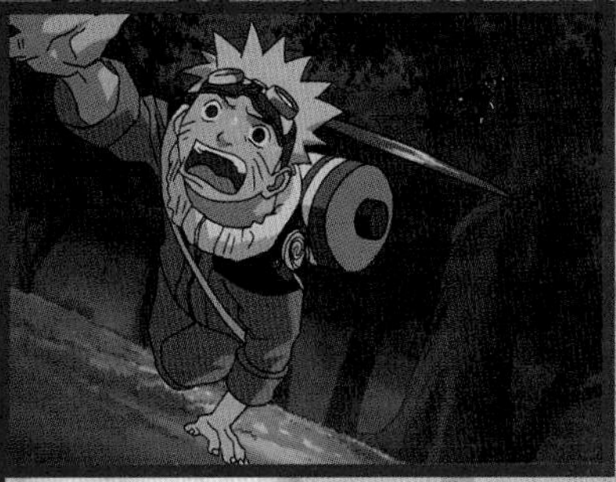

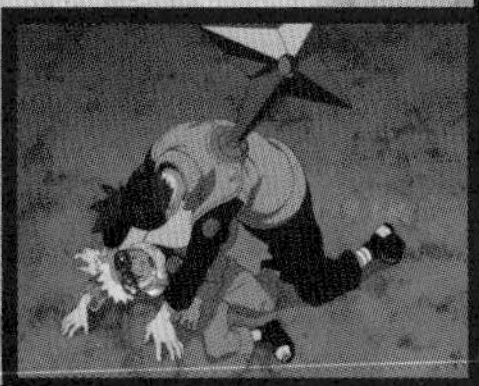

The moment Mizuki's shuriken is about to strike Naruto…

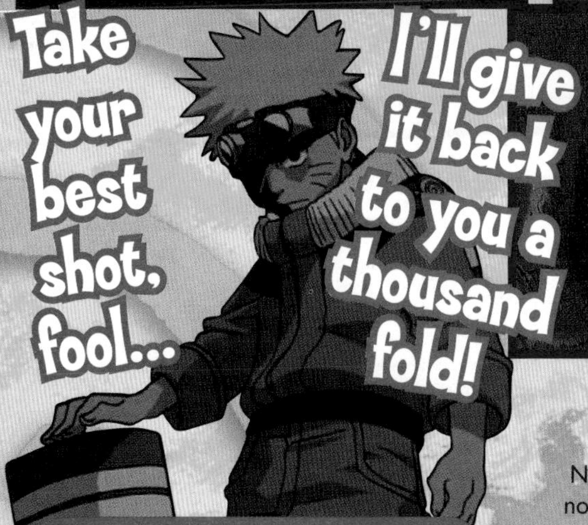
Take your best shot, fool...
I'll give it back to you a thousand fold!

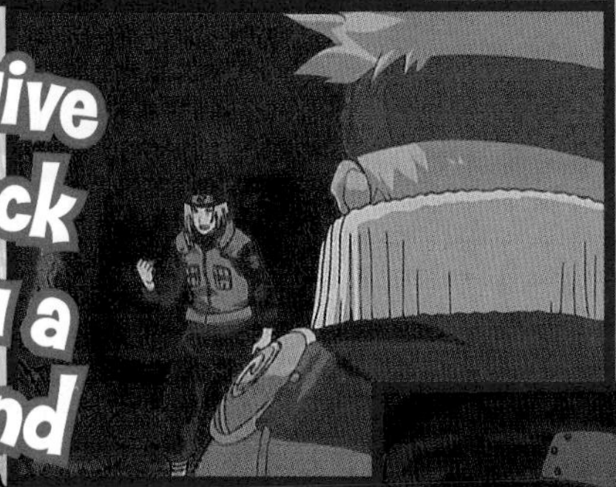

Mizuki turns his attacks on Iruka, who has just saved Naruto's life, and Naruto's anger explodes against Mizuki!

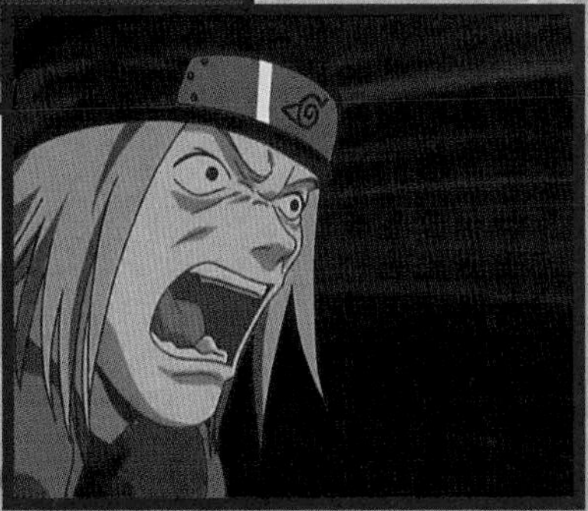

Mizuki refuses to acknowledge Naruto's humanity, no matter what. As he attacks Naruto, Mizuki wears a vicious expression!

Naruto's heretofore undiscovered power bursts forth!

Iruka throws his own body in the way of Mizuki's shuriken to protect Naruto. Naruto boils with rage at Mizuki's cruelty and finally releases the forbidden jutsu he just mastered!!

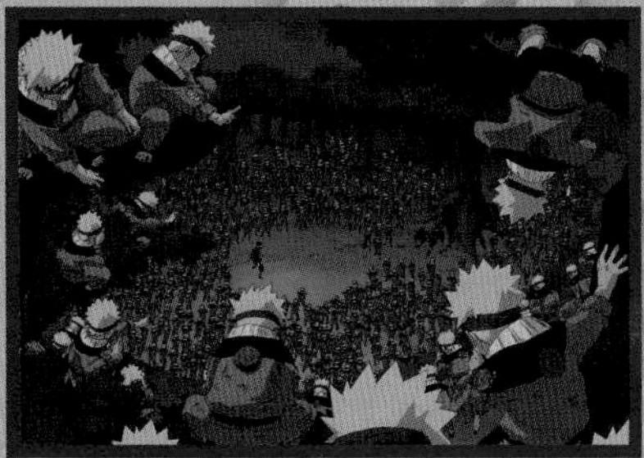

Shadow Clone Jutsu! Naruto brilliantly defeats Mizuki with the high-level ninjutsu he just learned!

The tragic events of Iruka's childhood…

Iruka's past

Iruka lost his parents 12 years ago when the Nine-Tailed Fox attacked the village. Because he experienced the desolation of growing up as an orphan, Iruka understands Naruto's emotions…

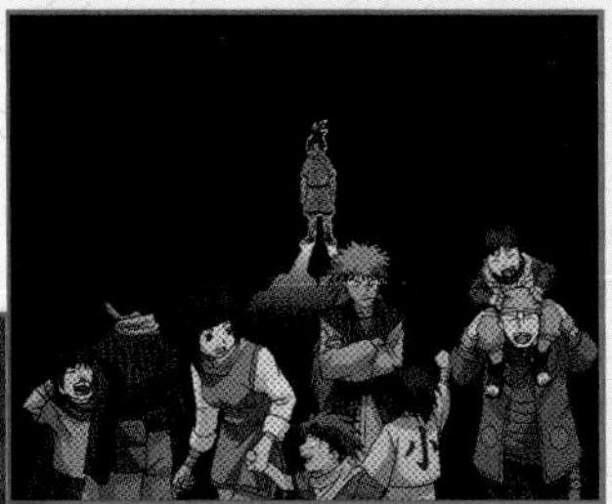

After losing the love and attention provided by his parents, Iruka endured many lonely years as a child.

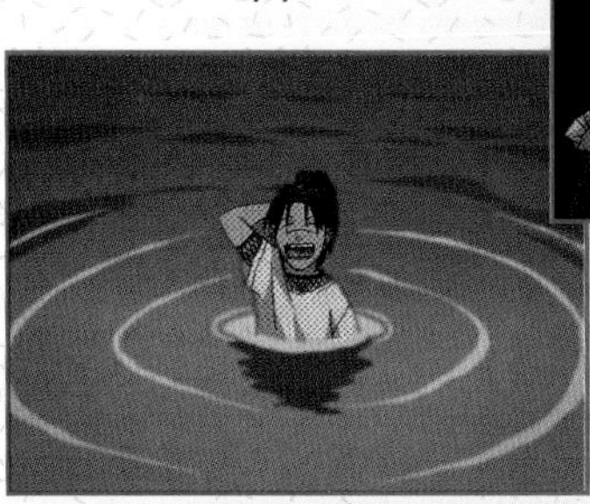

Iruka often did silly, outrageous things in an effort to get others to notice him… much like Naruto does today.

Episode Two

My Name Is Konohamaru!

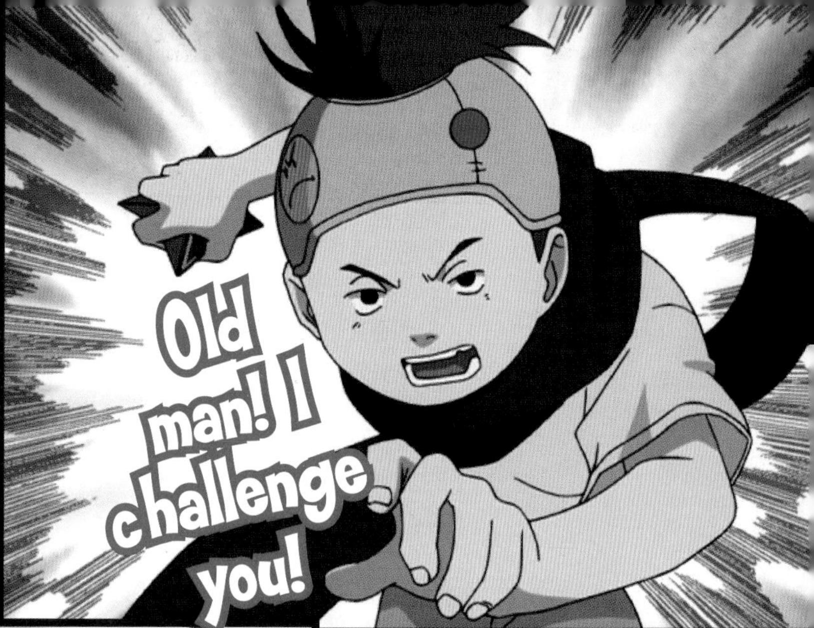
Old man! I challenge you!

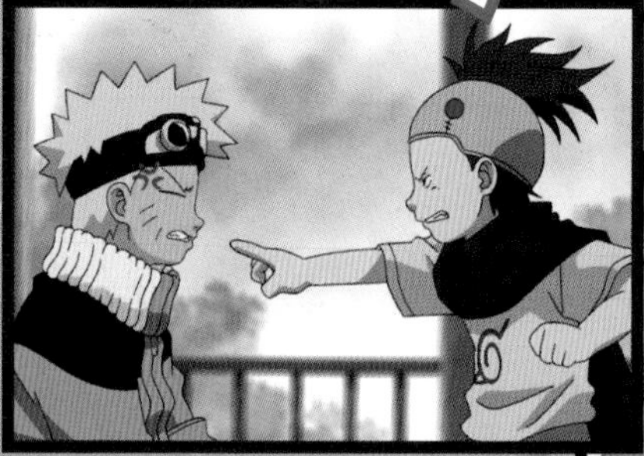

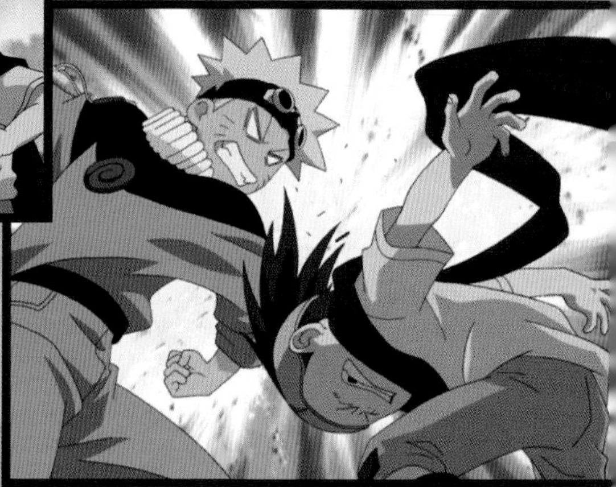

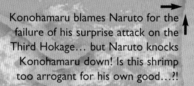

Konohamaru blames Naruto for the failure of his surprise attack on the Third Hokage… but Naruto knocks Konohamaru down! Is this shrimp too arrogant for his own good…?!

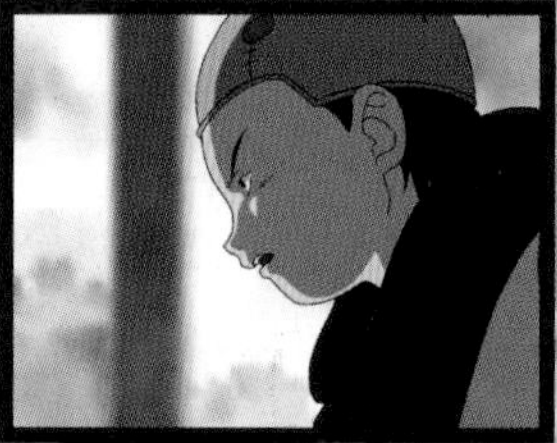

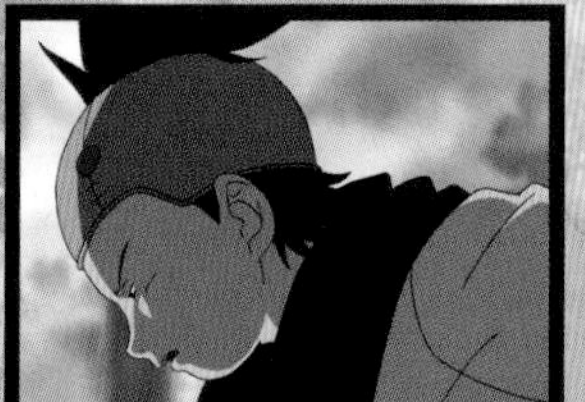

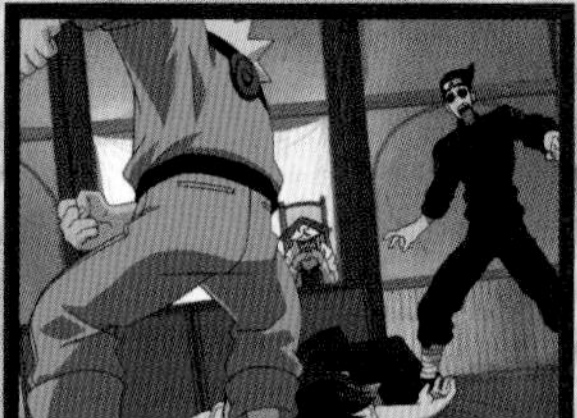

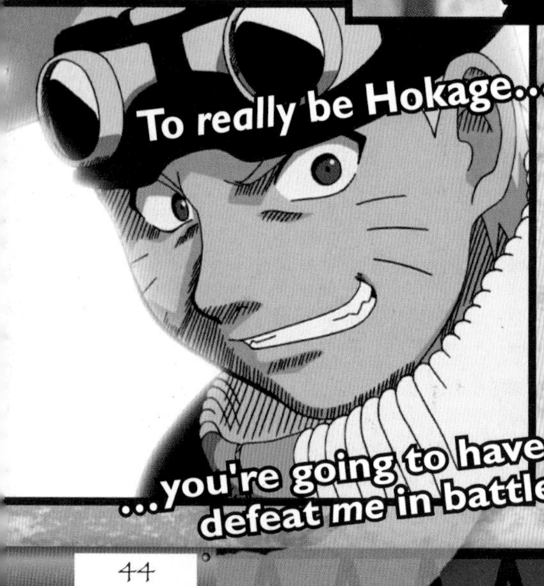
To really be Hokage…
…you're going to have to defeat me in battle!

To add more fuel to the fire of Konohamaru's passion to become Hokage, Naruto challenges him!

Naruto and Konohamaru's strange relationship!

Konohamaru becomes Naruto's student in order to defeat his grandfather, the Third Hokage, and eventually win the title of Hokage for himself. Naruto attempts to teach Konohamaru the Sexy Jutsu (the technique he used to incapacitate the Third Hokage), taking him to places like the bookstore and public bath for training…

Naruto refuses to back down against Ebisu, who only shows contempt for his opponent!

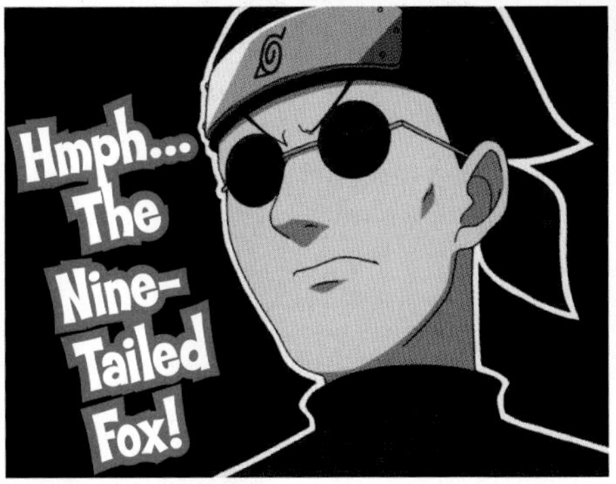
Hmph... The Nine-Tailed Fox!

Naruto reveals his special talents!

In order to re-exert his authority over his student Konohamaru, Ebisu goes head-to-head against Naruto…!! What move does Naruto unleash on Ebisu, elite ninja of the village?!

A new secret maneuver that's impossible to predict!

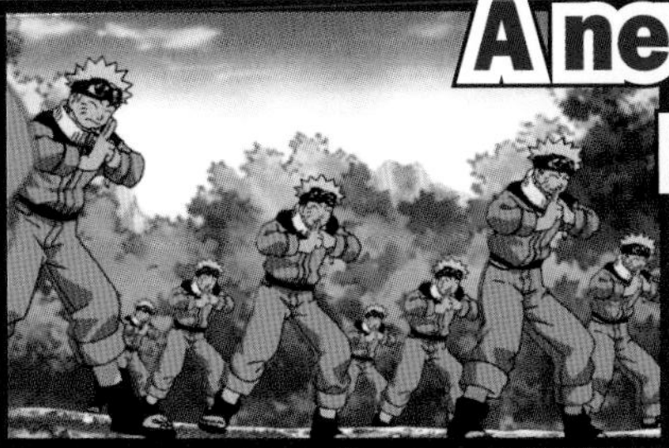

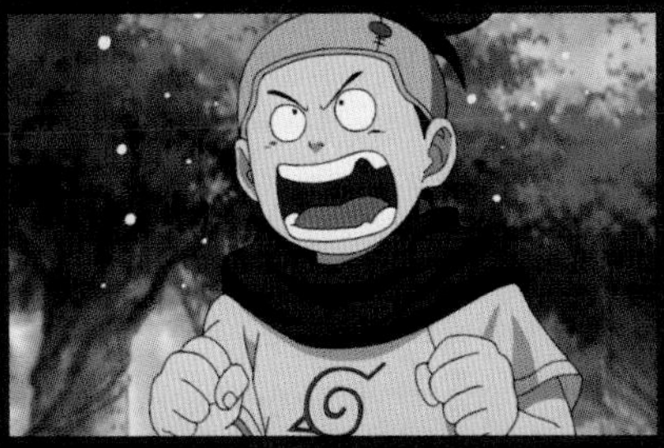

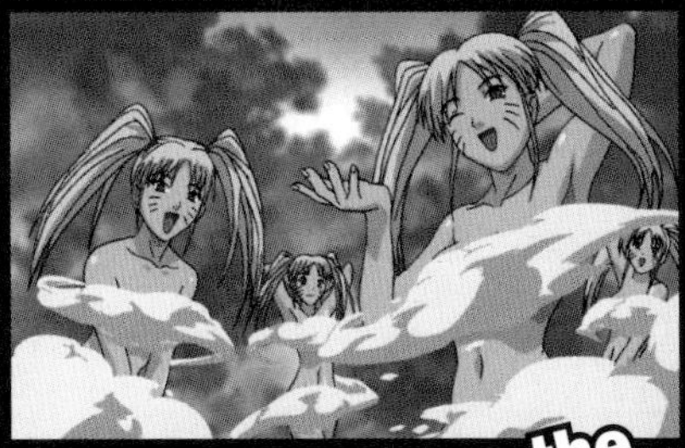

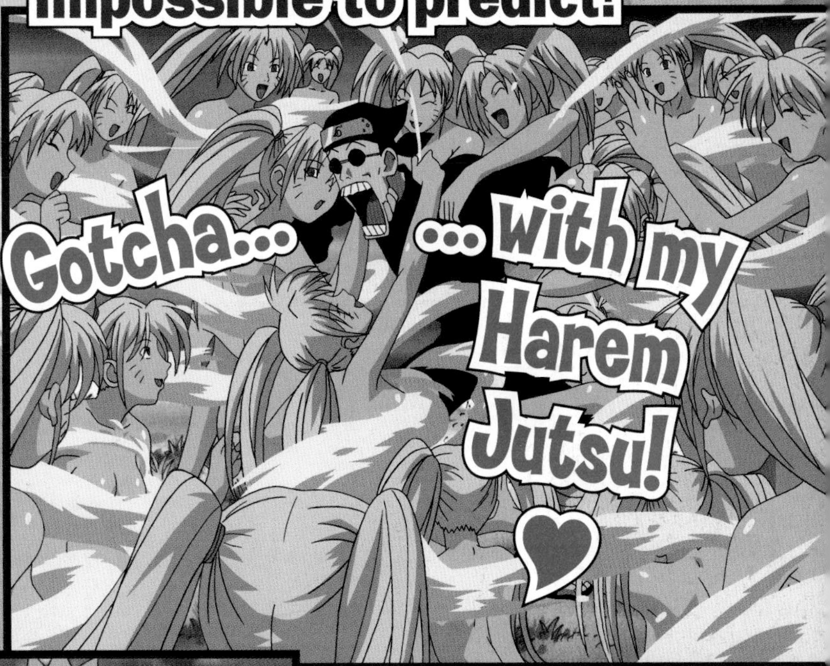
Gotcha...
...with my Harem Jutsu!

There are no shortcuts along the Ninja Way! For now, those are the only words of encouragement that Naruto can give!

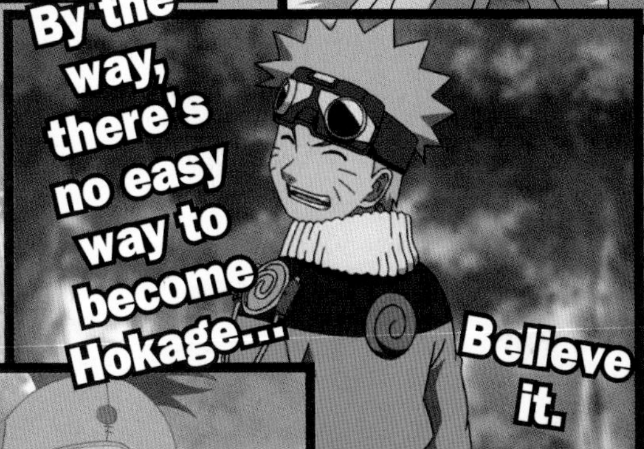
By the way, there's no easy way to become Hokage...
Believe it.

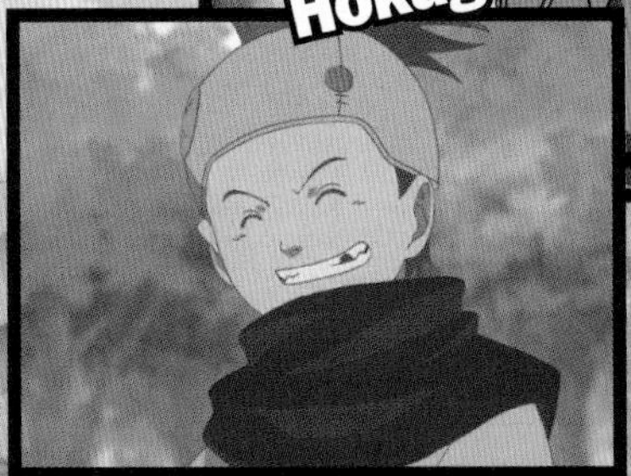

After hearing Naruto's heartfelt advice, Konohamaru is overwhelmed with feelings of affection.

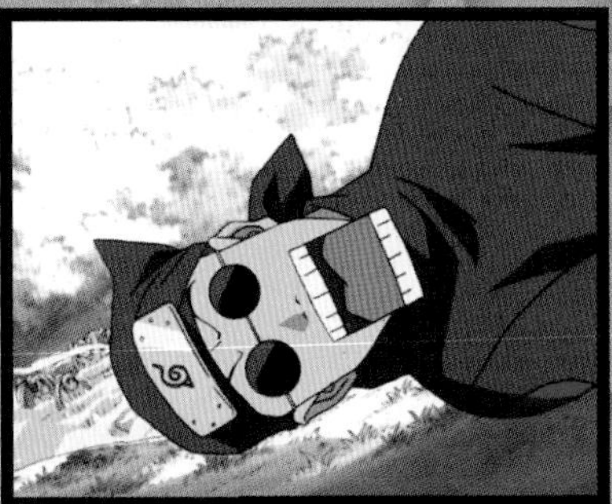

Naruto defeats Ebisu handily by using a new secret maneuver that combines Clone Jutsu with Sexy Jutsu! In the end, Ebisu was defenseless against feminine wiles…

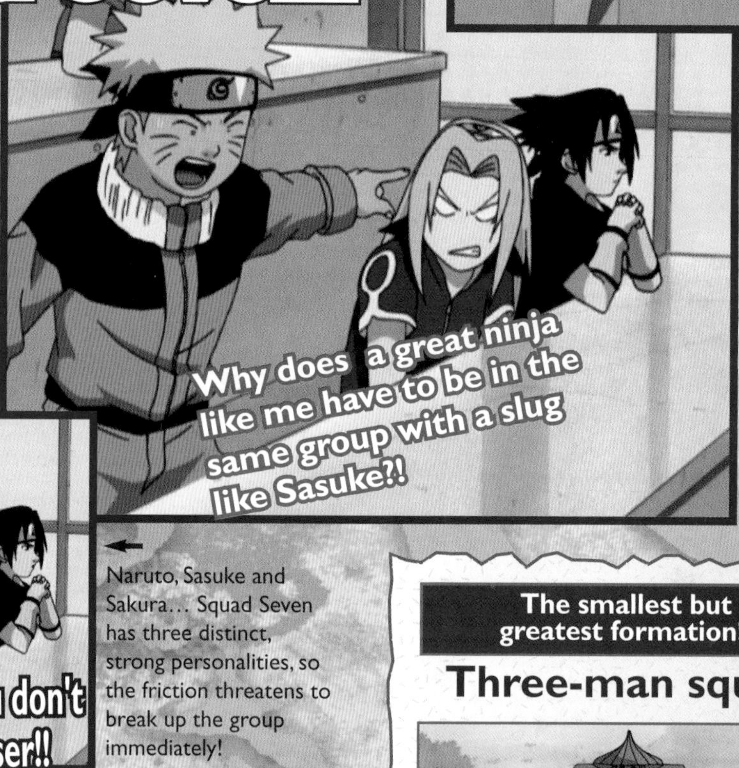

Episodes 3 to 5

The Formation of Leaf Genin Squad Seven!

The new Hidden Leaf Village genin assemble to hear Iruka announce the roster of three-man squads.

Why does a great ninja like me have to be in the same group with a slug like Sasuke?!

Naruto explodes with frustration when he learns his squad assignment!

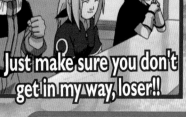

Just make sure you don't get in my way, loser!!

Naruto, Sasuke and Sakura… Squad Seven has three distinct, strong personalities, so the friction threatens to break up the group immediately!

The incompatible threesome have a rocky relationship from the start!

Naruto, proud to have finally become a genin, is thrilled about being assigned to the same squad as Sakura, the girl he likes! But he's extremely unhappy to be squadmates with Sasuke, whom he hates! The different dreams of the three members mingle and conflict, but for now, this group is a team!

The smallest but greatest formation!!

Three-man squads

Shinobi who become genin embark on missions in three-man squads and develop teamwork skills. Each squad is led by a shinobi of chunin rank or higher, and, during their missions, the squad members act in concert with their instructor as a four-person group.

The jonin in charge of Squad Seven is Kakashi Hatake!

Naruto gets frustrated with waiting for Kakashi, who is late to meet his new students. In retaliation, Naruto sets up a predictable prank, but...

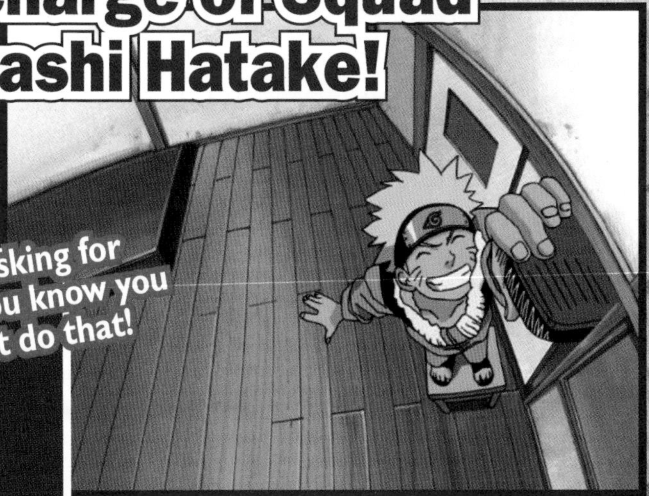

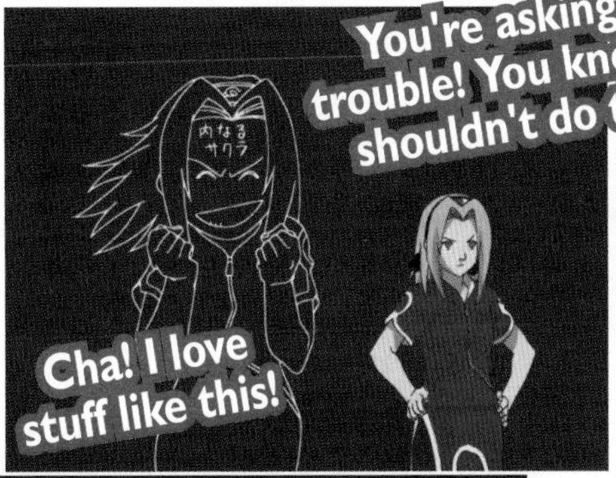
You're asking for trouble! You know you shouldn't do that!
内なる サクラ
Cha! I love stuff like this!

As an honor student, Sakura can't stand by silently while Naruto tricks their new sensei! But inside her heart, she can hardly contain her excitement!

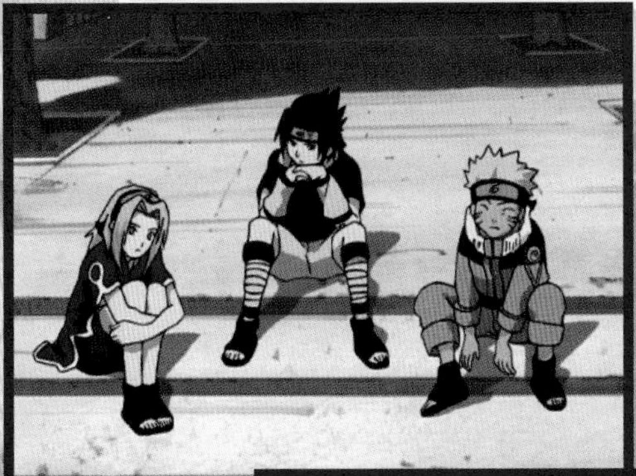

After the shock subsides, the three listen carefully to Kakashi's instructions for the following morning's mission.

Kakashi is assigned to be in charge of Naruto and the others, but because he arrives late and falls prey to Naruto's trap, he doesn't seem to be taking his responsibility seriously. However, after introductions are made, Kakashi suddenly springs a mission on Naruto and Squad Seven…!!

A survival exercise begins immedi-ately after their first meeting!

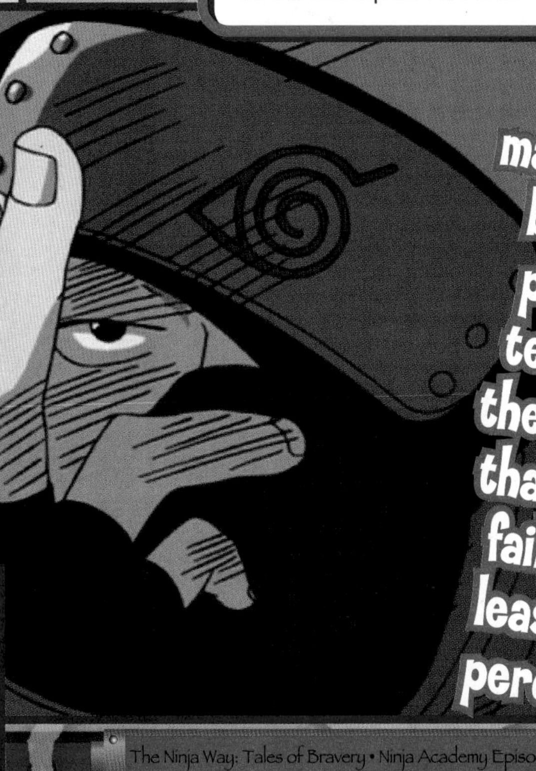

The mission is actually an ultra-difficult exercise in which only nine are chosen to be genin from the group of 27 Academy graduates!!

This is a make-it-or-break-it, pass-fail test. And the chance that you'll fail is at least 66 percent!

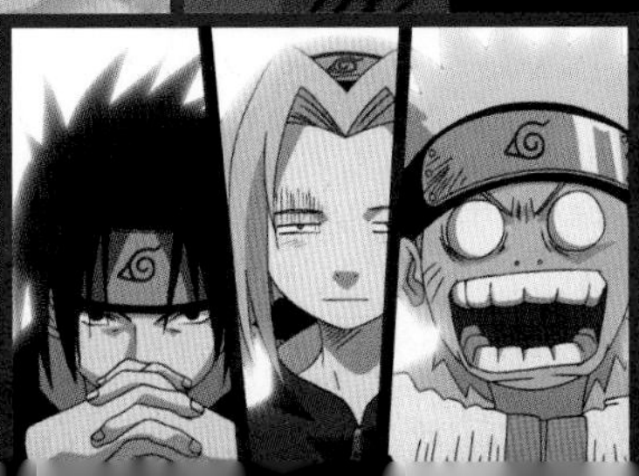

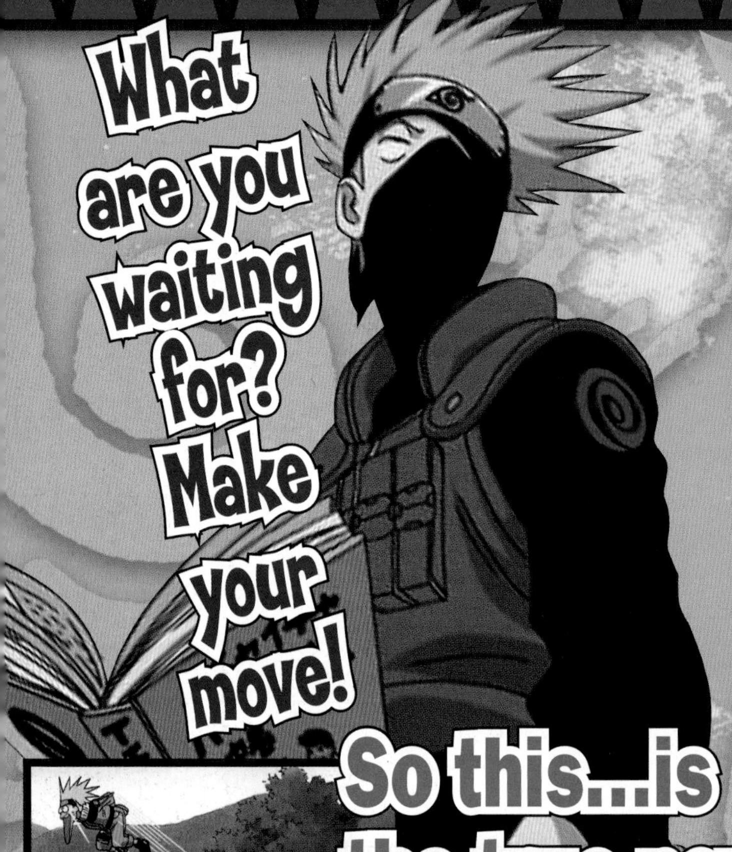

What are you waiting for? Make your move!

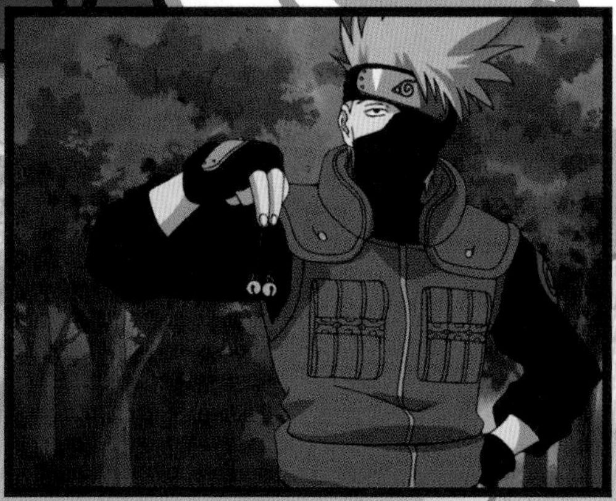

Only the two who grab the bells can pass the test.

Kakashi's decision!

The objective of the survival exercise is to snatch the bells away from Kakashi. But Kakashi's power is way beyond their expectations and the three are forced into a struggle they never expected!

So this...is the true power of a jonin!

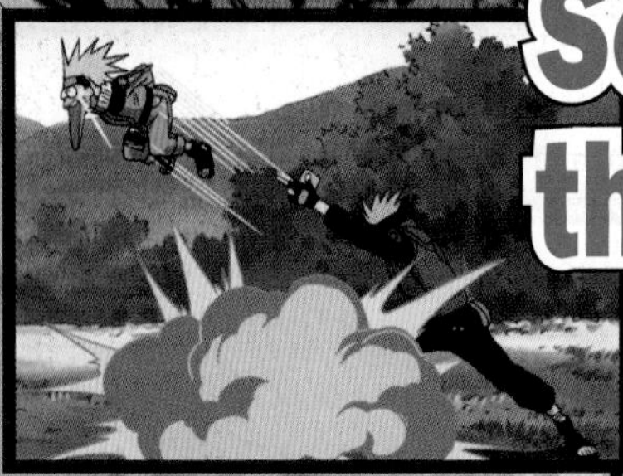

Naruto and Sakura don't even get a chance to counter Kakashi's attacks and are both dispatched handily!

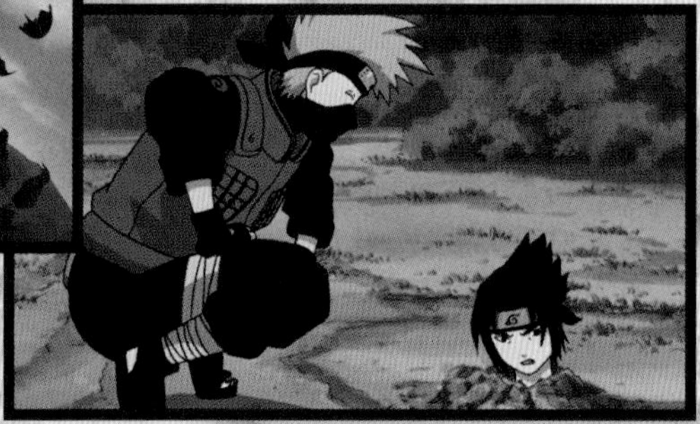

Even Sasuke, who boasts the top grades at Ninja Academy, is no match for Kakashi!

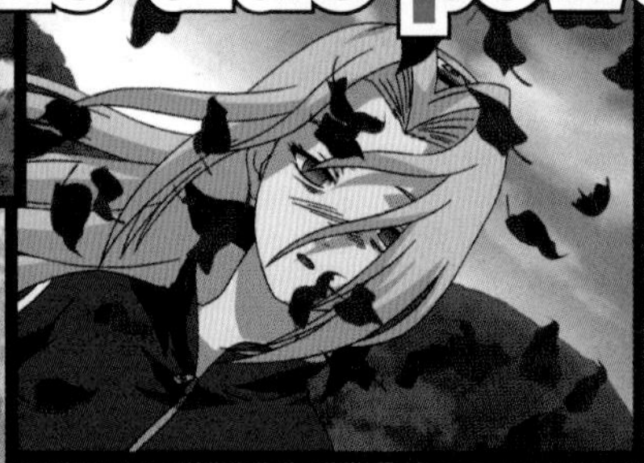

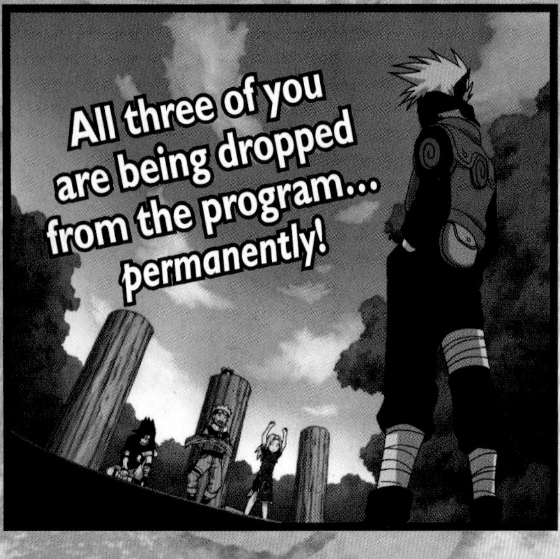
All three of you are being dropped from the program... permanently!

When the allotted time expires, Naruto and others gather together again. Kakashi stares them down and coldly says…

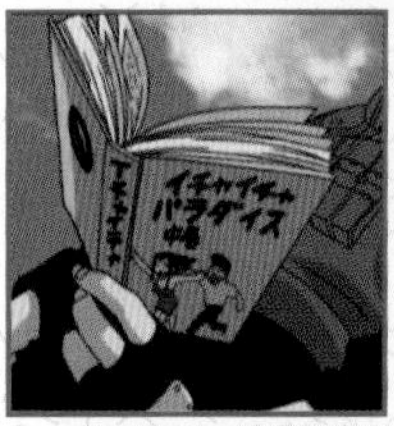

Make-out Paradise

A romance novel trilogy... for adults only!

The age 18-and-over novel that Kakashi loves to read. Comprised of three volumes, the content is rumored to be naughty! ♥

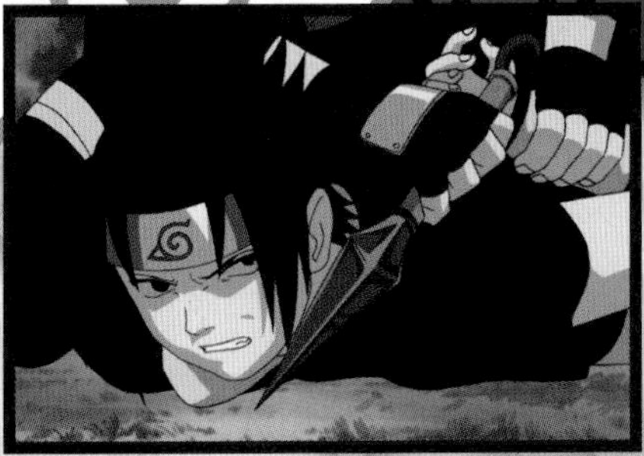

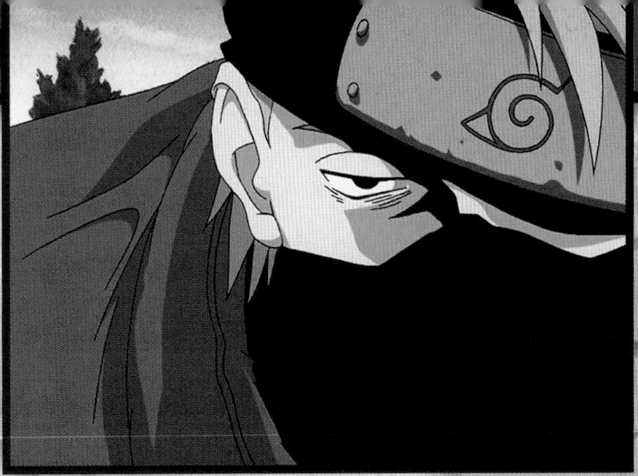

Kakashi is furious with the young ninja for acting selfishly instead of using teamwork to benefit the squad as a whole!

They must read beyond the obvious meaning of the test and uncover the real purpose of this exercise!

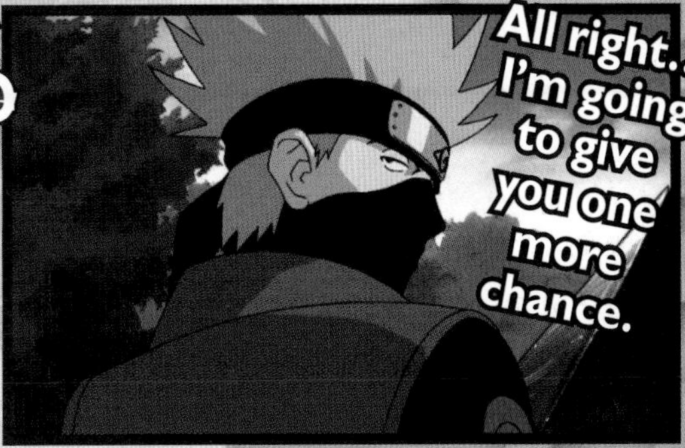
All right... I'm going to give you one more chance.

"Eat lunch now to build up your strength… but Naruto doesn't get any." During the break before the test continues in the afternoon, Kakashi's harsh words shock Sasuke and Sakura!

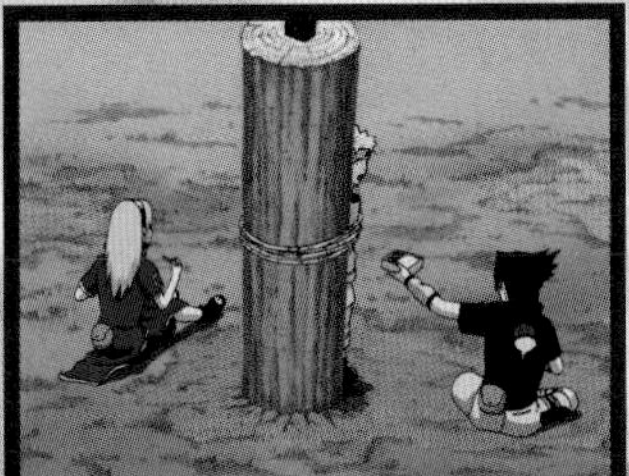

Sasuke daringly shares his lunch with Naruto in spite of Kakashi's warning!

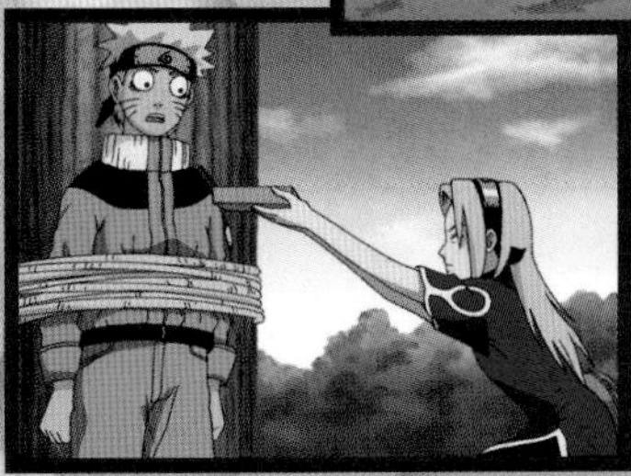

"We need to get those bells as a team." After hearing Sasuke's argument, Sakura agrees with the decision to defy Kakashi.

Even though they disobeyed his orders, Kakashi announces that all three have passed the test. "A ninja must see through deception." The order to not give any lunch to Naruto was another test of the squad's teamwork. And so… Kakashi's exercise reaches its conclusion!

The test is over! Is the result success... or failure?!

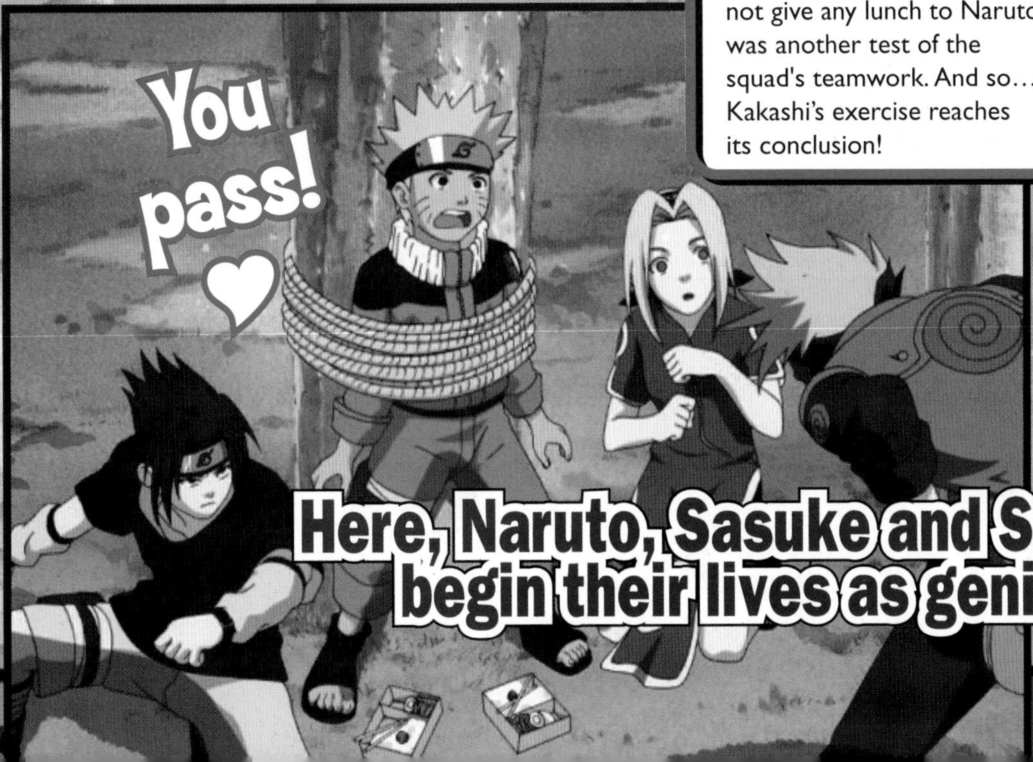
You pass! ♥

Kakashi can't help but smile when he sees the young ninja using teamwork!

Here, Naruto, Sasuke and Sakura begin their lives as genin!

Secret Shinobi Picture Album

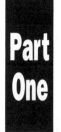

Part One

Ninja Academy

This Shinobi Picture Album introduces Naruto's world through never-before-seen design illustrations. Your guide to the Ninja Academy portion is, of course, Iruka-sensei!

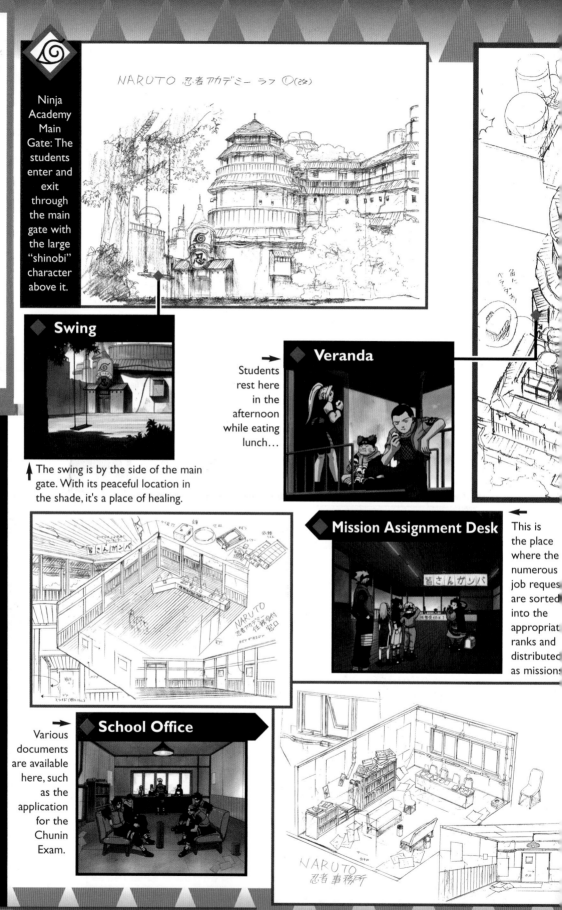

Ninja Academy Main Gate: The students enter and exit through the main gate with the large "shinobi" character above it.

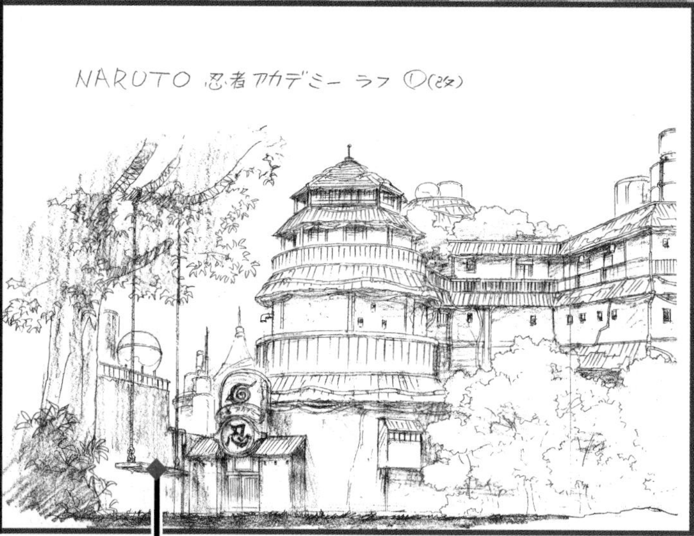
NARUTO 忍者アカデミー ラフ ①(改)

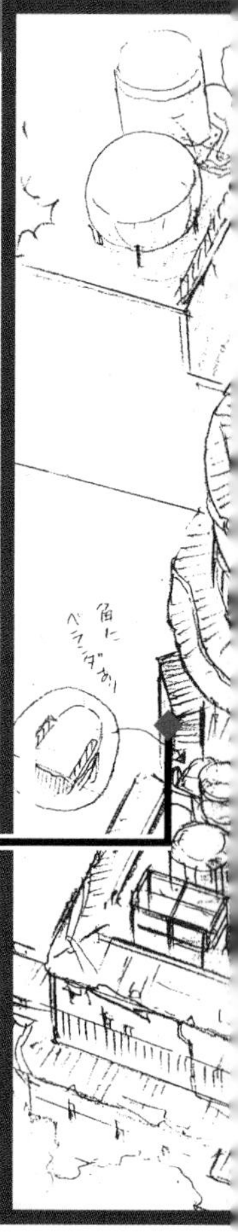

Swing

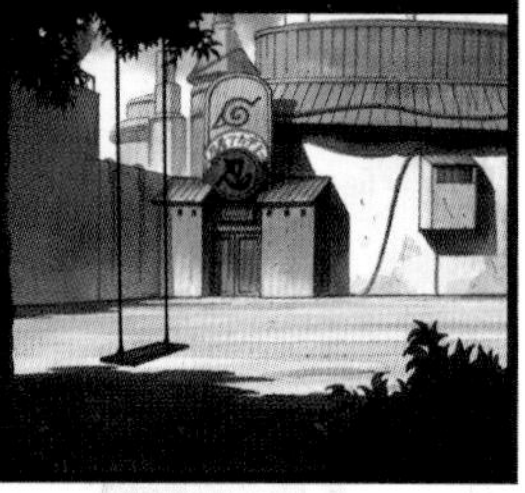

The swing is by the side of the main gate. With its peaceful location in the shade, it's a place of healing.

Veranda

Students rest here in the afternoon while eating lunch…

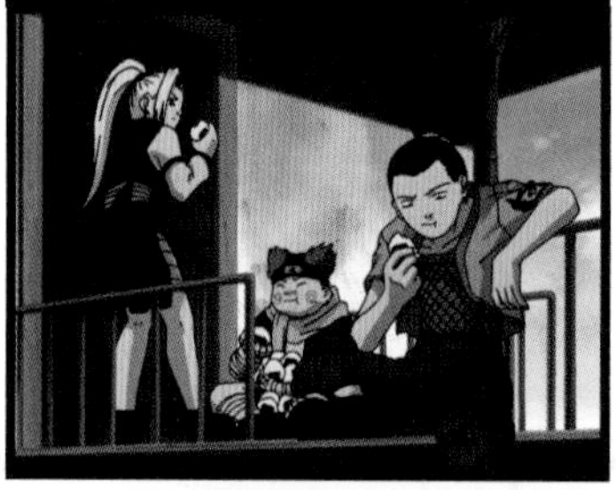

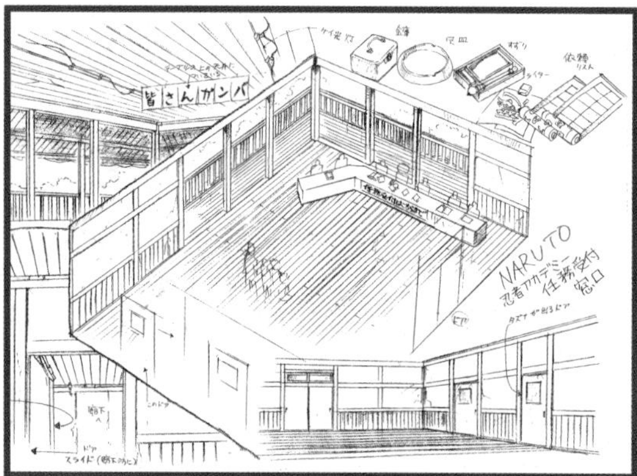
皆さんガンバ
NARUTO
忍者アカデミー
任務受付
窓口

Mission Assignment Desk

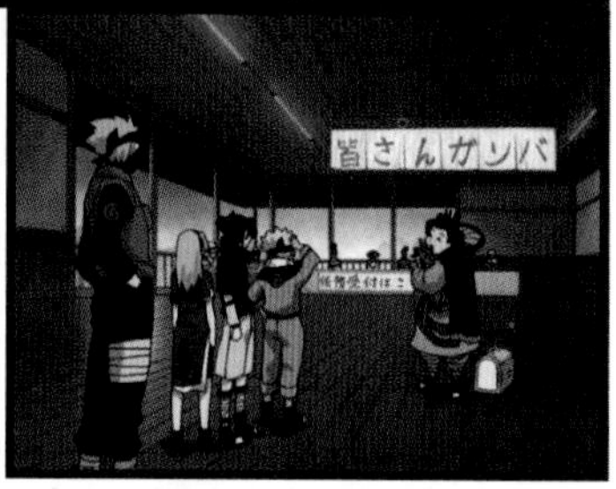
皆さんガンバ

This is the place where the numerous job reques are sorted into the appropriat ranks and distributed as mission

School Office

Various documents are available here, such as the application for the Chunin Exam.

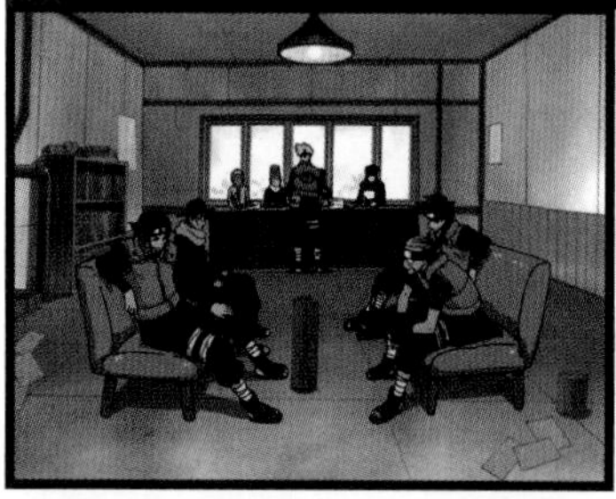

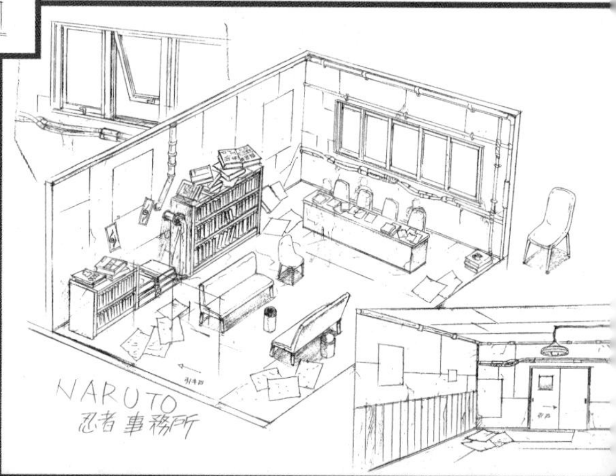
NARUTO
忍者事務所

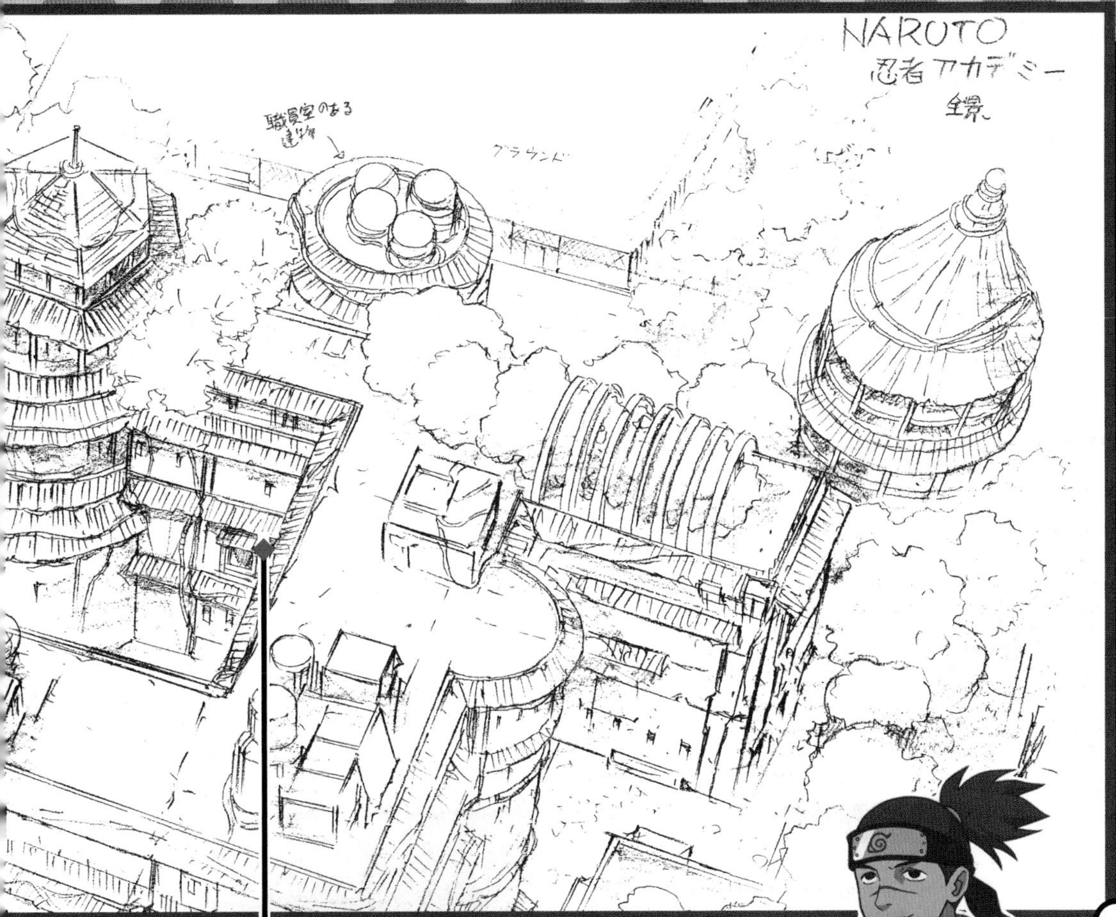
NARUTO
忍者アカデミー
全景
職員室のある建物
グラウンド

Bird's-eye view of Ninja Academy: the campus is composed of multiple buildings, and even the rooftops are used efficiently.

Storage

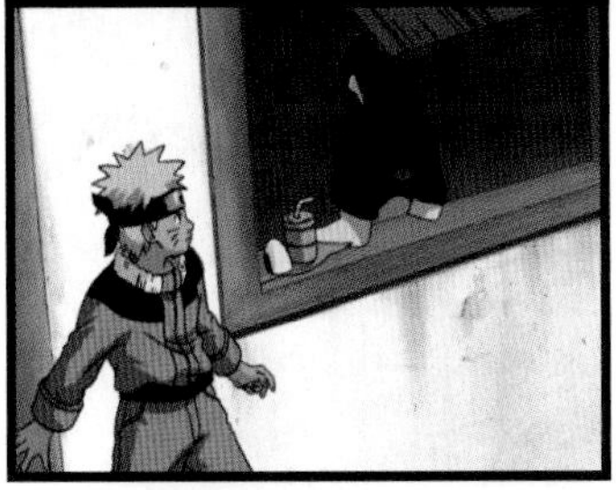

Vaulting horses are kept in the storage area where Naruto ambushed Sasuke.

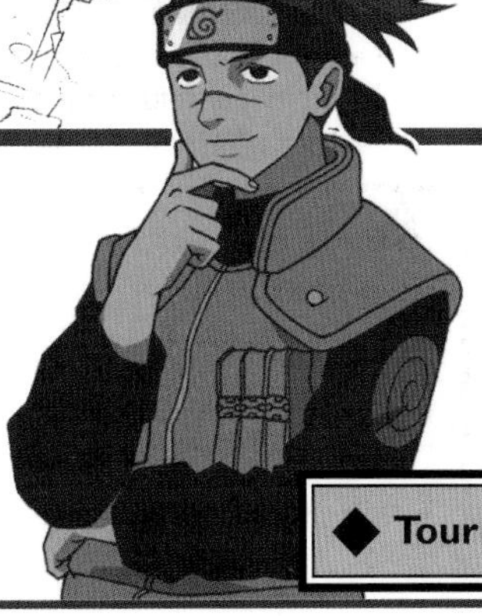
Okay, everybody! Listen carefully!

Tour Guide: Iruka

Guidance Office

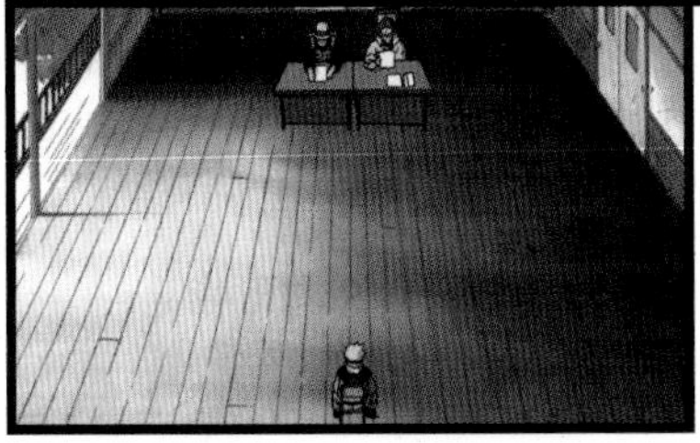

In this office, students are guided on what paths they should take. Sometimes, students come here to discuss their personal or academic concerns.

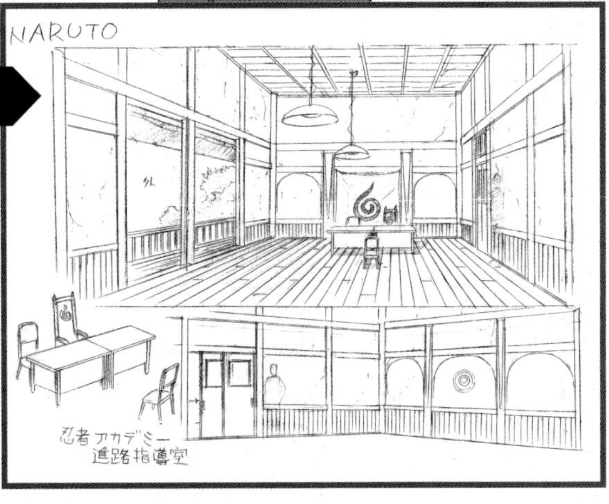
NARUTO
忍者アカデミー
進路指導室

Bird's-eye view of a Ninja Academy Classroom: A class at Ninja Academy usually consists of 27 students. The classrooms must be spacious so that demonstrations can be performed there.

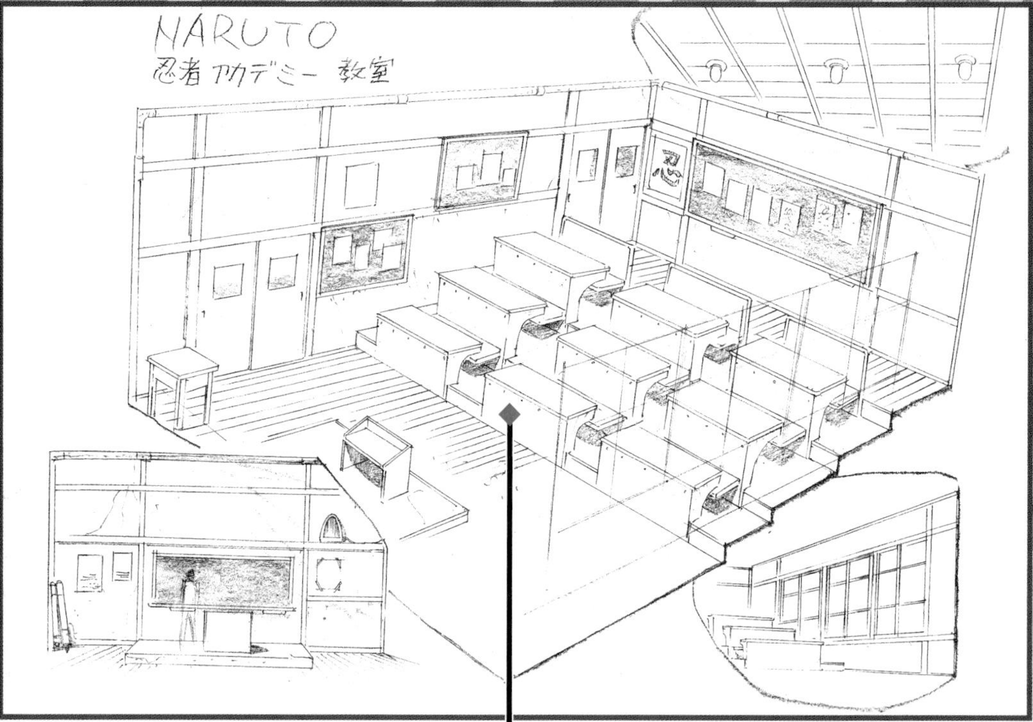
NARUTO
忍者アカデミー 教室

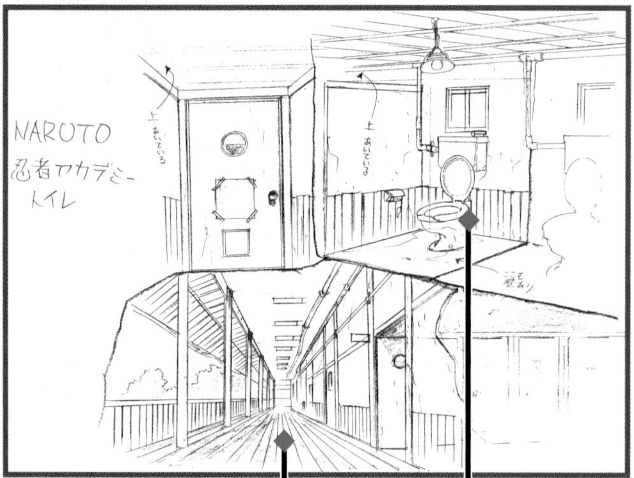
NARUTO
忍者アカデミー
トイレ

Desk

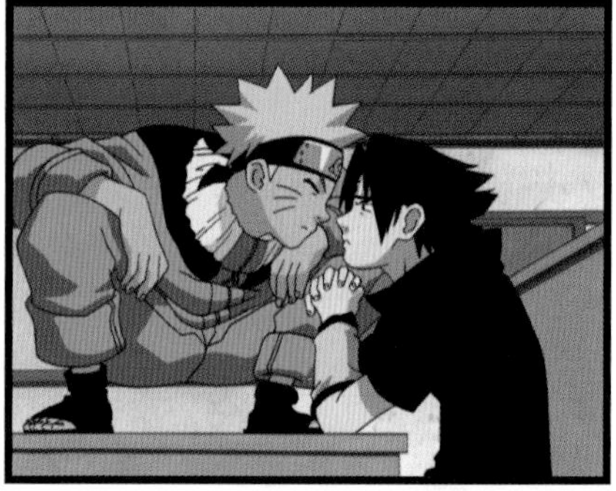

Each desk is shared by three students! Never stand on a desk like Naruto is doing here!!

Hallway outside the toilet

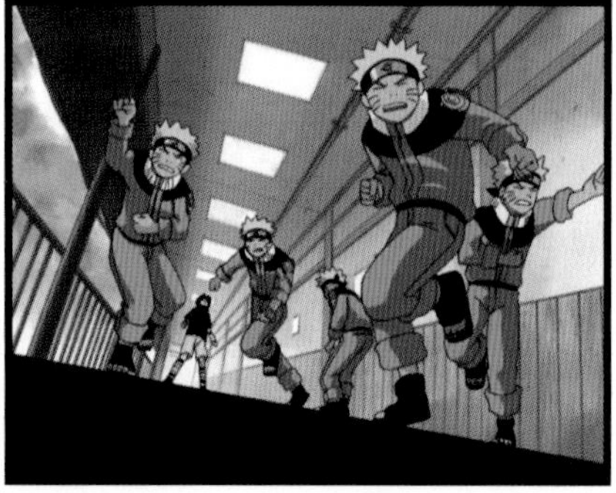

Never run in the hallway! Running while using the Clone Jutsu is completely out of the question!!

Toilet

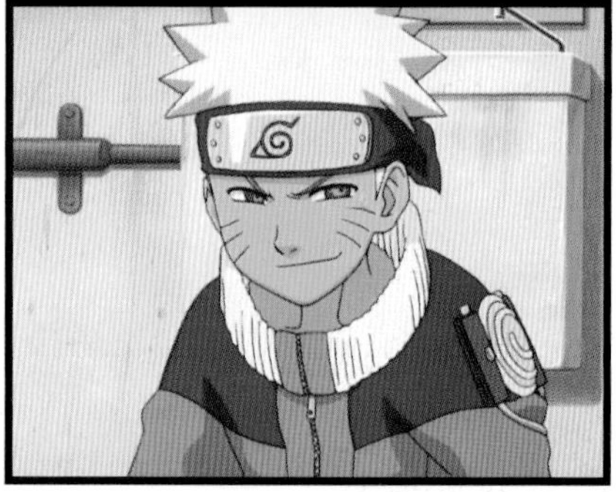

Only 15 cm of toilet paper should be used per bathroom visit. Got that, Naruto?!

Entrance Hall

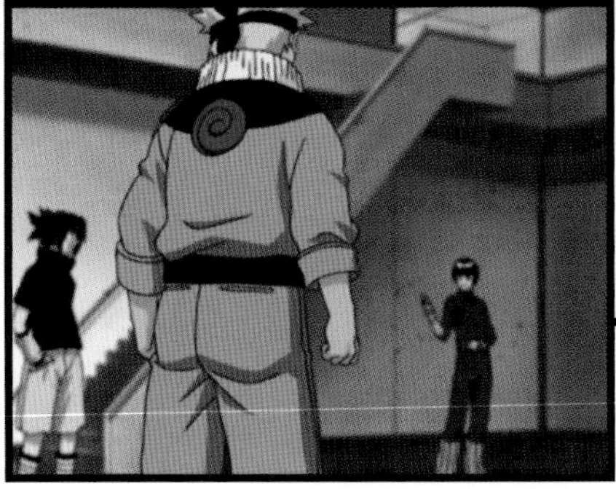

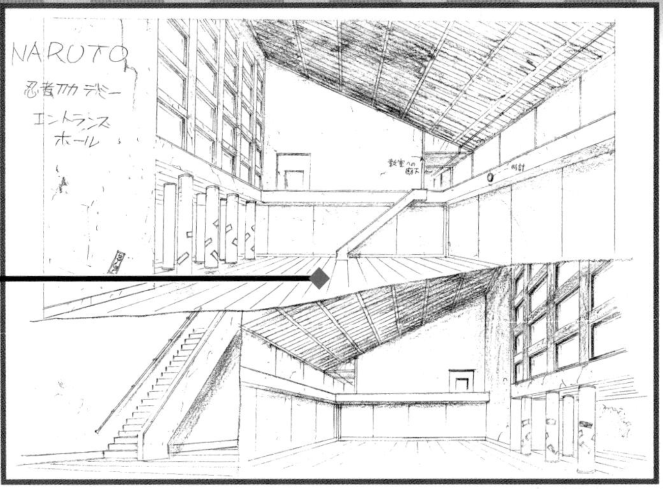
NARUTO
忍者アカデミー
エントランスホール

This multi-purpose hall is where Sasuke and Lee faced off. The second floor area is open and looks down on the first floor.

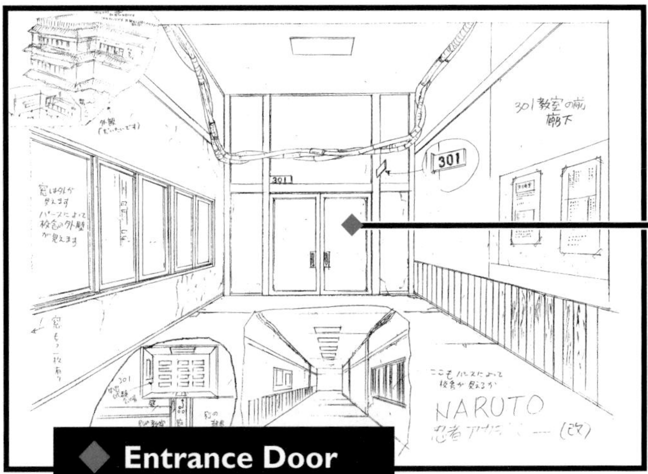
301
NARUTO

The hallway outside classroom 301

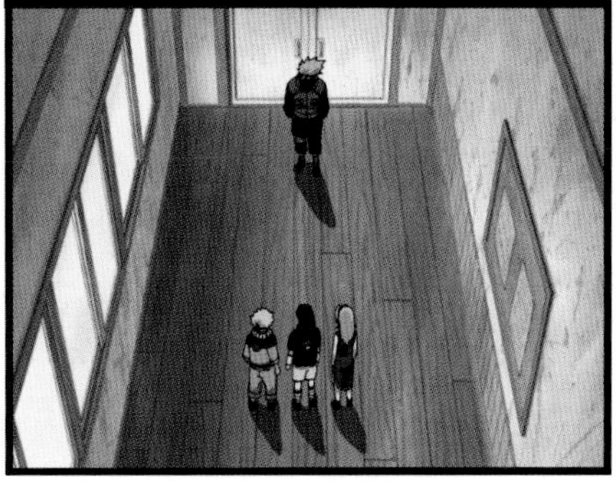

This is the hallway where Kakashi wished his students luck and sent them off to the Chunin Exam.

Entrance Door

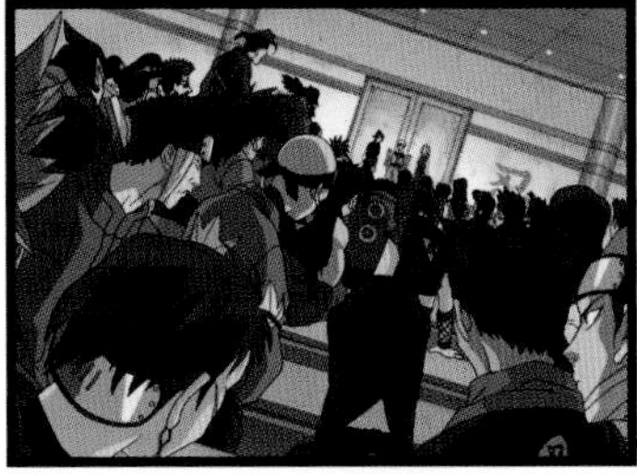

The entrance to room 301 is a double door and both doors open together. The design and size of this room is quite different from all the other classrooms.

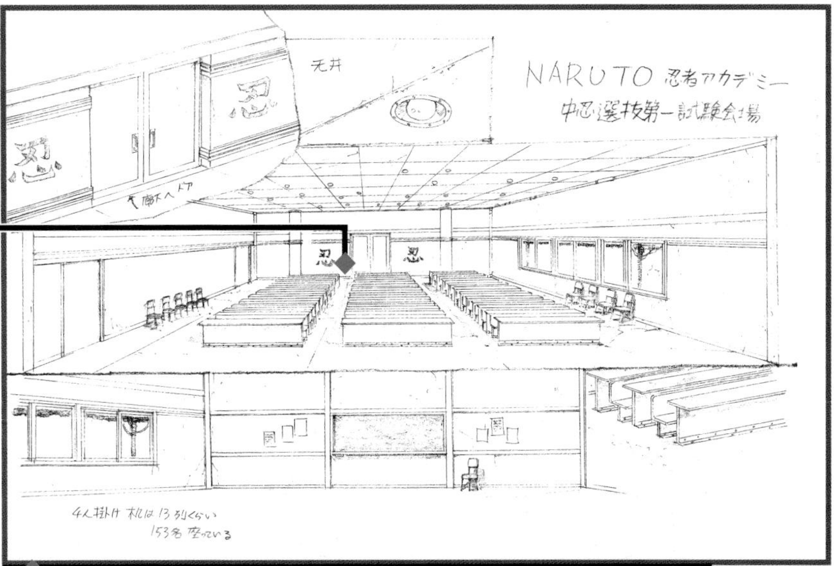
天井
NARUTO 忍者アカデミー
中忍選抜第一試験会場

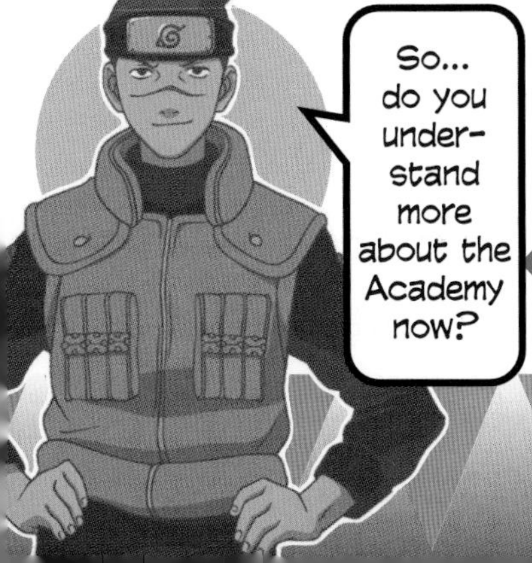
So... do you under-stand more about the Academy now?

Location of the Chunin Exam's First Stage: Classroom 301
became the site for the first portion of the Chunin Exam. The room's large size allows it to accommodate over 100 people.

See through it! False Imitation Jutsu!

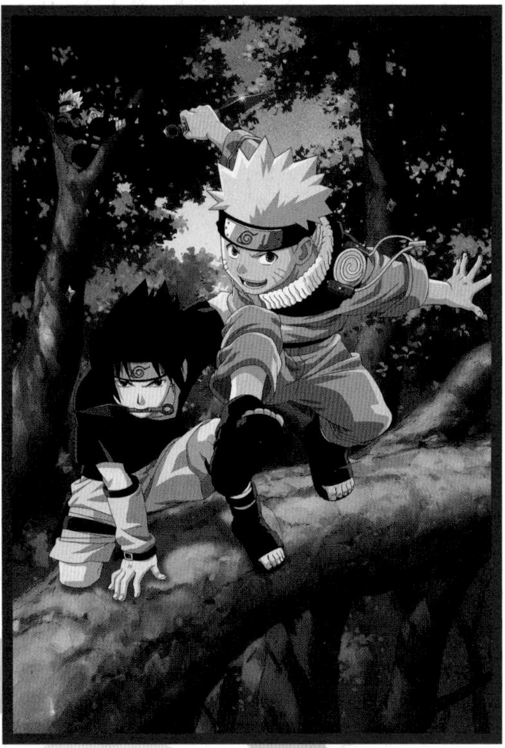

Some of the small images below (labeled A-J) were cropped from the large illustration on the left. But hidden within the group are images taken from a different illustration! There are four pieces that don't belong. Focus your chakra and see through the deceit to detect the fakes!

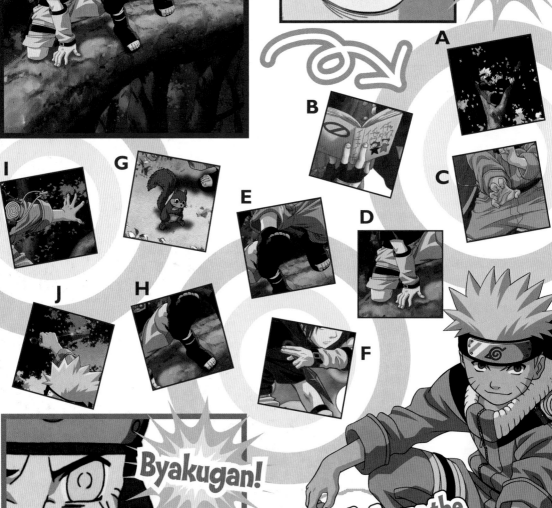

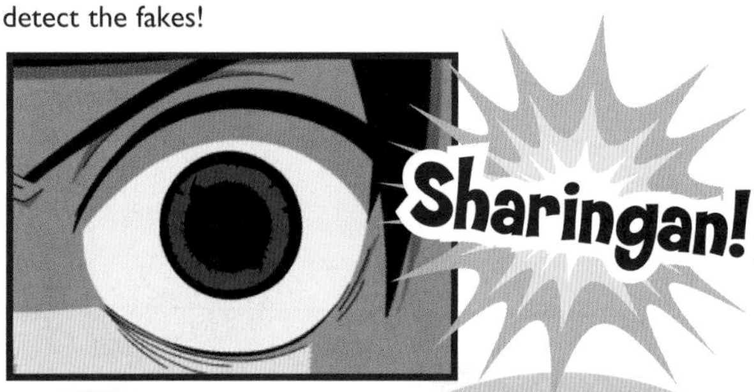
Sharingan!

A

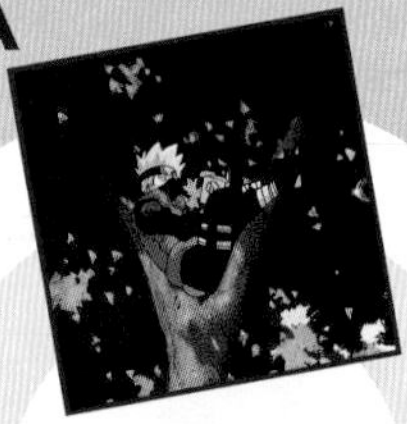

B

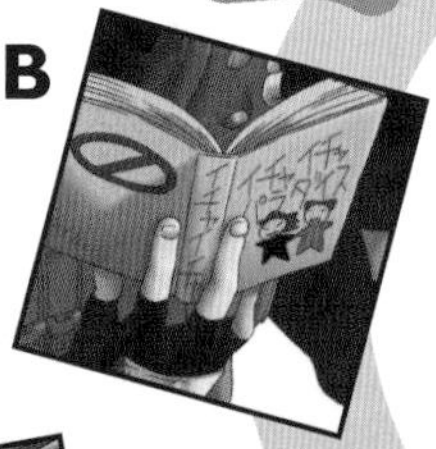

C

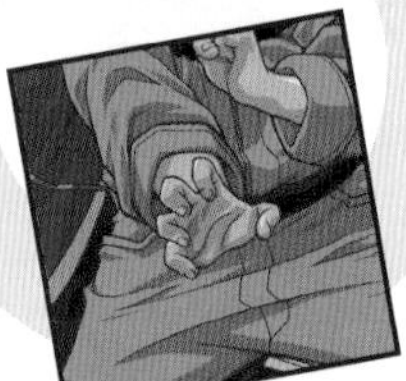

I

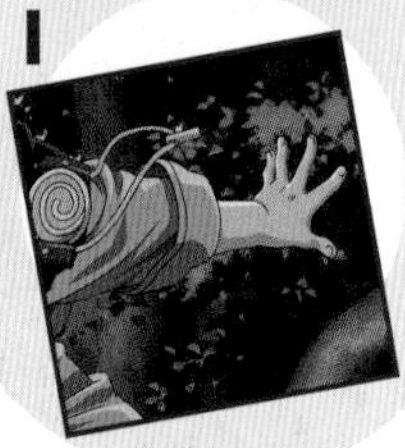

G

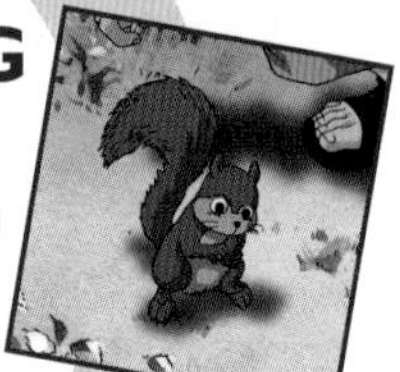

E

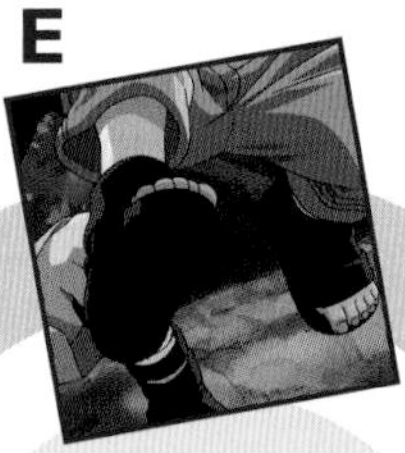

D

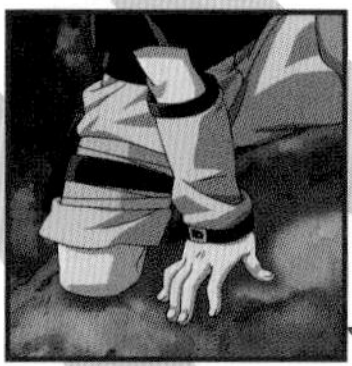

J

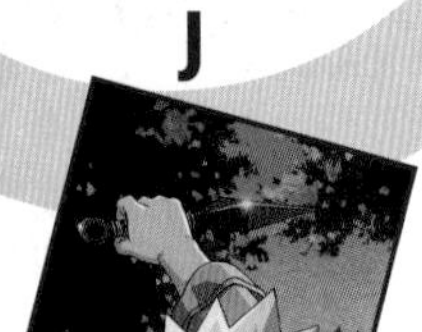

H

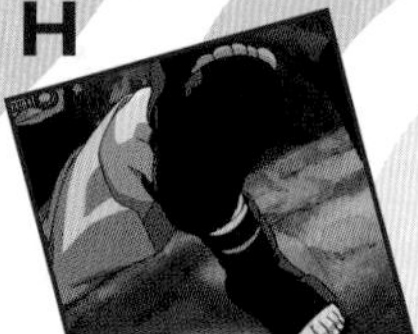

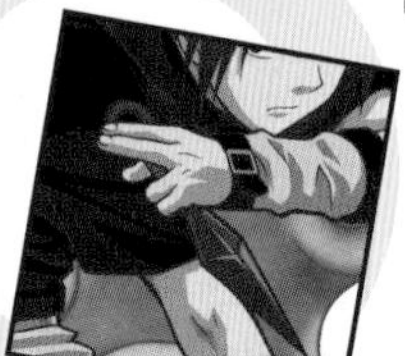

F

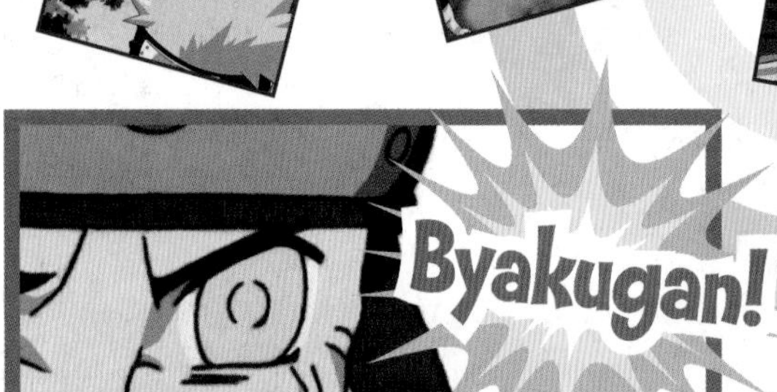
Byakugan!

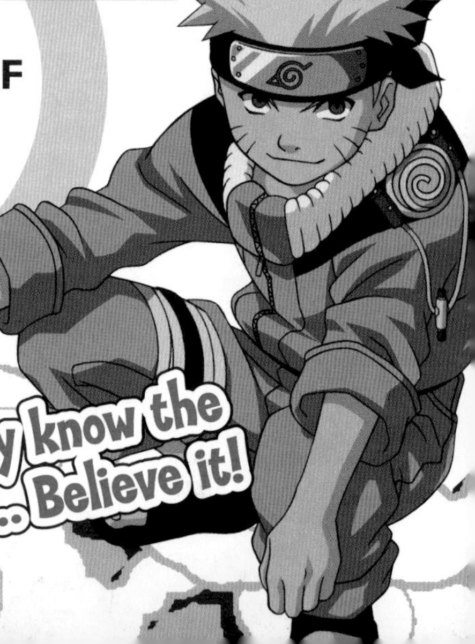
I already know the answer... Believe it!

Find the answer on page 228!!

A dangerous mission! Journey to the Land of Waves!

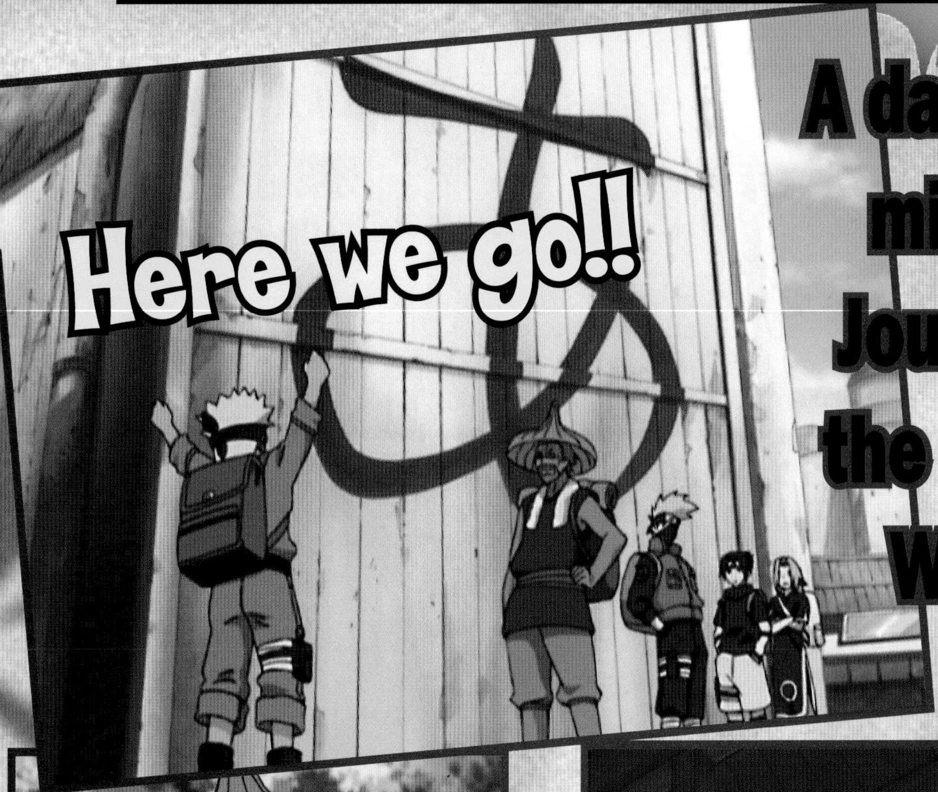
Here we go!!

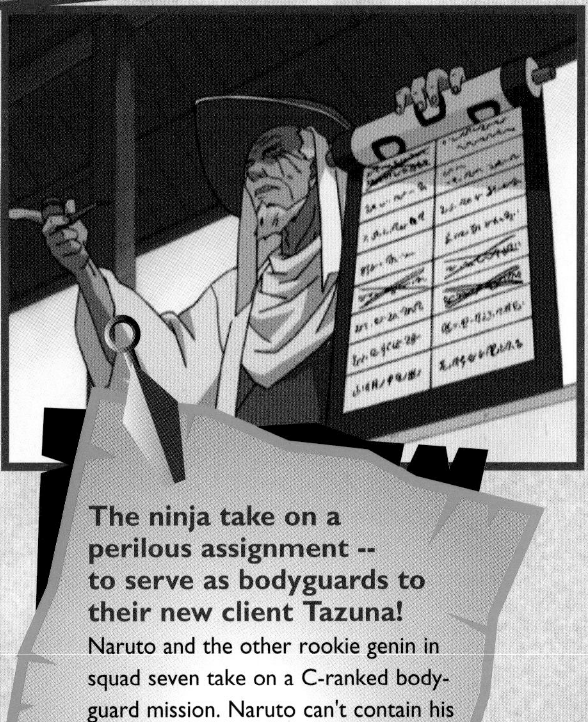

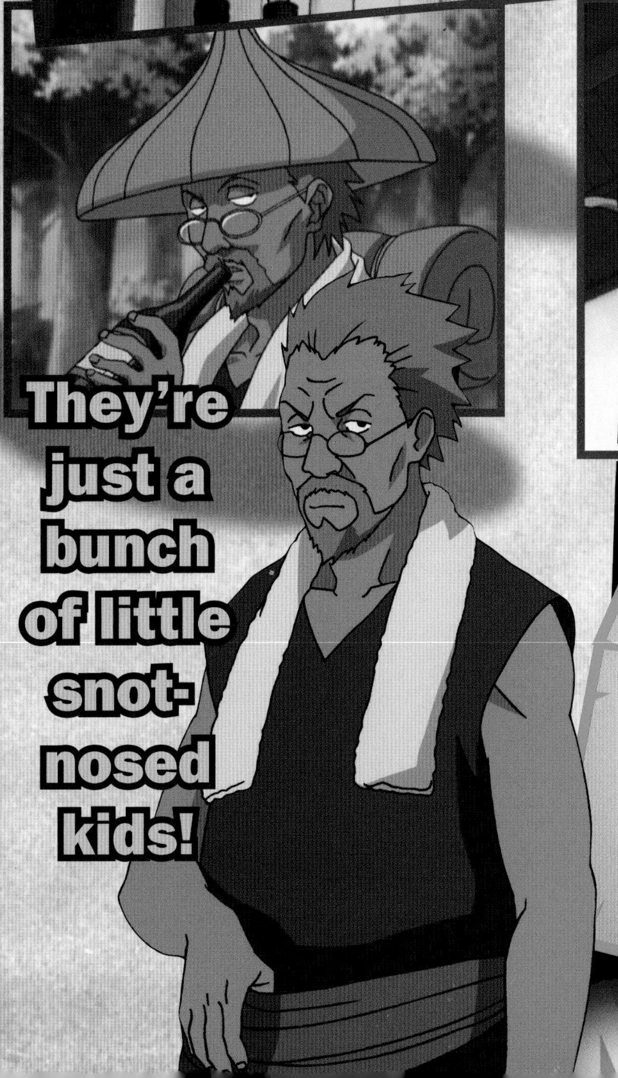
They're just a bunch of little snot-nosed kids!

The ninja take on a perilous assignment -- to serve as bodyguards to their new client Tazuna!

Naruto and the other rookie genin in squad seven take on a C-ranked bodyguard mission. Naruto can't contain his excitement about going on his first overseas trip. But Tazuna, the bridge builder whom the squad is assigned to protect, is a mysterious man. As the group steps out of the open village gate, they head toward the Land of Waves…

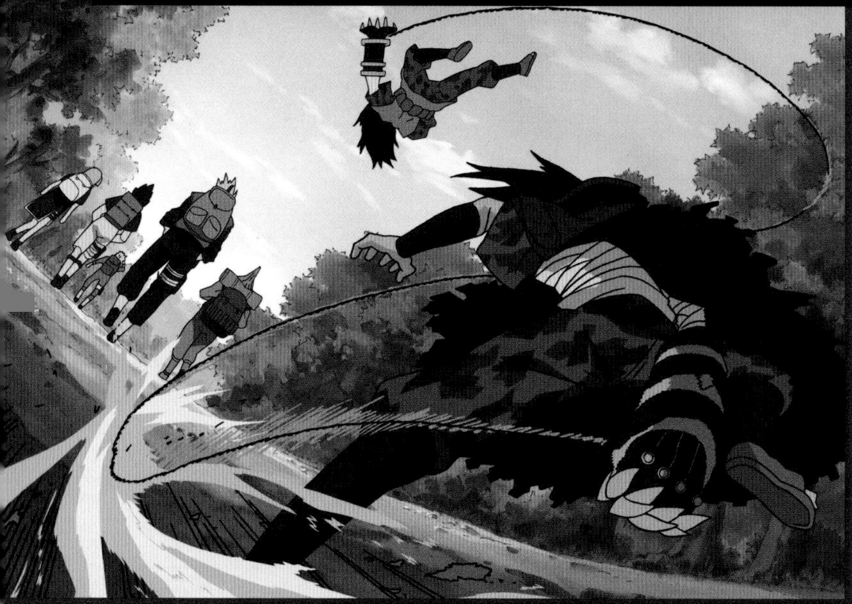

The group is suddenly thrown into crisis as the Demon Brothers attack!

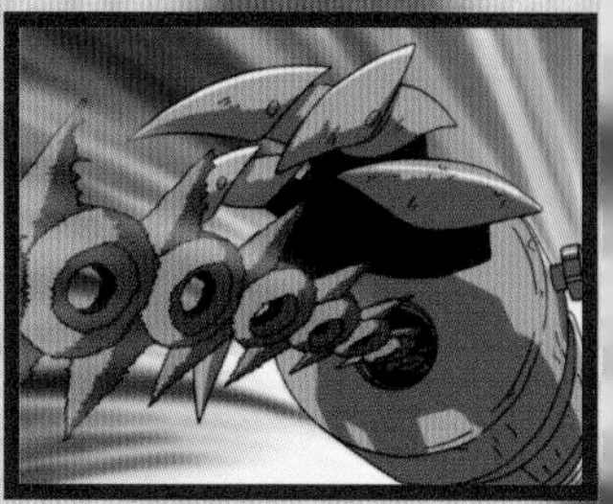
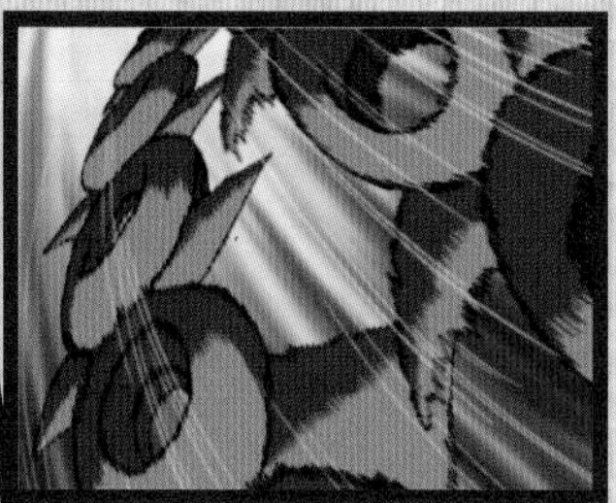
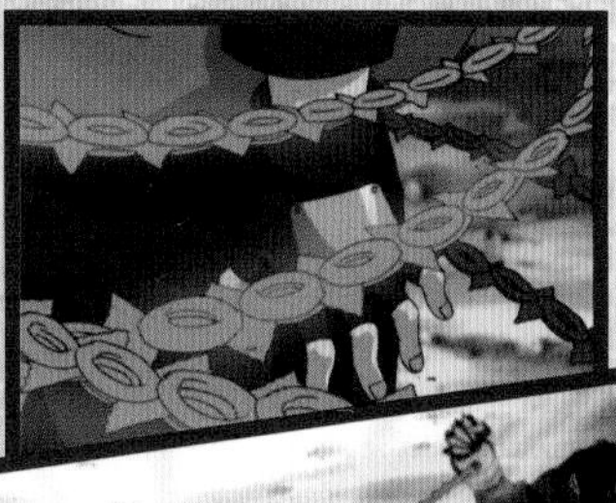
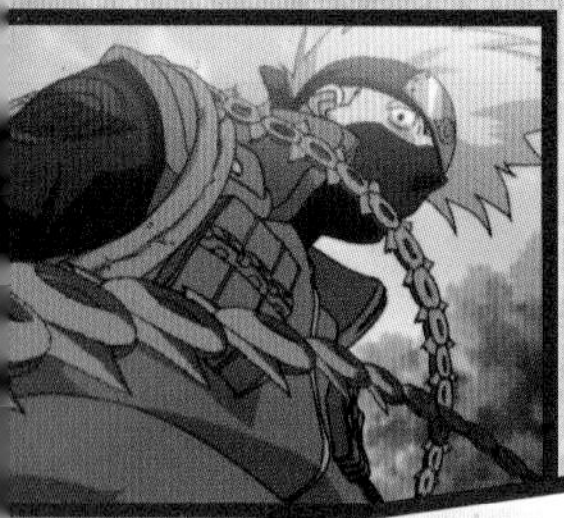

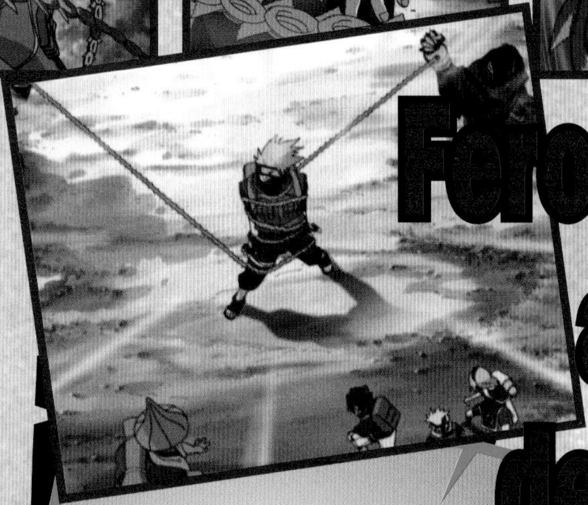

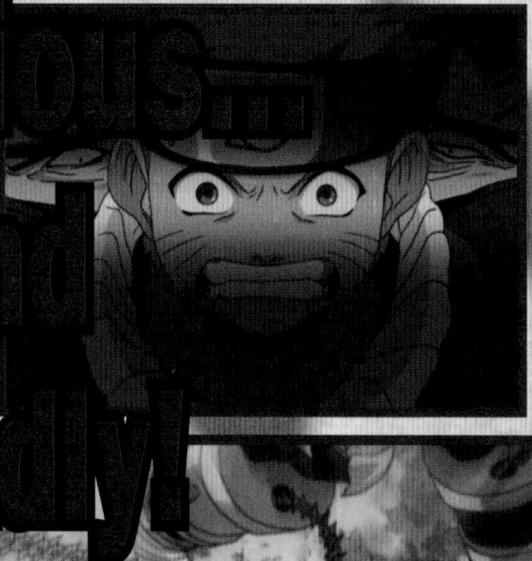

Ferocious... and deadly!

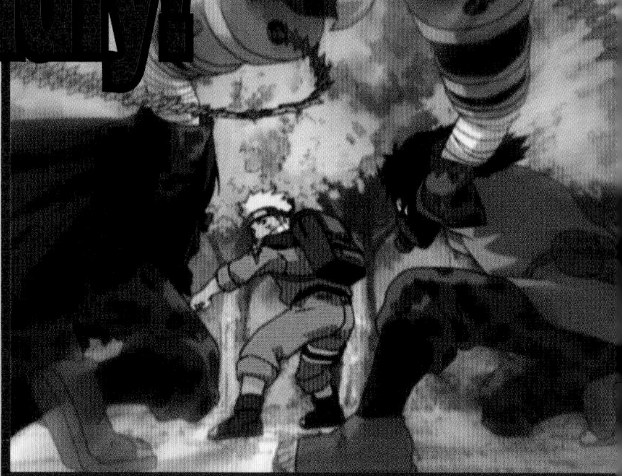

The Demon Brothers strike at Squad Seven with vicious blades!

A peaceful stroll is destroyed by the Demon Brothers' attack! Naruto is either too shocked or too scared to move as he faces his first real combat situation…but when Sasuke calls him a "scaredy-cat," the words pierce deep into Naruto's heart.

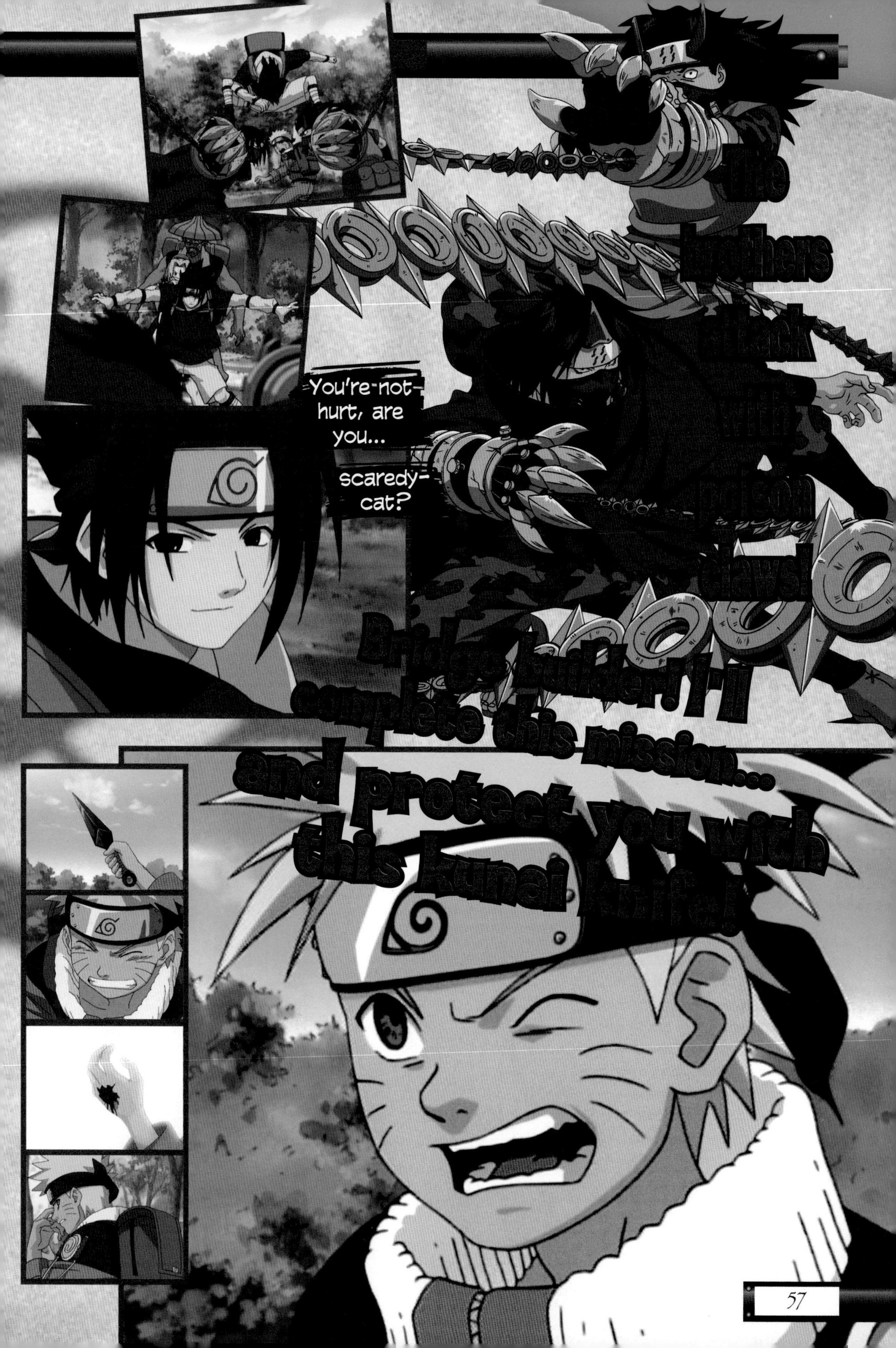
The brothers attack with poison claws!
You're not hurt, are you...
scaredy-cat?
Bridge builder! I'll complete this mission... and protect you with this kunai knife!

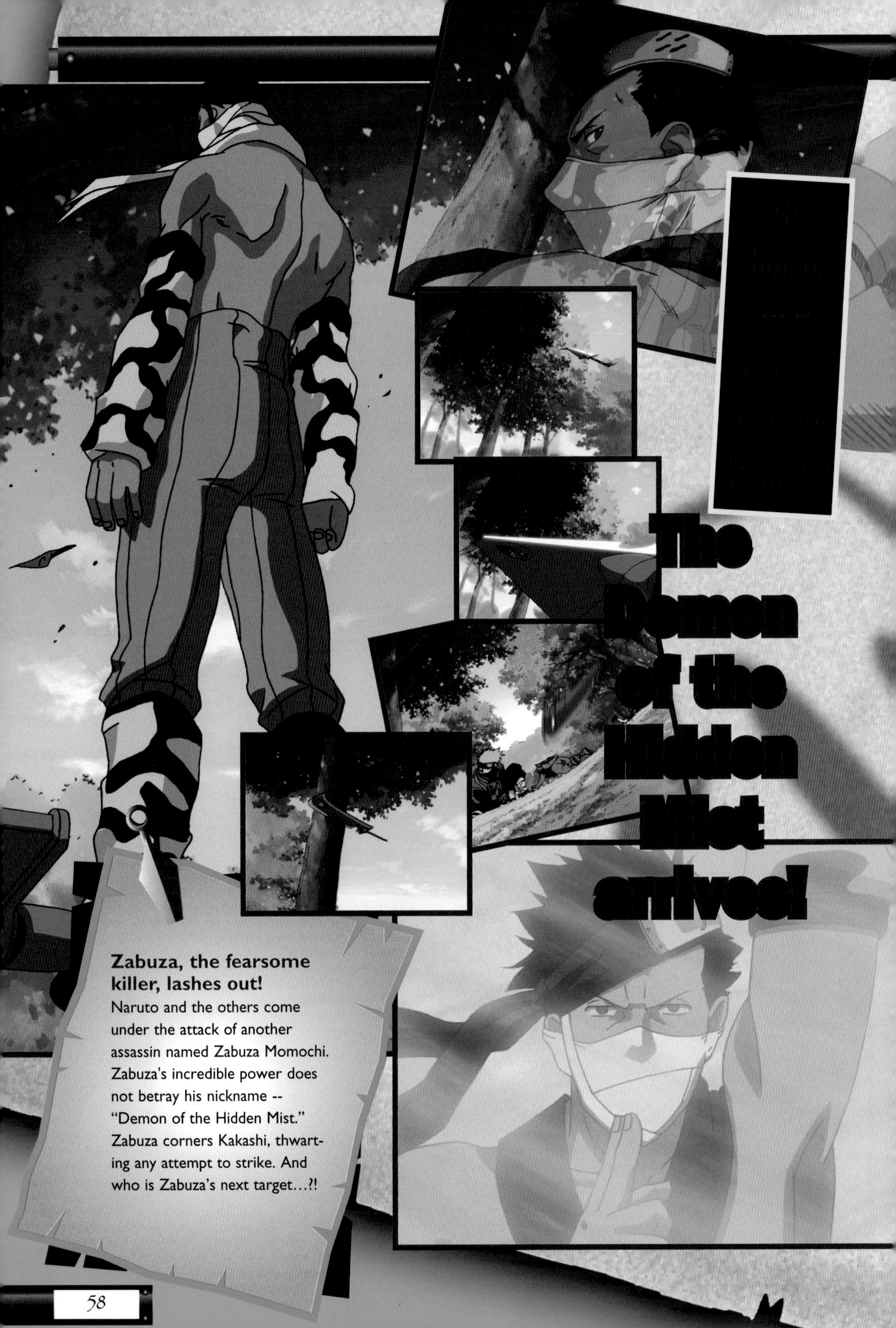

[redacted]

The Demon of the Hidden Mist arrived!

Zabuza, the fearsome killer, lashes out!

Naruto and the others come under the attack of another assassin named Zabuza Momochi. Zabuza's incredible power does not betray his nickname -- "Demon of the Hidden Mist." Zabuza corners Kakashi, thwarting any attempt to strike. And who is Zabuza's next target...?!

Put this in your Bingo Book...

"The ninja who will become Hokage of the Village Hidden in the Leaves... His name's Naruto Uzumaki!"

Demon Wind Shuriken... Windmill of Shadows!!

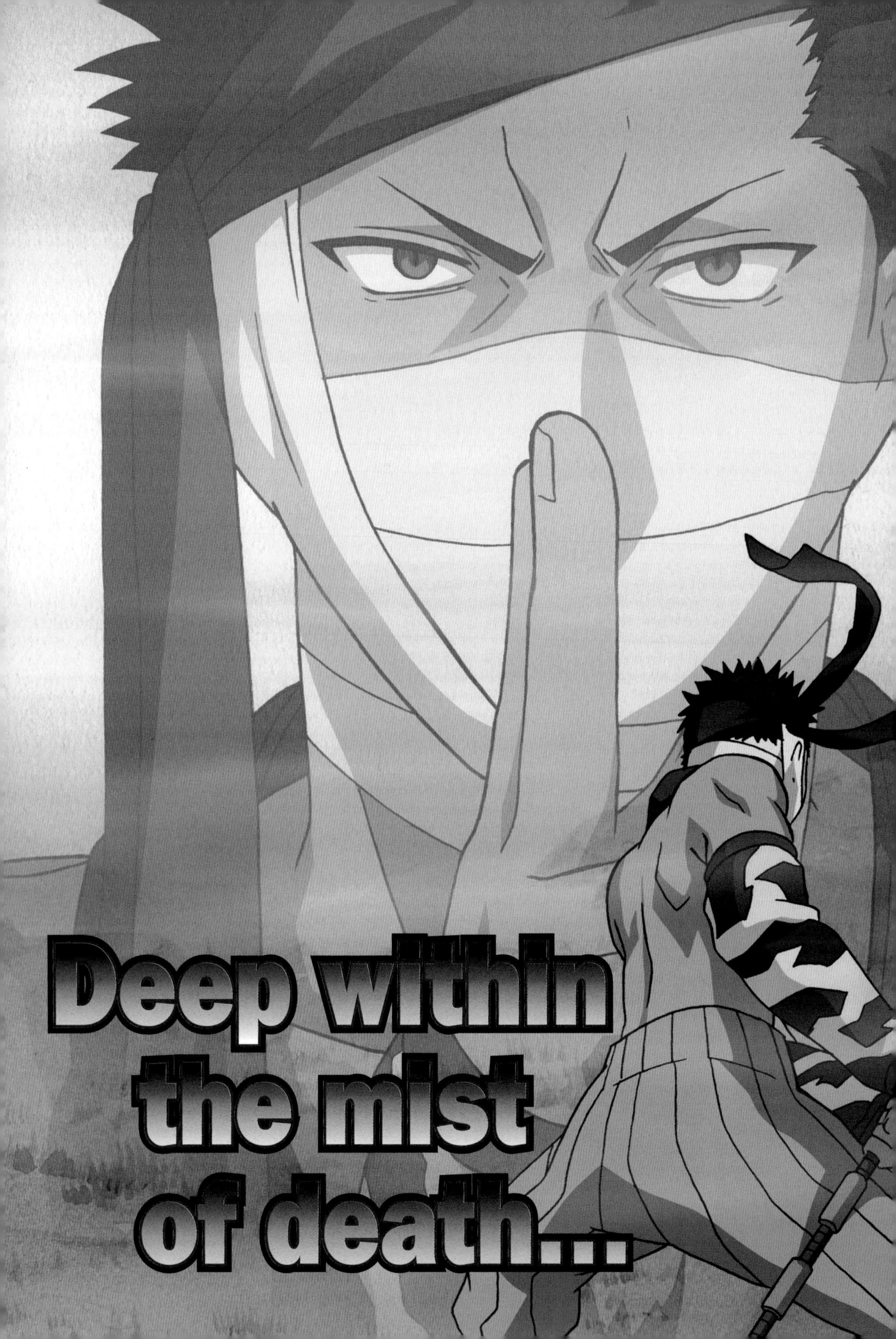
Deep within the mist of death...

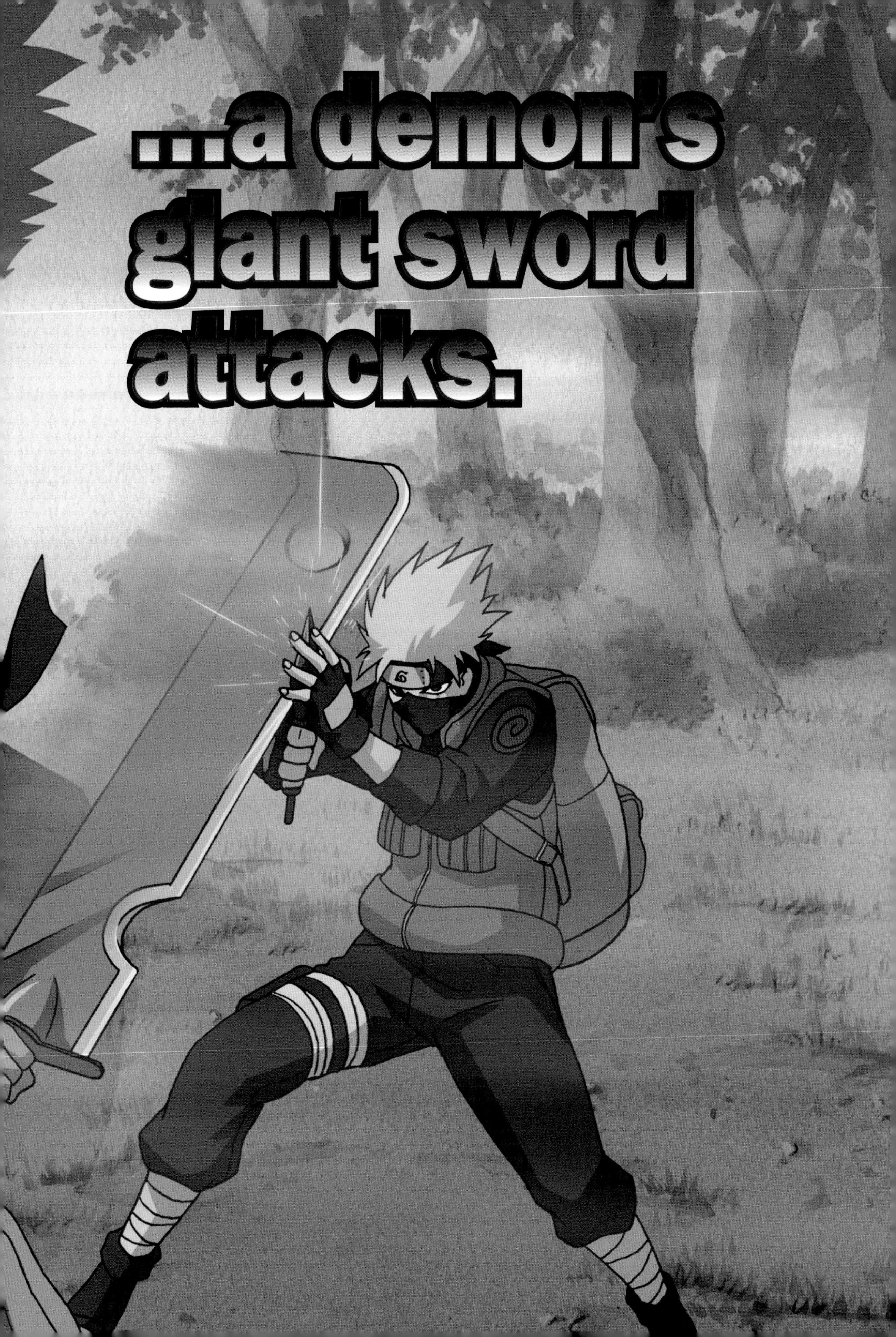
...a demon's giant sword attacks.

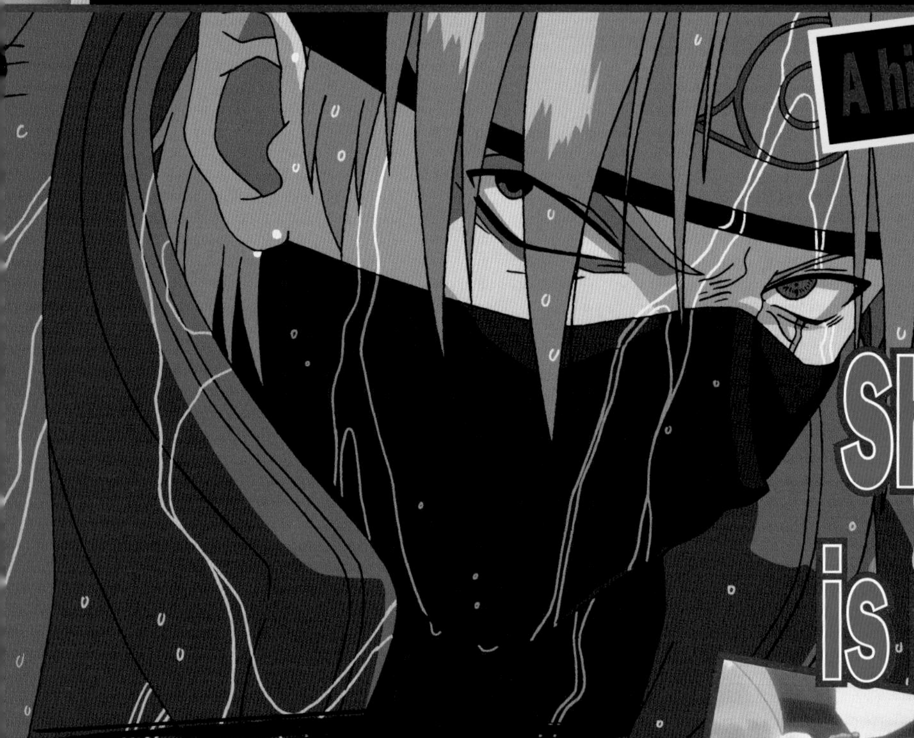

A hidden power...

The Sharingan is revealed!!

Your technique worked on me once, but it won't work again.

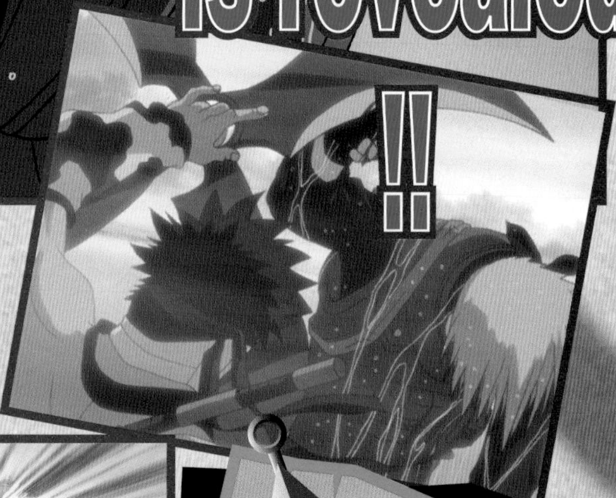

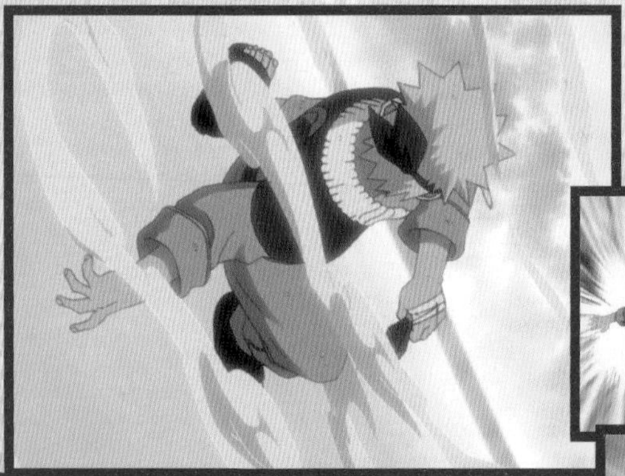

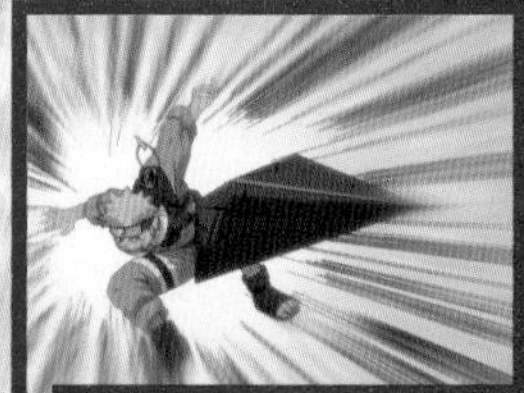

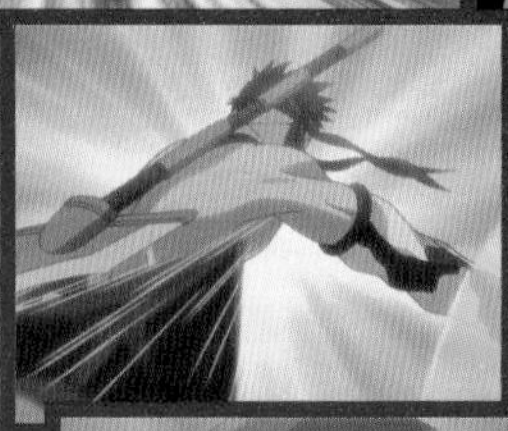

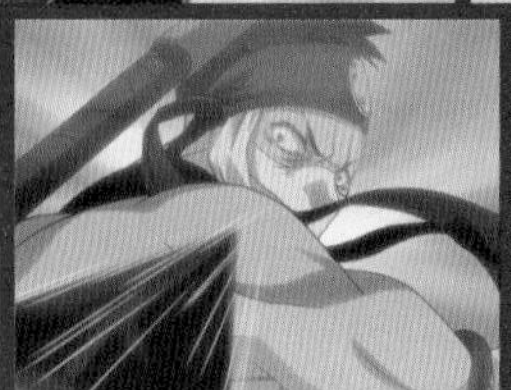

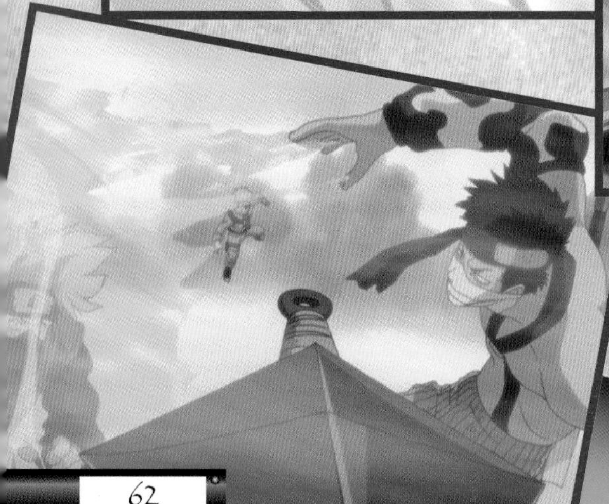

His students' teamwork allows Kakashi to escape Zabuza's trap!
The assassin's strength overwhelms Kakashi and he finds himself captured within Zabuza's Water Prison. With the pride of the Leaf Ninja on the line, Naruto and Sasuke cannot retreat! Their cleverness and skill allow them to launch a successful counterattack!

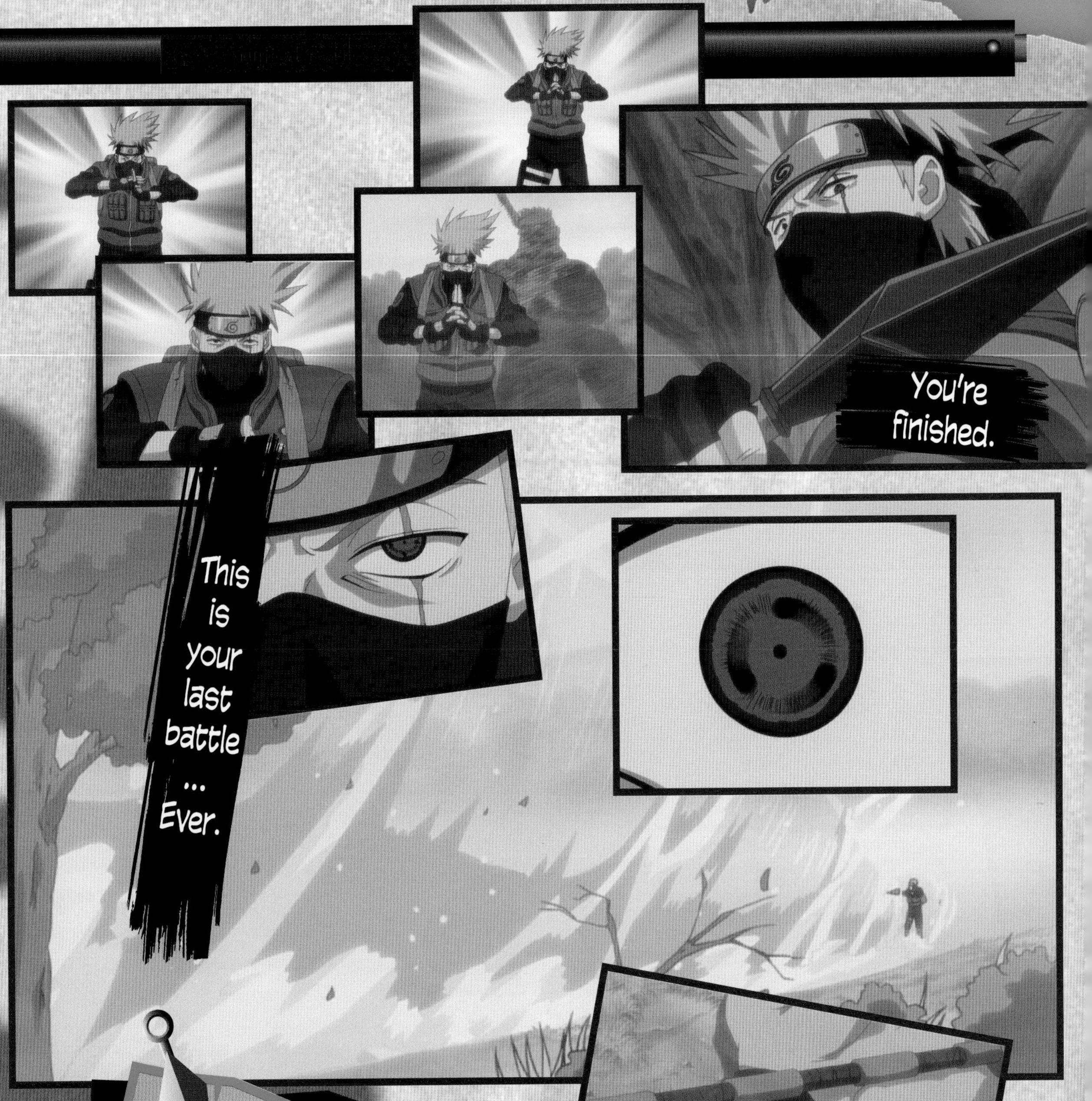
You're finished.
This is your last battle ... Ever.

Zabuza is killed...?!
A mysterious masked ninja appears!

Kakashi is known as the "Copy Ninja" because of his Sharingan eye. This secret skill allows him to imitate and steal jutsu, so Kakashi is able to strike back at Zabuza using his opponent's own techniques! The vicious battle looks like it might be coming to an end... But in the next instant, an attack comes from out of nowhere to fell the mighty assassin!

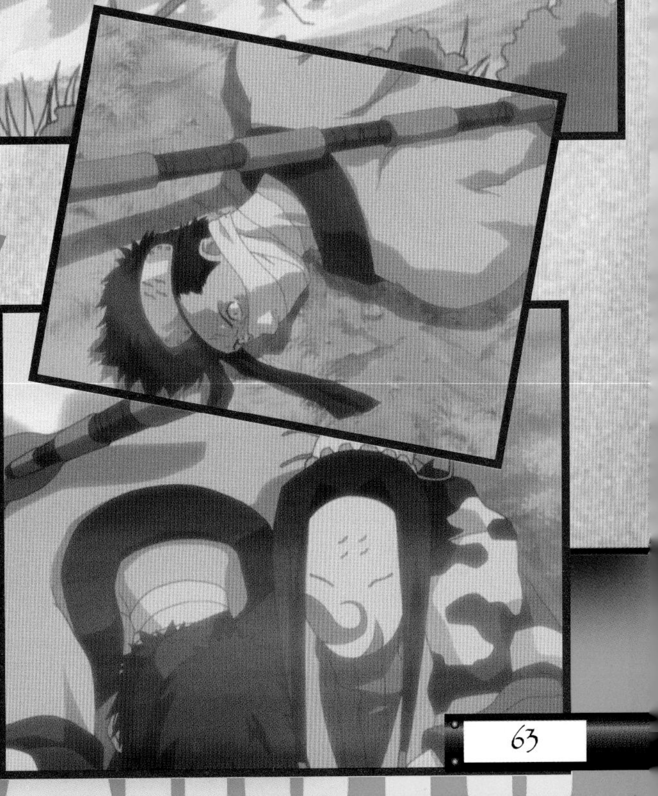

The astonishing Kekkei Genkai!

No move can counter his mysterious skills or his chilling bloodlust!

"Kekkei Genkai" -- bloodline traits -- are immensely powerful special abilities passed down genetically through certain families. Haku, a young warrior who is like a combat machine, has inherited this mystical blood…and he unleashes a fearsome hidden jutsu! Haku attacks Sasuke with cold, murderous intent and traps him inside Crystal Ice Mirrors!

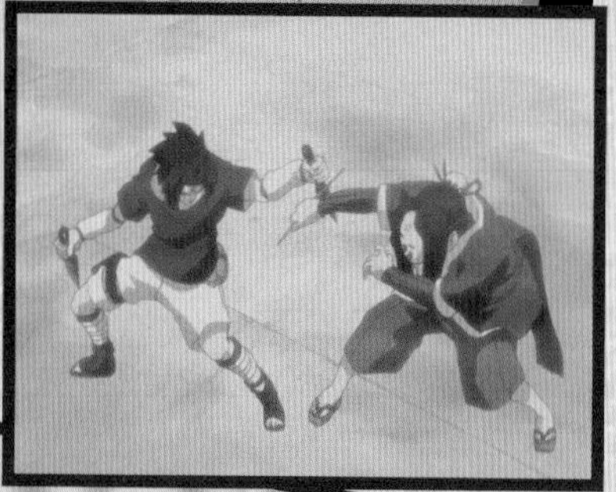

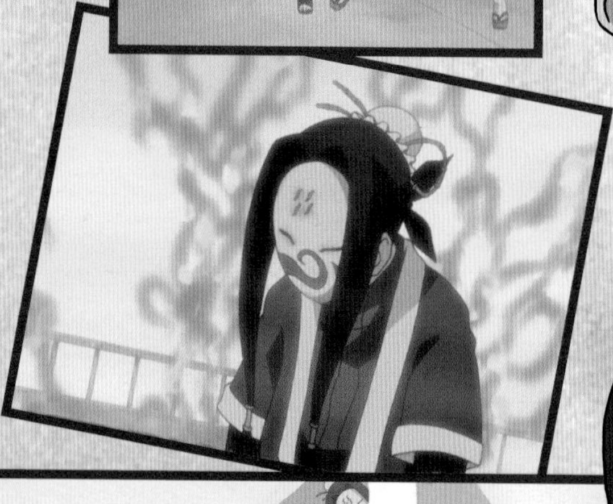

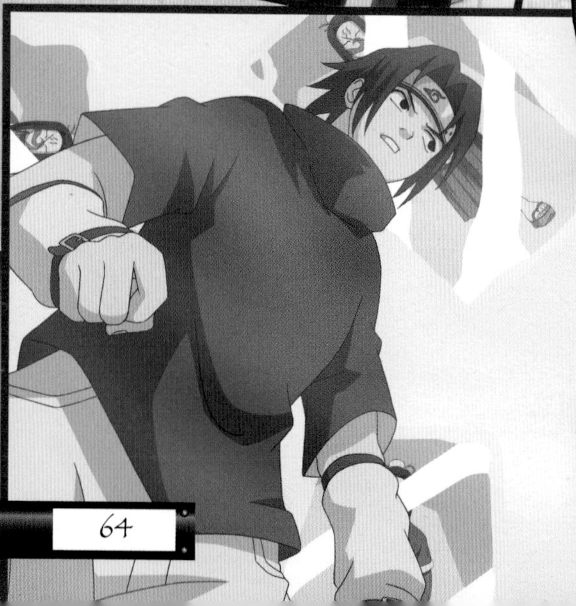

White blades slice through the wind!

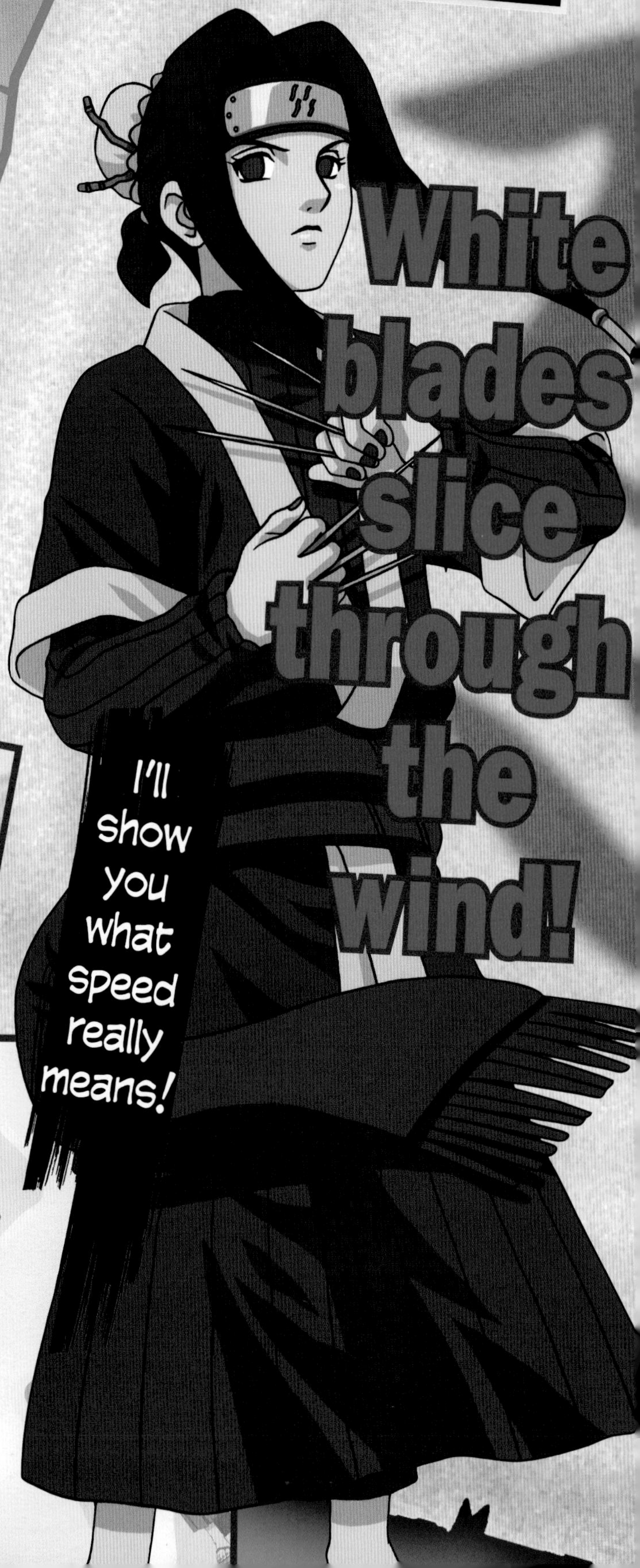
I'll show you what speed really means!

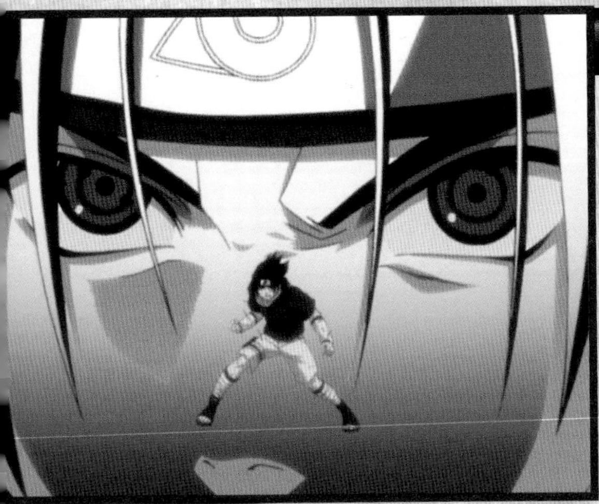

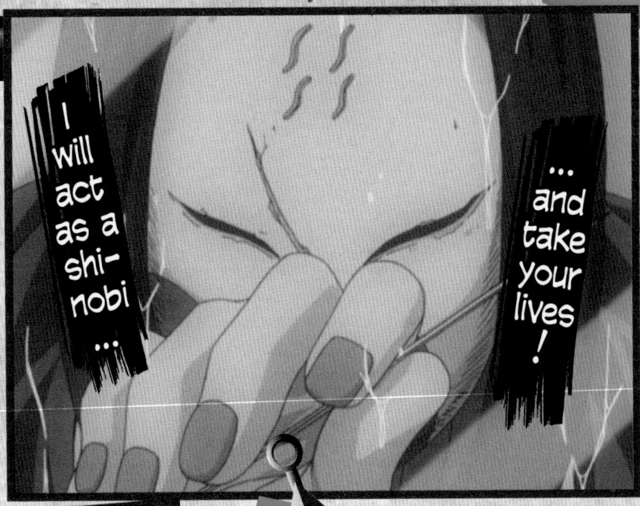
I will act as a shi-nobi...
...and take your lives!

Sasuke's Uchiha blood awakens...and his Sharingan eyes open!

In the midst of intense battle, with a paper-thin margin between life and death, the sleeping beast stirs to life! With the power of the Sharingan, Sasuke's vision is suddenly attuned to the motion of Haku's deadly senbon needles...and he throws himself into their path to protect Naruto!

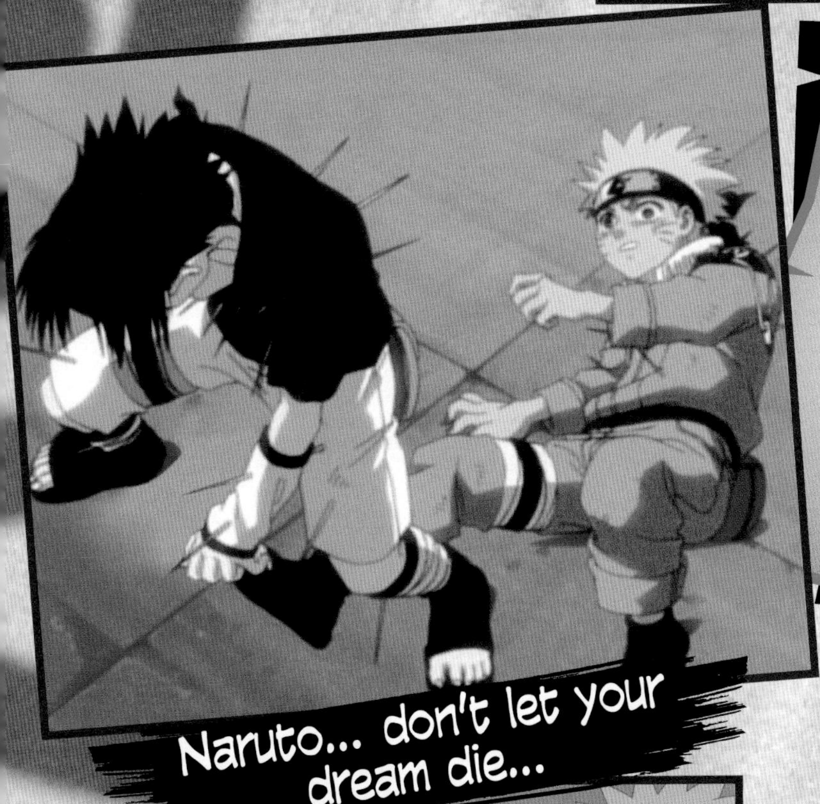
Naruto... don't let your dream die...

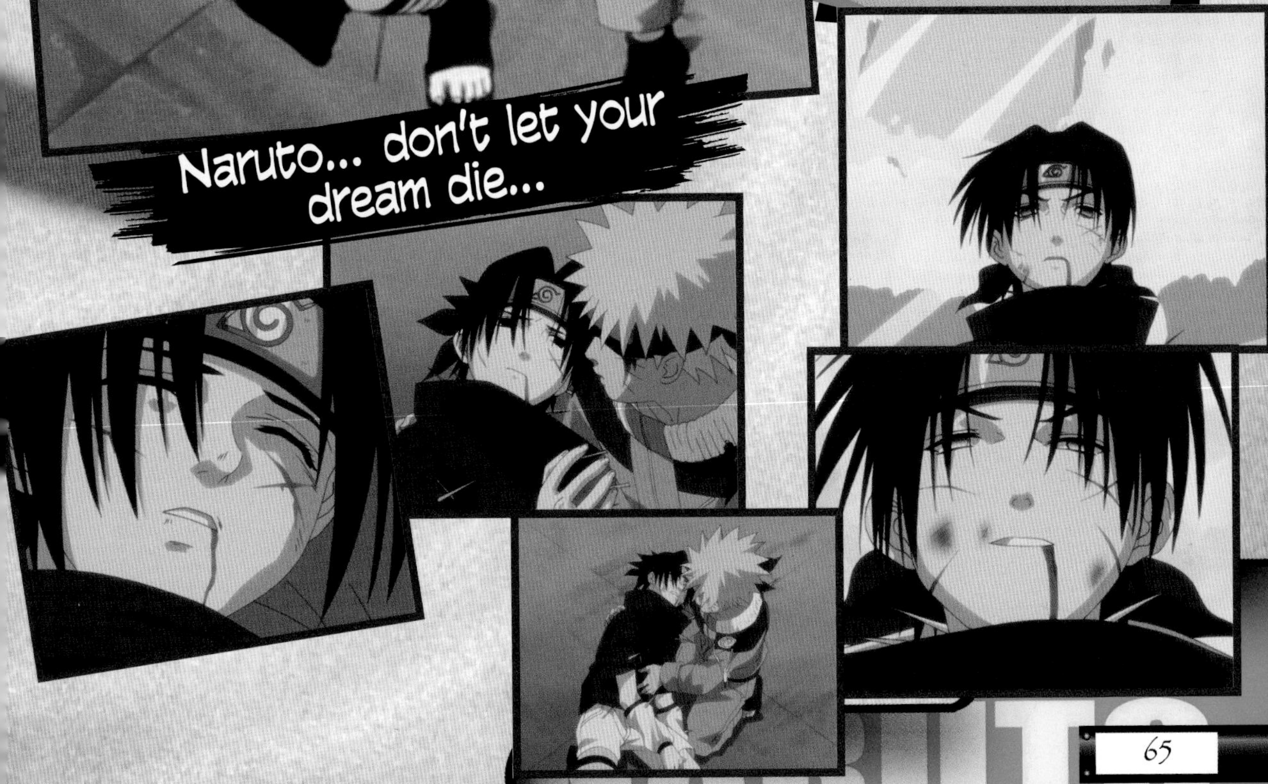

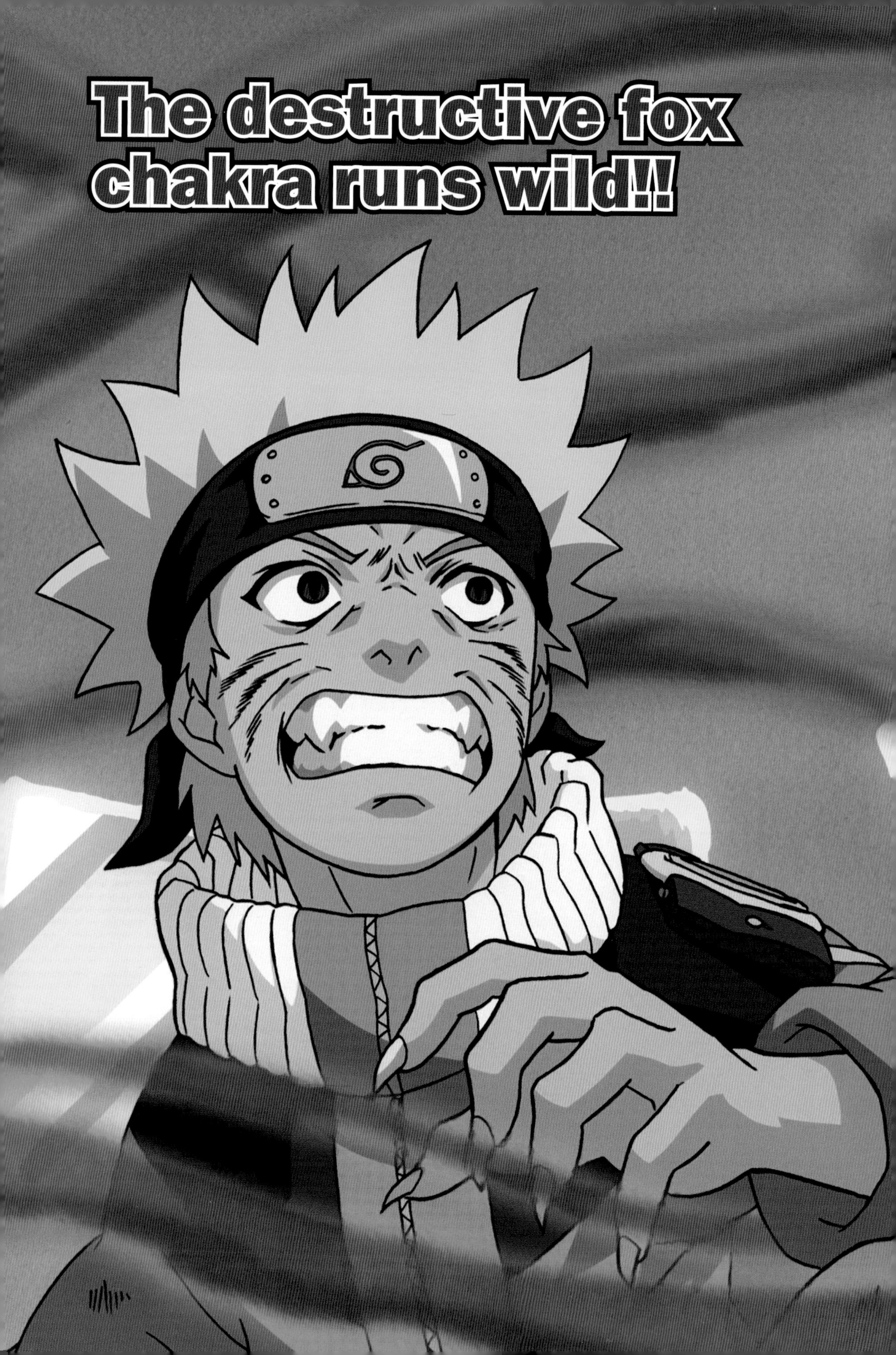
The destructive fox chakra runs wild!!

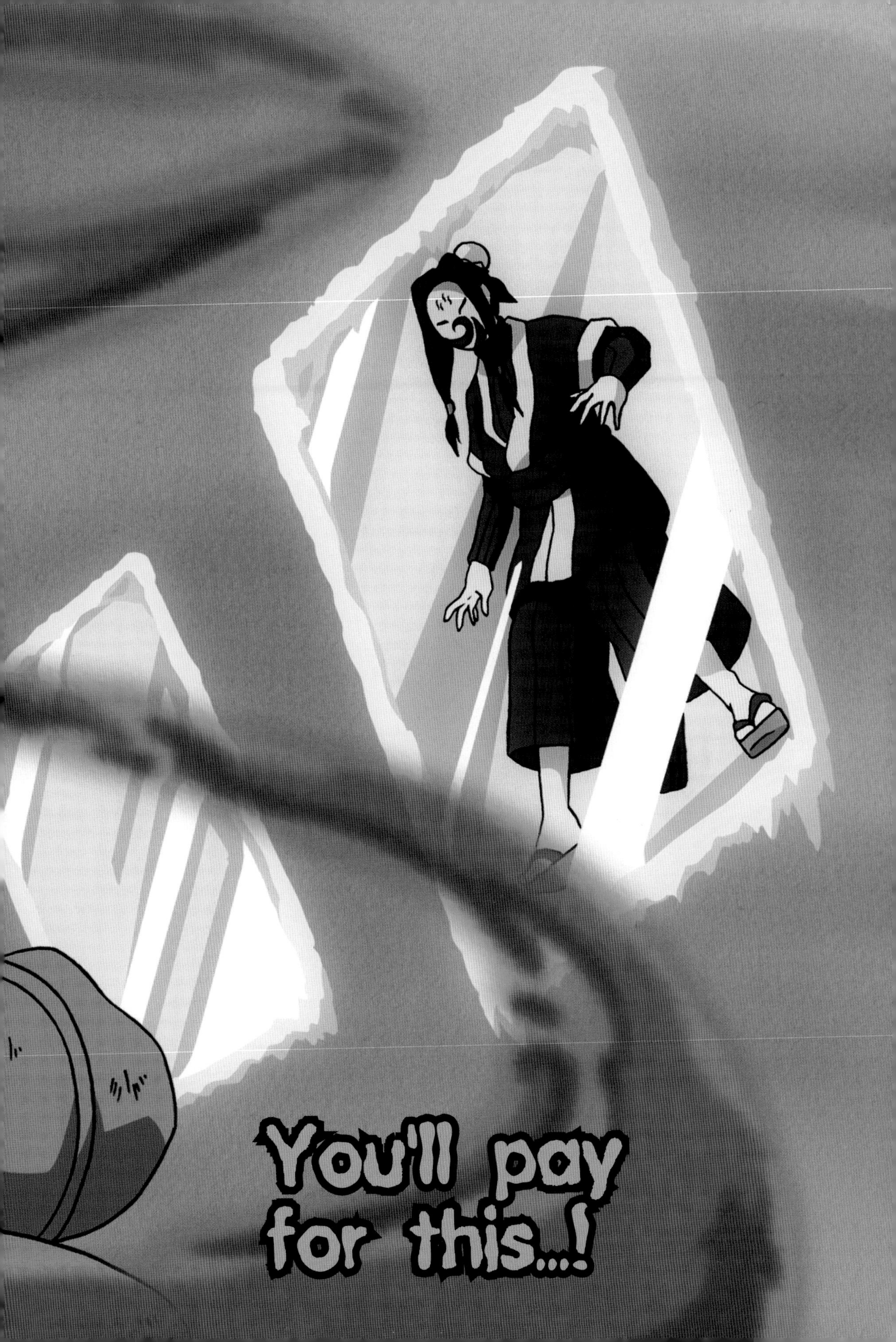
You'll pay for this...!

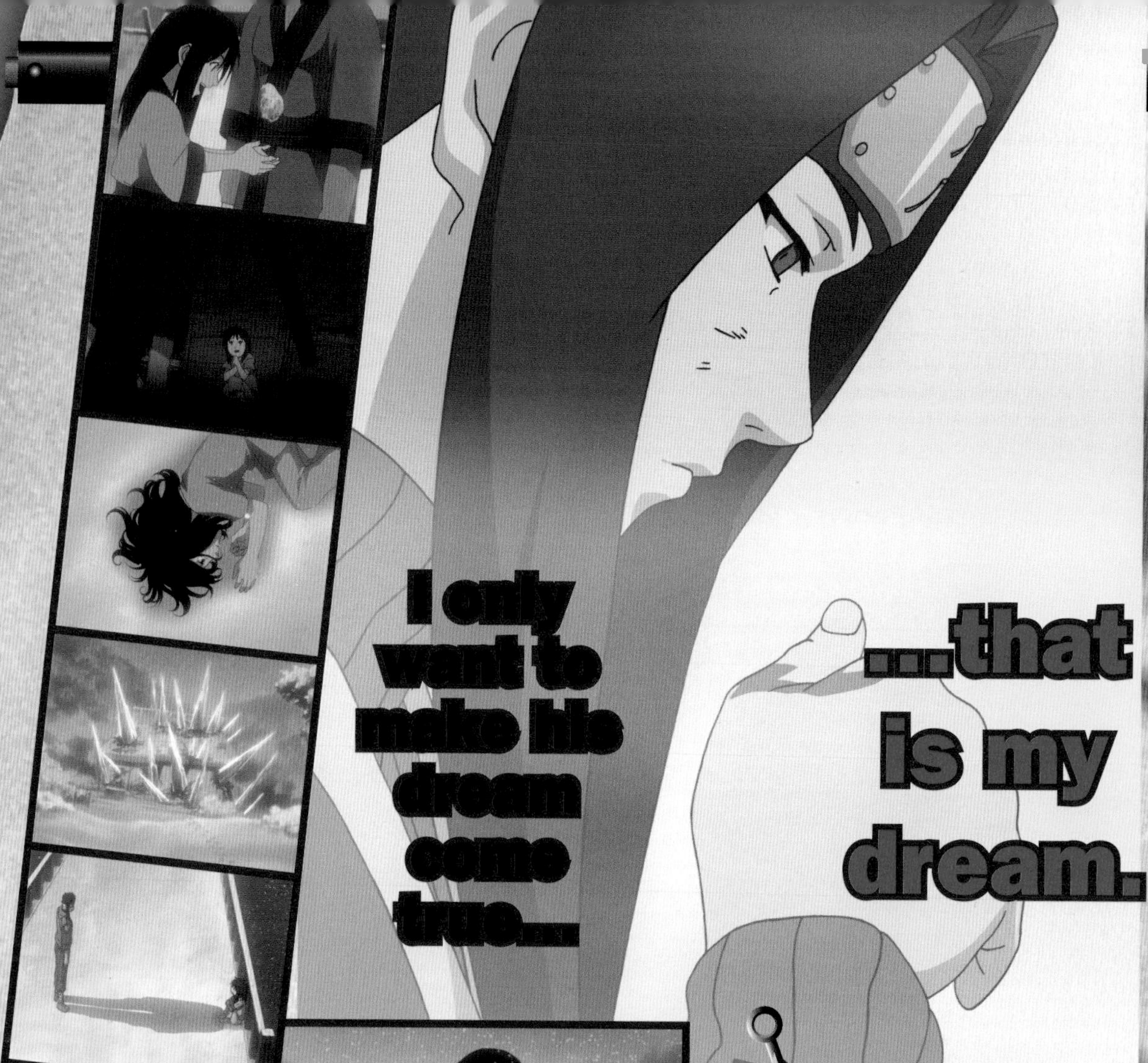
I only want to make his dream come true...
...that is my dream.

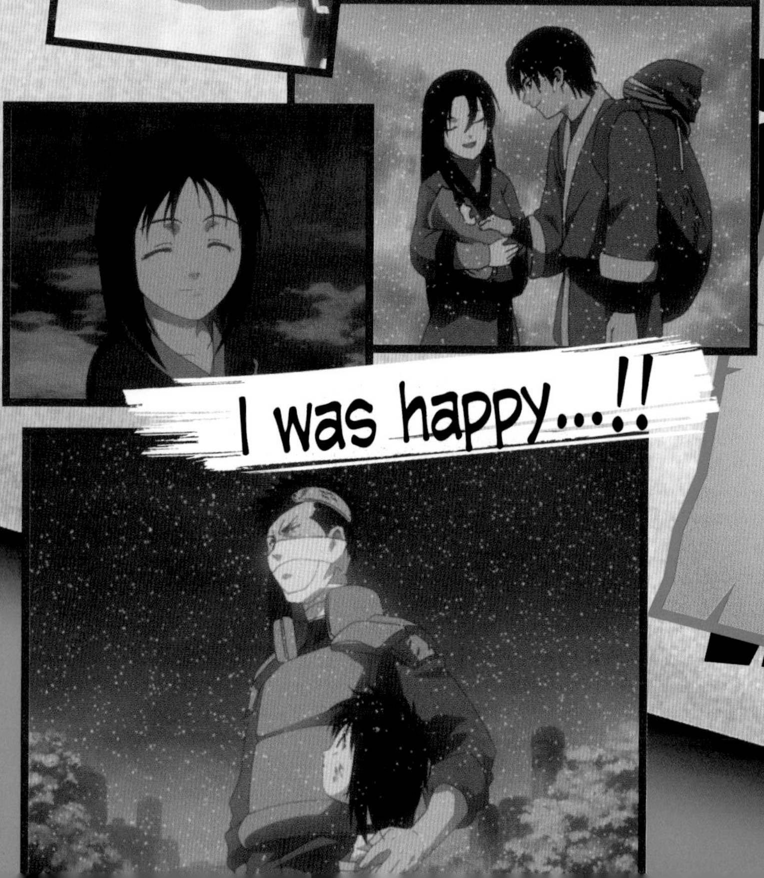
I was happy...!!

A tragic past and an innocent wish...

Because of the enormous stigma and fear surrounding his family's Kekkei Genkai, Haku's father killed his mother and almost killed Haku, too. But Zabuza valued Haku's bloodline power and took the boy under his wing. In order to act as a perfect weapon for his master, Haku suppresses his gentle nature and fights. Pleasing Zabuza becomes Haku's dream and his sole reason for existence.

The shield that protects the dream… and the blue blade that pierces through!

Haku feels that he has failed Zabuza and that the reason for his existence has been lost. He asks Naruto to end his life…but then Haku uses his own body as a shield to stop Kakashi's Lightning Blade from killing Zabuza. By saving the one person who matters to him, Haku is able to attain his ninja way before his brief existence is snuffed out.

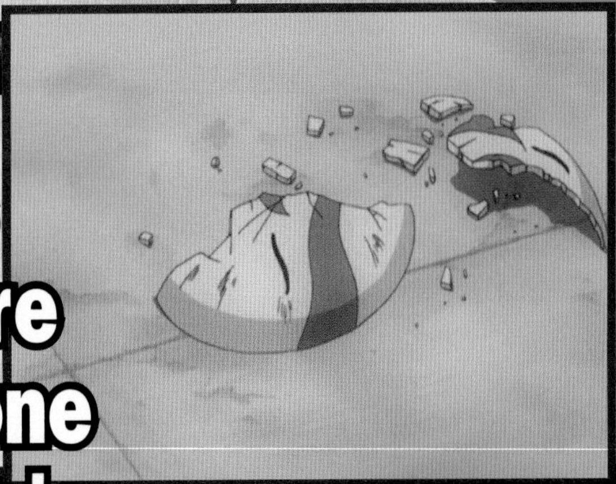

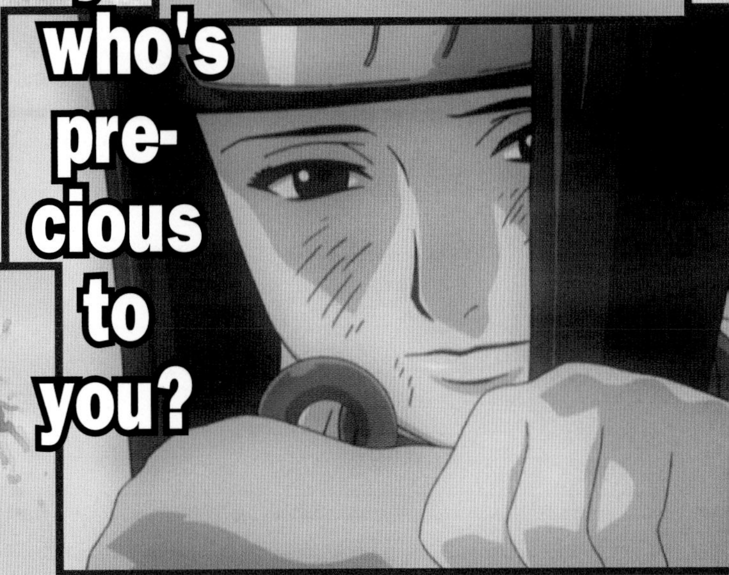
Is there anyone who's pre-cious to you?

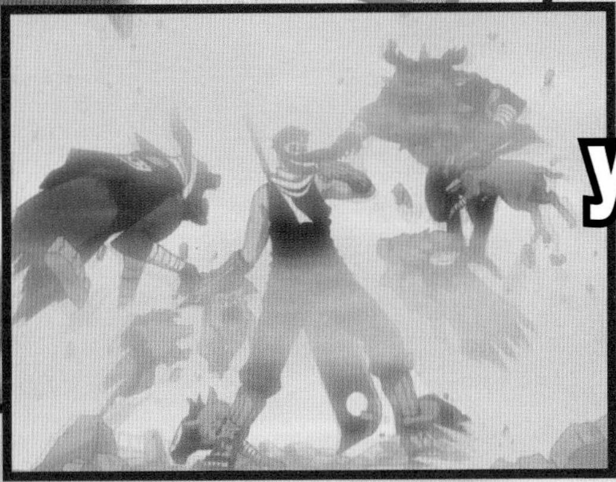

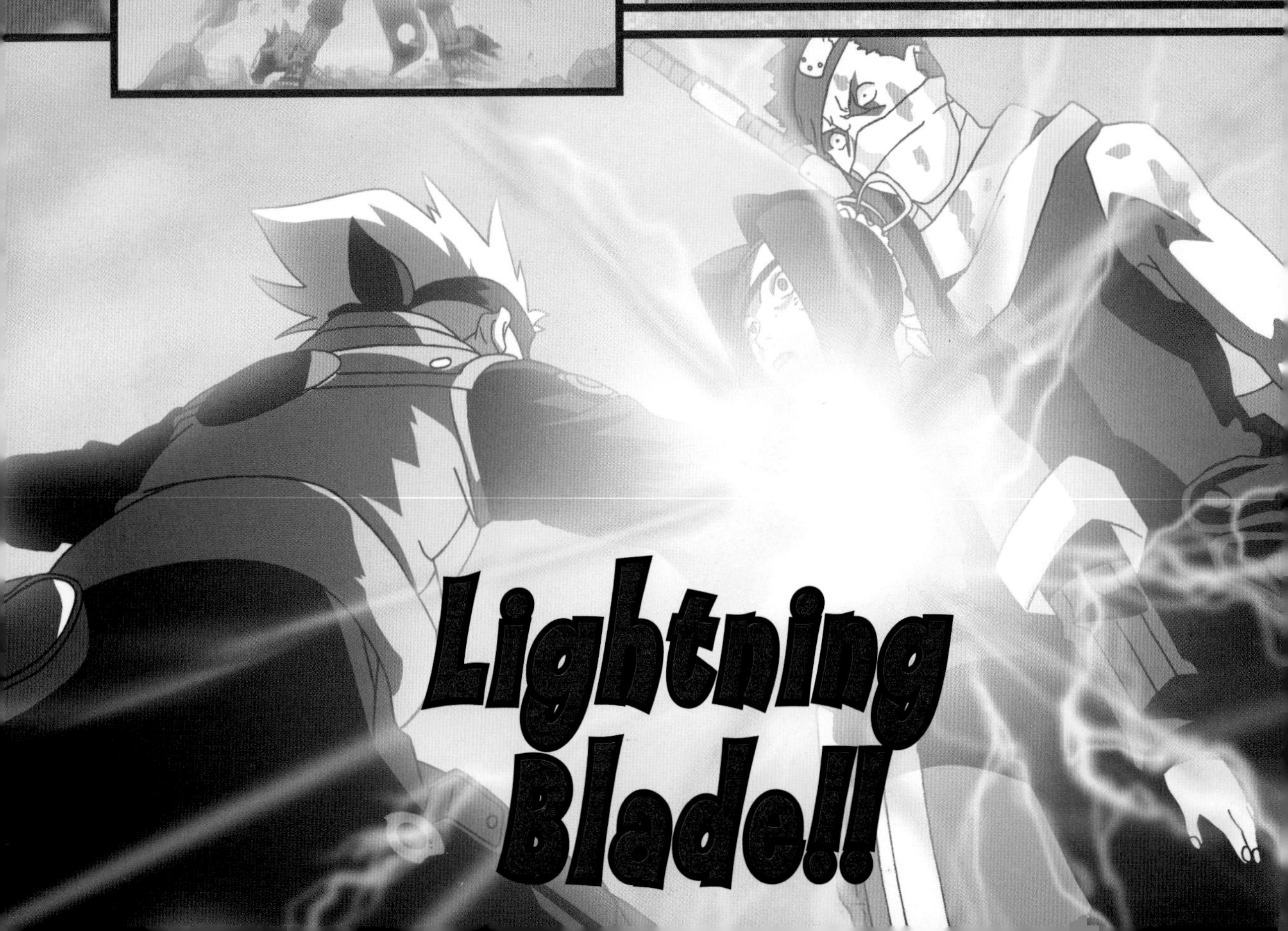
Lightning Blade!!

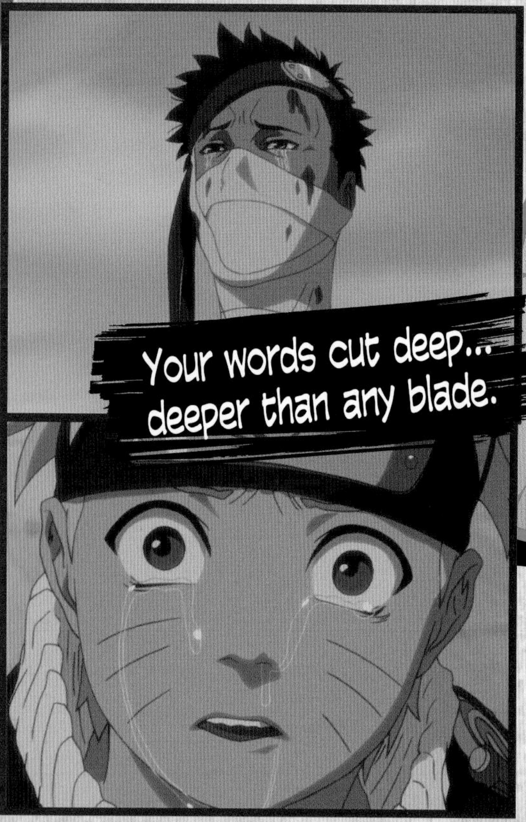
Your words cut deep...
deeper than any blade.

The desperate final battle!

With his pride as a shinobi on the line, Zabuza the demon launches one last attack!
Carrying the single kunai he received from Naruto in his mouth like a fang, Zabuza initiates a final attack. As he dashes atop the bridge, Zabuza's appearance truly becomes that of a horrible demon…one weighed down with violent anger and devastating grief!

Zabuza perishes with the snow!!

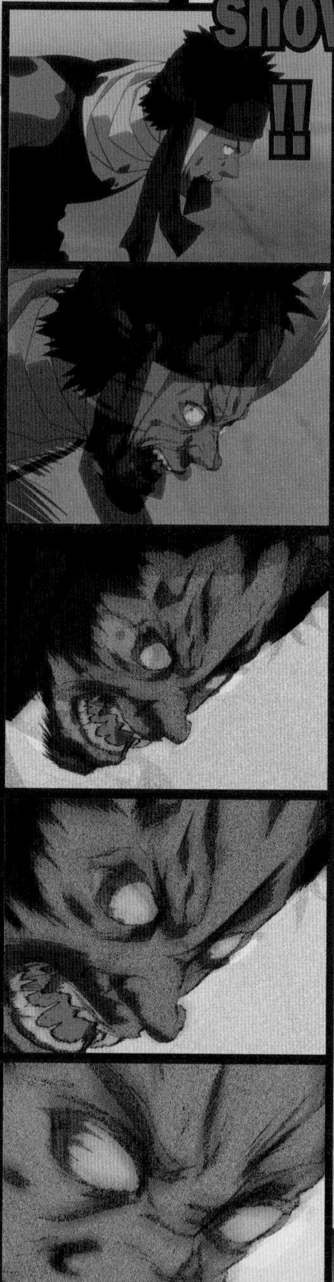

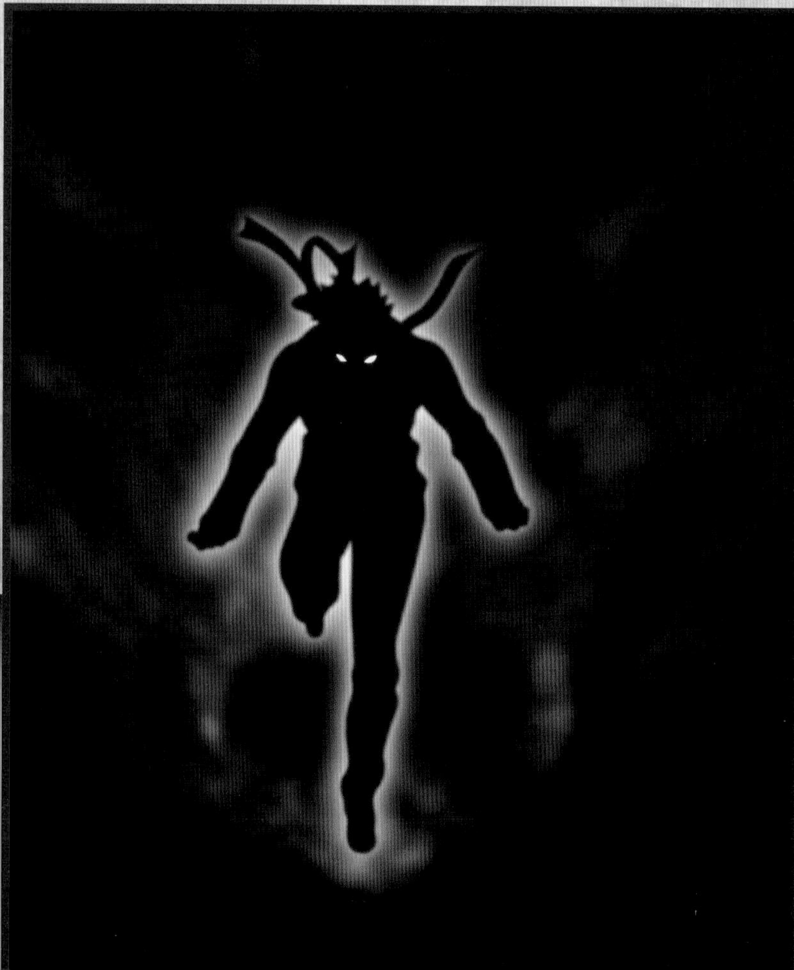

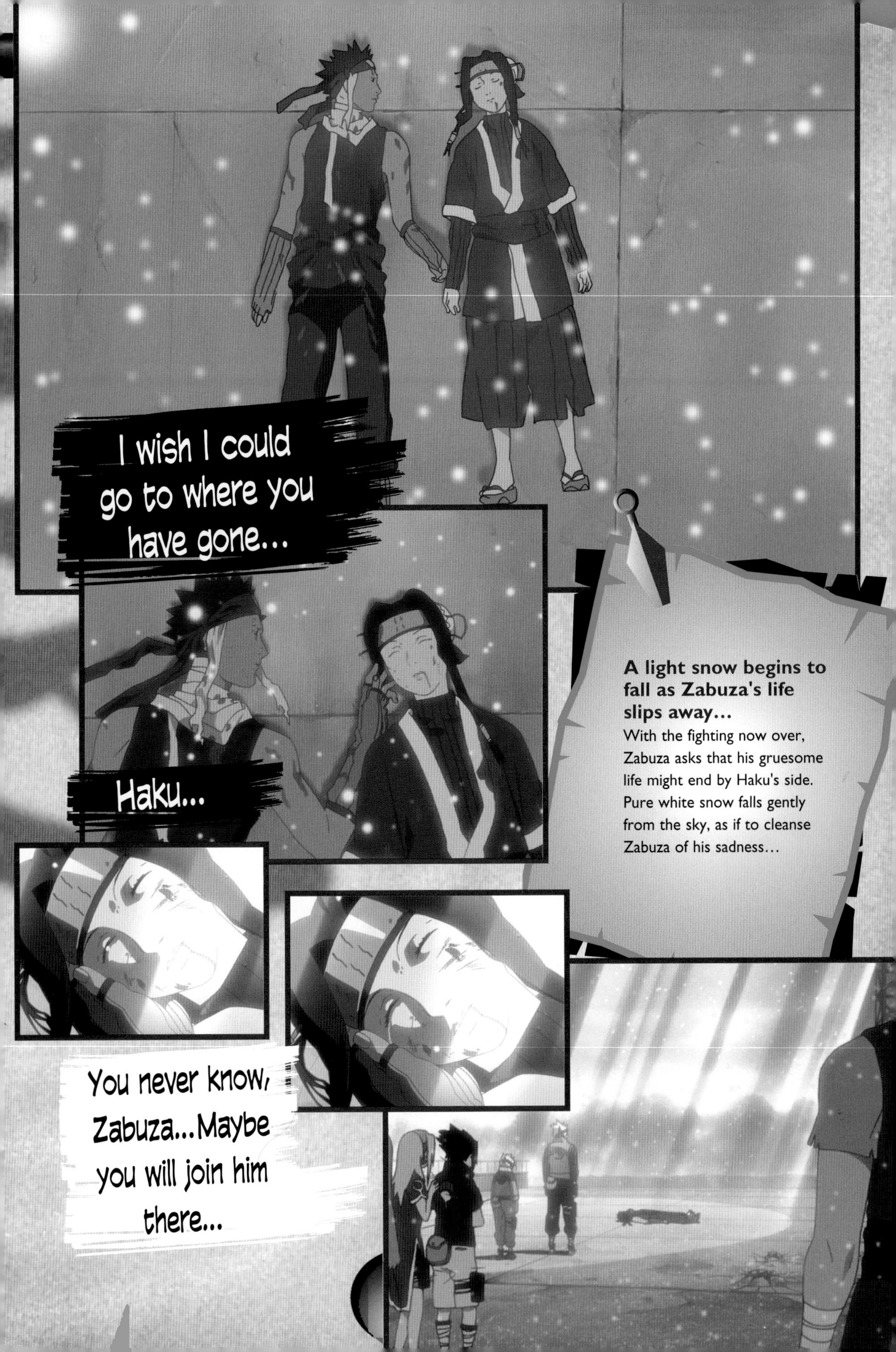
I wish I could go to where you have gone...
Haku...
You never know, Zabuza...Maybe you will join him there...

A light snow begins to fall as Zabuza's life slips away...

With the fighting now over, Zabuza asks that his gruesome life might end by Haku's side. Pure white snow falls gently from the sky, as if to cleanse Zabuza of his sadness...

"As a deadly battle ends, some light still shines...

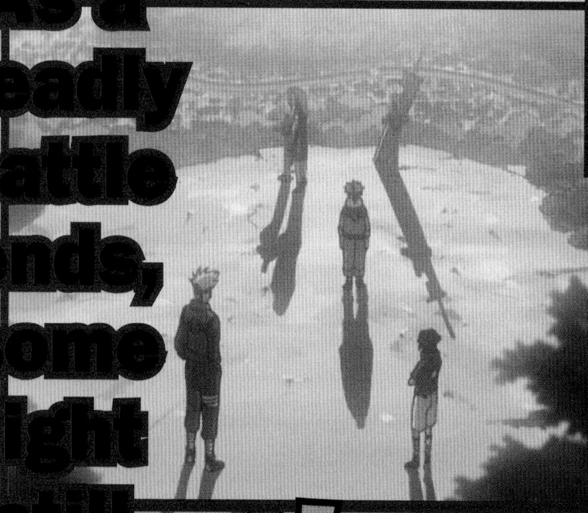

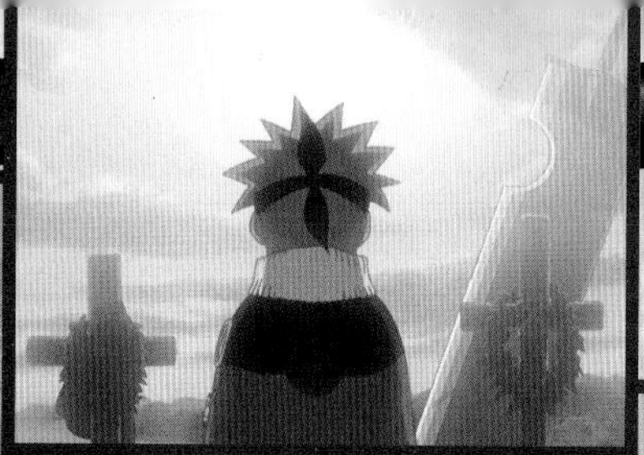

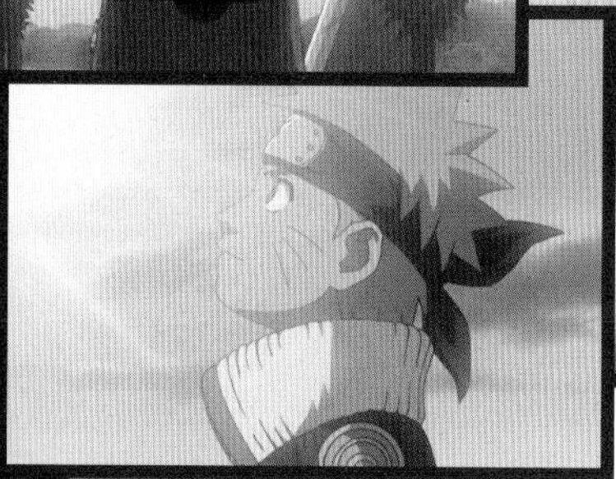

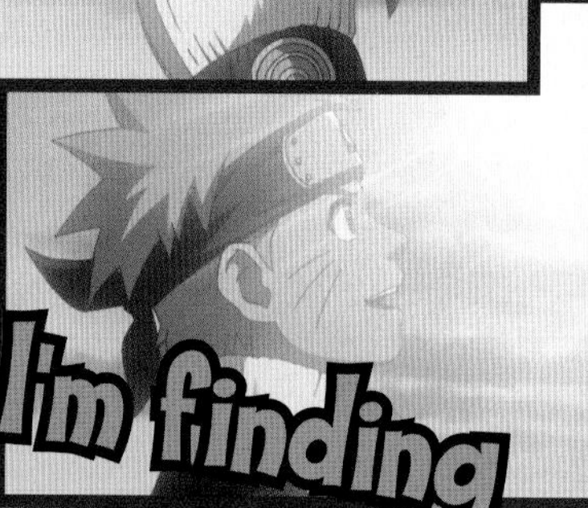

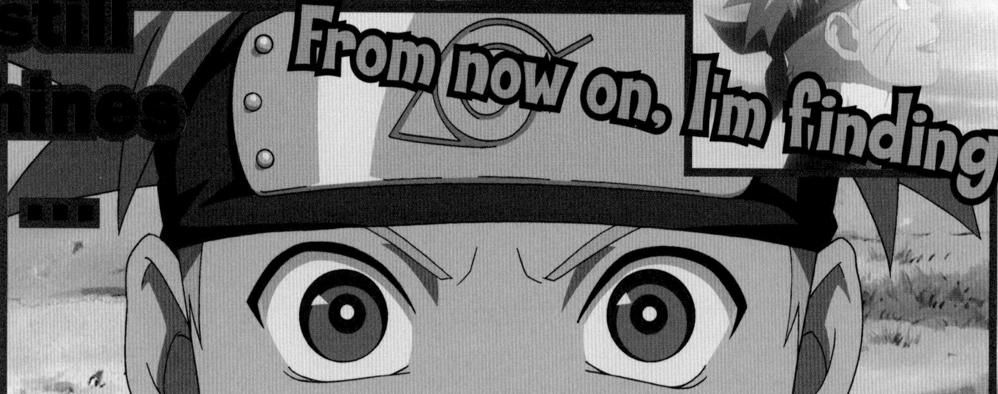
From now on, I'm finding
my own ninja way!

In the afterglow of intense combat, those who survived look to the future! Naruto and the others will always keep in their hearts the memory of Zabuza and Haku -- the "demon" shinobi and the boy who tried to become a weapon -- as they continue down the road ahead. Even if they stumble or lose their way, they'll follow a ninja way that is "straight and true and without any regrets!"

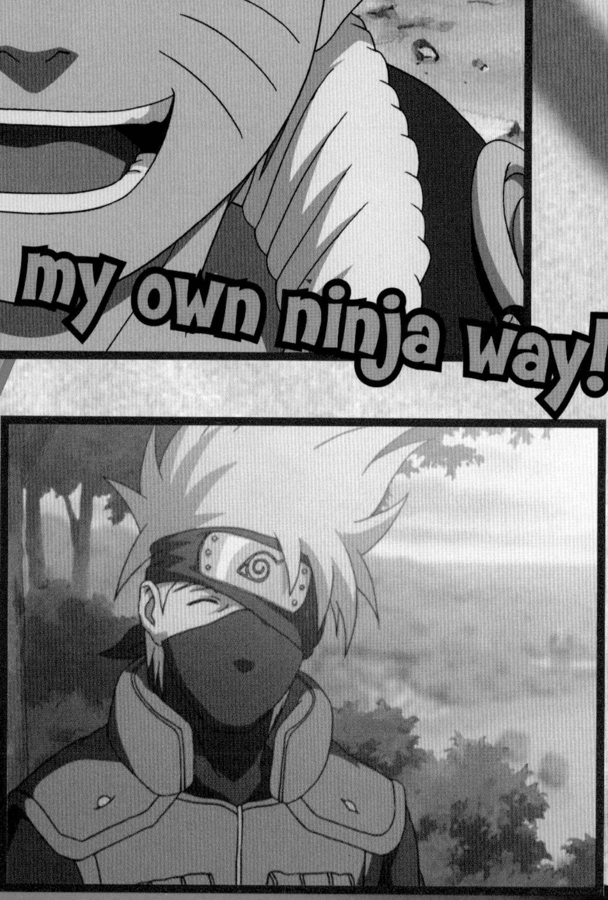

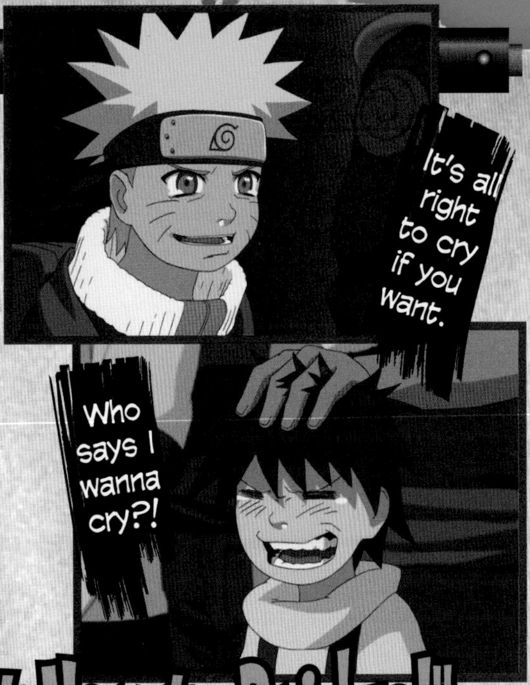
It's all right to cry if you want.
Who says I wanna cry?!

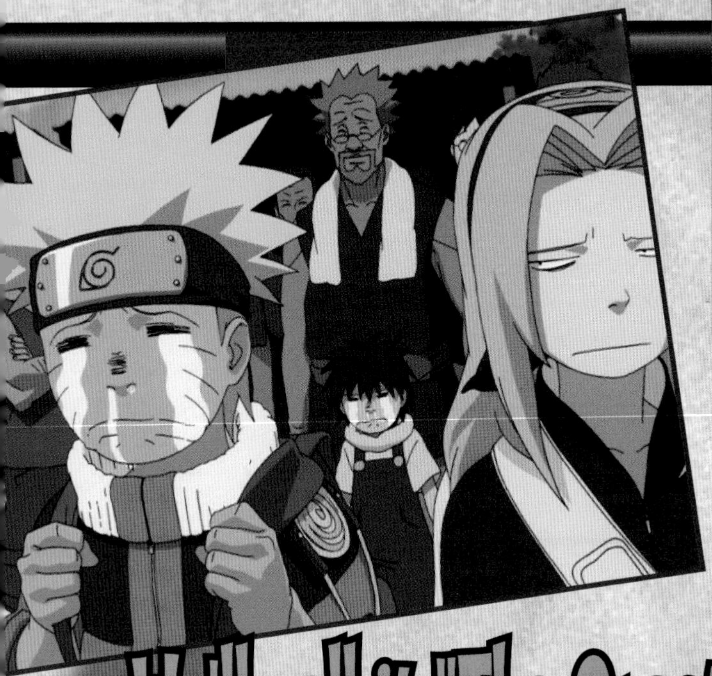

We'll call it "The Great Naruto Bridge!"

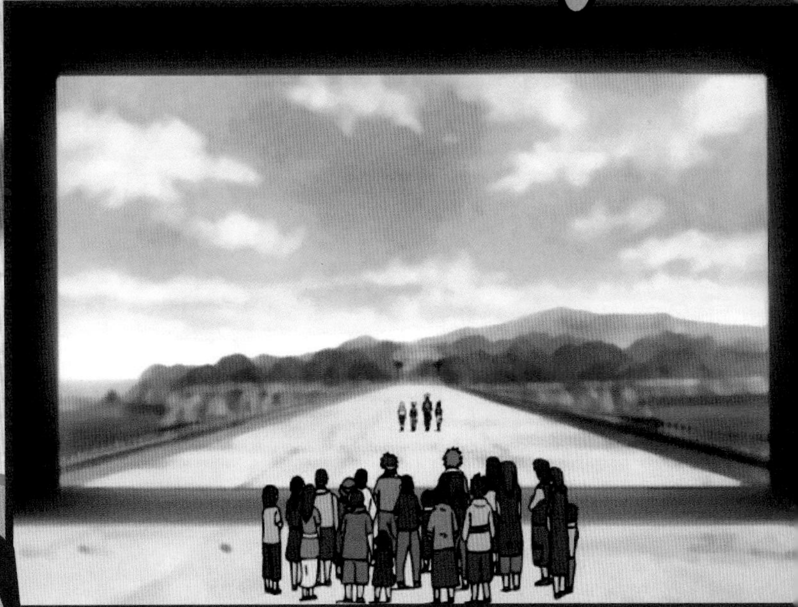

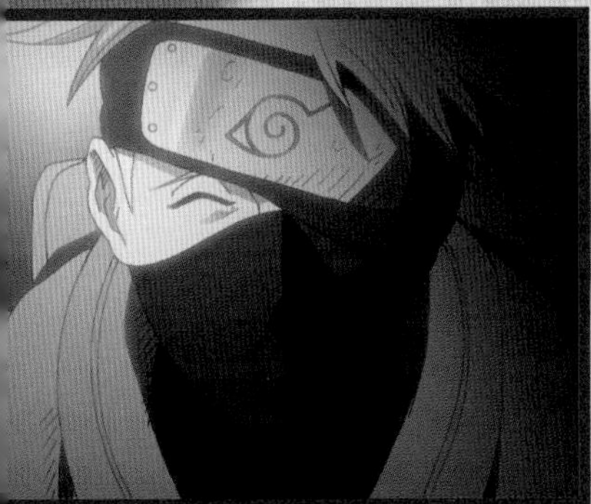

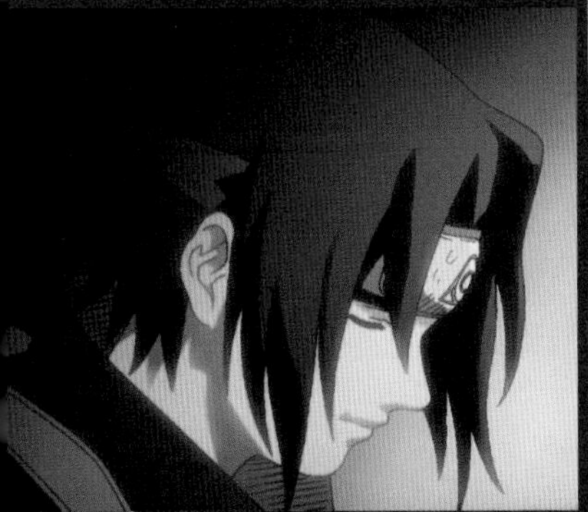

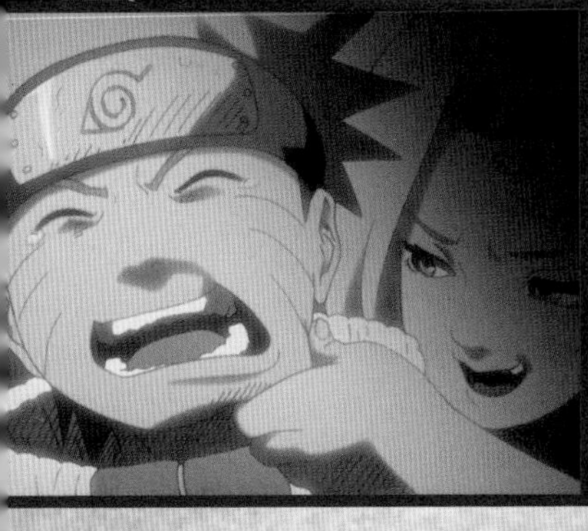

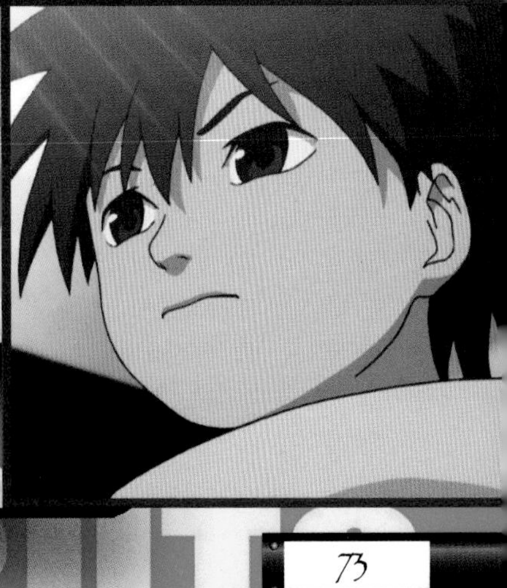

The Bridge of the Hero is finally complete!

Tazuna and his fellow workers achieve their goal of completing the bridge! Squad Seven's mission is now complete, as well. The people of the Land of Waves give Naruto and his party a rousing sendoff. A hope-filled future spreads out before them...

Zabuza Momochi

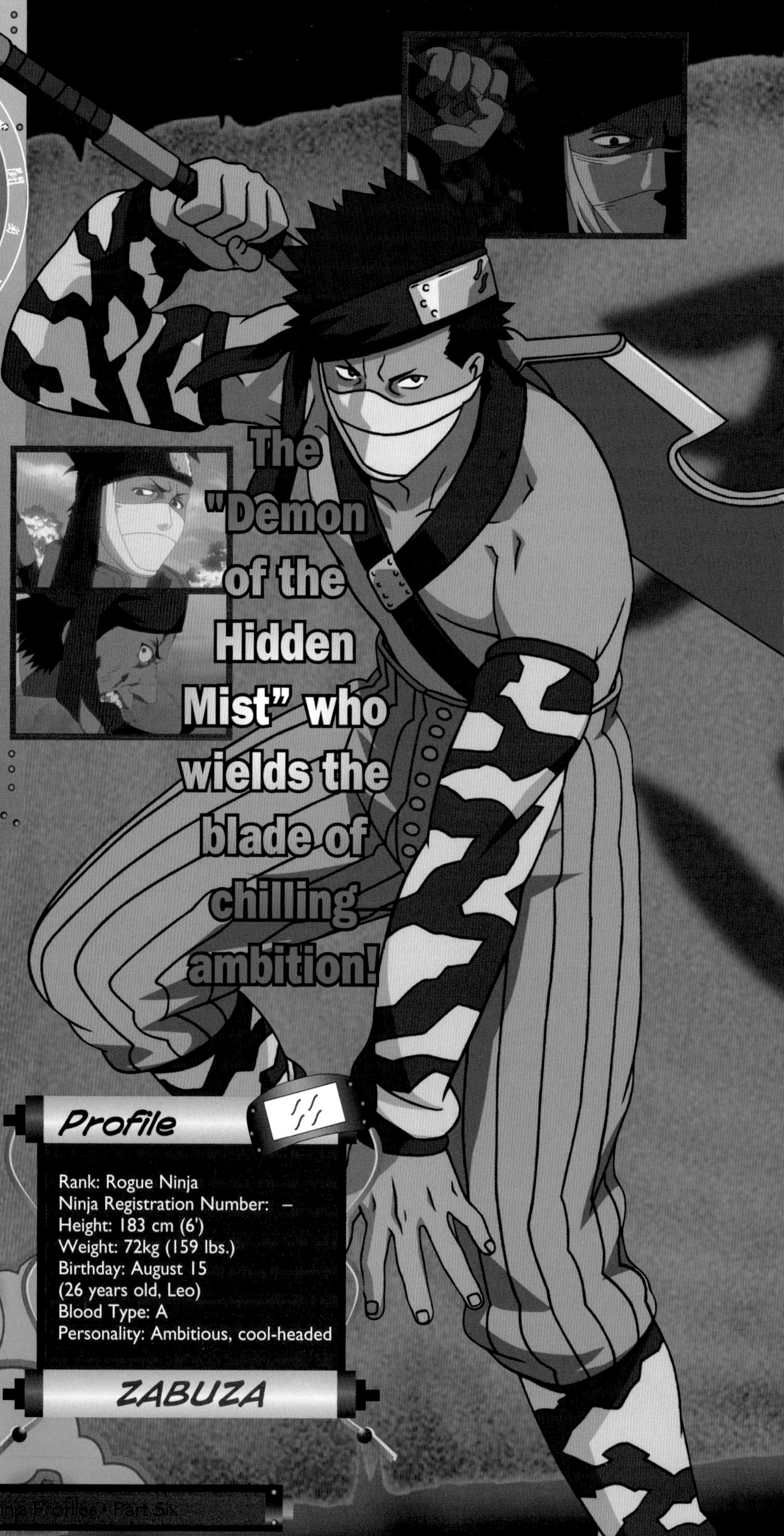

The "Demon of the Hidden Mist" who wields the blade of chilling ambition!

tai 体
nin 忍
gen 幻

Within him, he hides immense drive and formidable talents. His skill with the Guillotine Sword is amazing, and the sharpness of his ninjutsu and taijutsu is particularly impressive.

Profile

Rank: Rogue Ninja
Ninja Registration Number: –
Height: 183 cm (6')
Weight: 72kg (159 lbs.)
Birthday: August 15
(26 years old, Leo)
Blood Type: A
Personality: Ambitious, cool-headed

ZABUZA

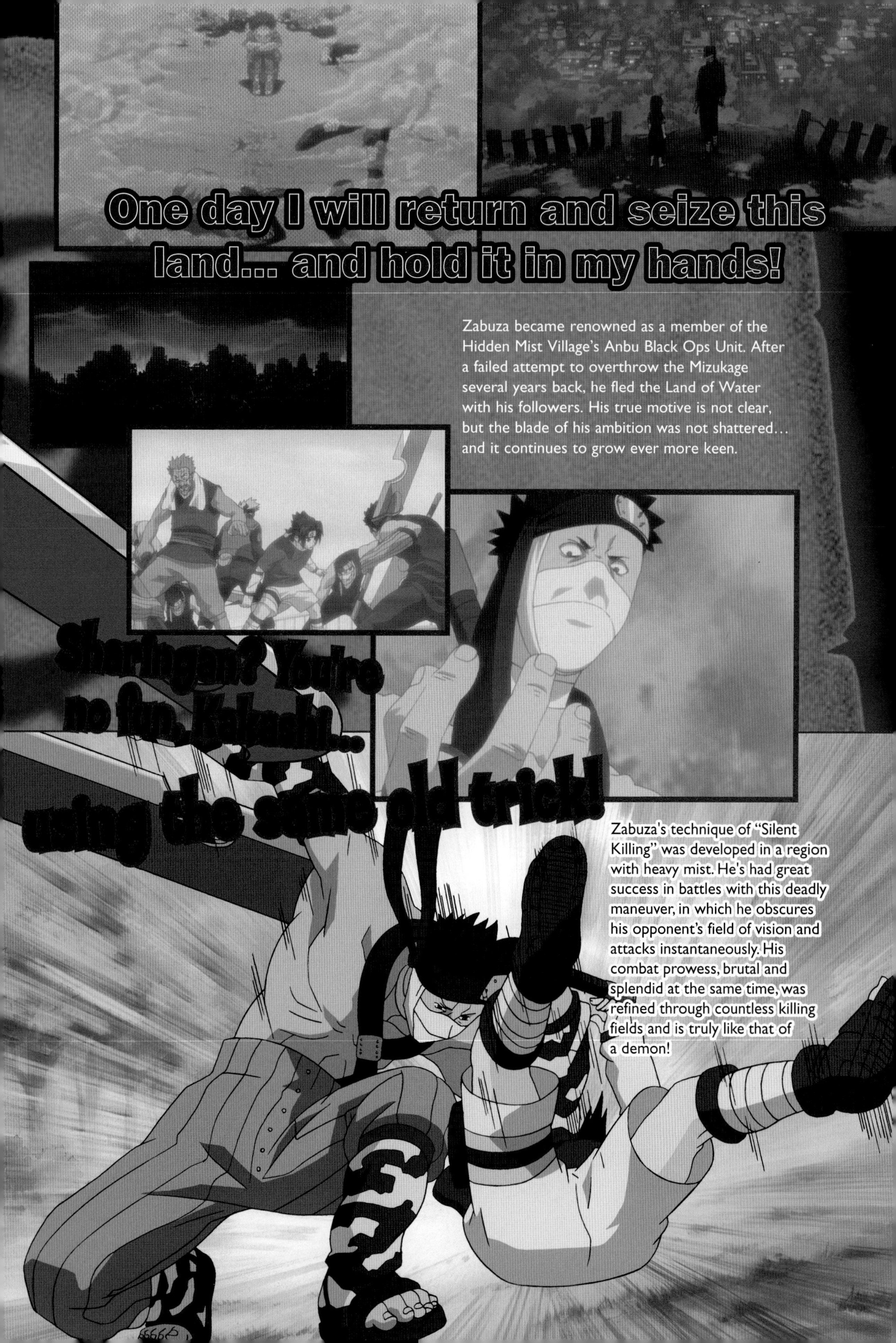
One day I will return and seize this land... and hold it in my hands!
Sharingan? You're no fun, Kakashi... using the same old trick!

Zabuza became renowned as a member of the Hidden Mist Village's Anbu Black Ops Unit. After a failed attempt to overthrow the Mizukage several years back, he fled the Land of Water with his followers. His true motive is not clear, but the blade of his ambition was not shattered... and it continues to grow ever more keen.

Zabuza's technique of "Silent Killing" was developed in a region with heavy mist. He's had great success in battles with this deadly maneuver, in which he obscures his opponent's field of vision and attacks instantaneously. His combat prowess, brutal and splendid at the same time, was refined through countless killing fields and is truly like that of a demon!

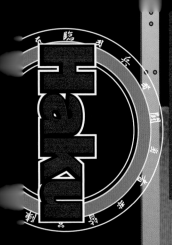

Haku

A fighting machine who has inherited the blood of tragedy...

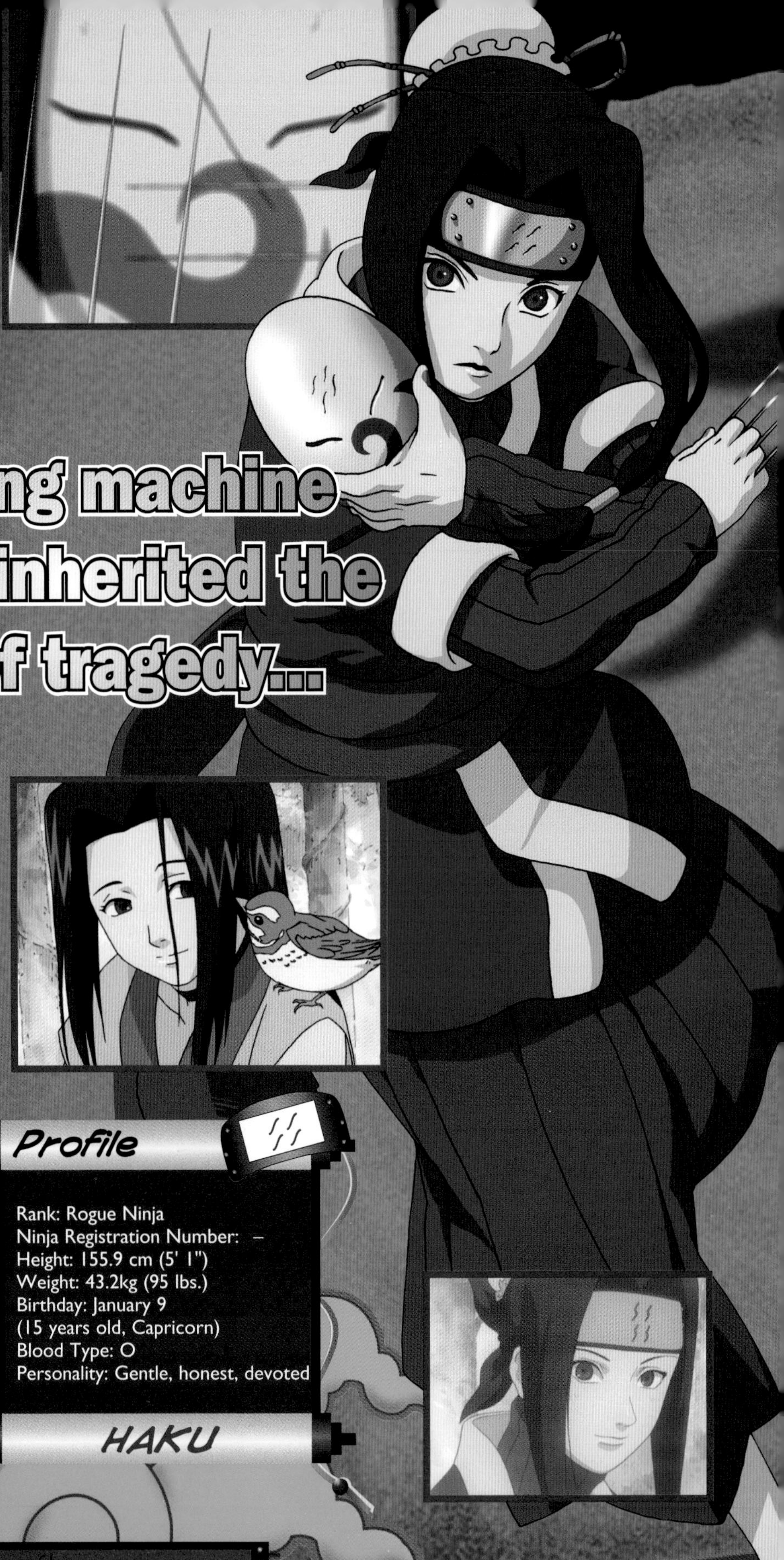

tai 体 nin 忍 gen 幻

He is an individual with a delicate appearance and gentle heart. He hides his face with a mask and uses the power of his Kekkei Genkai (bloodline trait) to become Zábuza's weapon...

Profile

Rank: Rogue Ninja
Ninja Registration Number: –
Height: 155.9 cm (5' 1")
Weight: 43.2kg (95 lbs.)
Birthday: January 9
(15 years old, Capricorn)
Blood Type: O
Personality: Gentle, honest, devoted

HAKU

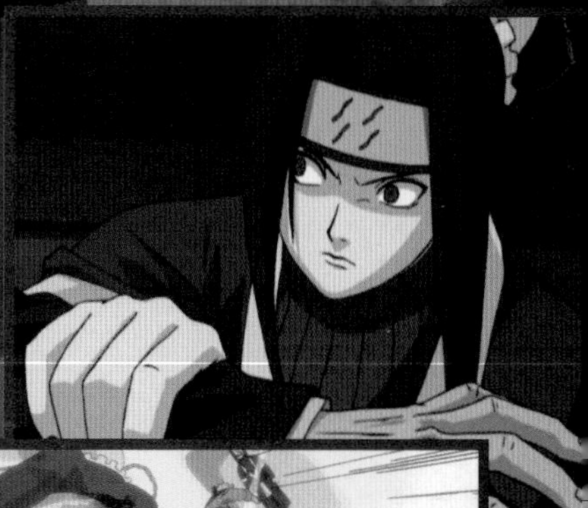

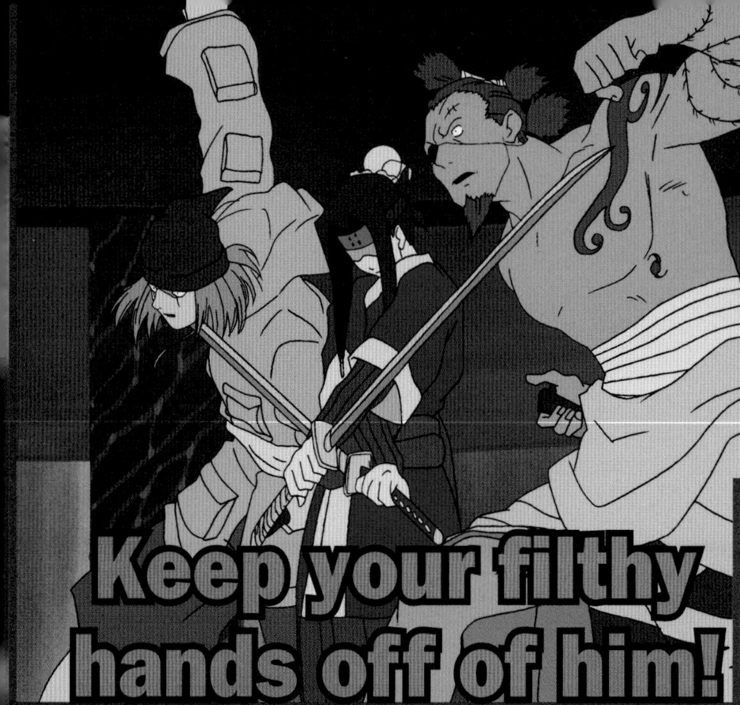
Keep your filthy hands off of him!

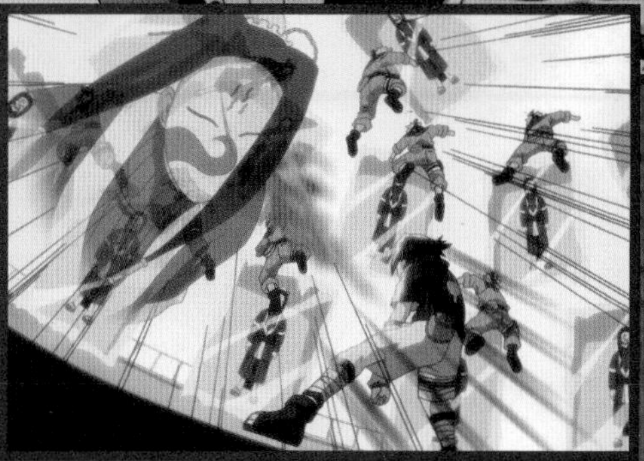

In addition to having amazing physical ability, Haku also possesses a Kekkei Genkai. Without any regrets, he commits his natural talent to the service of his master, Zabuza!

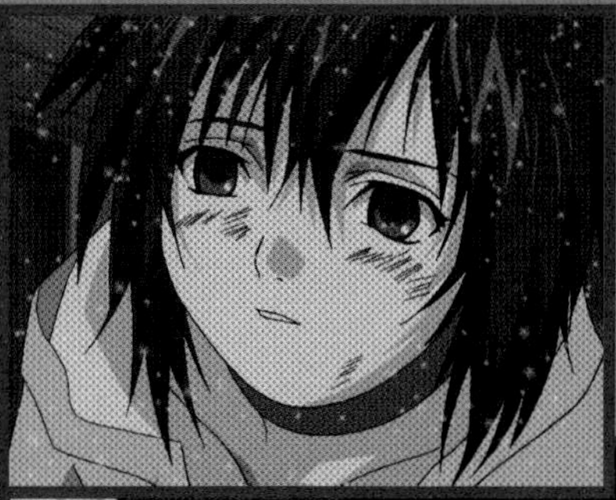

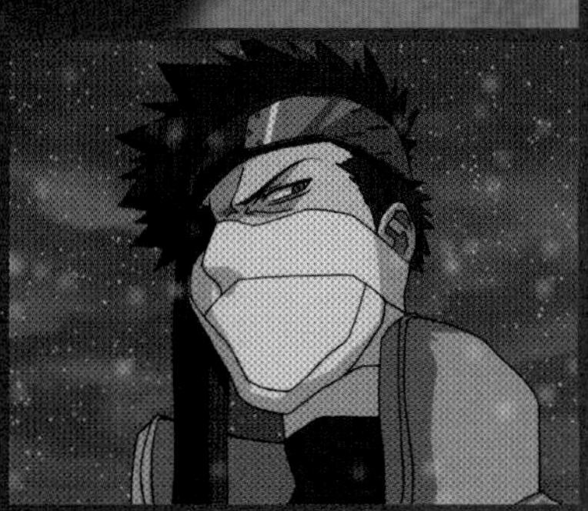

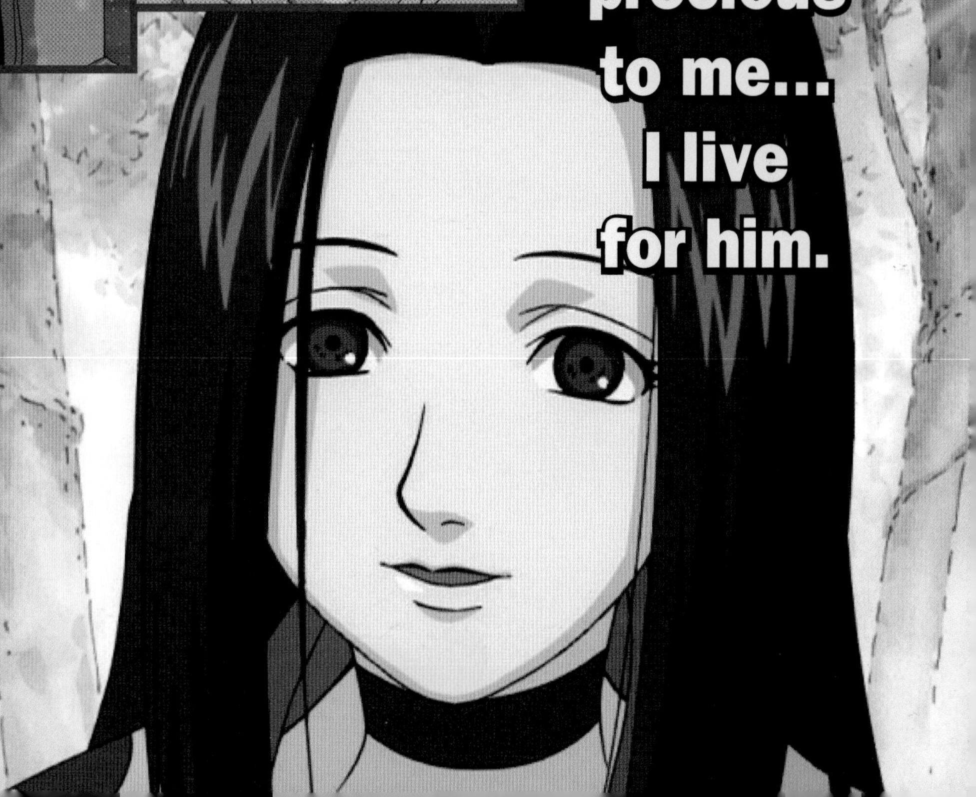
I fight for someone who is precious to me... I live for him.

Because of the Kekkei Genkai that flows in the blood of his body, Haku lost his family and therefore his reason for living. But it was those special genetic abilities that made Haku valuable to Zabuza...so Zabuza rescued Haku to use him as a tool in combat. Haku willingly risks his life to live as Zabuza's weapon, even if that means his path is brutal beyond all reason...

The Rise and Fall of...

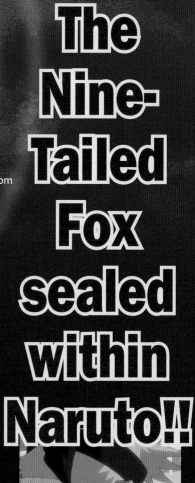

The Nine-Tailed Fox sealed within Naruto!!

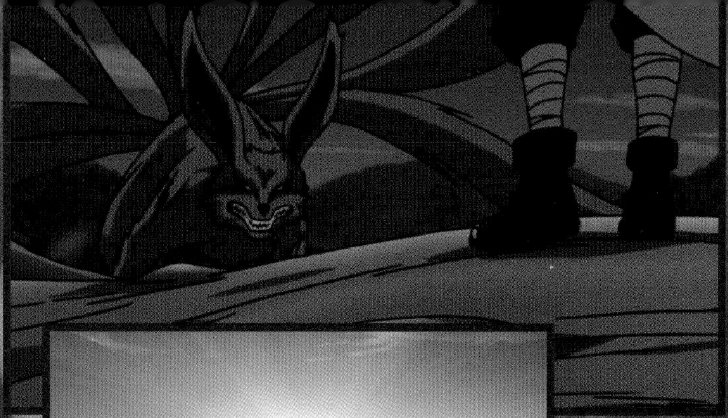

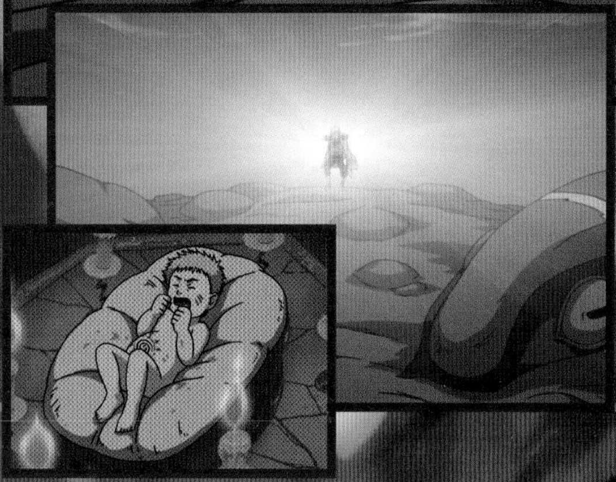

← ↑ The Fourth Hokage sacrificed himself to protect the village from the Nine-Tailed Fox.

↑ The fox's spirit was sealed in Naruto's belly by the Fourth Hokage's secret jutsu,

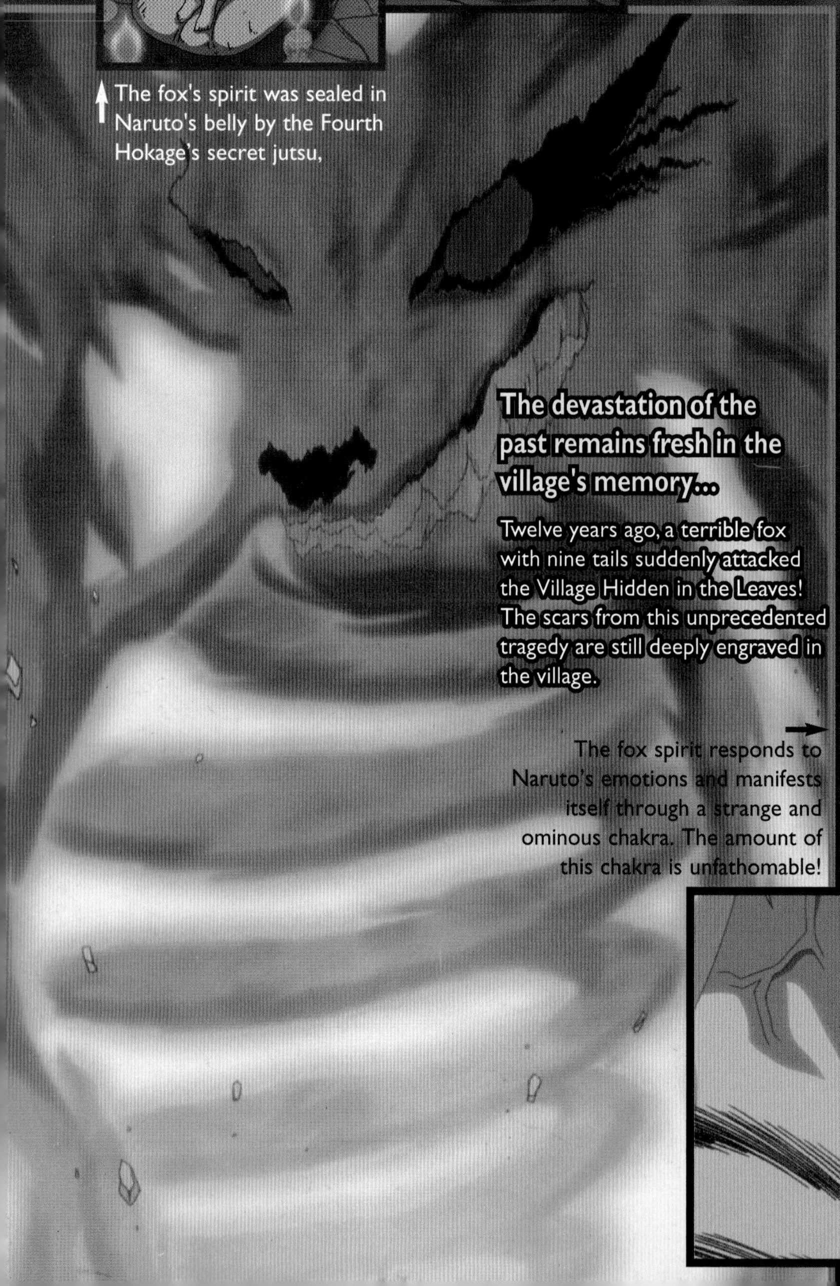

The devastation of the past remains fresh in the village's memory...

Twelve years ago, a terrible fox with nine tails suddenly attacked the Village Hidden in the Leaves! The scars from this unprecedented tragedy are still deeply engraved in the village.

→ The fox spirit responds to Naruto's emotions and manifests itself through a strange and ominous chakra. The amount of this chakra is unfathomable!

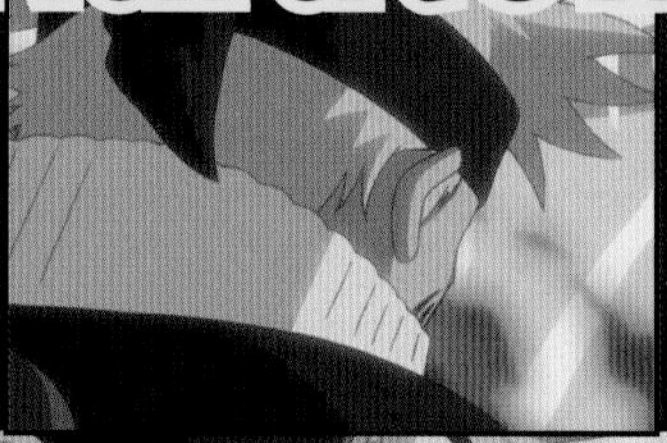

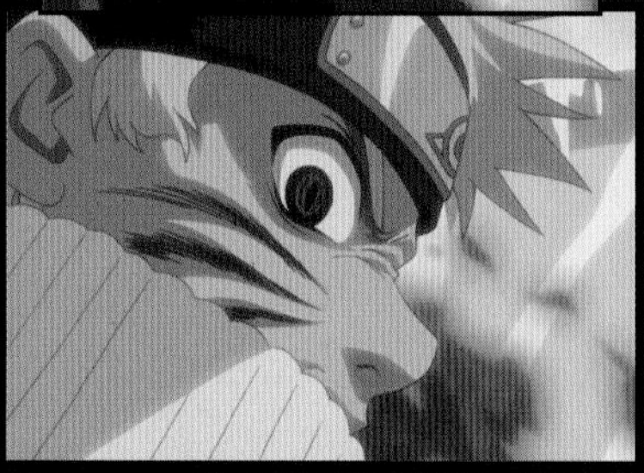

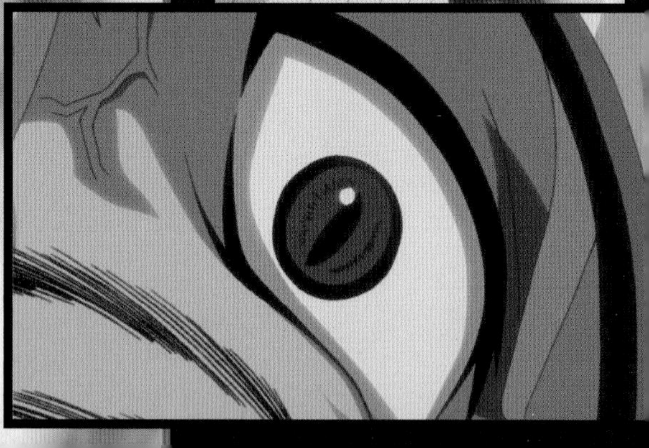

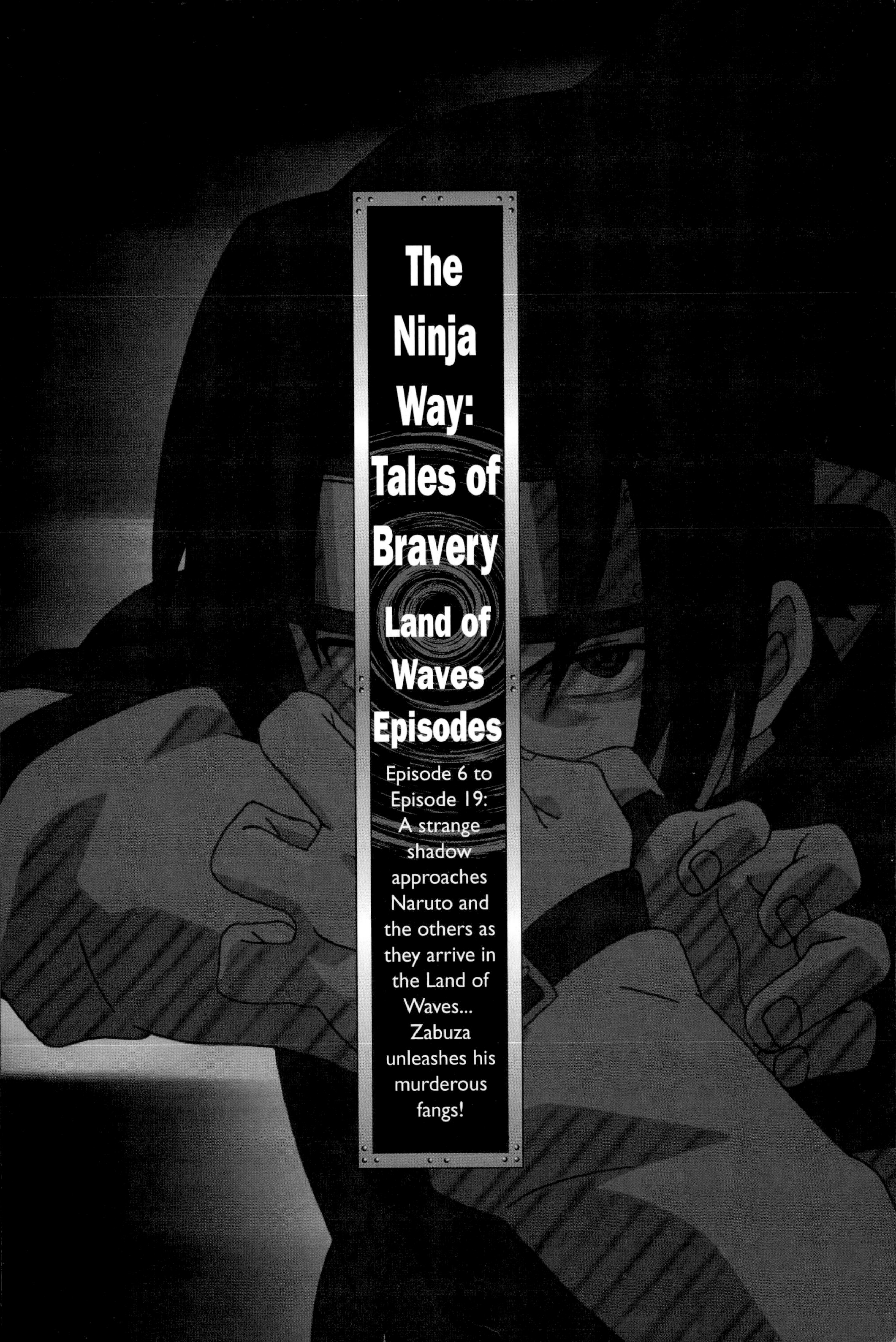

The Ninja Way: Tales of Bravery

Land of Waves Episodes

Episode 6 to Episode 19: A strange shadow approaches Naruto and the others as they arrive in the Land of Waves... Zabuza unleashes his murderous fangs!

Episodes 6 to 11

Is disaster inevitable?! The bodyguard mission begins!

No! I want to go on a real mission!

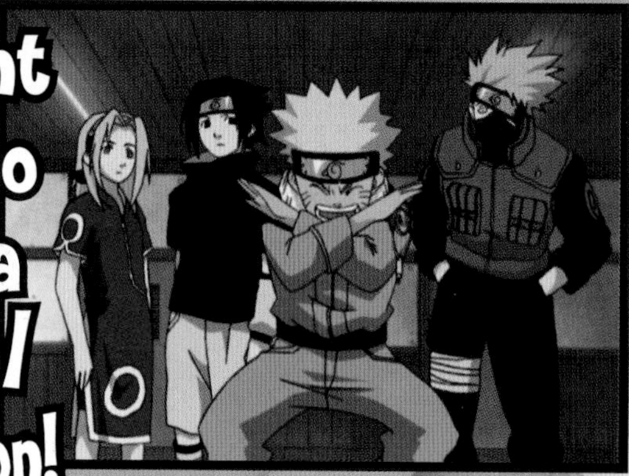

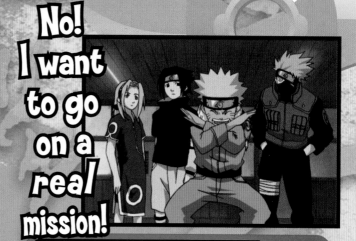

After becoming genin, Naruto and his squad have been completing a steady stream of missions. But they're sick of executing such boring tasks and demand a more important assignment! So the Hokage gives Naruto and the others a demanding C-ranked mission in which they must escort a man to the Land of Waves.

The highly anticipated bodyguard mission commences with a journey to the Land of Waves!

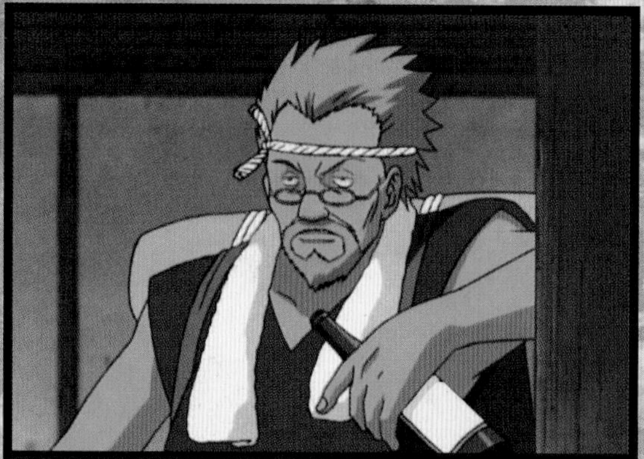

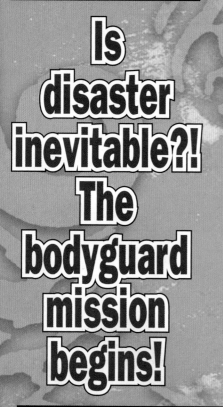

← Their client is Tazuna, a bridge builder from the Land of Waves. He has a mysterious air about him…so does this job spell trouble?

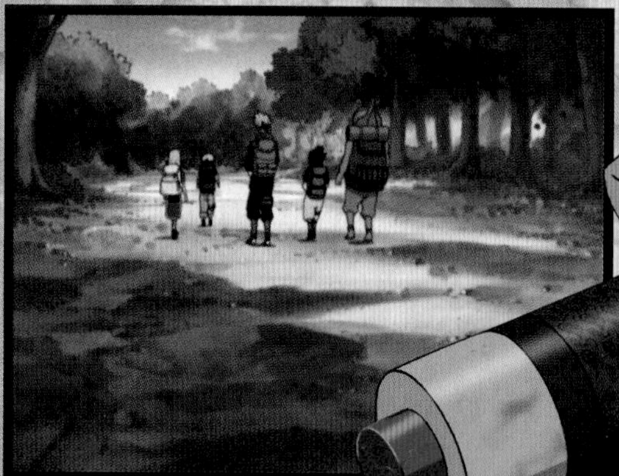

→ The mission: To protect Tazuna until the construction of his bridge is complete. The destination: The Land of Waves!

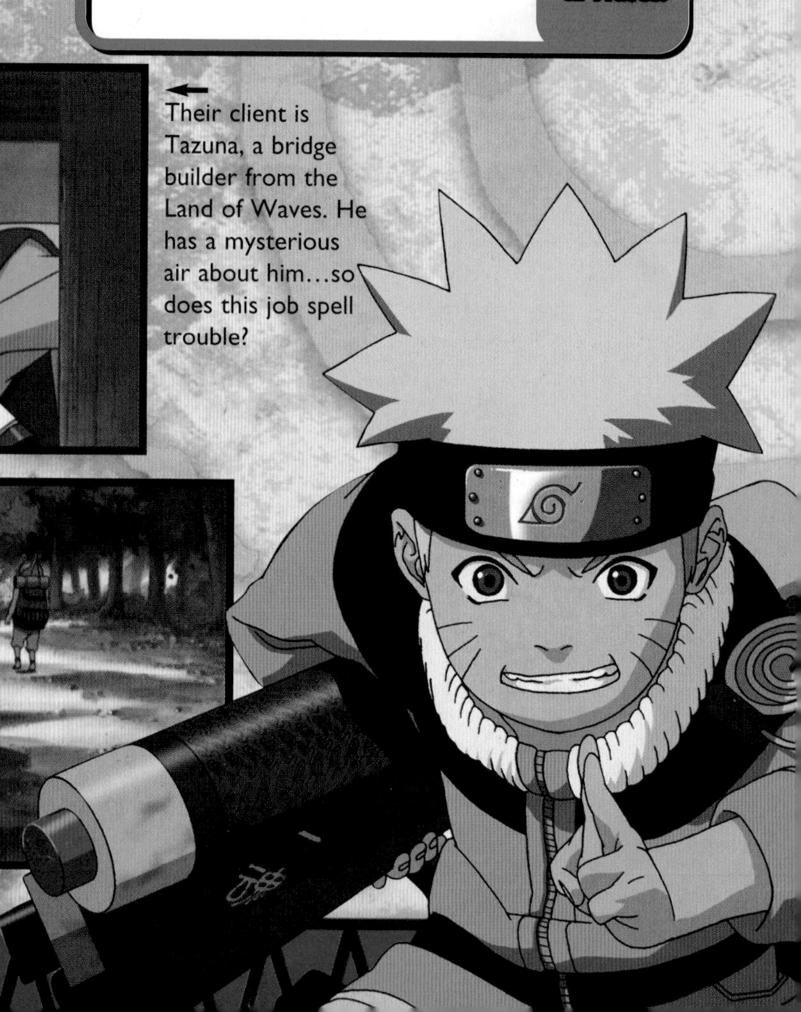

A vicious strike with a deadly goal!

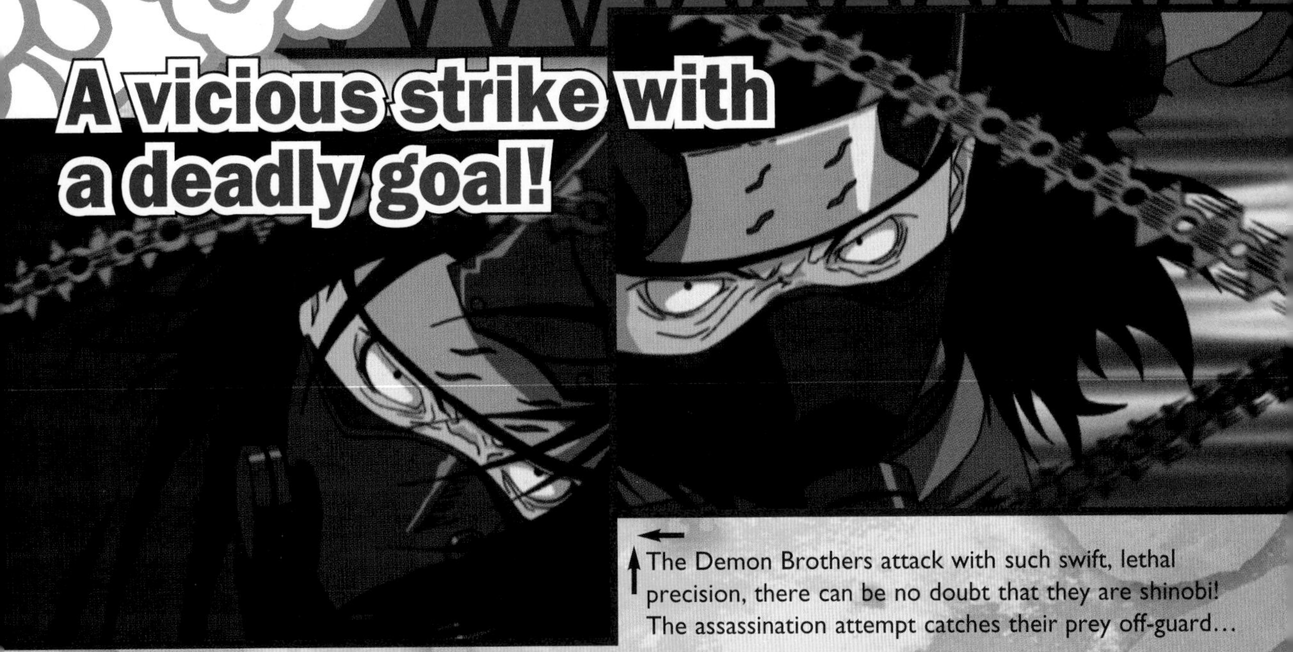

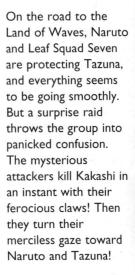

The Demon Brothers attack with such swift, lethal precision, there can be no doubt that they are shinobi! The assassination attempt catches their prey off-guard...

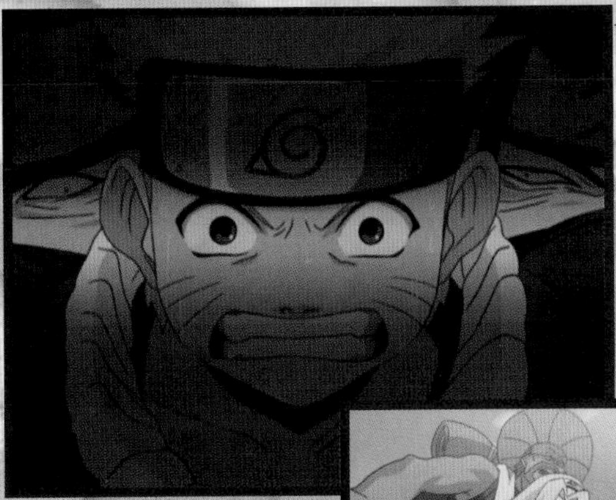

Right away, Naruto is cornered from behind! Does he have any way out?

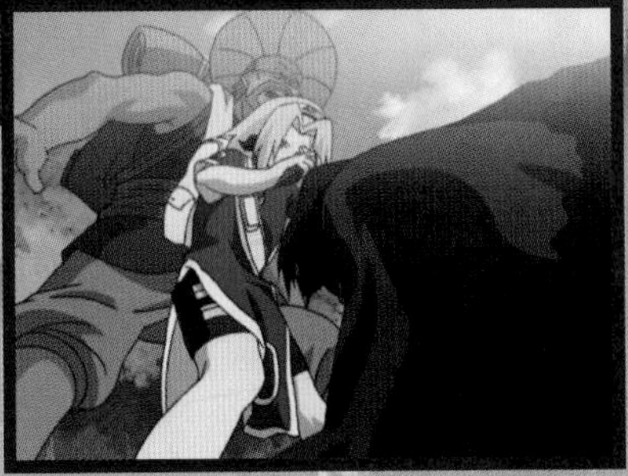

"I...I've got to stop them!" Using her body as a shield, Sakura desperately protects Tazuna!

A sudden, violent assault by the Assassins of the Mist!

On the road to the Land of Waves, Naruto and Leaf Squad Seven are protecting Tazuna, and everything seems to be going smoothly. But a surprise raid throws the group into panicked confusion. The mysterious attackers kill Kakashi in an instant with their ferocious claws! Then they turn their merciless gaze toward Naruto and Tazuna!

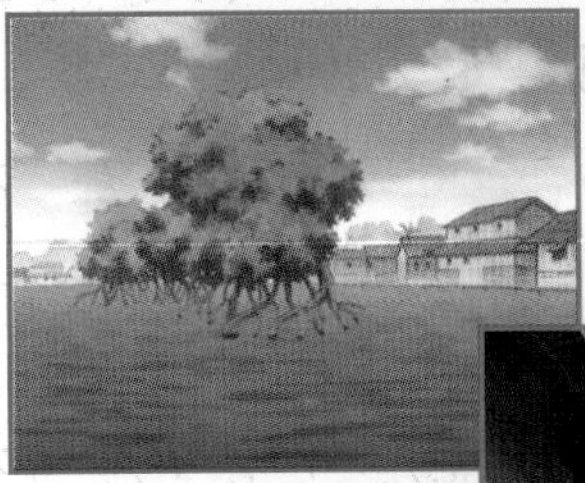

It is a land of breathtaking beauty, with clear rivers and lush foliage.

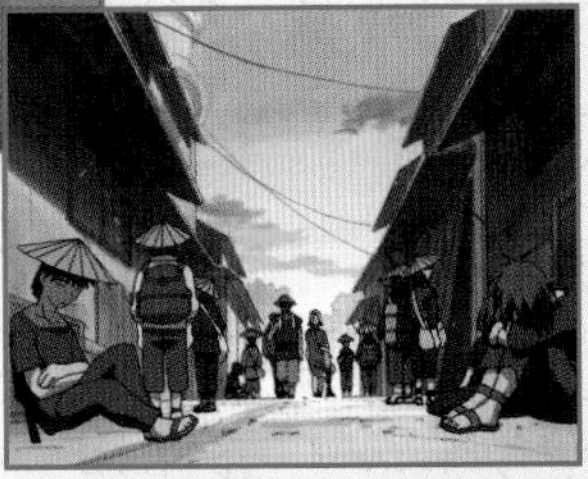

Gato's tyrannical rule has led to poverty, suffering and despair...

South of the Hidden Leaf Village...

A Small Nation, the Land of Waves

Although the Land of Waves lacks natural resources, mangrove trees flourish in the waterways that run throughout the island, and the vistas are beautiful and calm. Also, because this country has few conflicts with neighboring nations, it also has the distinction of not having a hidden ninja village. But this vulnerability has allowed the nefarious Gato to amass wealth, power and influence...

The Demon Brothers retreat, but...

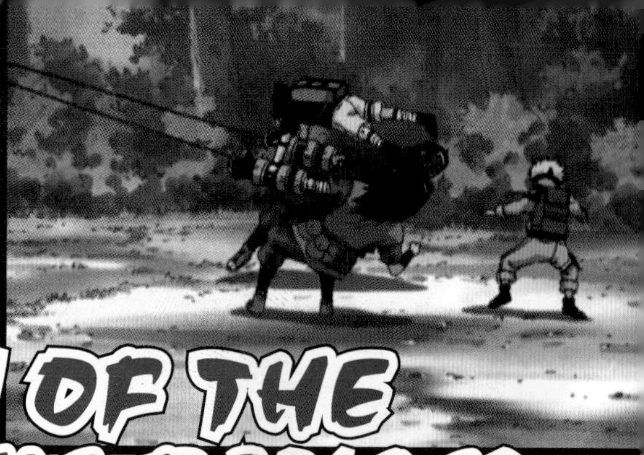

Although this is his first real combat situation, Sasuke displays exceptional skill! Meanwhile, Naruto stands paralyzed…

THE DEMON OF THE MIST BARES HIS FANGS!

Through Sasuke's quick thinking and Kakashi's careful strategy, the group manages to thwart the assassins. Kakashi wonders why they were attacked by shinobi, and Tazuna reluctantly provides the answer. Gato, the powerful and corrupt shipping tycoon, has put a price on Tazuna's head…

Surprise … The true enemy is revealed!

Kakashi only pretended he had been killed in order to observe the enemy's movements.

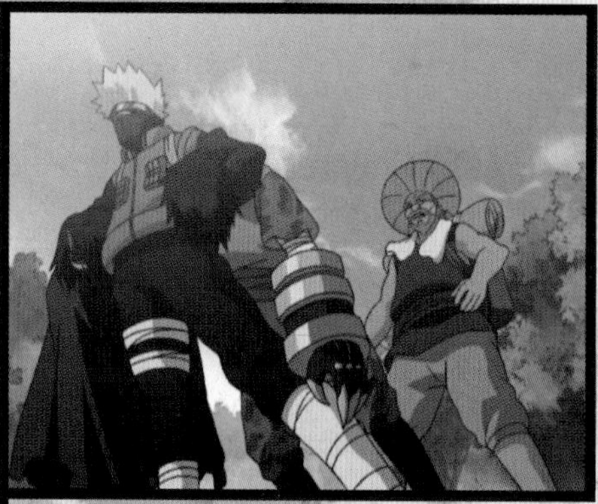

To prove his determination as a shinobi, Naruto cuts deep into the wound on his left hand, but…

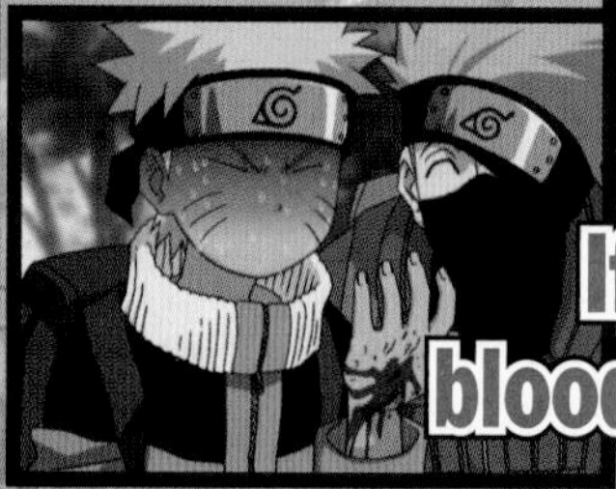

If you lose any more blood, you're going to die.♥

Could the men who attacked Tazuna be chunin from the Village Hidden in the Mist? No… they are rogue ninja -- exiles from the Hidden Mist Village -- hired by Gato. After hearing the report that the Demon Brothers' attempt has failed, Zabuza rises to the challenge!

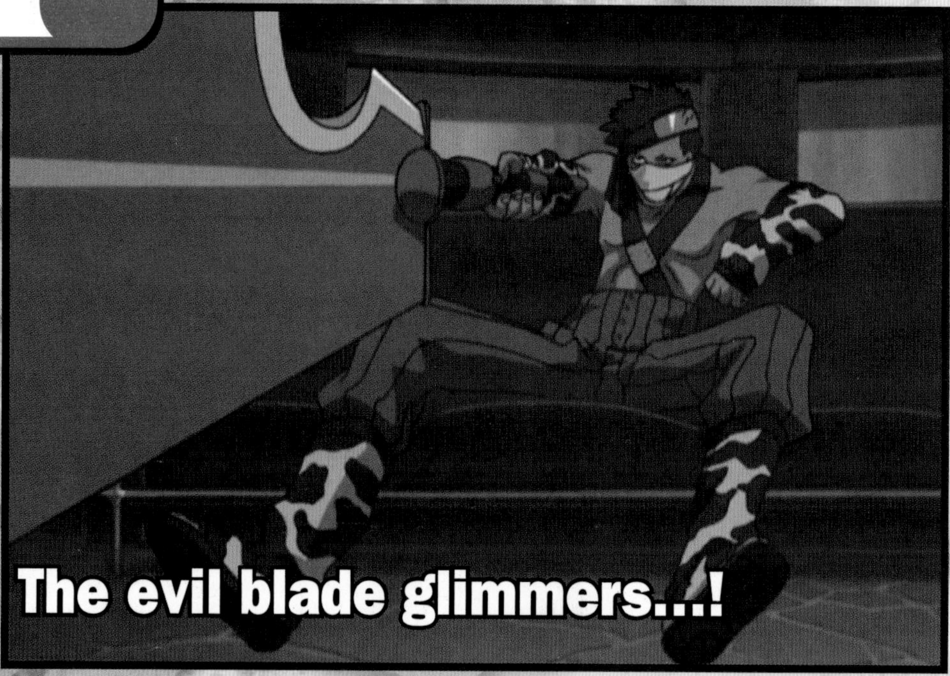

The evil blade glimmers…!

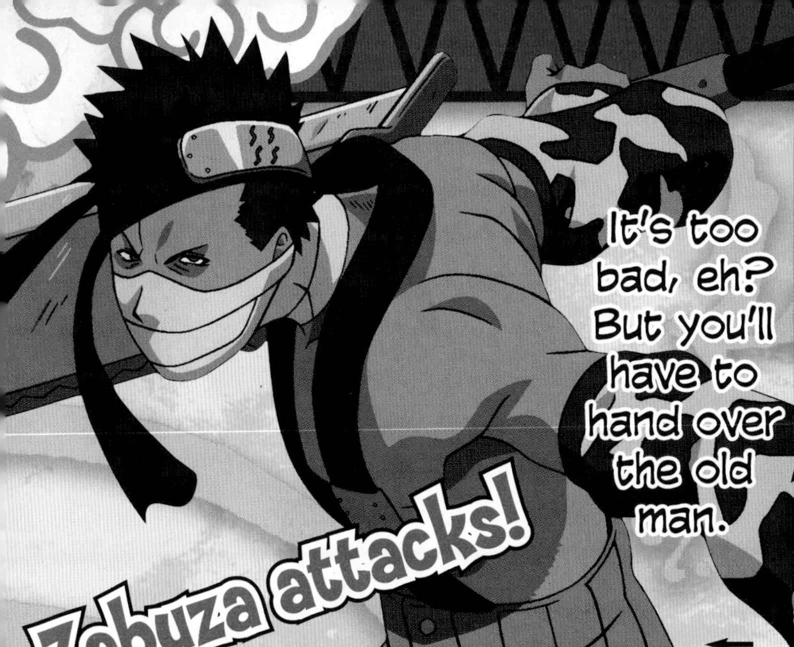
It's too bad, eh? But you'll have to hand over the old man.

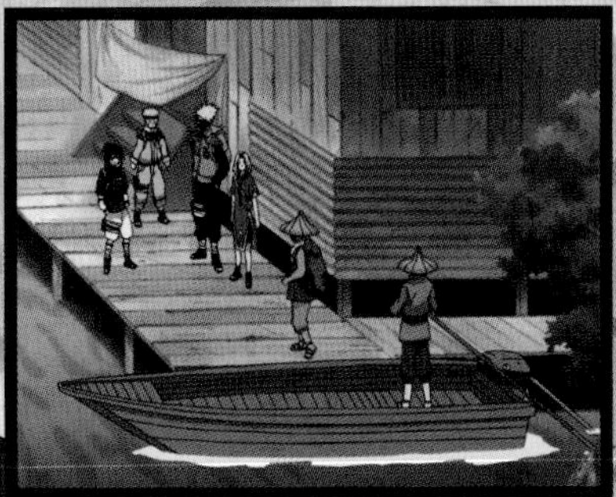

The group safely arrives in the Land of Waves…but lingering tension continues to gnaw at them as they prepare for another confrontation.

Zabuza attacks!

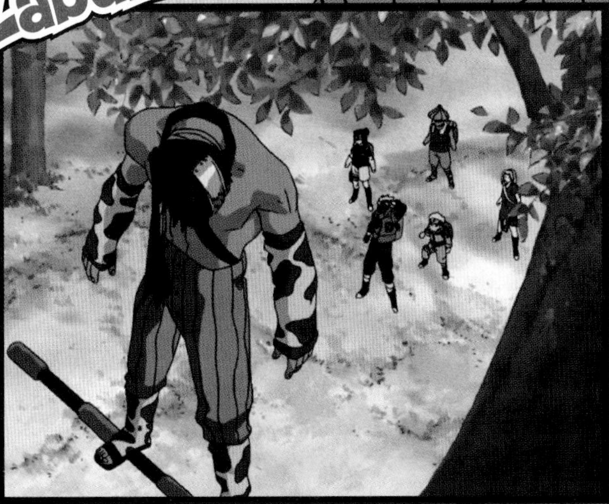

Zabuza observes his prey with a menacing gaze. Kakashi realizes immediately that Zabuza possesses a formidable level of power, so he unleashes his secret ability, the Sharingan, to engage Zabuza in a duel!

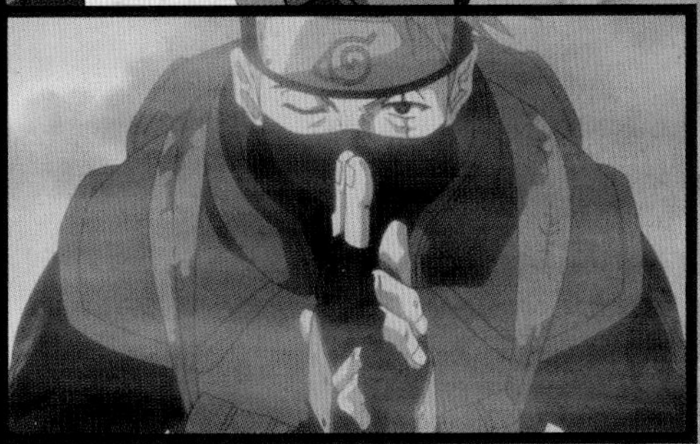

In the midst of the bloodthirsty Clone Jutsu battle, Zabuza takes the upper hand! Death sneaks coldly up Kakashi's back…

Squad Seven faces annihilation at the hands of the over-whelmingly powerful Zabuza!

Almost immediately after arriving in the Land of Waves, Naruto and the others are again thrust into life-threatening danger. Their new opponent brandishes a giant, blood-covered sword…He is an assassin named Zabuza Momochi, who is proud to be known as "Demon of the Hidden Mist"!

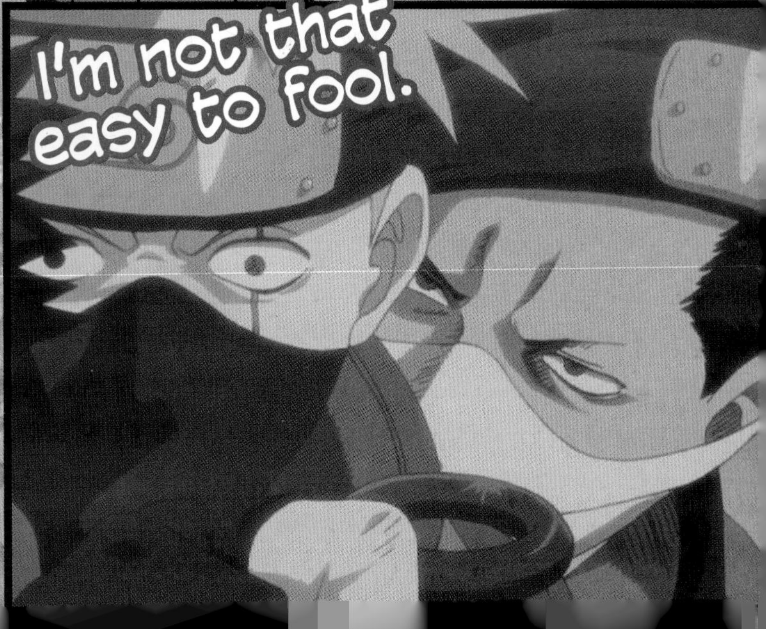
I'm not that easy to fool.

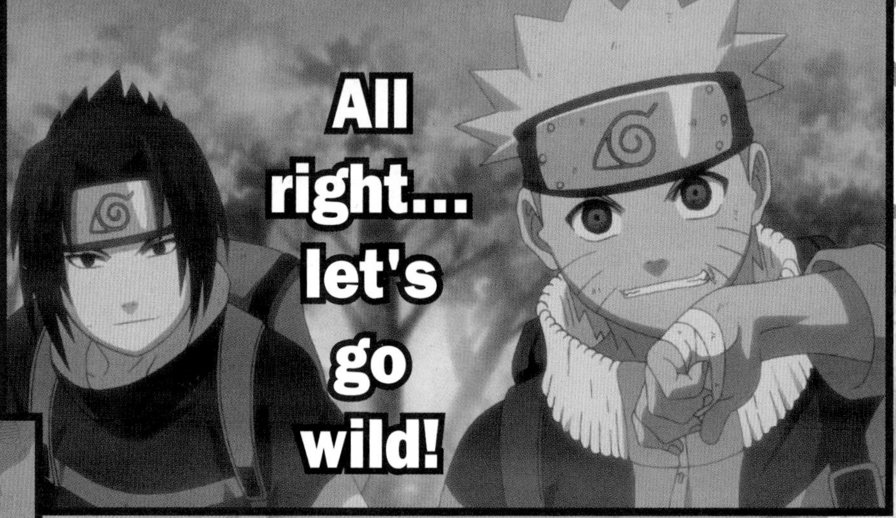

All right... let's go wild!

Naruto swore an oath on the pain of his left hand that he would "never run away." He never wants to feel the agony of shame and cowardice again...so now he must fight!

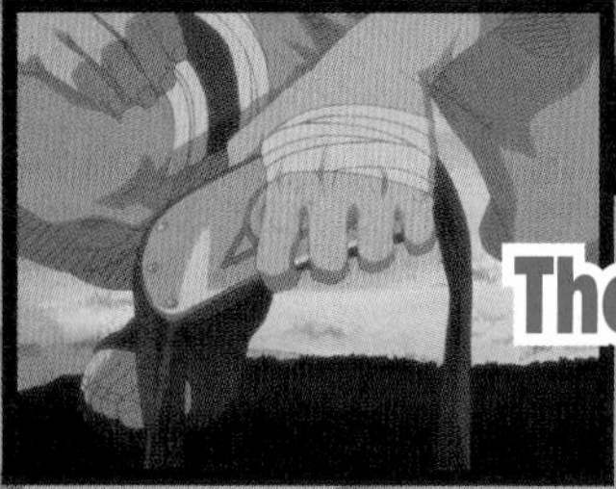

The inescapable Water Prison!

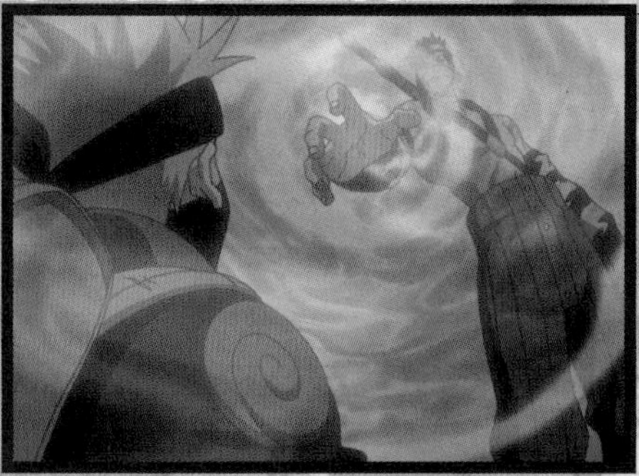

With Kakashi captured in the Water Prison Jutsu, Zabuza is convinced of his own victory...

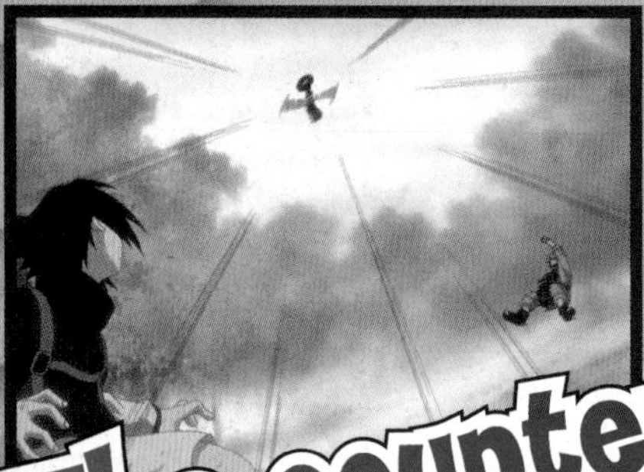

The counter-attack!

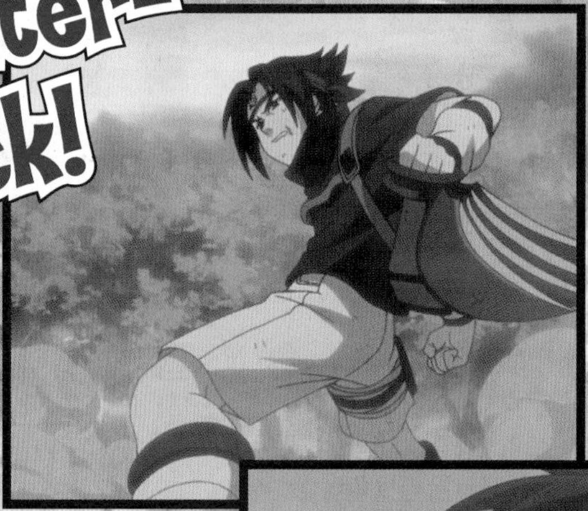

Even if Naruto and Sasuke coordinate their efforts, they have no hope of defeating this enemy. Their only choice is to rescue Kakashi from the Water Prison. At that moment, their two wills are forged into a single driving purpose!

With no room for error, Sasuke keeps his cool and hurls his shuriken at Zabuza with stunning accuracy. It's a huge gamble...the fate of Sasuke's comrades rests on the blade of his shuriken!

Rescue Kakashi! The burning determination of the shinobi!

Zabuza's incredible skill even overpowers Kakashi, who ends up trapped within the Water Prison Jutsu. In these desperate circumstances, there is only one path to follow. With heartfelt commitment not to retreat even a single step, Naruto and Sasuke face the demon!

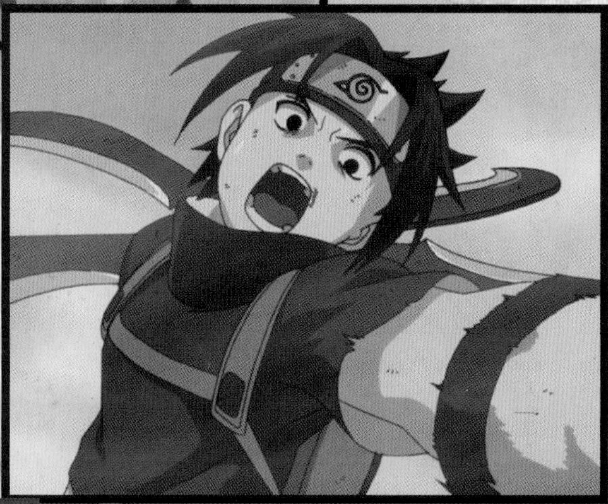

Sharingan!!

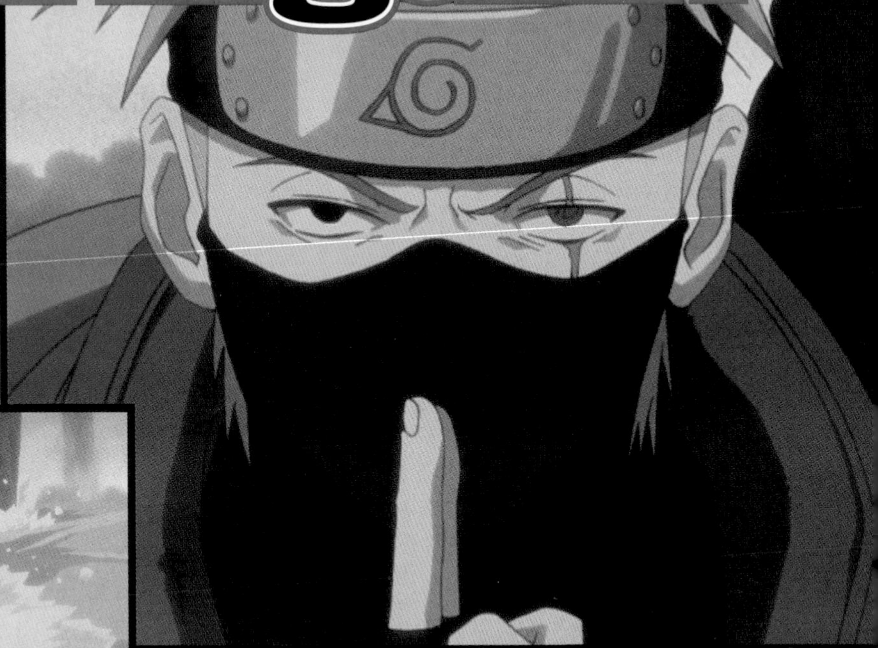

The Sharingan eye sees through all trickery and illusion, grasping Zabuza's jutsu as well as seeming to read his thoughts and the secrets of his very soul! With Kakashi unleashing Zabuza's own jutsu faster than he himself can, Zabuza has no moves left and must concede…

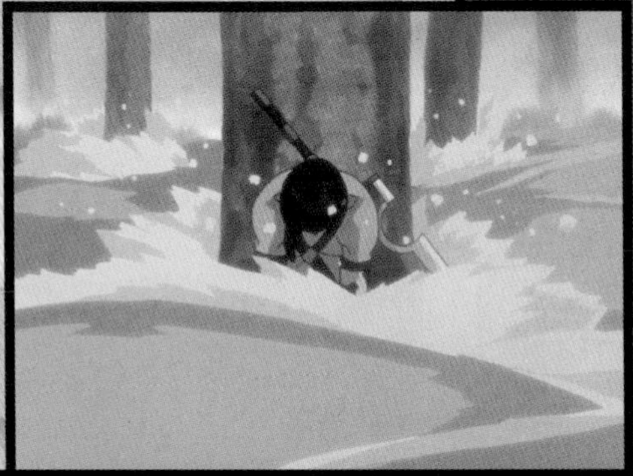

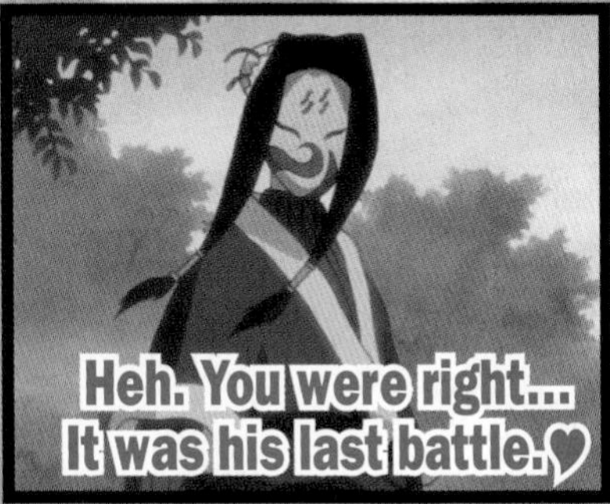
Heh. You were right... It was his last battle.♥

The mysterious shinobi who finishes off Zabuza claims that he is a member of the Elite Tracking Unit from the Hidden Mist Village and says he was on a mission to kill the rogue ninja.

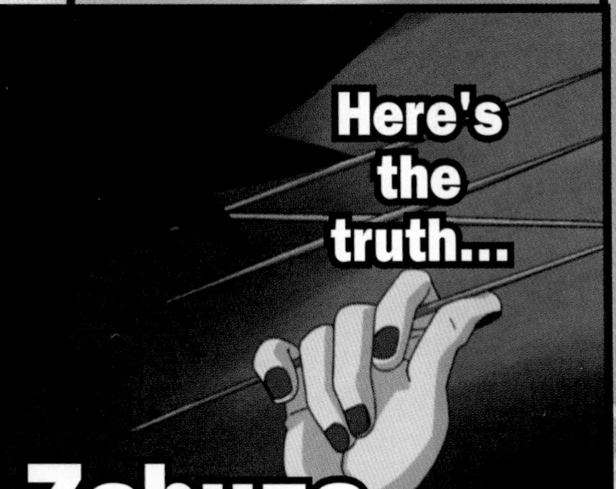
Here's the truth...

Could Zabuza have merely been in a deathlike state?!

Zabuza is still alive!

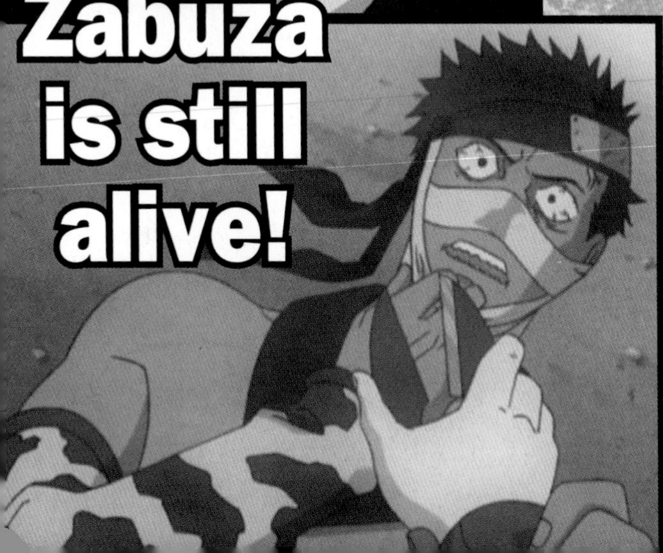

Zabuza is defeated! But...?

Naruto and Sasuke's combination attack destroys the Water Prison and they manage to release Kakashi. Kakashi turns his Sharingan on Zabuza, perceiving and copying his opponent's powerful Water Style jutsu. After an intense battle, Kakashi is finally on the brink of defeating Zabuza…!!

You need to apply the power of chakra through training!

Kakashi is proud of how his pupils acquitted themselves in the battle with Zabuza, but he knows they need more training. They must develop their chakra control by climbing trees…without using their hands!

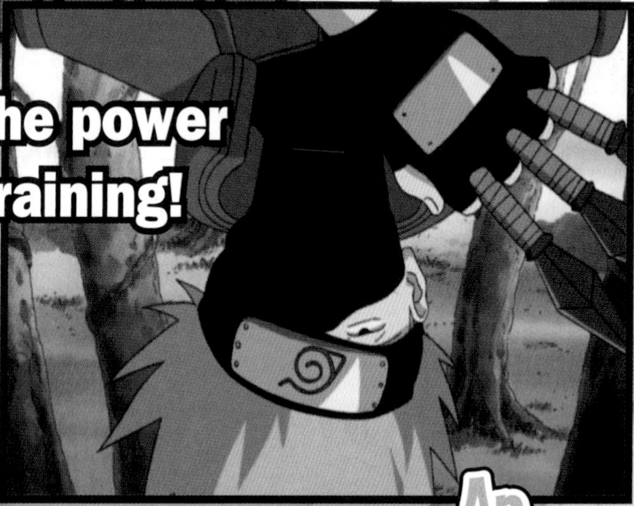

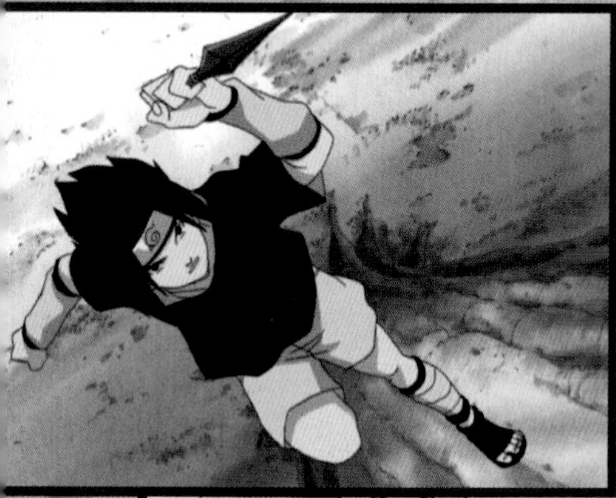

An intense new exercise!

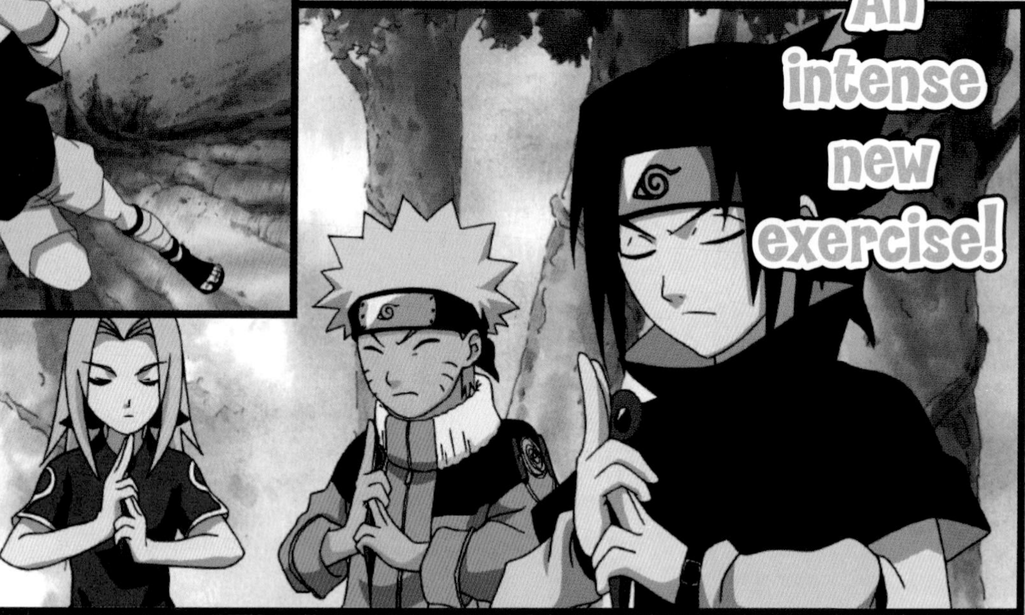

Although Sakura completes the task easily, Naruto and Sasuke have trouble with it. The two show their competitive spirit as they see who can climb up higher and faster!

Kakashi gives Naruto and the others a new training exercise to prepare them for Zabuza's return…he tells them to climb trees! Naruto and Sasuke struggle mightily, showing that they still have plenty of room to grow. They begin the task, aiming for the top!

The tree-climbing practice emphasizes the importance of chakra.

But…what about Zabuza?!

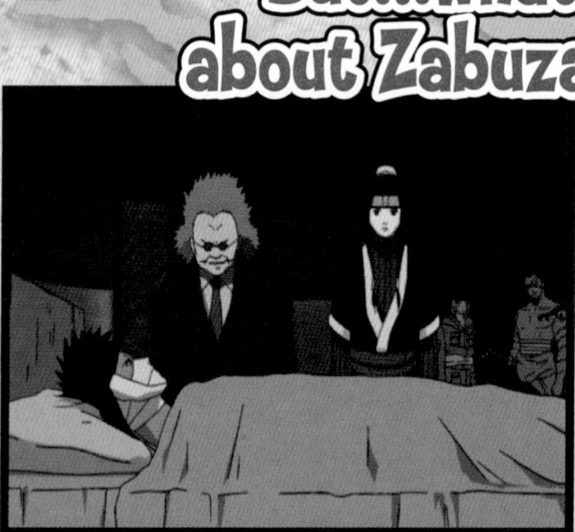

Zabuza must take time to recover from his near-death state. But he is fated to once again clash with Kakashi and his squad…

The Land Where a Hero Once Lived

Kaiza rescued Inari from drowning.

Because of his courage and strength, people recognized him as a hero.

Gato ordered Kaiza's execution. Inari's courage and the hope of the people died along with Kaiza...

The man who was called a hero...

Tazuna recounts the sad history of his family and his community...

This tragedy has left a deep wound in the Land of Waves.

The torn photograph that hangs in Tazuna's house symbolizes the sorrowful past that pulled Tazuna's family and the Land of Waves into despair. On the day that Gato killed their hero, the people of the Land of Waves lost hope...

Get to work on him!

Because of Gato's tyranny, the Land of Waves is plagued by epidemic poverty and crime.

The shipping company tainted by dark tactics

The Gato Corporation

On the surface, The Gato Corporation is one of the largest ocean transport companies in the world. But beneath that artifice, it is a corrupt organization that turns a massive profit by trafficking in narcotics and contraband and through takeovers of industries and nations. Gato turned his eyes to the small nation of the Land of Waves and controls the country's ocean transportation and rules like a dictator, monopolizing the shipping and transportation lanes.

Episodes 12 to 19

The Demon returns for a decisive, life-and-death battle on the bridge!

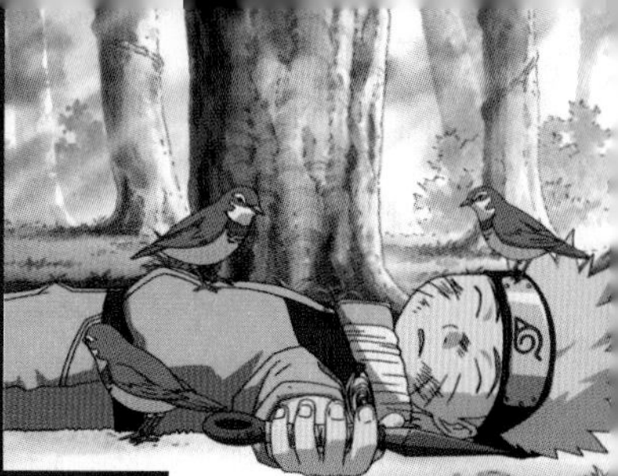

After exhausting himself with training exercises, Naruto lies deeply asleep in the forest. Rays of sunshine filter through the branches and dapple the ground with light…

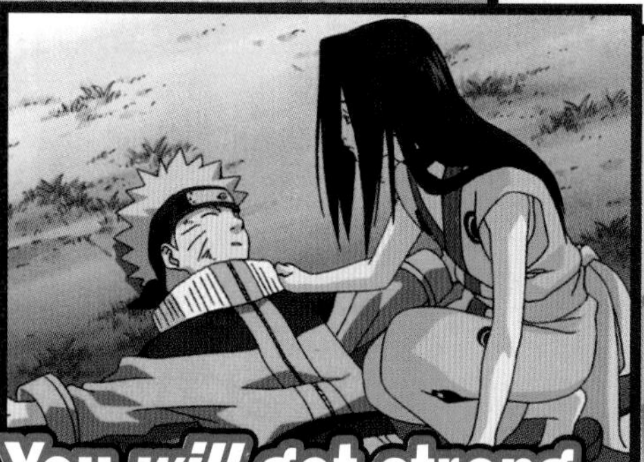

Haku leans over the sleeping Naruto and rouses him from sleep with his gentle voice. He asks Naruto, his enemy, why he is working so hard…

You *will* get strong…

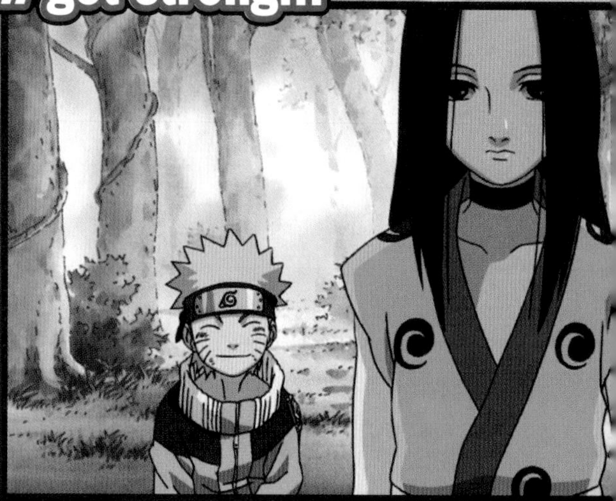

As Haku says, "we'll meet again somewhere," a murderous glare washes over his eyes. What will transpire when they meet next?

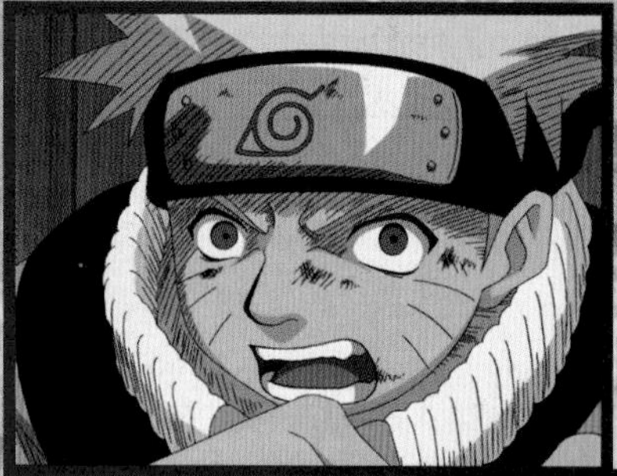

"You don't know what it's like to suffer and get treated like dirt!" Naruto roars at Inari, accusing him of cowardice. What could Inari be feeling…?

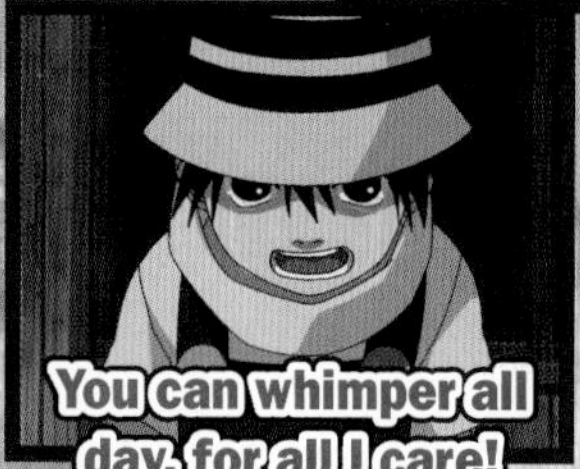

You can whimper all day, for all I care! You're just a coward!

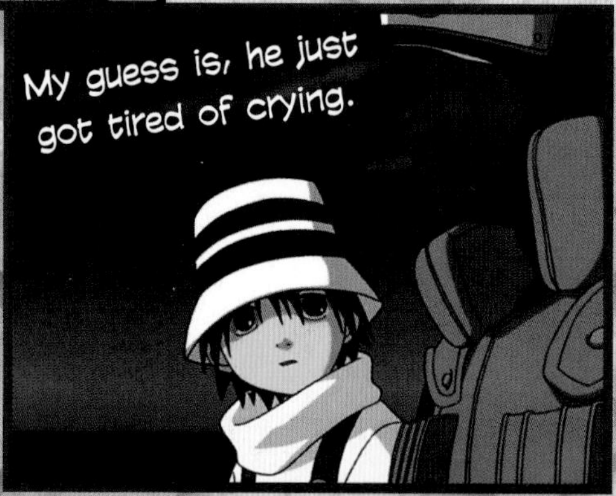
My guess is, he just got tired of crying.

After countless hours of diligent practice, Naruto and Sasuke complete their training. Meanwhile, Tazuna's bridge is nearing completion. Witnessing Naruto and his teammates' single-minded dedication and bold convictions reawakens Inari's sad memories…

The training is complete! The time for battle approaches…

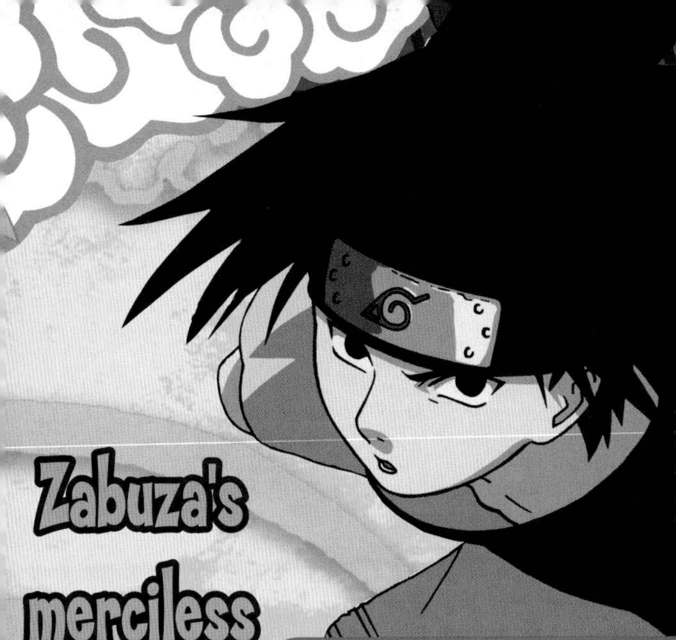

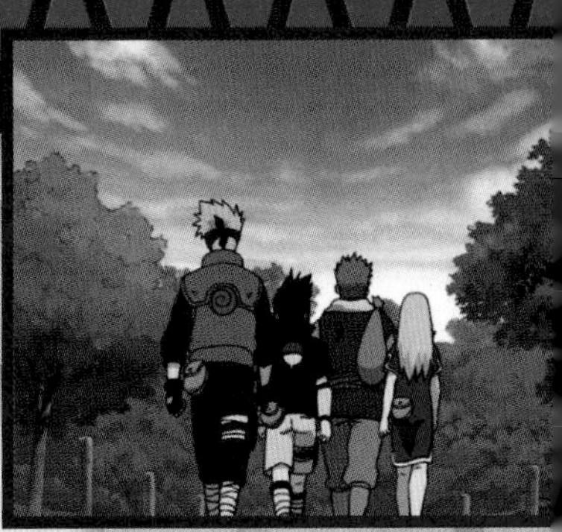

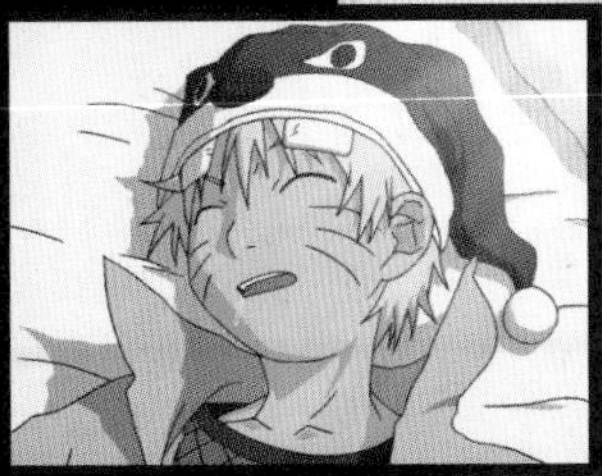

The group departs for the nearly finished bridge. But Naruto, exhausted from overexerting himself in training, is still asleep...

Zabuza's merciless attack... The fog of death envelops the four!

When they arrive at the bridge, a shocking sight greets them. Was it Zabuza who attacked Tazuna's workers? From a thick mist that reeks of blood, Zabuza emerges once again!!

The bridge of hope is awash with bloodlust... but Tazuna must be protected!

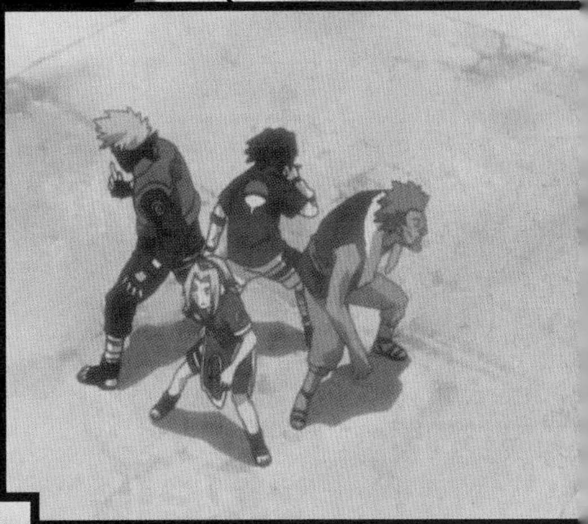

The air is blanketed in impenetrable fog... The Hidden Mist Jutsu! Zabuza is indeed alive!

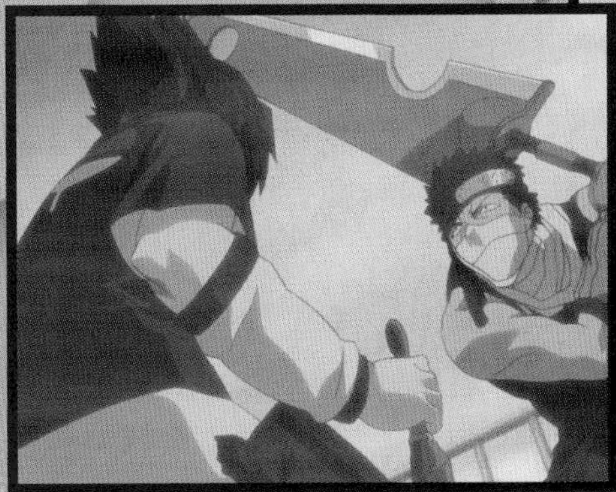

"I'm trembling with excitement!" The power of the Uchiha clan shines through the mist...and there is no more need to cower in fear of Zabuza's strength.

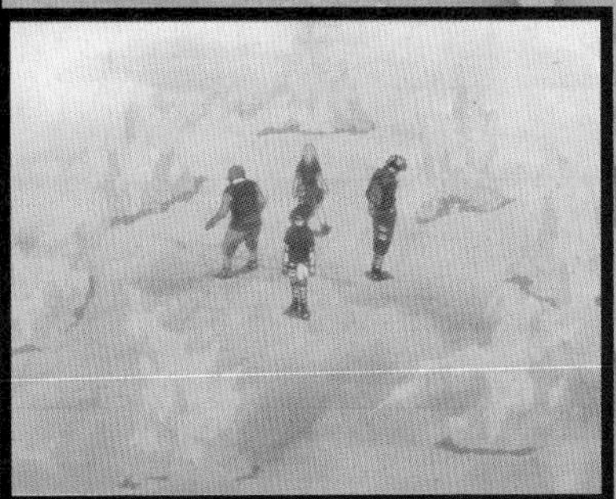

Zabuza's water clones are easily vanquished, proving how much Sasuke has grown!

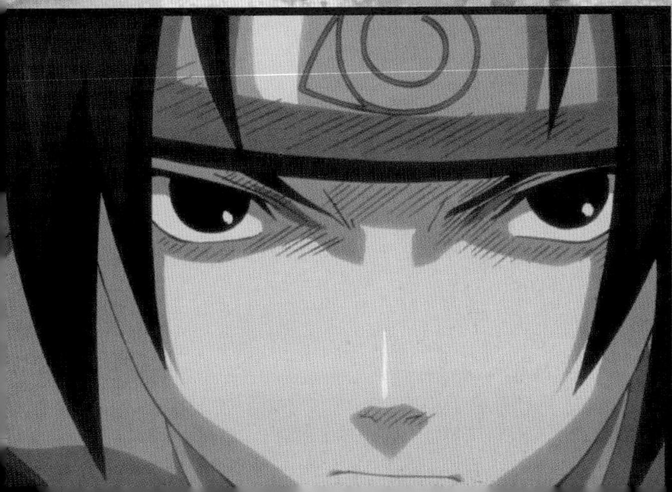

...I can see it!

↑ "Can I be that strong, too…?" If you care about something, protect it with both arms!

I was in the mood to cut something...

When you're happy,

it's okay to cry...!

↑ Naruto understands the rush of joy from finally being acknowledged and accepted.

Naruto Uzumaki...

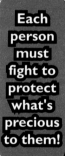

is here!

↑ Better late than never, Naruto finally arrives at the battle scene! Will he help turn the tide of the battle?

Each person must fight to protect what's precious to them!

Deep within the thick mist, the battle on the bridge finally begins. Sasuke has a fiery exchange with Haku, while Kakashi goes up against Zabuza. At the same time, Gato's hired assassins attack Tazuna's home. Inari musters up all his courage to protect his mother…and Naruto comes to his rescue!

→ Sasuke is trapped in the Crystal Ice Mirrors, a white world of illusion that is impossible to escape!

← Haku's needles travel faster than the eye can see and are impossible to dodge!

Sasuke shields Naruto from the deadly onslaught of Haku's senbon and ends up riddled with the needles. The blue fire of life begins to fade from Sasuke's eyes…

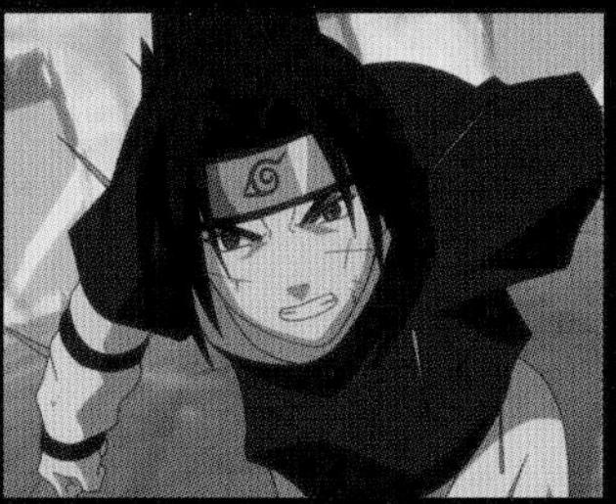

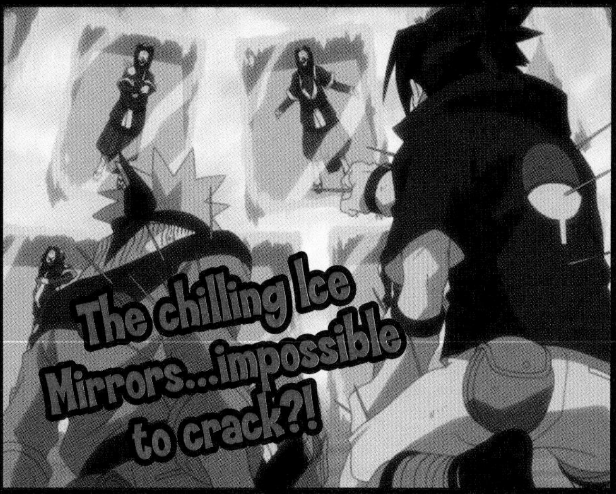
The chilling Ice Mirrors…impossible to crack?!

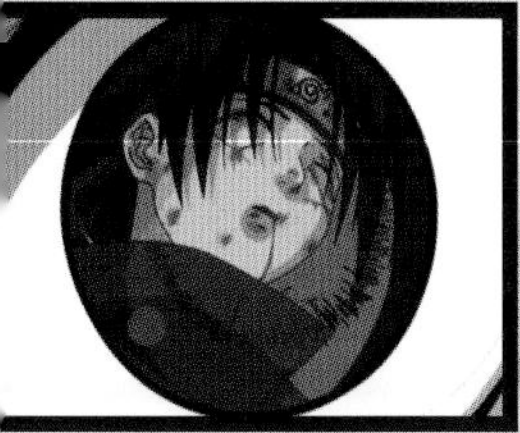

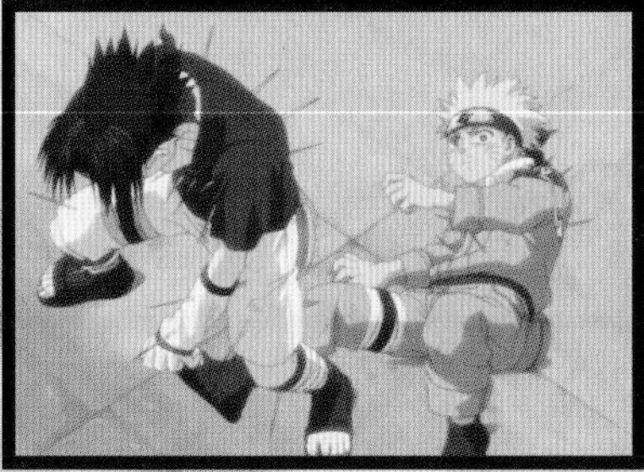

Ice needles pierce Sasuke! Then…

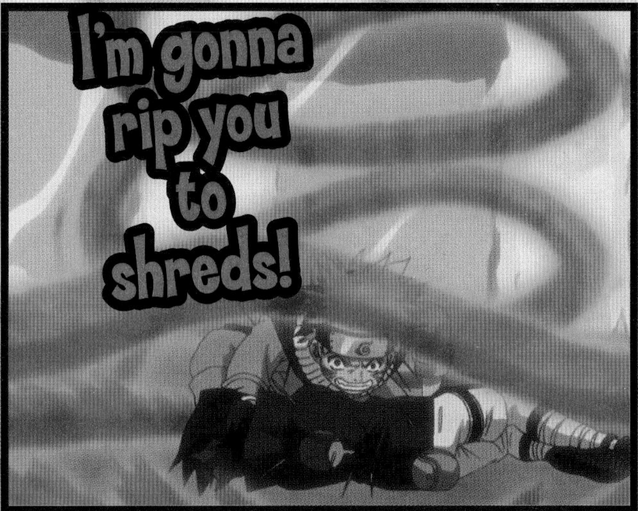
I'm gonna rip you to shreds!

"You'll pay for this!" Naruto swears he'll get revenge on Haku, who killed Sasuke and took away his future! The wretched power that has long slept inside Naruto now rises!

The fearsome Crystal Ice Mirrors… a secret inherited skill!

Haku buries his own emotions and fights for Zabuza. Under the extreme battle conditions, Sasuke's Sharingan power, passed down through the Uchiha clan, awakens. Inside the Ice Mirrors, a battle between two who possess Kekkei Genkai traits comes to a shocking end!

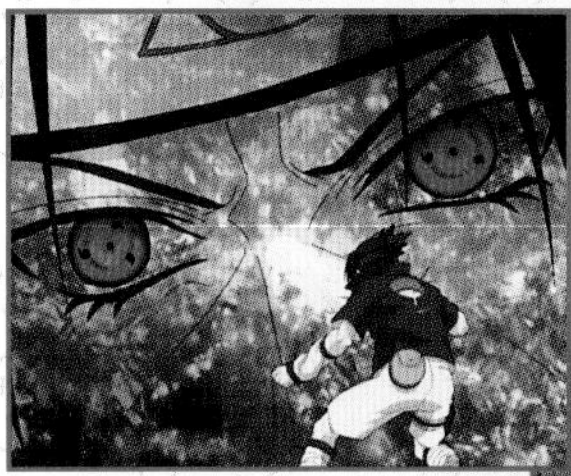

Sasuke's older brother Itachi is the object of his passionate desire for revenge. But how did this hatred arise?

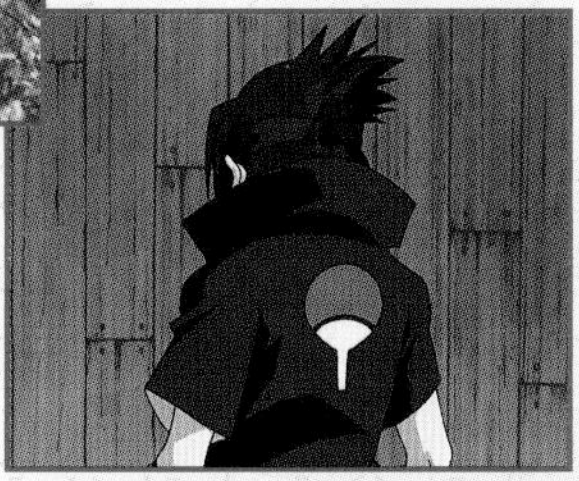

Sasuke's family name is like a blessing and a curse, representing abundant raw talent but also blood-soaked tragedy.

The Hidden Leaf Village's Most Powerful Bloodline

The Uchiha Clan

The greatest family in the Hidden Leaf Village, the Uchiha Clan not only boasted unmatched fighting skills but passed down the Sharingan eye through the family bloodline. But in a horrifying turn of events, the clan was destroyed and its reign of glory came to an abrupt end. Now it is viewed as the clan of misfortune, and the two brothers who survive are the last inheritors of the family name and blood.

Haku's reason for existence is shattered!

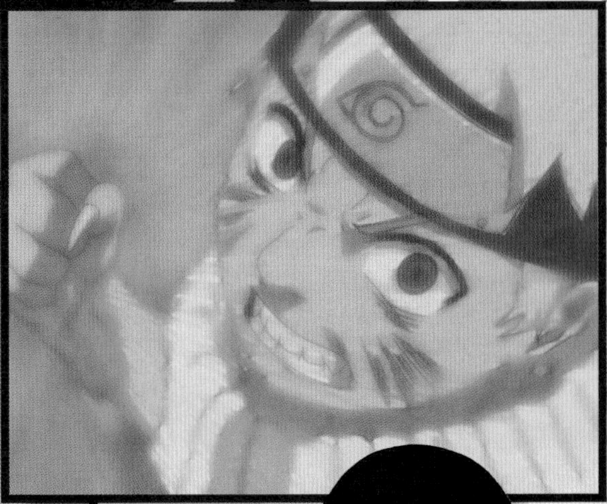

The Nine-Tailed Fox's chakra is set loose! The overwhelming, sinister power swallows Haku and breaks him!

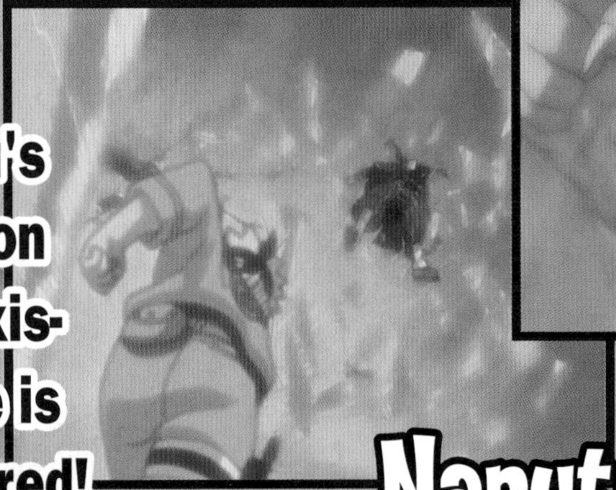

Naruto... kill me...

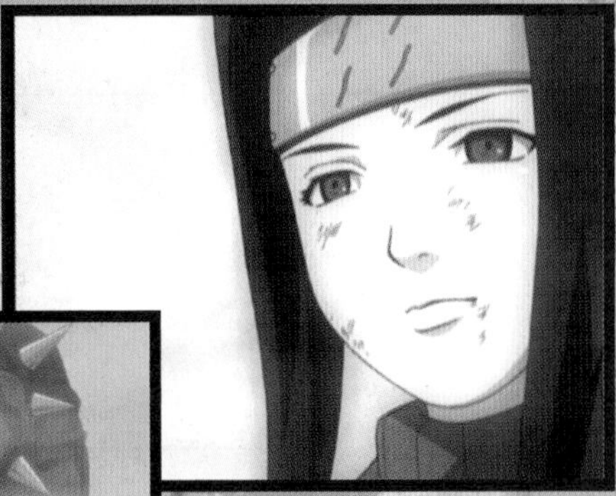

Haku tells Naruto, "My usefulness is over. The only thing that gave my life meaning... it's gone." His eyes are tranquil and at peace.

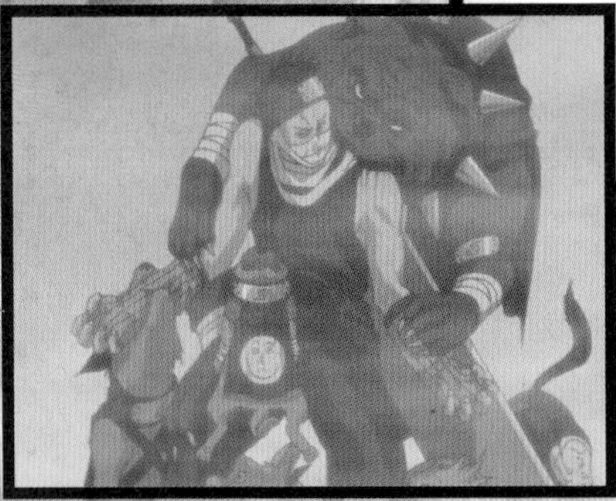

Zabuza succumbs to Kakashi's Summoning Jutsu, and the intense battle between the two approaches its conclusion.

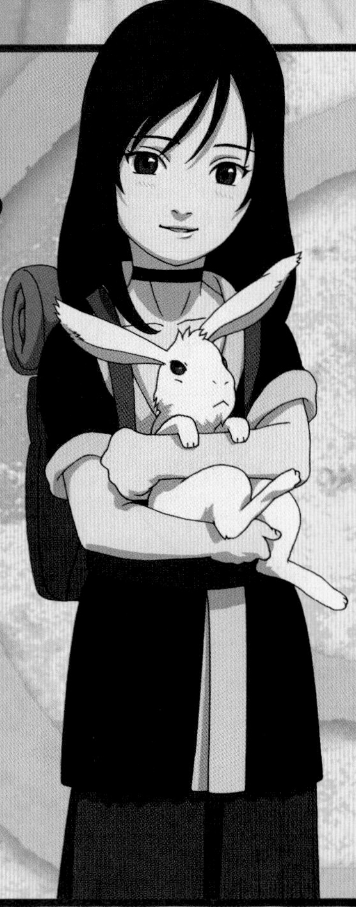

The Nine-Tailed Fox awakens, and Haku's innocent dream is destroyed!

After seeing Sasuke die, the explosion of Naruto's hatred, pain and anger rouses the fox spirit sleeping inside him, and this extreme, ferocious power obliterates the Ice Mirrors. Haku's sole purpose for living was to serve Zabuza as his most powerful weapon, and having been defeated by Naruto, he knows that he has failed.

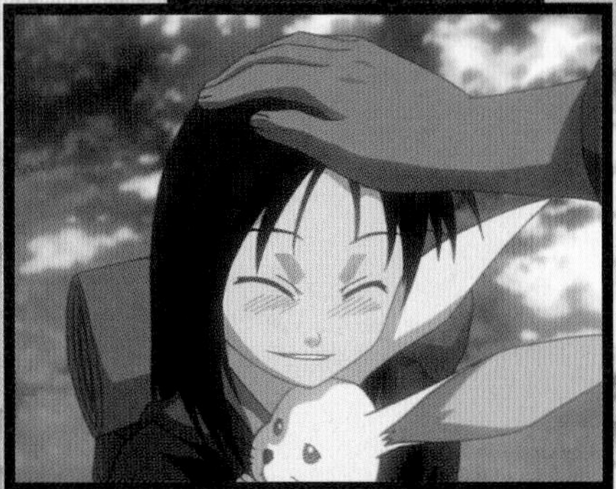

Even if he was only valued as a living weapon, Haku felt happy to be needed.

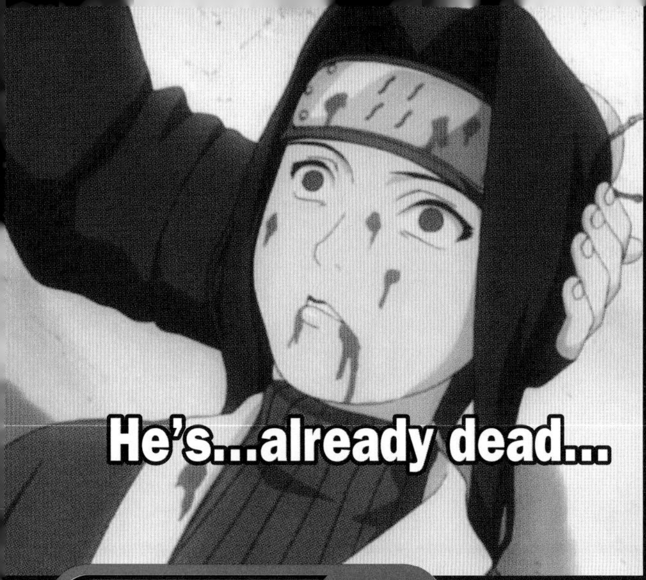
He's...already dead...

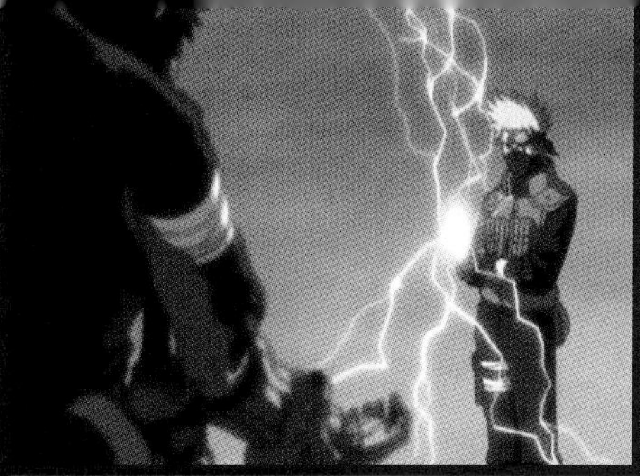

Kakashi unleashes his secret move, Lightning Blade, against Zabuza. But Haku throws himself in front of Kakashi's hand to protect his master and Kakashi's attack rips through him.

The Weapons Called Shinobi

Beyond his tragic fate... Haku achieves a valiant end!

After failing to vanquish Naruto, Haku has lost his reason to exist and he seeks out death. But destiny gives him one final purpose to serve: Haku acts as a shield for Zabuza, saving his master and perishing valiantly. Haku dies protecting the person most precious to him, and not serving as an emotionless tool.

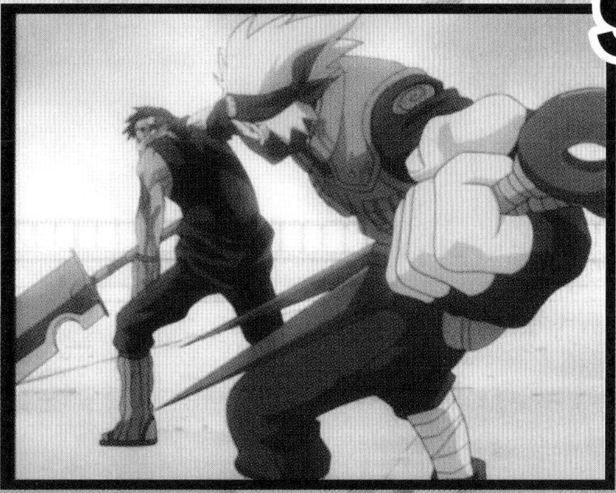

"You have no idea what real strength is." The sadness of losing Haku, who was only supposed to be his tool, dulls the blade of the "Demon."

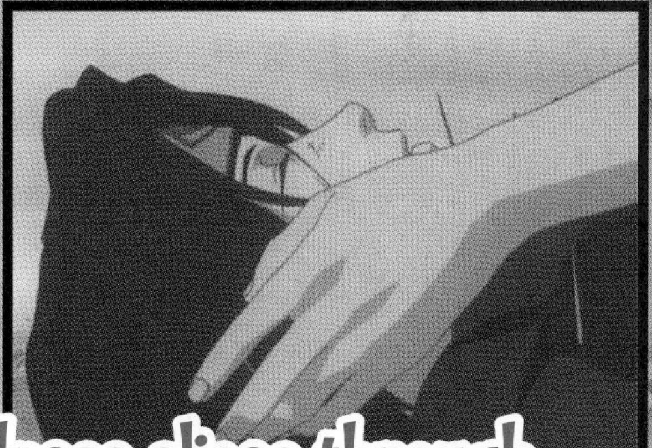
Sadness slices through

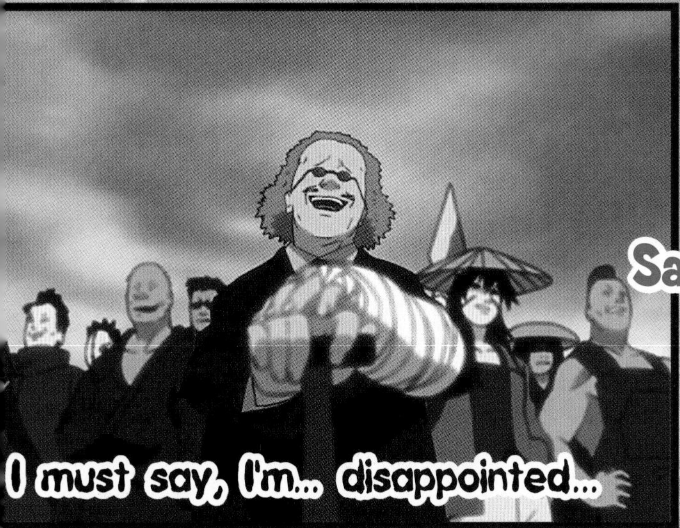
I must say, I'm... disappointed...

As the bloody mist whirls around the bridge, Gato suddenly appears with his army in tow and reveals that he always intended to kill off Zabuza along with Tazuna and the others!

Sakura touches Sasuke, and the cold reality of his death is crushing.

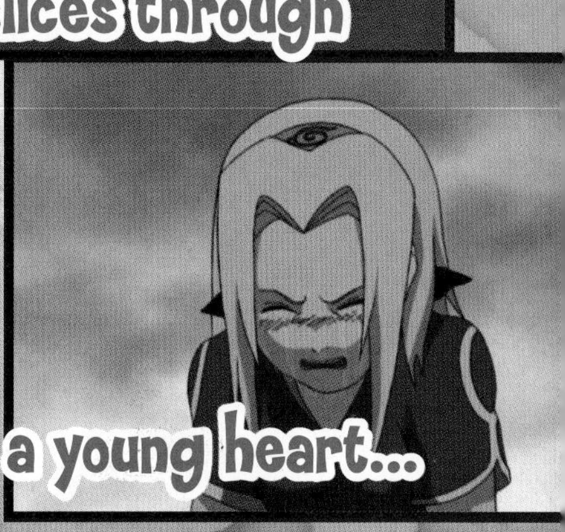
a young heart...

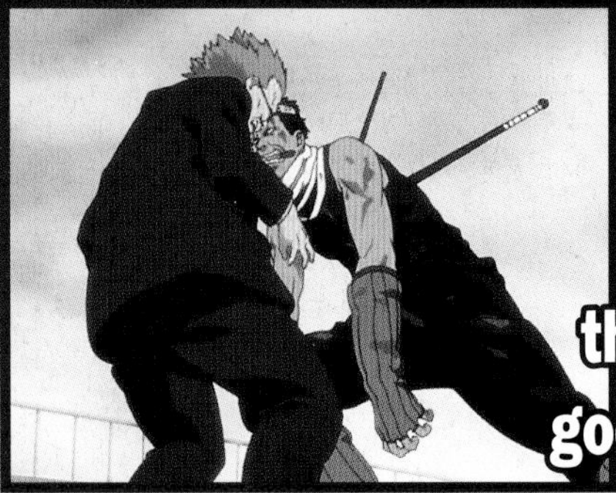

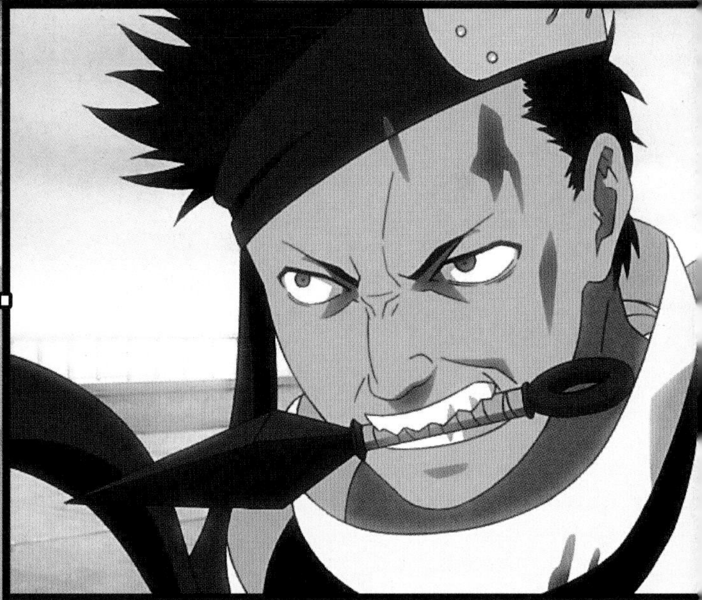

So this is... goodbye... at last.

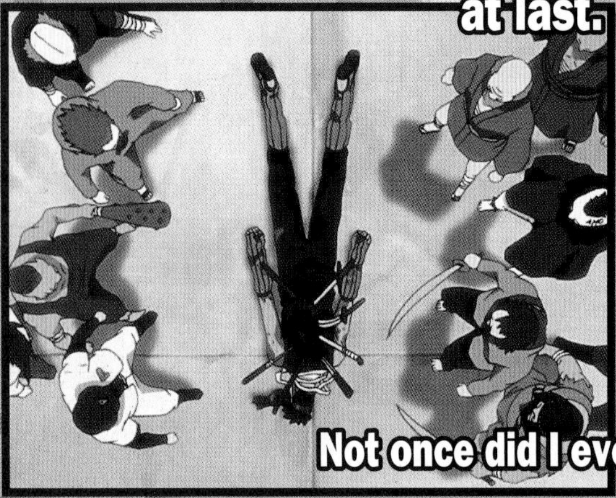

Zabuza the Demon perishes heroically. He attempts to honor Haku's death by killing Gato with his own hands...

Not once did I ever thank you, Haku... Forgive me for that...

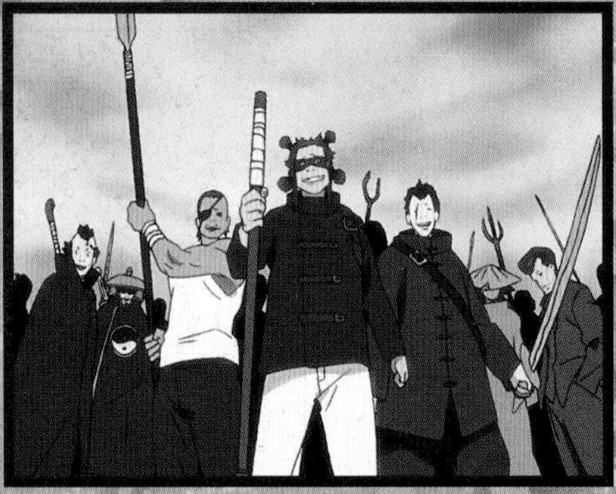

As Gato's restless army becomes a raging mob, Inari and others show up to face them head-on! Seeing Naruto's courage has changed the hearts of the people of the Land of Waves.

Sakura...

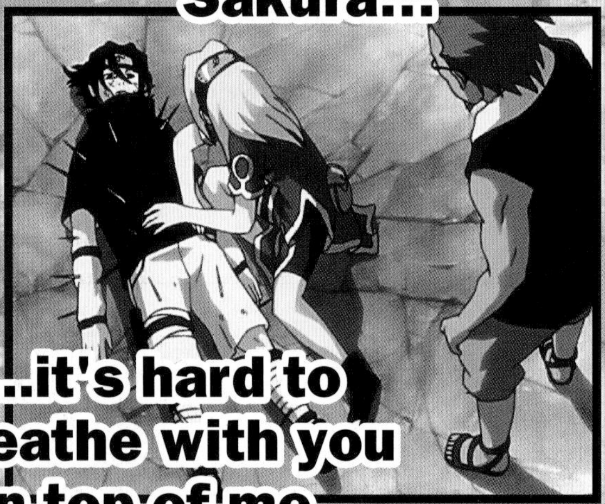

...it's hard to breathe with you on top of me...

Sasuke wakes from his slumber, spared from death by Haku, who could not extinguish his own gentle spirit and avoided hitting Sasuke's vital organs.

The demon's last dance!

Naruto is furious that Zabuza shows no reaction to Haku's death, and as his heartfelt tears fall, he demands answers from Zabuza. Does being a shinobi mean being so cold, hard and emotionless? Did Haku's life and his sacrifice mean nothing to Zabuza? Honest emotion fills Zabuza's eyes and, for his own pride as well as Haku's memory, he charges toward Gato. In killing Gato, Zabuza will surely die, but he attacks and, incredibly, his appearance changes to that of a true demon.

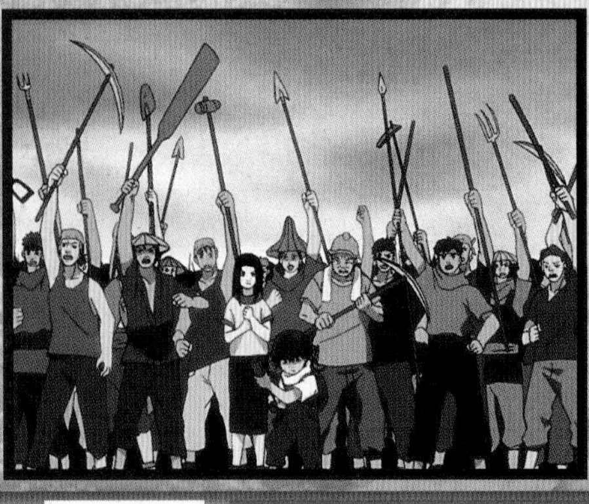

White snow falls, ushering in a dawn of hope...

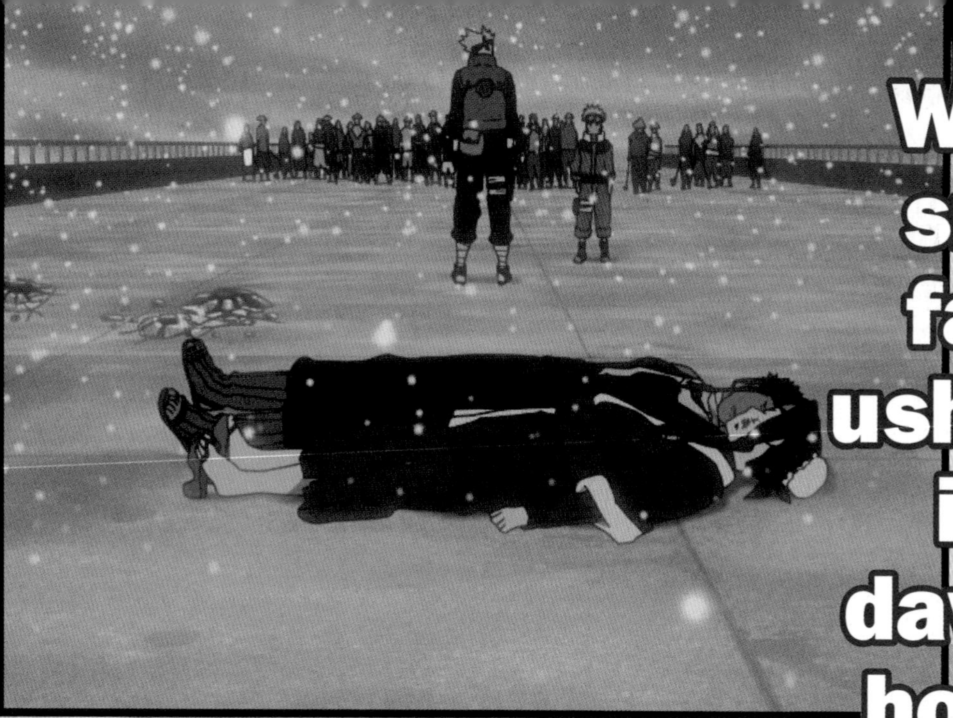

This is no false show of emotion... Zabuza's heart has genuinely melted.

Mission complete! Farewell to the Land of Waves...

Zabuza's life ended in the falling snow. The Land of Waves, which had been shrouded in a deep fog of despair, welcomed a new morning with a beautiful sunrise. The bridge, now finally complete, will connect the Land of Waves and its people to an open and hopeful future. And the bridge's new name -- the Great Naruto Bridge -- honors the person who opened their hearts.

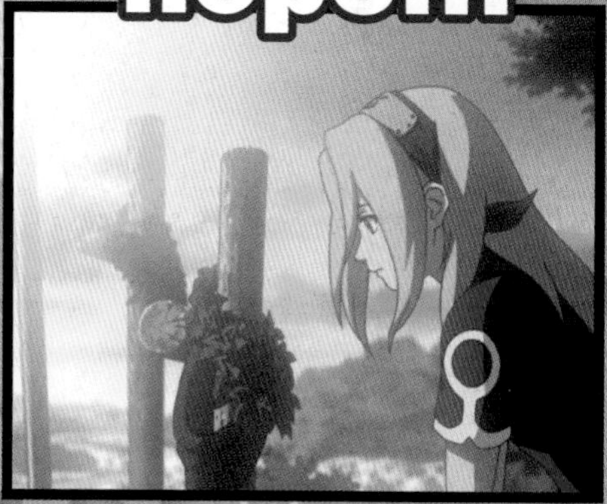

Zabuza and Haku are buried on a hill that overlooks the Land of Waves. Their lives and deaths made a deep and lasting impression on the hearts of the young shinobi.

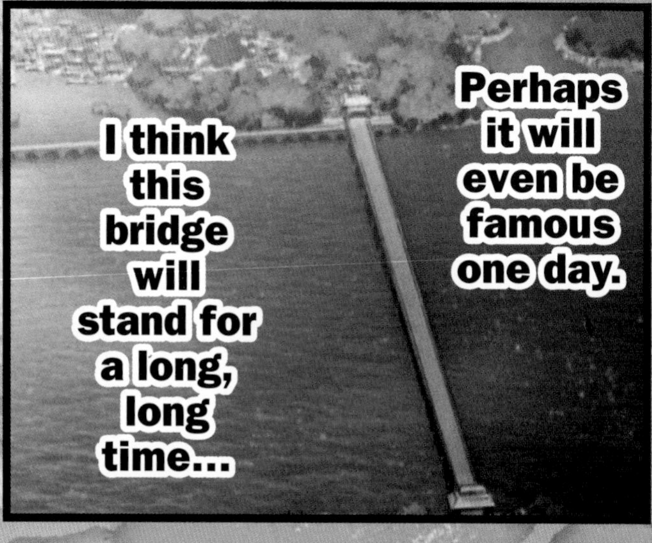
I think this bridge will stand for a long, long time...
Perhaps it will even be famous one day.

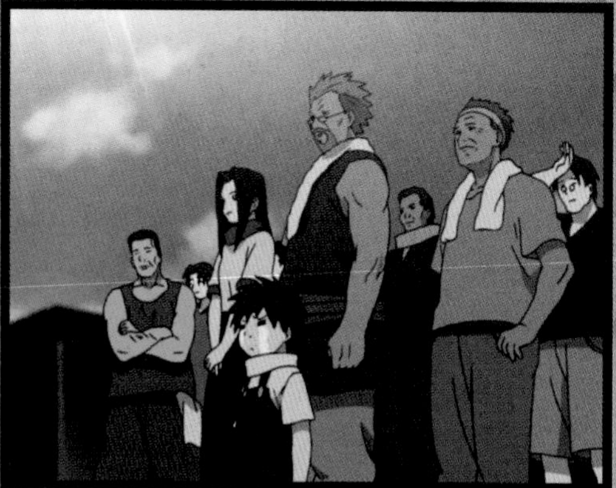

Inari, Tazuna and the people of the Land of Waves send off Naruto and his squad as they depart on their journey home.

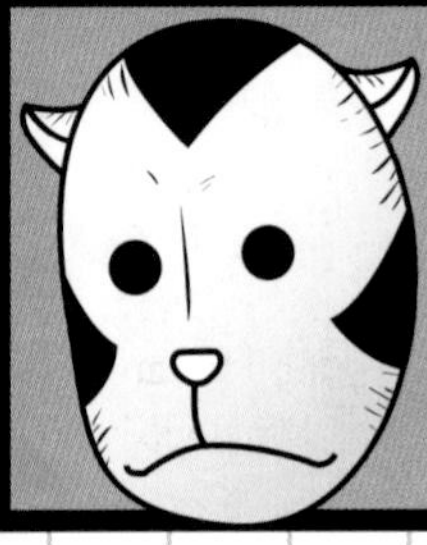

Part One

Anbu Black Ops Unit Special Report

Naruto Uzumaki

Naruto went from being a mischievous problem child to a true shinobi of the Hidden Leaf Village. We examine the core character of Naruto, who has exhibited rapid growth.

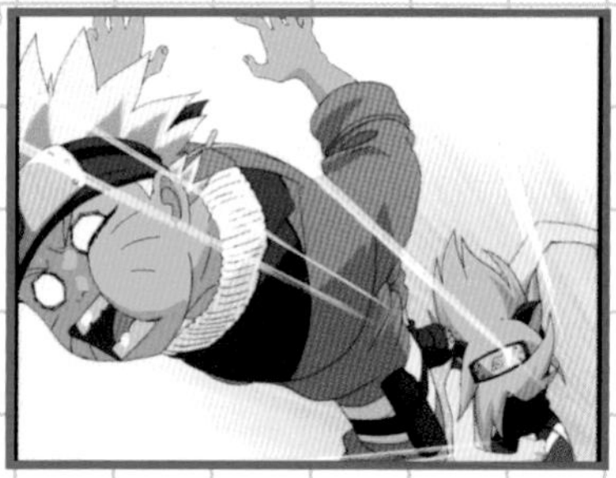

↑ A deep wound heals almost instantly because of the Nine-Tailed Fox's influence.

Report 1

His potential is limitless because of the enormous chakra locked within him!

The amount of chakra hidden inside Naruto is overwhelming. The Nine-Tailed Fox spirit sealed within his body seems to be the source of this potentially awesome power.

What I notice most about Naruto is his unpredictability. As a born prankster, he has an imaginative mind that allows him to develop creative strategies for outmaneuvering the enemy. The massive stores of power hidden inside him along with his surprising growth mean that he's constantly exceeding my expectations. But…in reality, his unpredictability tends to hurt him more than it helps…

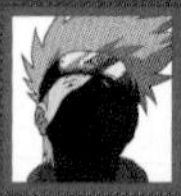

Testimony

Kakashi Hatake

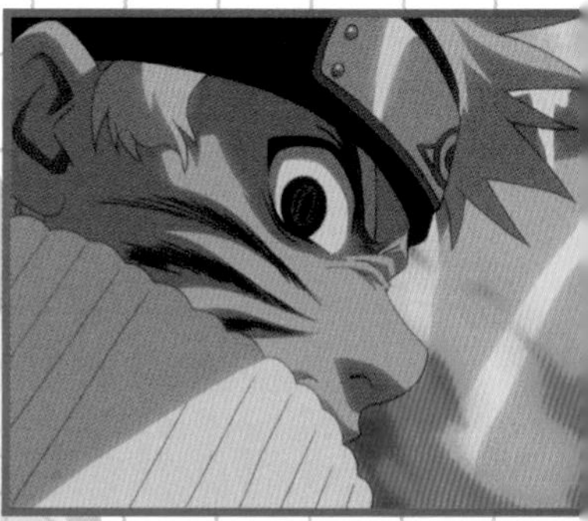

→ As the Nine-Tailed Fox began to awaken, it was horrifying yet exhilarating.

Report 2

When he sets his mind on something, he pursues it with steadfast devotion! Sakura is his life! Ichiraku Ramen is his life!

His passion for ramen and for Sakura Haruno goes beyond reason. Naruto can be single-minded to the point of stubbornness; his strong will is dedicated to following through with his convictions.

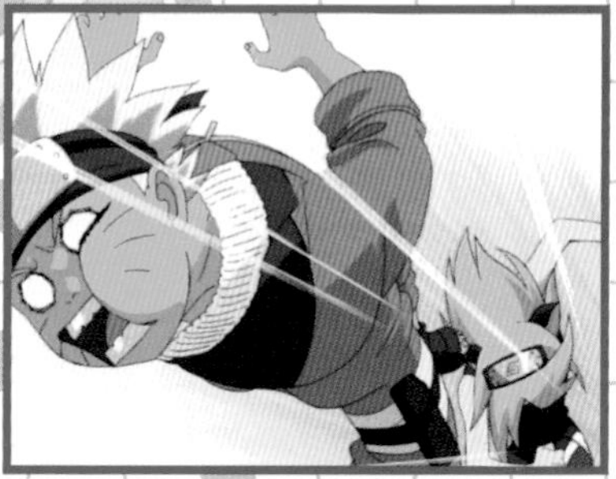

↑ Naruto's feelings toward Sakura are not reciprocated…but he continues his unyielding pursuit!

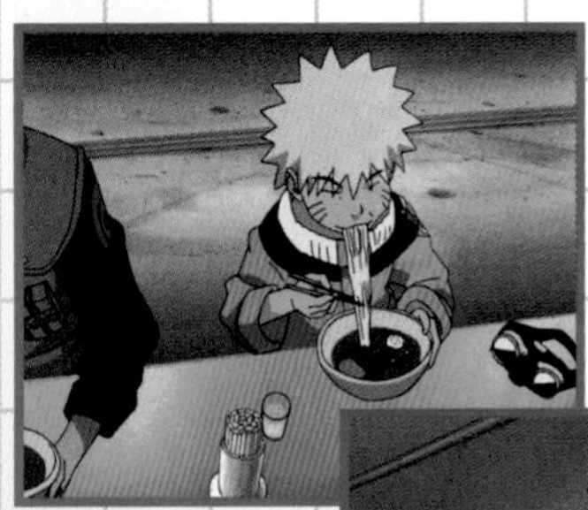

← His favorite thing of all is ramen from Ichiraku restaurant. You can often find him there with one of his old Ninja Academy instructors.

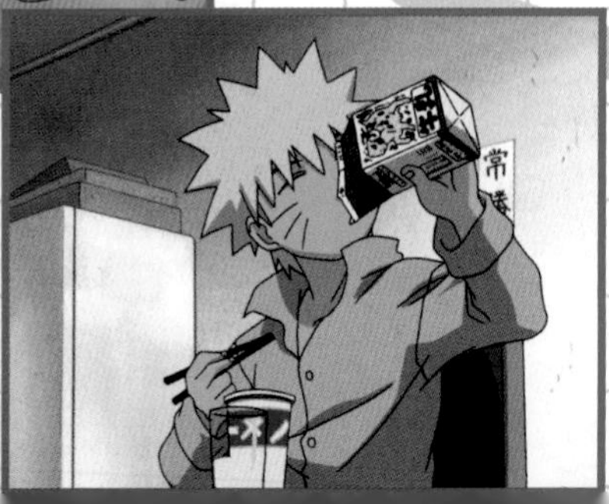

→ At home, he eats instant ramen. Miso flavor is his favorite.

No matter what, Boss's life is all about ramen, yeah! When he treated me to dinner the other day, I tried to order fried noodles, but he gave me this look like he might kill me! Oh, his relationship with Sakura? Of course, it's…hee hee! Uh… Aghhh! Help!!

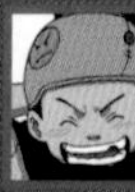

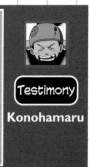

Testimony

Konohamaru

Report 3

There's no way to shake Naruto's determination to follow his path and become a truly great shinobi!
Naruto's powerful convictions, which do not bend or falter under any circumstances, are remarkable. No matter what he has to endure, he moves straight ahead on his path. The example he sets has had enormous influence on the other genin.

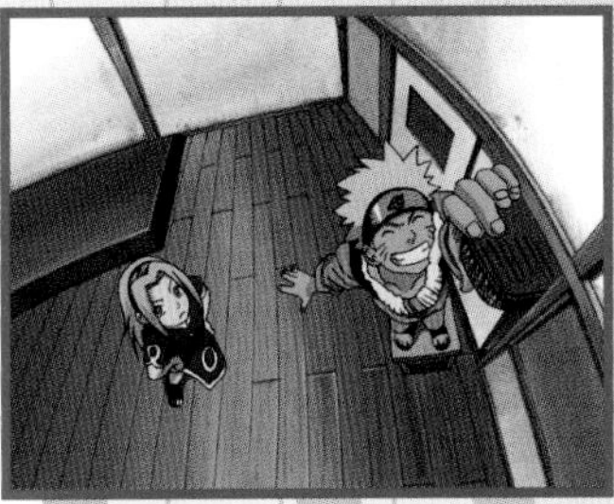

← He uses mischief as a way to make an impression.

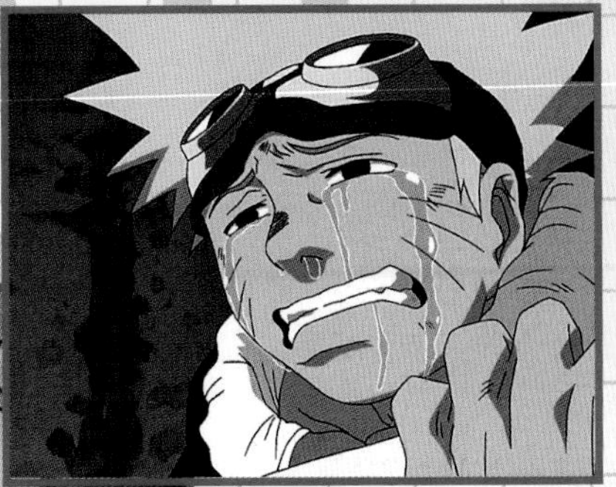

→ The first time he truly felt acknowledged and respected, he was overflowing with joy, and fat teardrops flowed down his cheeks.

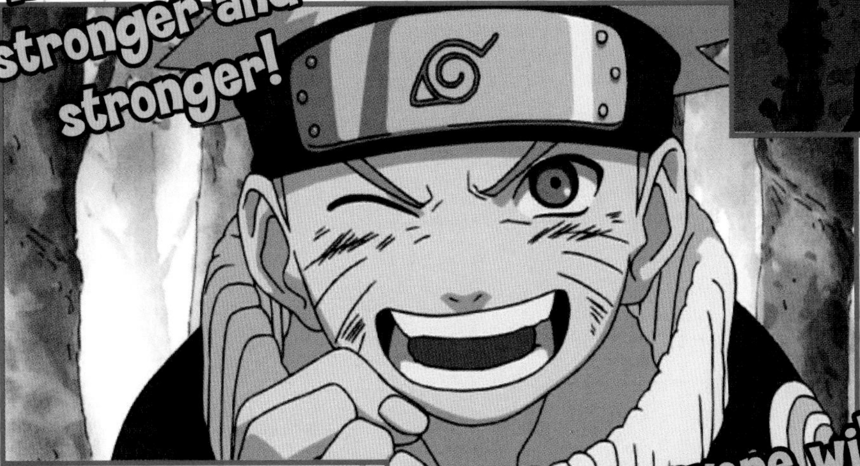
I need to get stronger and stronger!
Then everyone will know who I am, and they'll all respect me!

← "I'll be the next Hokage!" Naruto adamantly believes in his dream, and he is willing to work hard to make it come true.

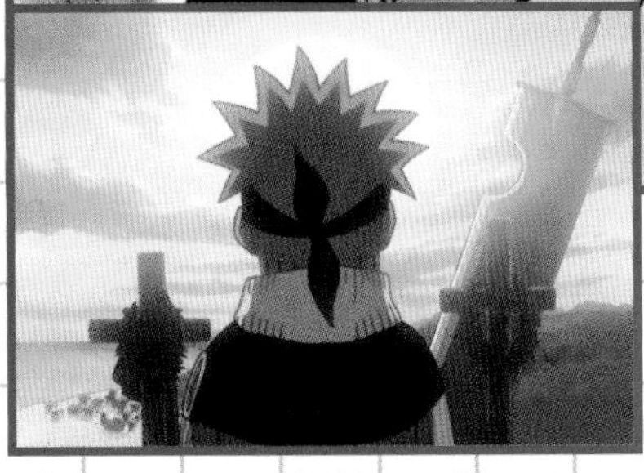

↑ In the Land of Waves, Naruto learned the harsh truth about the life of a shinobi.

Overall Results

His abilities as a shinobi are still immature, but his strong belief in himself and his attitude of dedication to hard work is deserving of praise. Especially noteworthy is the immeasurable potential hidden within him. He could very well make incredible strides in his development. We should keep tabs on his progress.

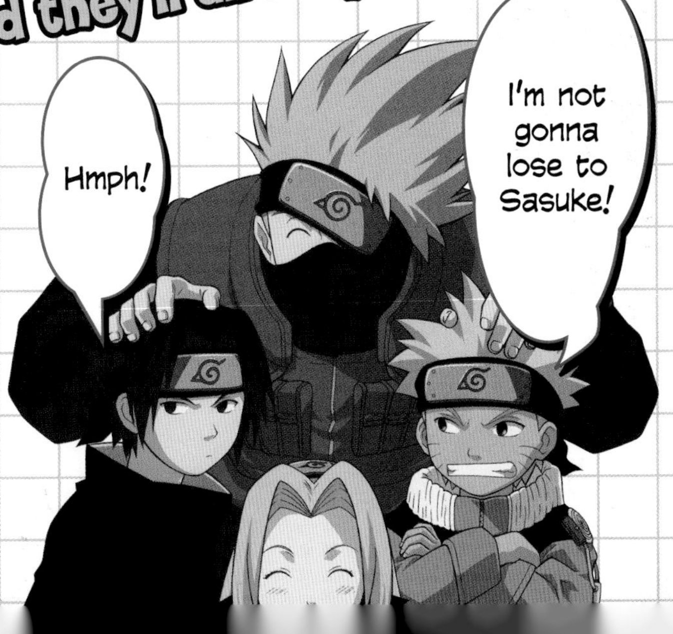
I'm not gonna lose to Sasuke!
Hmph!

Secret Shinobi Picture Album

Part Two

Naruto's House

The greatest ninja artisan of the Hidden Leaf Village, Kakashi, has arrived! He discerns the truth about Naruto's house using his incredible insight!

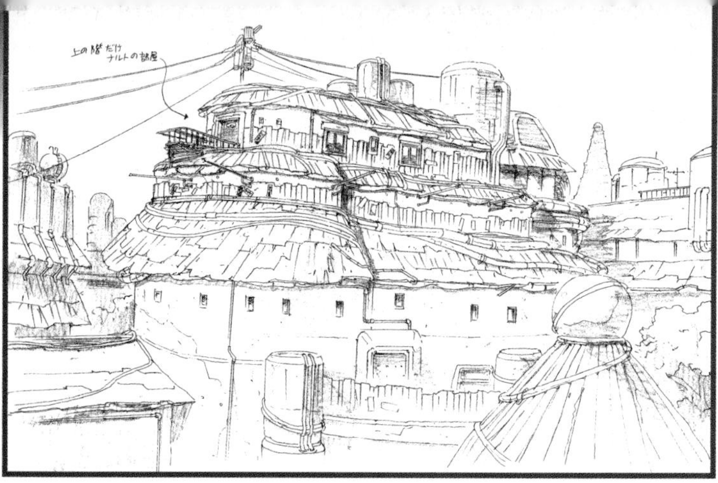

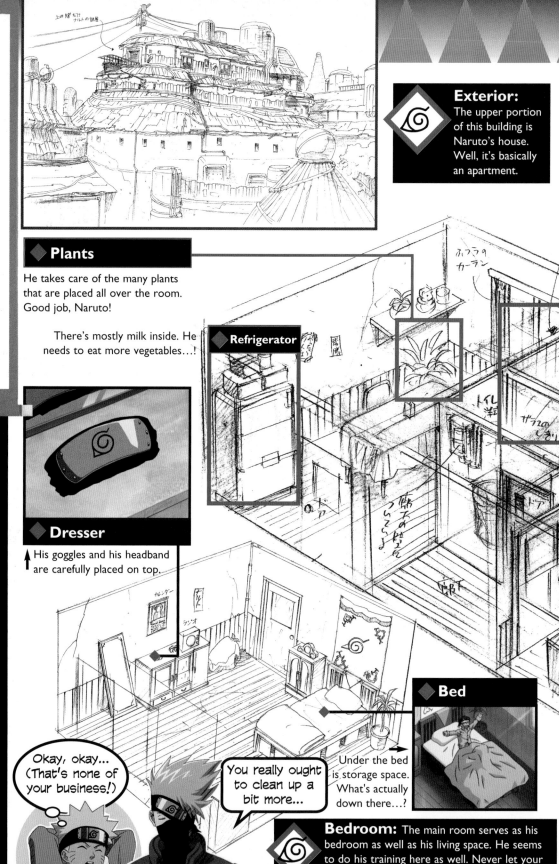

Exterior: The upper portion of this building is Naruto's house. Well, it's basically an apartment.

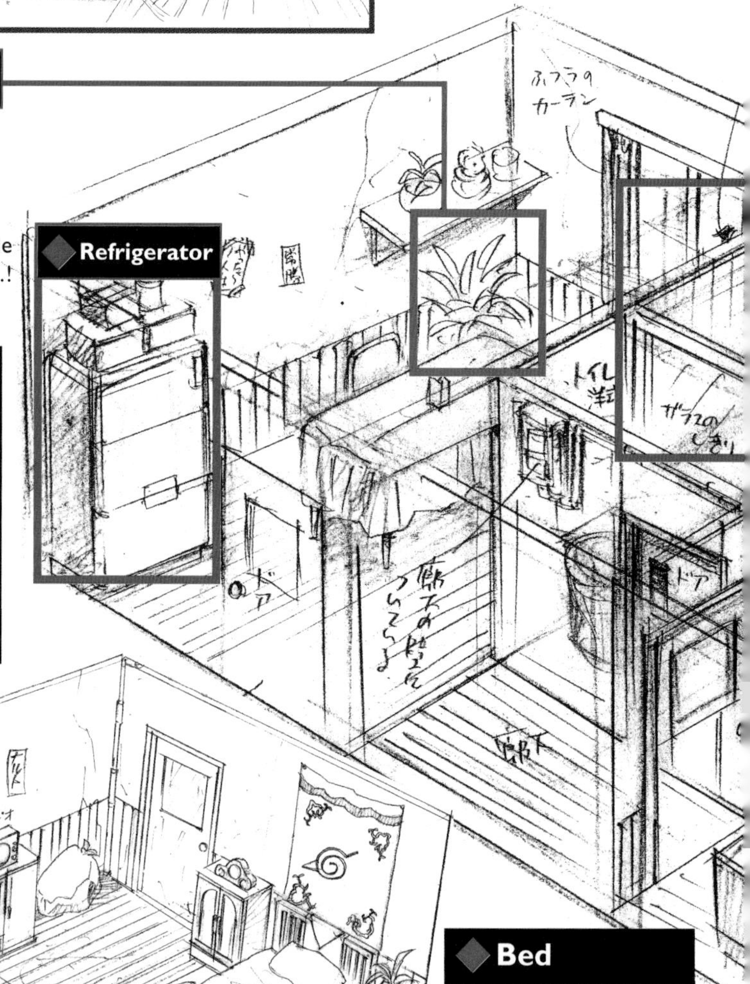

Plants

He takes care of the many plants that are placed all over the room. Good job, Naruto!

Refrigerator

There's mostly milk inside. He needs to eat more vegetables...!

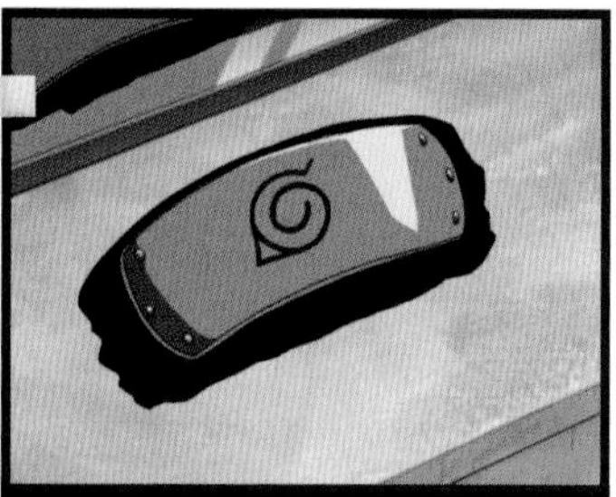

Dresser

↑His goggles and his headband are carefully placed on top.

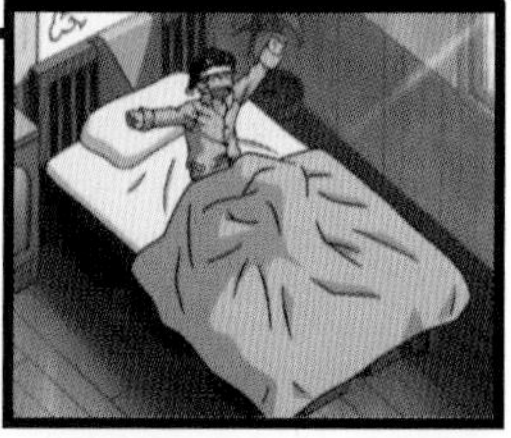

Bed

Under the bed is storage space. What's actually down there...?

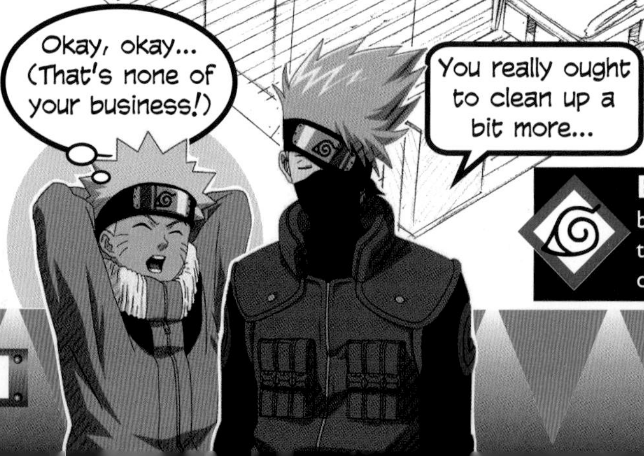
You really ought to clean up a bit more...
Okay, okay... (That's none of your business!)

Bedroom: The main room serves as his bedroom as well as his living space. He seems to do his training here as well. Never let your devotion to self-improvement fade, Naruto!

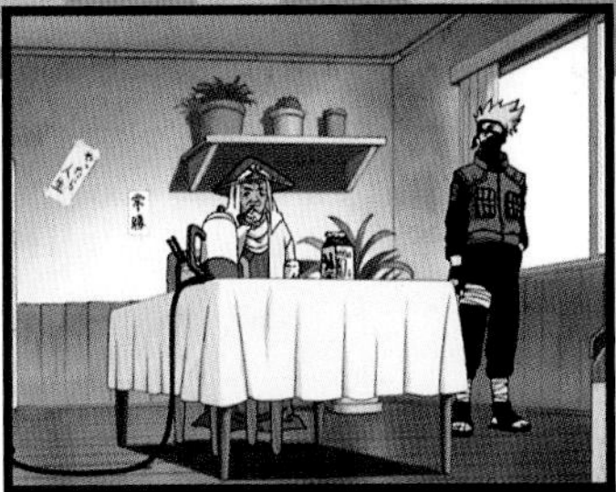

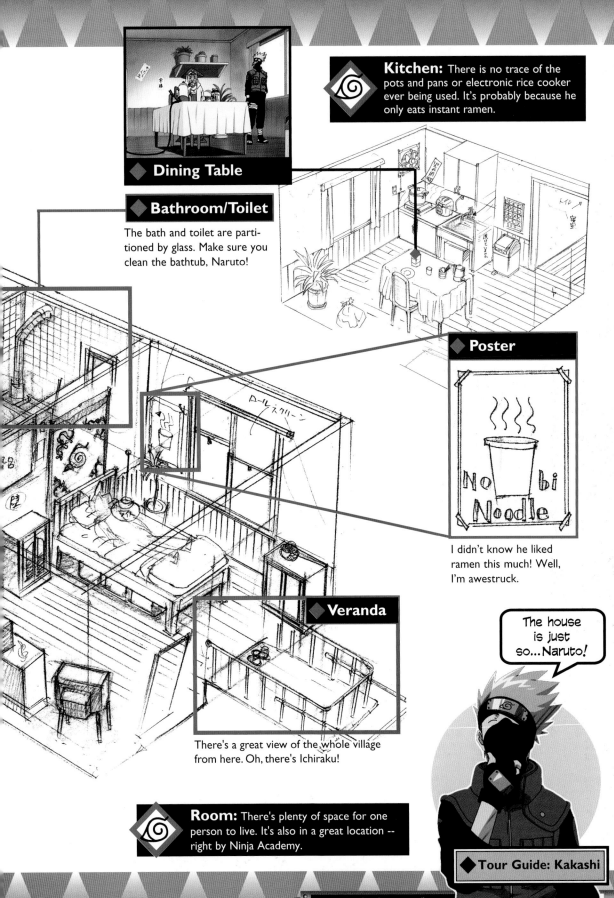

Dining Table

Kitchen: There is no trace of the pots and pans or electronic rice cooker ever being used. It's probably because he only eats instant ramen.

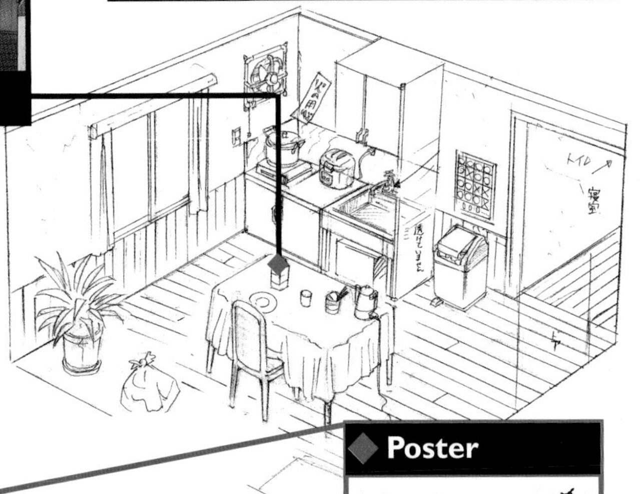

Bathroom/Toilet

The bath and toilet are partitioned by glass. Make sure you clean the bathtub, Naruto!

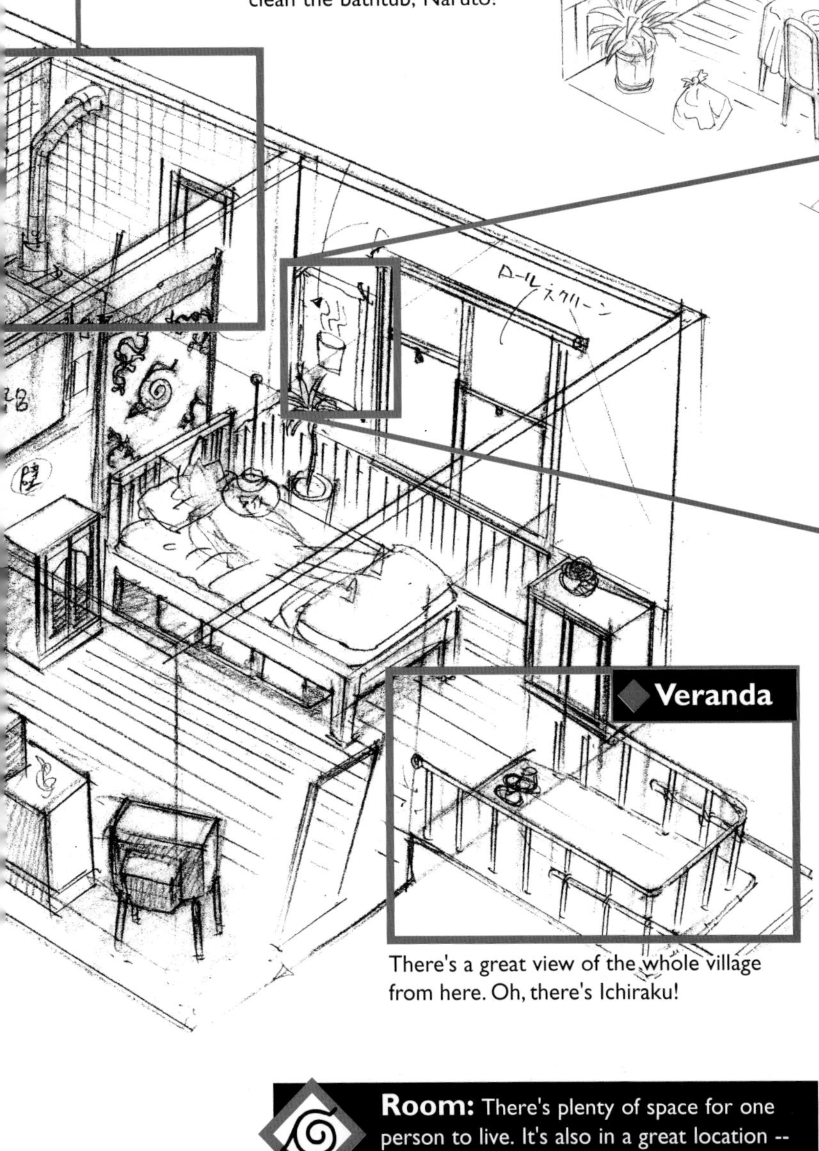

Poster

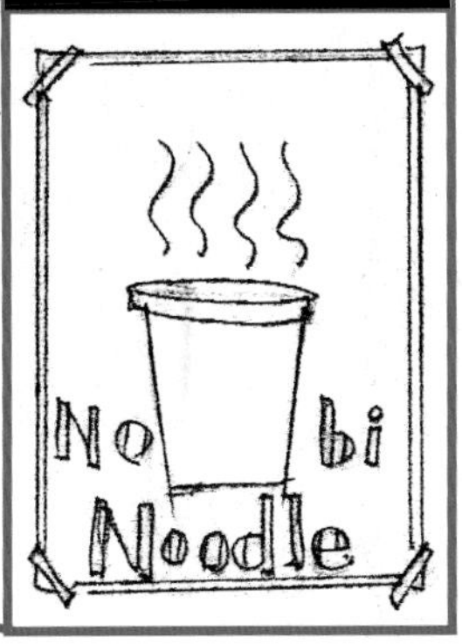
No bi
Noodle

I didn't know he liked ramen this much! Well, I'm awestruck.

Veranda

There's a great view of the whole village from here. Oh, there's Ichiraku!

Room: There's plenty of space for one person to live. It's also in a great location -- right by Ninja Academy.

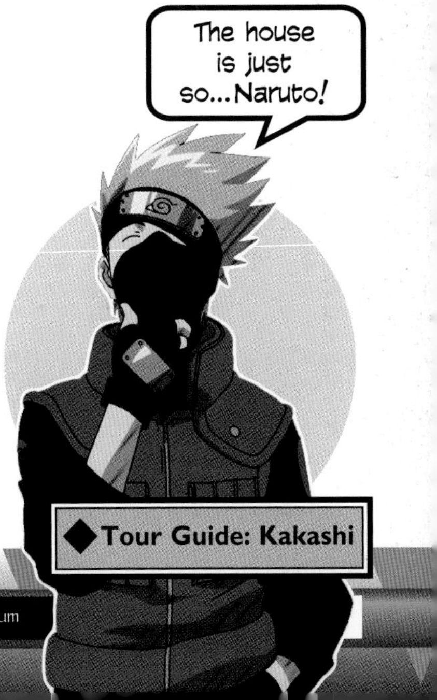
The house is just so...Naruto!

Tour Guide: Kakashi

Shinobi Picture Album

Part Three

Tazuna's House

Tazuna's house in the Land of Waves holds many memories…! With Naruto as our guide, we make a dramatic entrance …Believe it!

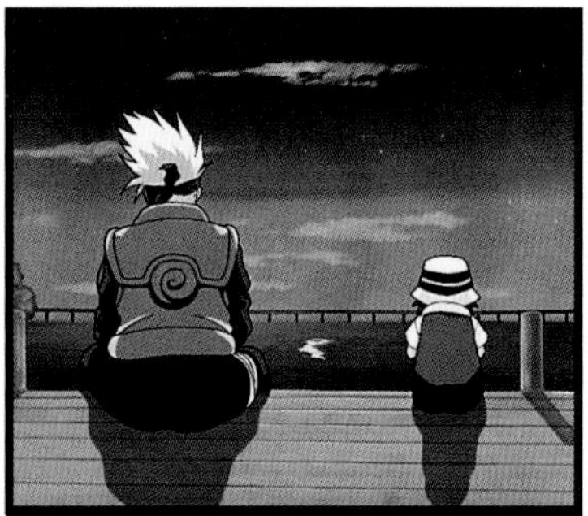

Porch

↑ The ocean is immediately beyond the porch. The view at night was really beautiful…

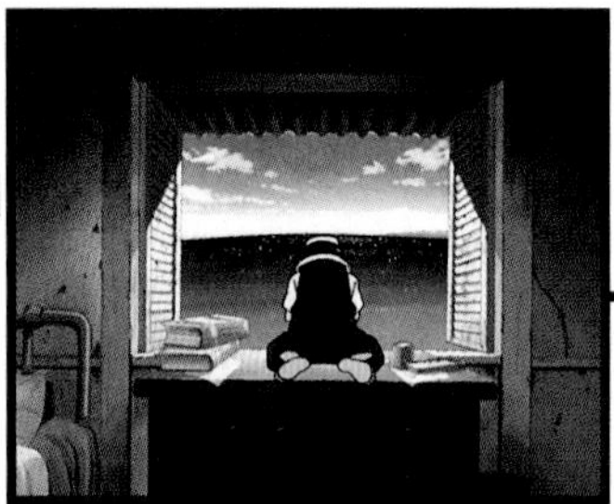

Window

↑ The view from this window was fantastic! I remember Inari was always staring at the sea.

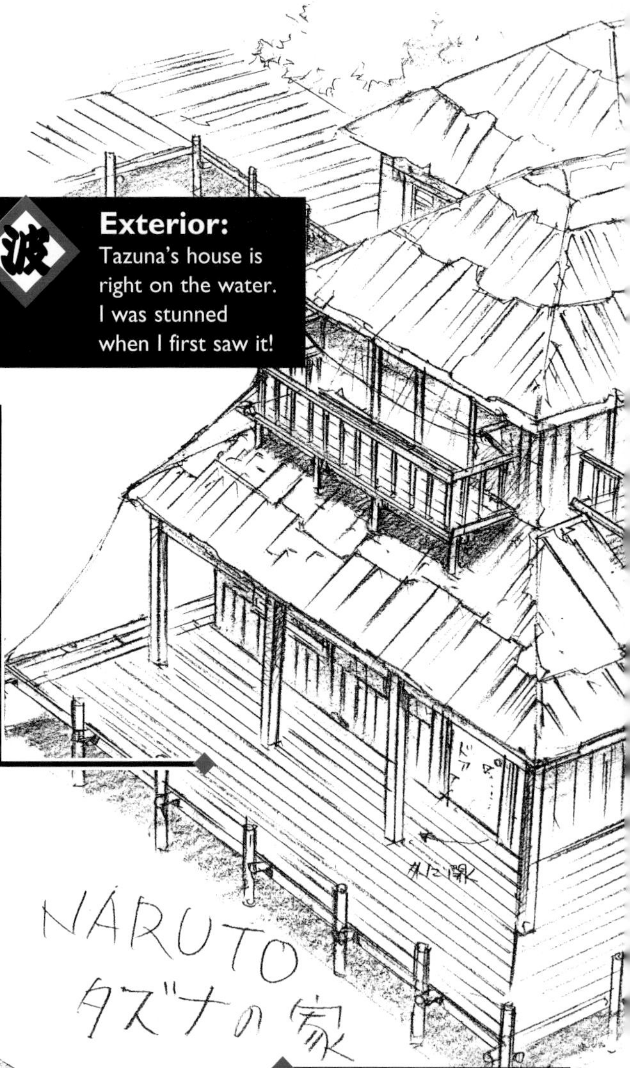

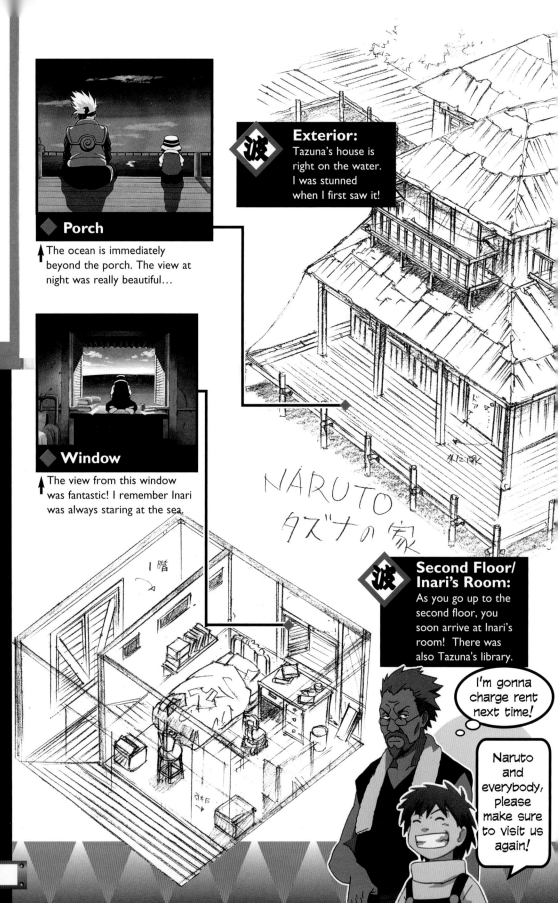

NARUTO
タズナの家

Exterior: Tazuna's house is right on the water. I was stunned when I first saw it!

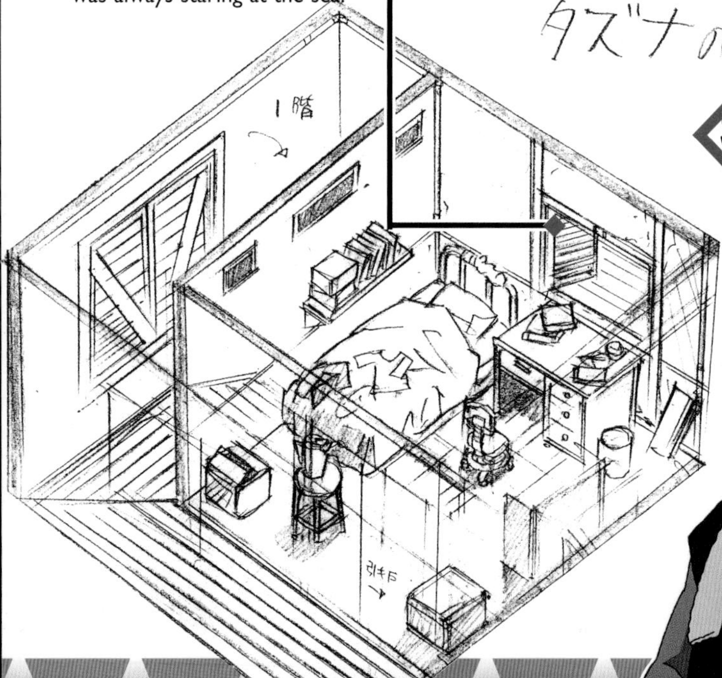

Second Floor/ Inari's Room: As you go up to the second floor, you soon arrive at Inari's room! There was also Tazuna's library.

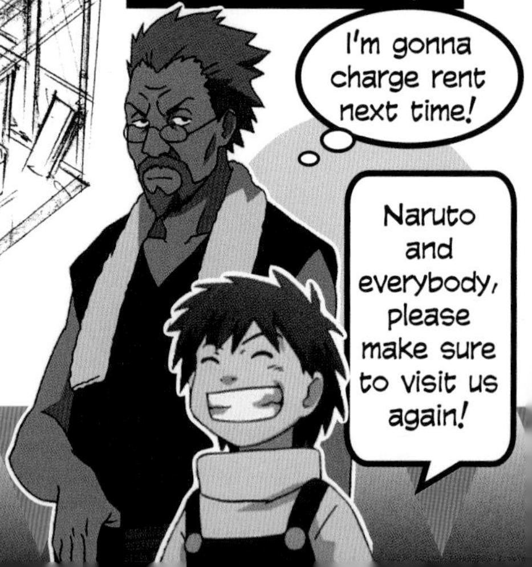

I'm gonna charge rent next time!
Naruto and everybody, please make sure to visit us again!

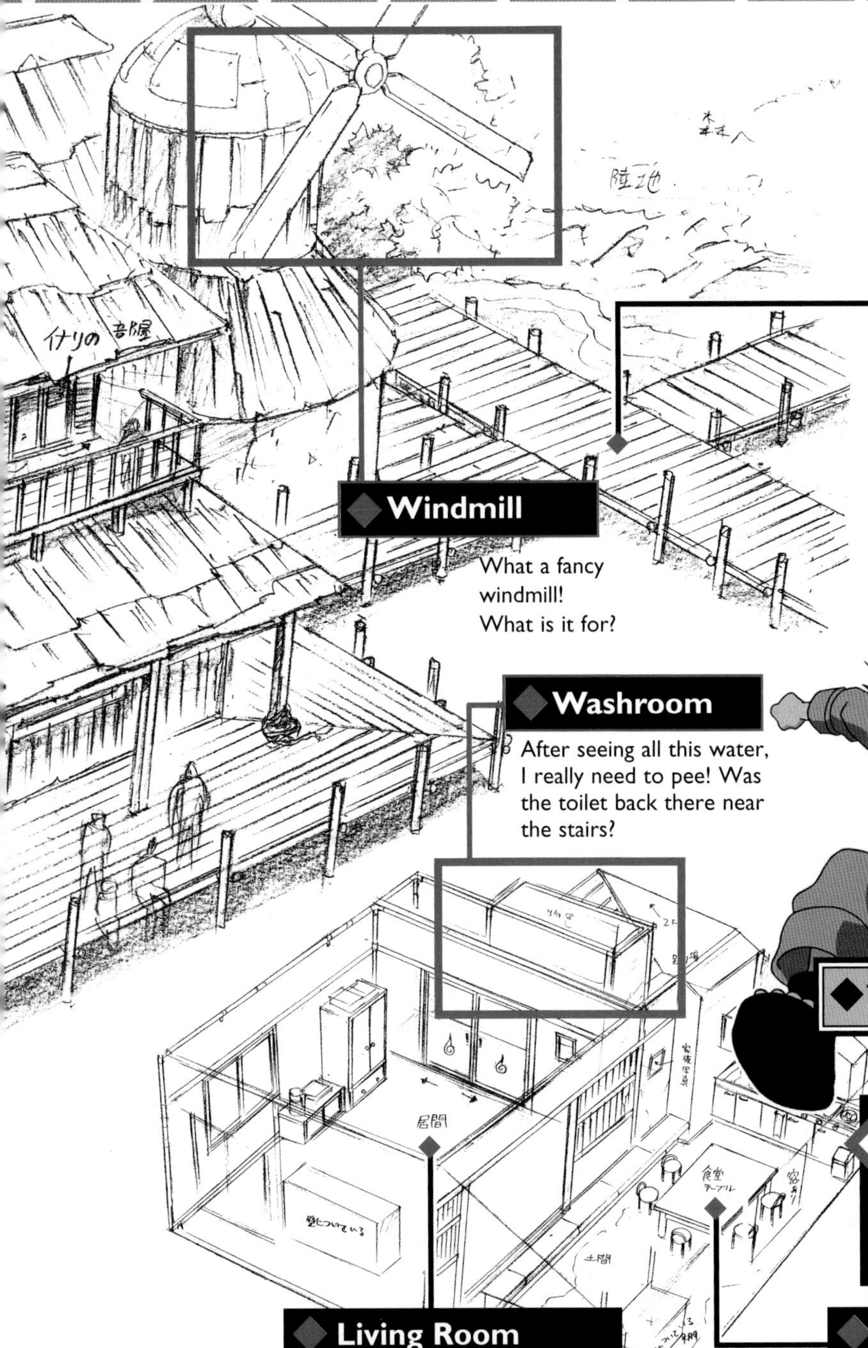

陸地
居間

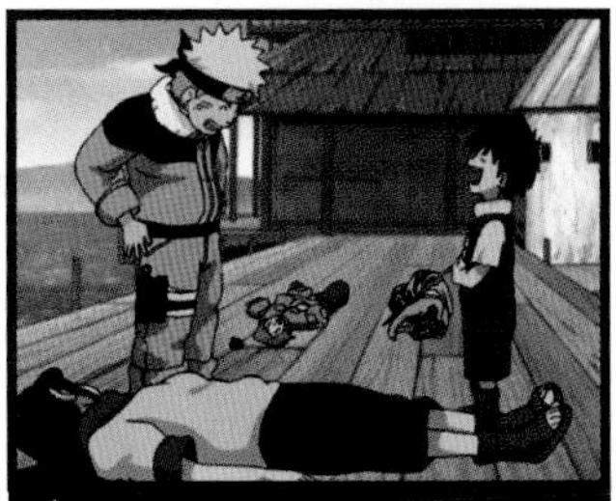

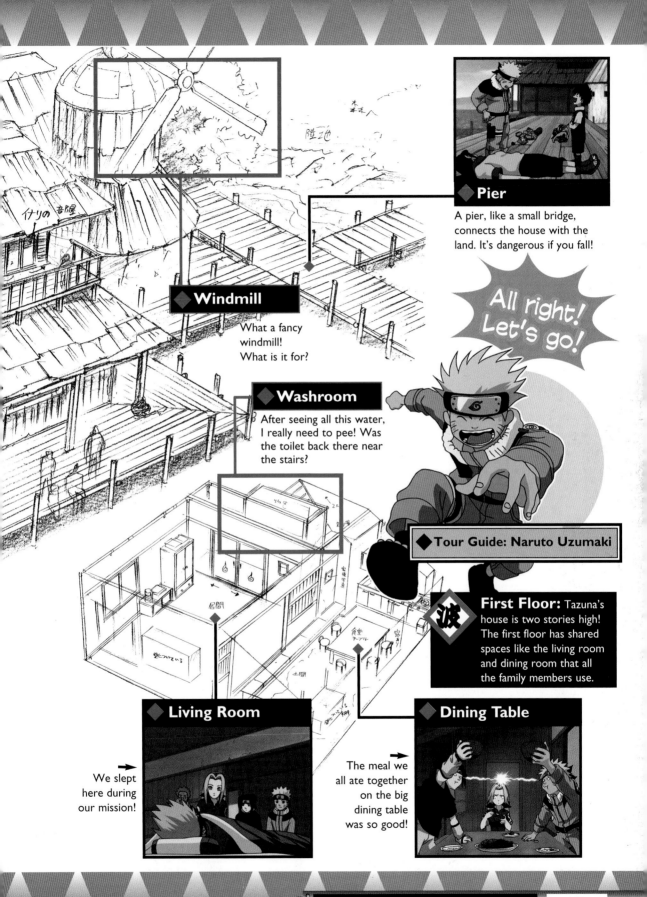

◆ Pier

A pier, like a small bridge, connects the house with the land. It's dangerous if you fall!

◆ Windmill

What a fancy windmill! What is it for?

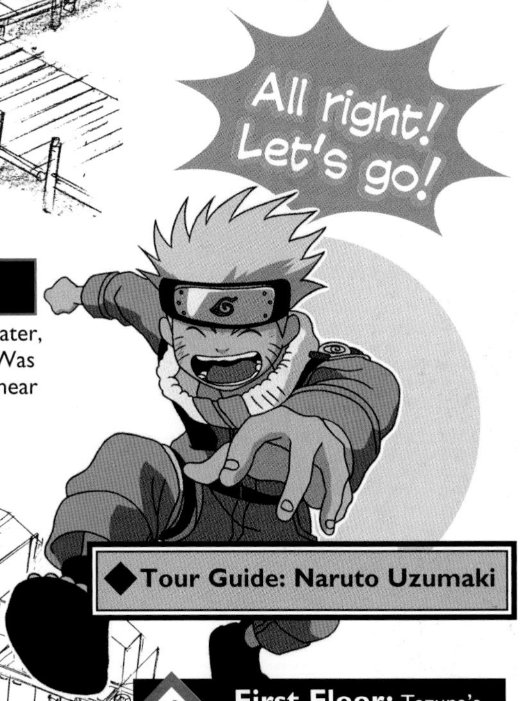

All right! Let's go!

◆ Washroom

After seeing all this water, I really need to pee! Was the toilet back there near the stairs?

◆ Tour Guide: Naruto Uzumaki

波

First Floor: Tazuna's house is two stories high! The first floor has shared spaces like the living room and dining room that all the family members use.

◆ Living Room

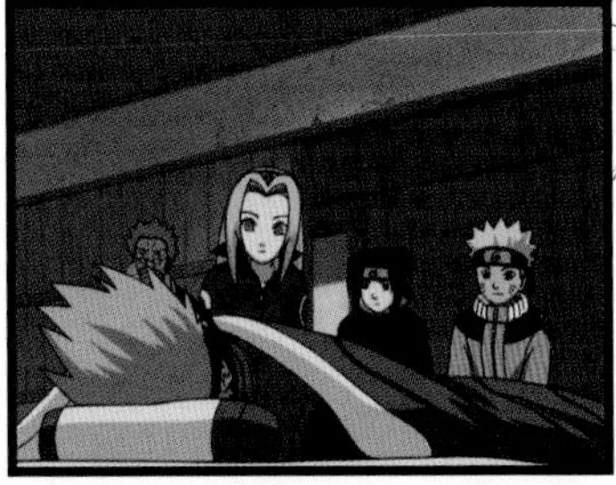

We slept here during our mission!

◆ Dining Table

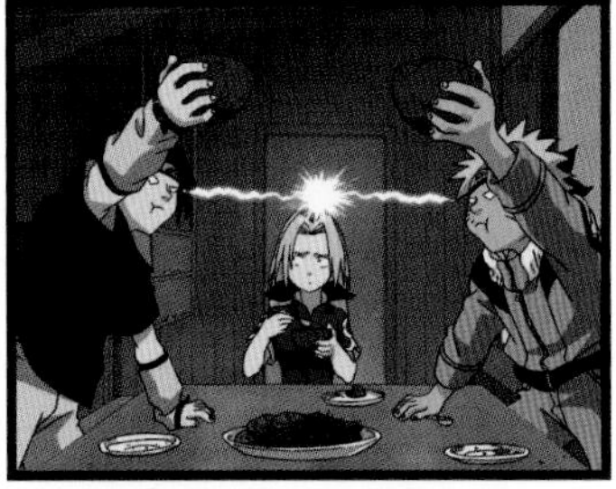

The meal we all ate together on the big dining table was so good!

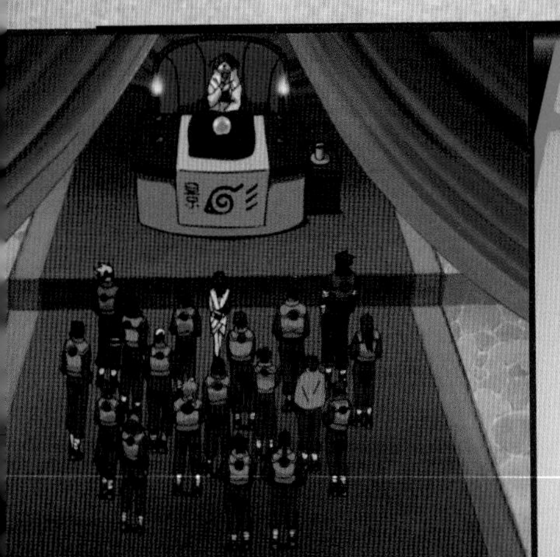

The Chunin Exams...

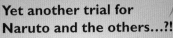

Yet another trial for Naruto and the others...?!

The Hokage summons all the squad leaders of the Hidden Leaf Village and informs them that the Chunin Exams will soon begin. This difficult series of tests will pit the genin against their finest counterparts from other nations for promotion to the rank of chunin. Who will be nominated by Kakashi, Asuma and Kurenai, the leaders of this year's rookies...?!

A tumultuous new journey begins!

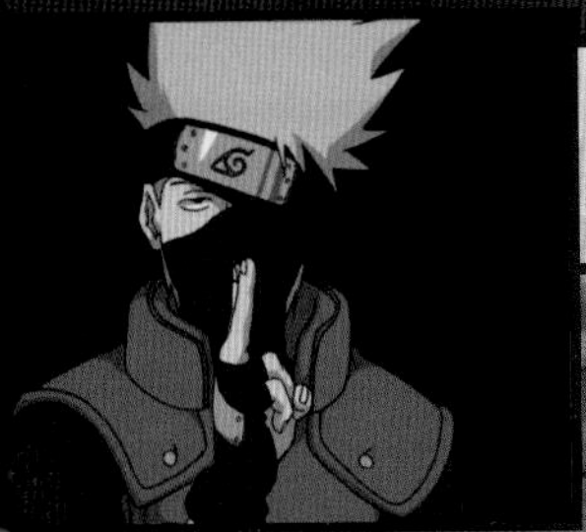

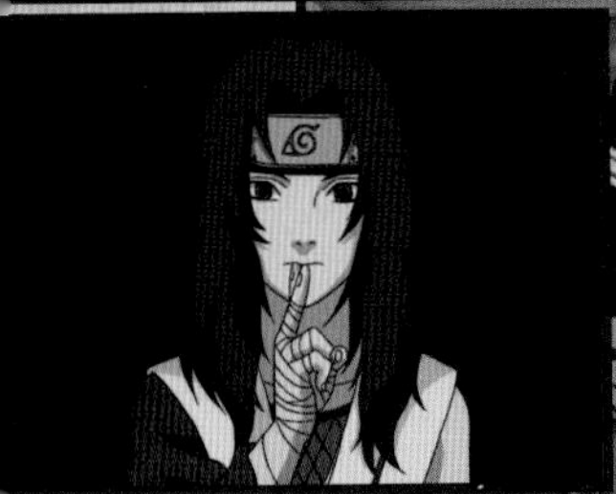

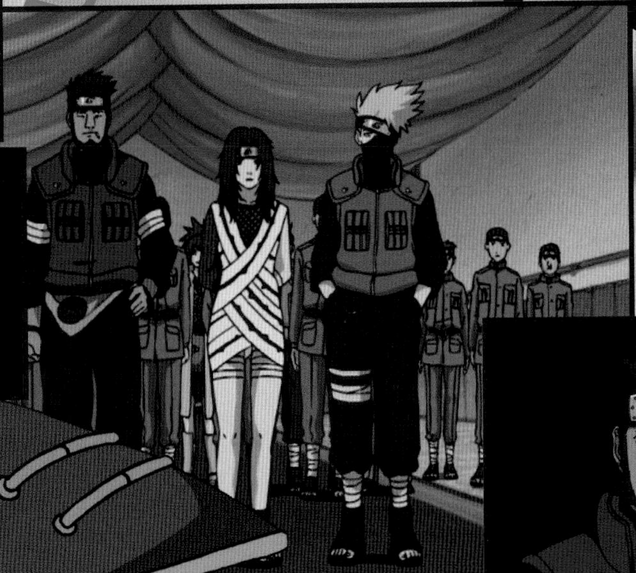

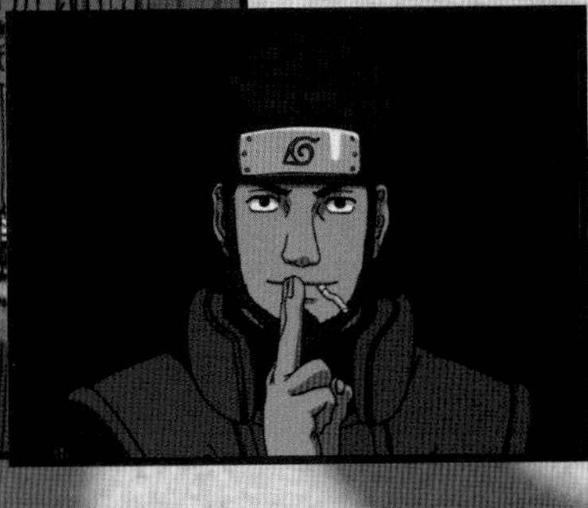

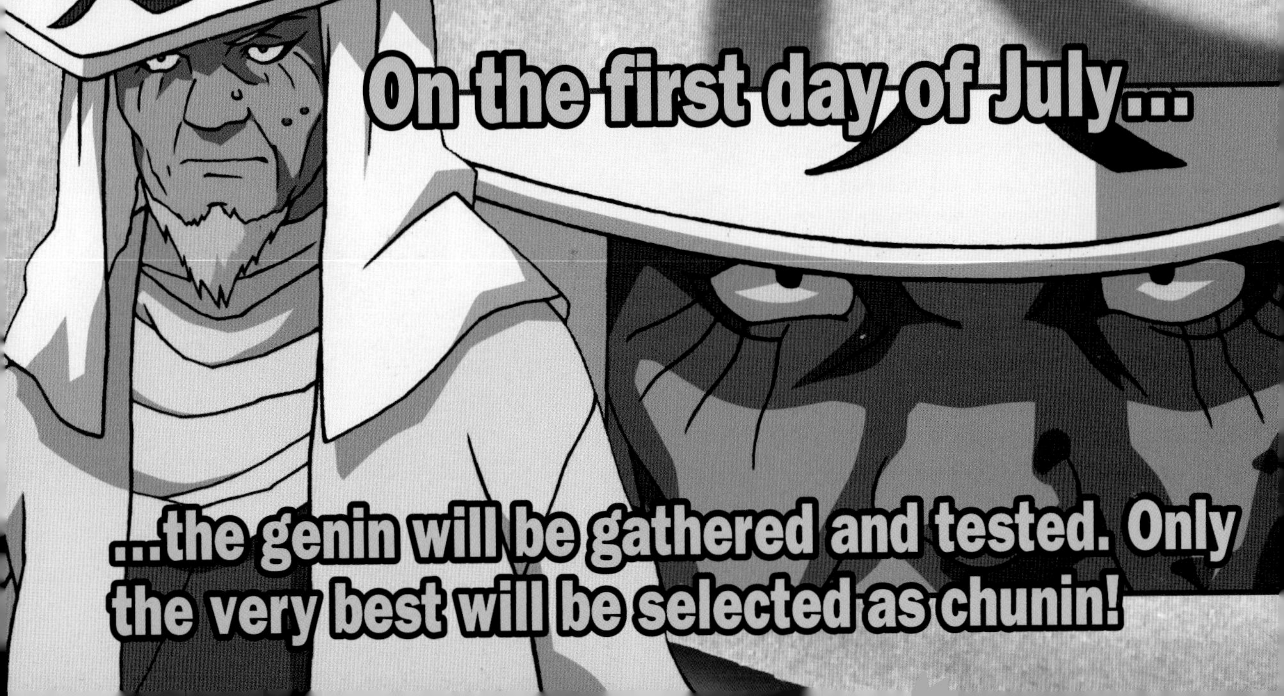

On the first day of July...

...the genin will be gathered and tested. Only the very best will be selected as chunin!

An explosive situation!

The most promising young talents arrive in the Hidden Leaf Village!

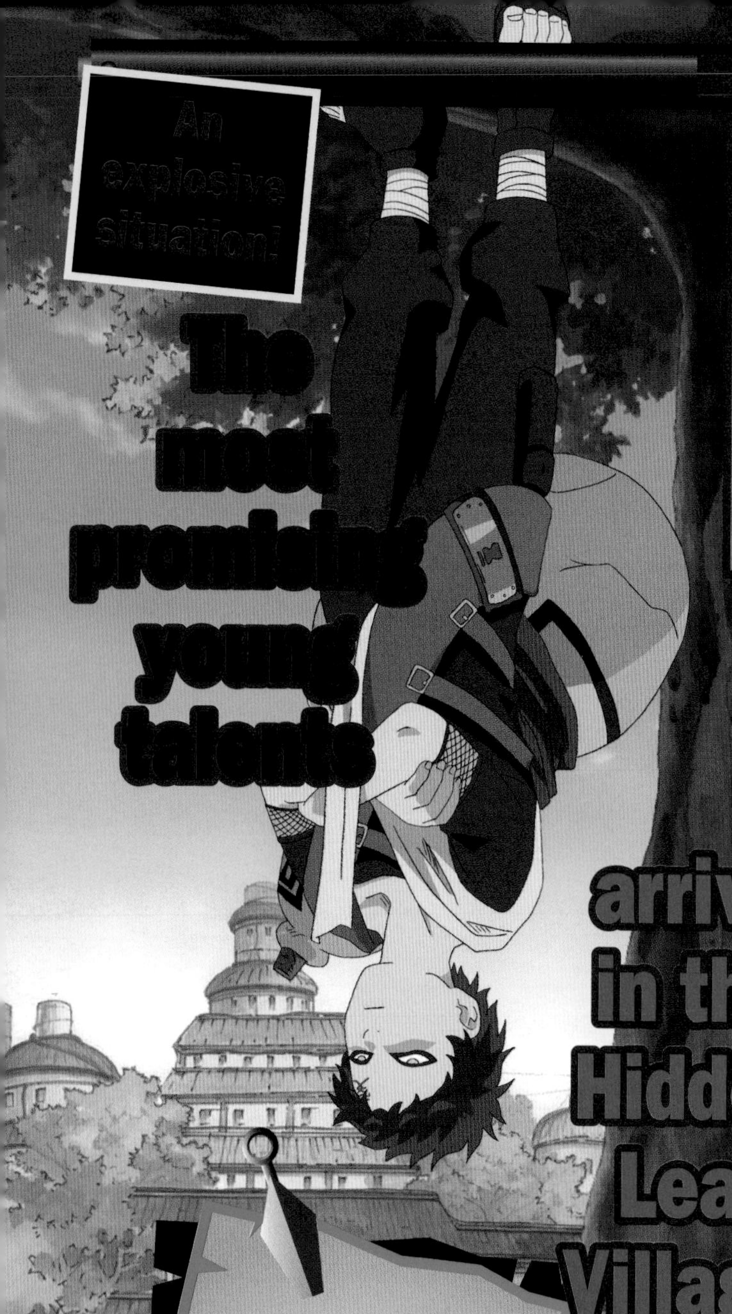

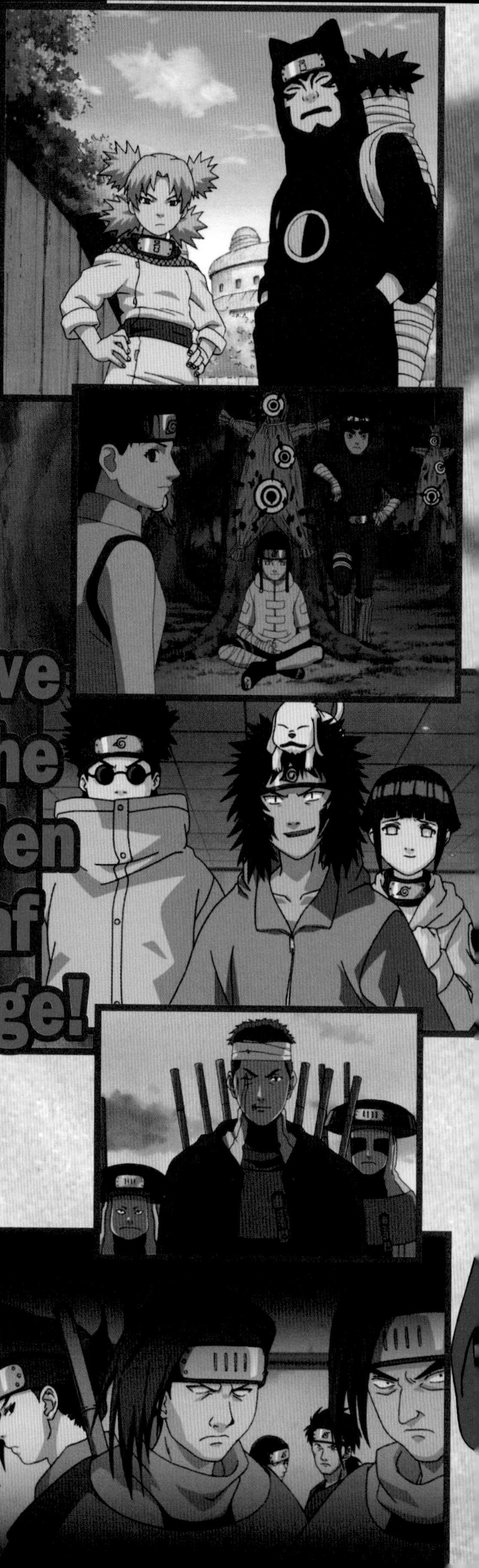

Naruto and the others now face countless rivals!
The many genin who have gathered in the Village Hidden in the Leaves assemble at the examination hall. Here, not only will they have to face off against shinobi from other nations, but from their own village as well! Facing unfamiliar eyes, full of defiance and hostility, what will Naruto and his squad do…?!

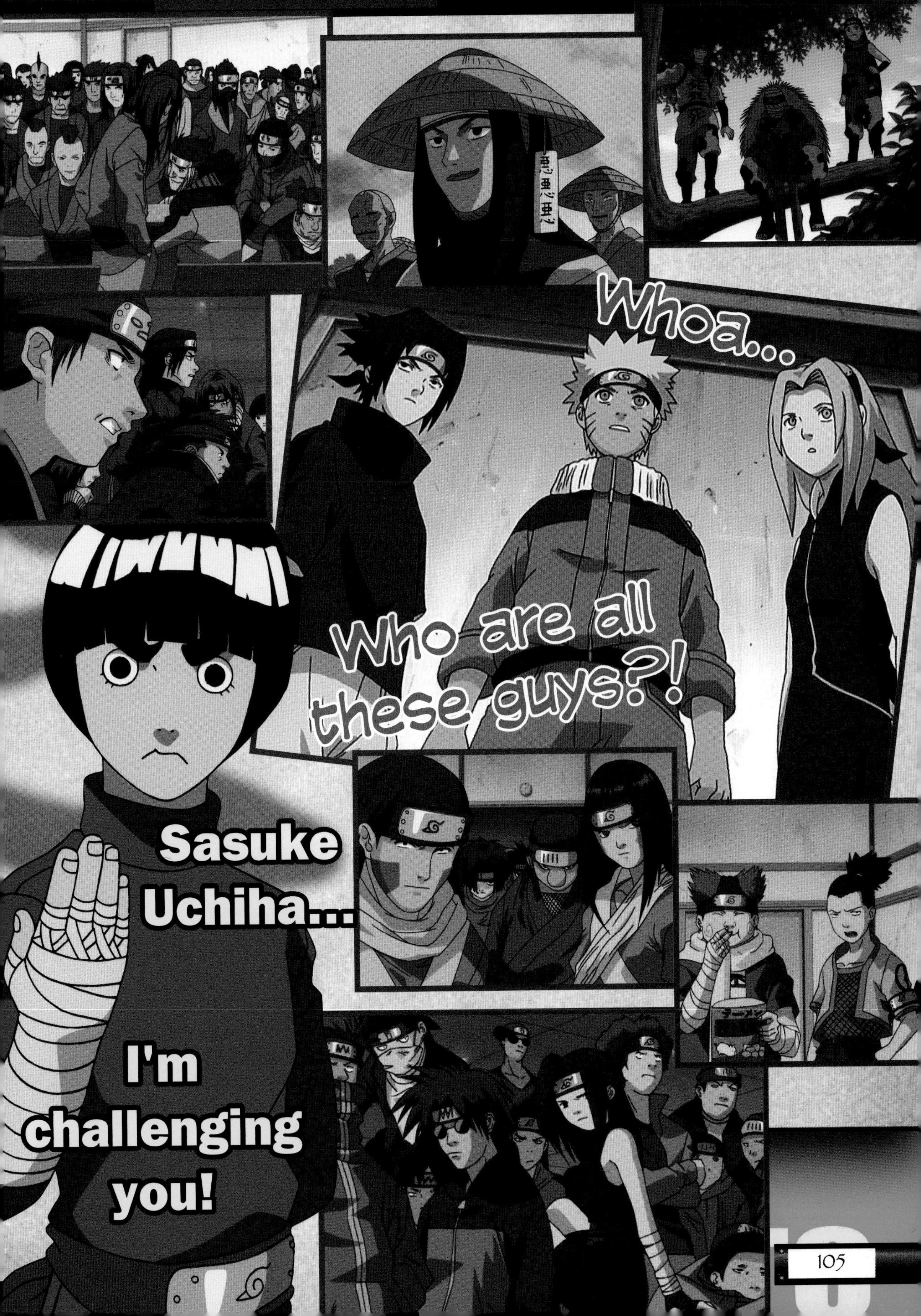
Whoa...
Who are all these guys?!
Sasuke Uchiha...
I'm challenging you!

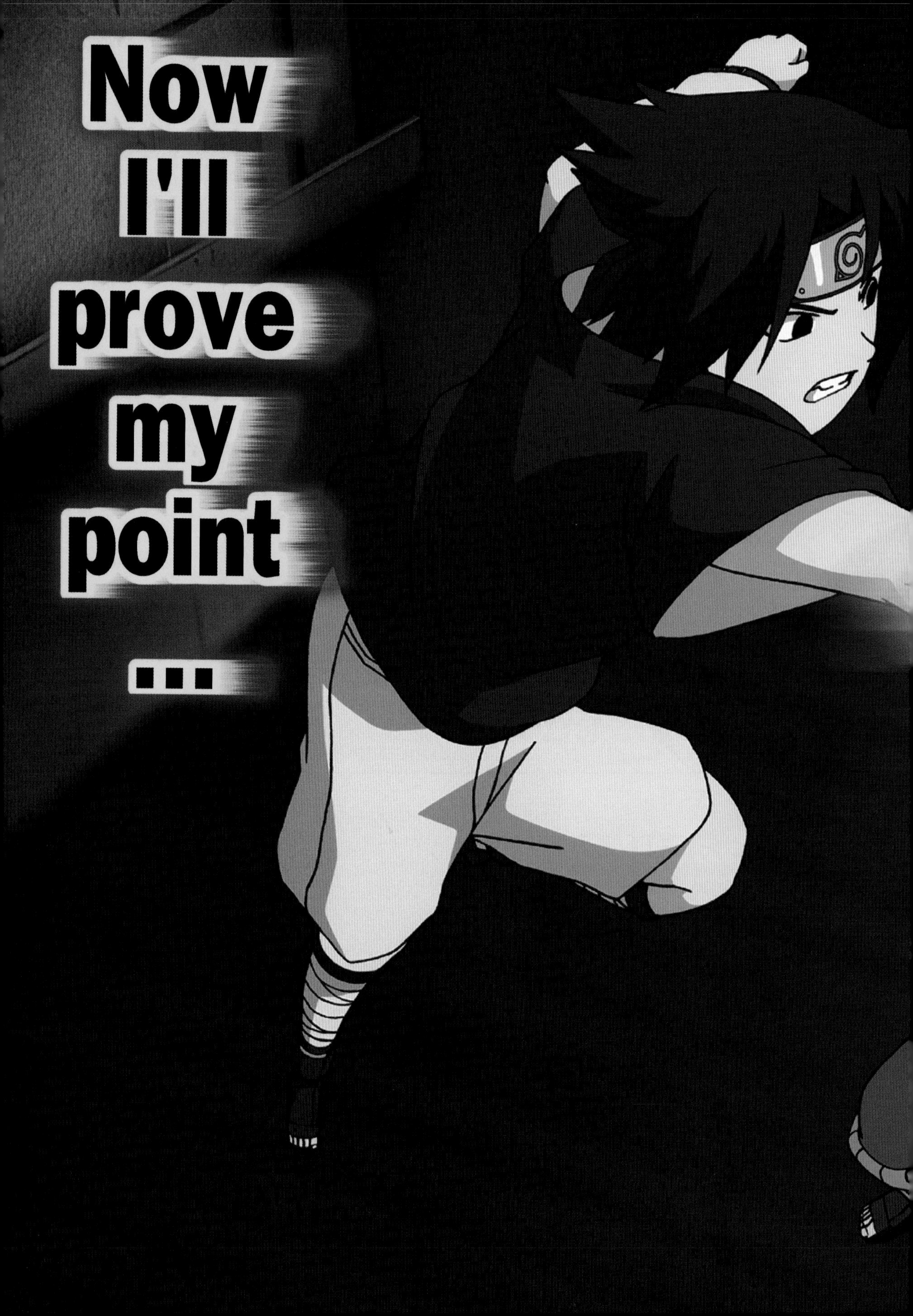
Now I'll prove my point ...

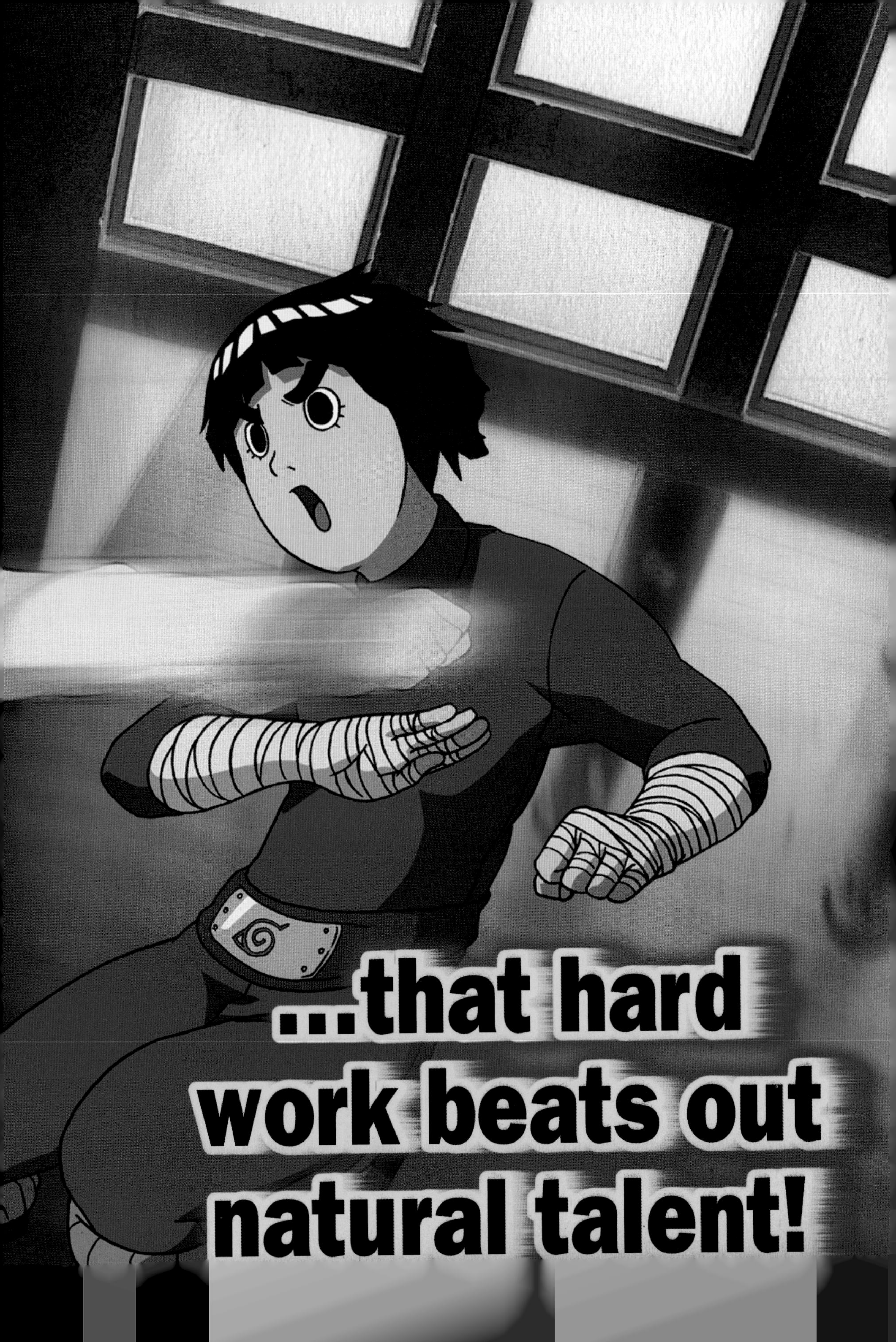
...that hard
work beats out
natural talent!

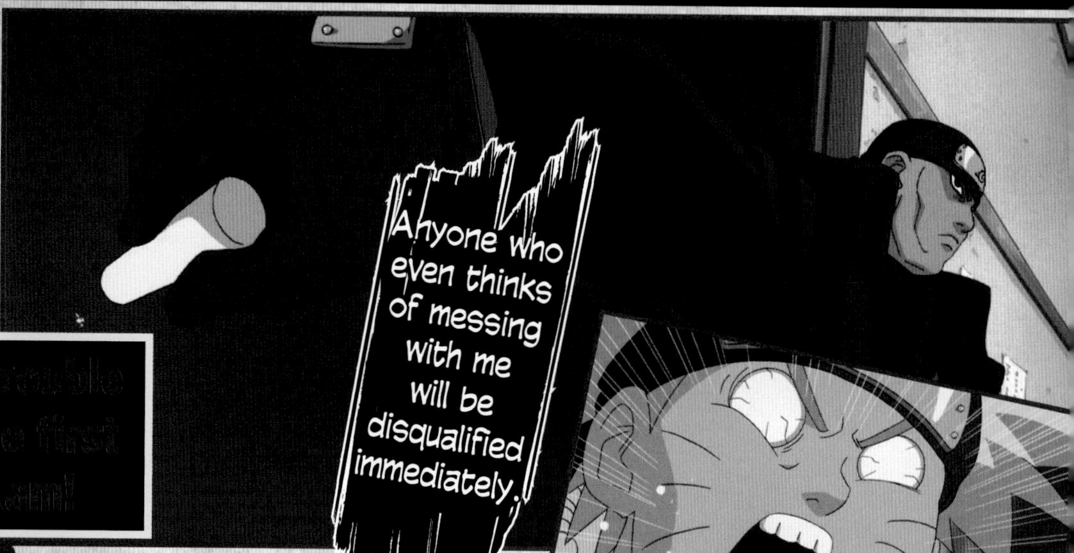
Anyone who even thinks of messing with me will be disqualified immediately.

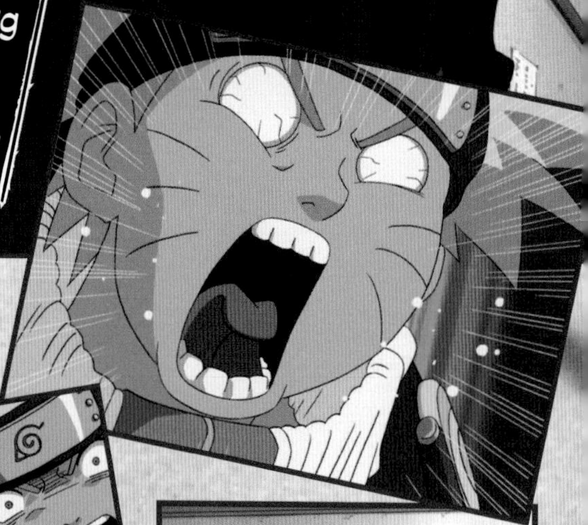

Big trouble in the first exam!

An ultra-difficult written test!

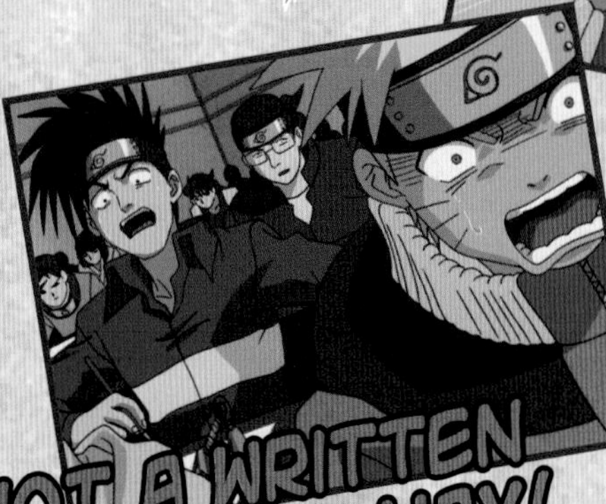
NOT A WRITTEN TEST... NO WAY!

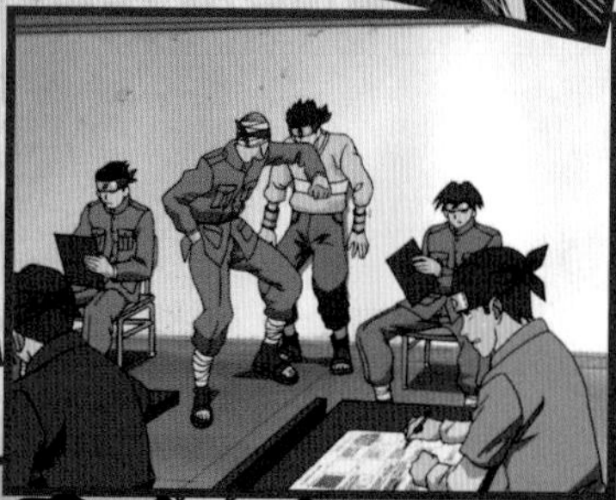

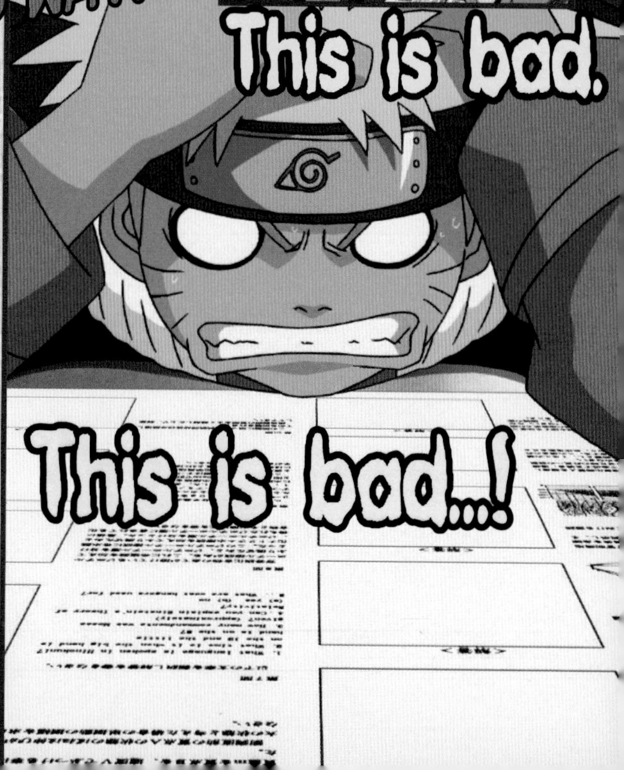
This is bad.
This is bad...!

What will Naruto do in this desperate situation?!
The first exam is a written test that presents an overwhelming obstacle for Naruto. No matter how much he stares at the questions, none of them make sense and he can't answer a single one. As the minutes tick by, Naruto feels more and more hopeless!

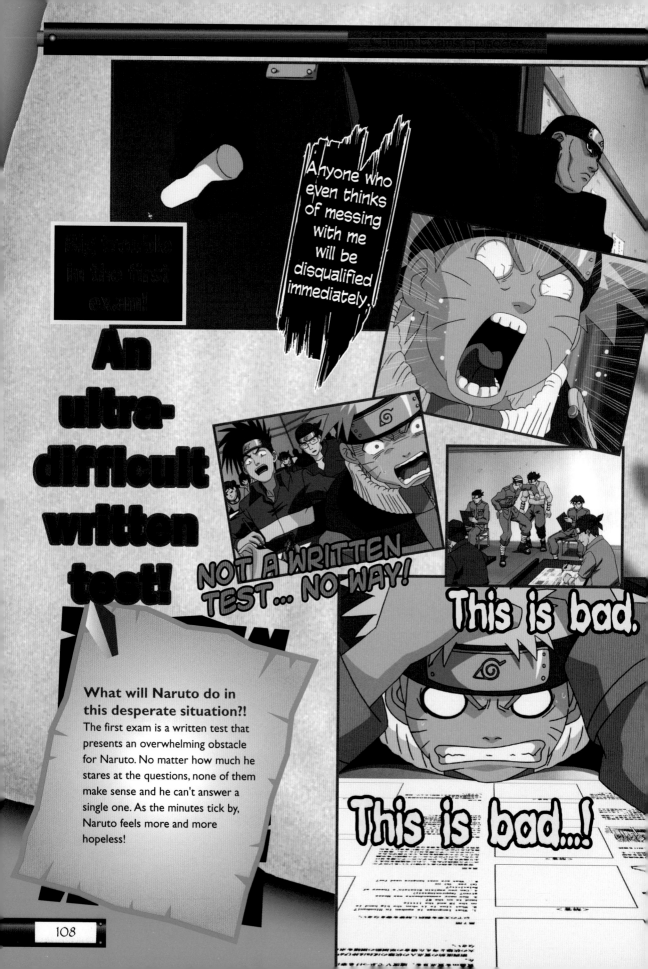

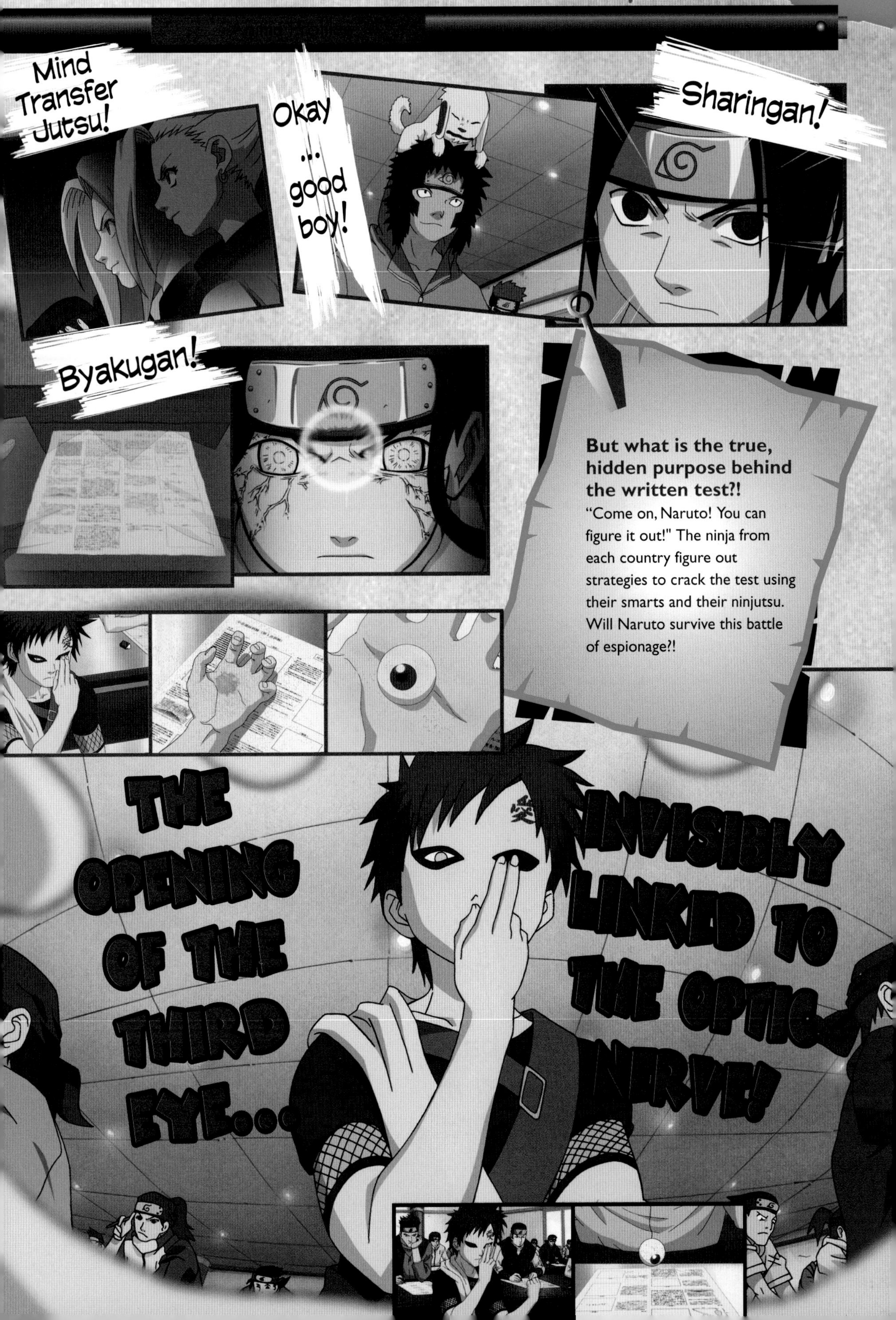
Mind Transfer Jutsu!
Okay ... good boy!
Sharingan!
Byakugan!
But what is the true, hidden purpose behind the written test?!
"Come on, Naruto! You can figure it out!" The ninja from each country figure out strategies to crack the test using their smarts and their ninjutsu. Will Naruto survive this battle of espionage?!
THE OPENING OF THE THIRD EYE...
INVISIBLY LINKED TO THE OPTIC NERVE!

The final question!

The decisive tenth question of the test!

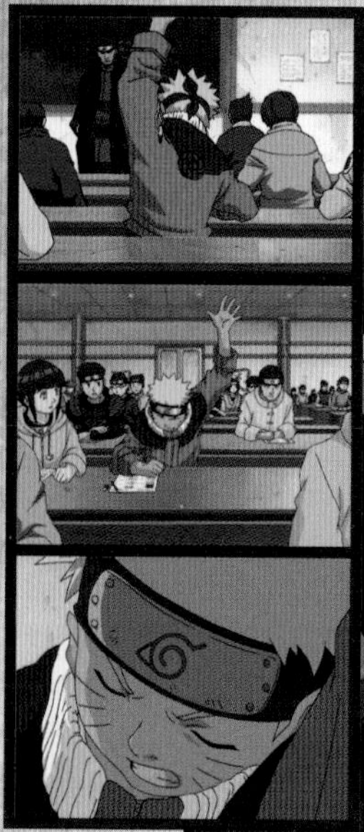

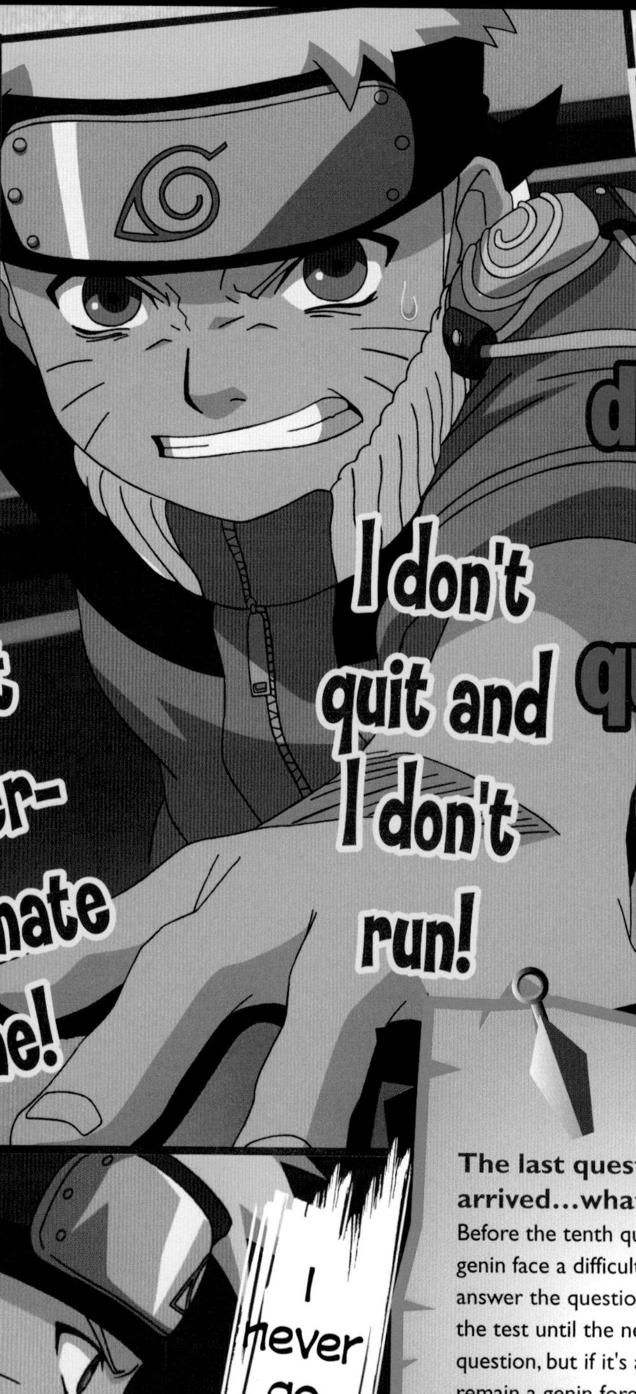
I don't quit and I don't run!
Don't under-estimate me!

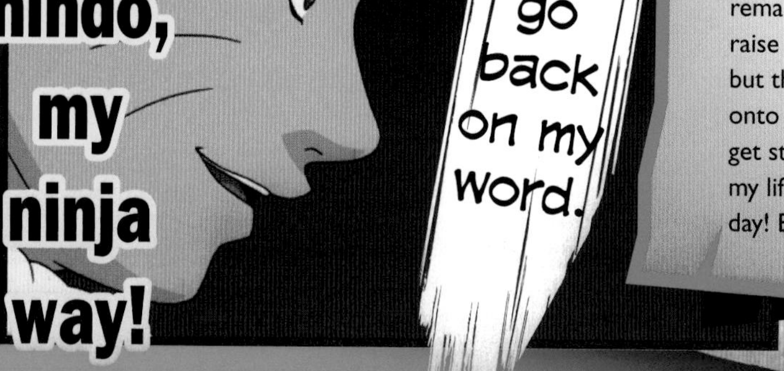
I never go back on my word.
That's my nindo, my ninja way!

The last question has arrived...what will Naruto do?!
Before the tenth question is presented, the genin face a difficult choice: decline to answer the question and withdraw from the test until the next year…or accept the question, but if it's answered incorrectly, remain a genin forever! Naruto begins to raise his hand as if to withdraw, but then he slaps his hand down onto the table! "I don't care if I do get stuck as a genin for the rest of my life… I'll still be Hokage some day! Believe it!"

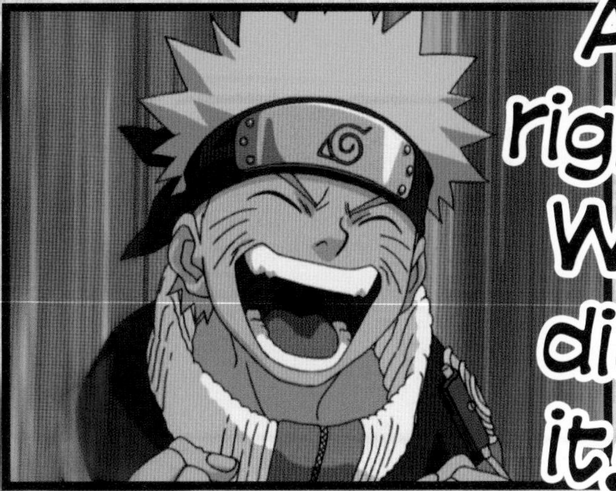
All right! We did it!

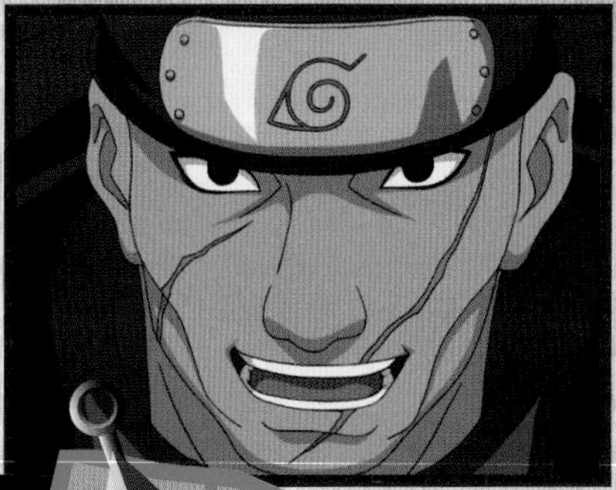

Naruto passes the first stage! But...

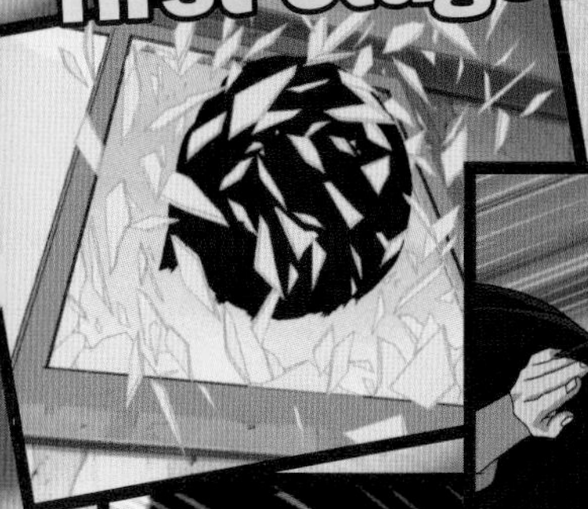

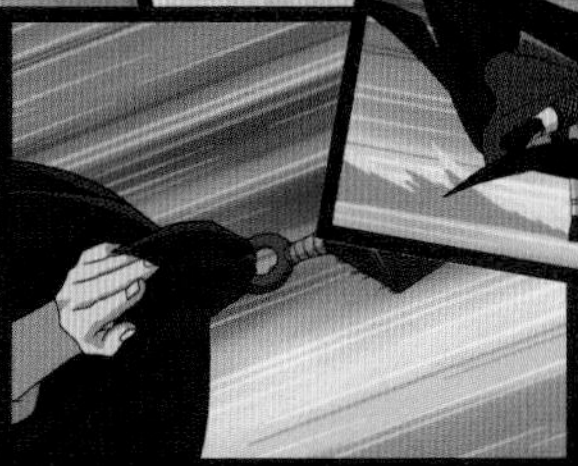

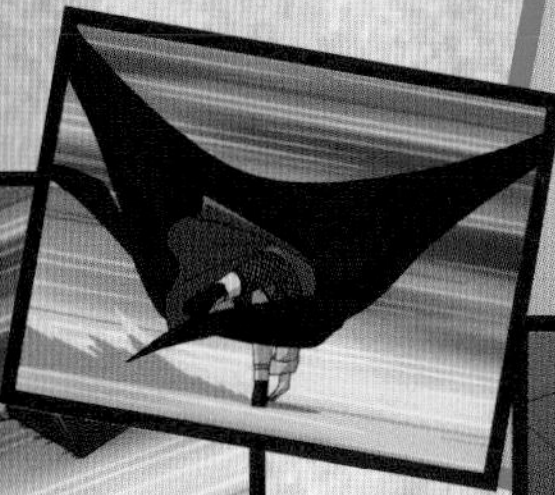

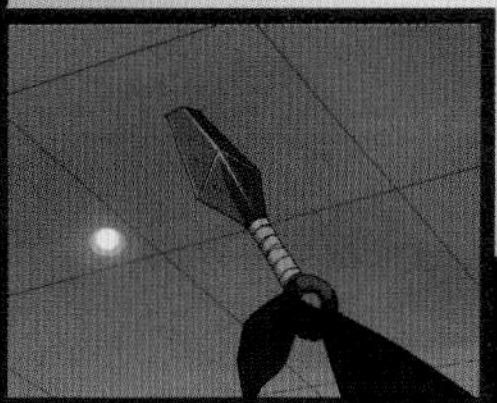

Accepting the tenth question means passing the test?!
Through his courage and the strength of his convictions, Naruto manages to pass the written test! But before he can celebrate his victory, the second phase of the exam begins with a bang!

Here comes the Second Test's Proctor: Anko Mitarashi.

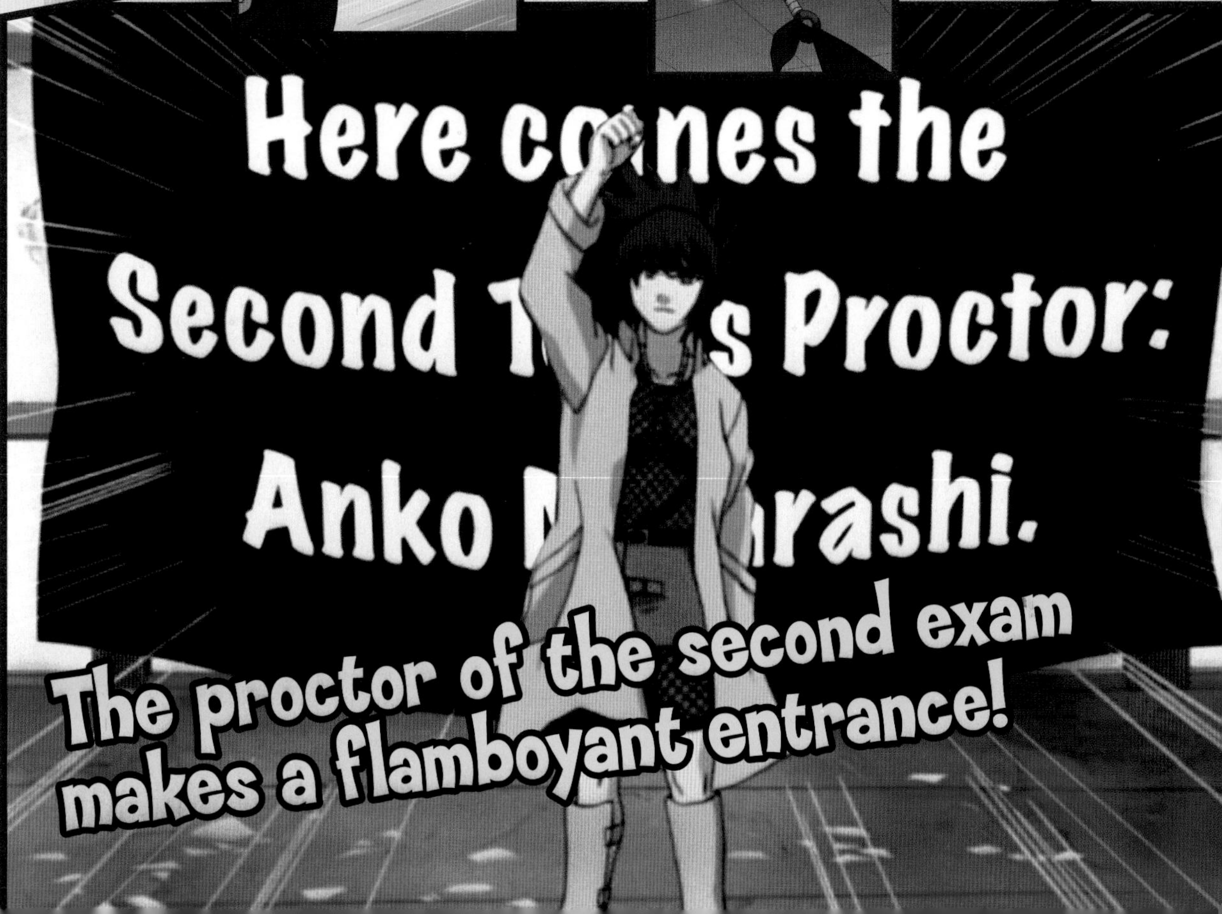

The proctor of the second exam makes a flamboyant entrance!

The Second Exam!

A harrowing test of survival in the Forest of Death!

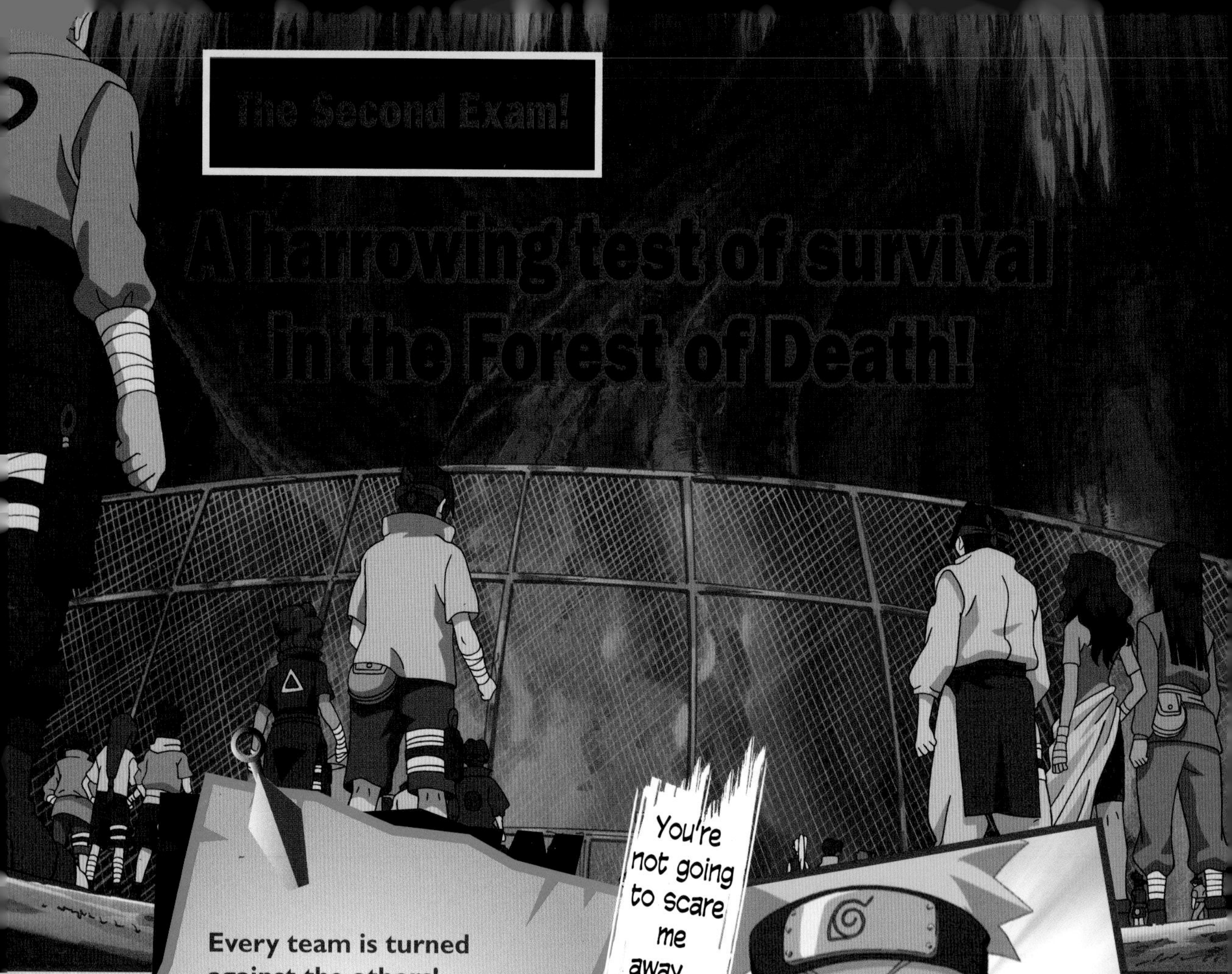

Every team is turned against the others!

In the dense, dark forest, the best ninja from each village are gathered. The site of the second exam is also known as the "Forest of Death," so what sorts of dangers await the candidates? With their pride and their villages' honor on the line, 78 shinobi tremble as they line up to face their fate!

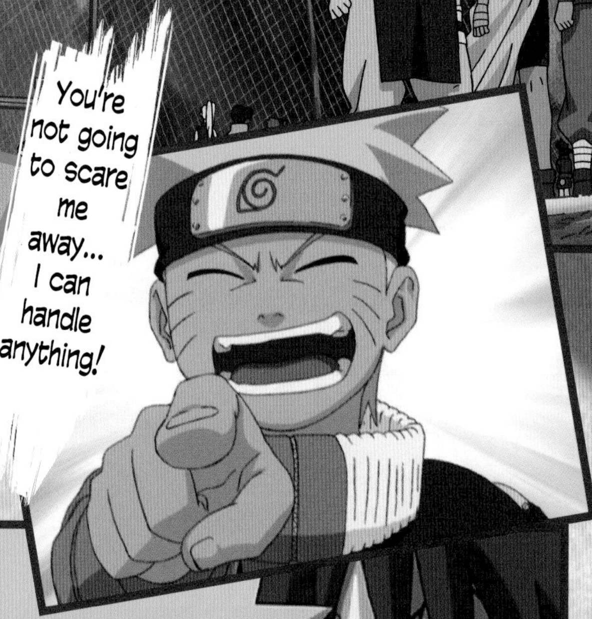
You're not going to scare me away... I can handle anything!

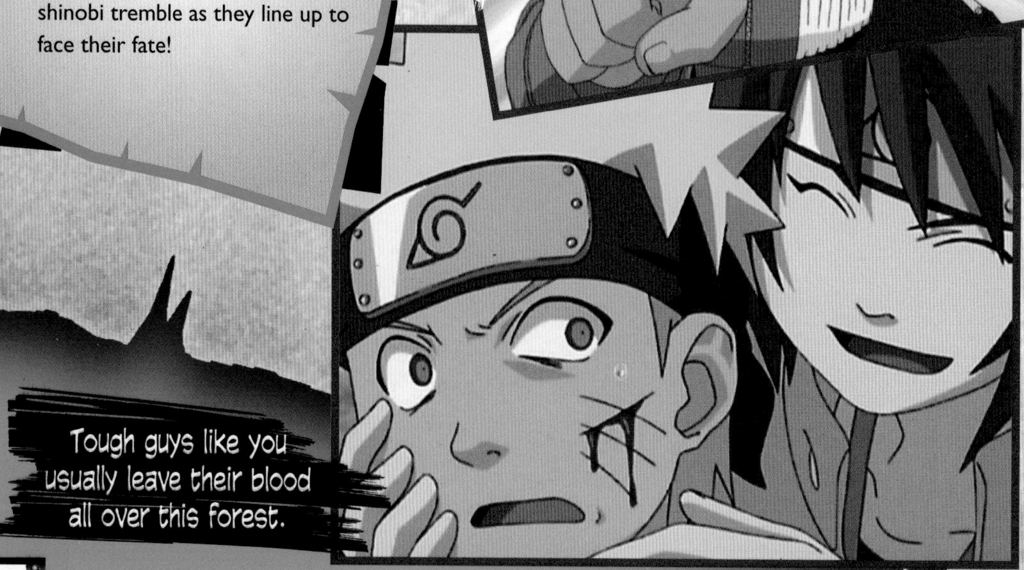
Tough guys like you usually leave their blood all over this forest.

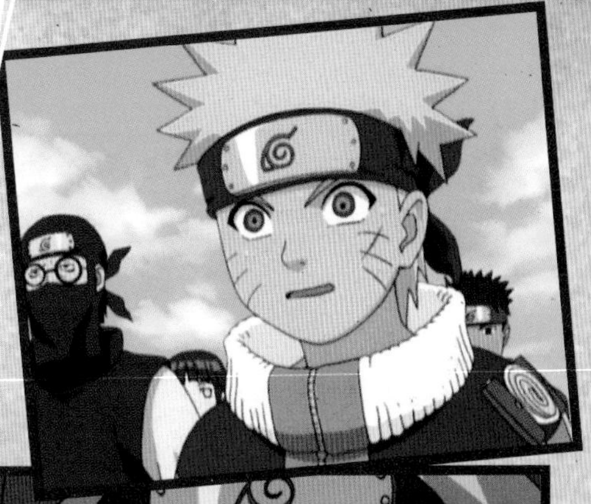

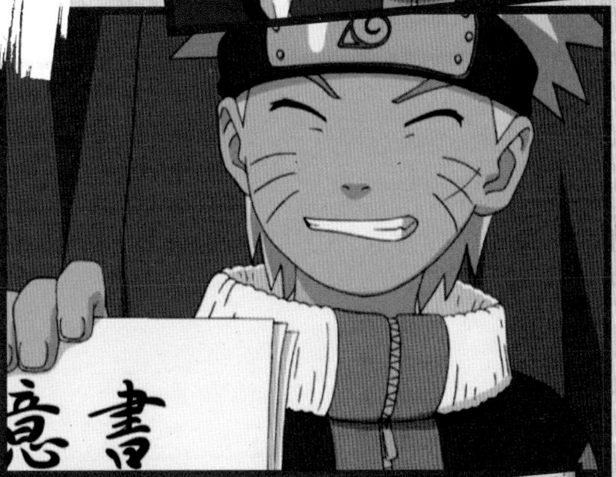

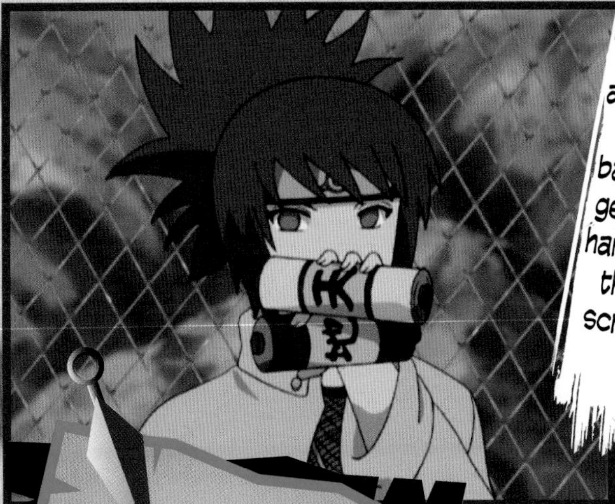
It's an anything-goes battle to get your hands on these scrolls!

The survival competition finally begins!

Each team is given one scroll, and to survive the test, they must reach the finish line with a pair of them! There are no rules to hold the participants back, so they can be merciless in their pursuit of the scrolls. Plus, the forest itself is full of life-threatening dangers! Brushing aside their fear, Naruto's squad prepares for battle.

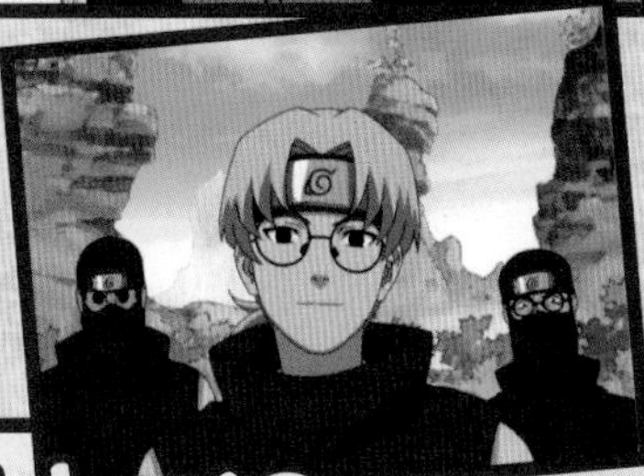

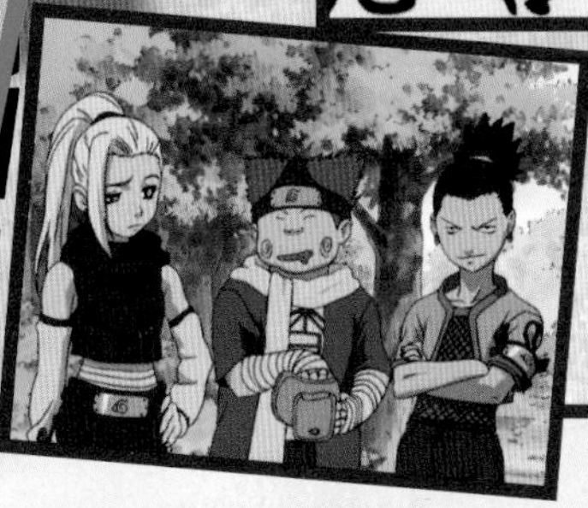

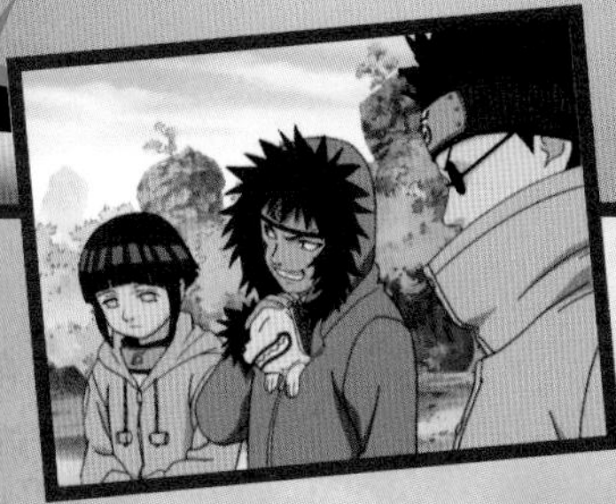

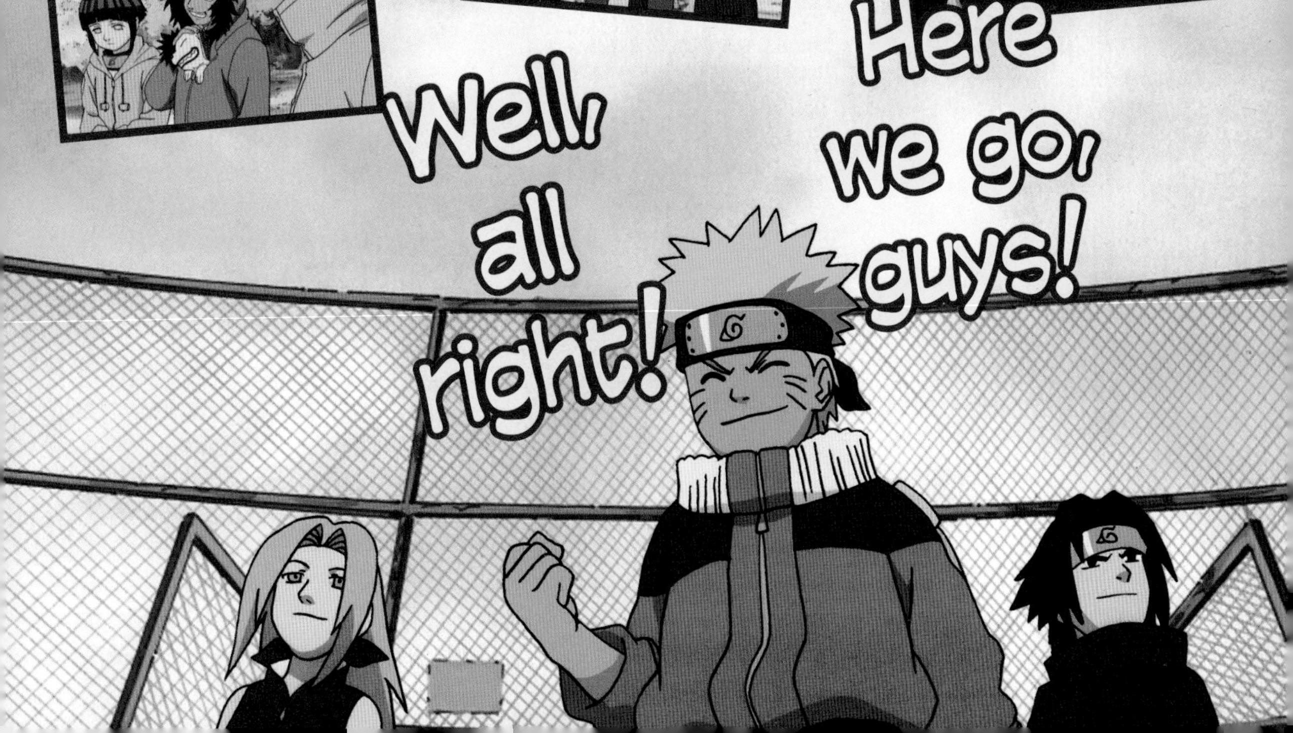
Here we go, guys!
Well, all right!

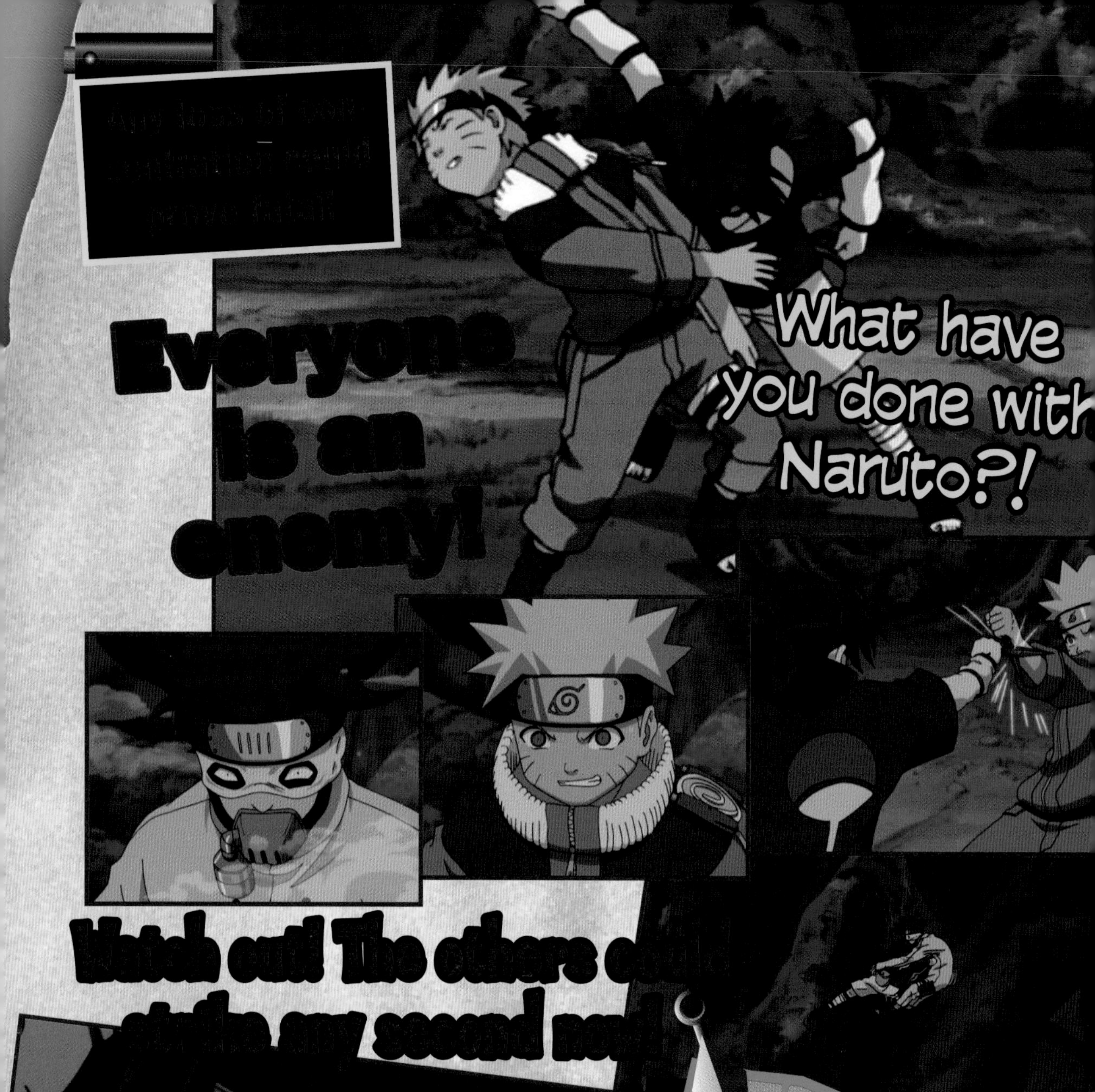

Any loss of our
confidence would
prove fatal.

Everyone
is an
enemy!

What have
you done with
Naruto?!

Watch out! The others could
strike any second now!

Kill or be killed...a cruel test!
An assassin from the Village Hidden in
the Rain tries to infiltrate the group by
transforming himself into Naruto! A
butcher from the Hidden Grass Village
attacks with brutal force! As Naruto
and others are pushed to the brink of
death, they learn how harsh the test
truly is...and are forced to face their
darkest fears!

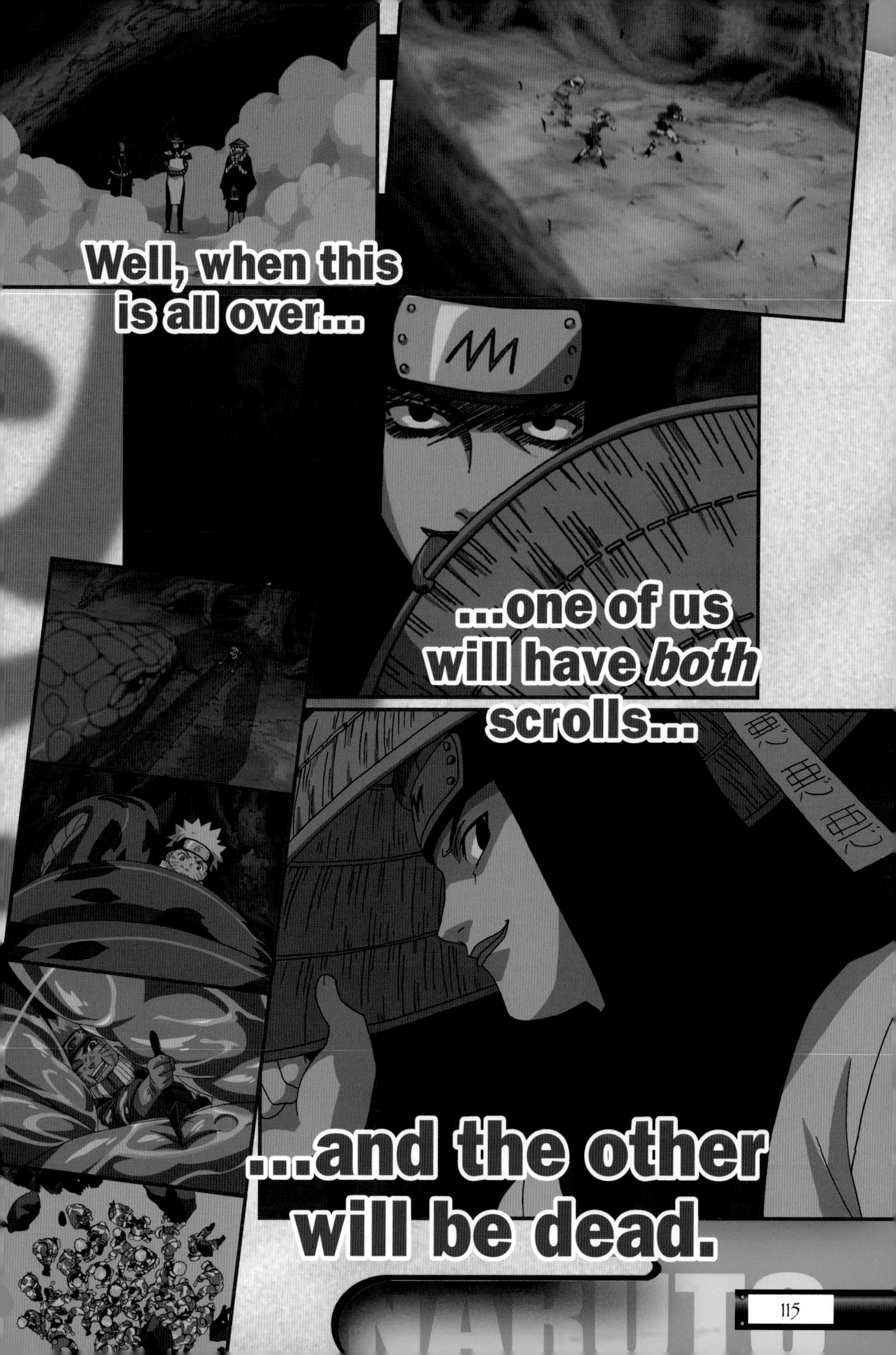
Well, when this is all over...
...one of us will have *both* scrolls...
...and the other will be dead.
NARUTO

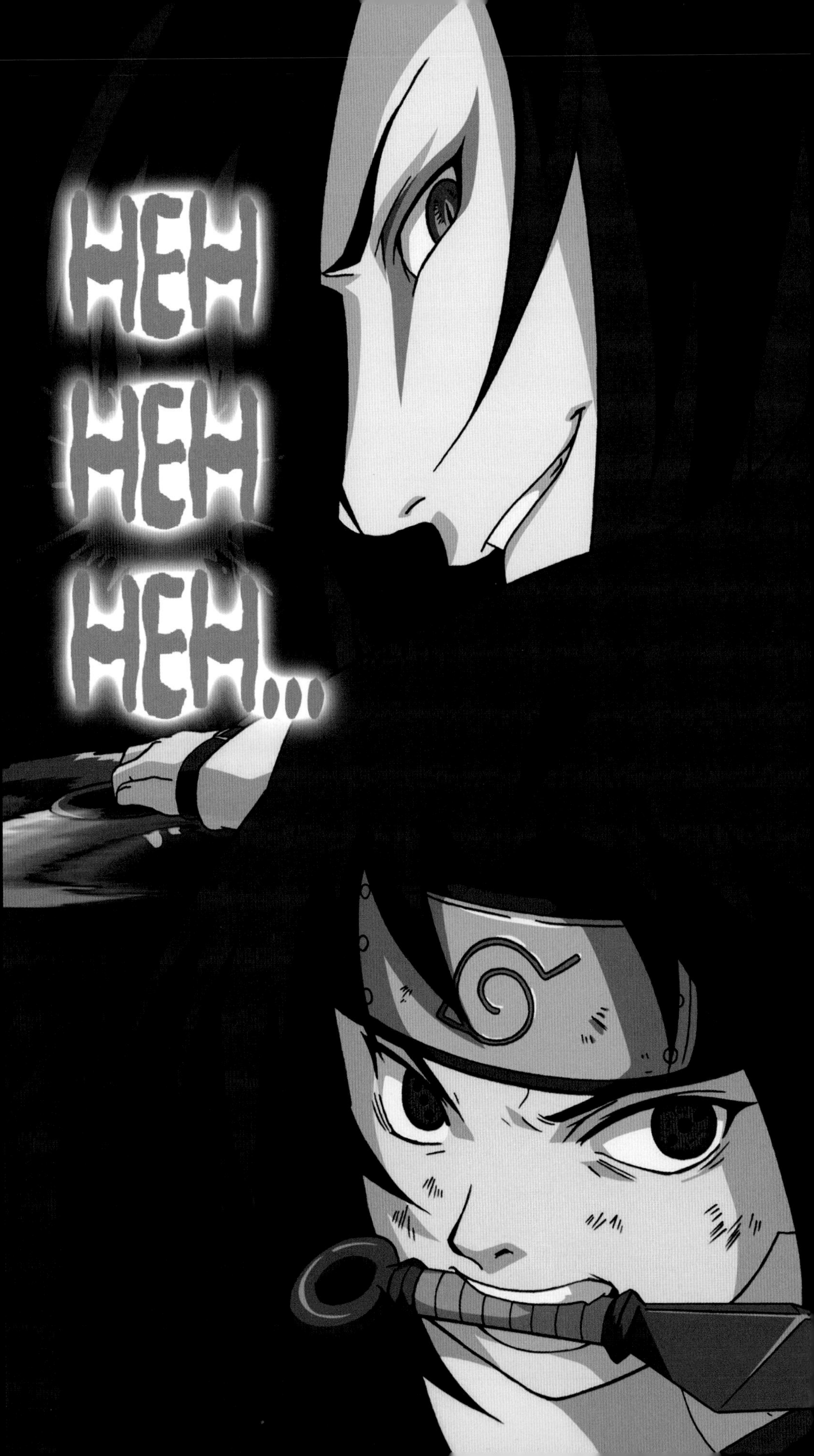
HEH HEH HEH...

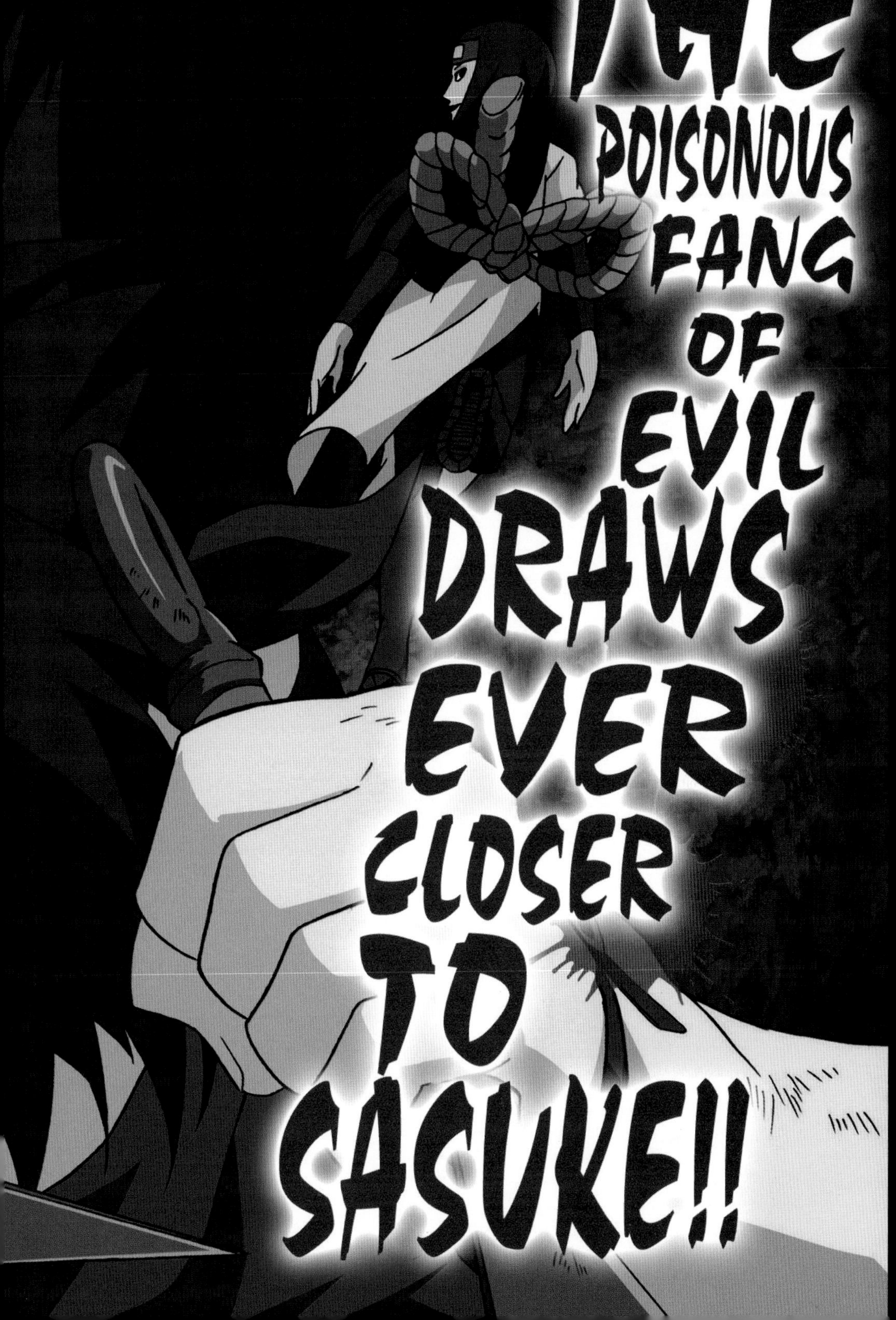
THE POISONOUS FANG OF EVIL DRAWS EVER CLOSER TO SASUKE!!

[redacted]

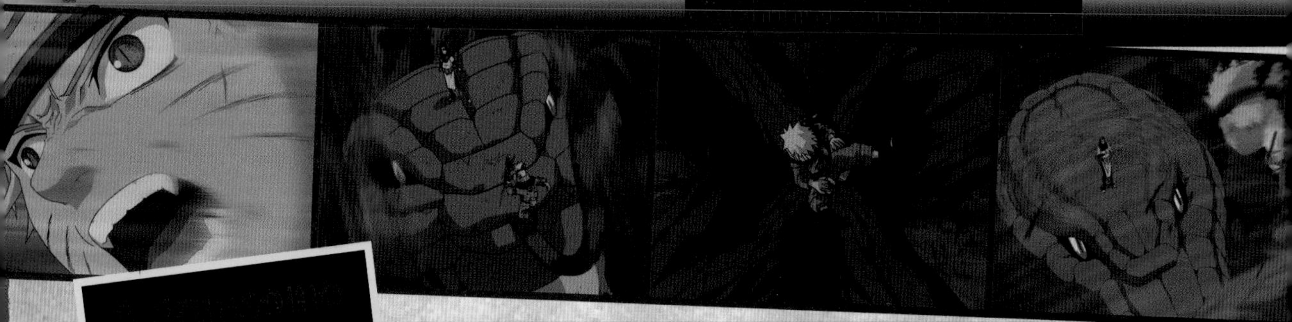

[redacted]

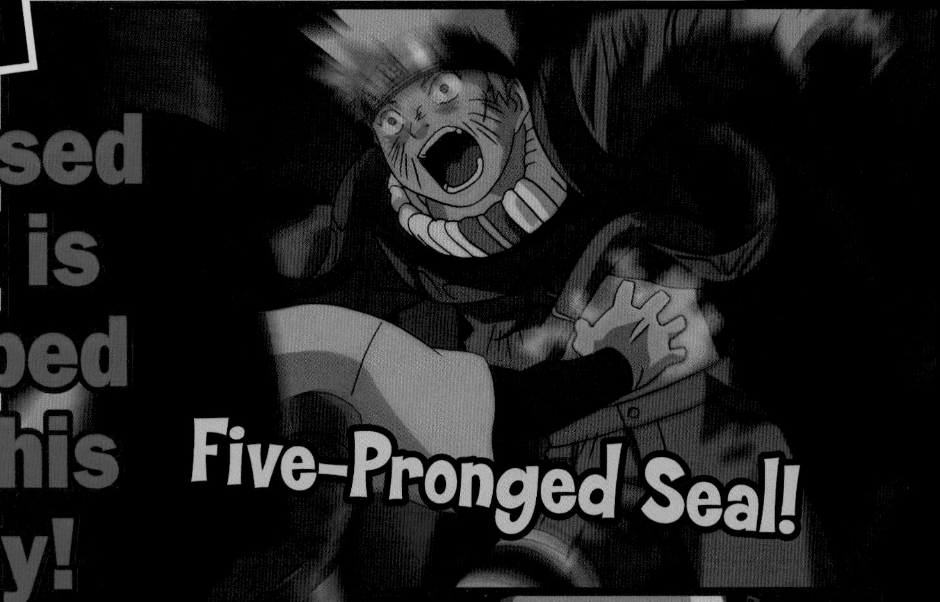
A cursed seal is stabbed into his belly!
Five-Pronged Seal!

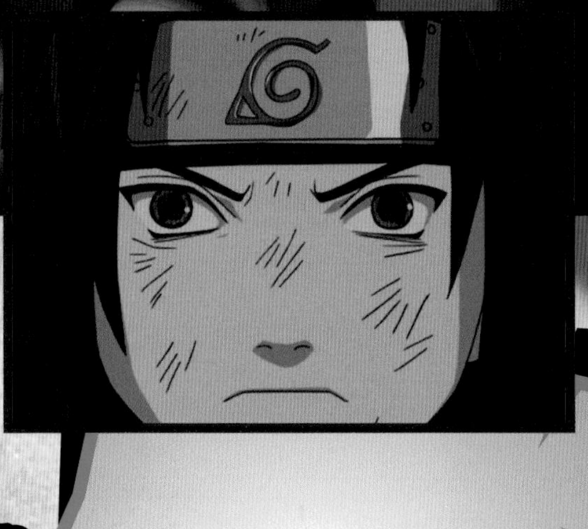

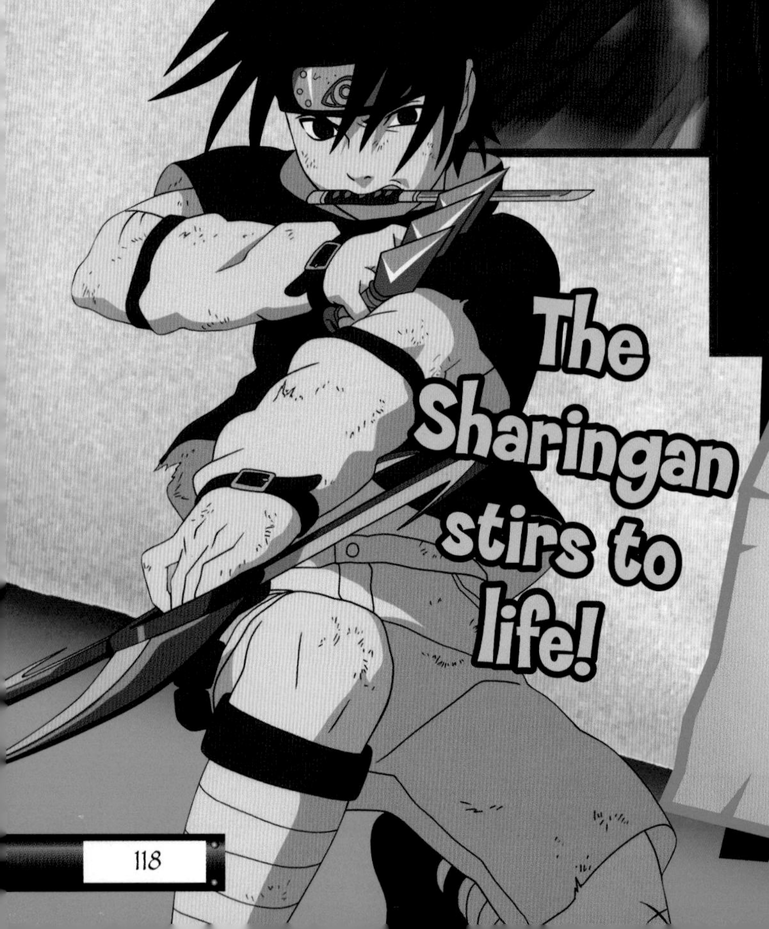
The Sharingan stirs to life!

Naruto's wrath awakens Sasuke!
Naruto explodes with power as the Nine-Tailed Fox's chakra begins to leak out. Orochimaru's sealing jutsu cripples Naruto and he collapses, unable to fight. But at that moment, Sasuke's Uchiha blood pushes him into action!

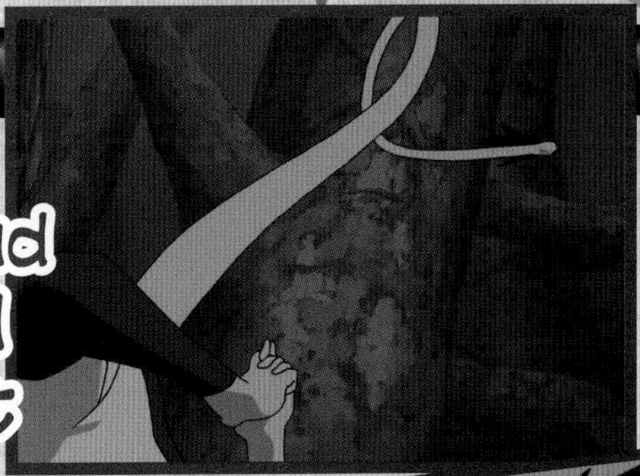

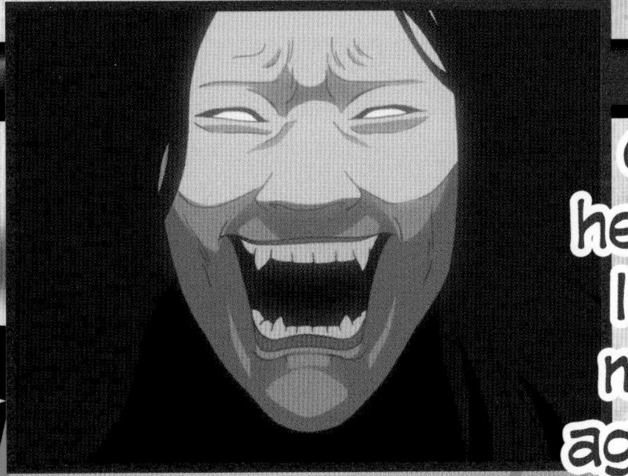
Oh, he and I will meet again...

What does Orochimaru want?!
Orochimaru's wicked fangs sink into Sasuke's neck! Sasuke writhes in pain and a curse mark appears on his skin. Orochimaru was once one of the Sannin (legendary three ninja), and he betrayed the Hidden Leaf Village. But why did he return…and why is he targeting Sasuke?

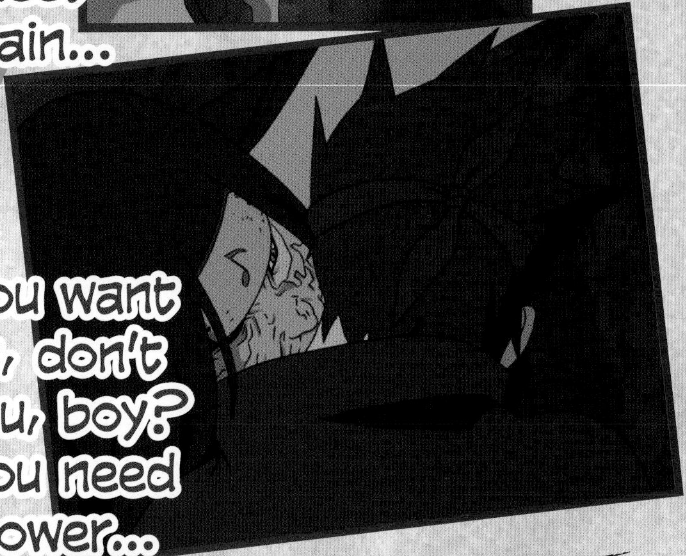
You want it, don't you, boy? You need power...

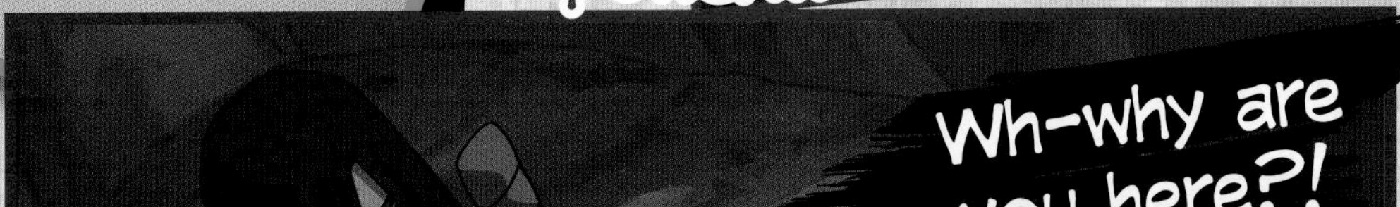
Wh-why are you here?!
There's a boy I want... a very promising prospect.

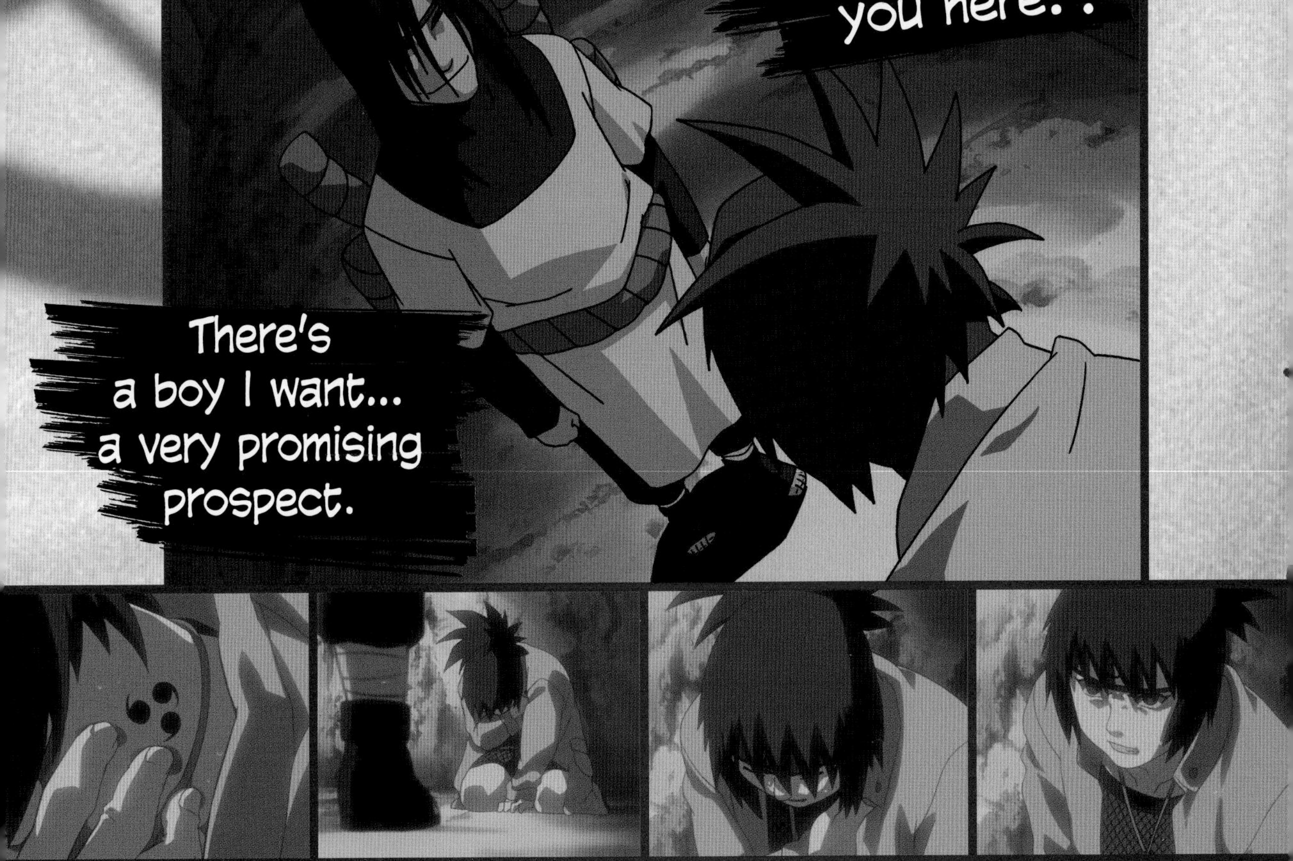

A whirlwind sweeps through the air!

Lee's spirit burns with determination!

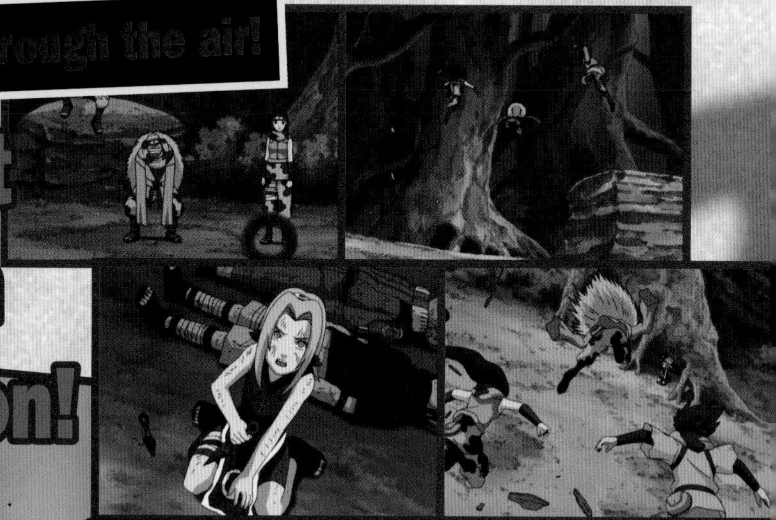

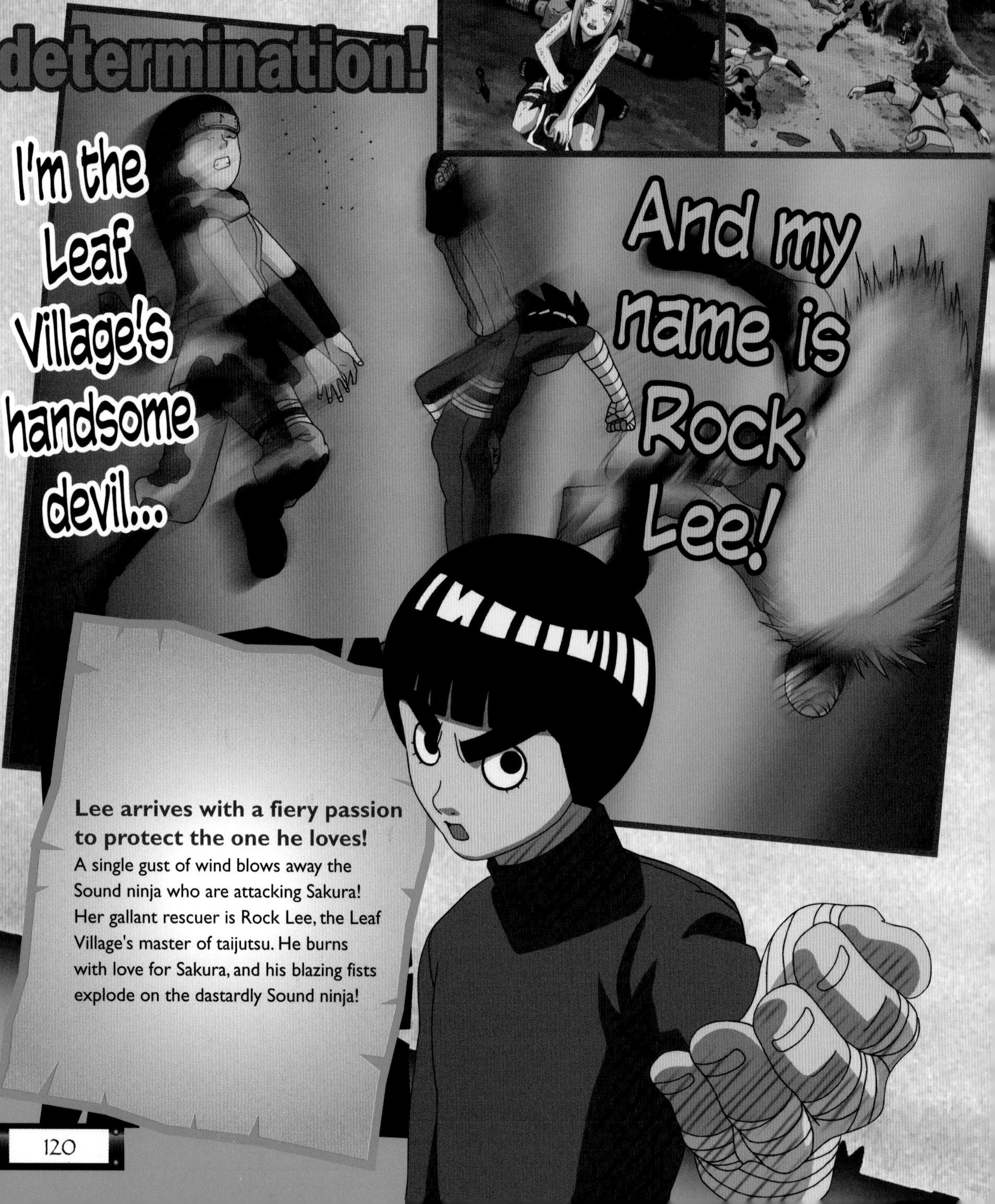
I'm the Leaf Village's handsome devil...
And my name is Rock Lee!

Lee arrives with a fiery passion to protect the one he loves!
A single gust of wind blows away the Sound ninja who are attacking Sakura! Her gallant rescuer is Rock Lee, the Leaf Village's master of taijutsu. He burns with love for Sakura, and his blazing fists explode on the dastardly Sound ninja!

Sakura works up her resolve...!

Helpless against the supersonic speed of the Sound ninja's attacks, Lee is badly wounded and can no longer fight. But Sakura bolsters her courage and determination and fights the Sound ninja. She is inspired by Lee, who risked his life to protect her, by her beloved teammates and, more than anything else, by her own ninja way!

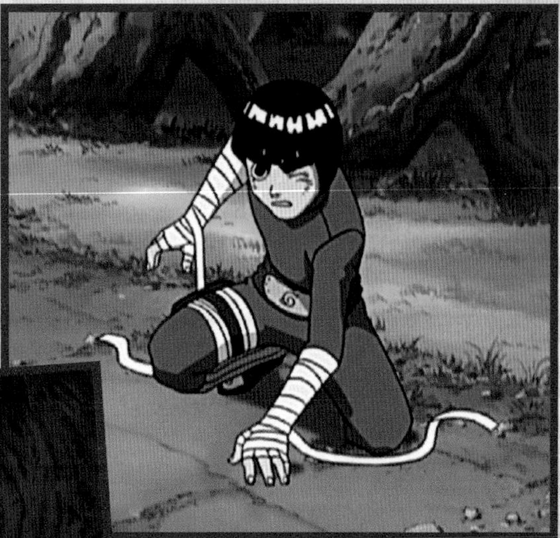

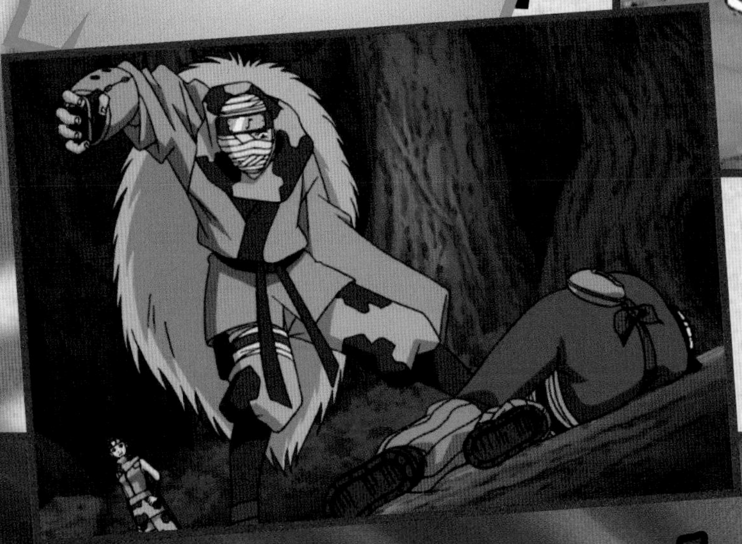

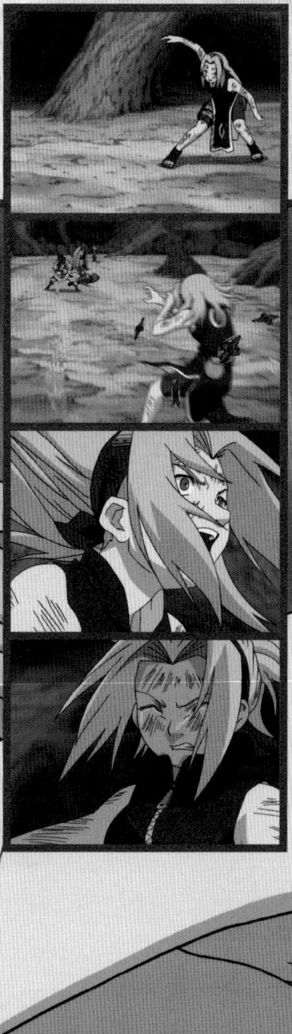

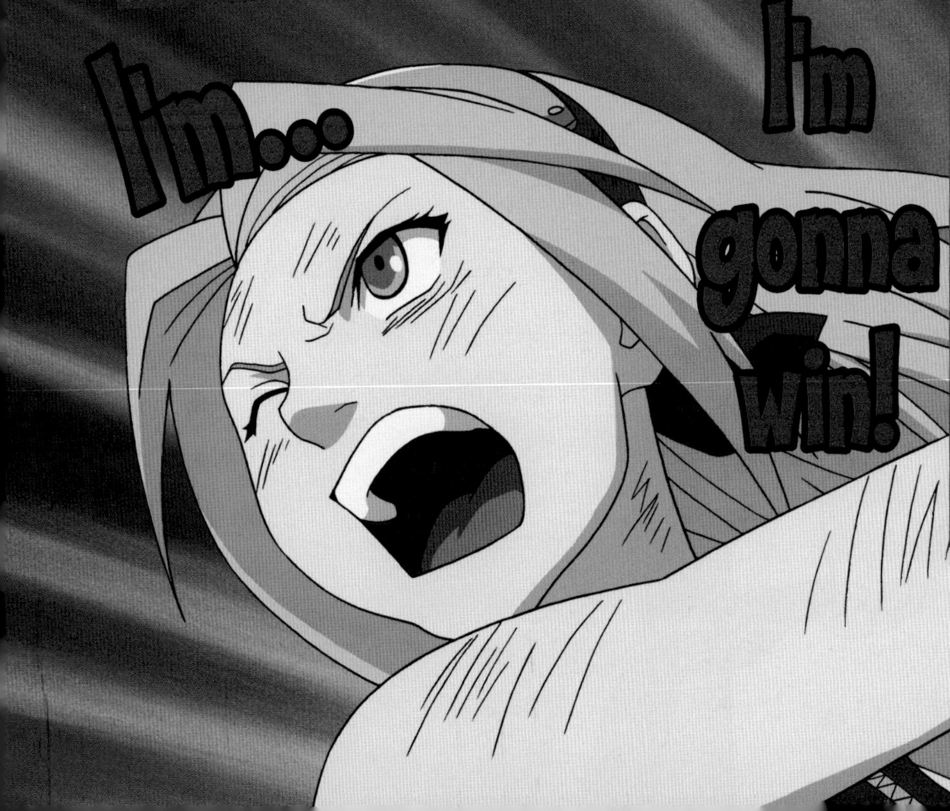
I'm...
I'm gonna win!

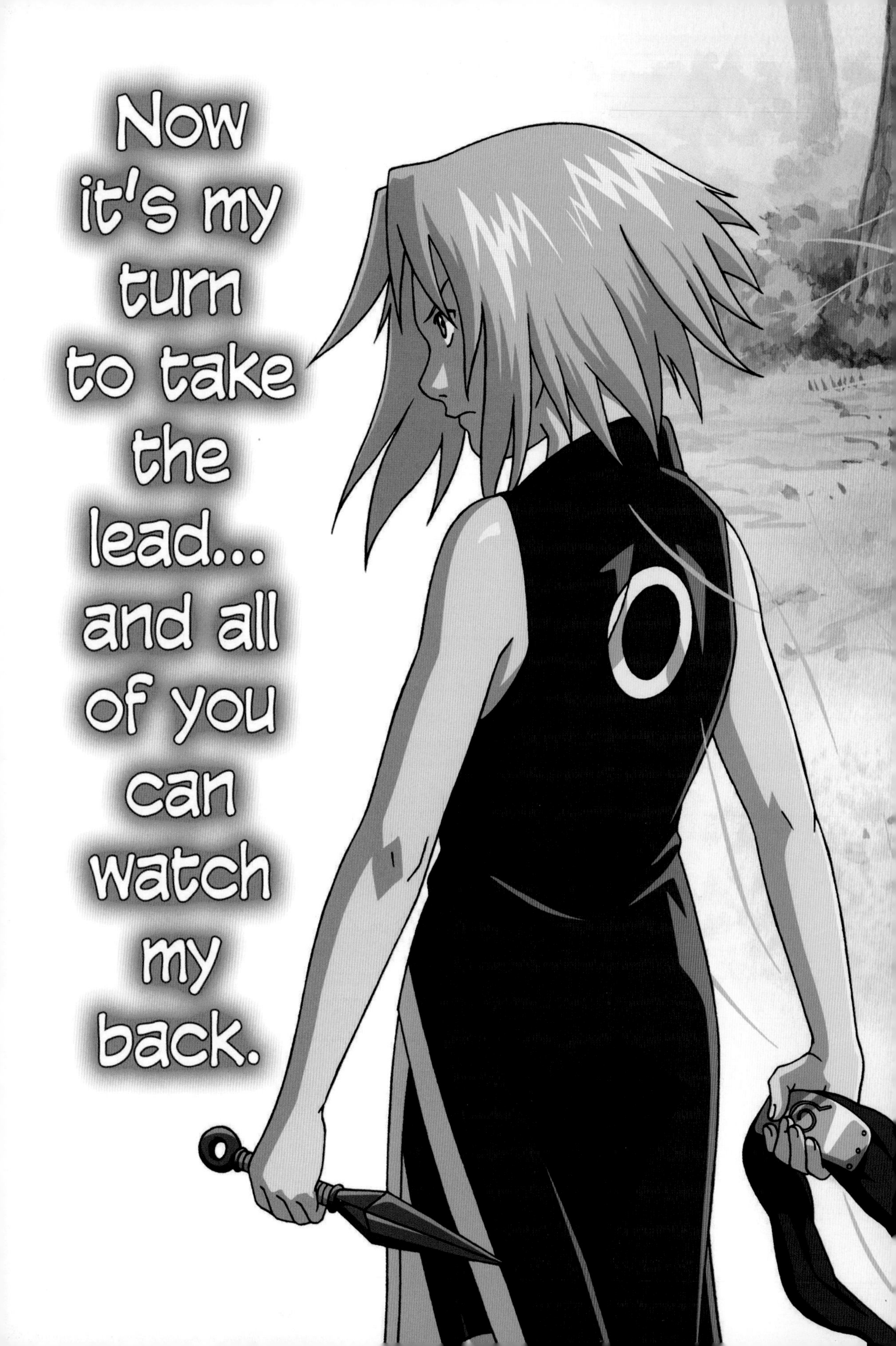
Now it's my turn to take the lead... and all of you can watch my back.

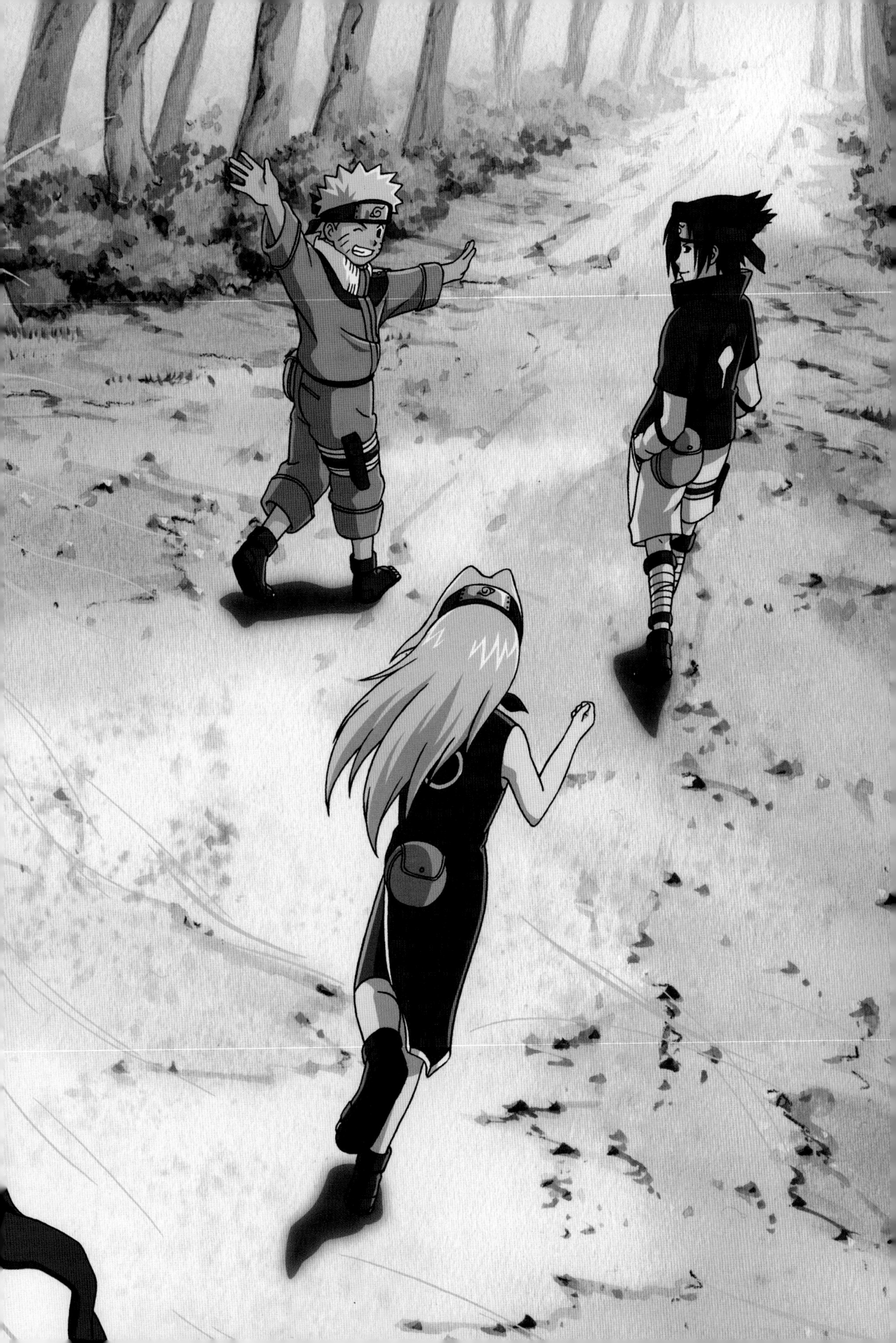

The cruel Sharingan...

Sakura's desperation calls out to Sasuke...

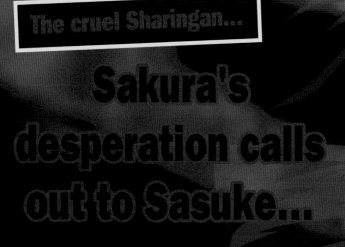

Sakura...

Who did this to you?!

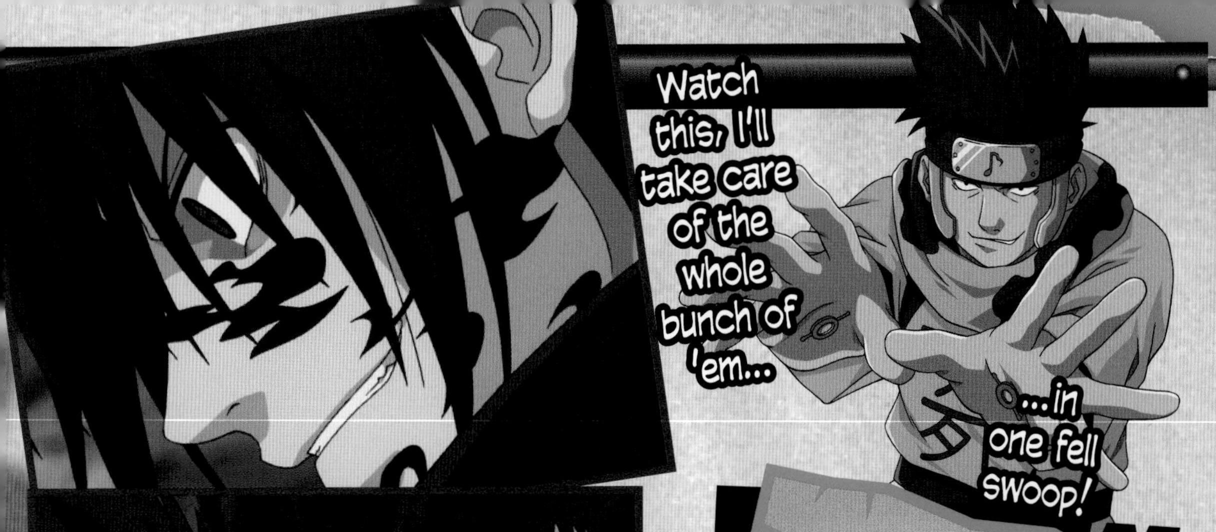
Watch this, I'll take care of the whole bunch of 'em...
...in one fell swoop!

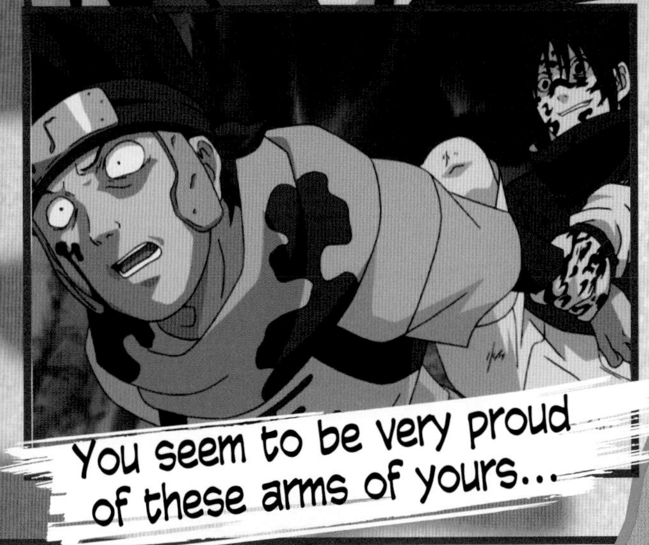
You seem to be very proud of these arms of yours...

The horrifying power of the curse mark begins to spread!
As Sasuke awakens, the effects of the curse mark are obvious. Strange, ominous patterns have appeared on his skin, and an eerie chakra surrounds his body, infected with the squirming shadow of Orochimaru! Terrified by this vision of a new, cold-blooded Sasuke, Sakura lets out a pained scream!

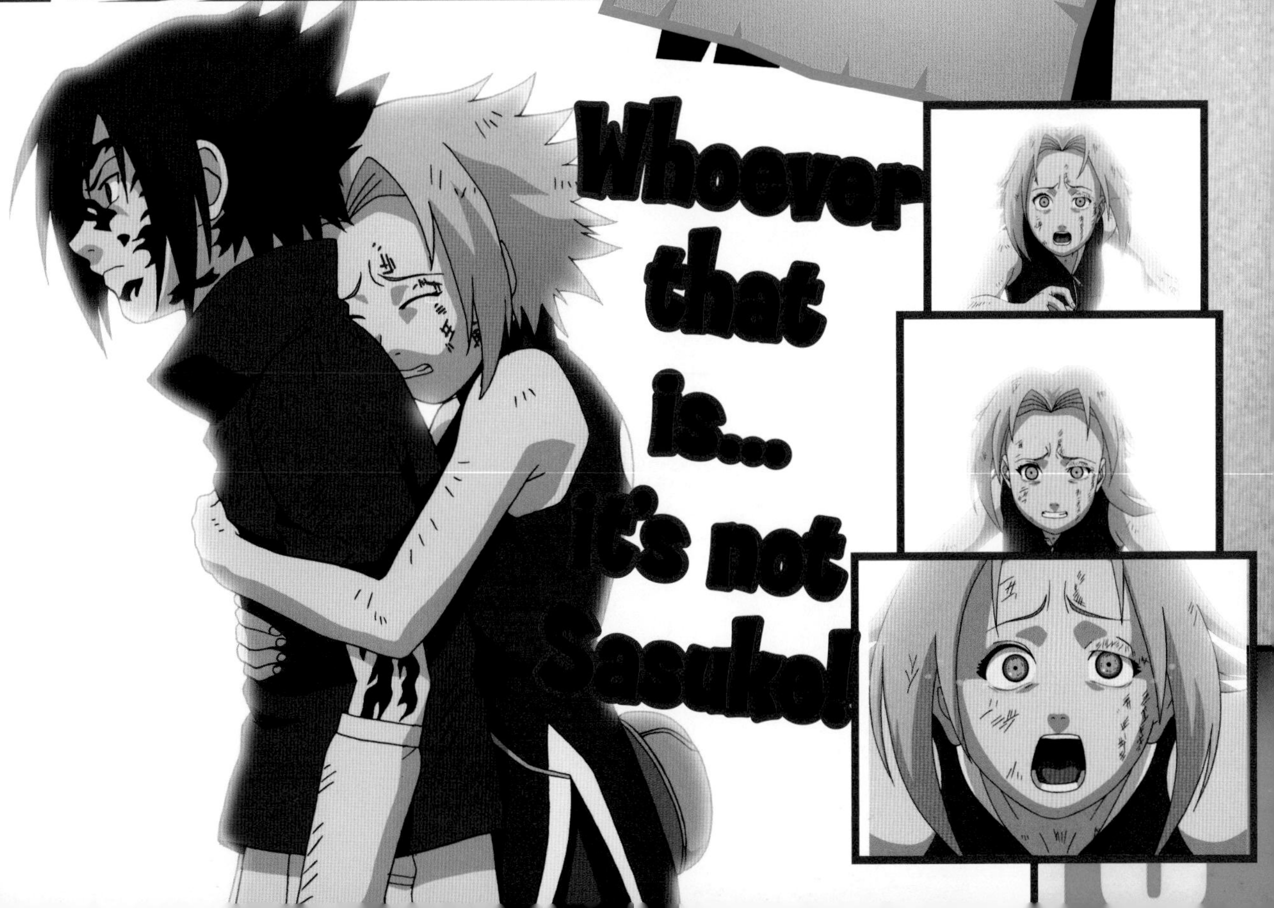
Whoever that is... it's not Sasuke!

The menace from the Sand village!

A massacre of bloody tears...!!

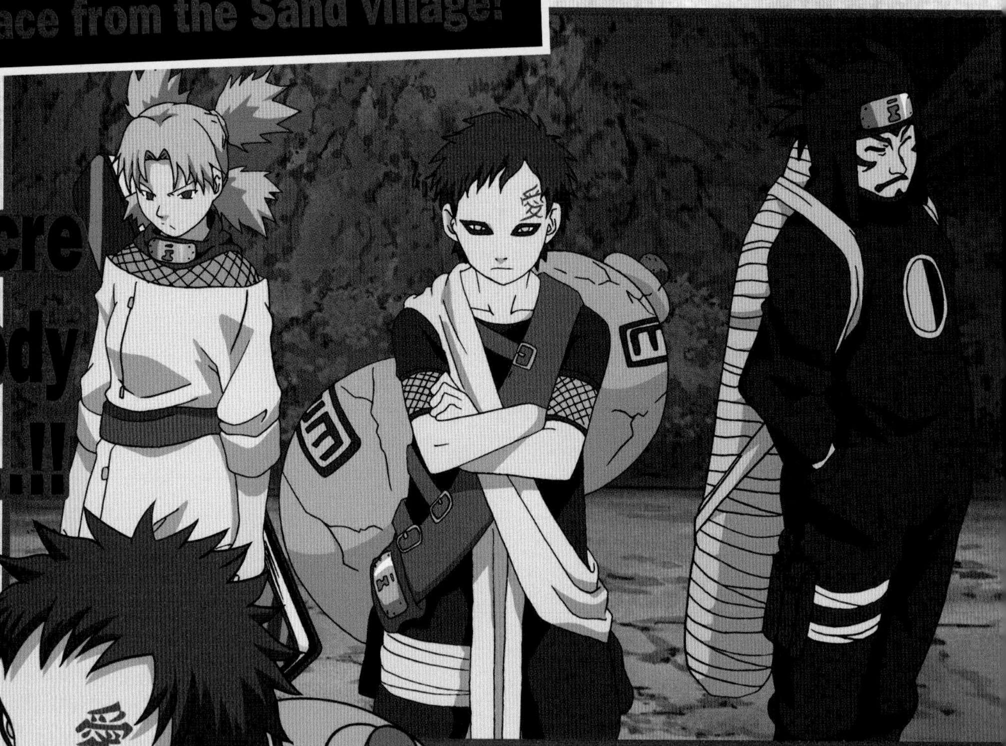

They looked at me the wrong way... so all of them will die.

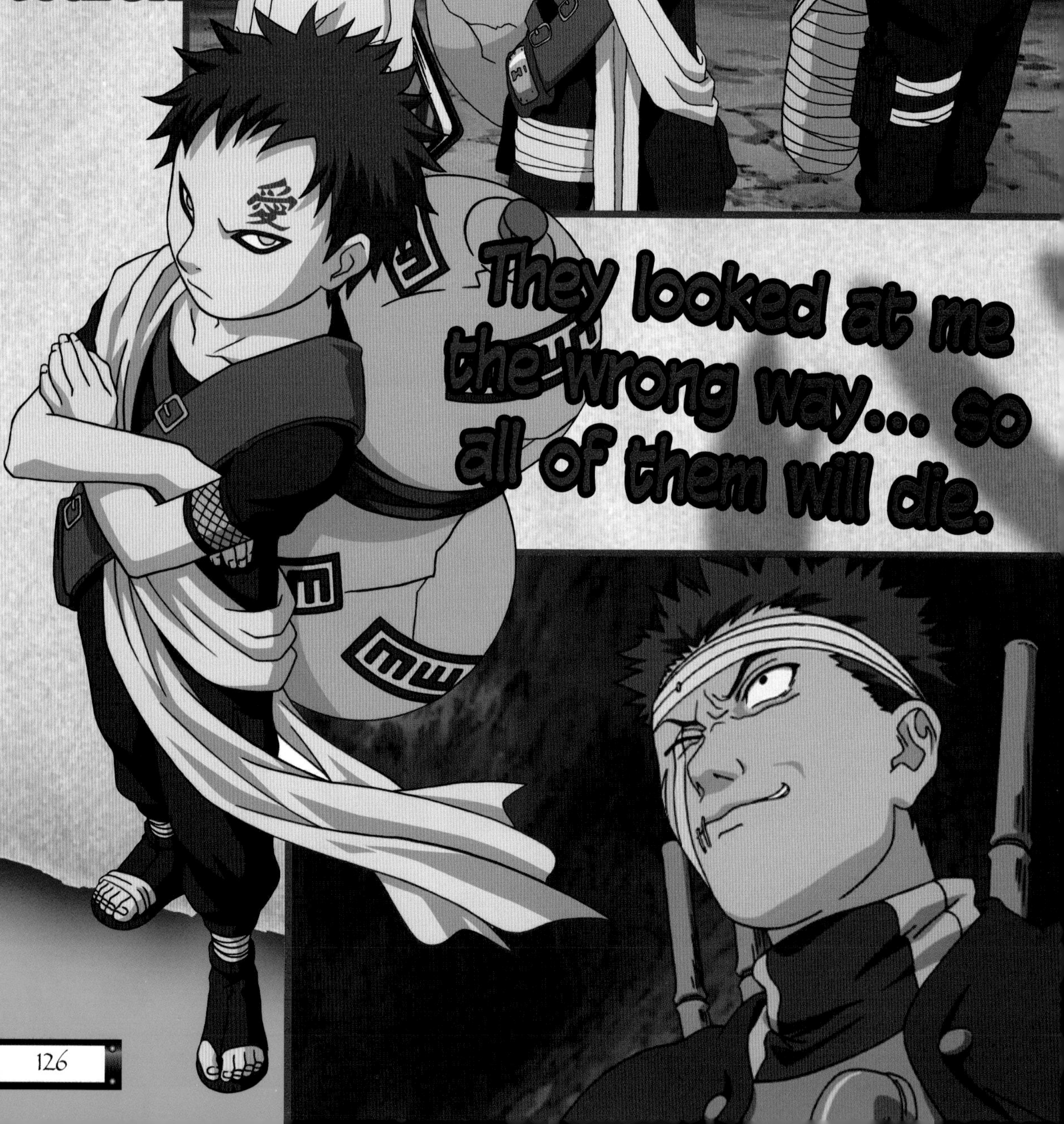

Even Gaara's teammates fear his power!

The Rain Ninja attack Gaara with a deluge of senbon needles… But in the instant before they strike, a wall of sand shields Gaara's entire body and the assault is thwarted!

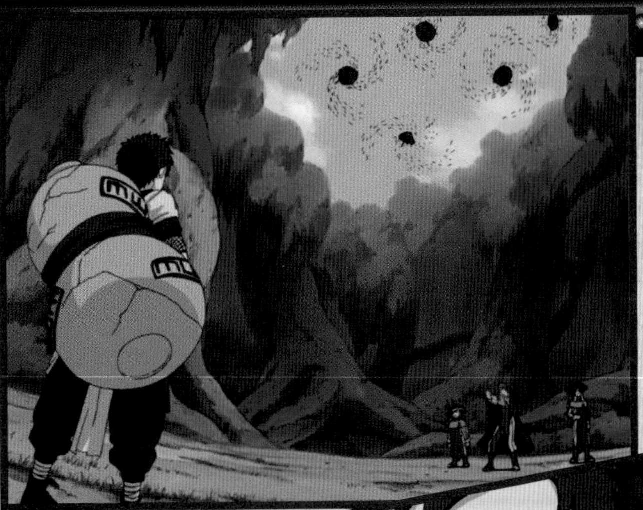

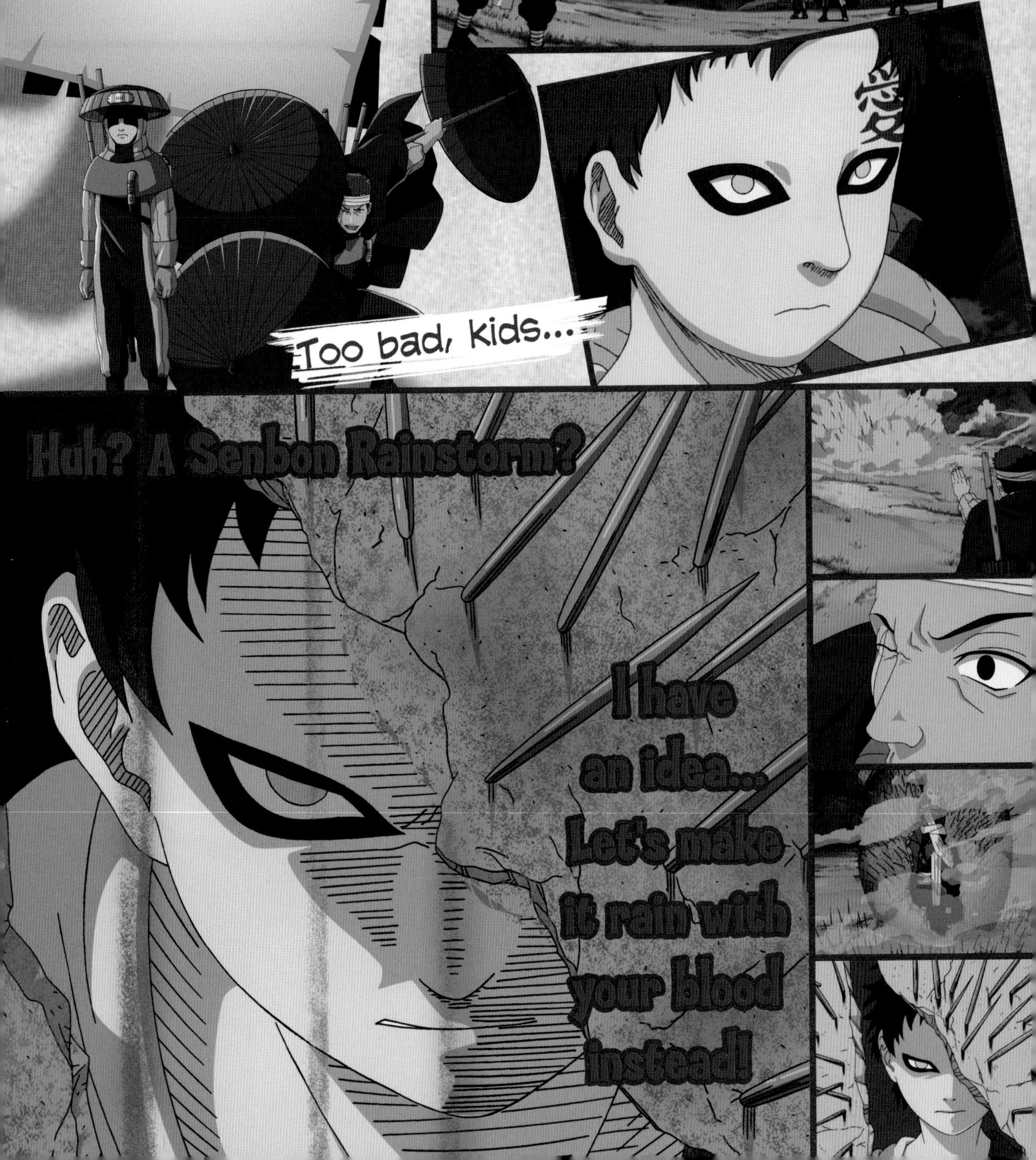
Too bad, kids...
Huh? A Senbon Rainstorm?
I have an idea... Let's make it rain with your blood instead!

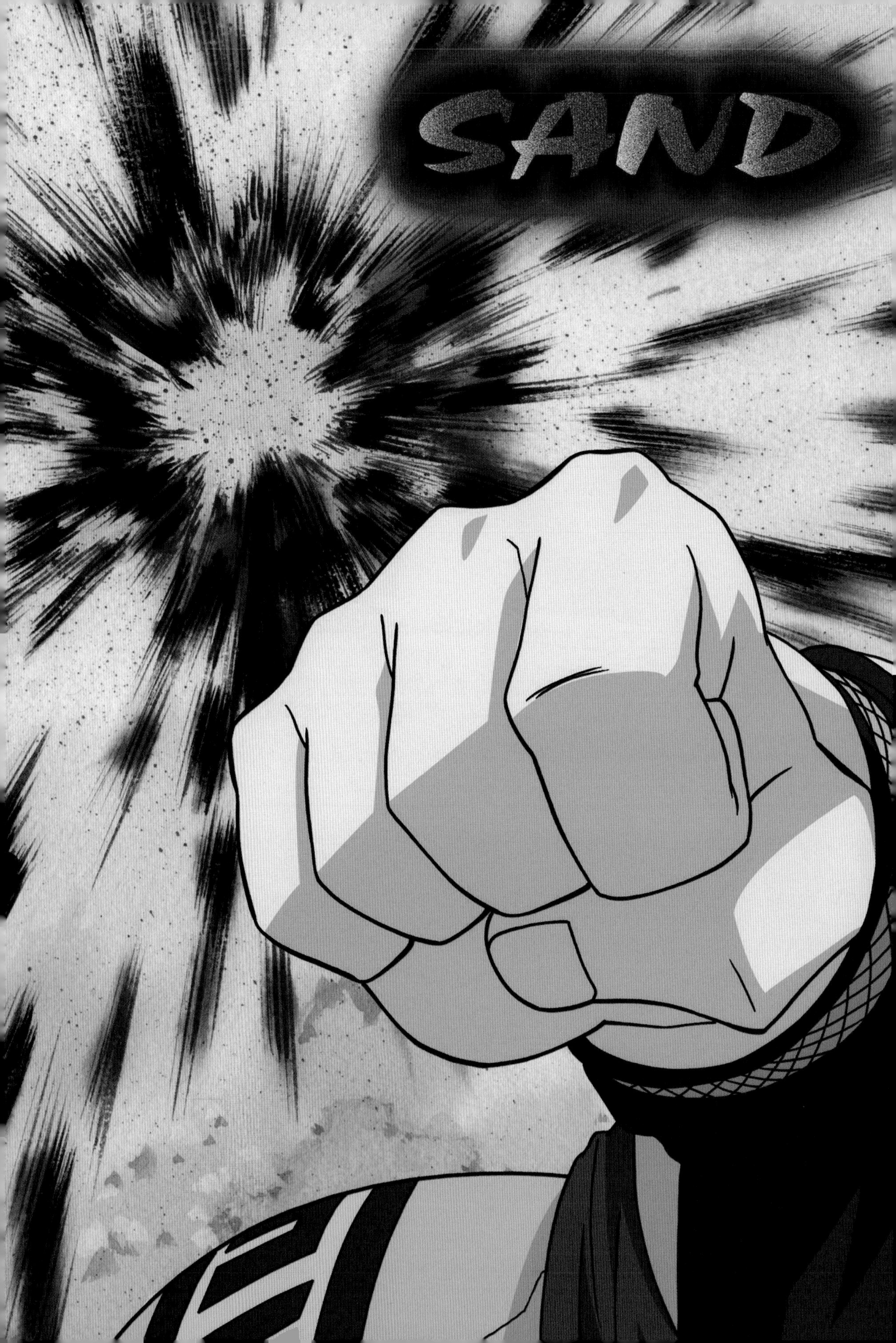
SAND

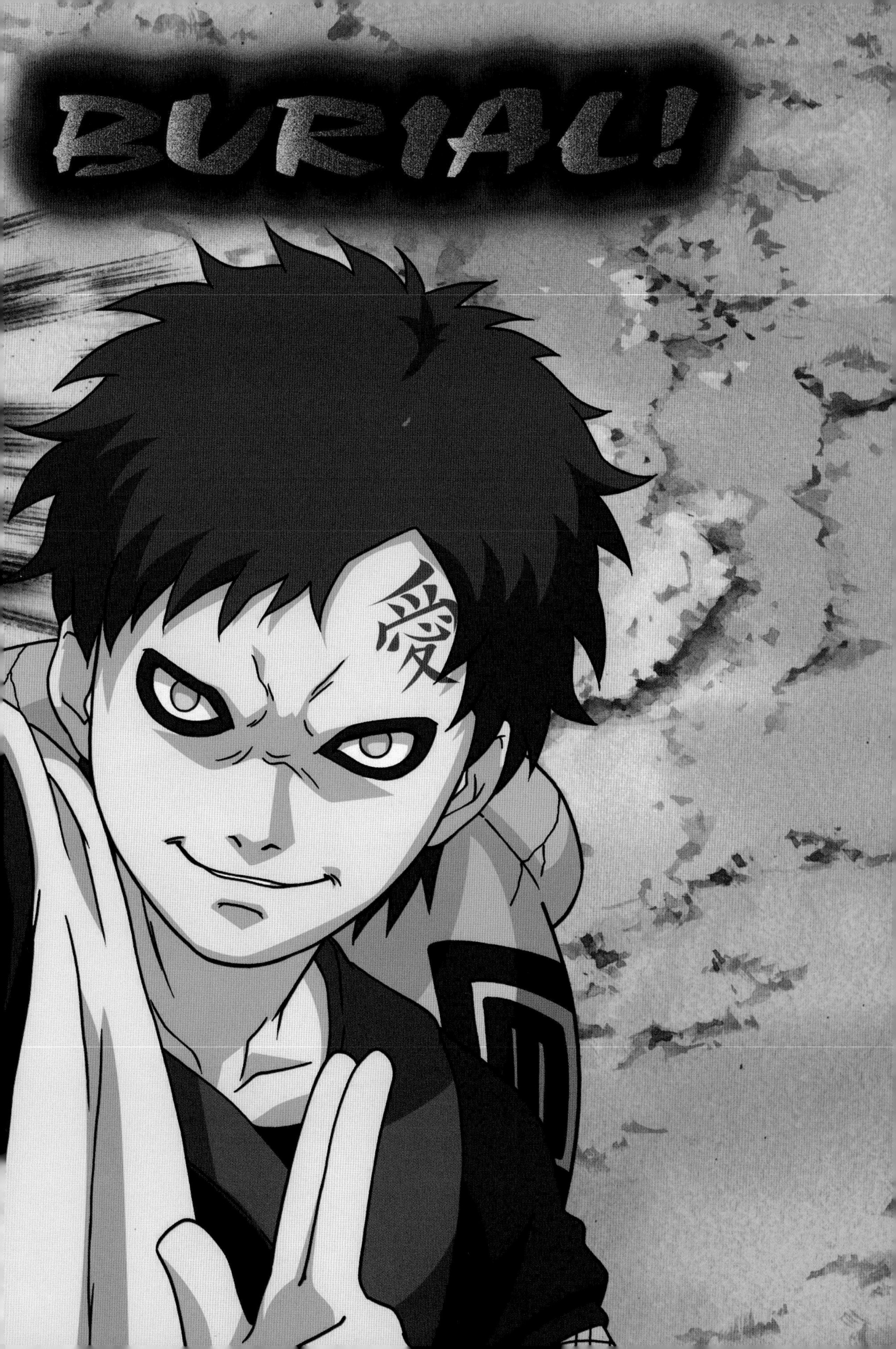
BURIAL!
愛

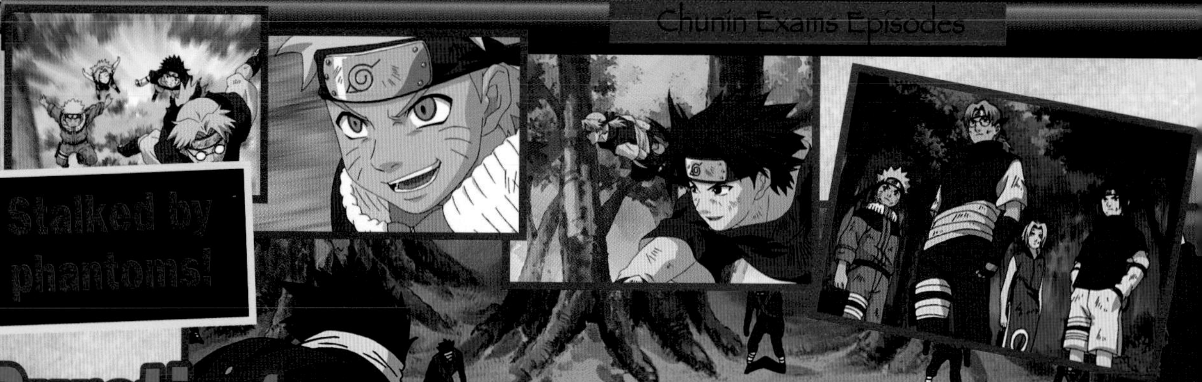

Stalked by phantoms!

Bursting free of a trap of violent rain!

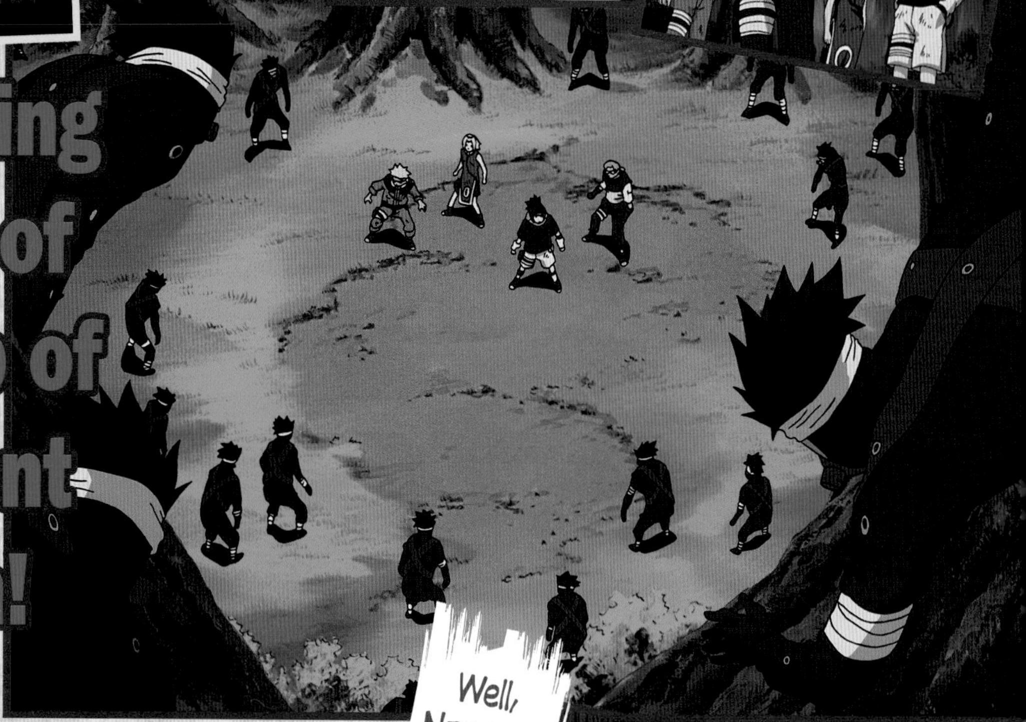

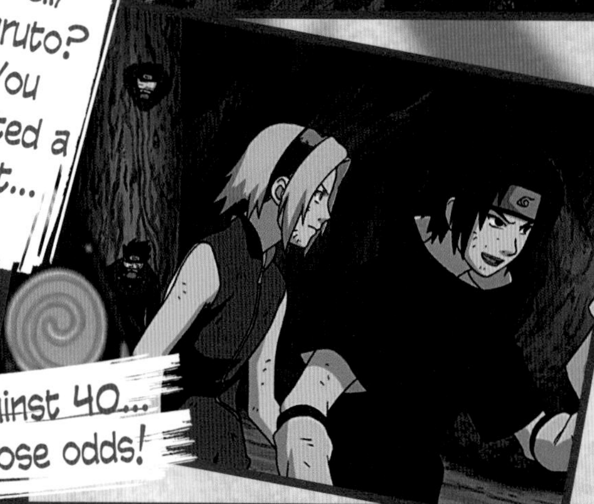
Well, Naruto? You wanted a fight...

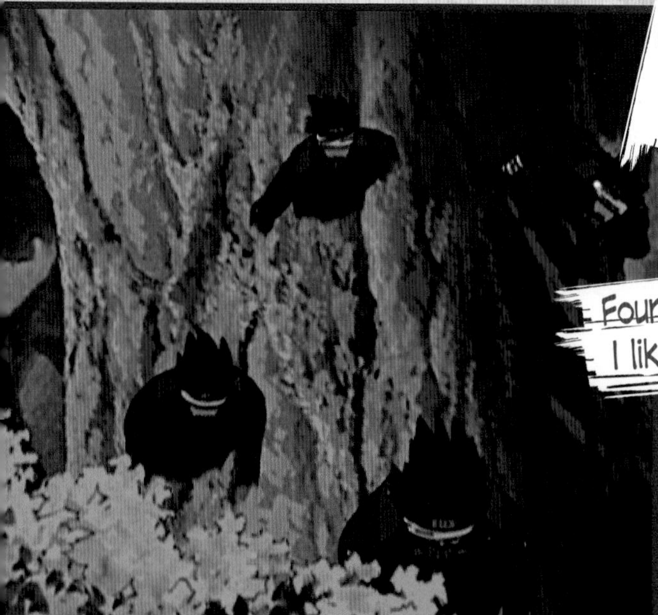
Four against 40... I like those odds!

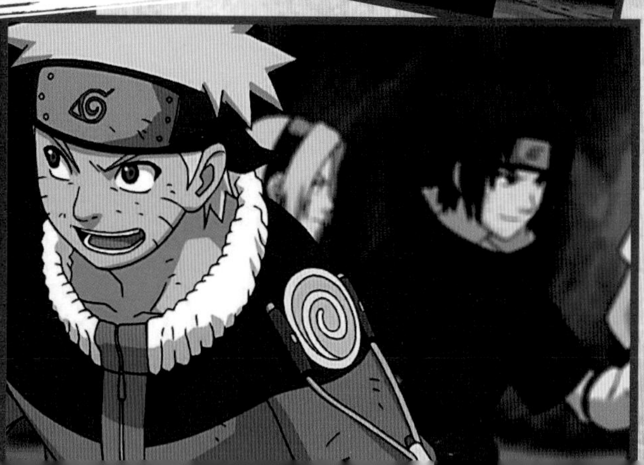

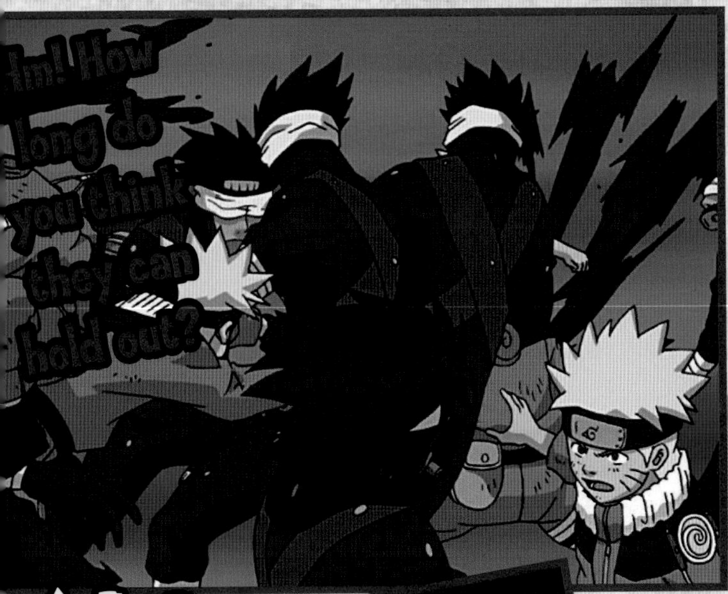
hm! How long do you think they can hold out?

Naruto tries to fight off the phantoms and grab their scroll!

As the darkness of night falls in the forest, Naruto and the others are surrounded by Rain ninja! Clones? Genjutsu? Unsure of what technique the enemy is using, their impatience and anxiety is heightened. But Naruto makes his move, using the Shadow Clone Jutsu to outmaneuver the Rain ninja!

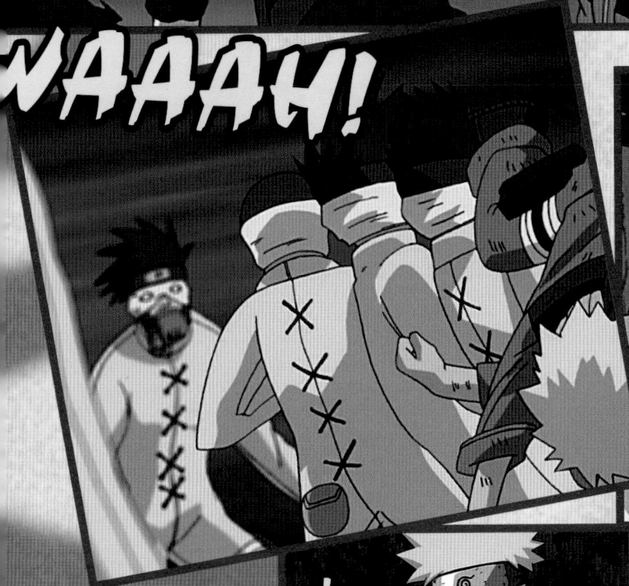
WAAAH!

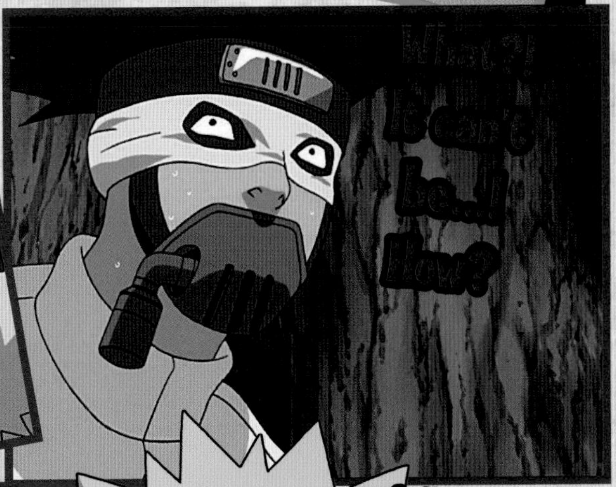
What?! It can't be...! How?

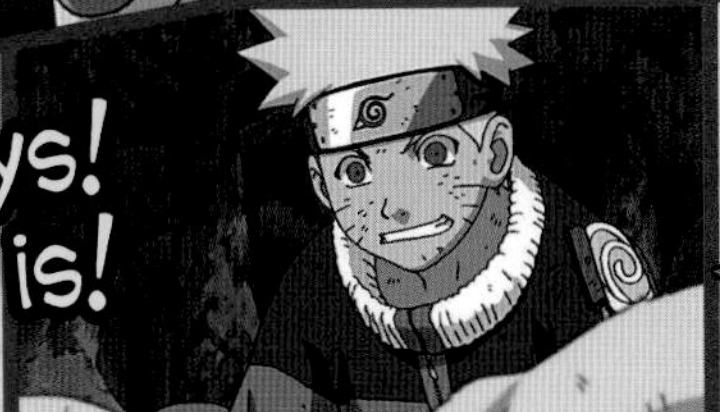
Hey, guys! Here it is!

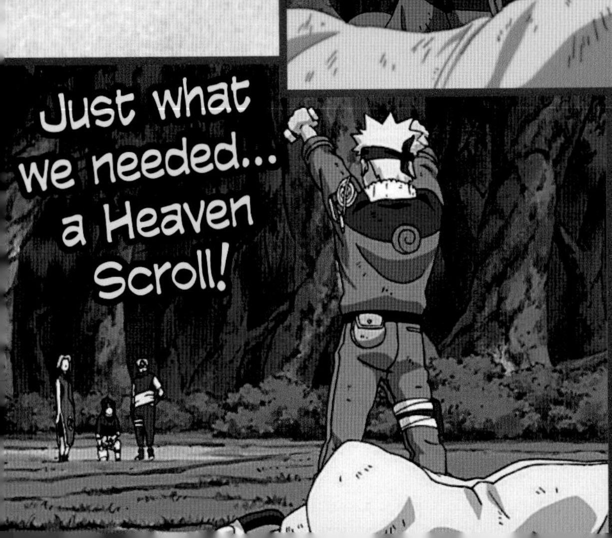
Just what we needed... a Heaven Scroll!

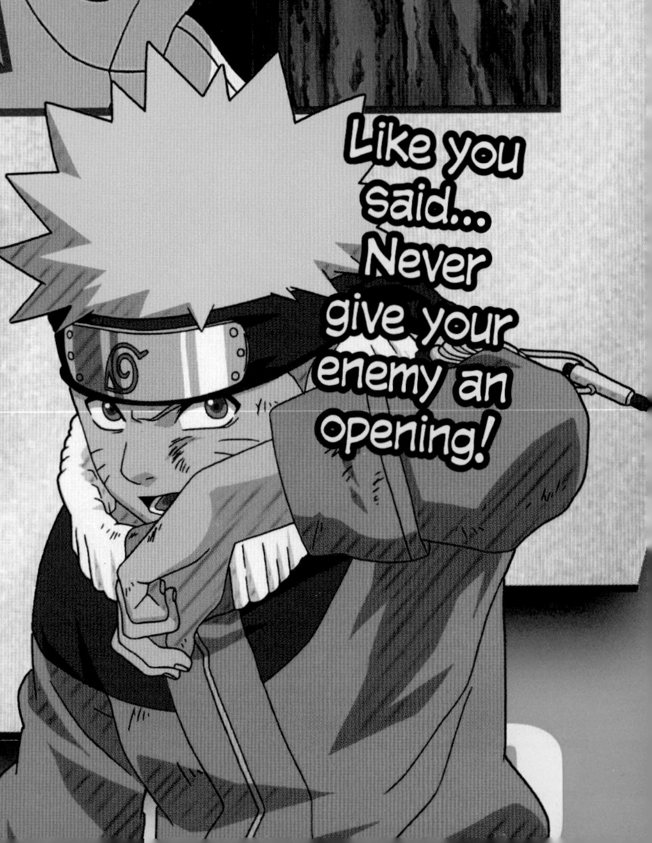
Like you said... Never give your enemy an opening!

The Second Exam reaches its conclusion!

The purpose of the Chunin Exams is revealed!

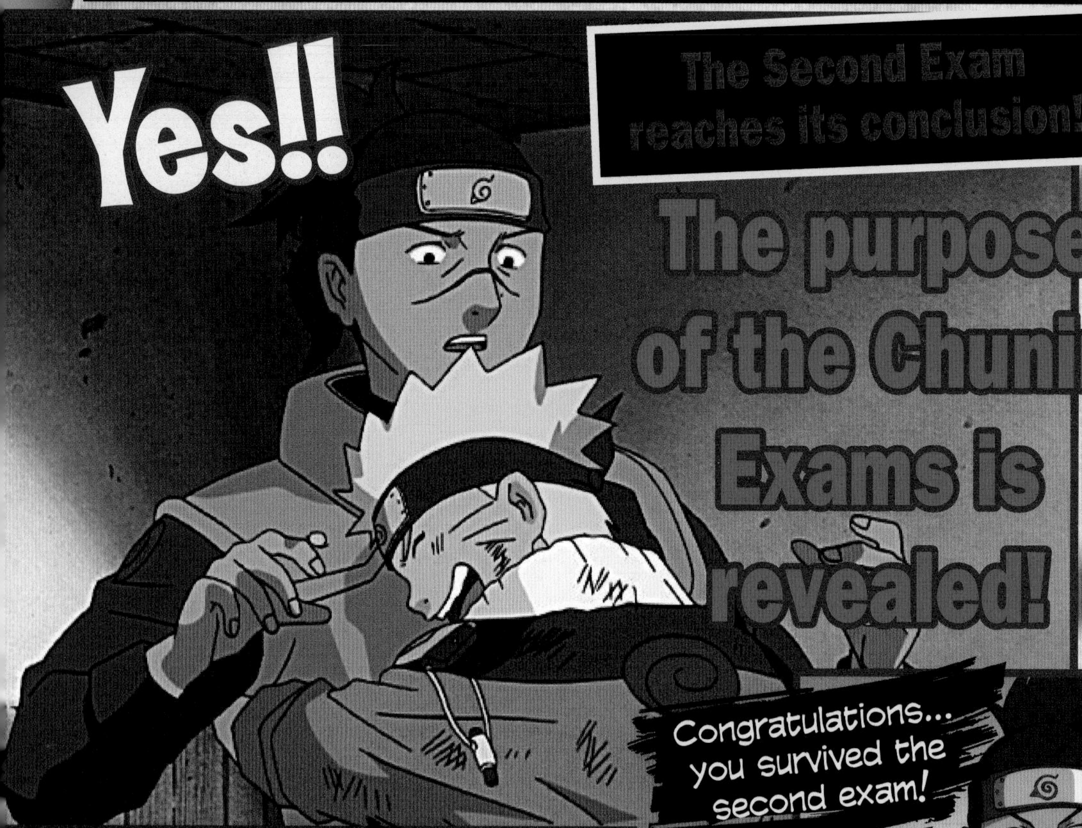
Yes!!

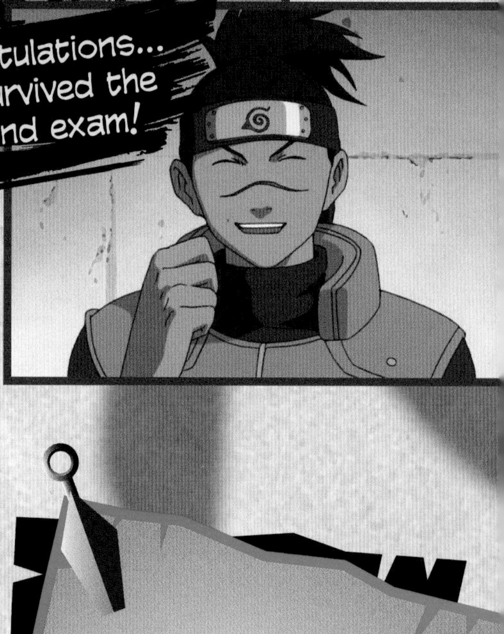
Congratulations... you survived the second exam!

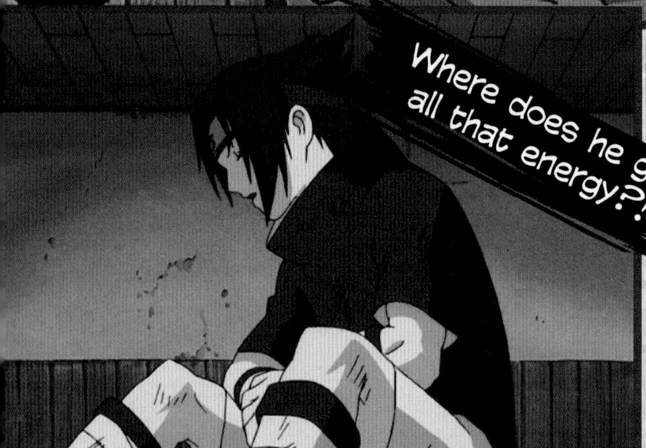
Where does he get all that energy?!

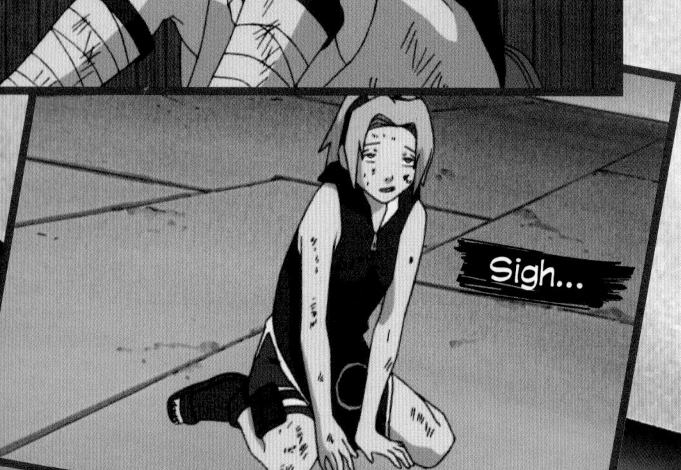
Sigh...

At the finish line, a surprise reunion with Iruka!

Waiting at the goal line for Naruto, Sasuke and Sakura is none other than Iruka, their former Academy teacher. With a gentle smile on his face, he informs them that they've passed the second exam. Overflowing with joy, Naruto charges into Iruka, hugging him with all his might!

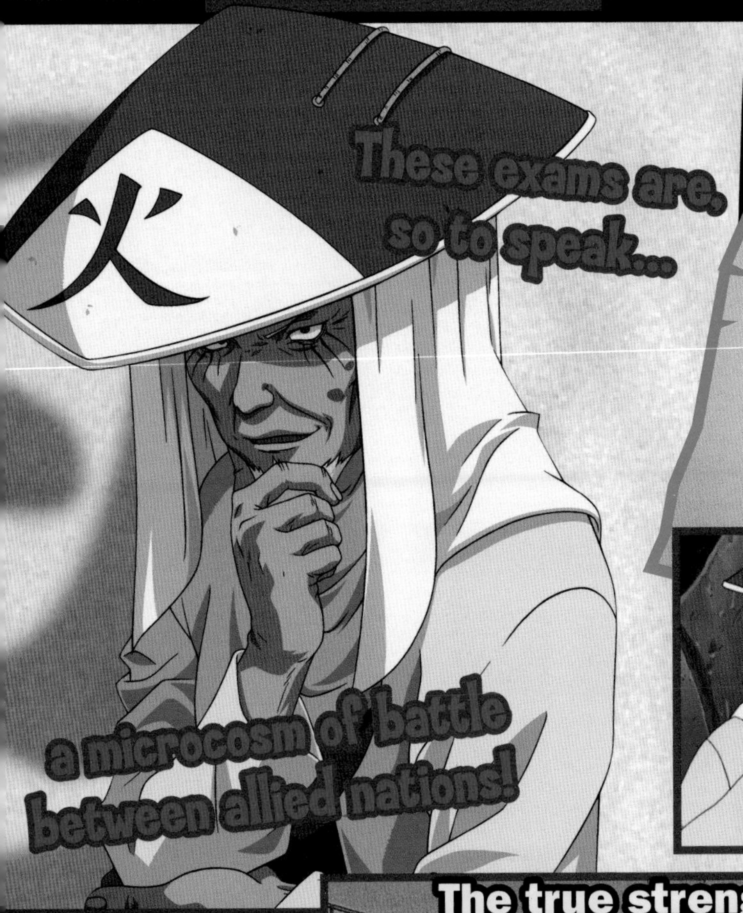
These exams are, so to speak...
a microcosm of battle between allied nations!

What is the real reason for conducting these exams?

The Hokage gives an earnest speech, revealing the truth behind the Chunin Exam. The candidates must put their lives on the line to defend the honor of their nations and to preserve their own dreams. The exam is a battlefield that allows each country to display its national power and demonstrate the threat it presents to other nations!

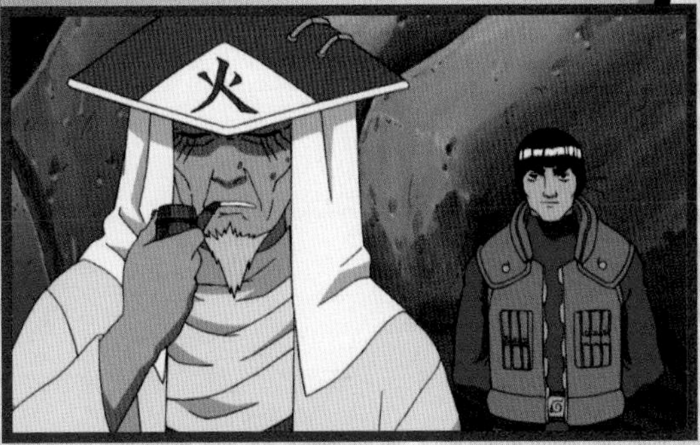

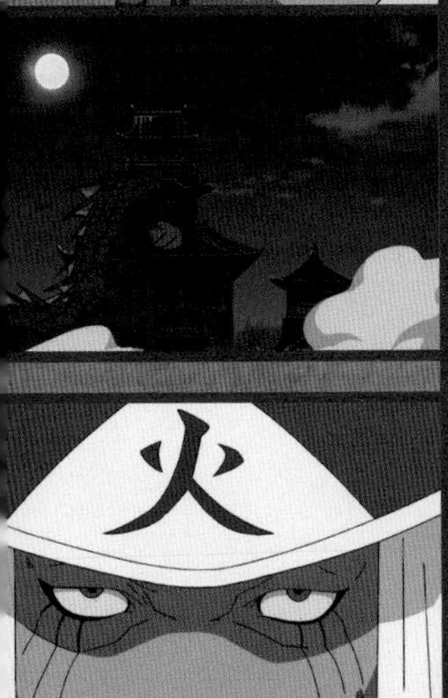

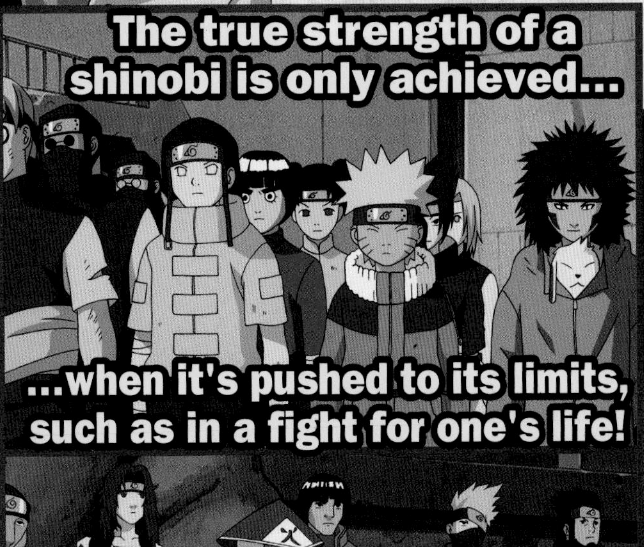
The true strength of a shinobi is only achieved...
...when it's pushed to its limits, such as in a fight for one's life!

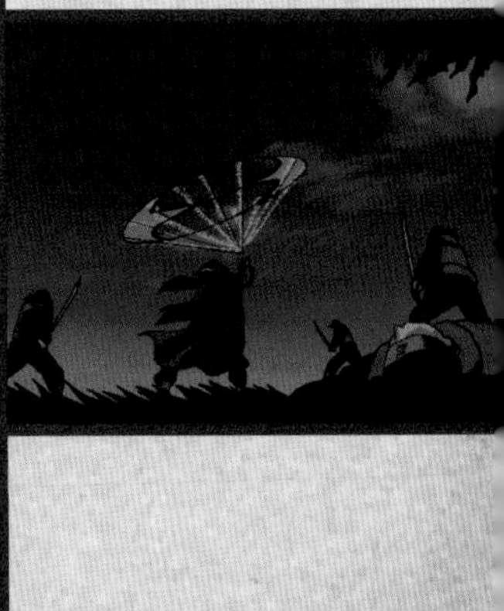

Three different personalities, three different strengths!

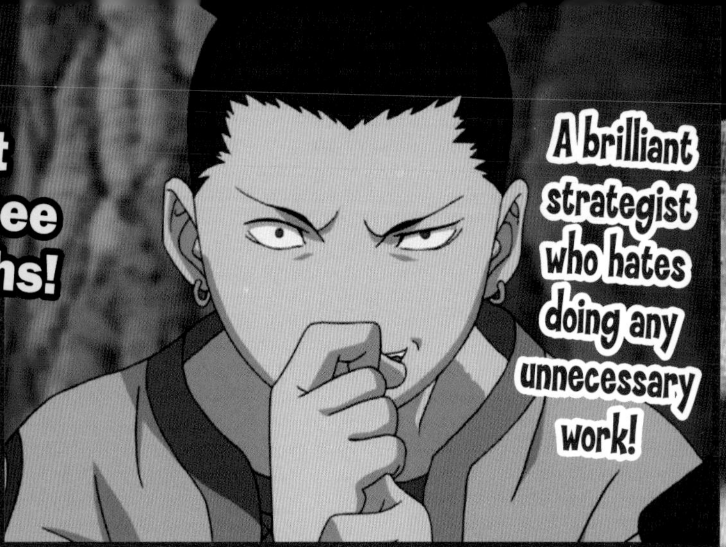

A brilliant strategist who hates doing any unnecessary work!

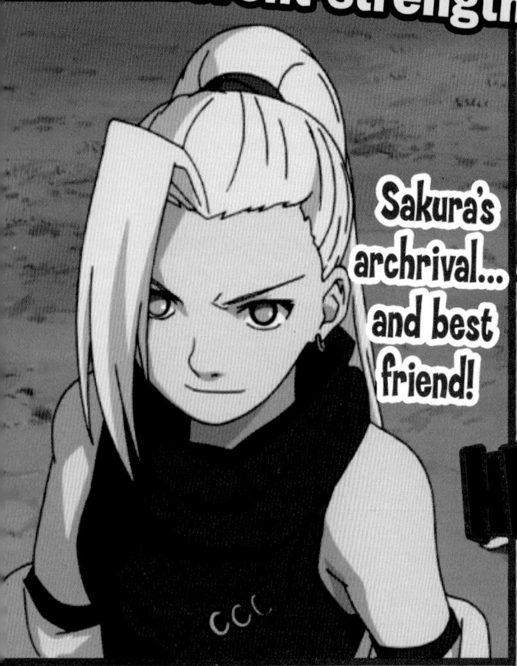

Sakura's archrival... and best friend!

THE WEAKEST TEAM IN THE HIDDEN LEAF VILLAGE!

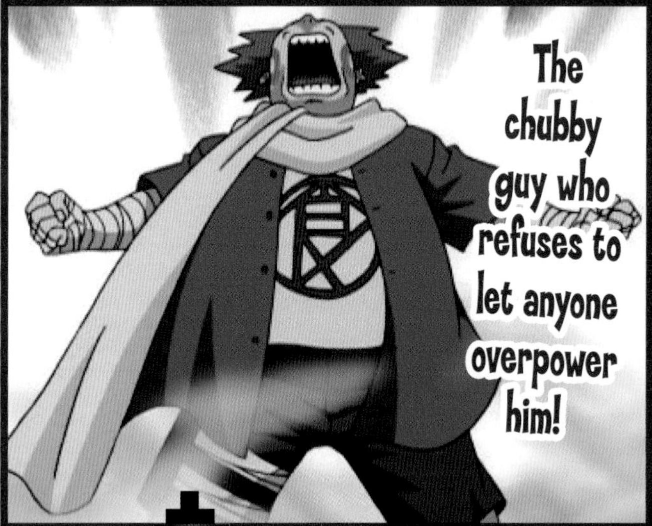

The chubby guy who refuses to let anyone overpower him!

When it matters most, their teamwork comes together!
Each member of the squad has distinct traits, but they're especially impressive when they combine their individual powers. When they work in concert, these three are unstoppable...and unbeatable!

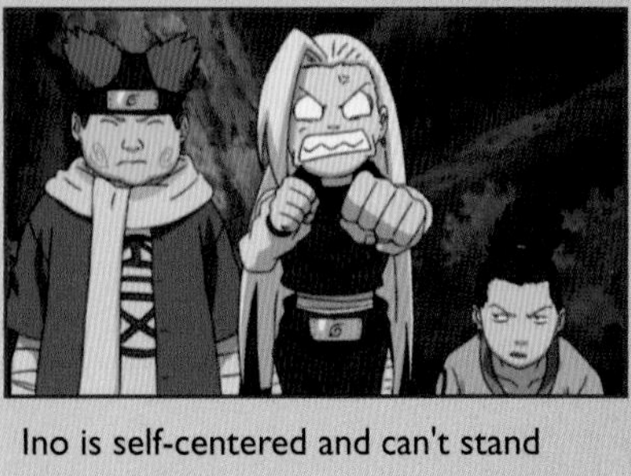

Ino is self-centered and can't stand losing. Choji is always stuffing his face. Shikamaru is smart but has no motivation. Well, little by little, they'll get more mature...

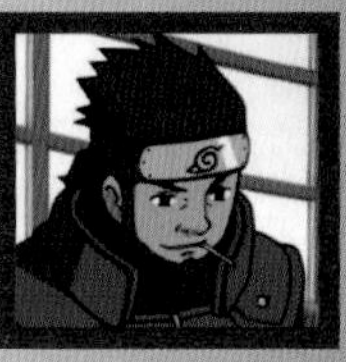

◆ Jonin Leader ◆

Asuma Sarutobi

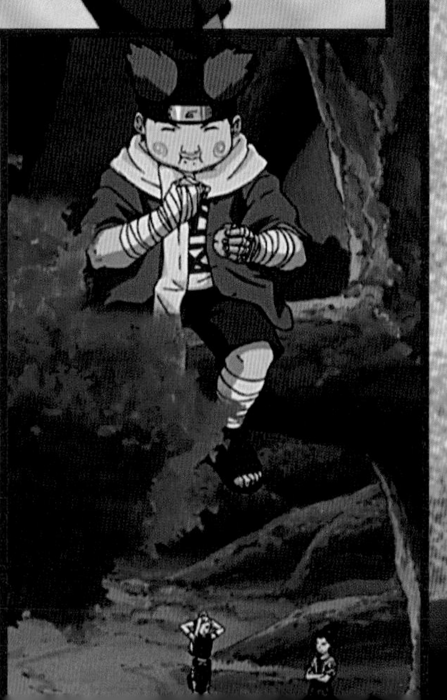

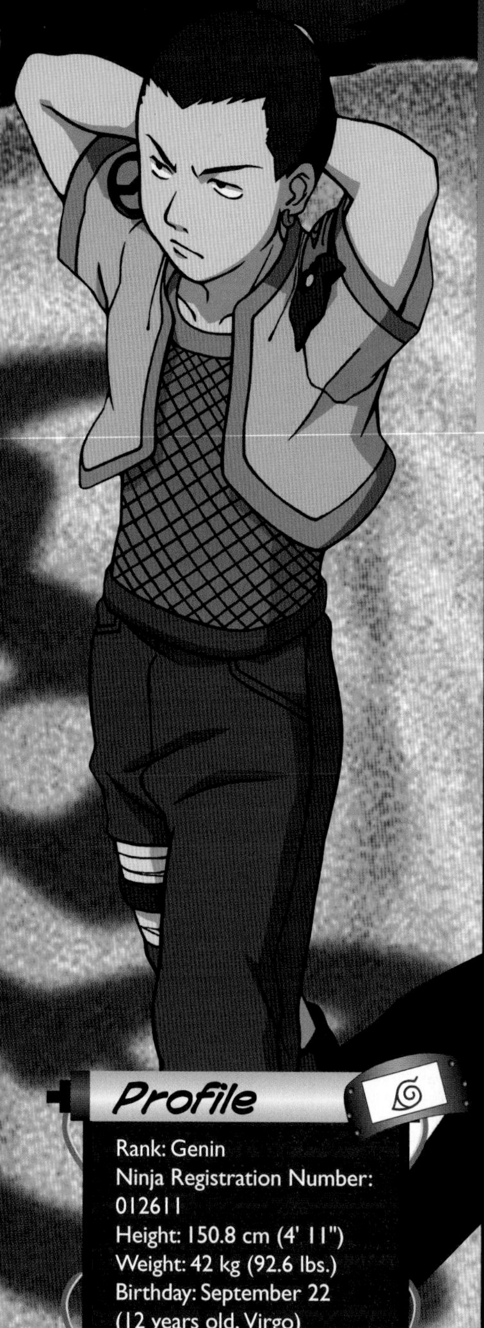

Profile

Rank: Genin
Ninja Registration Number: 012611
Height: 150.8 cm (4' 11")
Weight: 42 kg (92.6 lbs.)
Birthday: September 22
(12 years old, Virgo)
Blood Type: AB
Personality: Relaxed, lazy

SHIKAMARU

Shikamaru Nara

Ino Yamanaka

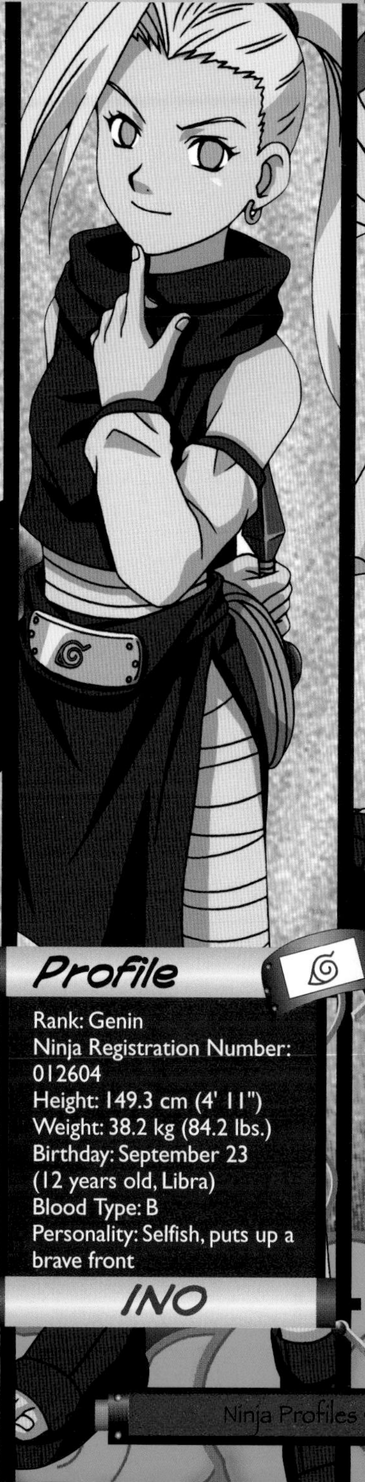

Profile

Rank: Genin
Ninja Registration Number: 012604
Height: 149.3 cm (4' 11")
Weight: 38.2 kg (84.2 lbs.)
Birthday: September 23
(12 years old, Libra)
Blood Type: B
Personality: Selfish, puts up a brave front

INO

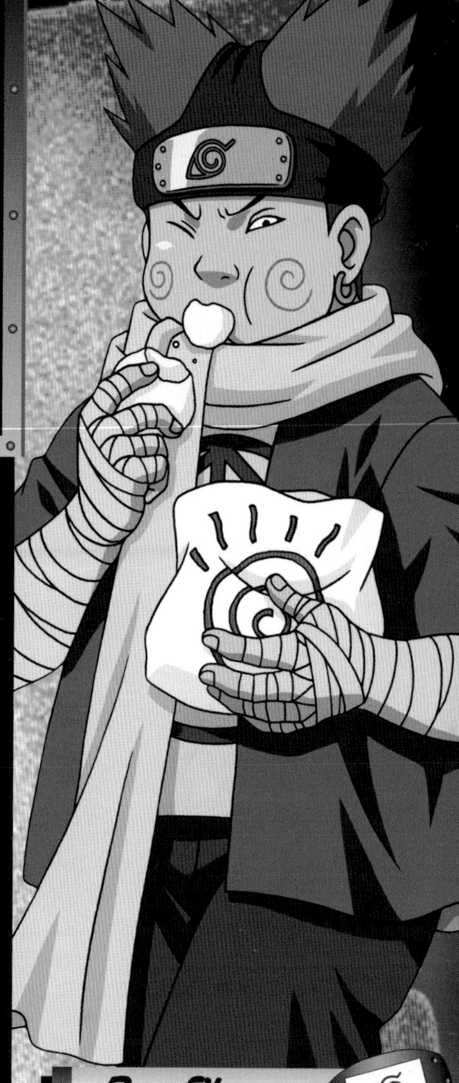

Profile

Rank: Genin
Ninja Registration Number: 012625
Height: 150.6 cm (4' 11")
Weight: 62kg (136 lbs.)
Birthday: May 1
(12 years old, Taurus)
Blood Type: B
Personality: Food-obsessed, laid-back

CHOJI

Choji Akimichi

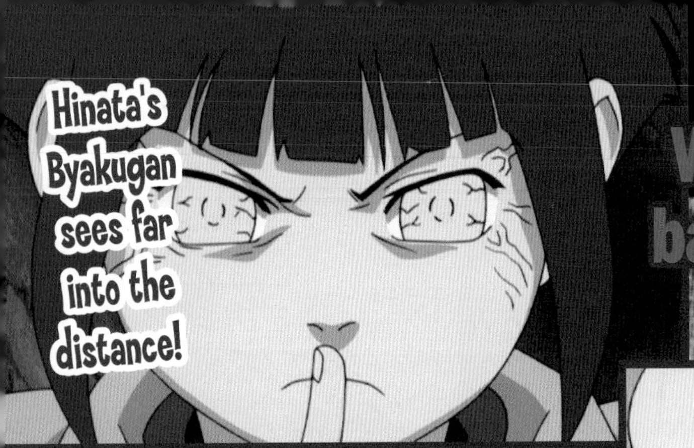
Hinata's Byakugan sees far into the distance!

With an excellent balance of offense and defense...

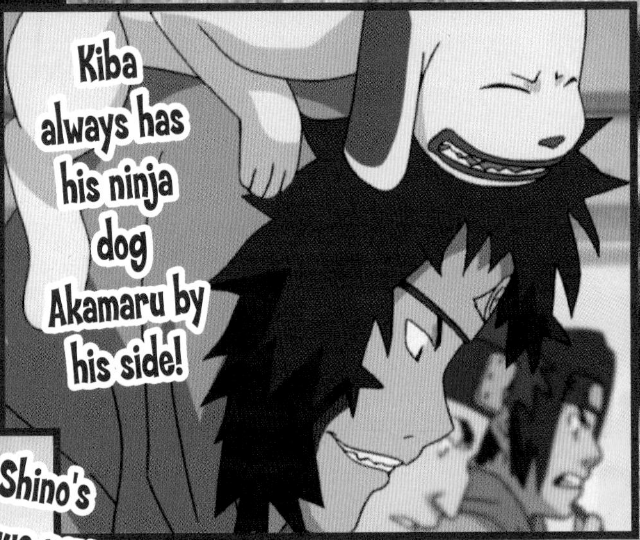
Kiba always has his ninja dog Akamaru by his side!

...and their excellent teamwork...

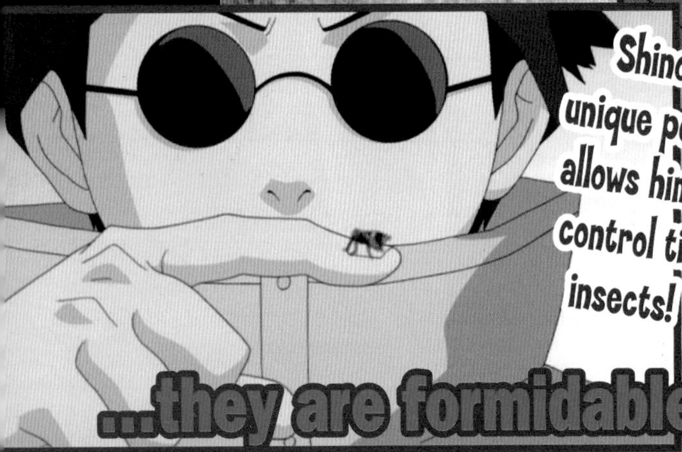
Shino's unique power allows him to control tiny insects!

...they are formidable contenders!

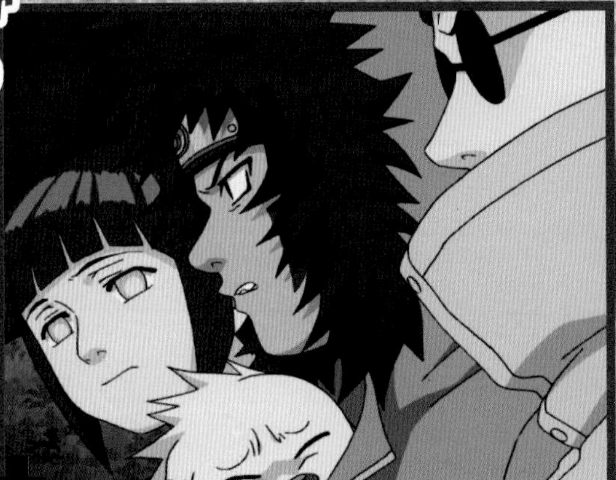

Squad 8

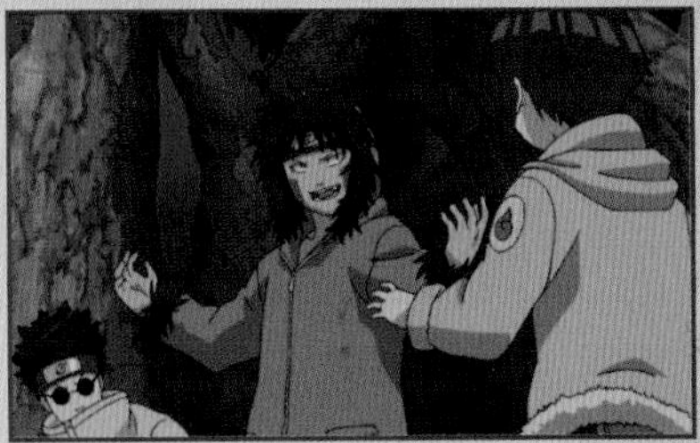

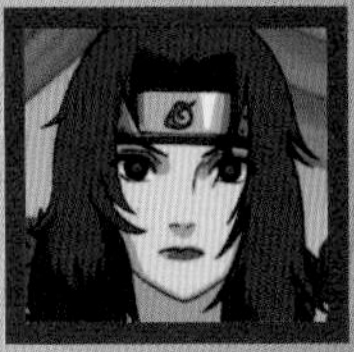

Jonin Leader

Kurenai Yuhi

Each one has a very different personality from the others, but I think they're a good squad -- all of them make up for what their teammates lack. And their recent growth has been surprisingly impressive…even to me!

This three-man squad successfully proceeds through the Forest of Death!

Kiba prefers to take swift, direct action while Shino favors analyzing a situation calmly. Hinata helps balance out the differences between those two, so the team has a good mix of defensive and offensive strengths. They might not be flashy, but their combined powers are very high.

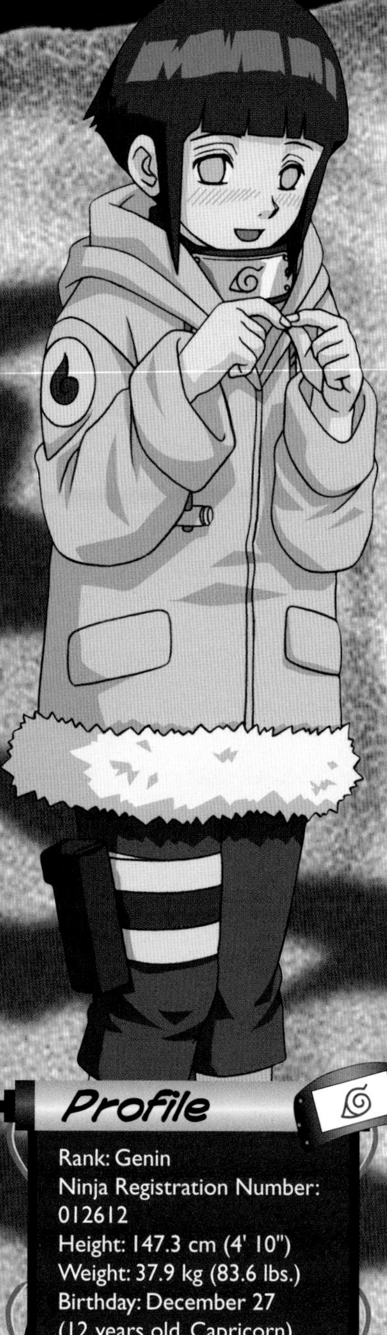

Hinata Hyuga

Profile

Rank: Genin
Ninja Registration Number: 012612
Height: 147.3 cm (4' 10")
Weight: 37.9 kg (83.6 lbs.)
Birthday: December 27
(12 years old, Capricorn)
Blood Type: A
Personality: Shy, withdrawn

HINATA

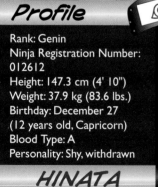

Kiba Inuzuka

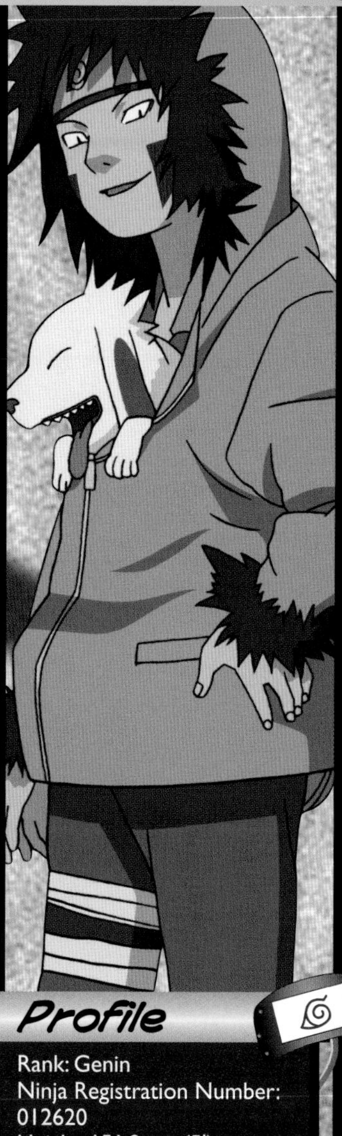

Profile

Rank: Genin
Ninja Registration Number: 012620
Height: 151.2 cm (5')
Weight: 43.3 kg (95.5 lbs.)
Birthday: July 7
(12 years old, Cancer)
Blood Type: B
Personality: Aggressive, hot-tempered, wild

KIBA

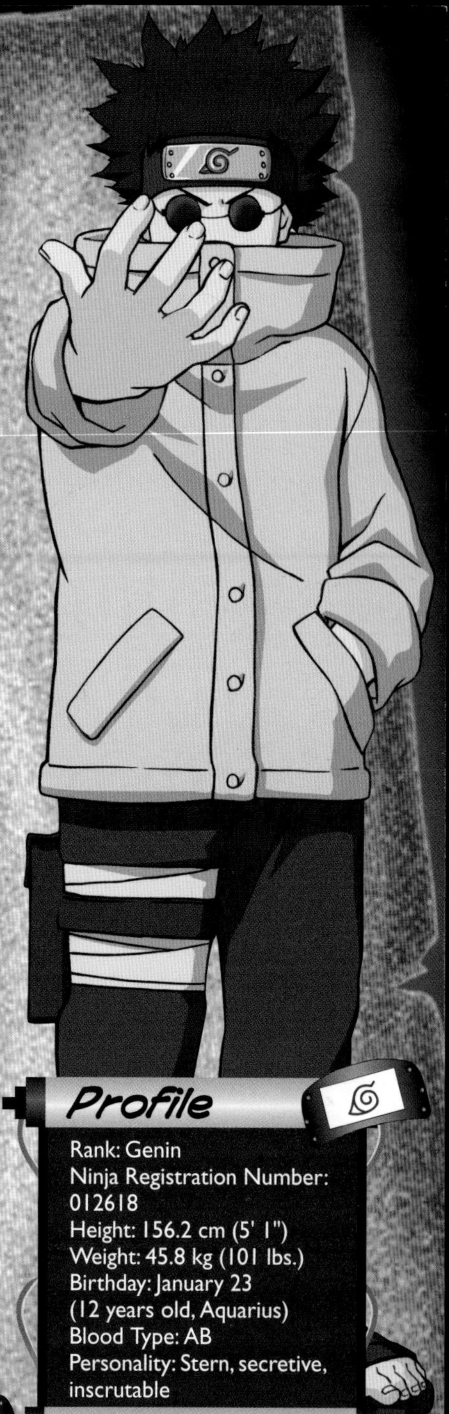

Shino Aburame

Profile

Rank: Genin
Ninja Registration Number: 012618
Height: 156.2 cm (5' 1")
Weight: 45.8 kg (101 lbs.)
Birthday: January 23
(12 years old, Aquarius)
Blood Type: AB
Personality: Stern, secretive, inscrutable

SHINO

Because it allows you to make your own body into a weapon...

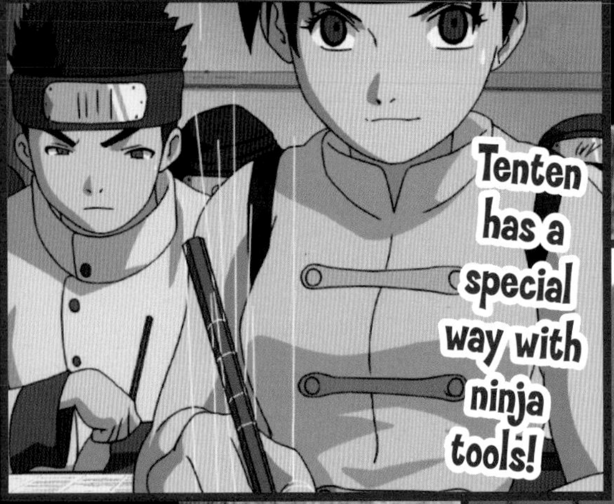

Tenten has a special way with ninja tools!

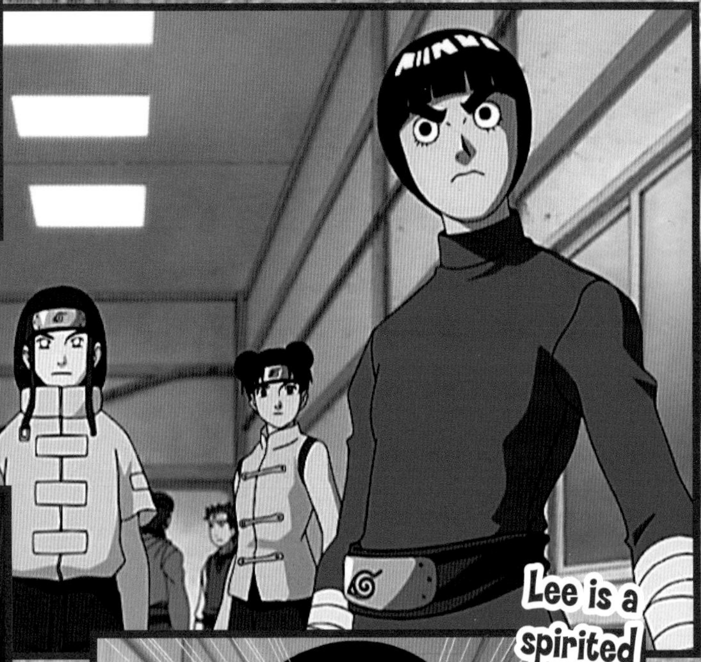

...taijutsu is truly the greatest!

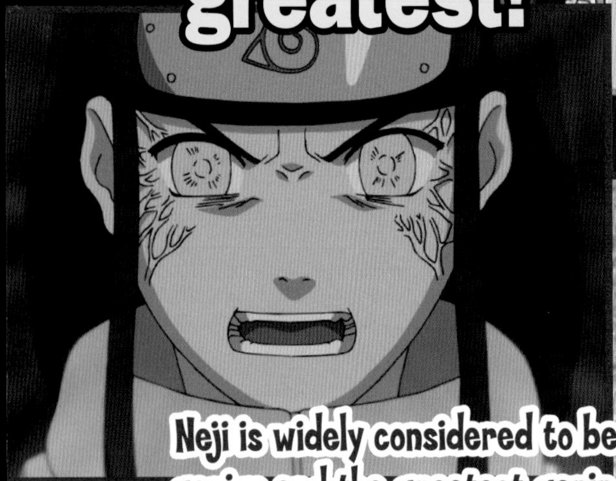

Neji is widely considered to be a genius and the greatest genin in the Hidden Leaf Village!

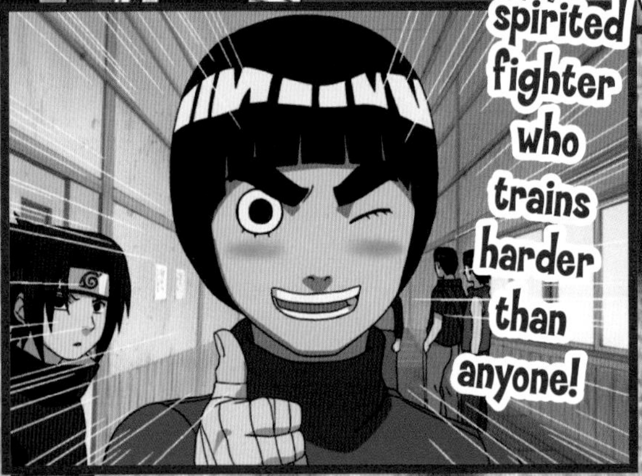

Lee is a spirited fighter who trains harder than anyone!

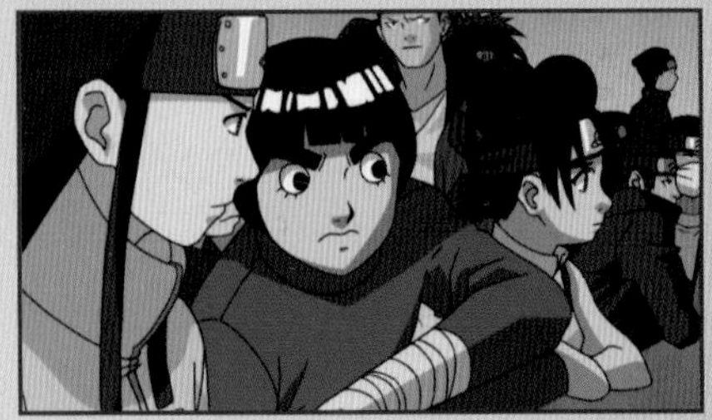

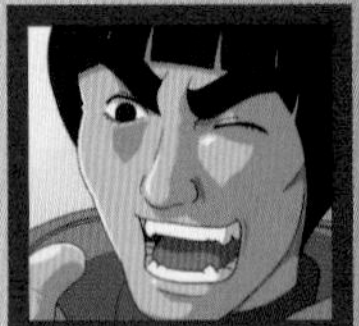

Jonin Leader

Might Guy

Training goes hand-in-hand with gutsiness, and gutsiness goes hand-in-hand with the bloom of youth! These kids are cute, and they respond passionately to my intense, strict training! You guys are the best, Neji, Tenten and Lee!

They keep their strengths hidden and don't show off, but they're the best and most talented team!

All three members of this squad have awesome power and are talented in taijutsu. They also have excellent teamwork because they trust one another. Their fighting strength as a three-man squad is extremely high, and they worked to refine their skills even further before entering the Chunin Exam!

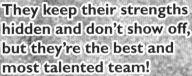

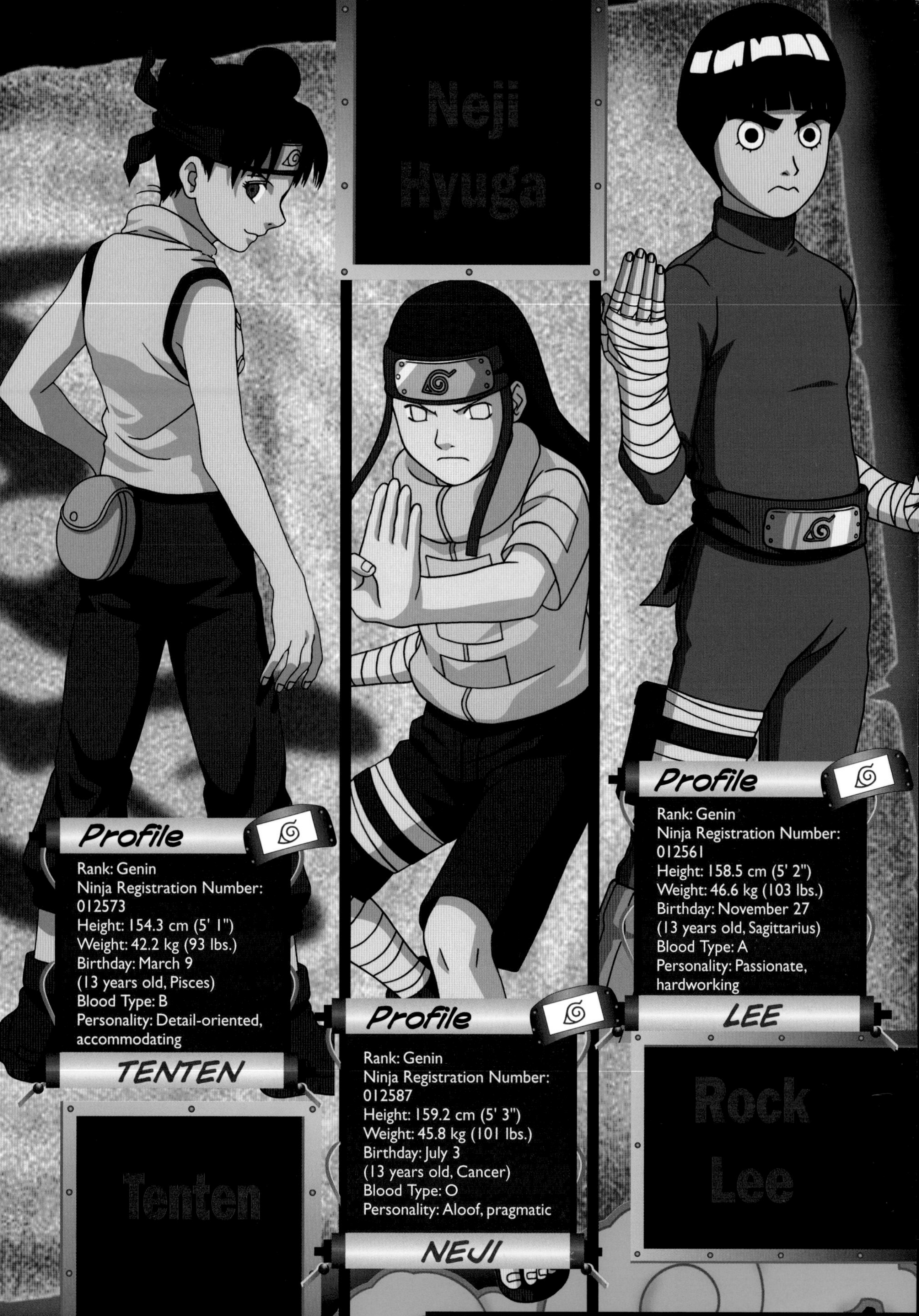

Tenten

Profile

Rank: Genin
Ninja Registration Number: 012573
Height: 154.3 cm (5' 1")
Weight: 42.2 kg (93 lbs.)
Birthday: March 9
(13 years old, Pisces)
Blood Type: B
Personality: Detail-oriented, accommodating

TENTEN

Neji Hyuga

Profile

Rank: Genin
Ninja Registration Number: 012587
Height: 159.2 cm (5' 3")
Weight: 45.8 kg (101 lbs.)
Birthday: July 3
(13 years old, Cancer)
Blood Type: O
Personality: Aloof, pragmatic

NEJI

Rock Lee

Profile

Rank: Genin
Ninja Registration Number: 012561
Height: 158.5 cm (5' 2")
Weight: 46.6 kg (103 lbs.)
Birthday: November 27
(13 years old, Sagittarius)
Blood Type: A
Personality: Passionate, hardworking

LEE

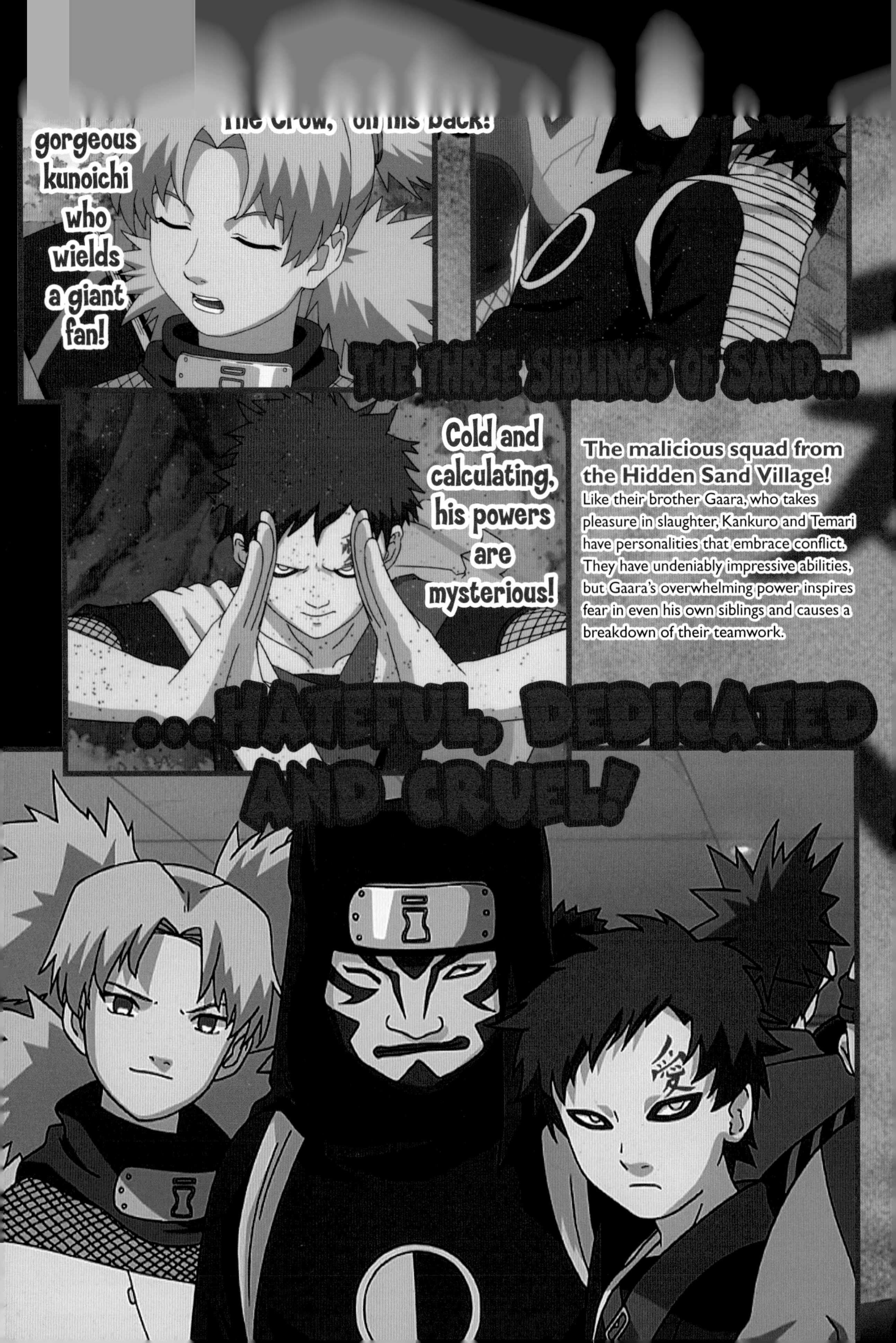
"The Crow," on his back!
gorgeous kunoichi who wields a giant fan!
THE THREE SIBLINGS OF SAND...
Cold and calculating, his powers are mysterious!
...HATEFUL, DEDICATED AND CRUEL!

The malicious squad from the Hidden Sand Village!
Like their brother Gaara, who takes pleasure in slaughter, Kankuro and Temari have personalities that embrace conflict. They have undeniably impressive abilities, but Gaara's overwhelming power inspires fear in even his own siblings and causes a breakdown of their teamwork.

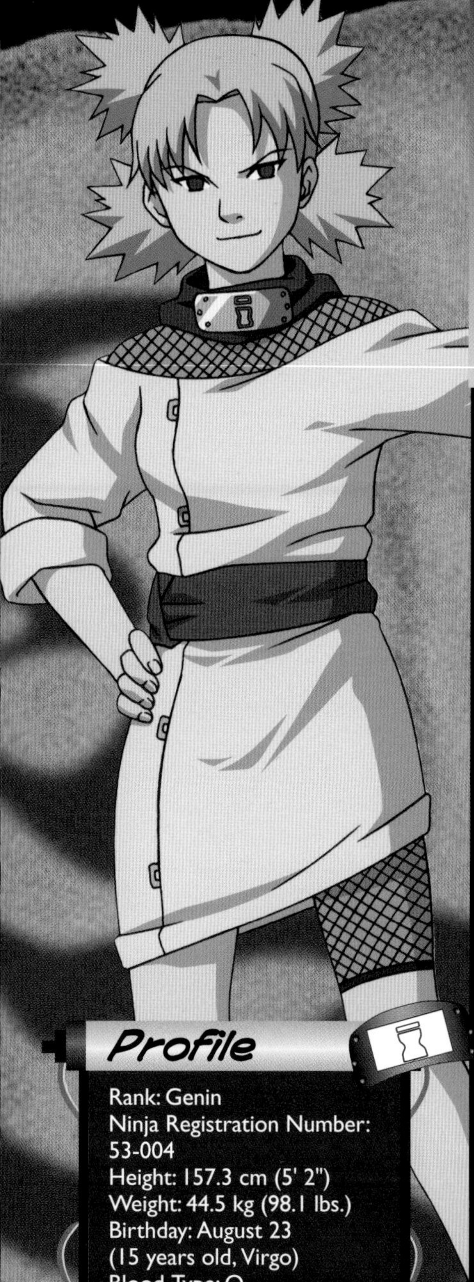

Profile

Rank: Genin
Ninja Registration Number: 53-004
Height: 157.3 cm (5' 2")
Weight: 44.5 kg (98.1 lbs.)
Birthday: August 23
(15 years old, Virgo)
Blood Type: O
Personality: Coldhearted, practical

TEMARI

Temari

Gaara

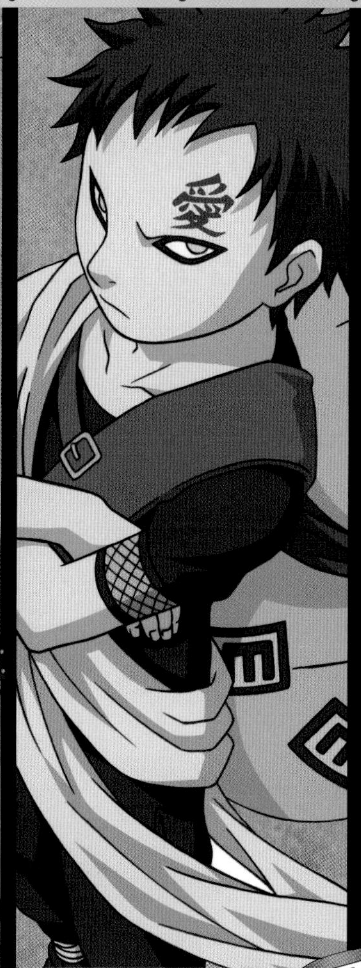

Profile

Rank: Genin
Ninja Registration Number: 56-001
Height: 146.1 cm (4' 10")
Weight: 39 kg (86 lbs.)
Birthday: January 19
(12 years old, Capricorn)
Blood Type: AB
Personality: Heartless, self-interested

GAARA

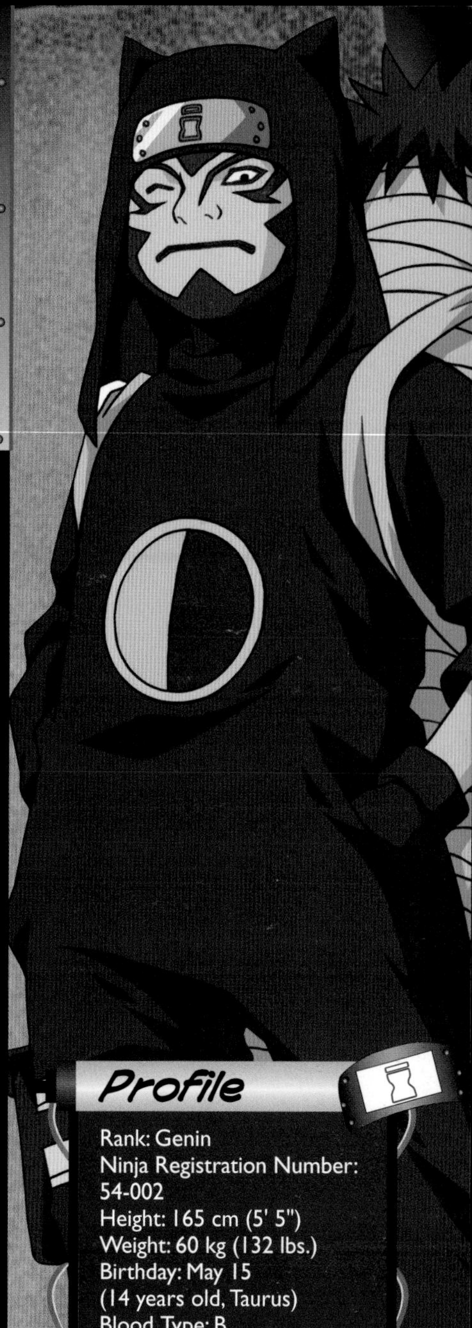

Profile

Rank: Genin
Ninja Registration Number: 54-002
Height: 165 cm (5' 5")
Weight: 60 kg (132 lbs.)
Birthday: May 15
(14 years old, Taurus)
Blood Type: B
Personality: Belligerent, simple

KANKURO

Kankuro

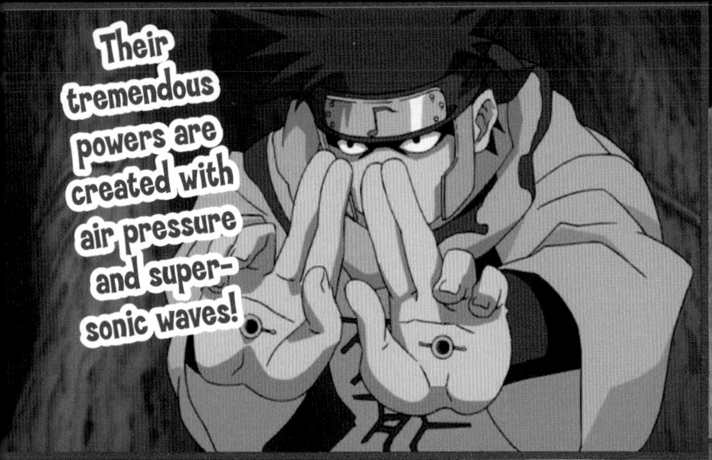
Their tremendous powers are created with air pressure and super-sonic waves!

These Sound ninja ruthlessly hunt down Sasuke!

Under Orochimaru's orders, the three ninja from the Village Hidden in the Sound try to assassinate Sasuke. Although they work together to complete their mission, they have little camaraderie. If the situation required it, they wouldn't hesitate to kill one another.

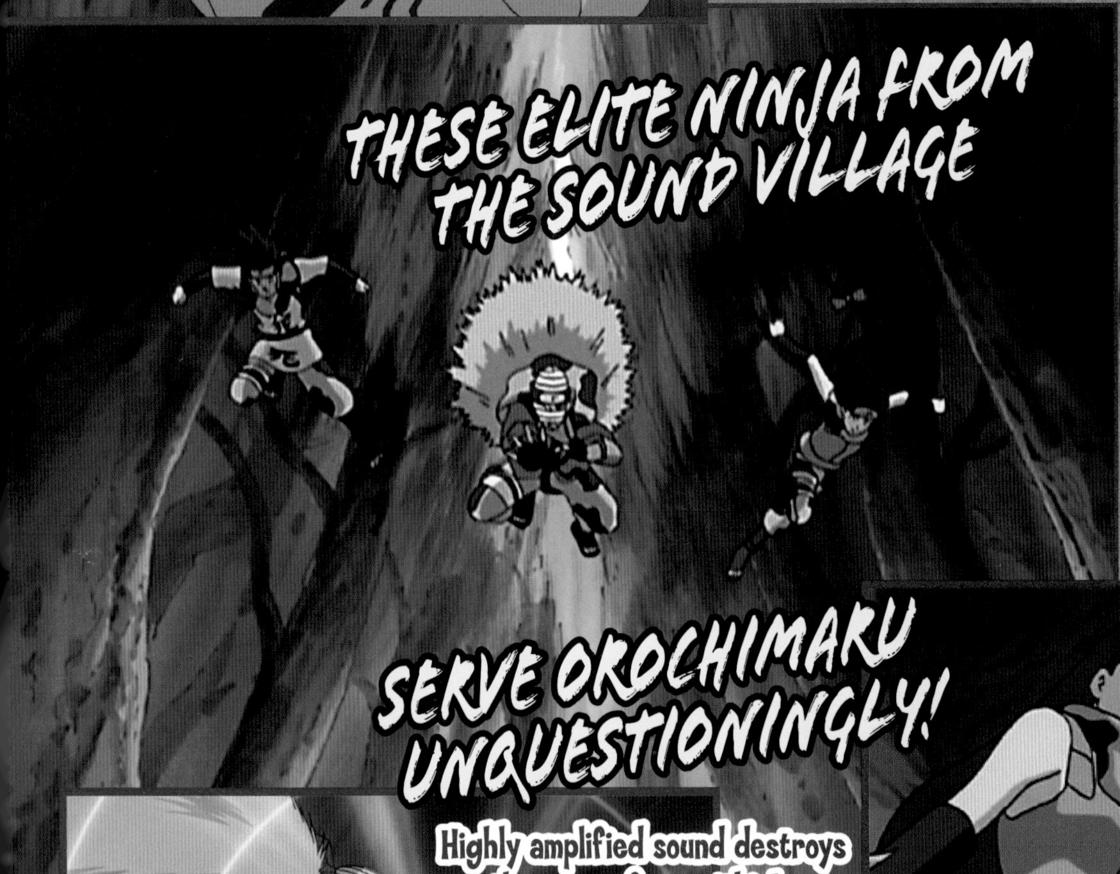

THESE ELITE NINJA FROM THE SOUND VILLAGE SERVE OROCHIMARU UNQUESTIONINGLY!

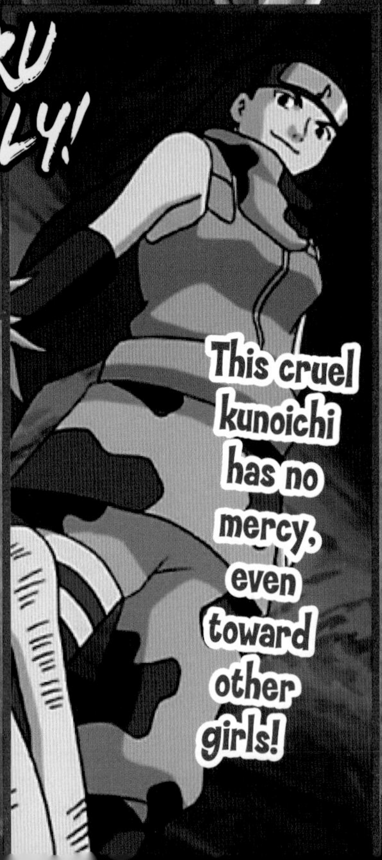
This cruel kunoichi has no mercy, even toward other girls!

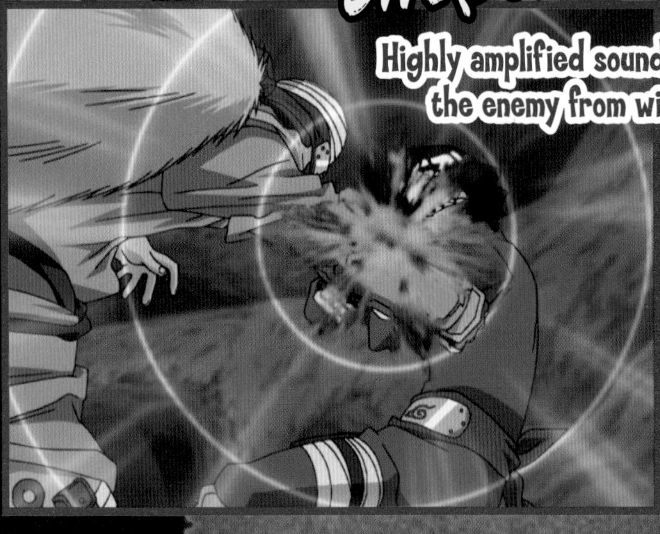
Highly amplified sound destroys the enemy from within!

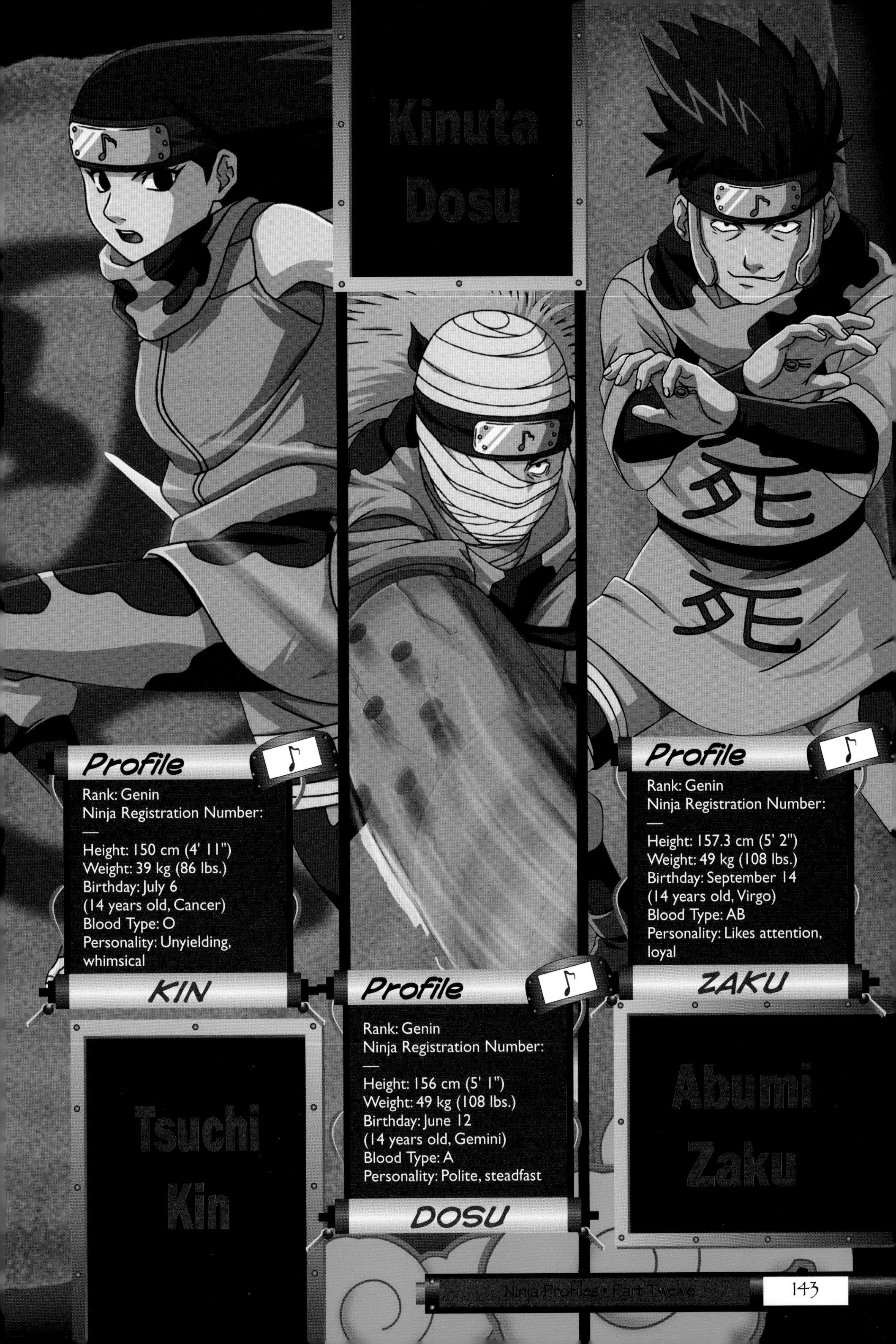

Tsuchi Kin

Profile

Rank: Genin
Ninja Registration Number:
—
Height: 150 cm (4' 11")
Weight: 39 kg (86 lbs.)
Birthday: July 6
(14 years old, Cancer)
Blood Type: O
Personality: Unyielding, whimsical

KIN

Kinuta Dosu

Profile

Rank: Genin
Ninja Registration Number:
—
Height: 156 cm (5' 1")
Weight: 49 kg (108 lbs.)
Birthday: June 12
(14 years old, Gemini)
Blood Type: A
Personality: Polite, steadfast

DOSU

Abumi Zaku

Profile

Rank: Genin
Ninja Registration Number:
—
Height: 157.3 cm (5' 2")
Weight: 49 kg (108 lbs.)
Birthday: September 14
(14 years old, Virgo)
Blood Type: AB
Personality: Likes attention, loyal

ZAKU

Ibiki Morino

The leader of the Torture and Interrogation Unit who has complete knowledge of the human soul!

I'm Ibiki Morino, your proctor...and from this moment, your worst enemy!

Evidence of his iron will is visible in the countless scars engraved on his body!

Ibiki is the proctor of the first portion of the Chunin Exams and is the leader of the Leaf Village's Torture and Interrogation Unit. He is a professional at exposing lies and the hidden secrets of the soul. His skills are recognized by all the jonin of the village.

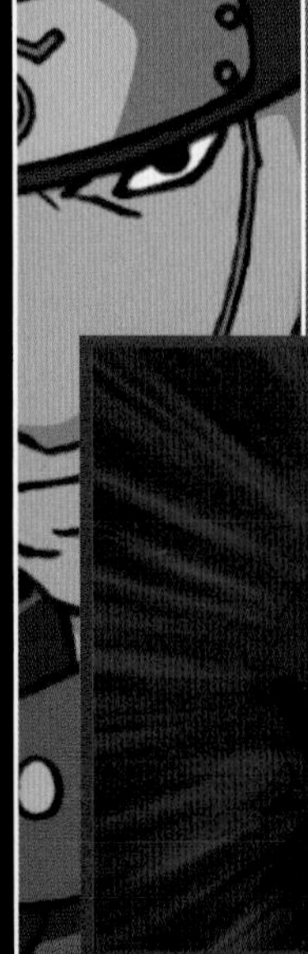

Profile

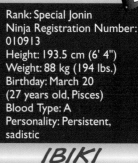

Rank: Special Jonin
Ninja Registration Number: 010913
Height: 193.5 cm (6' 4")
Weight: 88 kg (194 lbs.)
Birthday: March 20
(27 years old, Pisces)
Blood Type: A
Personality: Persistent, sadistic

IBIKI

Anko Mitarashi

Against her enemies, she's like a blazing inferno!

Why's he here? What's he doing at the Chunin Exams?

Profile

Rank: Special Jonin
Ninja Registration Number: 011226
Height: 167 cm (5' 6")
Weight: 45.8 kg (101 lbs.)
Birthday: October 24 (24 years old, Scorpio)
Blood Type: A
Personality: Playful, coarse, daring

ANKO

Beneath her fiery emotions lies a secret: Orochimaru's curse!

The proctor of the second test in the Chunin Exams, Anko has a straightforward personality similar to Naruto's. She takes action with brisk, furious intensity. Anko is such a strong shinobi that she became one of Orochimaru's targets, and for a while, she was his follower. She learned many horrifyingly destructive jutsu from him.

Passion! Intensity!

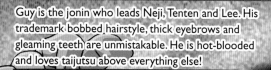

Guy is the jonin who leads Neji, Tenten and Lee. His trademark bobbed hairstyle, thick eyebrows and gleaming teeth are unmistakable. He is hot-blooded and loves taijutsu above everything else!

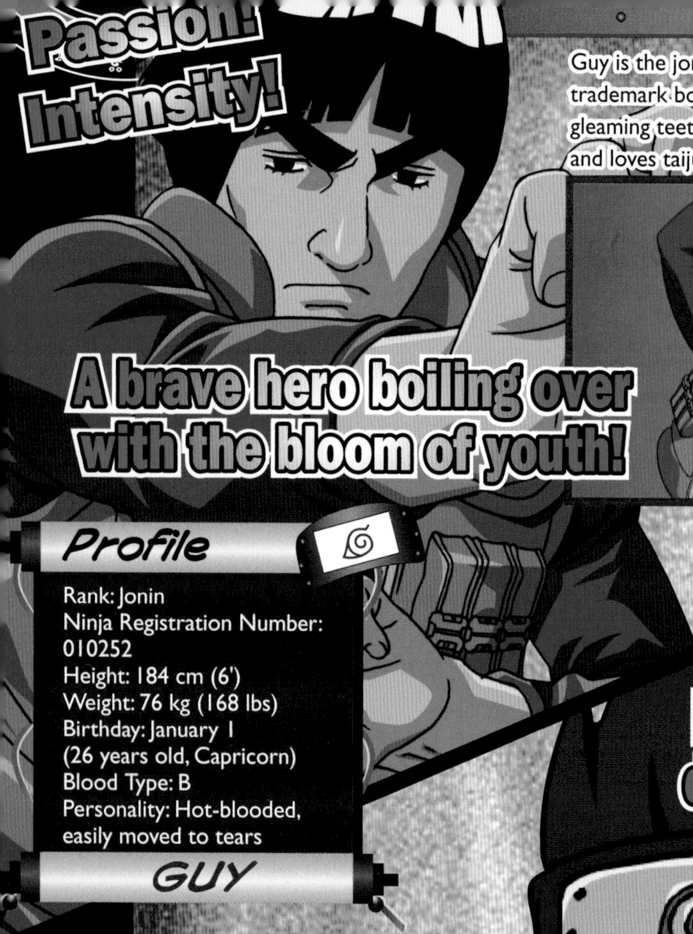

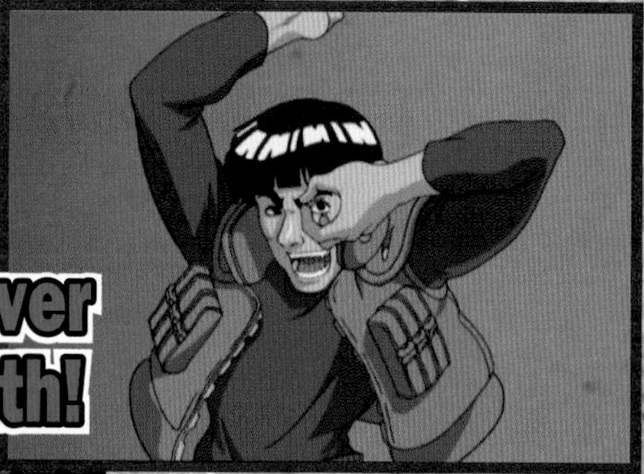

A brave hero boiling over with the bloom of youth!

Profile

Rank: Jonin
Ninja Registration Number: 010252
Height: 184 cm (6')
Weight: 76 kg (168 lbs)
Birthday: January 1
(26 years old, Capricorn)
Blood Type: B
Personality: Hot-blooded, easily moved to tears

GUY

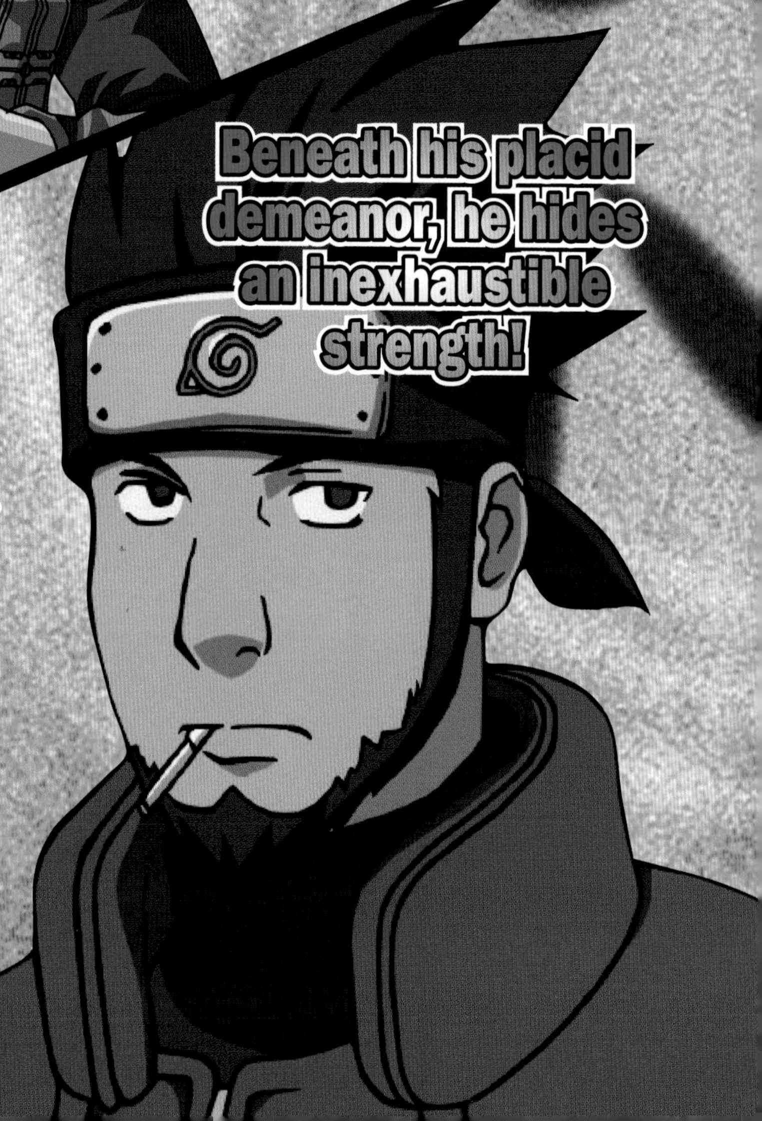

Beneath his placid demeanor, he hides an inexhaustible strength!

As the jonin leader of Squad Ten, Asuma oversees Ino, Shikamaru and Choji's training. He has a curt disposition and always has a cigarette dangling from his lip, but underneath, he's a capable ninja with some of the most extraordinary skills in the village.

Profile

Rank: Jonin
Ninja Registration Number: 010829
Height: 190.8 cm (6' 3")
Weight: 81.6 kg (180 lbs.)
Birthday: October 18
(27 years old, Libra)
Blood Type: O
Personality: Blunt

ASUMA

Kurenai Yuhi

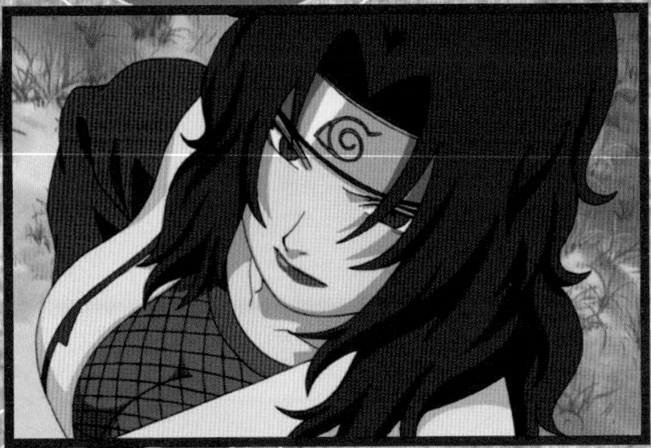

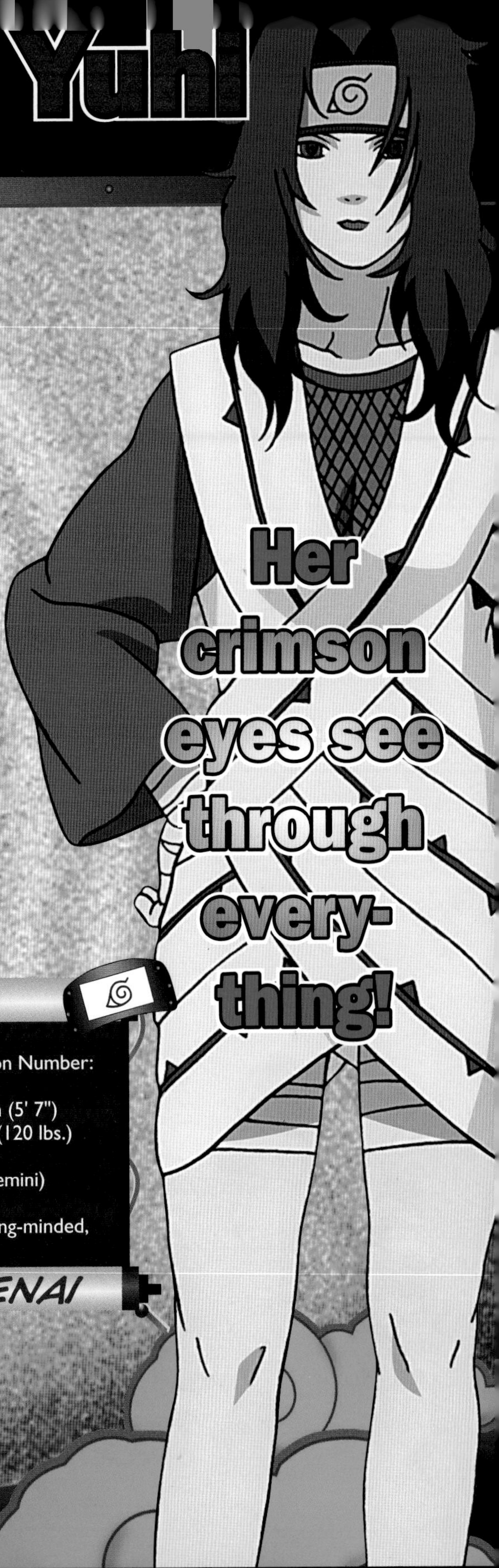

Asuma Sarutobi

Kurenai is a brand new Jonin in the Hidden Leaf Village and mentors Kiba, Hinata and Shino as the leader of Squad Eight. Far from timid, she is very firm as she intervenes in a disagreement between Kakashi and Iruka. But she certainly doesn't lack feminine graces and teaches her students with a gentle touch.

Her crimson eyes see through every-thing!

Profile

Rank: Jonin
Ninja Registration Number: 010881
Height: 169.1 cm (5' 7")
Weight: 54.4 kg (120 lbs.)
Birthday: June 11
(27 years old, Gemini)
Blood Type: AB
Personality: Strong-minded, precise

KURENAI

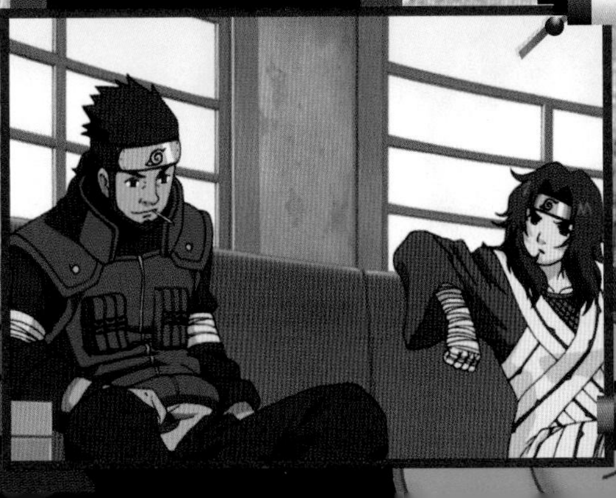

Orochimaru

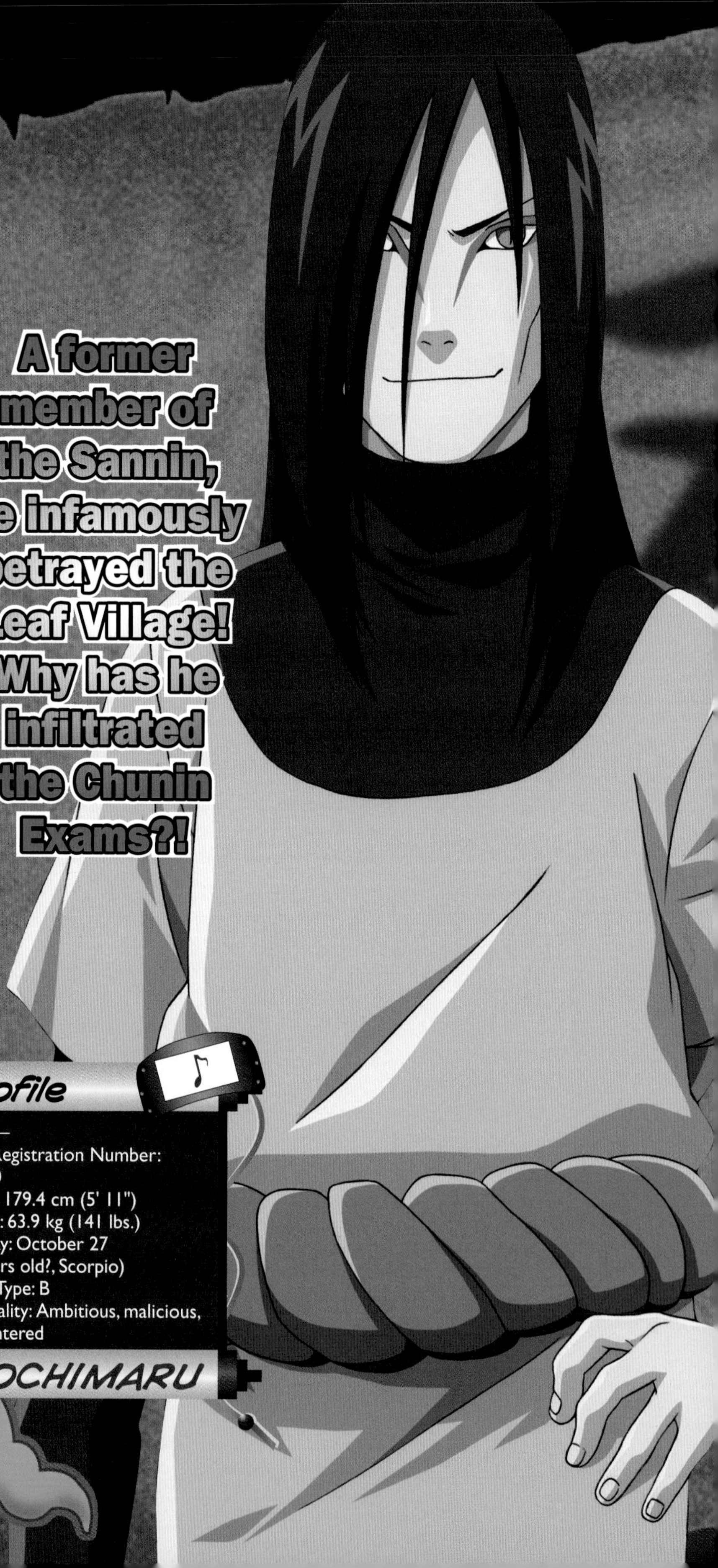

A former member of the Sannin, he infamously betrayed the Leaf Village! Why has he infiltrated the Chunin Exams?!

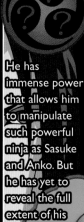

He has immense power that allows him to manipulate such powerful ninja as Sasuke and Anko. But he has yet to reveal the full extent of his strength...

Profile

Rank: —
Ninja Registration Number: 002300
Height: 179.4 cm (5' 11")
Weight: 63.9 kg (141 lbs.)
Birthday: October 27 (50 years old?, Scorpio)
Blood Type: B
Personality: Ambitious, malicious, self-centered

OROCHIMARU

Orochimaru is willing to do anything to achieve his goals, and he commits atrocities without a second thought. Although his power is terrifying, what is most alarming is his vicious tenacity and snakelike cold-bloodedness…

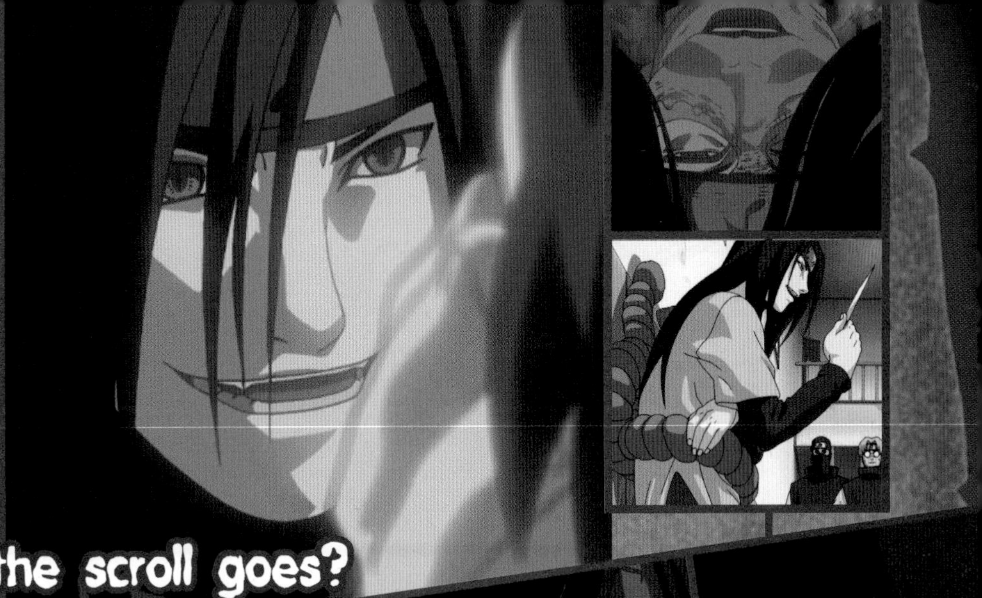

As far as the scroll goes?
I could simply kill you and *take* it.

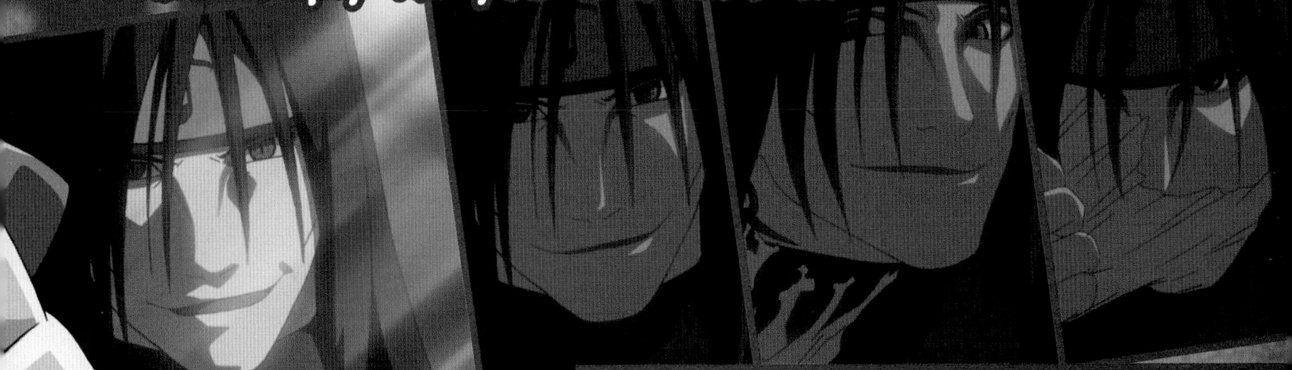

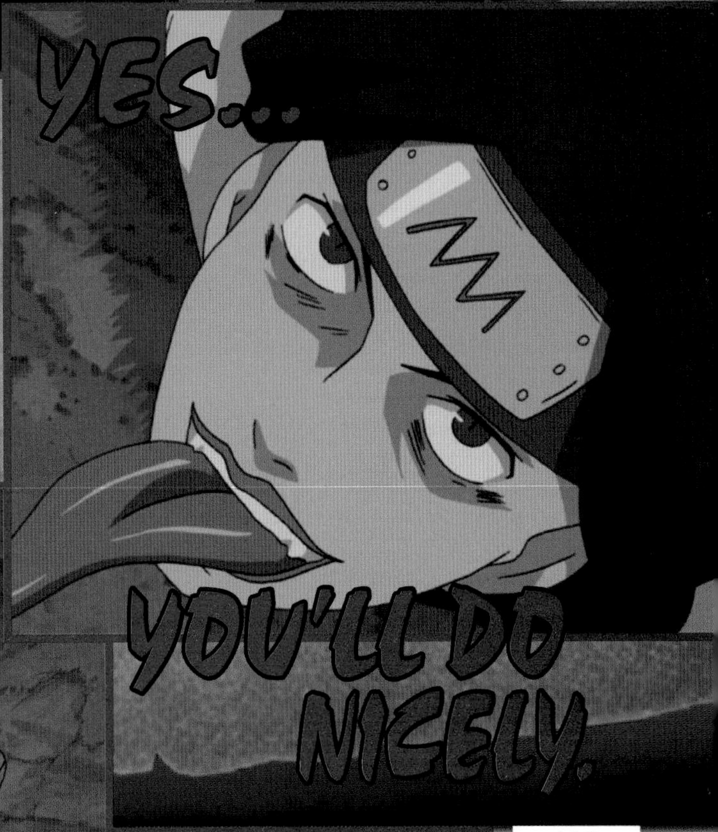

YES…
YOU'LL DO NICELY.

He created the Village Hidden in the Sound, assembling a group of talented shinobi to be his followers. He has latched his poisonous fangs onto Sasuke, heir to the greatest bloodline in the Hidden Leaf Village. Orochimaru took pains to conceal his identity in order to enter the Chunin Exams and gather information…but what are his true intentions? His motives are unclear, but his presence is bound to bring danger to his native Leaf Village…

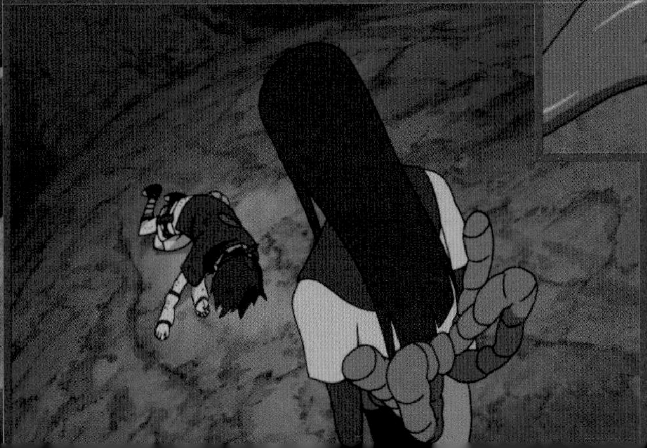

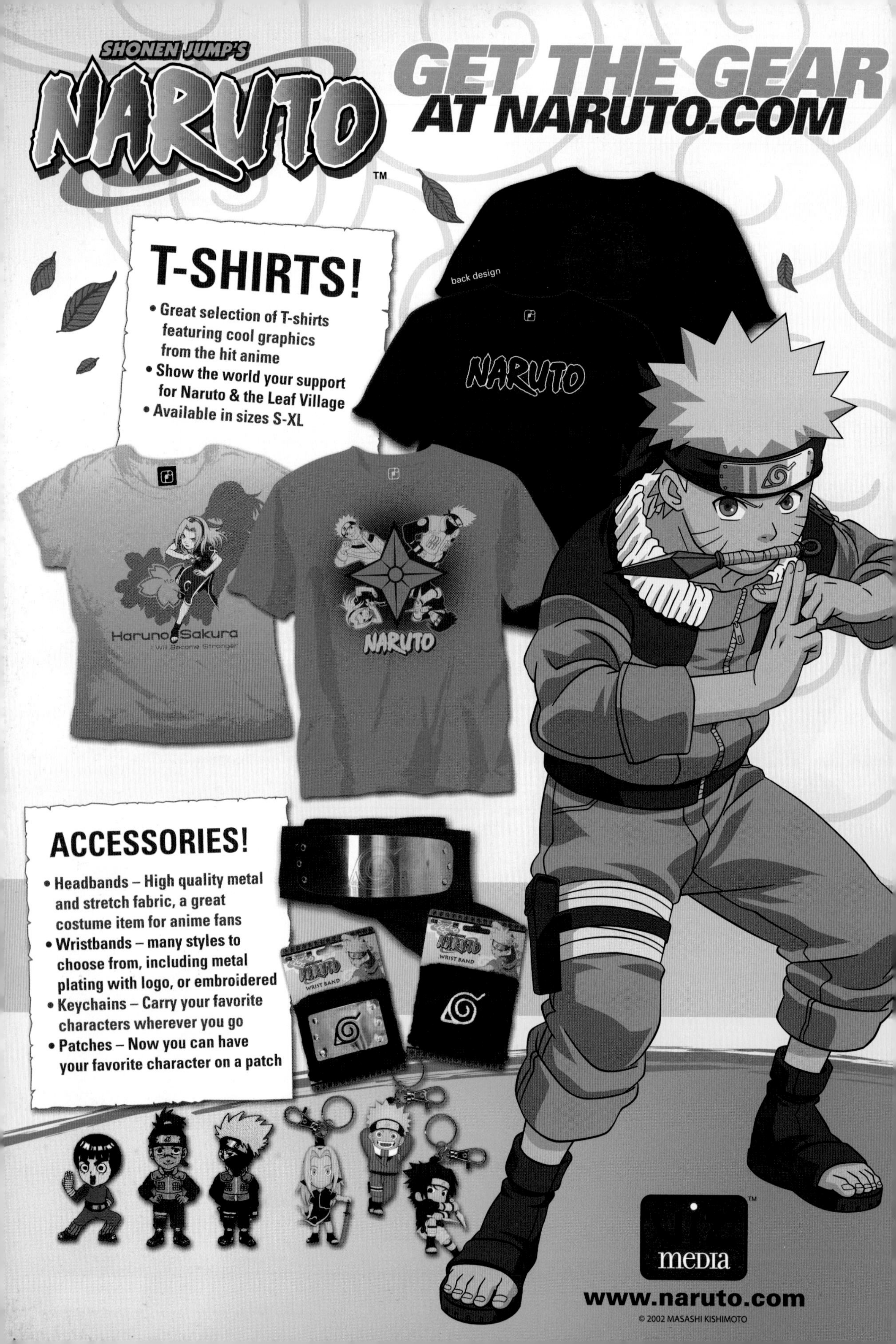
SHONEN JUMP'S
NARUTO™
GET THE GEAR
AT NARUTO.COM
T-SHIRTS!
• Great selection of T-shirts featuring cool graphics from the hit anime
• Show the world your support for Naruto & the Leaf Village
• Available in sizes S-XL
back design
NARUTO
Haruno Sakura
I Will Become Stronger!
NARUTO
ACCESSORIES!
• Headbands – High quality metal and stretch fabric, a great costume item for anime fans
• Wristbands – many styles to choose from, including metal plating with logo, or embroidered
• Keychains – Carry your favorite characters wherever you go
• Patches – Now you can have your favorite character on a patch
NARUTO
WRIST BAND
NARUTO
WRIST BAND
viz media™
www.naruto.com
© 2002 MASASHI KISHIMOTO

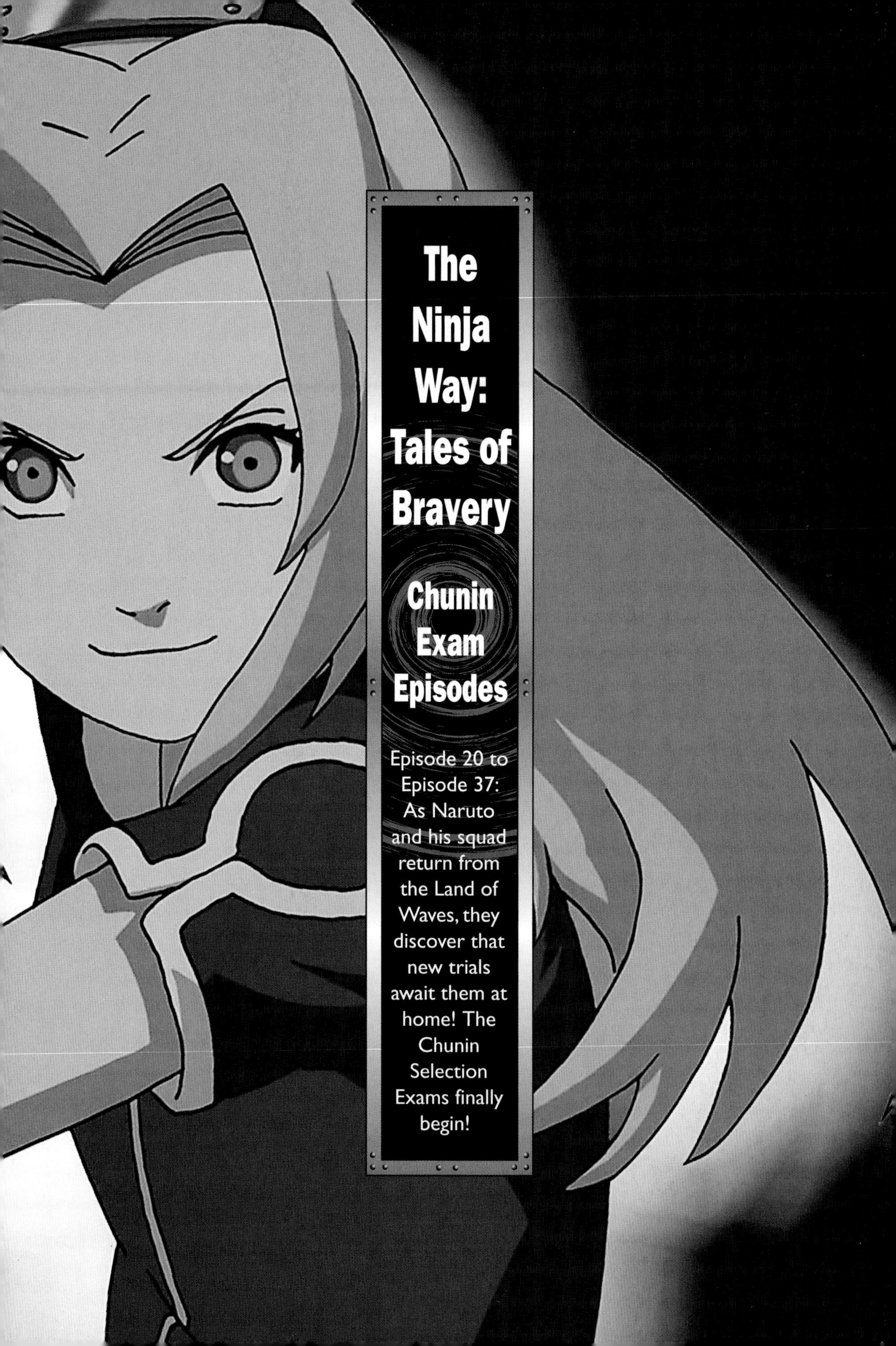

The Ninja Way: Tales of Bravery

Chunin Exam Episodes

Episode 20 to Episode 37: As Naruto and his squad return from the Land of Waves, they discover that new trials await them at home! The Chunin Selection Exams finally begin!

The dawn of a peaceful new day!

Episodes 20 to 25

A new awakening … What is Naruto's next mission?!

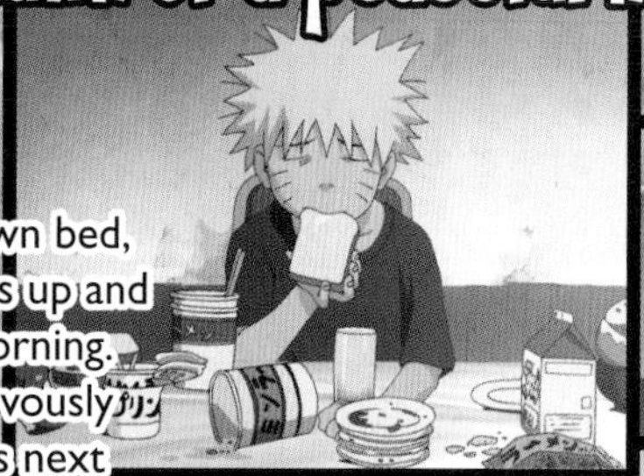

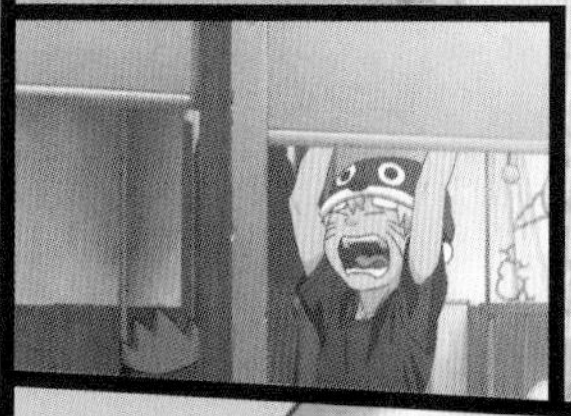

Back in his own bed, Naruto wakes up and greets the morning. But as he nervously anticipates his next mission, the excitement grows in his heart!

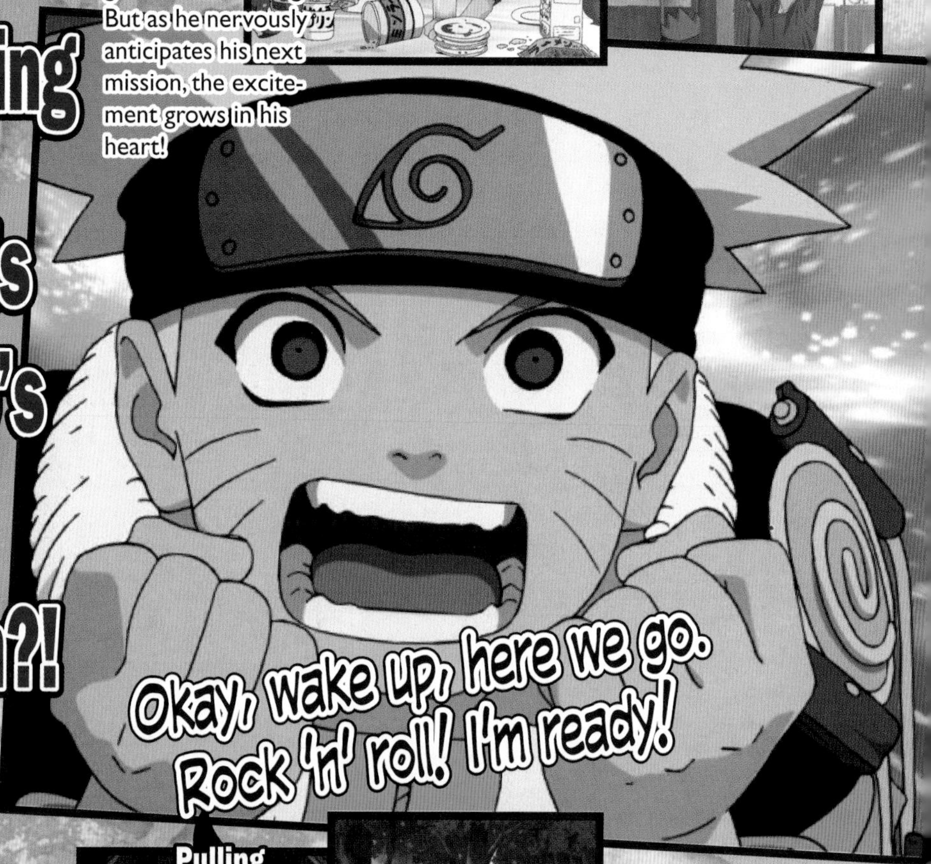
Okay, wake up, here we go. Rock 'n' roll! I'm ready!

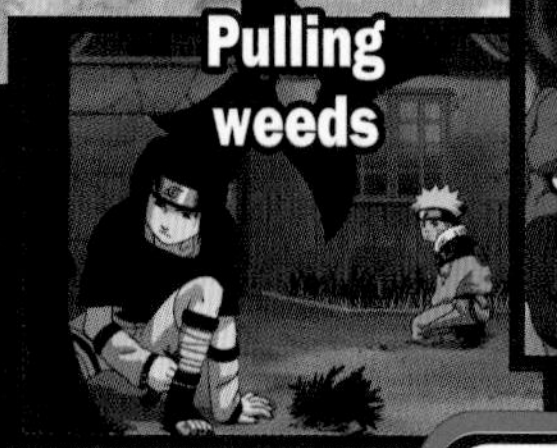
Pulling weeds

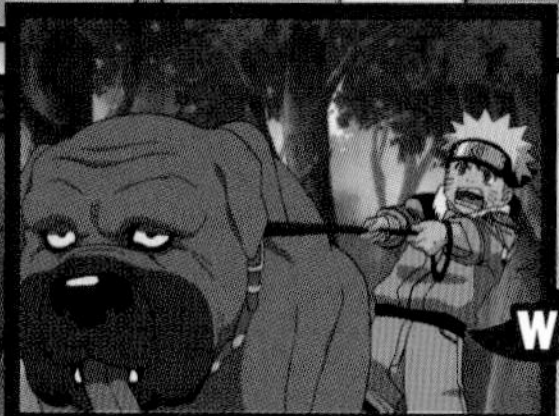
Dog walking

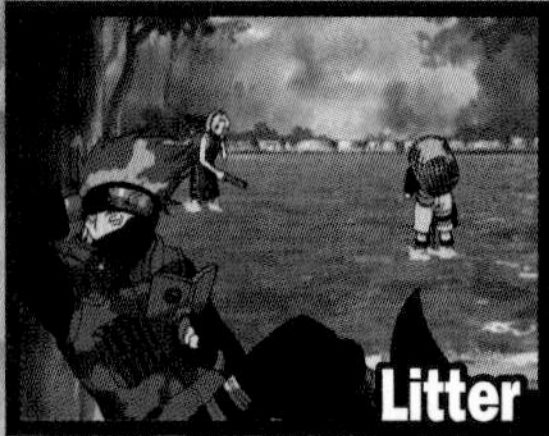
Litter collection

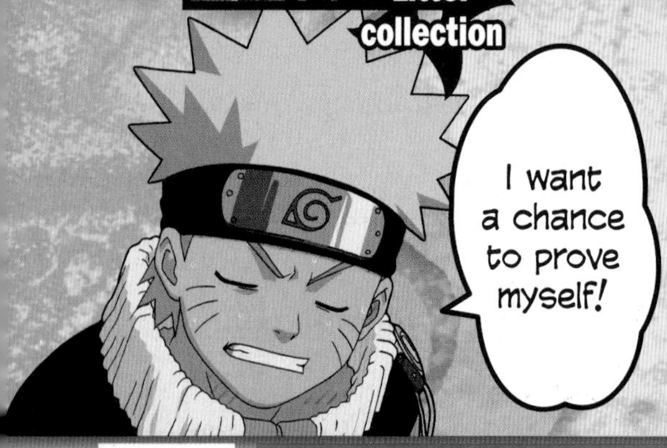
I want a chance to prove myself!

Back home in the Leaf Village, life returns to normal for Naruto…

After the conclusion of their harrowing battle in the Land of Waves, Naruto and the others come home to their own village. Having experienced significant growth on that mission, Naruto is full of drive and energy, but he is faced with boring tasks like walking dogs and picking up garbage! Naruto is extremely disappointed to be relegated to such assignments, especially after his thrilling experiences in the Land of Waves…

The peace is shattered...

Genin from the Village Hidden in the Sand appear suddenly, like they're looking for trouble!

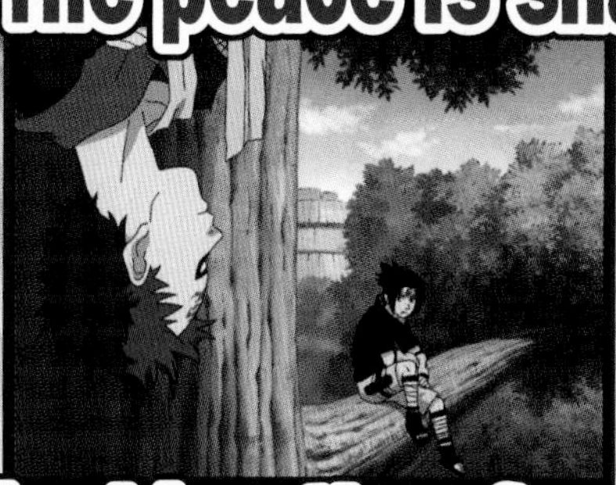

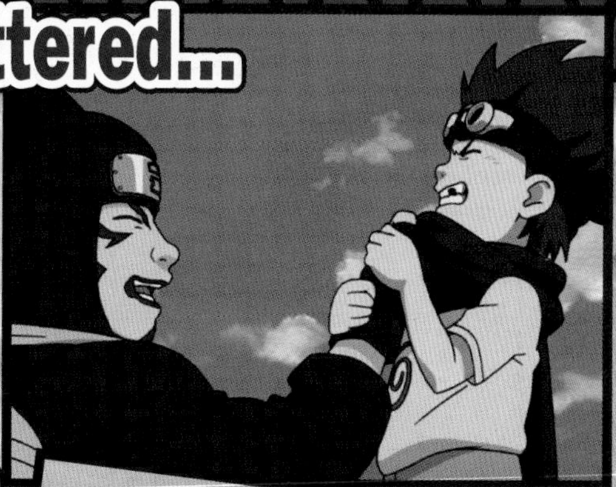

...Shinobi gather from lands far and wide...

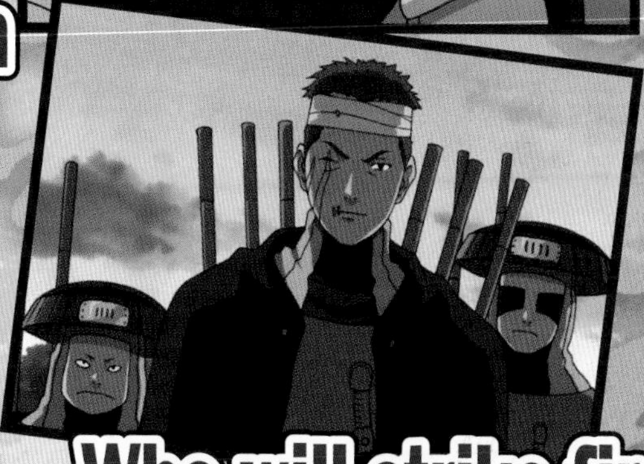

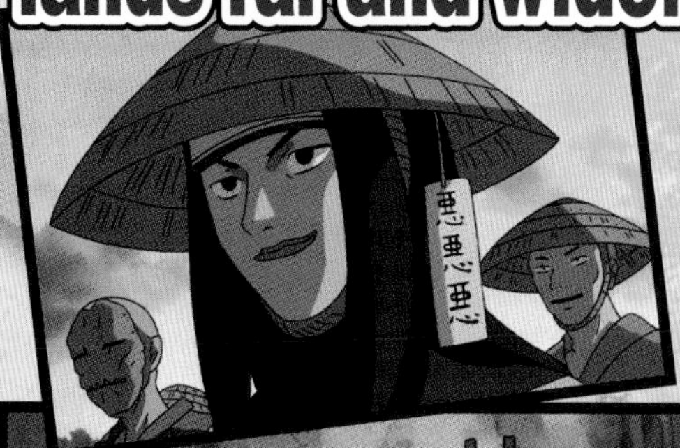

...Who will strike first?!

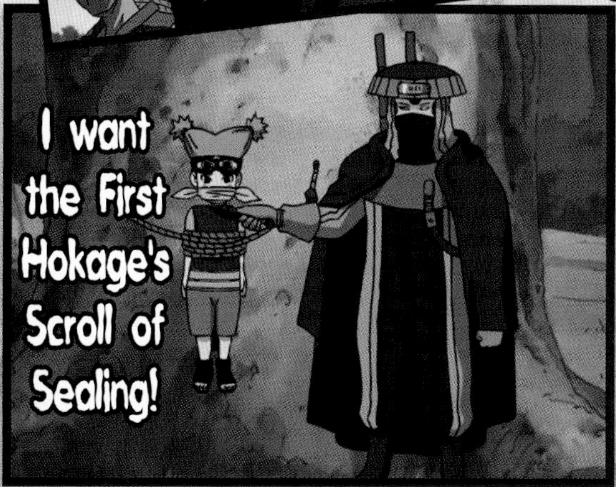
I want the First Hokage's Scroll of Sealing!

A mysterious foreign shinobi abducts Moegi! The blade closes in…what will be Moegi's fate?!

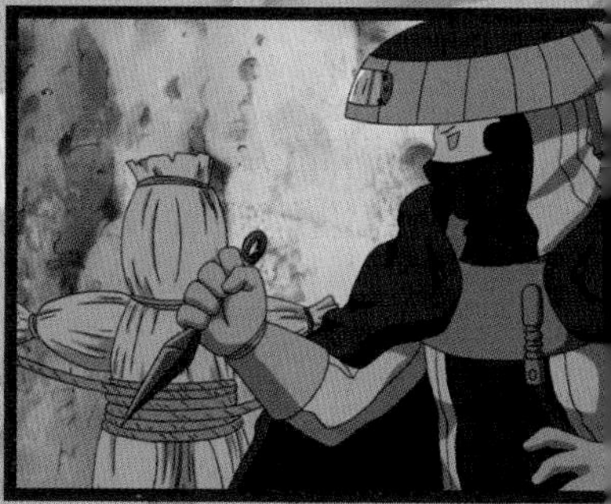

Naruto scoffs at the danger presented by the kidnapper and pulls off a surprise rescue! But the strange shinobi's true purpose lies beneath the surface…

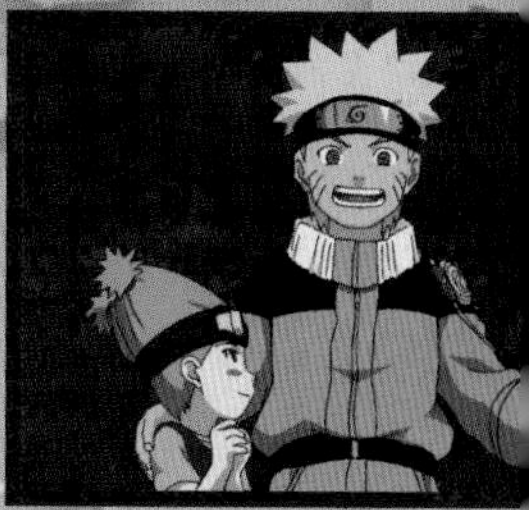

As the genin from other nations arrive, Naruto learns that the Chunin Selection Exams are going to be held. Soon, Naruto and the rest of his team come under the attack of an inscrutable ninja from the Village Hidden in the Rain! Is this an attempt to disrupt the exams?! Or is an enemy nation using the exams as cover to begin an invasion of the Leaf Village?! What is the truth…?!

An attack by the Rain ninja signals the start of the Chunin Exam!

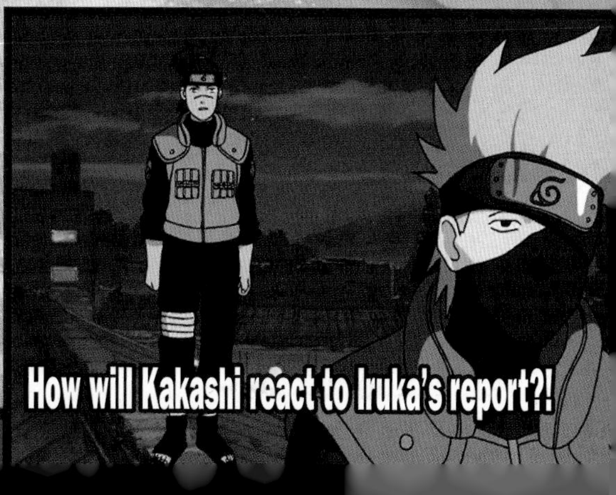

How will Kakashi react to Iruka's report?!

Sparks fly early at the examination site!

I want to fight … right here and right now!

vs. Sakura

Sakura nearly knocks herself out dodging Lee's wink/heart combo attack.

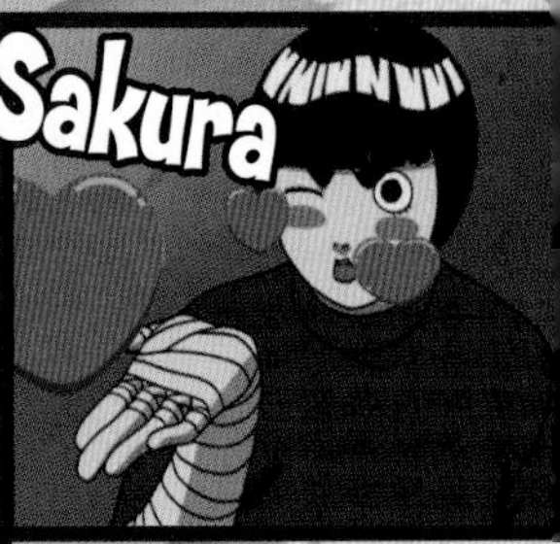

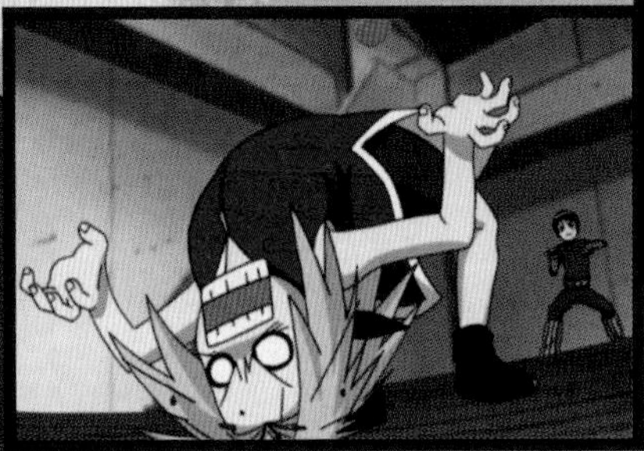

vs. Naruto

He strikes in a flash! Lee dodges an attack and unleashes the Leaf Hurricane! Naruto is down for the count.

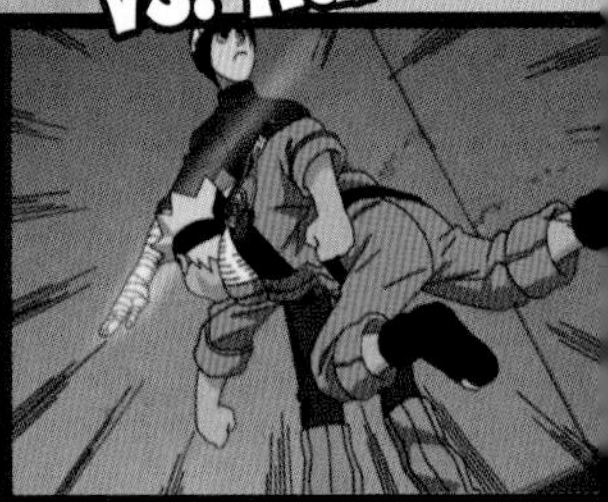

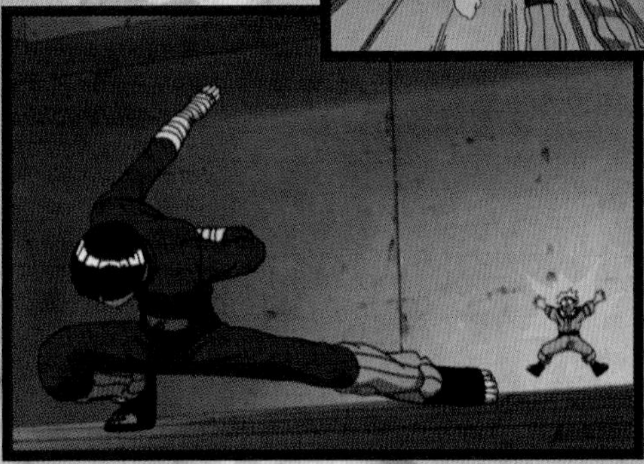

vs. Sasuke

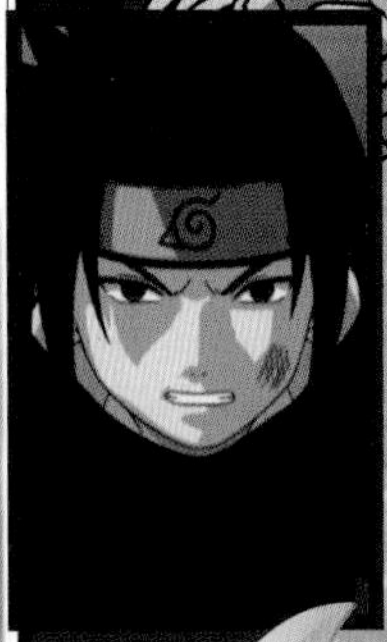

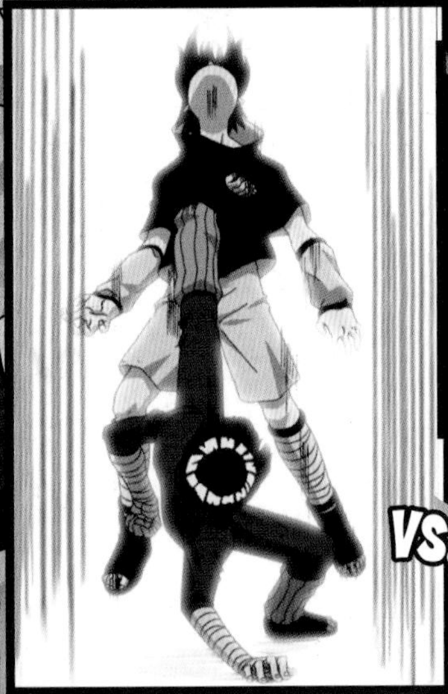

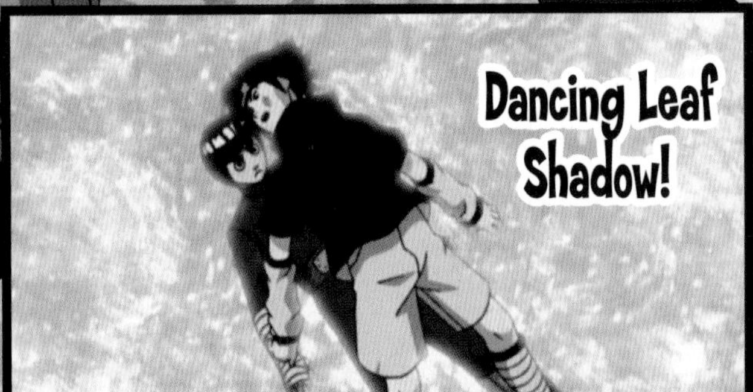

Dancing Leaf Shadow!

As Lee kicks up with his high-speed taijutsu, he captures his opponent in midair with the Dancing Leaf Shadow! Lee unleashes his ultimate taijutsu on Sasuke, who suddenly has no escape!

The ultimate clash of perseverance vs. brilliance!

The young Leaf ninja are filled with competitive spirit and rush to fight. Sasuke activates his Kekkei Genkai, the Sharingan, and Lee counters with his incredible speed! A victor is declared in the battle of innate genius versus hard work: Lee's high-speed taijutsu wins out, and Sasuke is trapped…

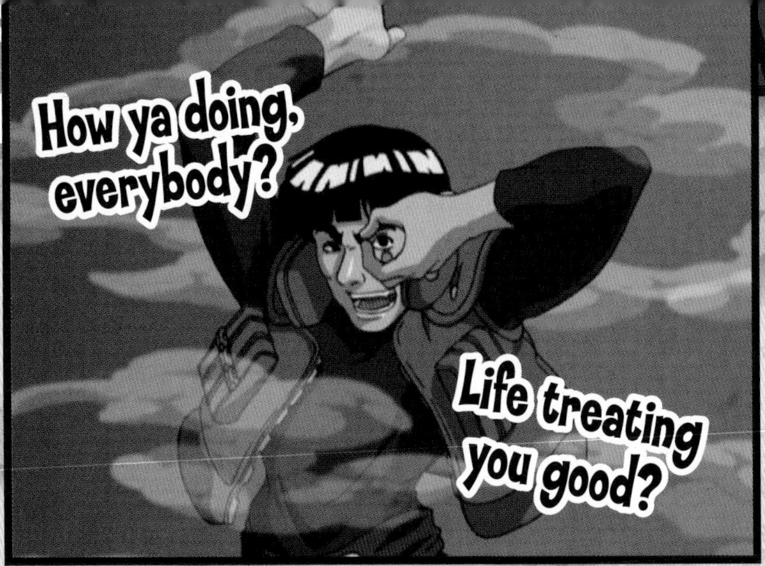
How ya doing, everybody?
Life treating you good?

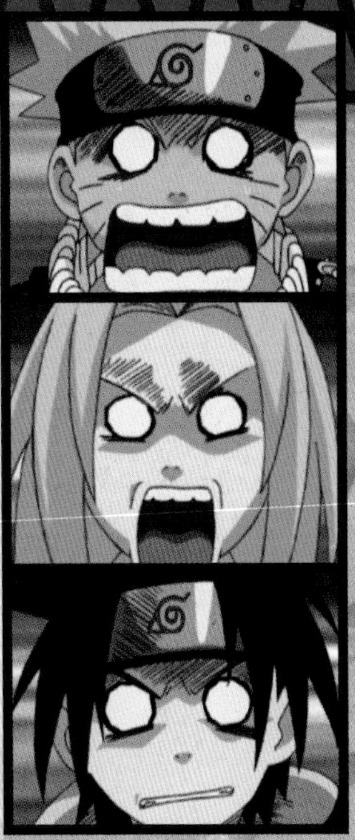

Guy shows up with his massive eyebrows, over-the-top personality, and shock of bobbed hair that all manage to surpass Lee's! Overwhelmed by this amazing vision, Naruto, Sakura and Sasuke are all stupefied!

Guy speaks with his fists!

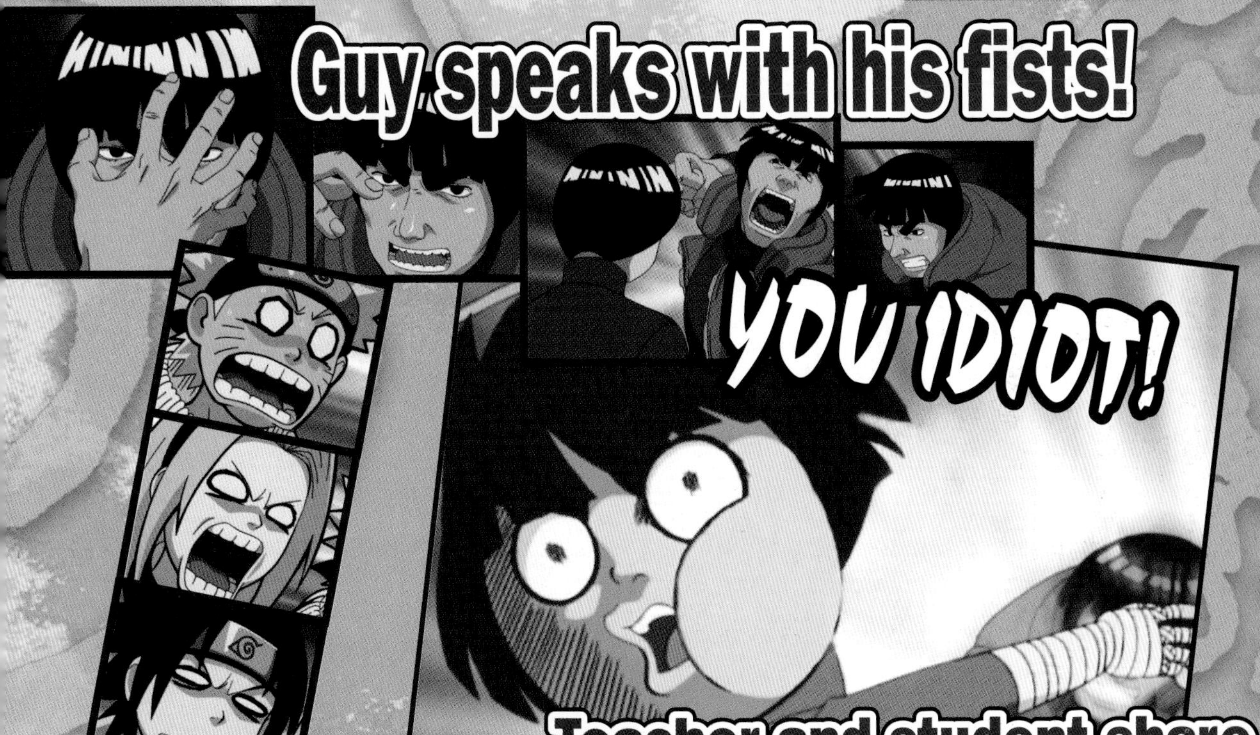
YOU IDIOT!

Teacher and student share an awe-inspiring bond!

What's this hot-blooded man's name?!

The scuffle between Sasuke and Lee is suddenly interrupted by the arrival of Might Guy! Guy and Lee are then swept away into a world that they alone share…

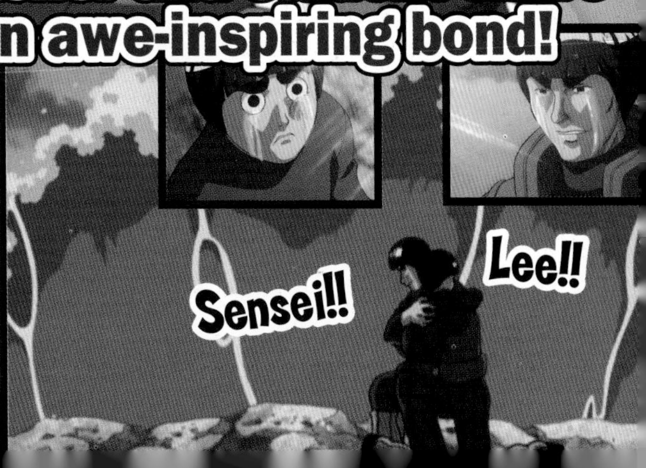
Sensei!!
Lee!!

Kabuto warns the rookies who are taking the exam for the first time…

A shockwave rumbles through the tense exam building!

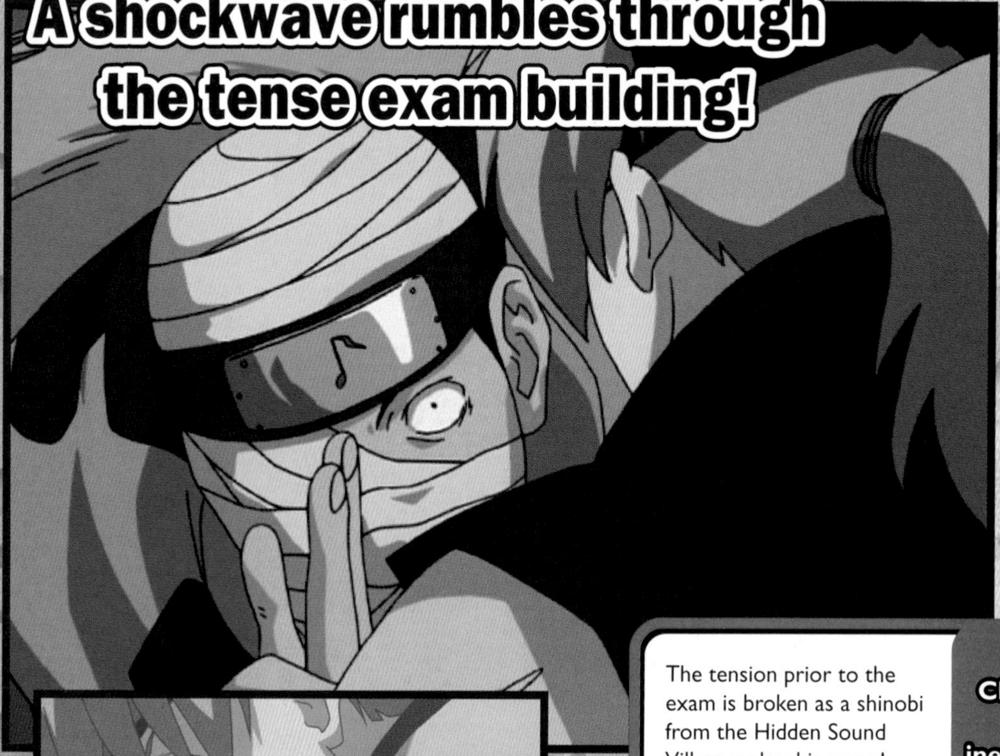

The tension prior to the exam is broken as a shinobi from the Hidden Sound Village makes his move! Kabuto avoids Dosu's blow…but in the next moment, Kabuto's glasses break and he vomits. He dodged the attack, so why did this happen?!

Clashes are inevitable as the fighters assemble in the arena!

This card displays data on the ninja from each village. It lists their special powers, the other members of their team, and the missions they have completed.

This card shows the number of students participating in this year's exam. As seen here, it's possible to create 3-D diagrams.

Shinobi Database

Ninja Info Cards

These cards are a type of ninja tool. Information can be burned on the card using chakra. The cards look blank to the naked eye, but when chakra is applied, various categories of data appear! However, only the person who originally burned the data onto the card is able to retrieve the information.

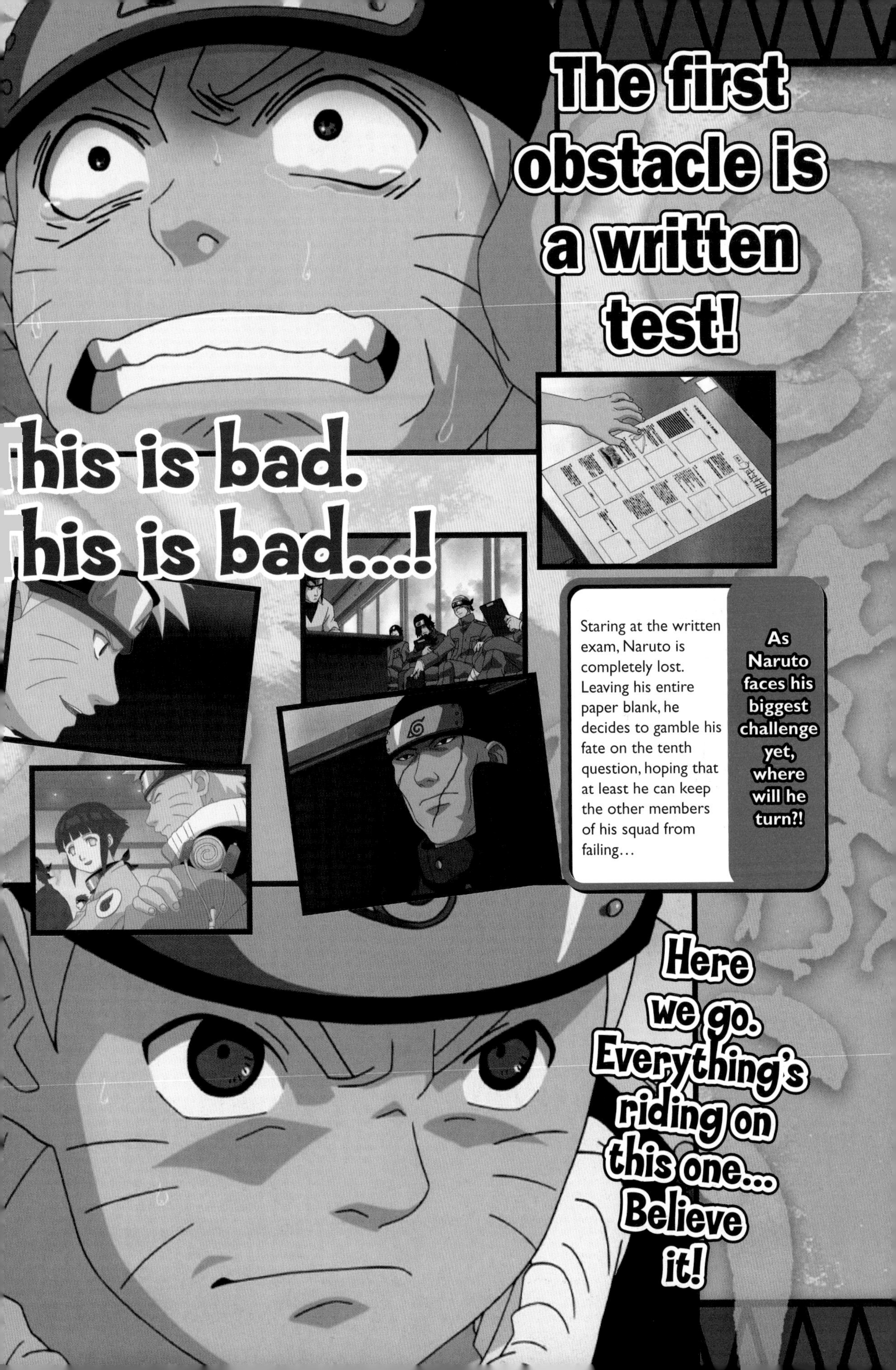
The first obstacle is a written test!
his is bad.
his is bad...!
Staring at the written exam, Naruto is completely lost. Leaving his entire paper blank, he decides to gamble his fate on the tenth question, hoping that at least he can keep the other members of his squad from failing…
As Naruto faces his biggest challenge yet, where will he turn?!
Here we go. Everything's riding on this one... Believe it!

Battle for survival! This extreme exam puts lives on the line!

↑ The object of the exercise is to reach the tower in the center of the forest with two scrolls in hand and all three team members alive.

→ The struggle for scrolls will occur deep in the forest, hidden from the gaze of the exam proctors. In these dire and shady circumstances, each squad's true colors rise to the surface!

This test will tax every one of your survival skills!

↓ The exam puts their teamwork to the test. Will Naruto and his squad pass?!

BELIEVE IT! WE'RE SO GOING TO WIN THIS!

After passing the first test, Naruto, Sasuke and Sakura take on the exam's second stage in the Forest of Death. Anko, the proctor, explains the rules and reveals that this portion of the exam is a no-holds-barred survival competition. Within five days, they must reach the finish line with a set of scrolls. But each team is given only one scroll, so they have to steal the second scroll using any means necessary. In this harsh test, every other team is an enemy!

The second exam is a life-and-death struggle for scrolls!

Diagram — The Forest of Death: Chart of each squad's departure gate!

The starting points of the 26 elite squads competing in the second exam are revealed here for the first time!

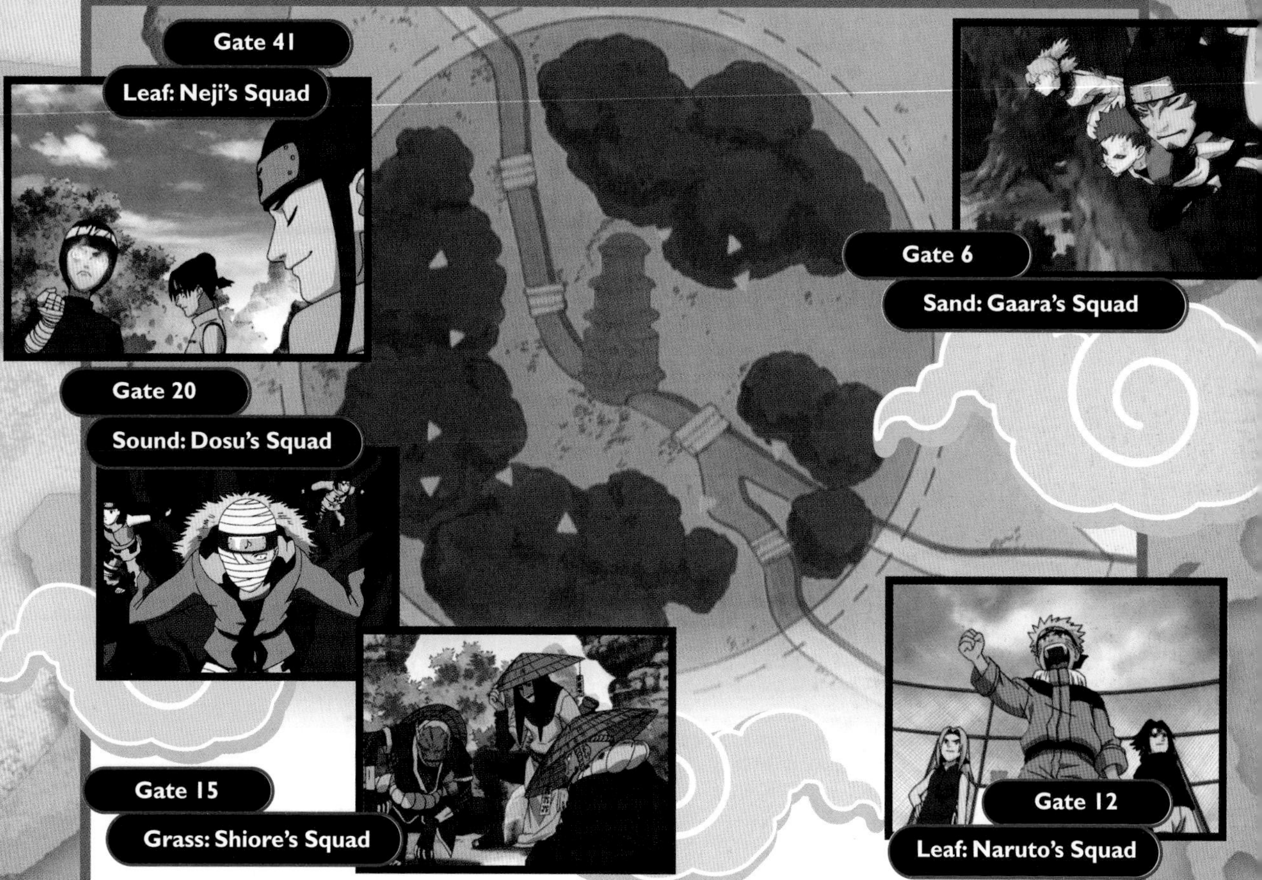

Gate 41

Leaf: Neji's Squad

Gate 6

Sand: Gaara's Squad

Gate 20

Sound: Dosu's Squad

Gate 15

Grass: Shiore's Squad

Gate 12

Leaf: Naruto's Squad

	Squad	Scroll		Squad	Scroll
3	Leaf – Toitsu's Squad	Heaven	24	Leaf – Tonbi's Squad	Earth
4	Sand – Kawaki's Squad	Heaven	25	Grass – Shigeri's Squad	Earth
6	Sand – Gaara's Squad	Earth	26	Leaf – Mebachi's Squad	Heaven
8	Rain – Shigure's Squad	Heaven	27	Leaf – Ino's Squad	Heaven
10	Leaf – Kyube's Squad	Heaven	29	Rain – Oboro's Squad	Heaven
12	Leaf – Naruto's Squad	Heaven	30	Rain – Kawazu's Squad	Heaven
15	Grass – Shiore's Squad	Earth	32	Sound – Genta's Squad	Earth
16	Leaf – Kiba's Squad	Heaven	34	Leaf – Kugiri's Squad	Earth
17	Leaf – Masao's Squad	Earth	35	Sand – Masago's Squad	Heaven
19	Sand – Jyari's Squad	Earth	37	Rain – Yudachi's Squad	Earth
20	Sound – Dosu's Squad	Earth	38	Leaf – Kabuto's Squad	Earth
21	Leaf – Mekabu's Squad	Heaven	41	Leaf – Neji's Squad	Earth
23	Waterfall – Kegon's Squad	Earth	44	Rain – Nezumi's Squad	Heaven

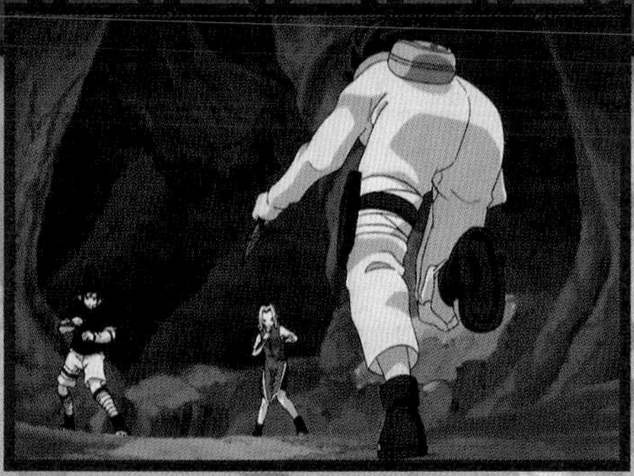

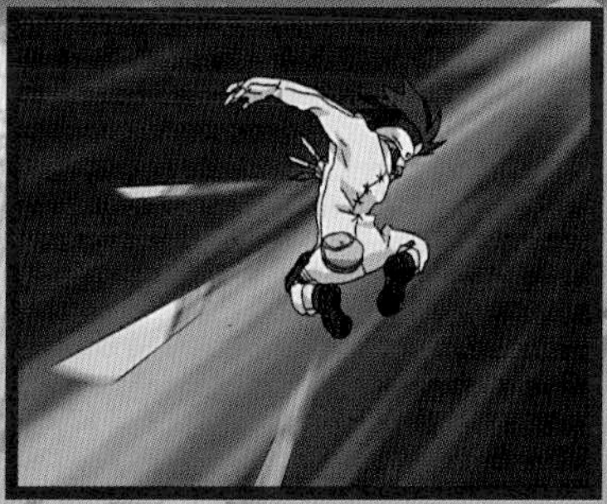

After a Rain ninja's sneaky attempt to disguise himself as Naruto fails, he changes tactics and tries a weapons attack!

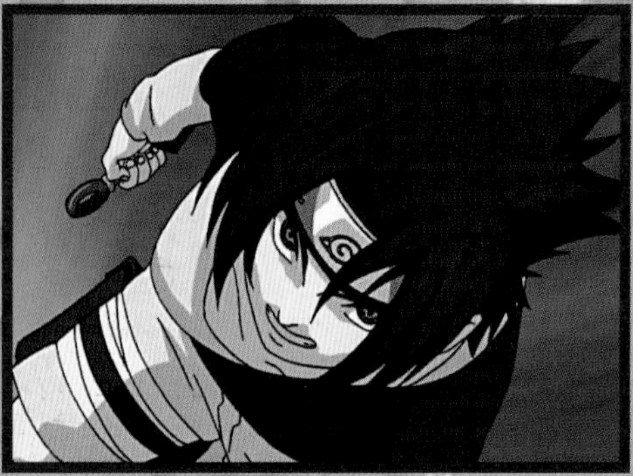

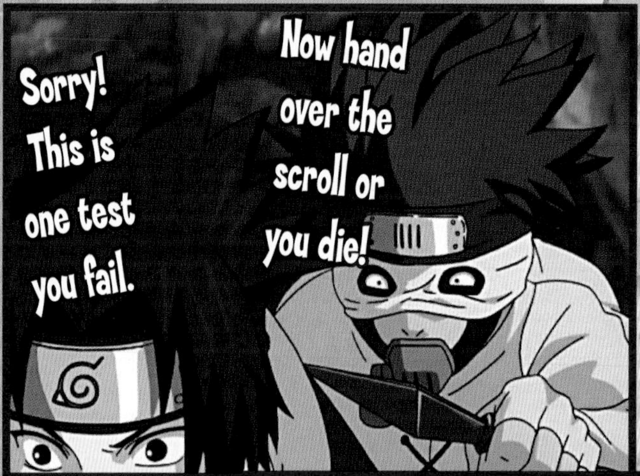
Now hand over the scroll or you die!
Sorry! This is one test you fail.

When Sasuke momentarily drops his guard, the Rain ninja sneaks up on him from behind! The kunai shines with a dull light as it hovers close to Sasuke's neck…

Naruto and his squad are beset by dangers from all sides!

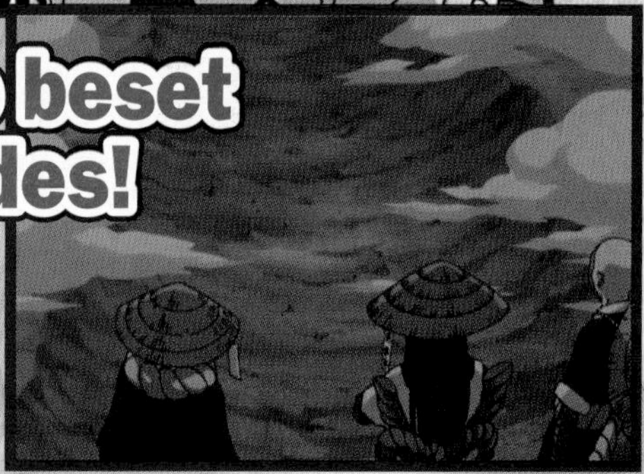

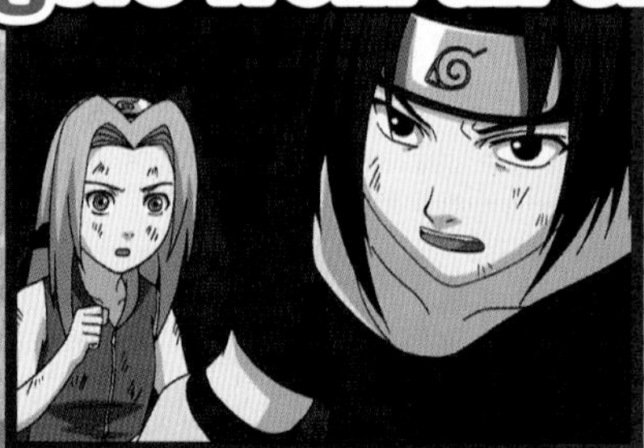

"What is it now?!" A mysterious, violent wind buffets Sasuke and Sakura as their next enemy approaches!

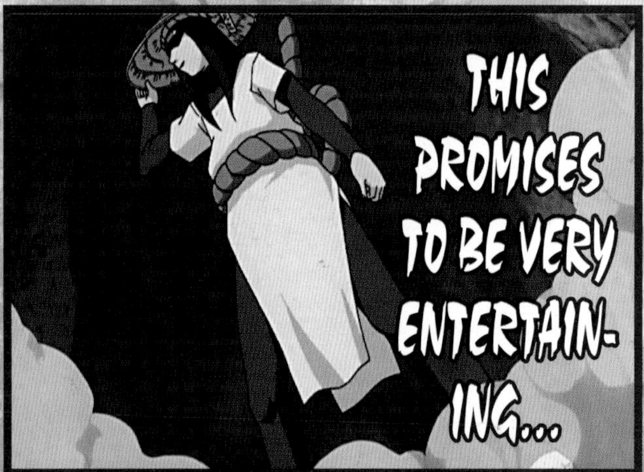
THIS PROMISES TO BE VERY ENTERTAIN-ING…

Immediately after they chase off the Rain ninja, a strange Grass ninja arrives!

As soon as the exam starts, an impostor takes the form of Naruto and attacks Sasuke and Sakura! Sasuke keeps a cool head, sees through the ruse and fights off the sly Rain ninja. But without a moment to rest, a creepy shadow descends upon them… Who is this new enemy?!

The fear of death draws near...!

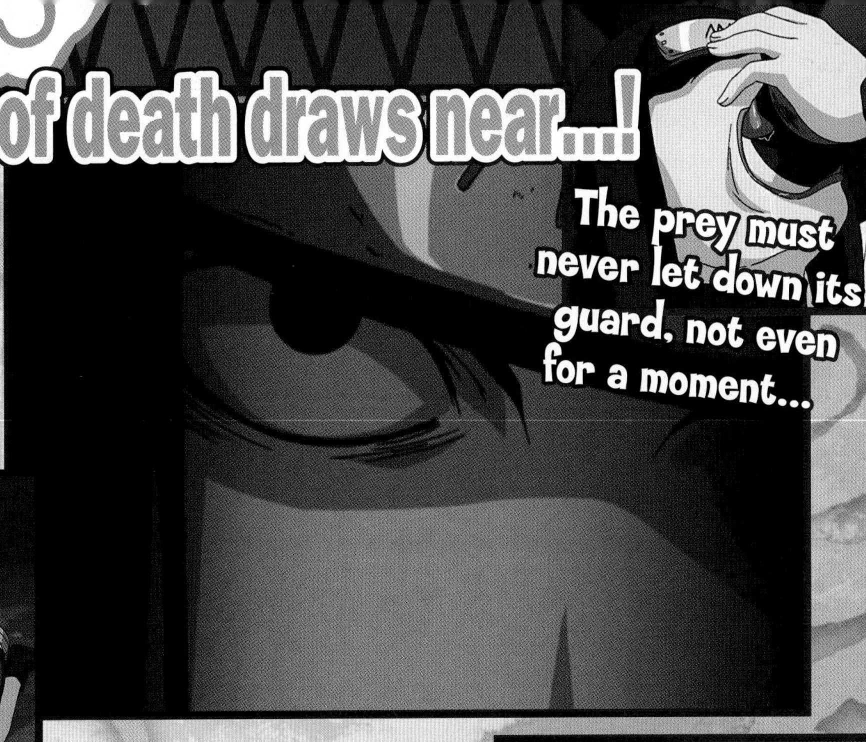

The prey must never let down its guard, not even for a moment...

Sasuke and Sakura are overcome by a sinister power that threatens to rip them apart! Do they have any chance of victory?

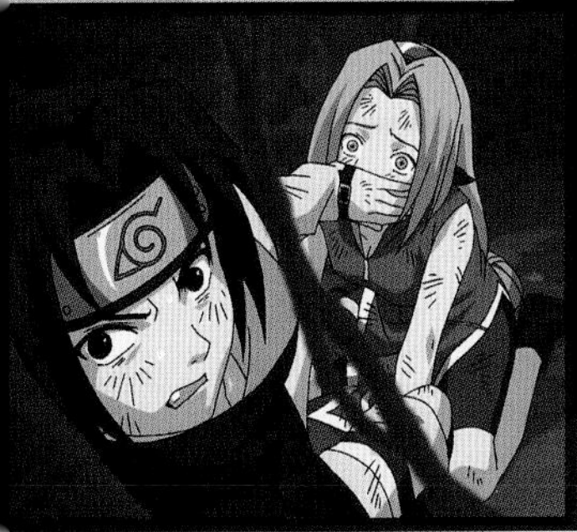

The mysterious Grass ninja's true identity is...

Anko has the same curse mark as Sasuke?! What happened in Anko's past...?!

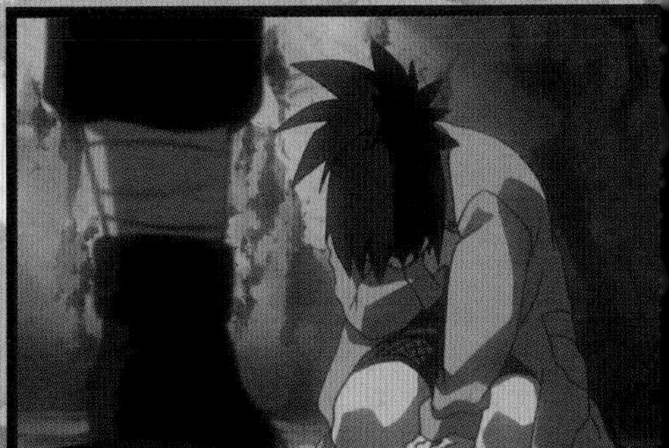

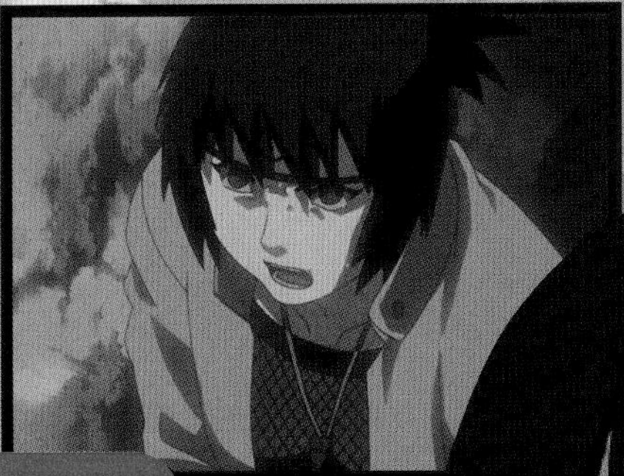

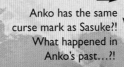

Spurred to action by Sakura's screams and Naruto's indignant rage, Sasuke fights valiantly against the Grass ninja. But the malicious ninja leaves a horrible curse mark on Sasuke's neck as a "parting gift!" Before slithering away, the evil impostor reveals his true identity: he is Orochimaru, once one of the Sannin—the legendary three ninja of the Hidden Leaf Village! But what does he want?!

A shiver runs through the Hidden Leaf Village as Orochimaru reemerges!

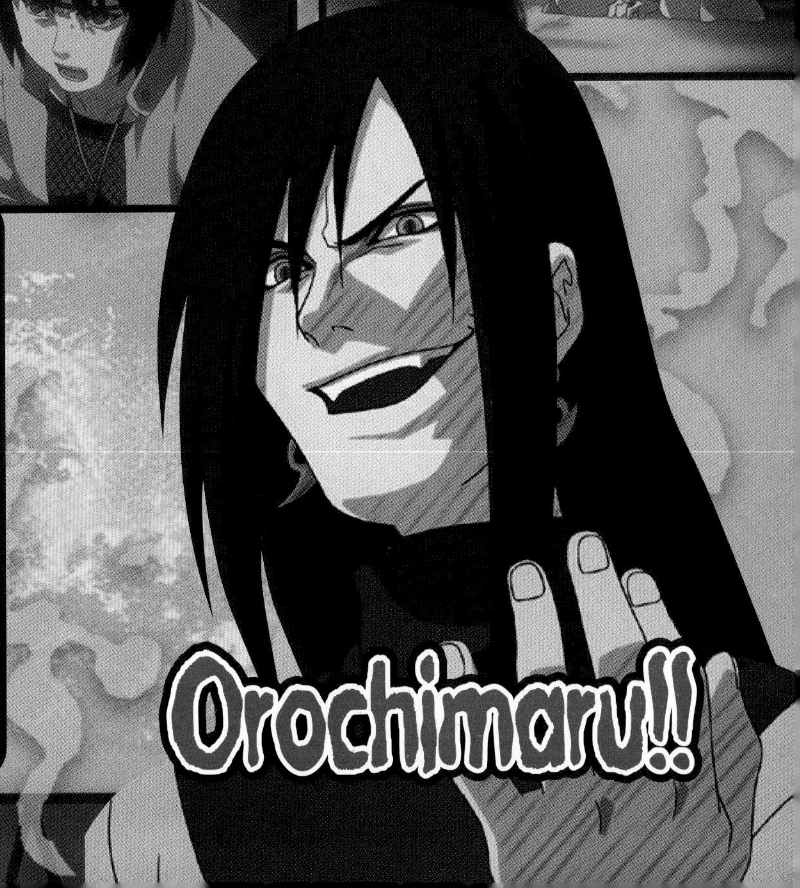

Orochimaru!!

ASSASSINS AMBUSH SAKURA!

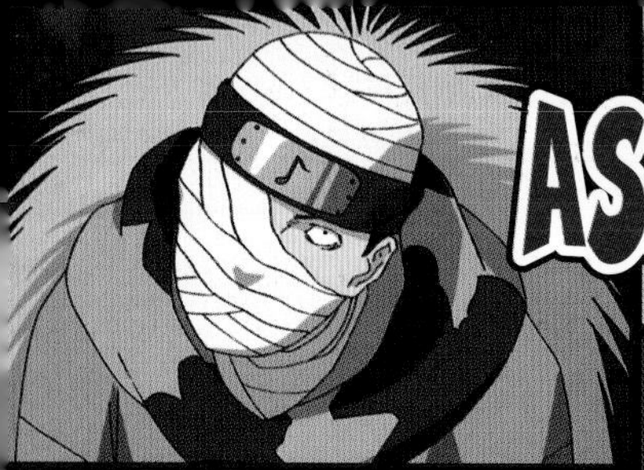

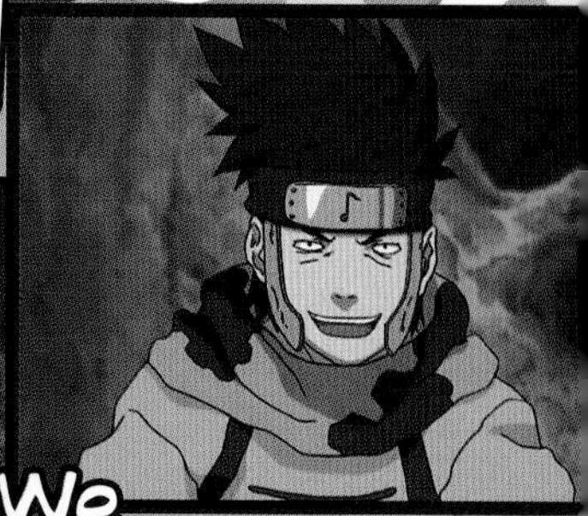

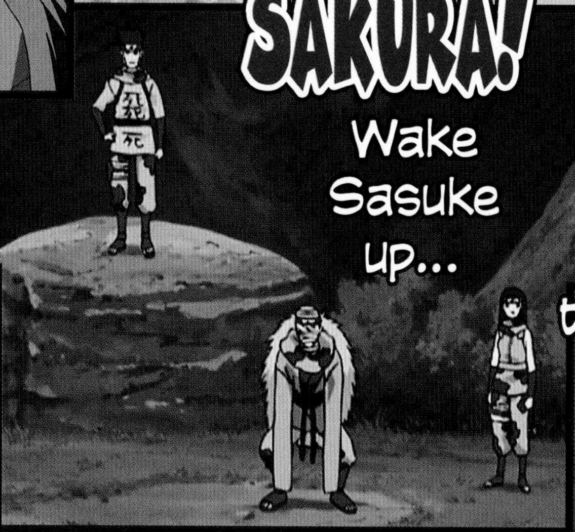

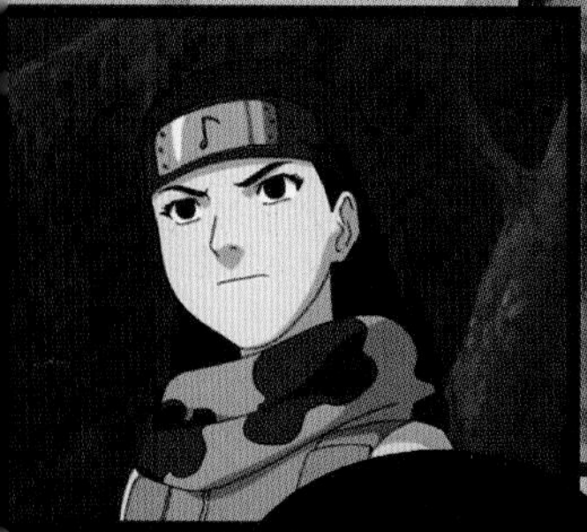

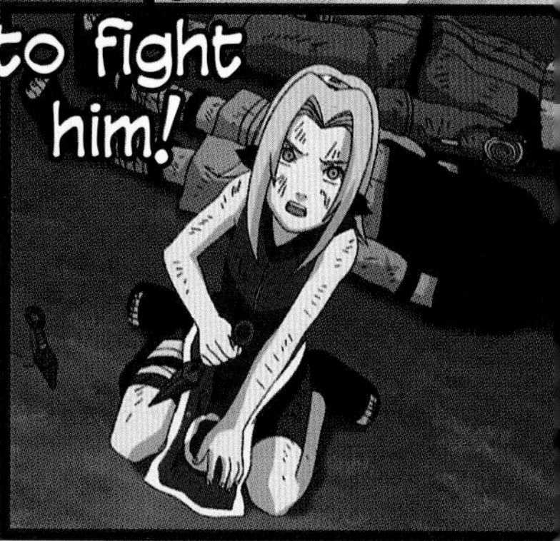

Wake Sasuke up...

We want to fight him!

Orochimaru has sent a team of his Sound ninja followers...and they're under orders to kill Sasuke!

The hurricane of Hidden Leaf makes a dashing entrance!

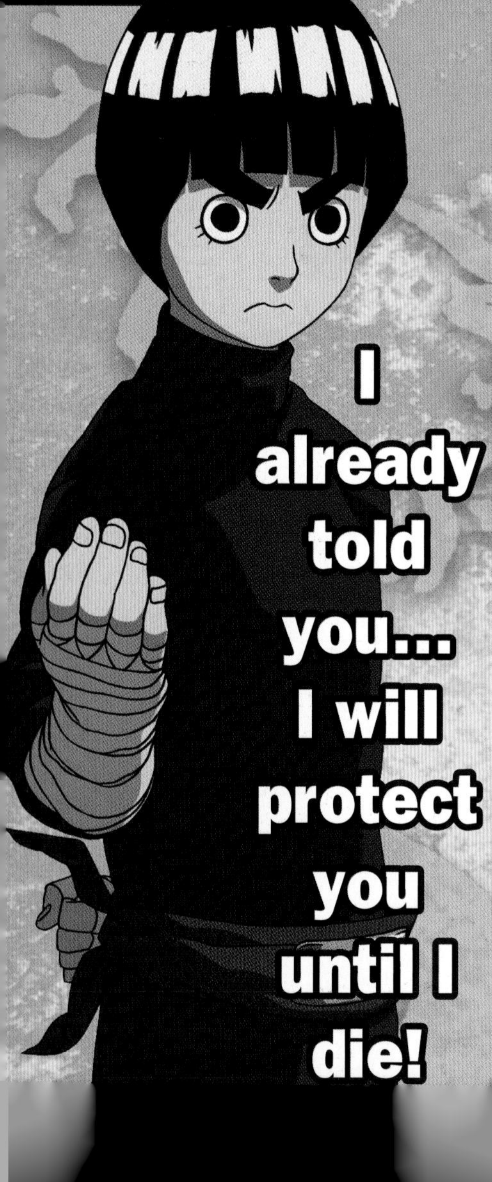

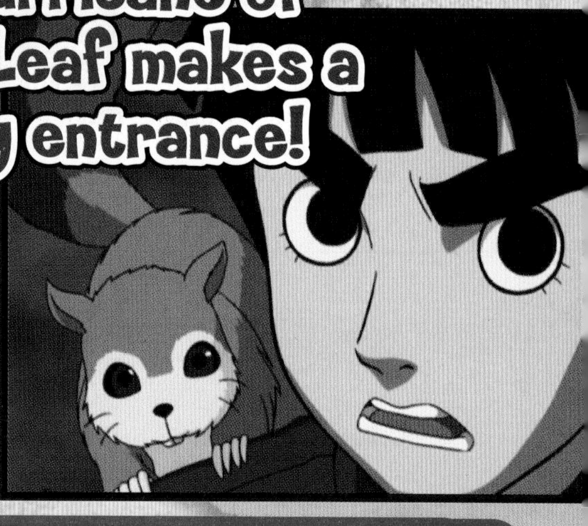

I already told you... I will protect you until I die!

"I will always appear, anytime and anywhere that you're in trouble, Sakura!" Lee is utterly serious!

After suffering grave injuries in battling with Orochimaru, Naruto and Sasuke lie unconscious and helpless on the forest floor. Sakura, now standing alone as sole defender of her squad, comes under attack by the vicious Sound ninja! In the intense standoff, Sakura realizes how inadequate she is as a fighter...but in her moment of utter panic, Lee arrives to save the day, like a ray of light through her clouds of despair!

Lee shows up in the nick of time!

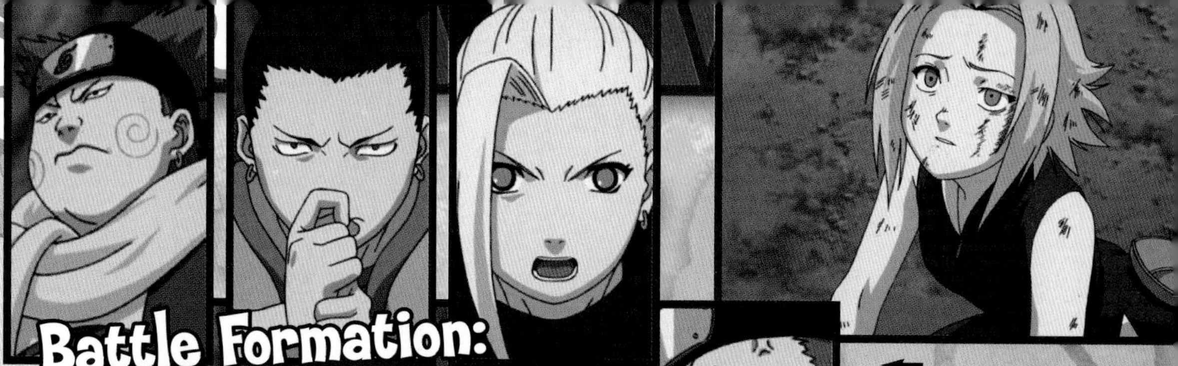

Battle Formation: Ino-Shika-Cho!

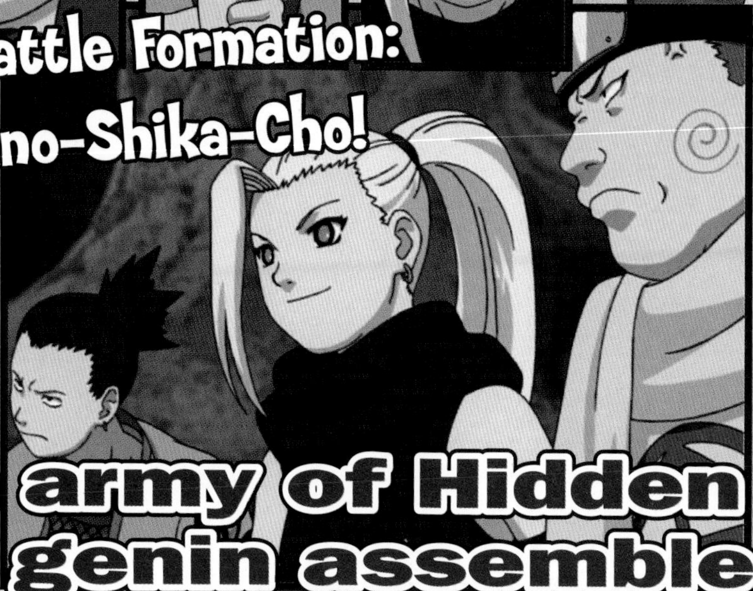

Despite being rivals, they can't hang back and allow other shinobi from their village to be bullied… or killed!

An army of Hidden Leaf genin assembles!

Lee and Sakura are both battered and bruised from fighting with the Sound ninja. Ino's squad, who had been watching from the bushes, suddenly bursts into the open! Lee's teammates Neji and Tenten also join the fray, and the tide of battle begins to turn. But then, a strange force comes over Sasuke…

The Hidden Leaf ninja gather to rally behind their own!

Neji, the top genin in the Hidden Leaf Village, rushes to defend his hometown… and to get revenge on the Sound ninja who wounded his comrades!

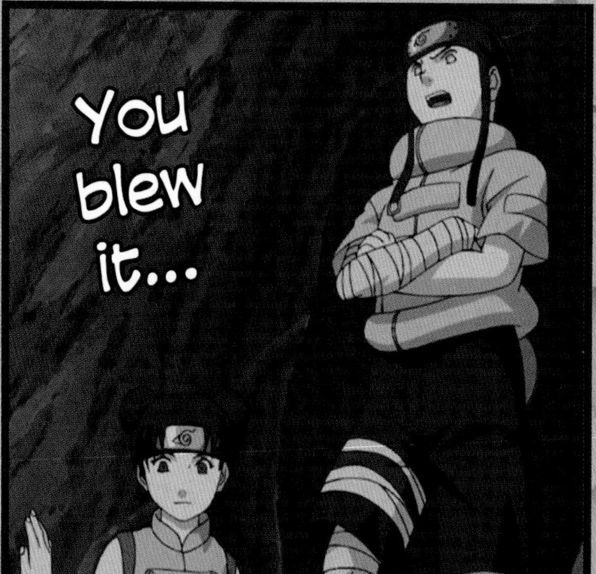
You blew it…

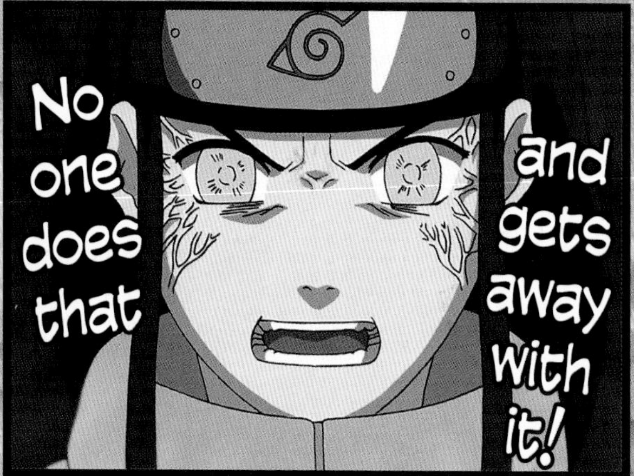
No one does that
and gets away with it!

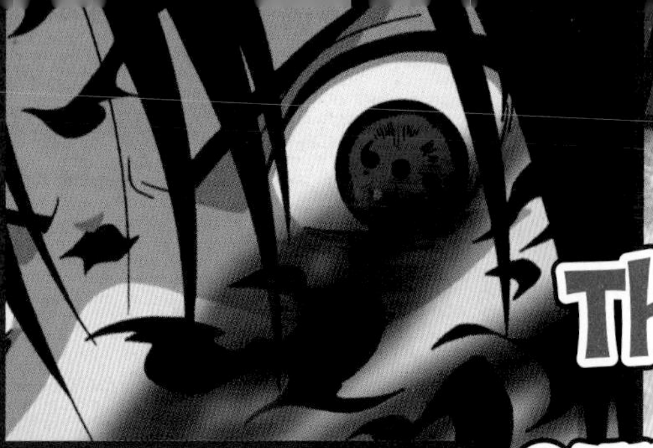

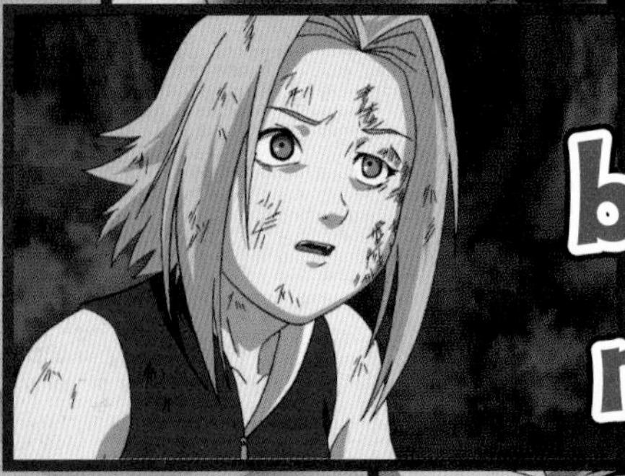

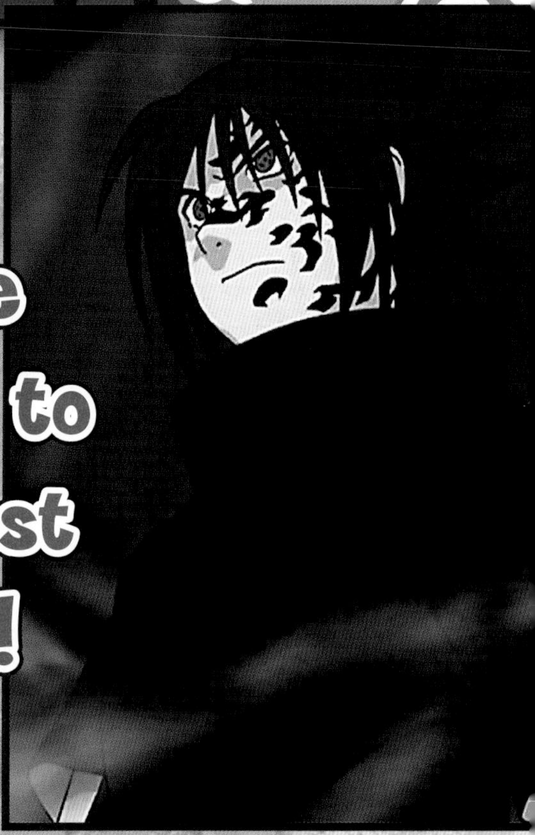

The curse begins to manifest itself!

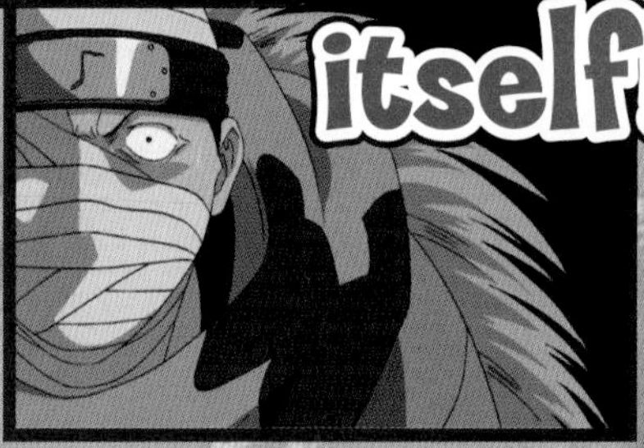

"I've never felt better…" Sasuke overflows with a strange, enormous chakra. Is this an effect of the curse mark?!

His lip curled with a sinister smile, Sasuke attacks with relentless force and merciless precision. He seems like a completely different person…

As Sasuke regains consciousness, the ominous curse marks spread across his body, signifying that he has surrendered himself to the monstrous power given to him by Orochimaru. He is filled with an enormous chakra that enables him to overwhelm the Sound ninja, but this gift carries a bitter price: Sasuke's soul starts to corrode with the power of limitless cruelty…

Everyone is taken aback as Sasuke rages with the power of the curse mark!

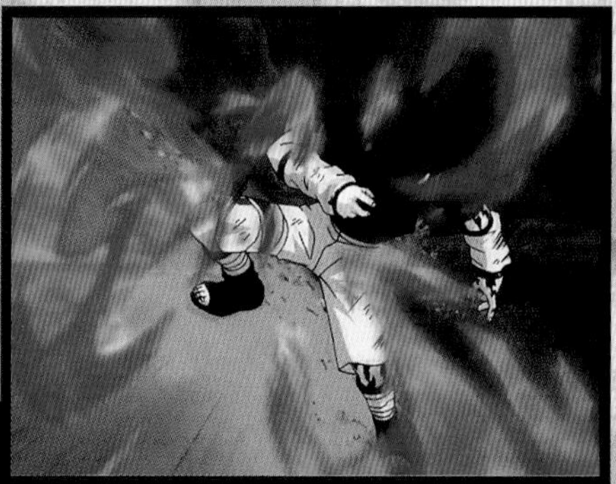

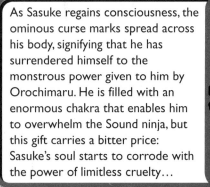

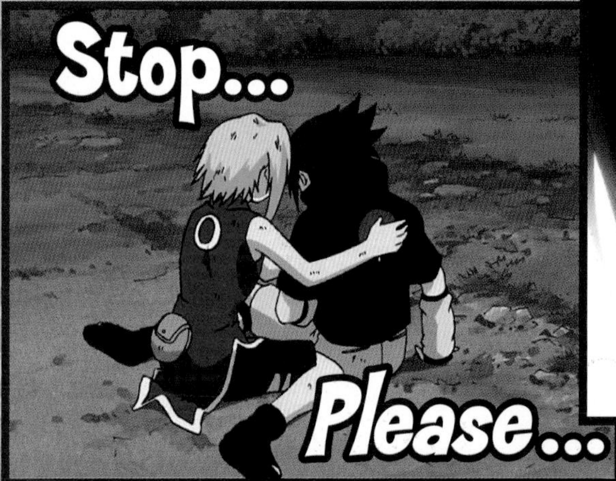
Stop…
Please…

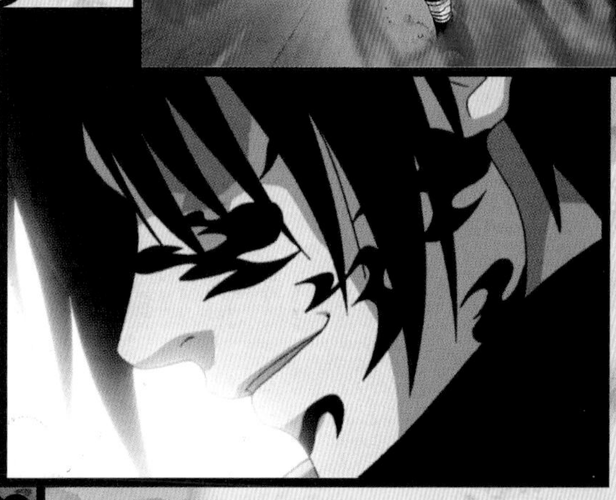

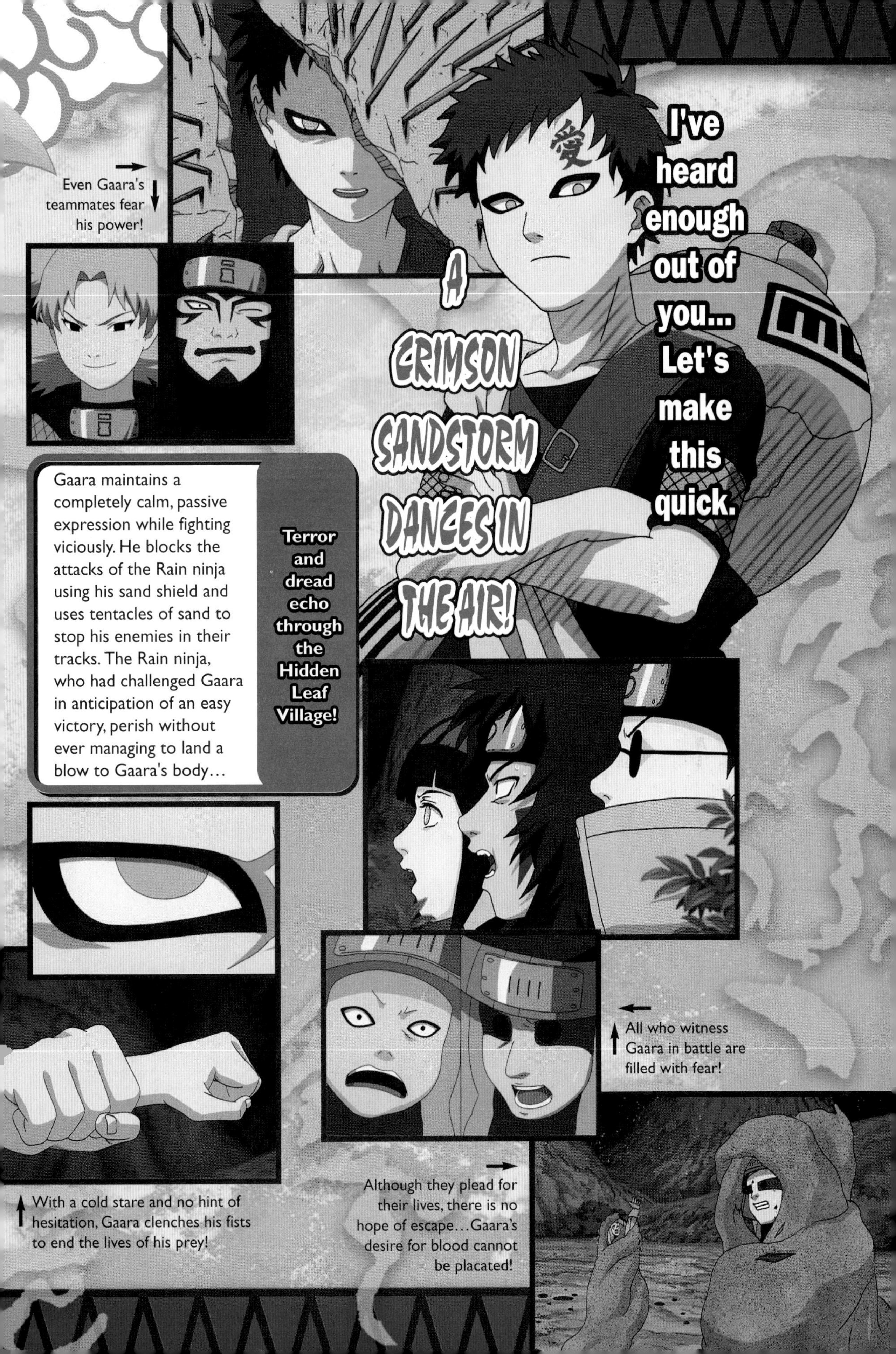
Even Gaara's teammates fear his power!
A Crimson Sandstorm Dances in the Air!
I've heard enough out of you... Let's make this quick.
Gaara maintains a completely calm, passive expression while fighting viciously. He blocks the attacks of the Rain ninja using his sand shield and uses tentacles of sand to stop his enemies in their tracks. The Rain ninja, who had challenged Gaara in anticipation of an easy victory, perish without ever managing to land a blow to Gaara's body…
Terror and dread echo through the Hidden Leaf Village!
All who witness Gaara in battle are filled with fear!
With a cold stare and no hint of hesitation, Gaara clenches his fists to end the lives of his prey!
Although they plead for their lives, there is no hope of escape…Gaara's desire for blood cannot be placated!

Naruto charges headlong at the mysterious illusions, but his fists just slice through air!

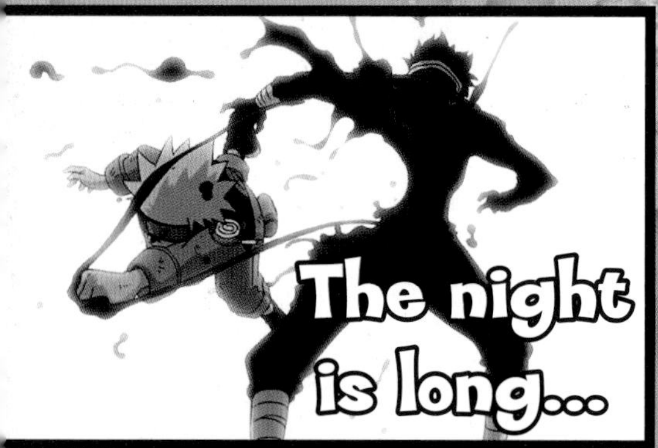
The night is long...

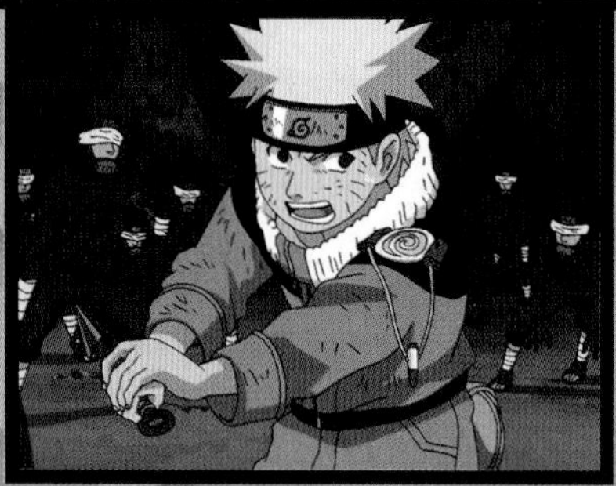

The illusions continue to emerge from the shadows... How do you fight an enemy when your attacks have no effect?!

Naruto and his squad are snared in a cunning trap!

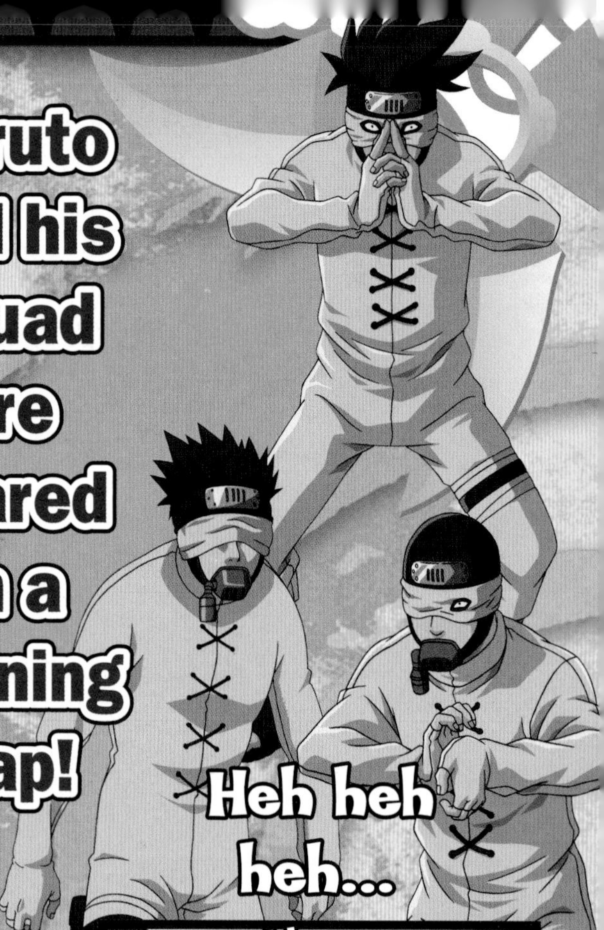
Heh heh heh...

Just when it seems like Naruto's crew is out of options, the real bodies of the Rain ninja are finally revealed!

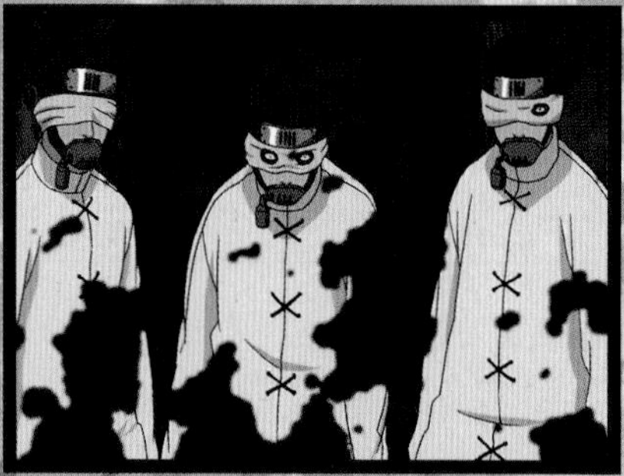

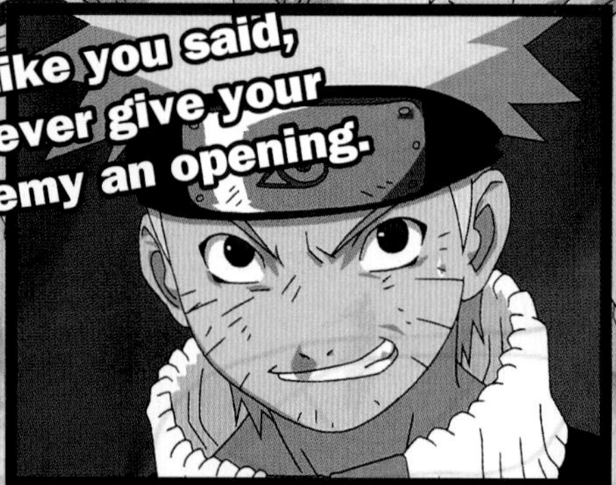
Like you said, never give your enemy an opening.

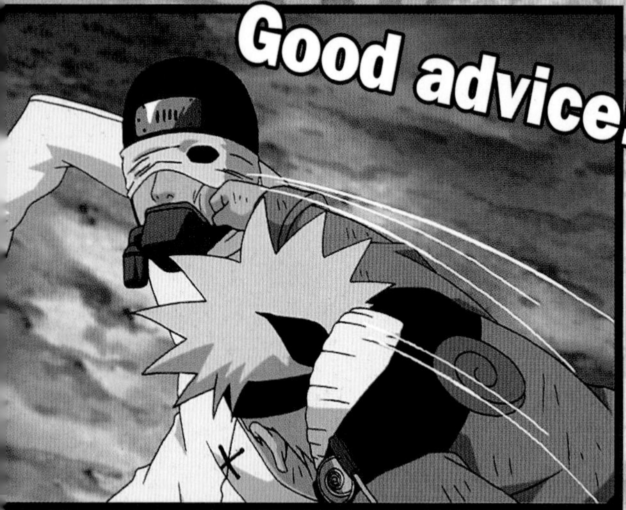
Good advice!

Still seeking a Heaven Scroll, Naruto and his squad head toward the tower in the center of the forest, but they get caught in the Rain ninja trap! Exhausted after defending themselves against the seemingly insurmountable attack, Naruto and his teammates appear to have reached the limits of their strength. But they manage to execute an elaborate plan...

No move can injure these shadowy, squirming illusions!

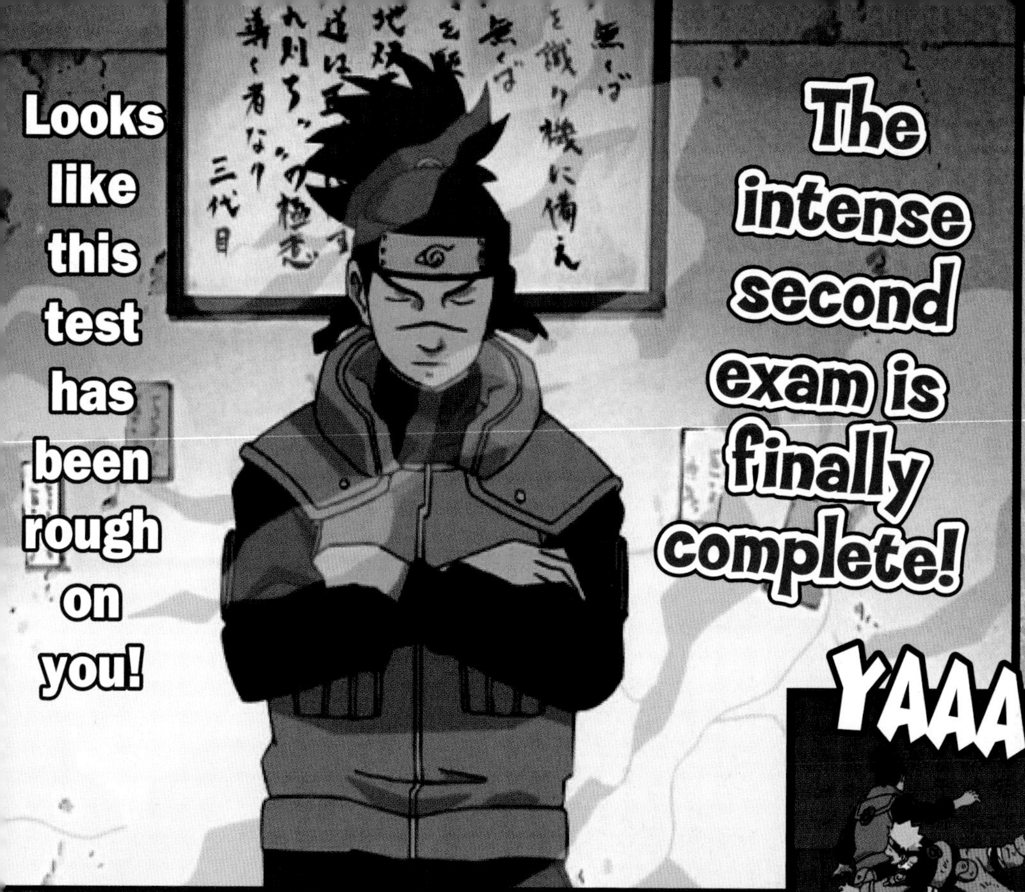

Looks like this test has been rough on you!

The intense second exam is finally complete!

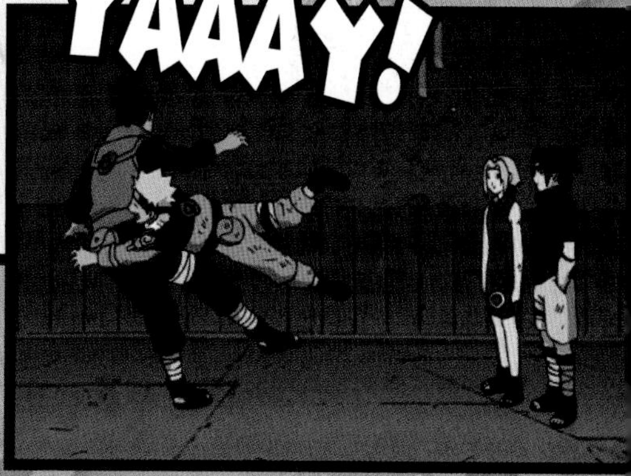
YAAAY!

Once the scrolls are opened, a summoning jutsu prompts Iruka to appear! Iruka acts as a messenger to greet Naruto and his squad and give them the good news: They've passed the second exam!

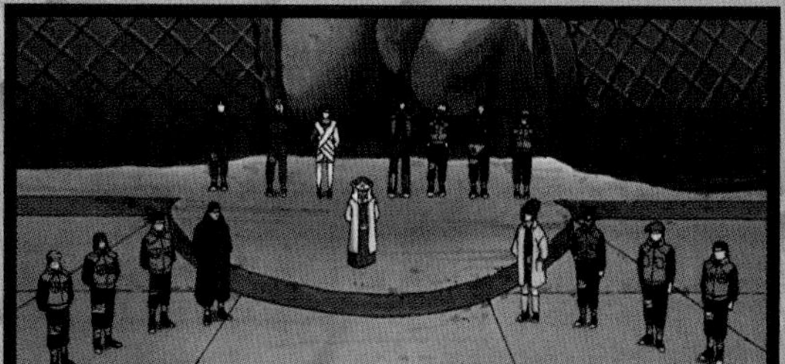

The ninja who passed the second test learn the true purpose of the Chunin Exam. As they weigh the Hokage's words, the third phase of the exam begins!

Naruto, Sakura and Sasuke arrive at the tower, and Iruka shows up to inform them that they have successfully completed the second exam. They are bewildered but joyful…after five days of staring death in the face, it's a relief to put the test behind them!

What awaits Naruto and his squad as they finish the test?!

What does the future hold for these ninja as they proceed to the third exam...and beyond?!

Part Two

Anbu Black Ops Unit Special Report

Sasuke Uchiha

Sasuke has the highest level of ability among this year's graduates from the Ninja Academy. We examine the extent of his true power and explore his troubling fate…

Report 1

The venerable Uchiha Clan is endowed with formidable talents!

Sasuke is one of the only surviving members of the Uchiha Clan, all of whose descendants possess advanced combat skills. Sasuke's Uchiha blood is surely part of the reason he graduated at the head of his Ninja Academy class. His obvious potential has quickly distinguished him from his peers.

Because of his famous name and his remarkable strength, the jonin of the village regard Sasuke with interest. He is also popular among the female students…

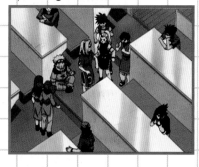

Sasuke Uchiha…? He's the guy from the Uchiha Clan who's inherited the Sharingan. I believe his power had not yet awakened during his Ninja Academy years. If the rumor is true that his abilities have now developed fully, I'd like a chance to fight him.

Testimony

Neji Hyuga

Report 2

The power that flows in the Uchiha blood…the Sharingan!

The Sharingan combines the powers of psychic perception, hypnosis and jutsu replication. Sasuke appears to have inherited these special powers, which only arise in select members of the Uchiha Clan.

Sasuke's power first awakened during the battle in the Land of Waves. Since then, he has been able to activate it at will and his combat skills have advanced significantly.

It is said that he has the power to anticipate his opponents' movements and see through any jutsu in an instant.

The effects of his own jutsu increase dramatically when used in tandem with the Sharingan.

Sasuke's powers are genuinely impressive. His abilities in taijutsu and ninjutsu are far above his peers, and despite his young age, he has full mastery of the Sharingan. But there is an air of impatience about him because of his passionate desire for strength. I hope it does not become troublesome…

Testimony

Hokage

Report 3

The avenger who burns with hatred!

The Uchiha Clan was tragically destroyed in a single night, leaving behind Sasuke and his older brother. Although the details are unclear, Sasuke seems to be haunted by a hidden secret of the atrocity...

These gruesome images are carved into his mind...

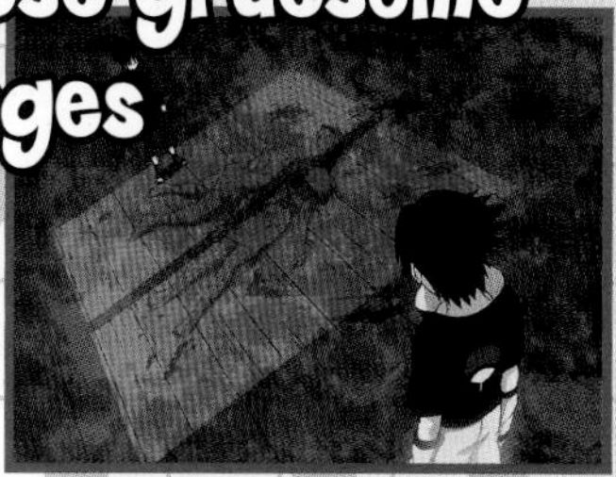

← When he was still a boy, his parents and his clan were annihilated.

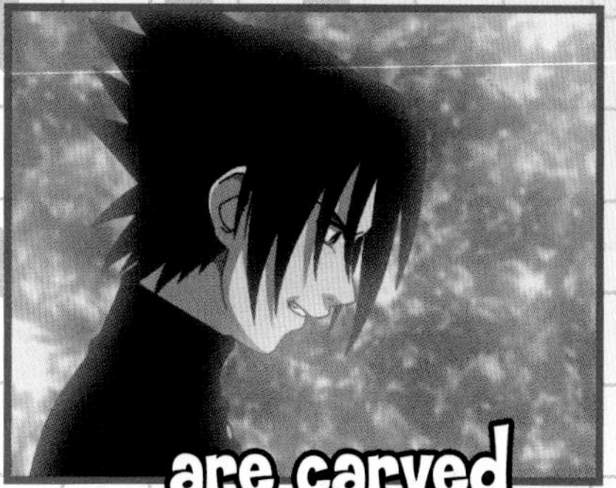

→ Those horrifying moments seem to have sparked Sasuke's lust for strength, and the grisly memories that eat away at his soul also fuel the fire of his obsession.

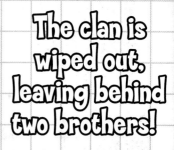

To defeat my brother, I must survive... I cannot allow myself to die!

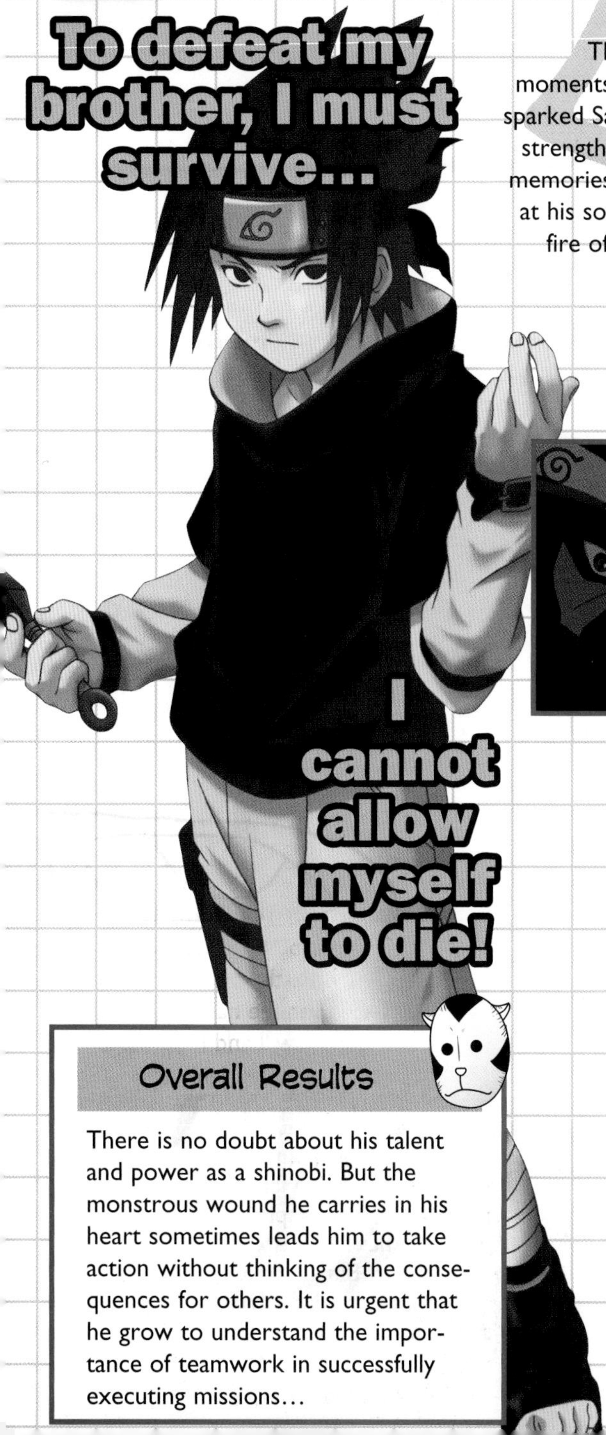

The clan is wiped out, leaving behind two brothers!

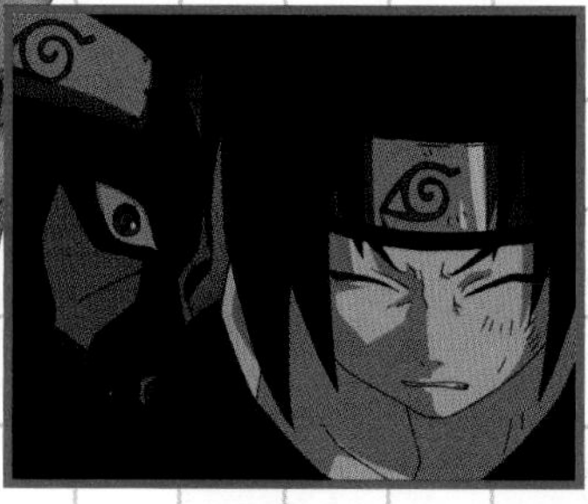

Orochimaru's curse mark is all too compatible with Sasuke's wicked thirst for revenge...

In the Forest of Death, Orochimaru infects Sasuke with his curse mark. As the effects of the curse take hold, a vicious chakra overwhelms Sasuke whenever he uses the Sharingan, and ominous black blotches spread all over his body...

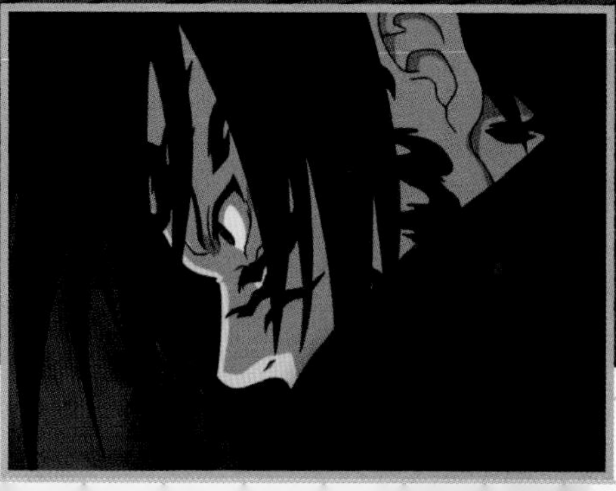

Overall Results

There is no doubt about his talent and power as a shinobi. But the monstrous wound he carries in his heart sometimes leads him to take action without thinking of the consequences for others. It is urgent that he grow to understand the importance of teamwork in successfully executing missions...

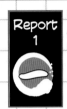

Anbu Black Ops Unit Special Report

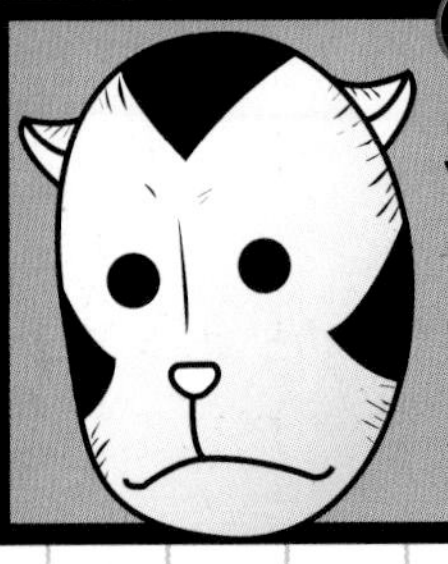

Sakura Haruno

Starting in her Ninja Academy days, Sakura established herself as one to watch because of her standout grades. How is she faring these days, now that she's a genin?

She is exceptionally knowledgeable, far beyond the genin level!

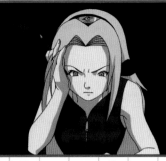

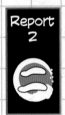

Report 1

Despite being weak in taijutsu, Sakura is clearly the most intelligent of the Hidden Leaf genin!

Although Sakura is a bit lacking in physical strength, she has an incredibly sharp mind. It would be advisable to keep an eye on her excellent analytical abilities. She can quickly assess her enemy's strengths and grasp the details of any situation. Under the guidance of a top-notch instructor, Sakura has the potential for immeasurable growth.

She masters the chakra control training exercise without breaking a sweat.

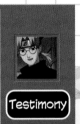

Testimony

Kabuto Yakushi

According to the information on my Ninja Info Card, Sakura is much smarter than any of the other genin in the Leaf Village. It seems she correctly solved every question on the written portion of the Chunin Exam, which is supposed to be basically impossible for a genin. Apparently she has something of a complex about her own strength (or lack thereof), but in my opinion, an amazing mind is perhaps the most valuable ninja weapon!

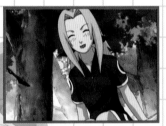

Report 2

Sasuke comes first, no matter what... Sakura is more devoted to her crush than to her ninja training!

Sakura is completely infatuated with her teammate Sasuke. This is not an admirable quality in a shinobi. But because her desire to impress Sasuke inspires her toward greater achievement, it actually seems to be a source of strength...

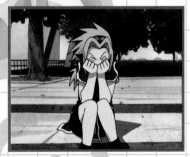

When Sasuke is involved, Sakura has a tendency to lose sight of everything else. One can't help but feel uneasy about her ability to collaborate effectively with her teammates.

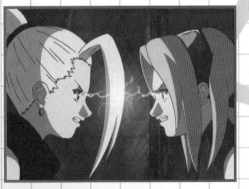

Ino Yamanaka is her rival for Sasuke's affections. If only Sakura would channel this passion into energy for her missions...

Testimony

Ino Yamanaka

Argh! How unfair is it that Billboard Brow is on the same squad as Sasuke?! I'm prettier, I'm better at ninjutsu...and basically I'm just way more Sasuke's type than she is. I guess Sakura's been working pretty hard lately...in her own pathetic way. But Sasuke is, was and forever shall be mine!!

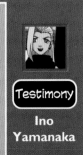

Report 3

"Cha!" is the scream of her soul! Is there another Sakura within Sakura?!

There seems to be another personality called "Inner Sakura" that exists inside Sakura but never shows outwardly, no matter the circumstances. We deduce that this unique phenomenon results from Sakura's dual nature as someone who is girly and demure but who possesses wild, raw emotions.

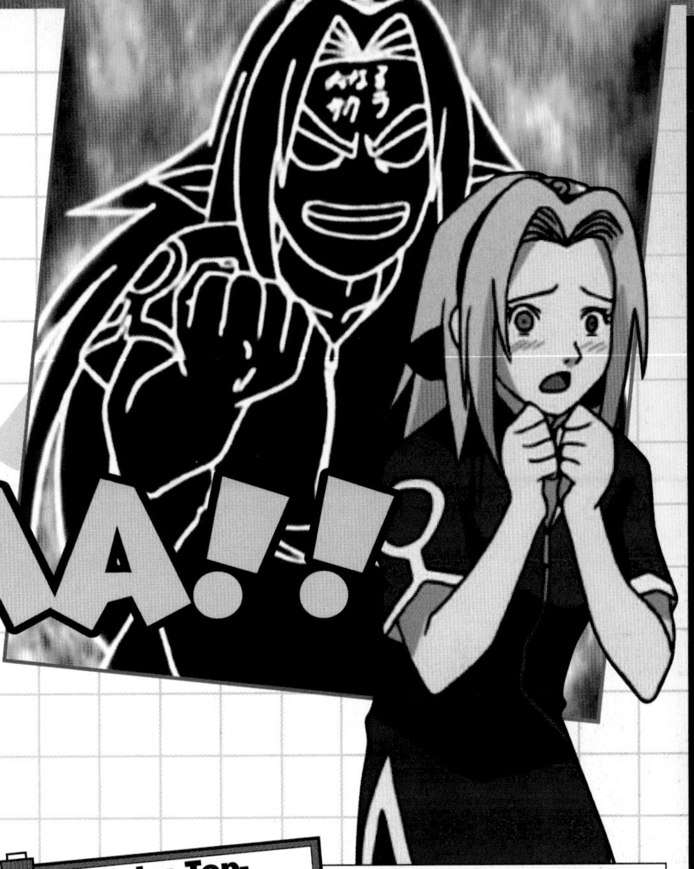
CHAAA!!

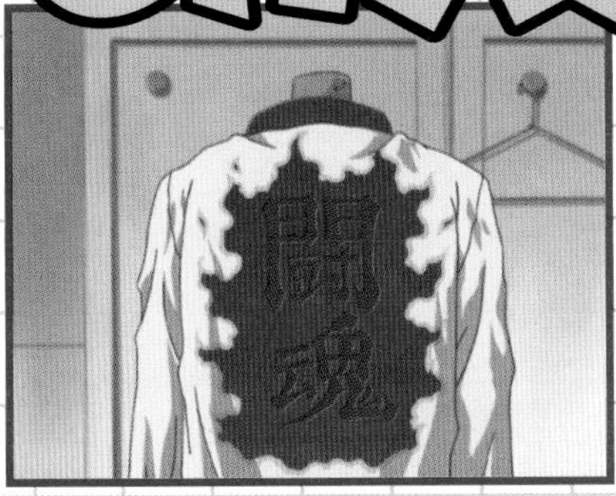

One clue to Inner Sakura's personality is evident in the characters printed on a robe hanging in Sakura's room: they say "tokon" (fighting spirit).

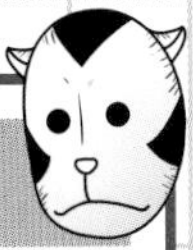

Overall Results

Sakura's keen intellect is worthy of praise, but her overwhelming affection for Sasuke betrays a softness unbecoming of a shinobi. She showed real tenacity and resolve while battling the Sound ninja in the Forest of Death; her goal now must be to seize upon and nurture those qualities so they become intrinsic to the real Sakura...not just the Inner Sakura.

Anbu Top-Secret Data

Inner Sakura Eyewitness Account!

Ep. 1:	0 times	Ep. 20:	4 times
Ep. 2:	0 times	Ep. 21:	0 times
Ep. 3:	5 times	Ep. 22:	0 times
Ep. 4:	2 times	Ep. 23:	0 times
Ep. 5:	3 times	Ep. 24:	0 times
Ep. 6:	1 time	Ep. 25:	0 times
Ep. 7:	0 times	Ep. 26:	2 times
Ep. 8:	0 times	Ep. 27:	1 time
Ep. 9:	0 times	Ep. 28:	0 times
Ep. 10:	0 times	Ep. 29:	0 times
Ep. 11:	0 times	Ep. 30:	0 times
Ep. 12:	2 times	Ep. 31:	0 times
Ep. 13:	1 time	Ep. 32:	0 times
Ep. 14:	0 times	Ep. 33:	0 times
Ep. 15:	0 times	Ep. 34:	0 times
Ep. 16:	3 times	Ep. 35:	0 times
Ep. 17:	0 times	Ep. 36	1 time
Ep. 18:	0 times	Ep. 37:	1 time
Ep. 19:	0 times		

Through the conclusion of the second phase of the Chunin Selection Exams, Inner Sakura has been witnessed 26 times in all. Naturally, most of these appearances were linked to Sasuke.

Secret Shinobi Picture Album

Part Four

Shinobi Tools

Armor and weapons are the keys to a shinobi's life! They protect the body from attack and provide methods to strike the enemy. Our guide on this topic is ace student Sakura!

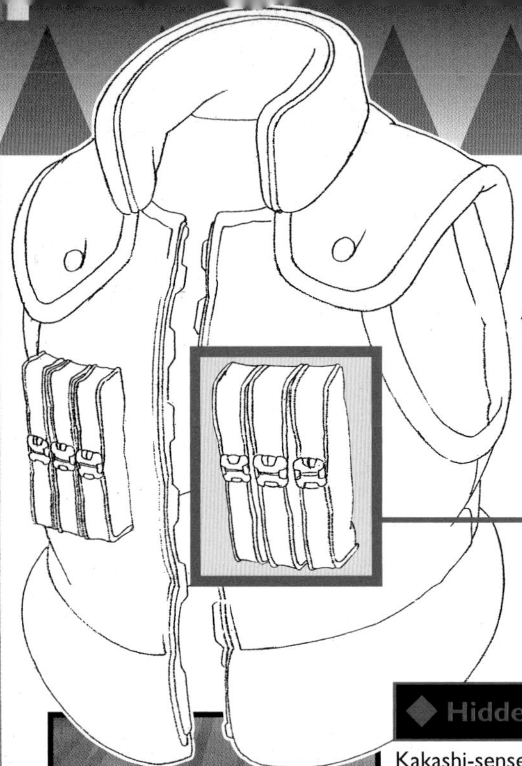

Protection: Protective gear is essential for preserving the life of a shinobi. Each piece is designed with flexibility, durability and convenience in mind!

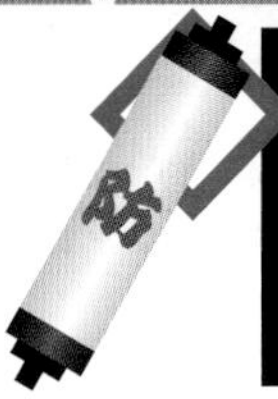

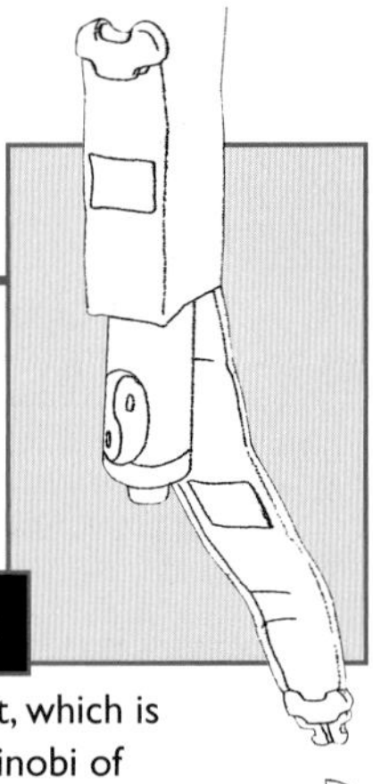

The scroll pouch is designed so it can be opened with one hand.

Hidden Leaf Vest

Kakashi-sensei wears this vest, which is standard equipment for all shinobi of chunin rank and above.

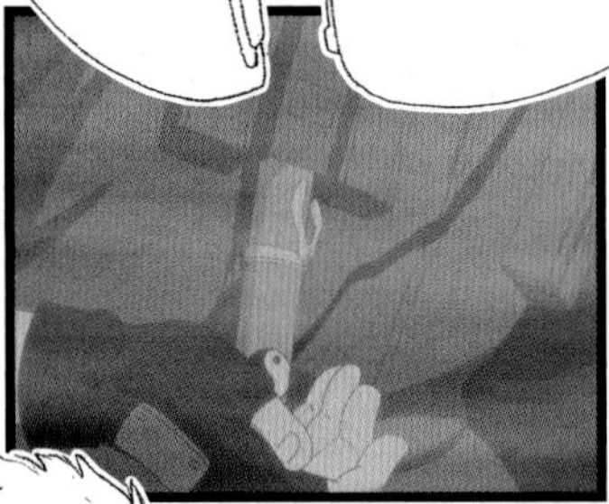

It's easy to pull out a scroll during battle without lowering your guard!

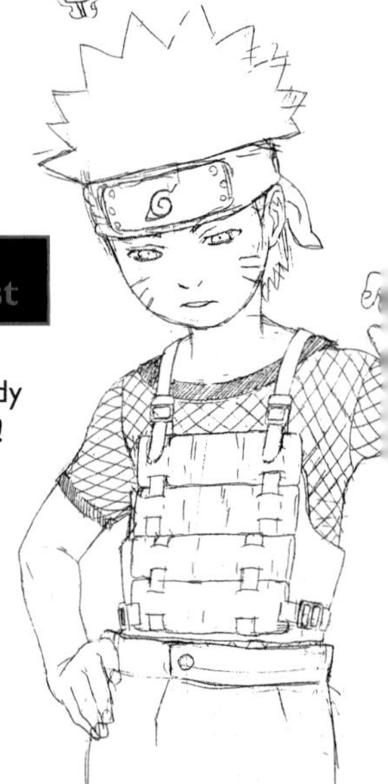

Chain mail + protective vest

This gear is worn under clothes to protect the body from any swords or kunai!

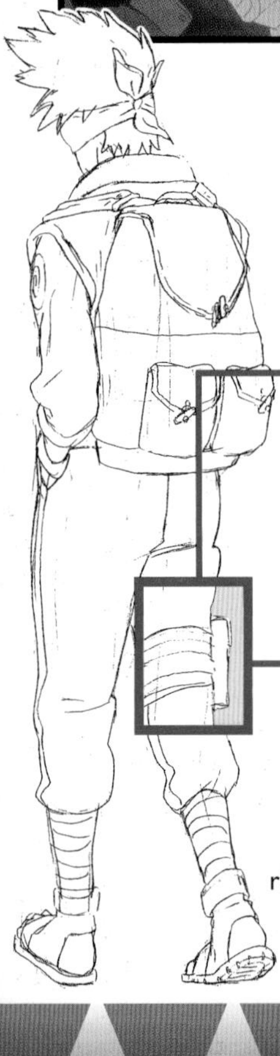

Shuriken Holster

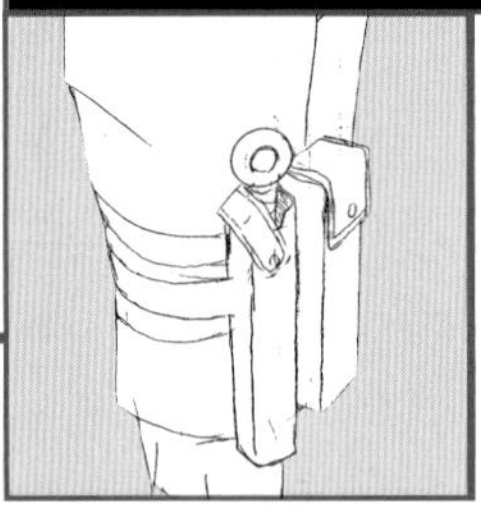

This is a case to store your shuriken and kunai. It's most commonly attached to the thigh.

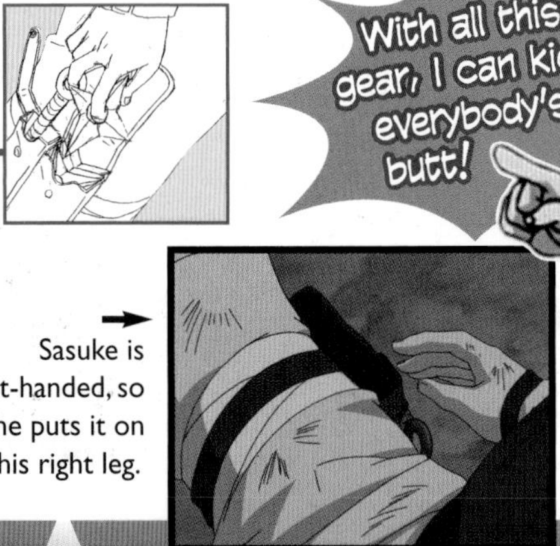

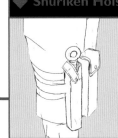

Sasuke is right-handed, so he puts it on his right leg.

Tour Guide: Sakura Haruno

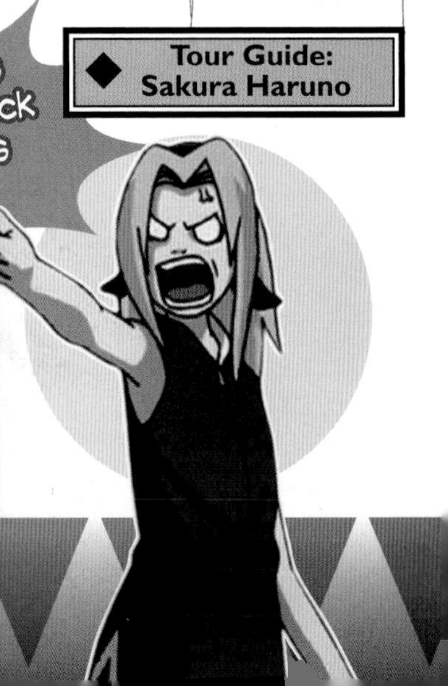
With all this gear, I can kick everybody's butt!

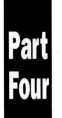

A Lesson From Beautiful Kunoichi Sakura ♥

Bonus Edition

♥ How to grip a weapon

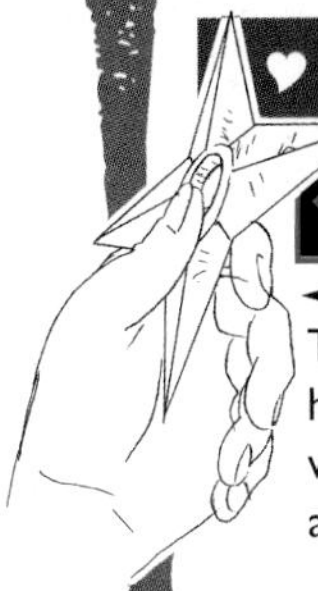

◆ Shuriken

← The trick is to hold it gently with your thumb and index finger.

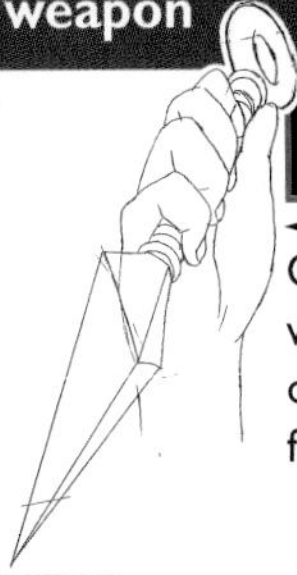

◆ Kunai

← Grip it tightly with the point of the blade facing down.

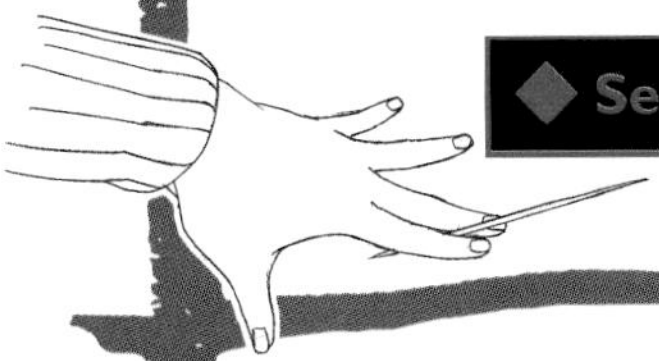

◆ Senbon

← Put it delicately between two fingers… it's quite difficult.

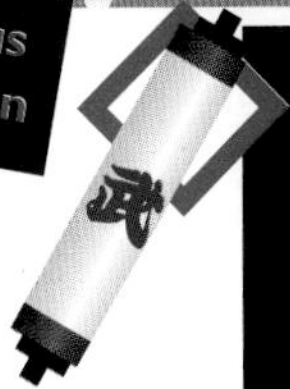

Weapons: Kunai and shuriken aren't a shinobi's only weapons. Arms come in an infinite variety of shapes and sizes. My weapon of choice is, of course, my ravishingly good looks. ♥

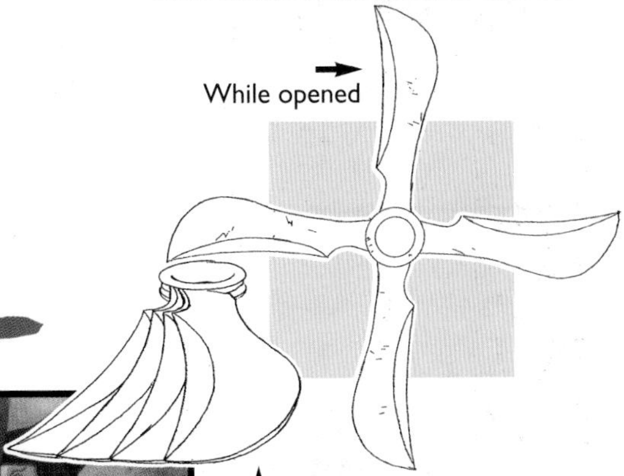

While opened →

↑ While closed

◆ Demon Wind Shuriken

This is a large shuriken—nearly a meter in diameter—that is collapsible. It's Sasuke's favorite weapon!

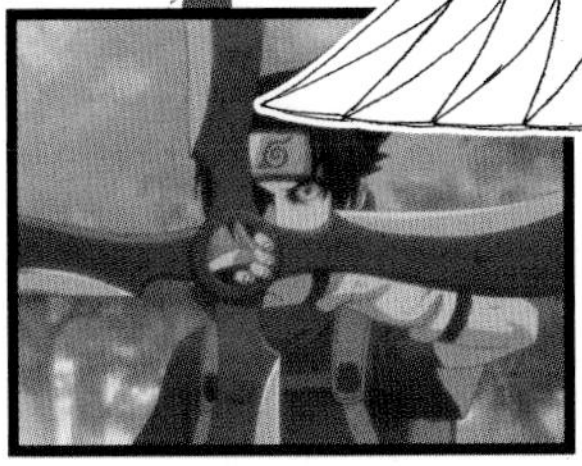

↑ This weapon saved Kakashi-sensei in the Land of Waves!

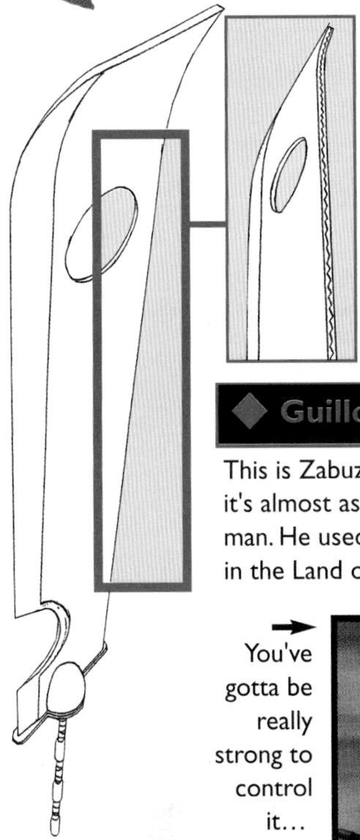

← It weighs about 30 kg (66 lbs.)! Its destructive force would even mow down a large tree!

◆ Guillotine Sword

This is Zabuza's huge sword—it's almost as tall as a full-grown man. He used it when we fought in the Land of Waves.

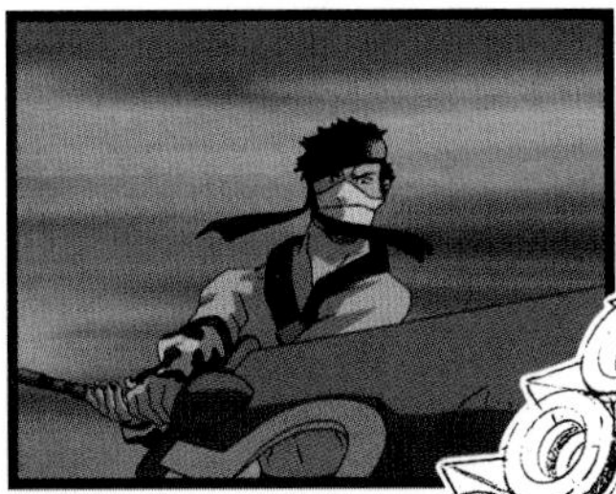

You've gotta be really strong to control it… →

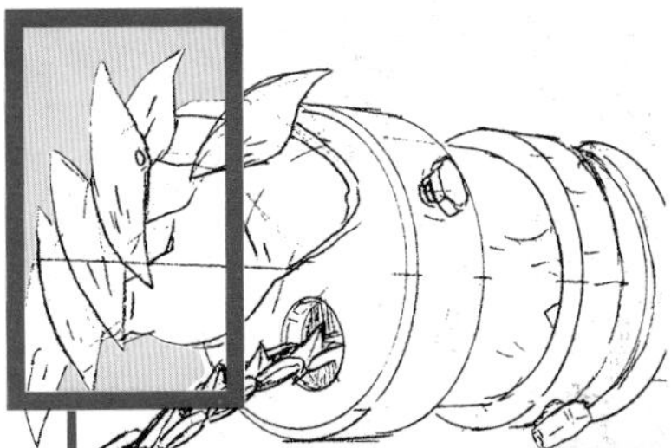

◆ Demon Brothers' Poison Claws + Bladed Chains

This is the special weapon of the Demon Brothers from the Hidden Mist Village. It's a dangerous device that shoots out chains with razor-like blades.

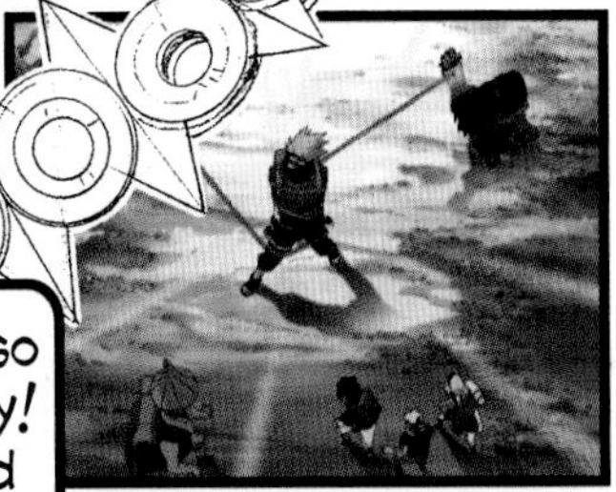

← Any enemy caught in the chains is sliced to bits by the blades!

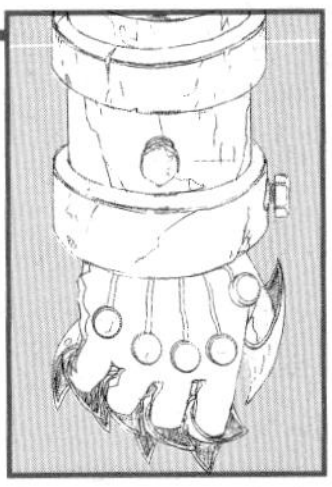

↑ The claws are smeared with poison. Terrifying!

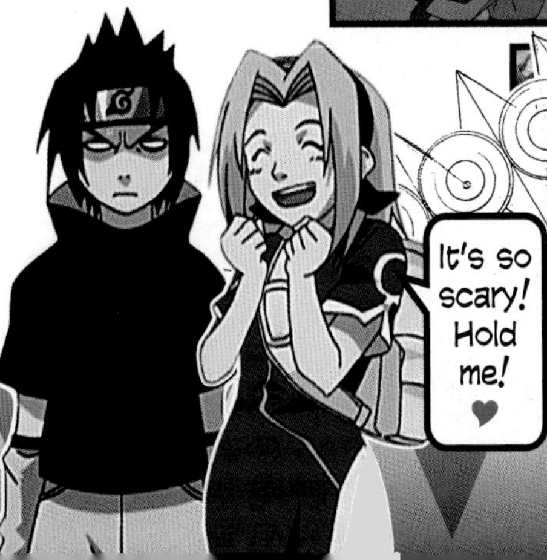
It's so scary! Hold me! ♥

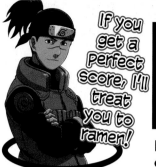

If you get a perfect score, I'll treat you to ramen!

Chunin Exam Study Guide

It's vital for all shinobi to be well educated! If you can solve all the problems on this practice test, you're sure to pass the Chunin Exam!

(Part 1) Read the paragraph below and answer the questions that follow.

Shinobi fighting skills can be divided into three basic categories: ninjutsu, taijutsu and (A). Ninjutsu is a special power that can be used by building up chakra inside the body, and can be identified according to attributes like (B) and Water Style. In addition, by (C) combining multiple ninjutsu, it is possible to create even more powerful jutsu. Taijutsu are attacks that use your own body, and the power of any taijutsu move largely depends on the user's stamina and level of training. In contrast to taijutsu, (A) is a type of jutsu that damages the opponent's mind using illusion.

Question 1. Choose the term that most appropriately fits the spaces marked (A) in the sentence.
(I) jujitsu, (II) genjutsu, (III) karate, (IV) ramenjutsu

Question 2. Choose the answers that fit the space marked (B) in the sentence (select all that apply).
(I) Fire Style, (II) Earth Style, (III) Futon Style, (IV) Sushi Style

Question 3. Related to the underlined portion (C), pick the answer that represents the combination of jutsu that result in the Harem Jutsu.
(I) Clone Jutsu + Sexy Jutsu, (II) Multi Shadow Clone Jutsu + Sexy Jutsu, (III) Expansion Jutsu + Sexy Jutsu, (IV) Shadow Possession Jutsu + Foxy Lady Jutsu

(Part 2) Answer the questions below by choosing the correct letter.

Question 1. Which grouping represents the names of the ninja villages that belong to the Five Great Nations?
(A) Leaf, Clouds, Rain, Sand, Stones
(B) Leaf, Mist, Waves, Rain, Sand
(C) Leaf, Mist, Clouds, Sand, Stones
(D) Sun, Shine, Rain, Water

Question 2. What is the other name for the 44th Battle Training Zone, where the second phase of the Chunin Exam was held?
(A) Forest of Death
(B) Forest of Fire
(C) Petrified Forest
(D) Forrest Gump

Question 3. Which scroll was Naruto's squad given at the beginning of the second stage of the Chunin Exam?
(A) Heaven Scroll
(B) Earth Scroll
(C) Dead Sea Scroll
(D) Rock 'n' Scroll

Question 4. According to Sasuke, he is...
(A) An avenger
(B) An adventurer
(C) An esteemed heir
(D) A criminal offender

Question 5. What is the jutsu that Orochimaru used to seal away the power of the Nine-Tailed Fox?
(A) Twin Snake Sacrifice Jutsu
(B) Five-Pronged Seal
(C) Elephant Seal Jutsu
(D) Tummy Tickling Jutsu

Question 6. What does Rock Lee call himself?
(A) The dark emperor who reigns over the Hidden Leaf Village
(B) The glowing angel who fell to earth and landed in the Hidden Leaf Village
(C) The handsome devil of the Hidden Leaf Village
(D) Brad Pitt of the Hidden Leaf Village

Question 7. What was Sakura's nickname during her childhood?
(A) Billboard Brow
(B) Forehead Supreme
(C) Baldy
(D) Brad Pitt of the Hidden Leaf Village

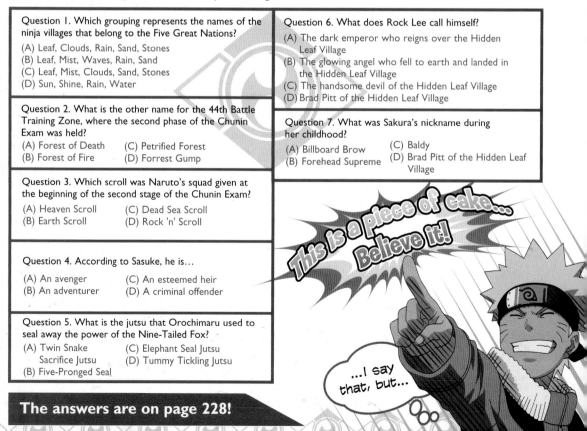

This is a piece of cake... Believe it!
...I say that, but...

The answers are on page 228!

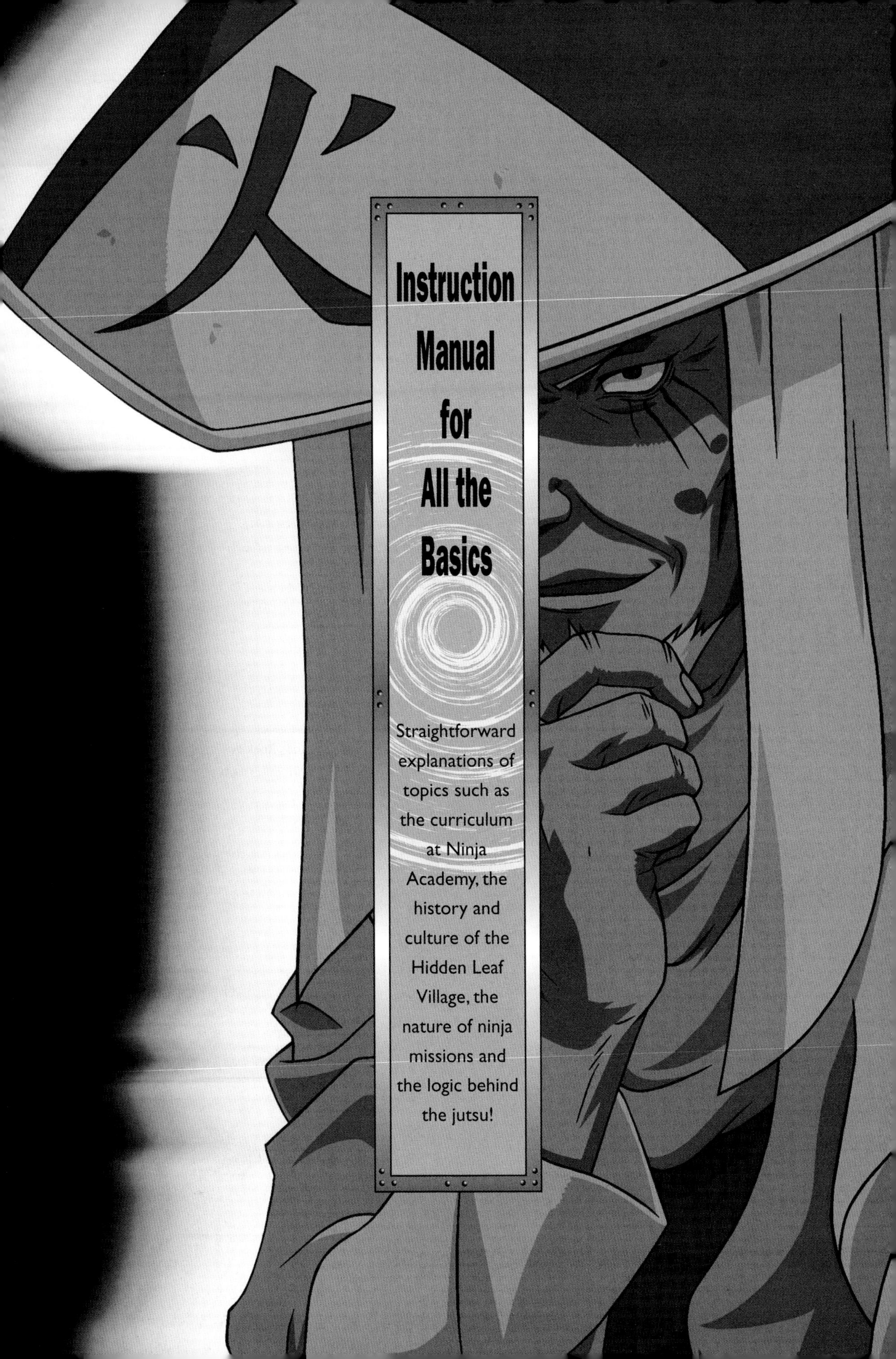

Instruction Manual for All the Basics

Straightforward explanations of topics such as the curriculum at Ninja Academy, the history and culture of the Hidden Leaf Village, the nature of ninja missions and the logic behind the jutsu!

The Village Hidden in the Leaves

Many other countries are also located on the same expansive continent as the Land of Fire. Among them are the countries known as the Five Great Nations, each of which are home to large shinobi villages.

Land of Earth
Village Hidden Among the Stones
Land of Lightning
Village Hidden in the Clouds
Land of Fire
Village Hidden in the Leaves
Land of Wind
Village Hidden in the Sand
Village Hidden in the Mist

This large hidden ninja village is located in the center of the Land of Fire.

Under the strong, authoritative command of its leader, the Hokage, the Hidden Leaf Village has become unified and prosperous. All of the military resources and strength of the Land of Fire are concentrated within the village, and many of its elite ninja are famous throughout the neighboring countries.

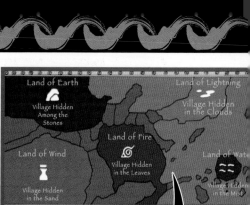

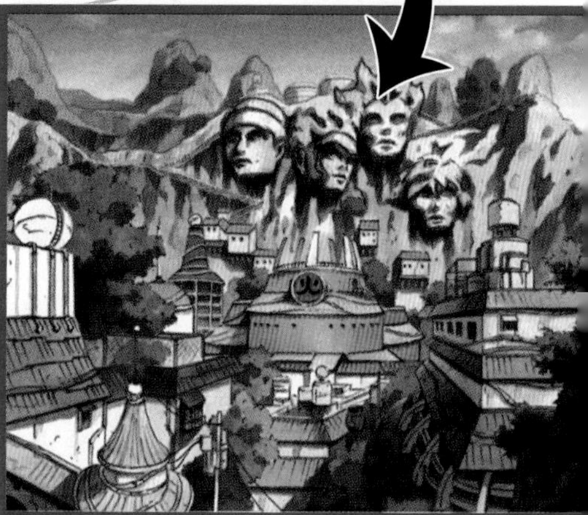

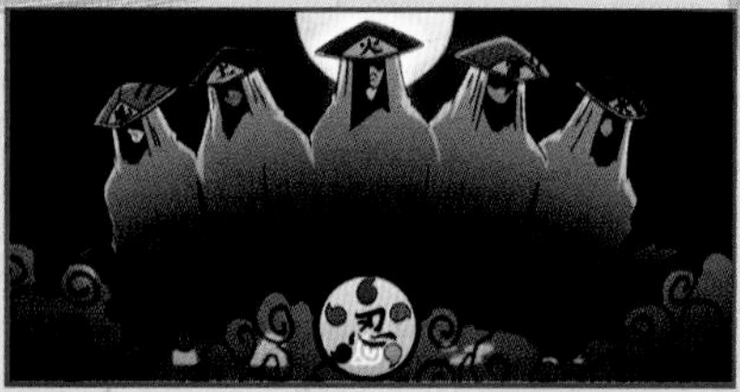

Located at the center of the Five Great Nations, the Hidden Leaf Village has benefited from open cultural exchange with the surrounding countries.

The Five Shadows—the Leaders of the Five Great Nations

The Five Kage or Shadows guide and rule over the tens of thousands of shinobi all over the world. It is no exaggeration to say that they are responsible for maintaining the equilibrium of the universe!

Country	Land of Fire	Land of Wind	Land of Water	Land of Lightning	Land of Earth
Hidden Village	Village Hidden in the Leaves	Village Hidden in the Sand	Village Hidden in the Mist	Village Hidden in the Clouds	Village Hidden Among the Stones
Village leader	Hokage	Kazekage	Mizukage	Raikage	Tsuchikage

The History of the Village Hidden in the Leaves

The Hidden Leaf Village was established about 60 years ago. It was founded when one gifted shinobi called a group of ninja together deep in a forest, away from civilian villages, and formed a unit. Early on, an overwhelming majority of the inhabitants were shinobi, but after the Ninja World War, the town began to diversify. Now there are many residents who are employed in a wide variety of occupations.

A One-Day Walking Tour of the Hidden Leaf Village!

Welcome to the Village Hidden in the Leaves! Our village covers a large area and has many places of interest. Since this is your first visit to the village, we have created a special itinerary that will allow you to see all the sights in one day!

10:00 a.m. Bursting with native flora!

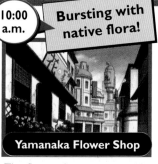

Yamanaka Flower Shop

This flower shop is operated by the Yamanaka family. Inside, the store is an explosion of color, with many rare flowers that can't be found in other countries.

11:00 a.m. A breathtaking view!

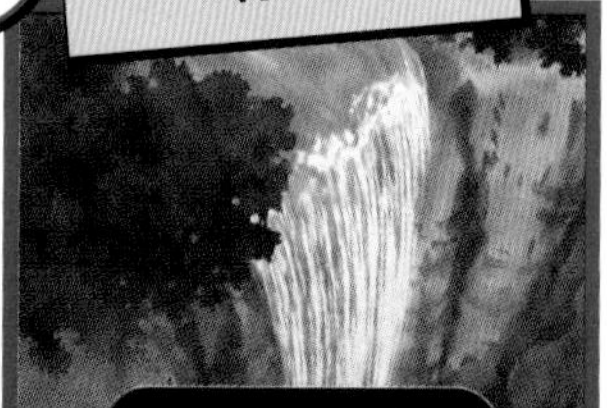

Hidden Falls

This great spot in the village isn't well known to the public. The view is truly superb…and since shinobi often train here, you just might run into one!

Annals of successive Hokage of the Hidden Leaf Village

"Love your village and become the pillar that protects and supports those who believe in you." This is the teaching that successive Hokage have passed down from generation to generation.

Second Hokage — Younger brother / Older brother — **First Hokage**

Mentor

The younger brother of the First Hokage. After the death of his older brother, he set up the infrastructure of the Leaf Village.

The founder of the Hidden Leaf Village, he built the village with his comrades about 60 years ago.

Third Hokage

A genius trained by the First and Second Hokage, he has held his title for a greater number of years than any other Hokage in the village's history.

Mentor

Jiraiya

Mentor

Fourth Hokage

He studied under a pupil of the Third Hokage and became Hokage himself at a young age. He perished after battling the Nine-Tailed Fox.

Leaf Village Shinobi Government

This chart represents the organizational basis for the command of high-level ninja. The Hokage reigns at the top and can give direction to the units beneath him very swiftly and efficiently.

Hokage

Head Advisors

After consulting with his Head Advisors, the Hokage, who stands at the top of the organization, communicates his decisions to each unit.

Routine Ops Unit

Most of the shinobi in the Hidden Leaf Village belong to this unit, which provides day-to-day support.

Medical Unit

The Medical Unit follows and supports the combat units. It has specialized subdivisions like the emergency care squad and research group.

Anbu Black Ops Unit

A secret unit under the direct supervision of the Hokage. They execute special, highly technical missions such as interrogation and assassination.

Akimichi Clan

This clan passes down a jutsu that allows them to dramatically enlarge their bodies for attack or for defensive purposes.

Aburame Clan

Members of this strange clan carry tiny parasitic insects inside their bodies.

Hyuga Clan

The Byakugan can see things happening a thousand leagues away and perceive the Keirakukei (chakra network) that exists inside the body.

Uchiha Clan

The Sharingan can see through an opponent's jutsu and immediately copy it.

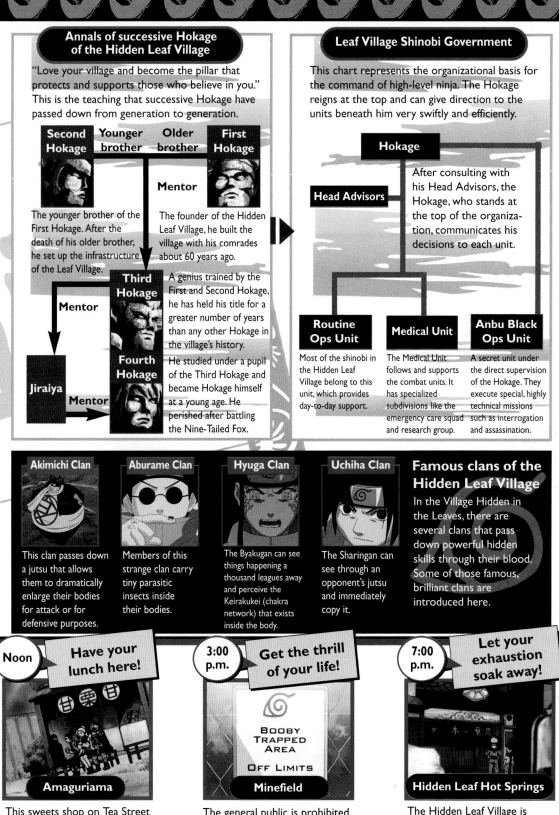

Famous clans of the Hidden Leaf Village

In the Village Hidden in the Leaves, there are several clans that pass down powerful hidden skills through their blood. Some of those famous, brilliant clans are introduced here.

Noon — **Have your lunch here!**

甘 栗 甘

Amaguriama

This sweets shop on Tea Street specializes in chestnut candies, such as chestnut jellies and jams.

3:00 p.m. — **Get the thrill of your life!**

BOOBY
TRAPPED
AREA
OFF LIMITS

Minefield

The general public is prohibited from entering this training ground. If you want a bit of a thrill, it has to be here!

7:00 p.m. — **Let your exhaustion soak away!**

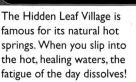

Hidden Leaf Hot Springs

The Hidden Leaf Village is famous for its natural hot springs. When you slip into the hot, healing waters, the fatigue of the day dissolves!

Ninja Academy

These students, their future one of unlimited potential, represent the future of the village itself.

This school trains students who will become the leaders of the Hidden Leaf Village!

Candidates who intend to become shinobi must attend Ninja Academy. The students learn and practice jutsu in hopes of growing up to become the shinobi who support the village.

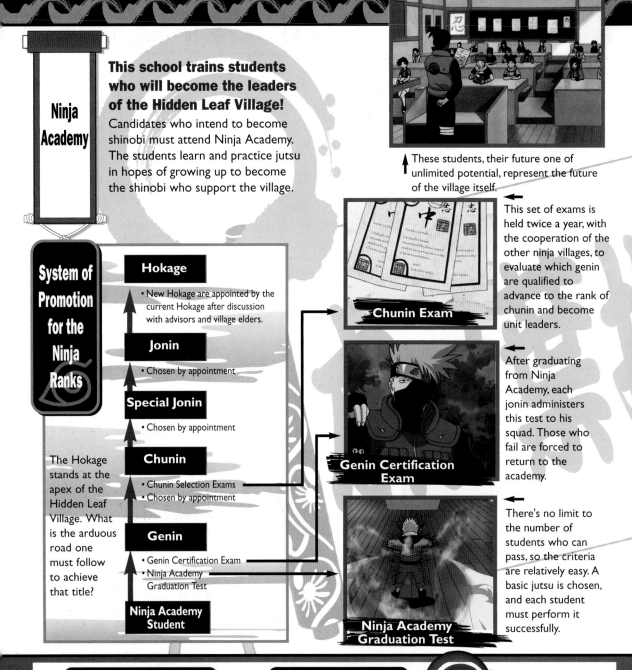

System of Promotion for the Ninja Ranks

The Hokage stands at the apex of the Hidden Leaf Village. What is the arduous road one must follow to achieve that title?

Hokage
- New Hokage are appointed by the current Hokage after discussion with advisors and village elders.

Jonin
- Chosen by appointment

Special Jonin
- Chosen by appointment

Chunin
- Chunin Selection Exams
- Chosen by appointment

Genin
- Genin Certification Exam
- Ninja Academy Graduation Test

Ninja Academy Student

Chunin Exam

This set of exams is held twice a year, with the cooperation of the other ninja villages, to evaluate which genin are qualified to advance to the rank of chunin and become unit leaders.

Genin Certification Exam

After graduating from Ninja Academy, each jonin administers this test to his squad. Those who fail are forced to return to the academy.

Ninja Academy Graduation Test

There's no limit to the number of students who can pass, so the criteria are relatively easy. A basic jutsu is chosen, and each student must perform it successfully.

The prime lounging spots for academy students!

During recess at Ninja Academy, the students can choose how to spend their time…so where do they go to relax when they get a break from their intense training?

Campus Veranda

The beautiful view from the open veranda will calm your soul and make your lunch taste better.

Campus Bench

Sitting on this comfortable bench, maybe you'll have a fascinating conversation with someone who shares your dreams…

Missions

These "ninja jobs" are the foundation for the existence of the village.

From babysitting to assassination, requests of all types are submitted to the village every day. The requests are evaluated, categorized and distributed to the shinobi, and the payment that is received upon completion of these missions maintains the livelihood of the shinobi and the operations of the village.

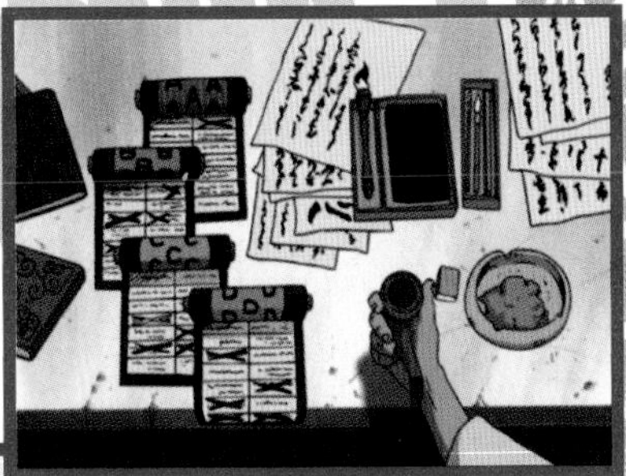

The Hokage and village elders assign the requests to shinobi according to their aptitude.

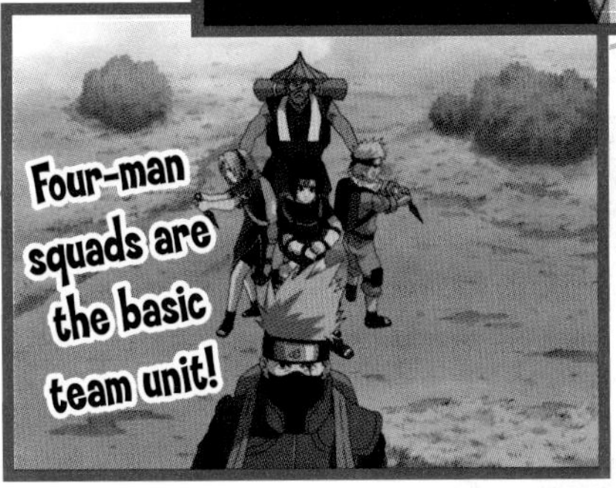
Four-man squads are the basic team unit!

Missions are usually carried out by a small four-man unit. This is the most suitable squad size for maximizing power while maintaining secrecy and maneuverability.

Leaf Village Top-Secret Mission Data

Rank	Level	Mission Content
S	Jonin	These are highly sensitive missions, such as assassinations of important persons and transportation of classified documents, that could affect the fates of nations. Since these missions are extremely dangerous, the payment is accordingly high.
A	Jonin, Special Jonin	Involving relations between nations, these vital missions include escorting important persons and suppressing the advance of other ninja forces. The assignments almost always involve combat.
B	Special Jonin, Chunin	Missions that fall into this category are ones such as providing a protective escort, gathering intelligence on a foreign nation and killing a ninja. Generally, open battle is not expected during missions of this rank.
C	Chunin, Genin	These missions include providing protective escorts and gathering intelligence, and involve some chance of injury to the ninja carrying out the assignment. Capturing wild animals and clearing mines also fall under this category.
D	Genin	No combat or direct danger is involved in these missions, which vary greatly in scope but include babysitting, potato digging and searching for missing pets. The payment is low.

The missions are split into five ranks according to their intricacy and the danger involved. As the rank of the mission travels up the scale, the danger and the payment both increase and the number of shinobi qualified to carry them out becomes smaller.

Shinobi Mission Experience: A Comparison

The differences in mission experience between the jonin, chunin and genin levels are undeniable. Compare for yourself!

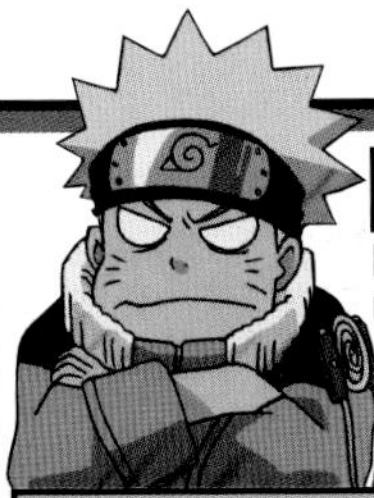

Genin
Naruto Uzumaki

D-rank:	7
C-rank:	1
B-rank:	0
A-rank:	0
S-rank:	0

Missions for Genin are mainly D-ranked. The early missions are mostly for gaining experience and developing teamwork.

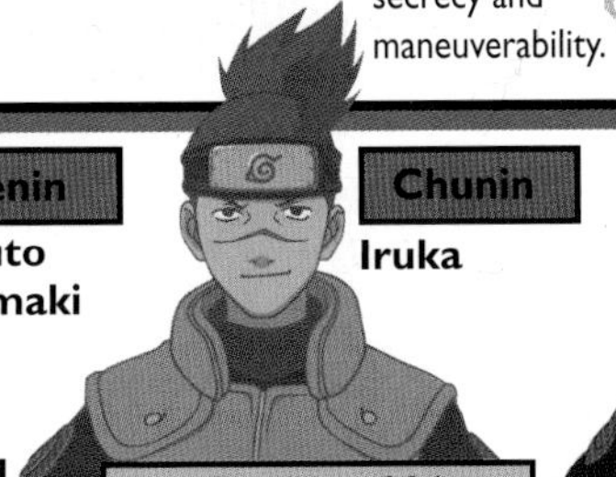

Chunin
Iruka

D-rank:	284
C-rank:	177
B-rank:	73
A-rank:	11
S-rank:	0

Iruka has completed many combat missions. Besides his missions, he is employed as a teacher and directs the education of younger shinobi.

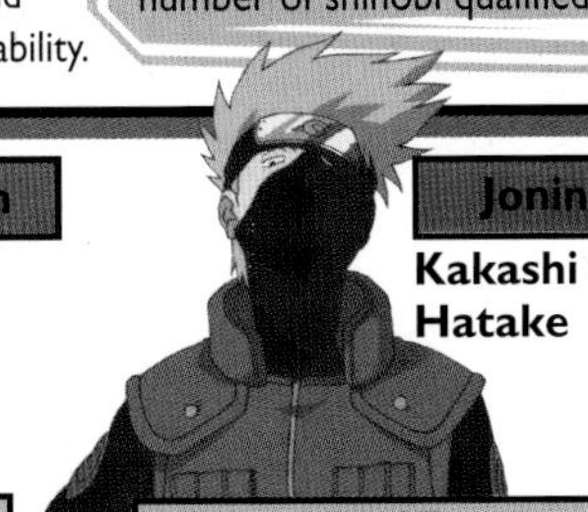

Jonin
Kakashi Hatake

D-rank:	197
C-rank:	189
B-rank:	413
A-rank:	276
S-rank:	38

Kakashi has an overwhelming amount of experience in battle. Because he has survived them all, he is a jonin.

* The numbers represent missions completed at the time the Chunin Exams commenced.

Jutsu

A shinobi's secret moves, which combine mental energy with physical power

Jutsu are a unique ability only accessible to shinobi. These astonishing skills are activated by building up chakra in the body and then using hand signs to convert the chakra into a jutsu.

Hand Signs

Both hands are used to create signs which change chakra into jutsu!

There are specific sequences of hand signs that, when made accurately and rapidly, result in the activation of particular jutsu. For higher-level jutsu, the sequence of hand signs becomes longer and more complicated because the activation is more difficult.

Tiger
Snake
Dragon
Dog
A SECRET MOVE IS UNLEASHED!
Earth Style: Fanged Pursuit Jutsu!

Chakra

The energy source for jutsu!

Jutsu
Hand Sign

Chakra is created by building up the energies of the mind and body. Besides being used to activate jutsu, this built-up chakra can also be channeled to the performance of superhuman feats, such as walking on water and lightning-fast running.

ENERGY SPIRITUAL/PSYCHIC
+
ENERGY BODY/PHYSICAL

← These two elements are combined to create chakra. Chakra control is vitally important.

Ninja training involves endless days of practice!

The only way to develop the ability to use advanced, jonin-level jutsu is intense training!

Mental training
Boost concentration!

↑ Did Naruto develop this exercise himself?! He balances a flower vase on the top of his head until the pressure is hard to bear…but he keeps on bearing it!

Tree climbing exercise
Increase chakra control!

→ This exercise heightens chakra control by requiring you to focus chakra in your feet to run up a tree without using your hands.

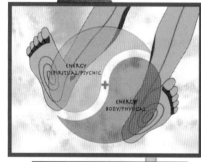

Bloom of Youth exercise
Develop taijutsu and tenacity!

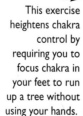

← Continuously putting body and soul to the test…this is also the bloom of youth!

I'm wiped out… Believe it…

Ninjutsu, taijutsu and genjutsu make up the range of powerful moves in a shinobi's arsenal!

Jutsu are subdivided into the categories of ninjutsu, taijutsu and genjutsu. What are the characteristics of each type?

Ninjutsu

There are many kinds of ninjutsu (stealth arts) and they serve a variety of purposes, including attacking, defending and escaping. The shinobi of each village often use unique ninjutsu that their own community has developed.

Taijutsu

Taijutsu (physical arts) employ one's own body to deliver kicks and punches. Neither chakra nor hand signs are fundamentally necessary for these moves, and they can be executed swiftly and continuously.

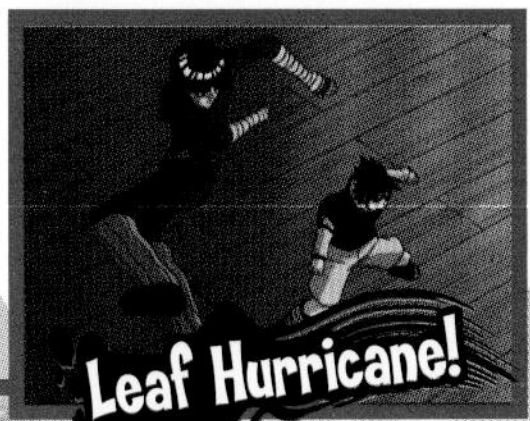
Leaf Hurricane!

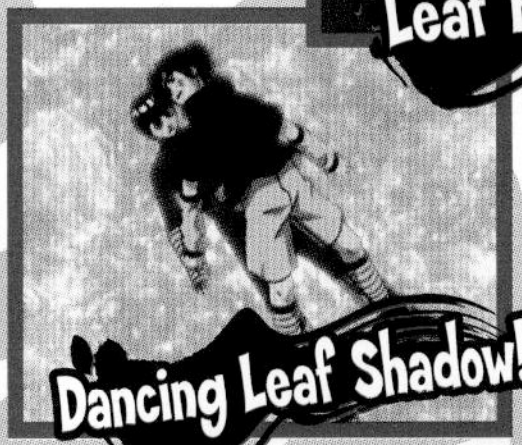
Dancing Leaf Shadow!

Since anyone can learn these moves, training makes all the difference in ability.

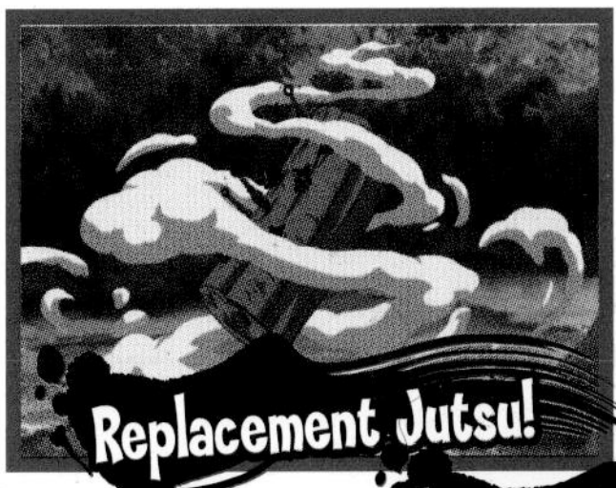
Replacement Jutsu!

The Clone Jutsu and Transformation Jutsu are basic ninjutsu that consume little chakra and can be deployed with simple hand signs.

Genjutsu

Genjutsu (illusion arts) trick the enemy by using a type of hallucination-inducing hypnosis. By confusing and exhausting his opponent's mind, the user of the jutsu gains an advantage.

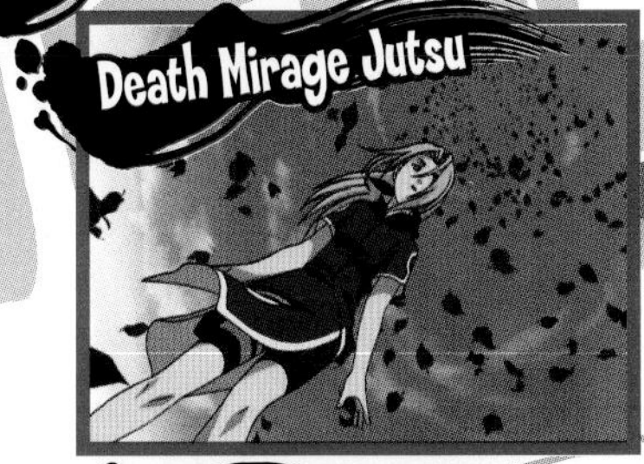
Death Mirage Jutsu

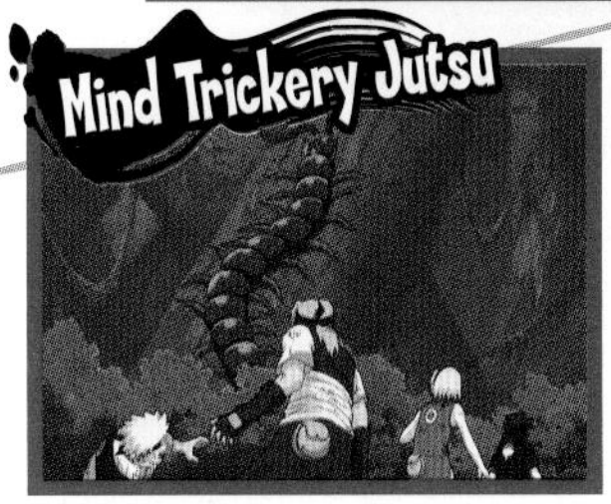
Mind Trickery Jutsu

A genjutsu's effects cover a wide area and can affect multiple opponents.

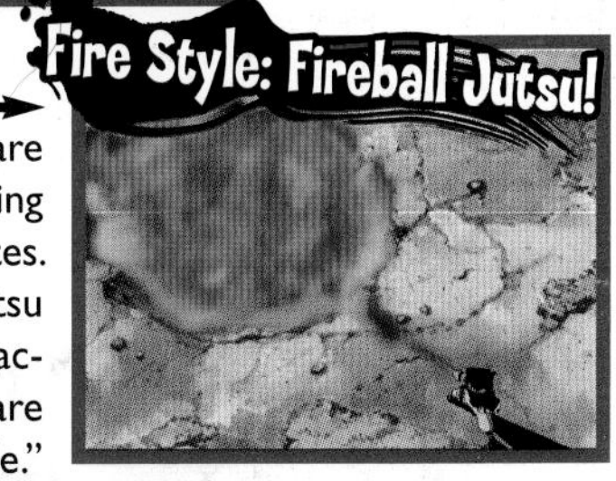
Fire Style: Fireball Jutsu!

Most ninjutsu are subdivided according to their attributes. For example, jutsu that reflect characteristics of fire are called "Fire Style."

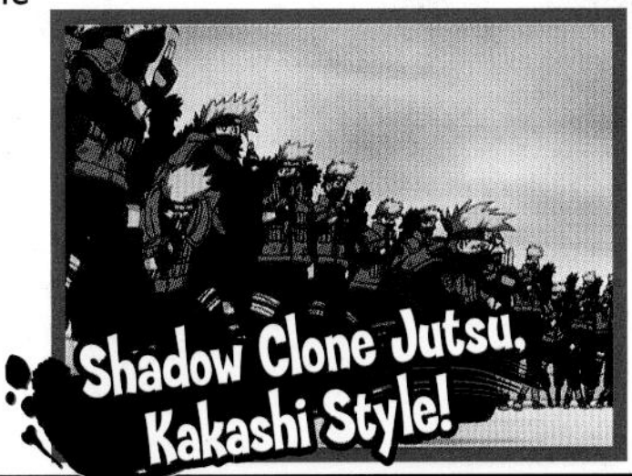
Shadow Clone Jutsu, Kakashi Style!

At the jonin level, shinobi are able to use complex ninjutsu in rapid succession. Their combat power seems superhuman.

Laugh-out-loud jutsu stories!

Tales of two jutsu… Here are the stories of a pair of jutsu that had memorable results!

The most seductive hidden jutsu of all! Some say it grants every man's wish!

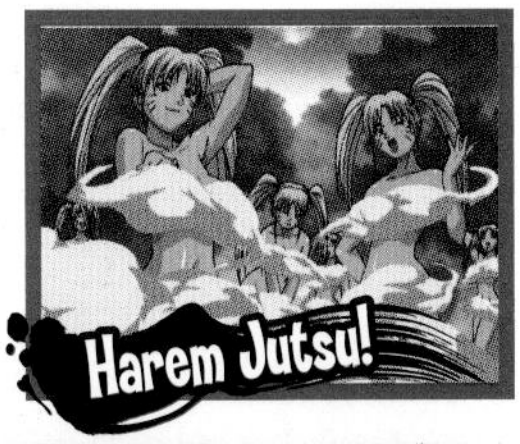
Harem Jutsu!

Leaf Special Jonin, Mr. E

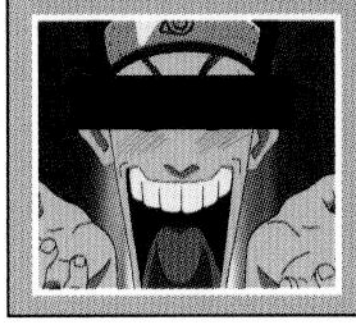

That jutsu won't work on me anymore! Just *try* to use it on me again…please!!

Kakashi's hidden move, which is "a huge pain in the butt!"

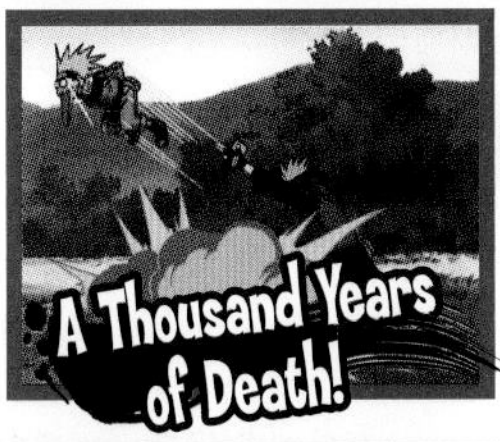
A Thousand Years of Death!

Leaf Genin, Mr. N

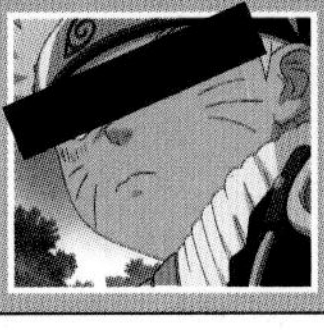

After that, it hurt to use the bathroom for three days! It was horrible! Believe it!

Kekkei Genkai

When a ninja's Kekkei Genkai awakens, his fighting power increases dramatically!

The special powers bestowed by fate and inherited through blood!

Kekkei Genkai (bloodline traits) are extraordinary powers that develop like genetic mutations. They are passed down from generation to generation within a family, and those who possess Kekkei Genkai can execute amazing hidden jutsu.

WHITE SECRET JUTSU

This trait is passed down in the Hyuga Clan, which has imposed various rules to protect the purity of their bloodline.

BYAKUGAN

SHARINGAN

Haku's secret jutsu is passed down within his family in the Land of Mist, but sometimes the trait skips a generation, so inheritance of the power is not guaranteed.

The Kekkei Genkai of the Uchiha Clan, this unique trait is visible in the eyes of the ones who possess it.

In the Land of Mist, bloodline powers were exploited in the conflicts of influential men and the warfare became relentless.

Because of the secret of their blood, Haku's father killed his mother and almost killed Haku as well.

It can be a curse to possess these powers, often seen as harbingers of calamity and horror!

Those who possess Kekkei Genkai are sometimes taken advantage of in battles and have even inspired wars themselves. Many families with bloodline traits suffer under persecution and end up on a road of destruction...

Curse Jutsu	Sealing Jutsu	Forbidden Jutsu	Secret Jutsu	
Victims of this jutsu suffer under a spell placed on their body and soul, and they exhibit a mark of the curse on their skin.	These jutsu use hand signs to seal an opponent's chakra. Not only can they contain an overly large chakra, but they can seal the rampage that results from a Curse Jutsu.	Jutsu that, because of their tremendous power, damage the body and soul of the user are considered Forbidden Jutsu. This class also includes jutsu that go against natural laws.	Secret Jutsu are taught only to families or groups living in a particular region. In the Hidden Leaf Village, the Nara Clan's Shadow Possession Jutsu falls into this category.	Beyond ninjutsu, taijutsu, genjutsu and Kekkei Genkai, there exist many other types and categories of jutsu.
• The curse restricts the victim's actions by inflicting enormous pain.				

Mandatory Lesson! More about jutsu!

The Secret Scroll That Shakes Heaven and Earth

These secret jutsu roar across heaven, shake the earth and rumble through the oceans. Countless splendid but violent jutsu are now revealed!

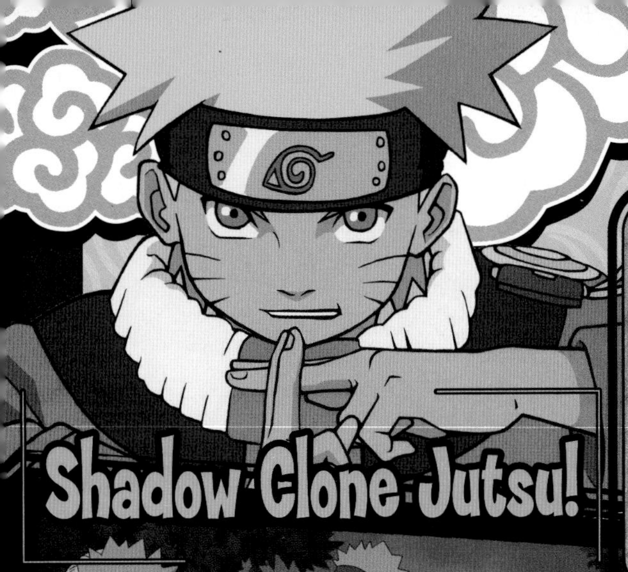

Shadow Clone Jutsu!

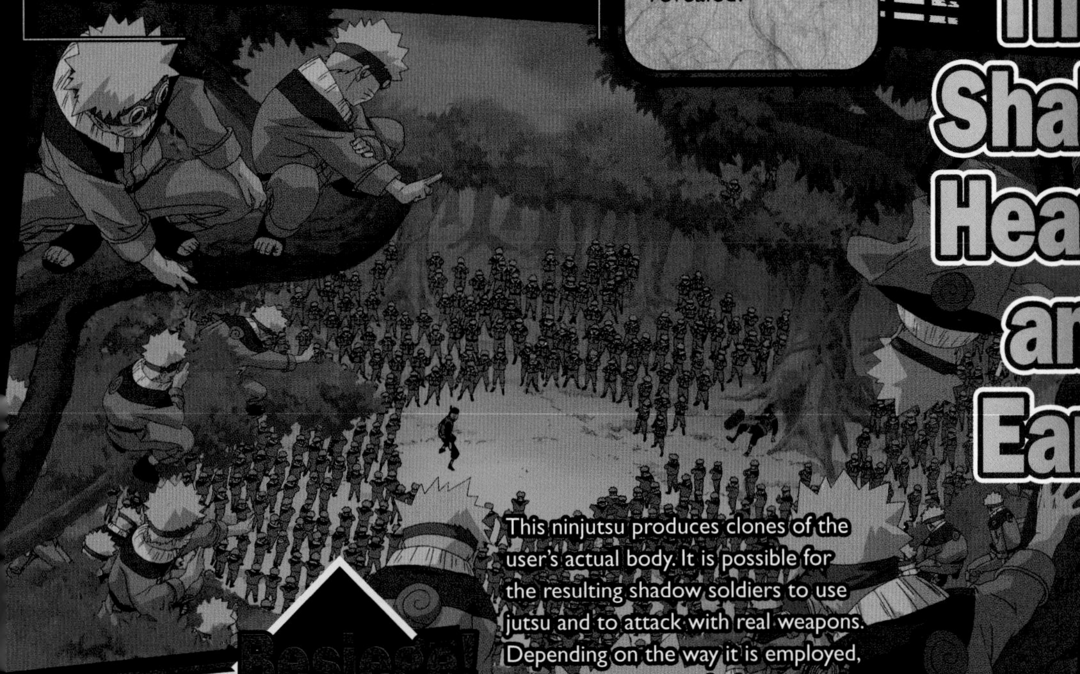

This ninjutsu produces clones of the user's actual body. It is possible for the resulting shadow soldiers to use jutsu and to attack with real weapons. Depending on the way it is employed, this technique expands the range of a shinobi's tactics infinitely.

Besiege!

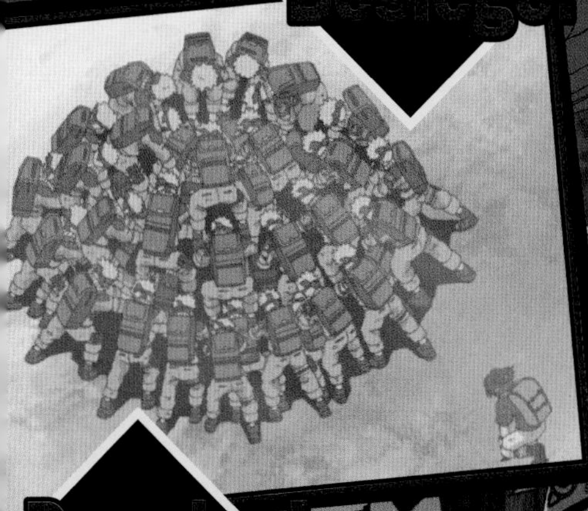

Destroy!

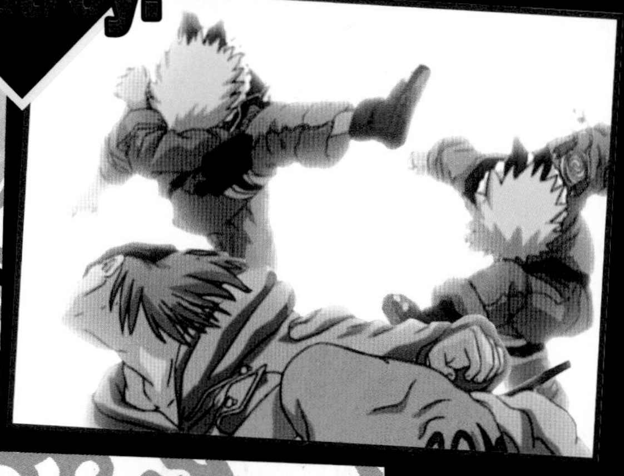

Deceive!

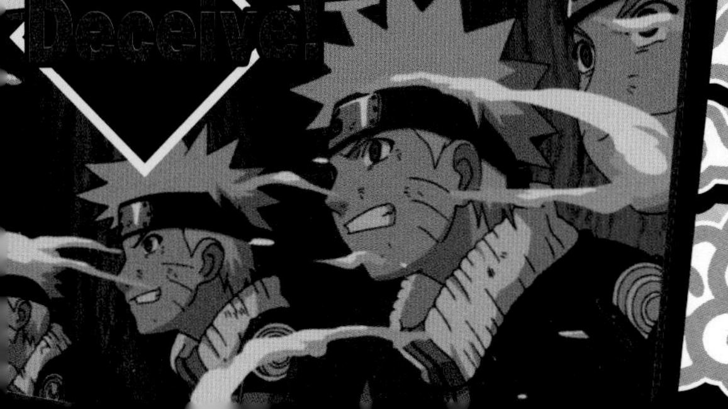

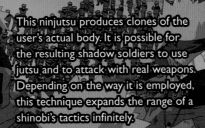

Sand Burial!

After capturing his foe within the Sand Coffin, Gaara's deadly, masterfully brutal ninjutsu crushes his enemy with the pressure of sand. The sand of death stirs as it seeks blood…to satisfy Gaara's thirst.

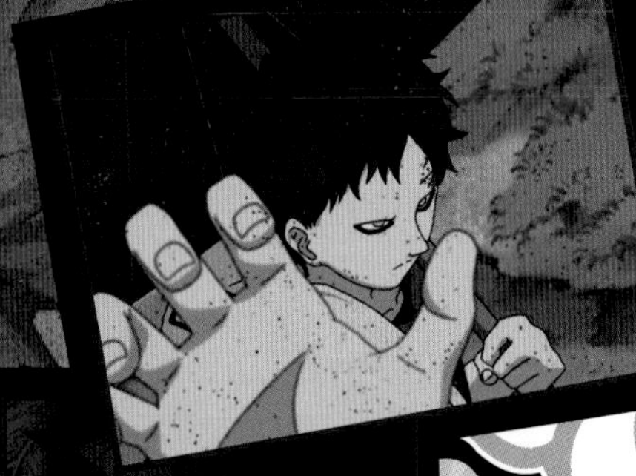

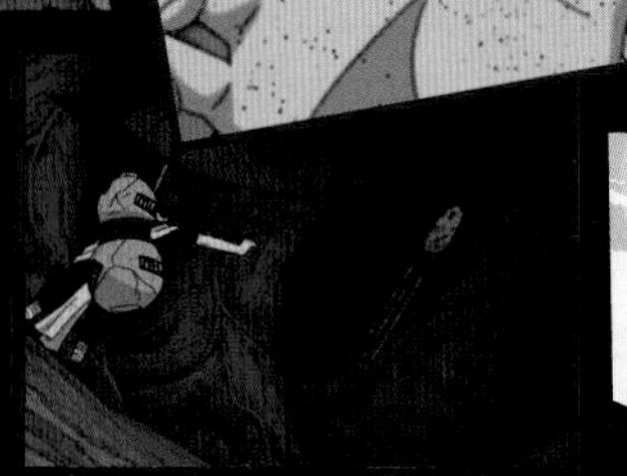

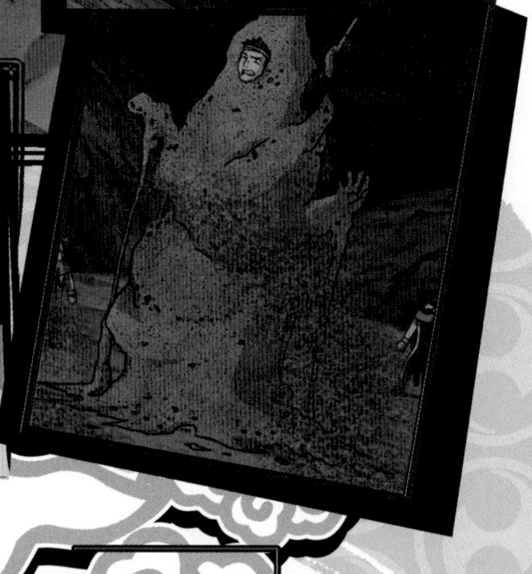

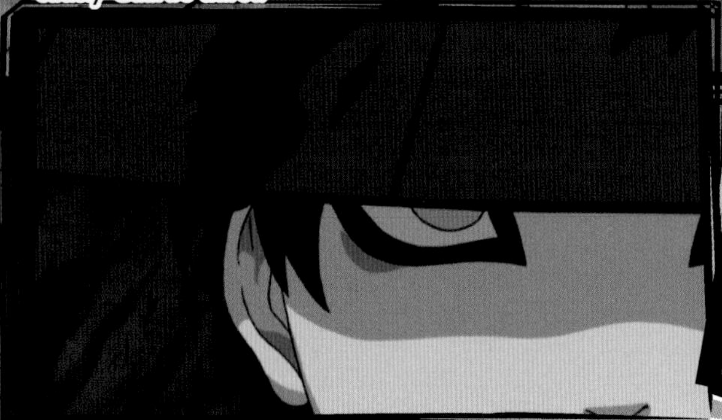

Water Prison Jutsu!

This jutsu immobilizes the enemy within a spherical wall of water. Inside this prison, it is a struggle to even move one's fingers, and escape is impossible!

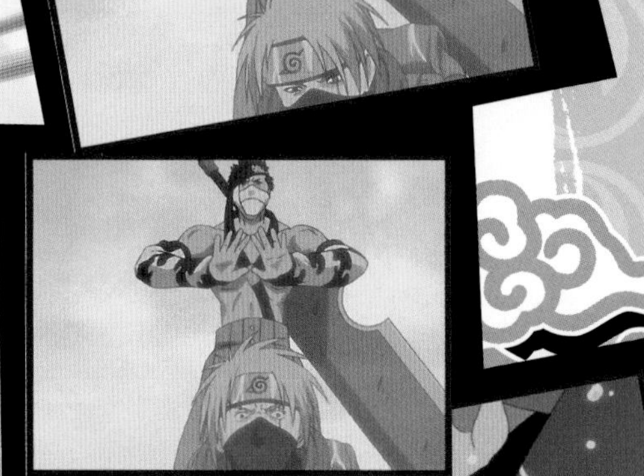

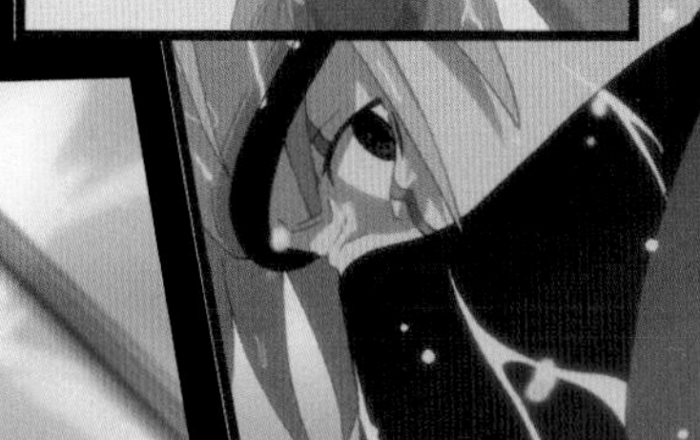

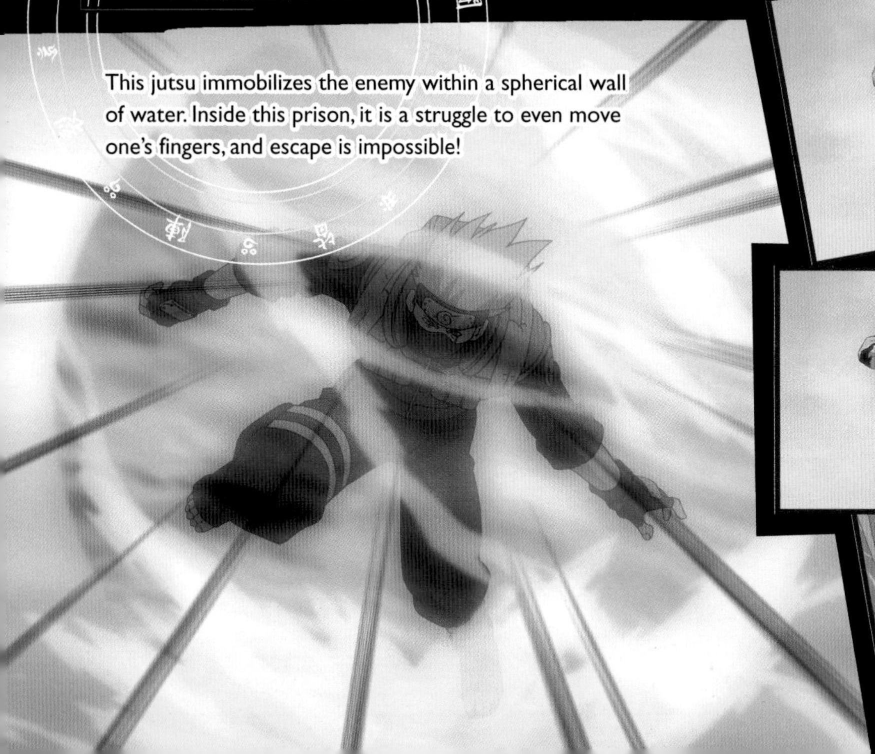

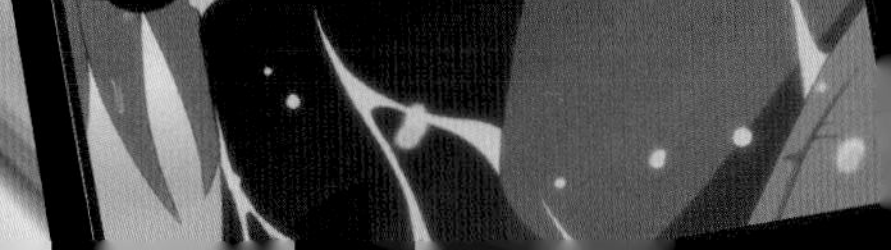

Fire Style: Fireball Jutsu!

This jutsu converts the chakra inside the body to flame and incinerates the enemy with a giant fireball. The amount of chakra used can be adjusted to control the sphere of attack. The scorching blaze has such a force that it plows up the earth.

Destroy the enemy using power drawn from all things in the universe!

Fire Style: Phoenix Flower Jutsu!

The spitballs of fire that shoot from the user's mouth are controlled by chakra and attack the enemy in pursuit. Within its beauty and brilliance, like exploding balsam flowers, it hides relentless, destructive power!

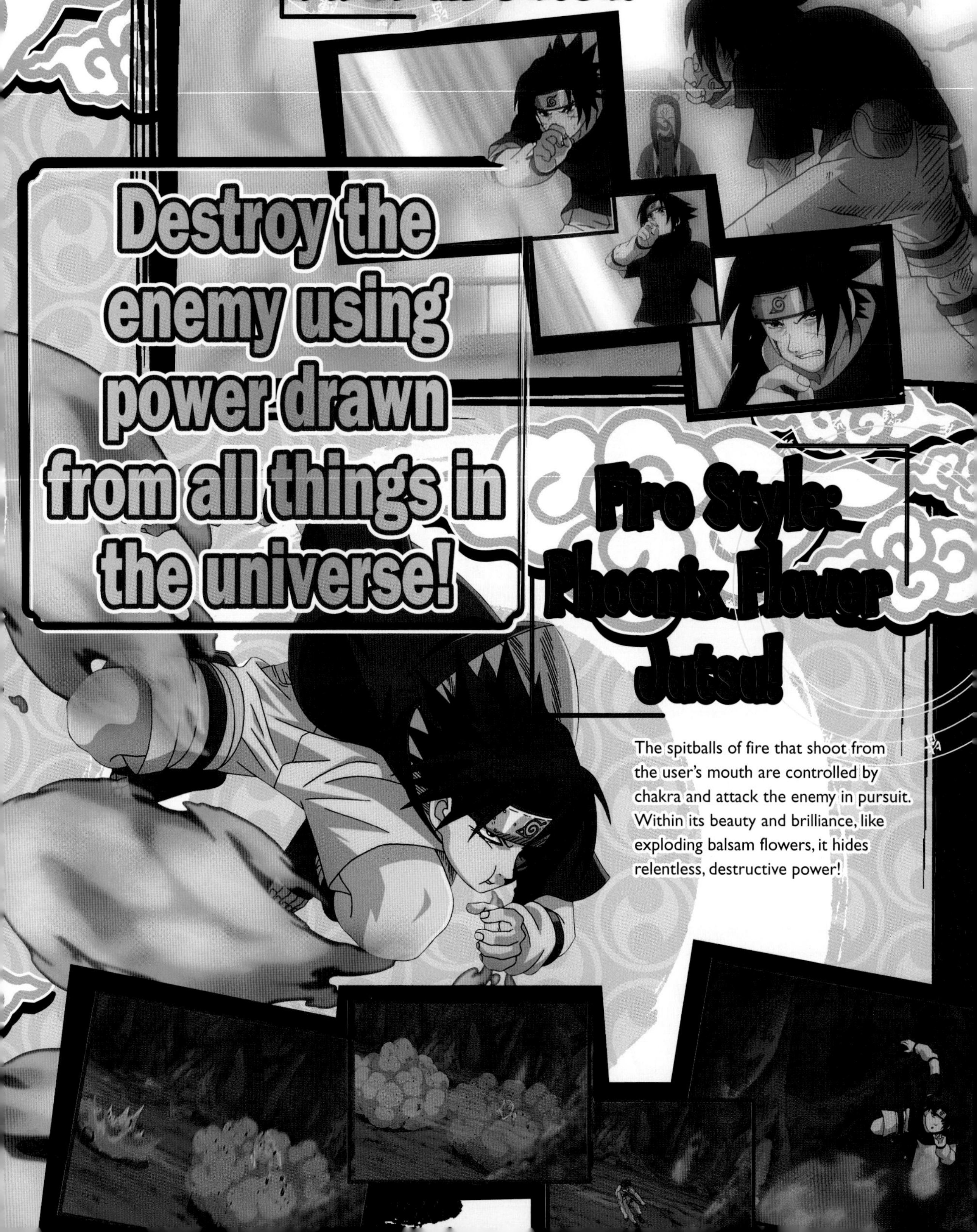

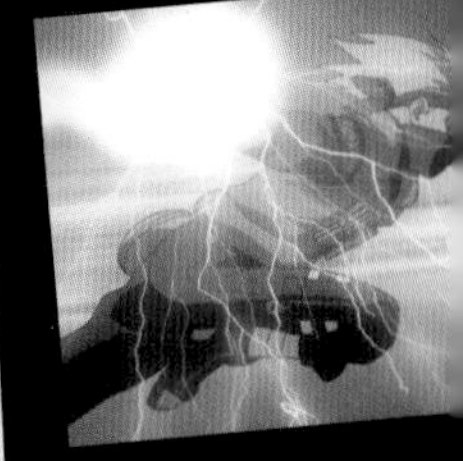

The Lightning Blade is a move that has been honed to the limit. This straight-ahead charge is very dangerous because it opens the user to an easy counterattack. Only those who have inherited the Sharingan can safely see the track to victory with this move.

Lightning

Those who are blessed with heaven's eyes may boast unmatched bravery...

Using a leading wire, a sharp line of flame is shot toward the enemy, as if a dragon is breathing flame. Sasuke used the power of both of his eyes to anticipate his enemy's next move and successfully target the dragon fire at his opponent.

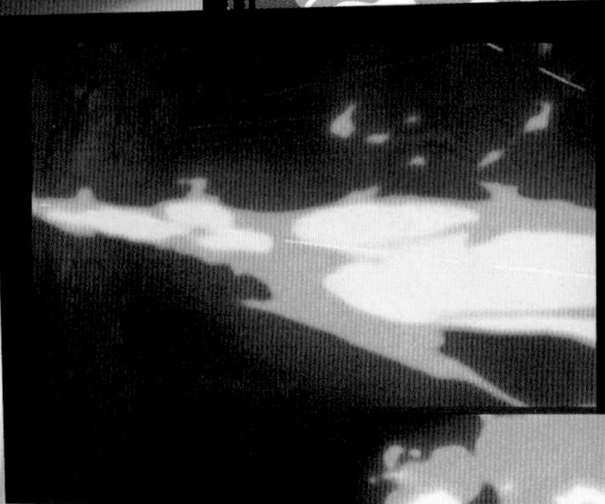

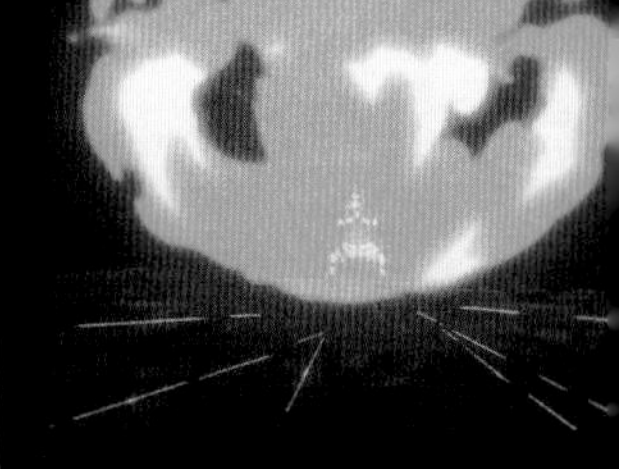

Fire Style: Dragon Flame Jutsu!

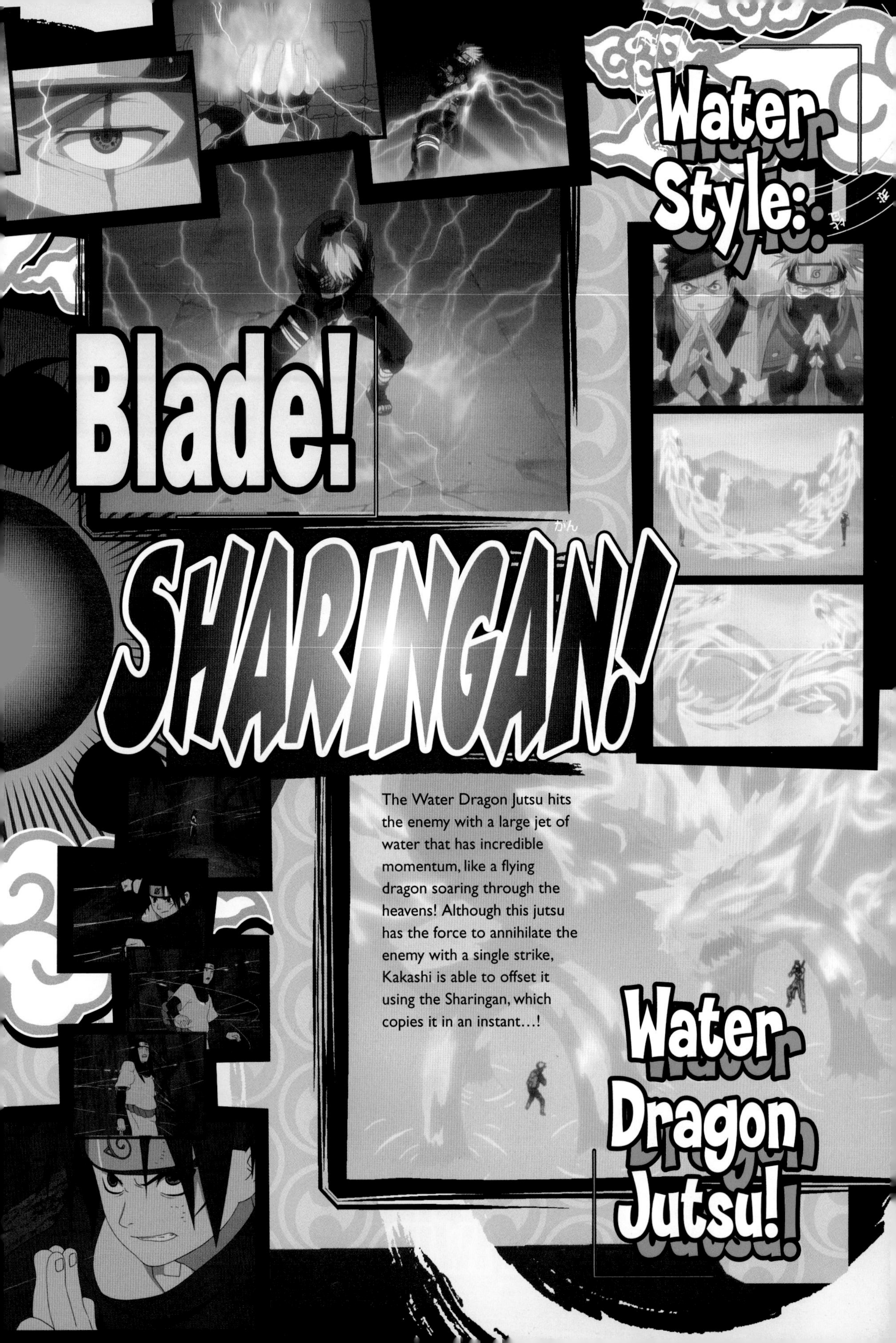
Water Style:
Blade!
SHARINGAN!
Water Dragon Jutsu!

The Water Dragon Jutsu hits the enemy with a large jet of water that has incredible momentum, like a flying dragon soaring through the heavens! Although this jutsu has the force to annihilate the enemy with a single strike, Kakashi is able to offset it using the Sharingan, which copies it in an instant…!

Primary Lotus!

Lee catches his enemy in midair and throws him down, adding high-speed rotation to drill his opponent's head into the ground! This technique is a deadly product of Lee's passionate, self-sacrificing training!

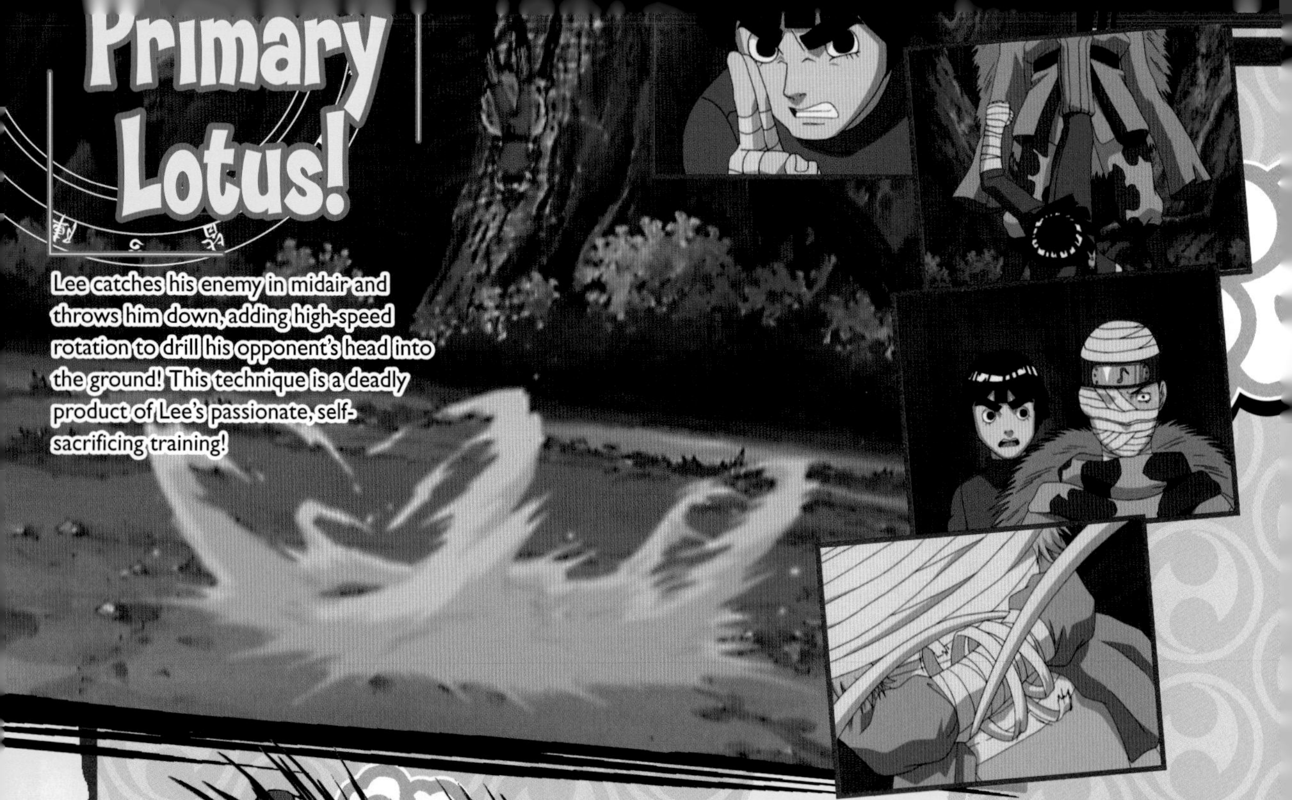

This move is a vicious, low, spinning kick that possesses a destructive power like a raging wind. Even a simple kick can become a deadly strike when it's unleashed with enough speed and power by a person highly trained in taijutsu!

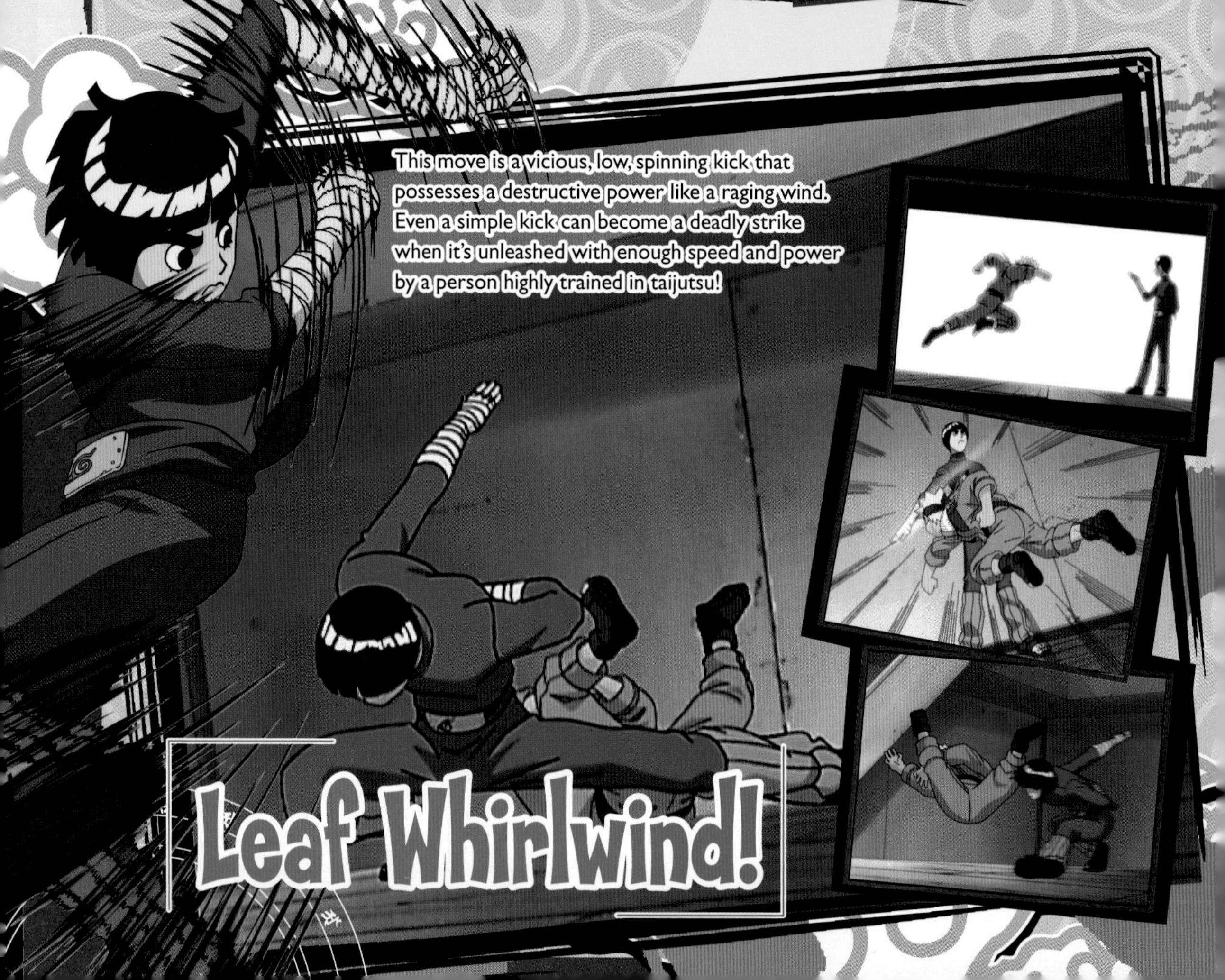

Leaf Whirlwind!

Leaf Style Secret Techniques that distinguish the greatest of the elite!

Byakugan!

This Kekkei Genkai is passed down through the Hyuga Clan, the oldest, most legendary family in the Hidden Leaf Village. These white eyes are able to perceive things happening a thousand miles away, and they can also see through barriers in front of them.

Formation: Ino-Shika-Cho!

Yamanaka, Nara, Akimichi...each clan takes pride in its honorable name, and each has a secret move that was refined and strengthened through arduous, excruciating training. These jutsu, which are like symbols for each clan, cause even more light to radiate on the Hidden Leaf Village.

Human Boulder!

After enlarging his body with the Expansion Jutsu, Choji uses his flesh as a weapon, hitting his target with a massive, spinning attack!

Mind Transfer Jutsu!

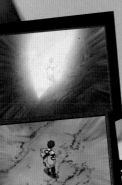

Ino uses this jutsu to project her soul into her enemy's body. She takes over the mind and body of her opponent and then can manipulate her foe at will!

Shadow Possession Jutsu!

In this secret jutsu, Shikamaru seizes control of his enemy's movement by stealing his foe's shadow and attaching his own shadow to it. Any movement Shikamaru makes is mimicked by his opponent!

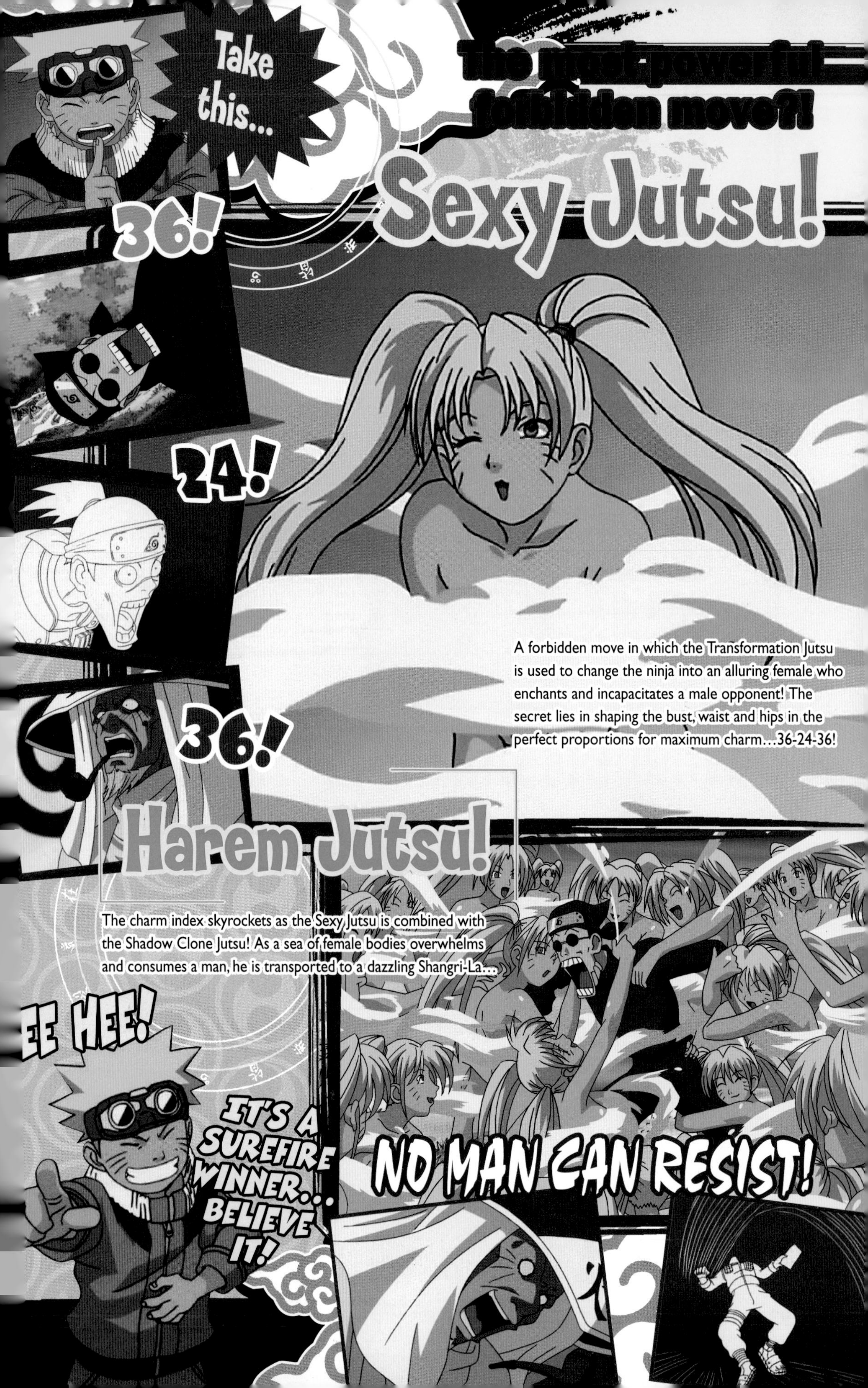
Take this...
The most powerful forbidden move?!
36!
24!
36!
EE HEE!
IT'S A SUREFIRE WINNER... BELIEVE IT!
NO MAN CAN RESIST!

Sexy Jutsu!

A forbidden move in which the Transformation Jutsu is used to change the ninja into an alluring female who enchants and incapacitates a male opponent! The secret lies in shaping the bust, waist and hips in the perfect proportions for maximum charm...36-24-36!

Harem Jutsu!

The charm index skyrockets as the Sexy Jutsu is combined with the Shadow Clone Jutsu! As a sea of female bodies overwhelms and consumes a man, he is transported to a dazzling Shangri-La...

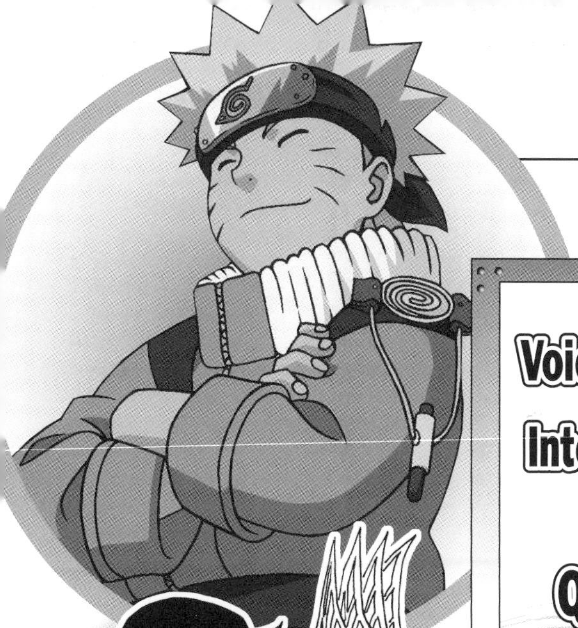

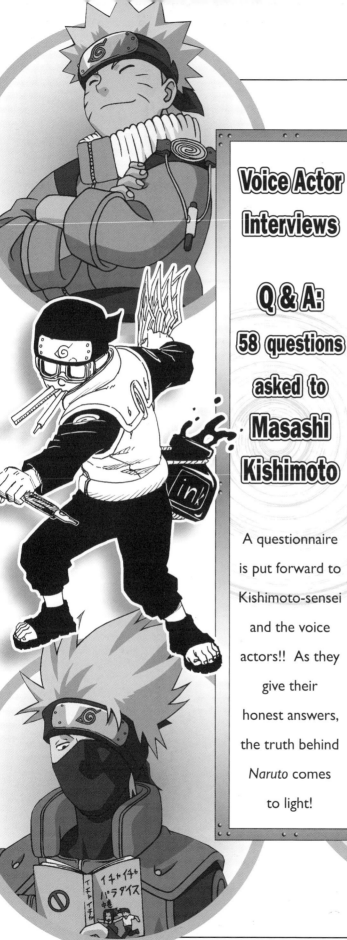

NARUTO

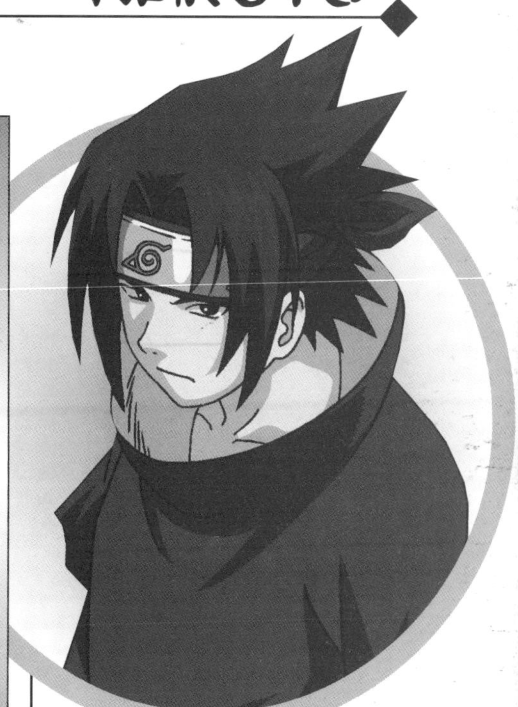

SASUKE

Voice Actor Interviews

Q & A: 58 questions asked to Masashi Kishimoto

A questionnaire is put forward to Kishimoto-sensei and the voice actors!! As they give their honest answers, the truth behind *Naruto* comes to light!

SAKURA

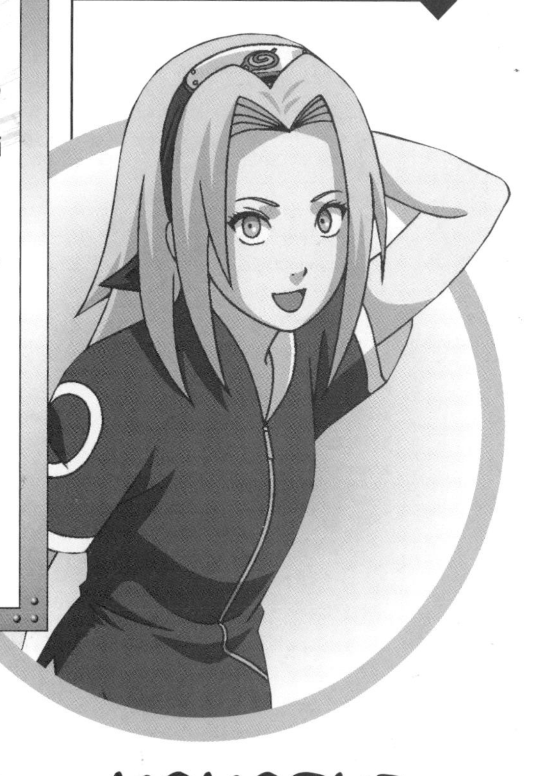

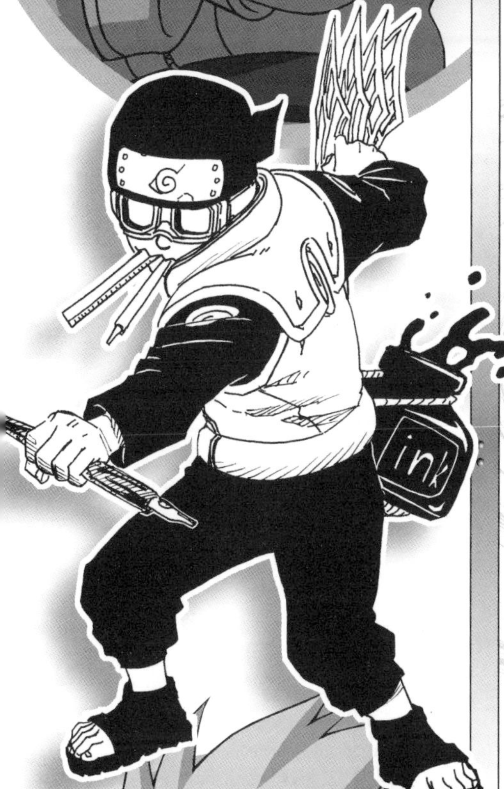
ink

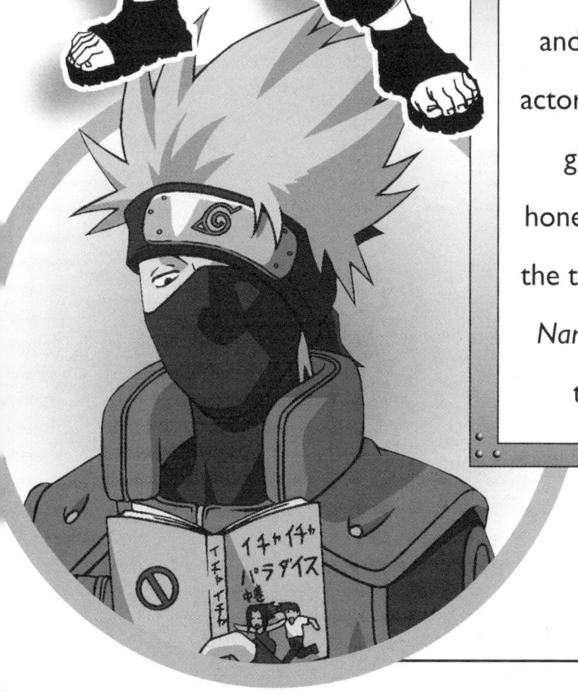
イチャイチャ
パラダイス
中巻

KAKASHI

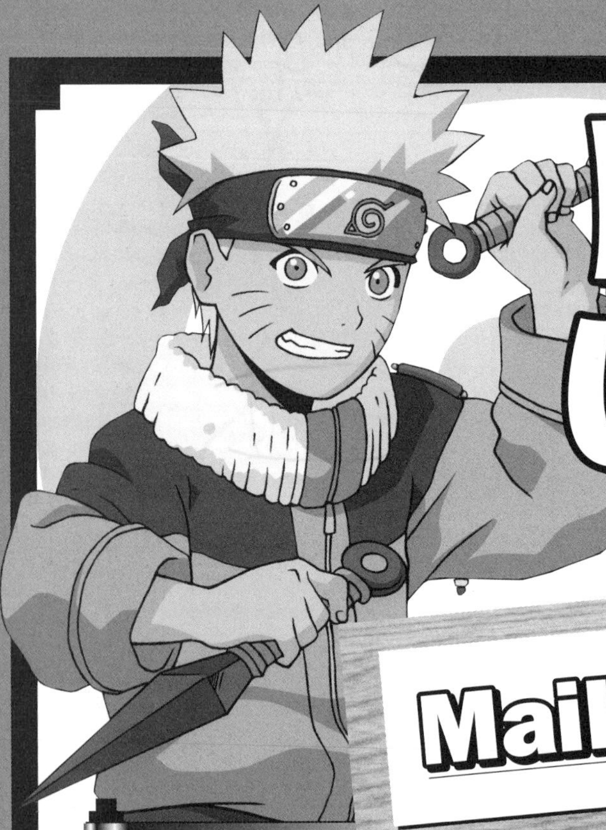

NARUTO UZUMAKI

Maile Flanagan

What did you think when you saw the anime?

I thought *Naruto* was cute and looked different from other anime I had seen before as it had a lot more detail to it.

If you could do one jutsu in real life, which one would it be?

Shadow Clone Jutsu.

What's your favorite *Naruto* weapon?

I like the kunai, but I can't wait to see some more new weapons.

Besides yourself, who is your favorite *Naruto* character?

Iruka-sensei. I like that he teaches Naruto how to be a ninja, but allows him to make his own mistakes, which are often quite hilarious.

Any interesting things happen while recording?

When we first listened to the original Japanese version, every time Naruto bugged out, it made everyone in the studio laugh.

Any tips on being a voice actor?

Learn how to do improv. Be flexible with your voice delivery and practice different voice sounds and reactions, getting hit, running and landing hard.

What's your favorite Japanese food?

Unagi, ebi and tekka sushi, edamame and, of course, ramen!

Sasuke Uchiha

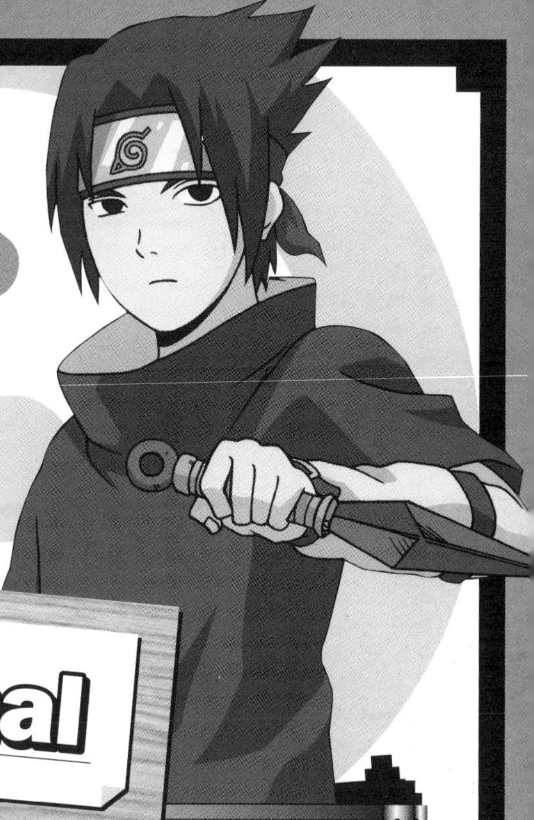

Yuri Lowenthal

Q What did you think when you saw the anime?

A It had a really cool look to it. I saw a couple of episodes and really enjoyed the quickness and crispness of it.

Q If you could do one jutsu in real life, which one would it be?

A Shadow Clone Jutsu.

Q What's your favorite *Naruto* weapon?

A I like Zabuza's sword, but I love Sasuke's kunai.

Q Besides yourself, who is your favorite *Naruto* character?

A It would have to be Kakashi. He's got this playful, irreverent side that balances out his coolness.

Q Any interesting things happen while recording?

A In the beginning, I didn't realize how popular the show was. As soon as I started to understand the fans' excitement, I was a bit nervous, but exhilarated at the same time.

Q Any tips on being a voice actor?

A First, find someone who can help you study voice acting and more importantly, record a demo reel. Also, find a city where they record a lot of commercials and shows.

Q What's your favorite Japanese food?

A Okonomiyaki, which is popular in Osaka.

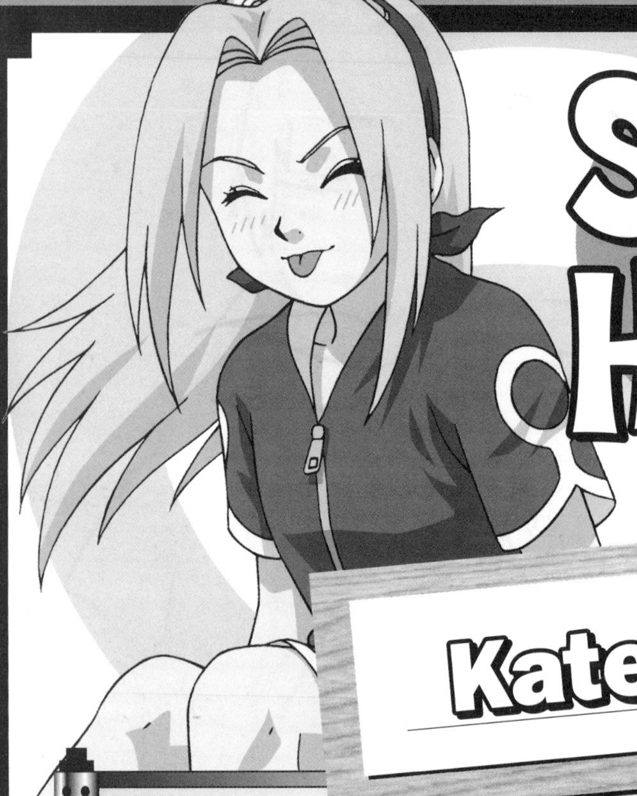

Sakura Haruno

Kate Higgins

Q What did you think when you saw the anime?

A I really liked the dialogue, how they got into the psyche of each of the characters. I liked the action and the relationship between Sakura and Sasuke as well as Sakura's strength and vulnerability. I also liked the camaraderie between Sakura, Sasuke and Naruto.

Q If you could do one jutsu in real life, which one would it be?

A Shadow Clone Jutsu.

Q What's your favorite *Naruto* weapon?

A The shuriken.

Q Besides yourself, who is your favorite *Naruto* character?

A Sasuke.

Q Any interesting things happen while recording?

A For a while, we couldn't figure out what to say [for Inner Sakura's catchphrase] instead of "Cha!" [The director] asked me what people say in the south when they're upset and they say "Grits!" But that didn't work after a while. So we went back to "Cha!"

Q Any tips on being a voice actor?

A Take a voice acting class, because it's the acting that is key to the voice. Since you're not onscreen, you have to get it all to come out of your voice. In terms of getting work, be a nice person. Because if you leave your ego at the door, you will get more work.

Q What's your favorite Japanese food?

A Teriyaki Chicken Bowl.

KAKASHI HATAKE

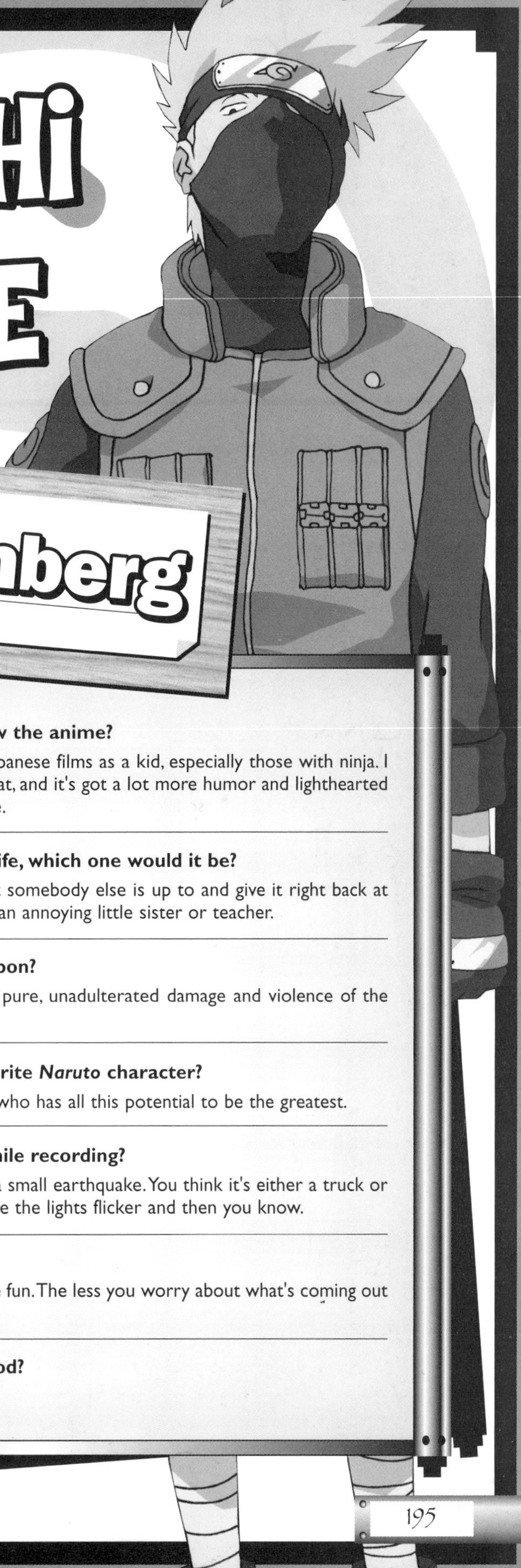

Dave Wittenberg

Q What did you think when you saw the anime?

A It was really cool. I was always into Japanese films as a kid, especially those with ninja. I thought the action on the show is great, and it's got a lot more humor and lighthearted moments than I thought it would have.

Q If you could do one jutsu in real life, which one would it be?

A The Sharingan. To be able to see what somebody else is up to and give it right back at them in an instant would be great on an annoying little sister or teacher.

Q What's your favorite *Naruto* weapon?

A I like the subtlety of senbon and the pure, unadulterated damage and violence of the bladed chain that rips up the body.

Q Besides yourself, who is your favorite *Naruto* character?

A I like Naruto 'cause he's like a savant who has all this potential to be the greatest.

Q Any interesting things happen while recording?

A While we were recording, there was a small earthquake. You think it's either a truck or moving equipment outside, but you see the lights flicker and then you know.

Q Any tips on being a voice actor?

A Have no fear. Just try to relax and have fun. The less you worry about what's coming out of your mouth, the easier it is.

Q What's your favorite Japanese food?

A Albacore Sashimi.

HIDDEN LEAF Q&A

58 QUESTIONS asked to MASASHI KISHIMOTO

The creator of *Naruto*, Masashi Kishimoto-sensei!

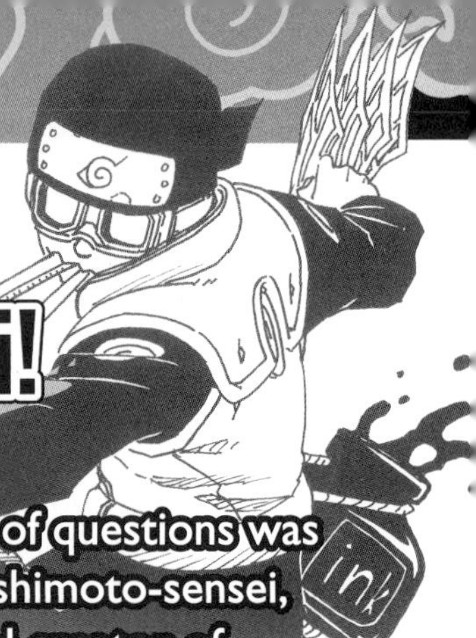

ink

Birthday: November 8, 1974
Blood Type: O
Hobby: Watching movies
Favorite type of ramen: Tonkotsu (pork-bone soup ramen)
Favorite word: Bochi-bochi (so-so)

A barrage of questions was fired at Kishimoto-sensei, the original creator of *Naruto!* We're now happy to present his answers!

Q What is the anime that influenced you the most?
A ***Akira.***

Q As you draw the manga, are you influenced at all by the anime version of *Naruto*?
A **Absolutely, very much.**

Q Do you have a favorite episode of the *Naruto* anime?
A **Episodes 17, 19 and 30.**

Q Were you a fan of any of the Japanese voice actors before they were involved with *Naruto*?
A **Yes, I was a fan of Jyurota Kosugi, who plays Asuma, and Nozomu Sasaki, who plays Hayate.**

Q For which character did you have the most trouble choosing colors?
A **Naruto.**

Q Who is the voice actor that you admire the most?
A **Akio Otsuka.**

Q In regards to the sound design in the anime production, what was most memorable?
A **The series of sounds during Zabuza's appearance.**

Q If you were to create an original story for the anime, what kind of story would it be?
A **I'd want to feature a generous robber like Goemon Ishikawa.**

Q Since *Naruto* has become an anime, has your level of motivation changed?
A **I thought, "I have to work even harder. If I take a break, the story on TV is going to catch up to the manga!" I was sweating!**

Q **Which *Naruto* character is the most fun to draw?**
A **Rock Lee.**

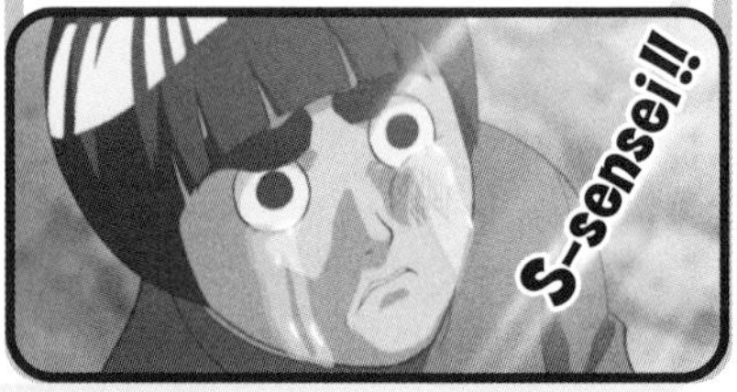

S-sensei!!

Q **What will happen in the love lives of Ino, Sakura and Hinata?**
A **I hope something happens! Ha ha!**

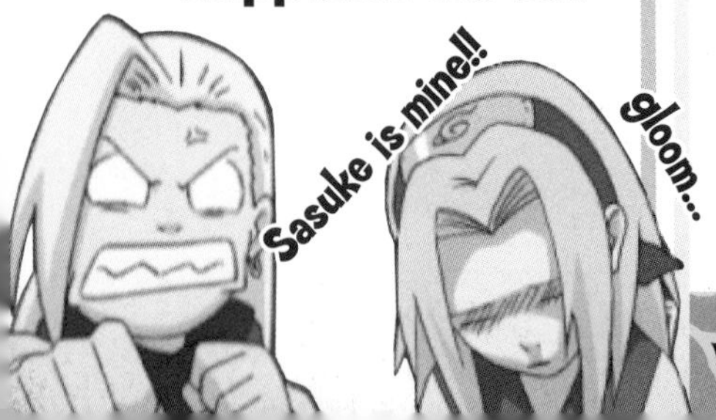

Sasuke is mine!!
gloom...

Q Do you watch the anime every week without missing an episode?
A **Of course!**

Q Who would you be most proud to know watches the *Naruto* anime?
A **Prime Minister Junichiro Koizumi.**

Q Please tell us about the top-secret episodes you've created with the anime production staff!
A **Oh! I hope we can make some in the future... Right now, there's nothing to tell (really!).**

Q If you were to do a voice for the anime, which character would you like to perform?
A **Tsunade.**

Q If you were to become involved in the anime production, what would you like to be in charge of?
A The original-picture guy.

Q Who are the scariest people involved in the anime?
A Tetsuya Nishio and Hirofumi Suzuki (their drawings are so good, it's scary!).

Q Do you sing the anime's opening and ending theme songs at karaoke?
A I haven't been to karaoke since the serialization began...eep!

Q Have you ever wanted to apologize to the anime staff for any of your designs?
A Yes...for Naruto's design, the chunin vest, the headbands and the pattern of the curse marks.

Q Who is your favorite musician or band?
A Oasis.

Q If you could be any person in history, who would you choose to be?
A John Manjiro (the first Japanese person to travel to the United States in the 1840s).

Q What is your most precious treasure?
A Two sets of animation storyboards from *Akira*.

Q Please tell us your favorite movie, movie actor and actress, and movie director.
A My favorite movie is *The Matrix*, my favorite actor and actress are Tom Hanks and Christina Ricci, and my favorite directors are James Cameron and Shinya Tsukamoto.

Q Who is your favorite painter?
A Monet.

Q What is your favorite novel and who is your favorite novelist?
A My favorite novel is *Run, Merosu* and my favorite novelist is Shinichi Hoshi.

Q If you were to take a character from the *Naruto* anime and write a spinoff story, which character would you choose and what kind of story would you write?

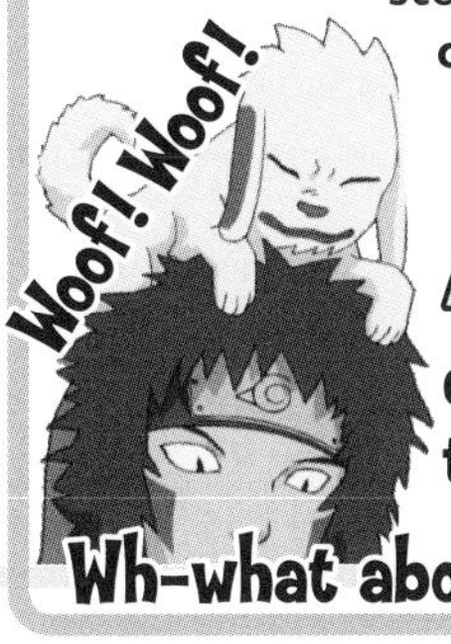
Woof! Woof!
Wh-what about me...?

A I'd like to write a story just about dogs with Akamaru as the star.

Q What are your favorite manga?
A My favorites are *Dragon Ball* and *Akira*.

Q If you could choose to switch places with a character from *Naruto* for a day, whom would you choose and why?
A Naruto. I'd use the Clone Jutsu to finish my work faster!

Q What kinds of people do you admire?
A I really admire people who are good at drawing.

Q What was the biggest crisis in your life so far?
A When a monkey attacked me.

Q If the earth were about to be destroyed, what would you do?
A I'd work hard to stop the destruction!

Q What is your favorite video game?
A The *Zelda* series.

Q If you were reincarnated, what would you want to do in your next life?
A I'd be a detective.

Q If there were an earthquake, what would you grab before evacuating?
A I'd take my licensing paperwork and my legal signature stamp. Ha!

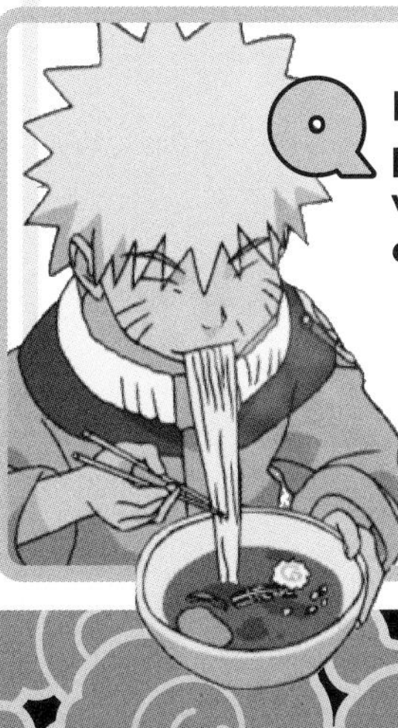

Q Is there a *Naruto* product that you would personally endorse?

A Bowls!

Q If you were an athlete, which sport would you play?
A Baseball.

Q How do you spend your days off?
A I watch movies.

Q What are your favorite and least favorite animals?
A I love dogs and I hate monkeys.

Q Do you have a top-secret stamina recipe or something that keeps your energy up like Kiba's rations pills?
A Aspara Drink.

Q Please tell us one manga artist you like.
A **Akira Toriyama.**

Q Ninja Tortoise, Ninja Dog, Ninja Toad...what is the next ninja beast you're planning to create?
A **Ninja cat.**

Q Where do you come up with your ideas?
A **My room.**

Q In your opinion, who is the scariest person in the manga industry?
A **Mr. Torishima (former editor in chief of *Weekly Shonen Jump*).**

Q What is your most important ninja tool for drawing the manga?
A **Soul.**

Q **How did you react when you found out your work would be made into an anime?**

A **Manly tears of joy!**

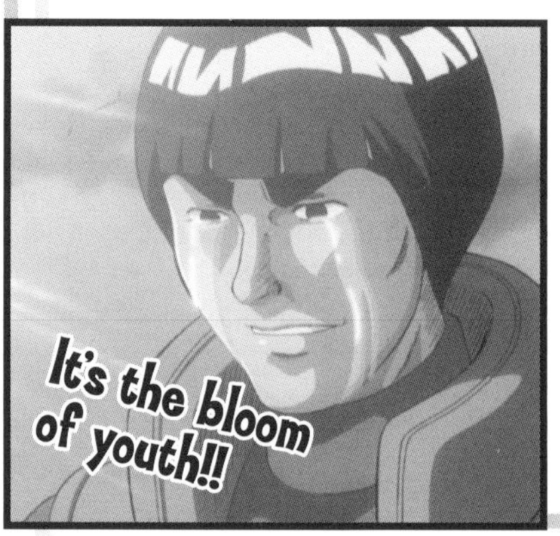
It's the bloom of youth!!

Q What's your philosophy for coming up with the characters' names?
A **I get my inspiration for the names from traditional Japanese style.**

Q When you just can't come up with any new ideas, what do you do?
A **I get up and move around to refresh myself.**

Q Is there anyone whom you talk to for advice or to work out your ideas for the manga?
A **Mr. Yahagi (my editor) and my younger brother.**

Q Are you friends with any other manga artists?
A **Yes, many.**

Q **Who is the most difficult character to draw?**

A **Sasuke.**

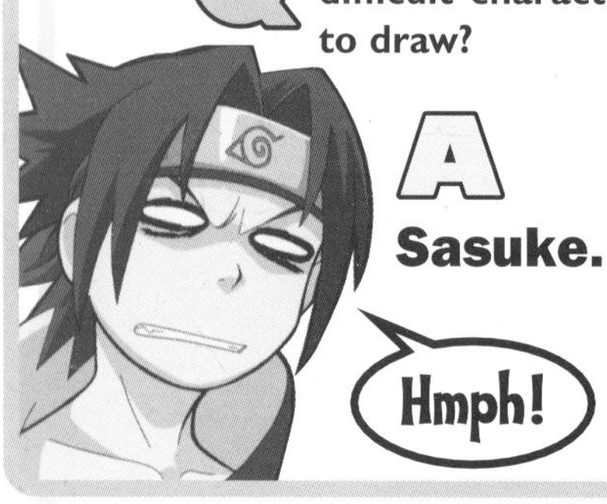
Hmph!

Q What animal do you wish you could summon?
A **Gamakichi and Gamatatsu (two of the small ninja toads).**

Q If you were a resident of the Leaf Village, what would your occupation be?
A **Movie director.**

Q Is there a real person whom Naruto was modeled after?
A **Not at all.**

Q Which present from your fans did you appreciate the most?
A **All of them.**

Q Which teacher would you like to learn ninjutsu from?
A **Iruka.**

Q If you were to draw a special, extra story in the manga, who would be the main character (other than Naruto)?
A **Kakashi.**

Q Who is your favorite female character in the series and why?
A **Anko, because of her relationship with Orochimaru...**

Q What is the longest and shortest amount of time it ever took you to complete one chapter?
A **The longest was five days. The shortest was two days. That's just for the pictures...phew!**

Assisted by Ibiki Morino
This interview was conducted by the leader of the Torture and Interrogation Unit. Kishimoto-sensei was reeling!

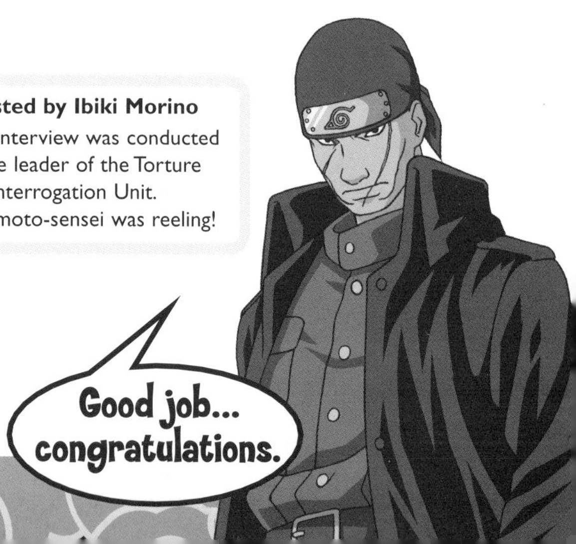
Good job... congratulations.

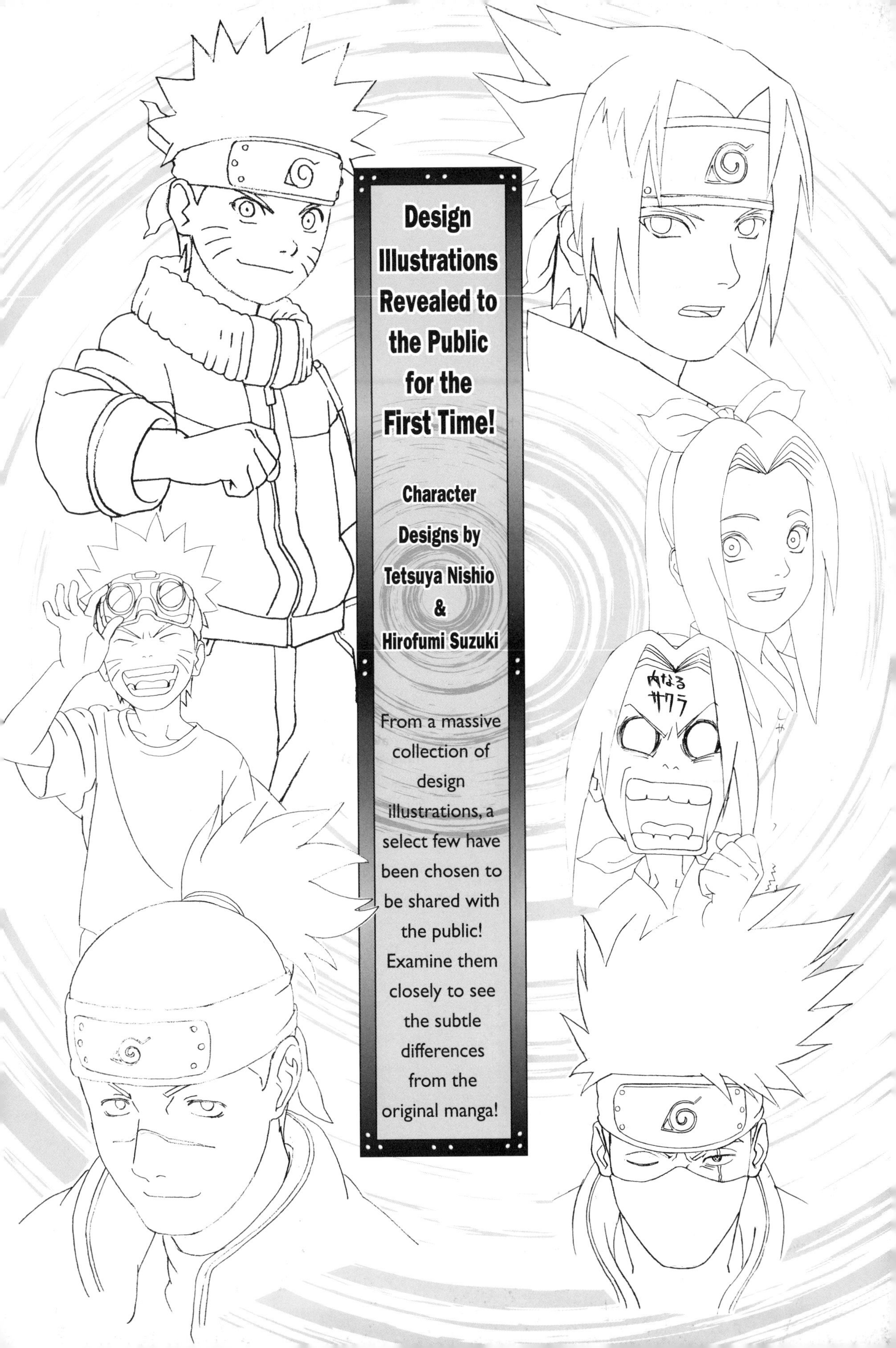
Design Illustrations Revealed to the Public for the First Time!
Character Designs by Tetsuya Nishio & Hirofumi Suzuki
From a massive collection of design illustrations, a select few have been chosen to be shared with the public! Examine them closely to see the subtle differences from the original manga!
内なるサクラ

Naruto Uzumaki

As the biggest troublemaker in the Hidden Leaf Village, Naruto is a misfit, so his clothes reflect that. He wears a jacket with a large collar and he likes to roll up his pants legs.

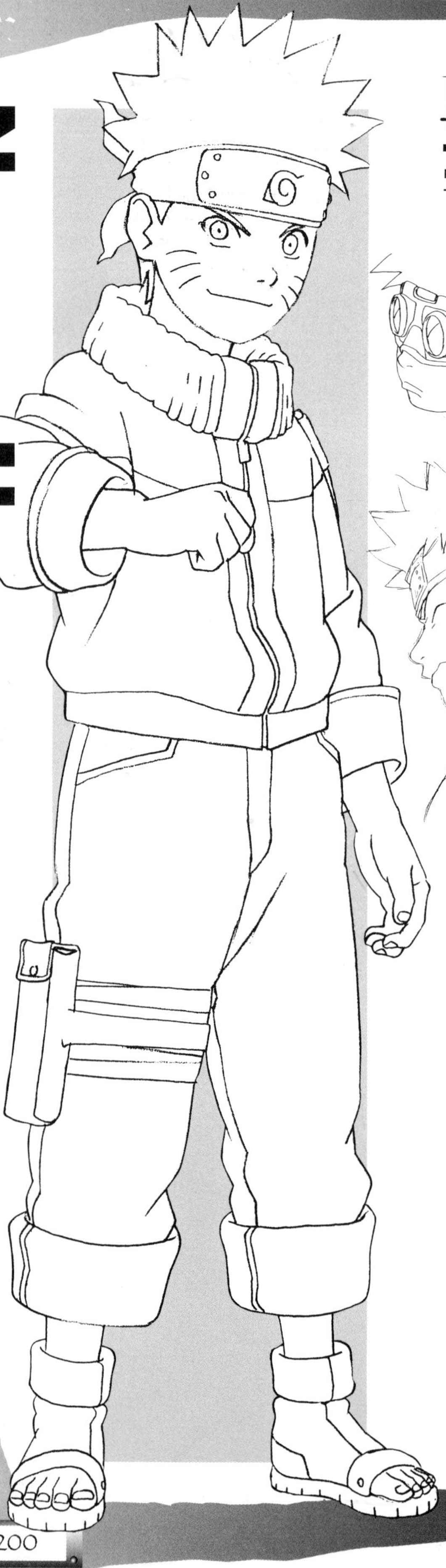

Goggles

➡⬇ The strap of his goggles is made of flexible, stretchy rubber. They fit his head perfectly!

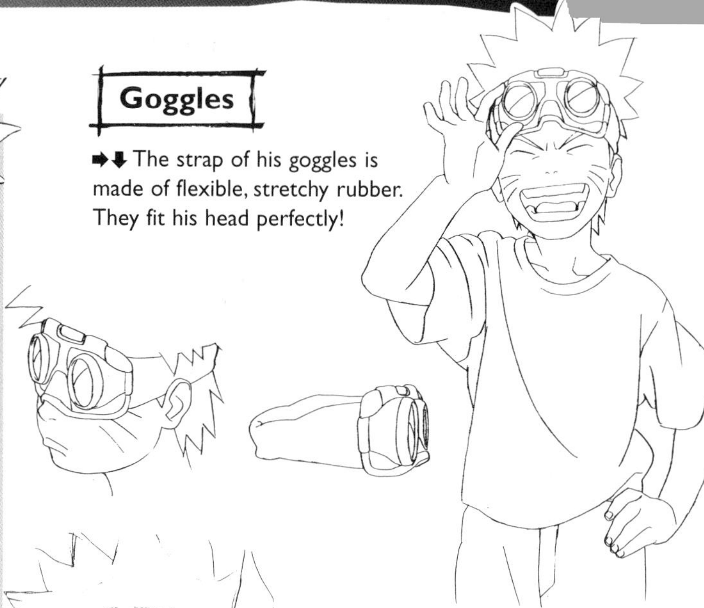

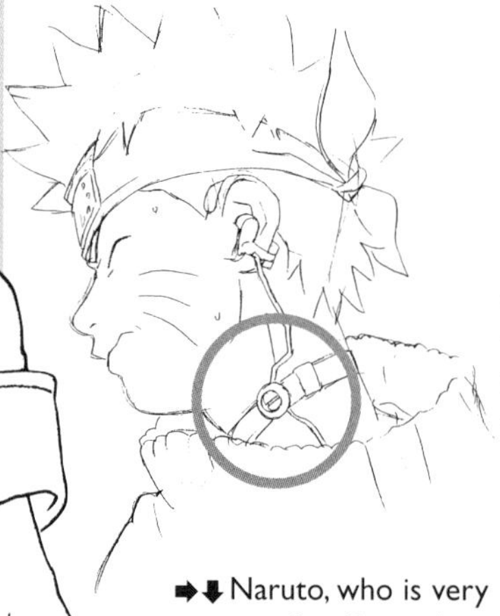

Transmitter

⬅This ultra-small communications device clips on to a collar-like strap with a wire extending into the ear. It's designed to not get in the way of movement.

➡⬇ Naruto, who is very emotionally effusive, has many different facial expressions for showing how he feels. He stays busy, sulking, laughing and exposing the whites of his eyes!

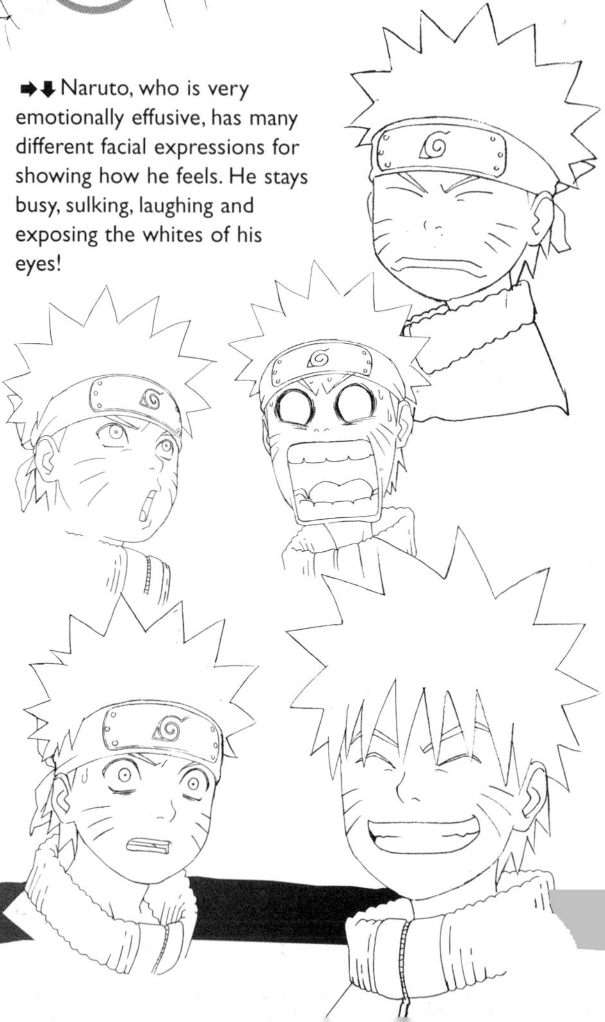

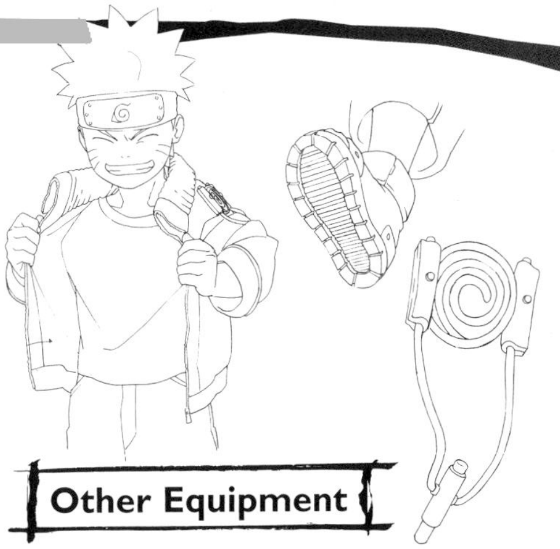

Other Equipment

⬆ The equipment on his left shoulder is made of soft material. The sandals Naruto wears are standard issue for all shinobi in the Hidden Leaf Village.

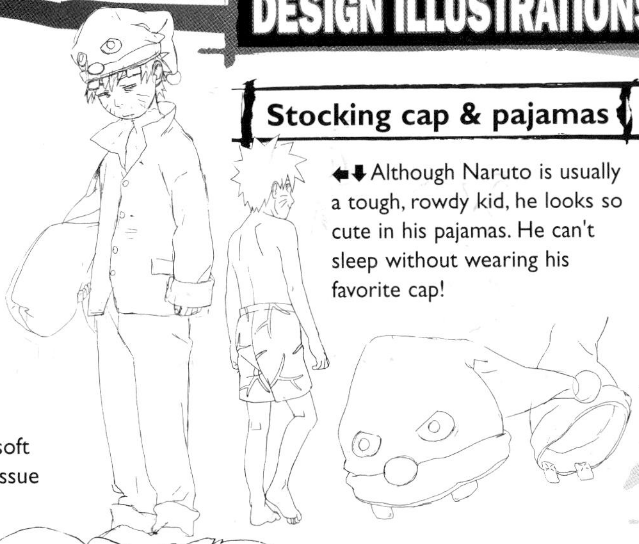

Stocking cap & pajamas

⬅⬇ Although Naruto is usually a tough, rowdy kid, he looks so cute in his pajamas. He can't sleep without wearing his favorite cap!

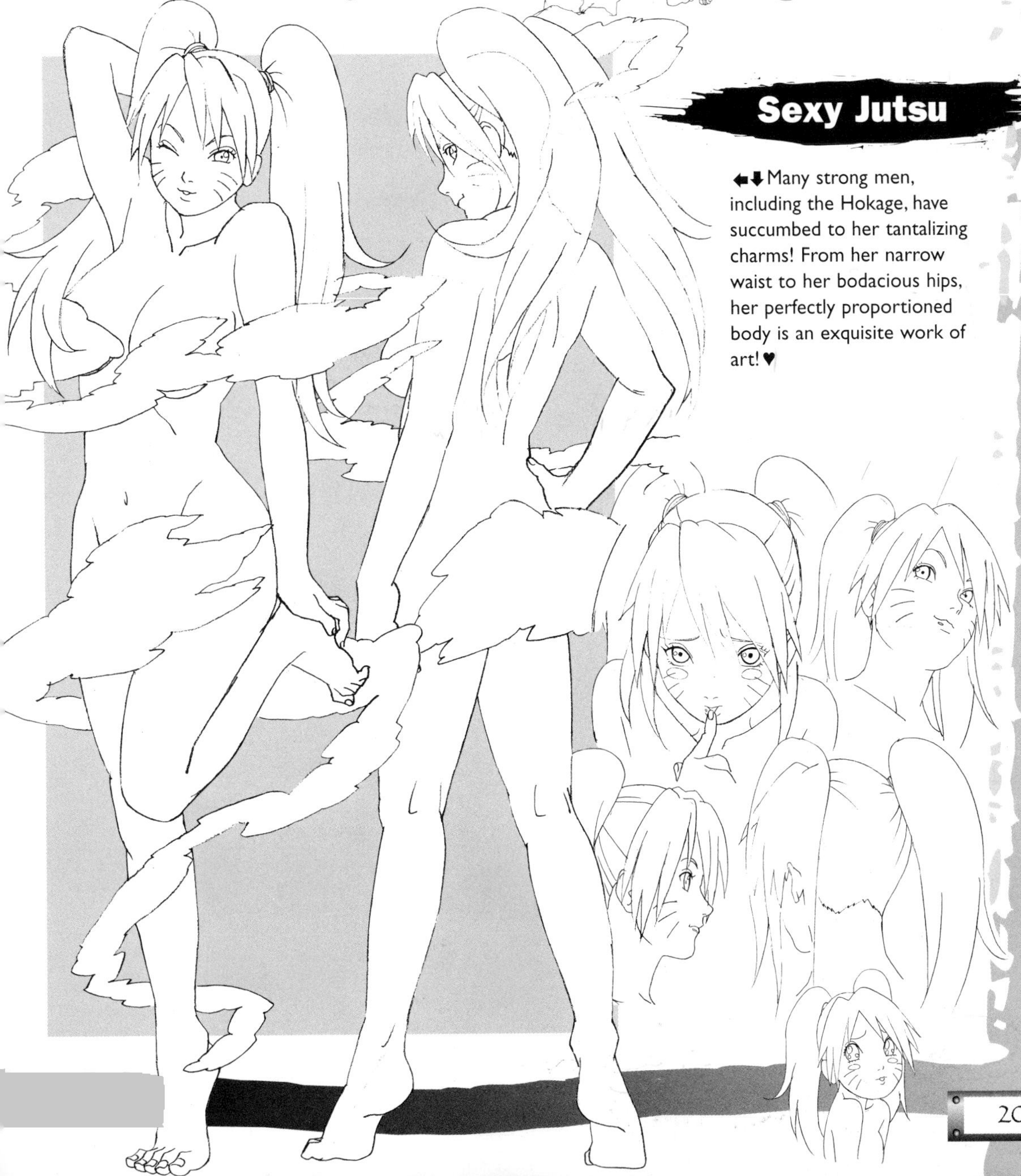

Sexy Jutsu

⬅⬇ Many strong men, including the Hokage, have succumbed to her tantalizing charms! From her narrow waist to her bodacious hips, her perfectly proportioned body is an exquisite work of art! ♥

Sasuke Uchiha

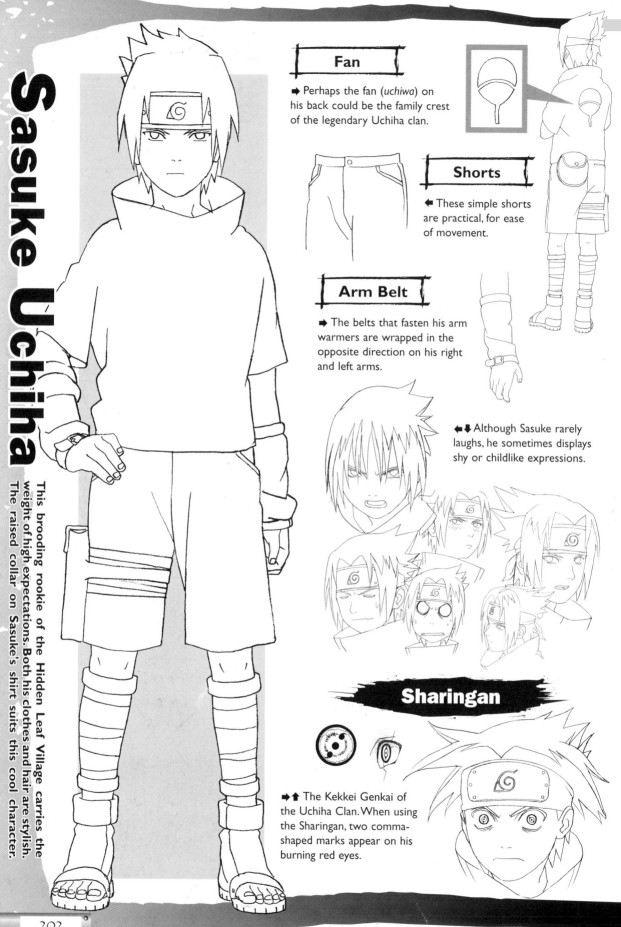

This brooding rookie of the Hidden Leaf Village carries the weight of high expectations. Both his clothes and hair are stylish. The raised collar on Sasuke's shirt suits this cool character.

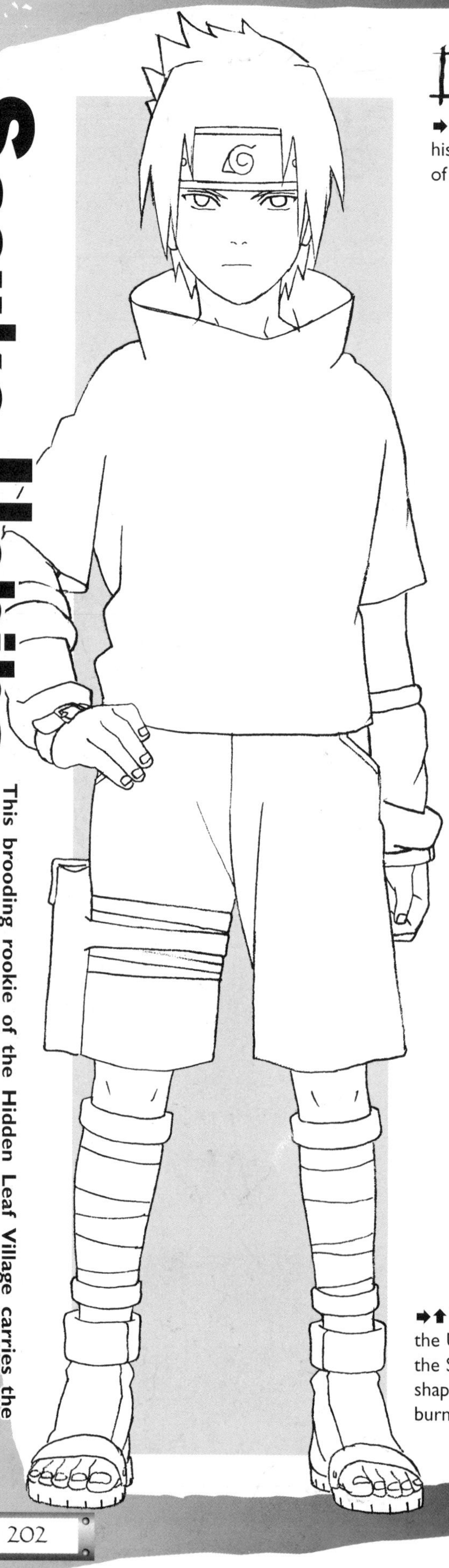

Fan

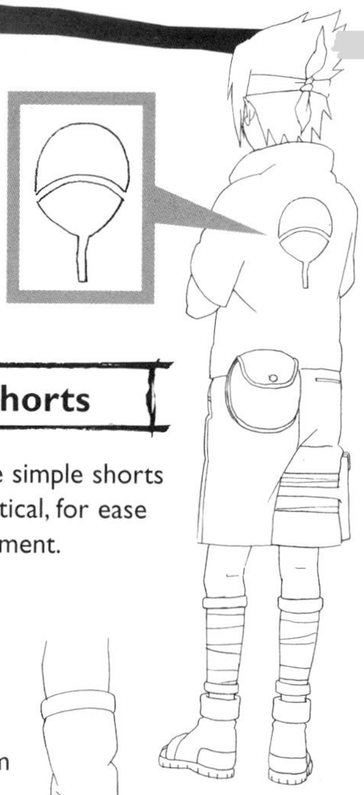

➡ Perhaps the fan (*uchiwa*) on his back could be the family crest of the legendary Uchiha clan.

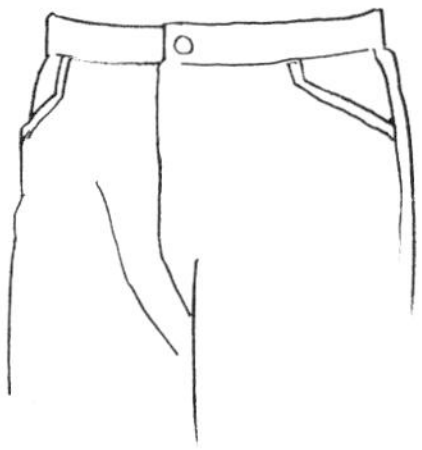

Shorts

⬅ These simple shorts are practical, for ease of movement.

Arm Belt

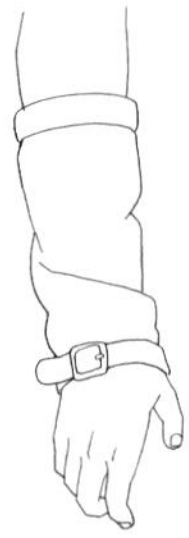

➡ The belts that fasten his arm warmers are wrapped in the opposite direction on his right and left arms.

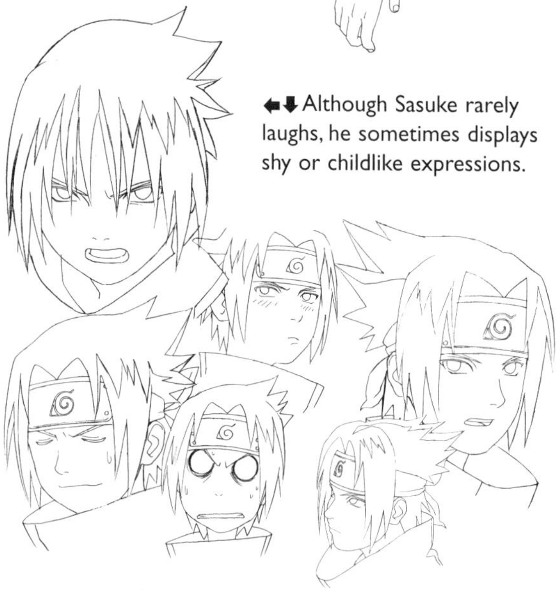

⬅⬇ Although Sasuke rarely laughs, he sometimes displays shy or childlike expressions.

Sharingan

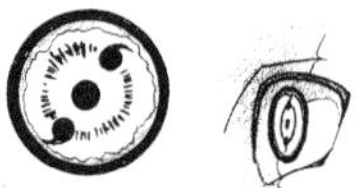

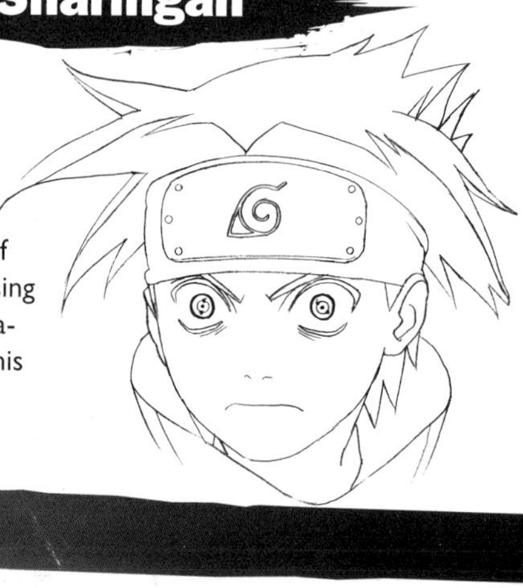

➡⬆ The Kekkei Genkai of the Uchiha Clan. When using the Sharingan, two comma-shaped marks appear on his burning red eyes.

Sakura Haruno

Sakura is a clear-headed and wise kunoichi. Like many girls, she devotes a lot of attention to her hair and her clothes. The circles that appear on the front, back and shoulders of her dress seem to be her family's crest.

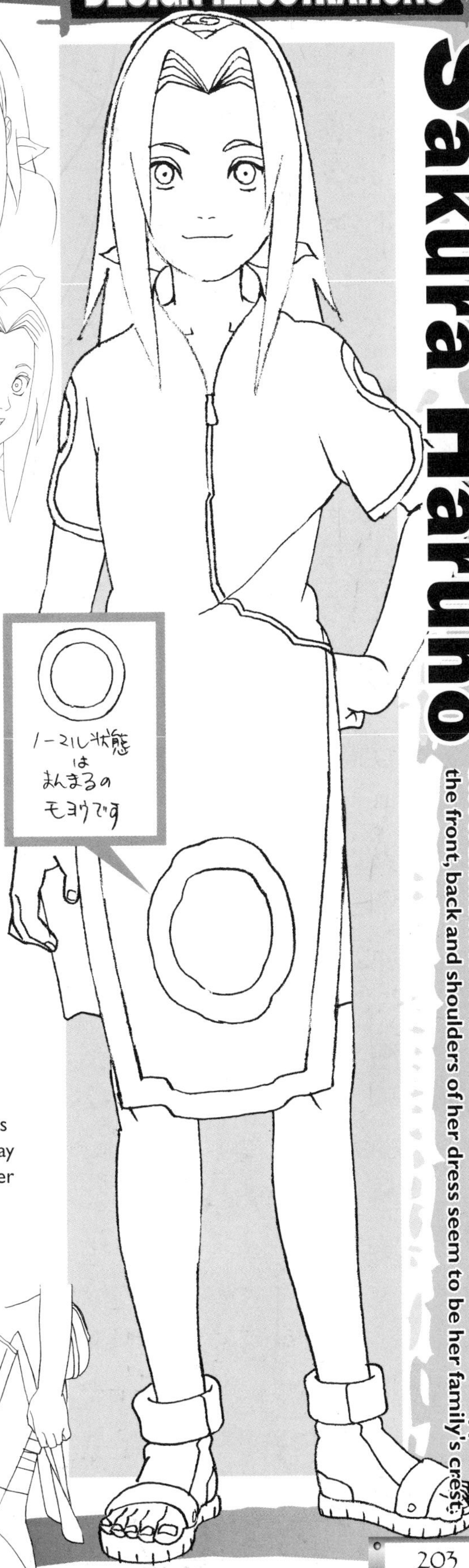

➡⬇ Sakura has a colorful array of facial expressions. When she ties her hair back with the ribbon Ino gave her, she looks very feminine.

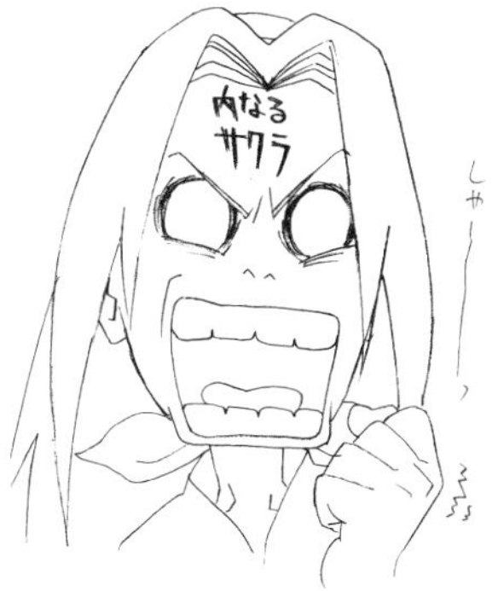

内なる
サクラ

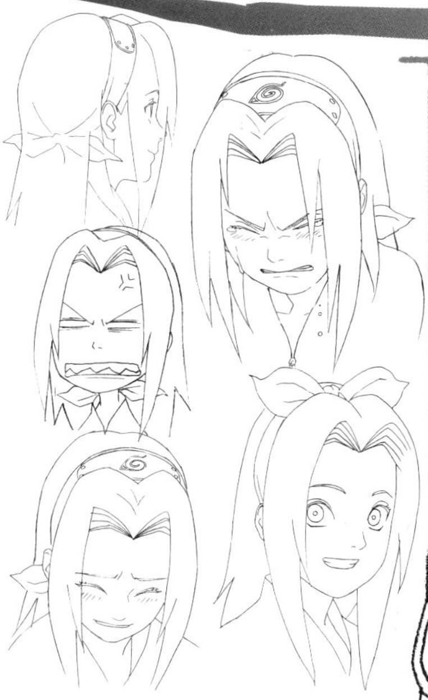

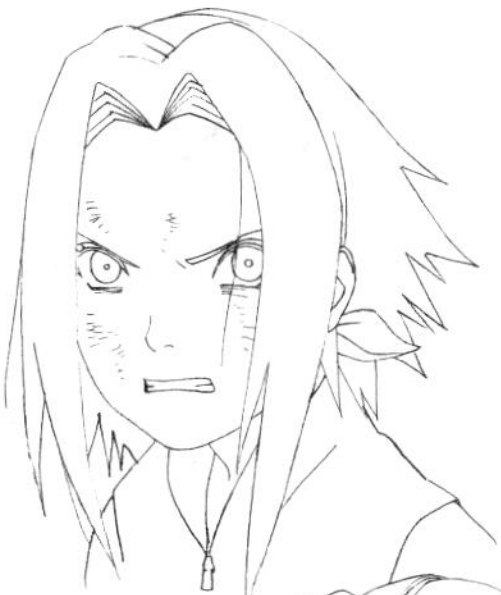

⬅⬇ Sakura's look changes after she cuts off her own hair and becomes more mature. She seems even spunkier and more energetic.

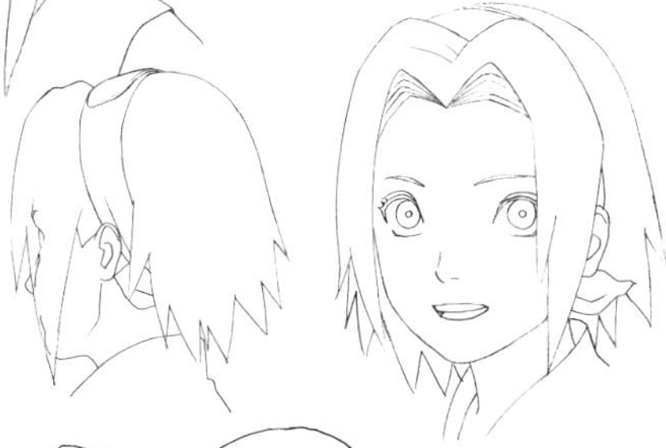

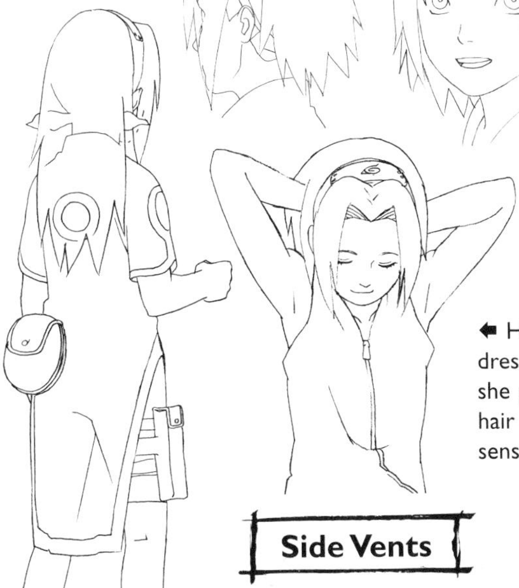

⬅ Her sleeveless dress and the way she pulls back her hair are kind of sensual.

Side Vents

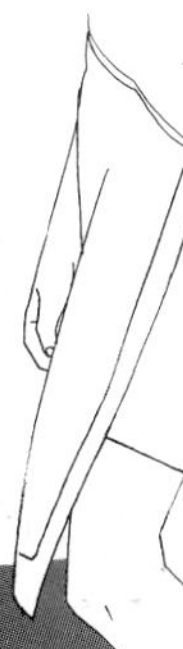

➡ The slits in the sides of her dress allow her to move quickly in intense combat. Because she wears leggings underneath, her modesty is not compromised, even if the dress flips over.

Kakashi Hatake

Kakashi is a jonin in the Hidden Leaf Village who leads Naruto and his squad. His normal pose, with his hands in his pockets, shows his calm and composed personality. Tying his headband slanted to conceal his Sharingan is Kakashi's special style.

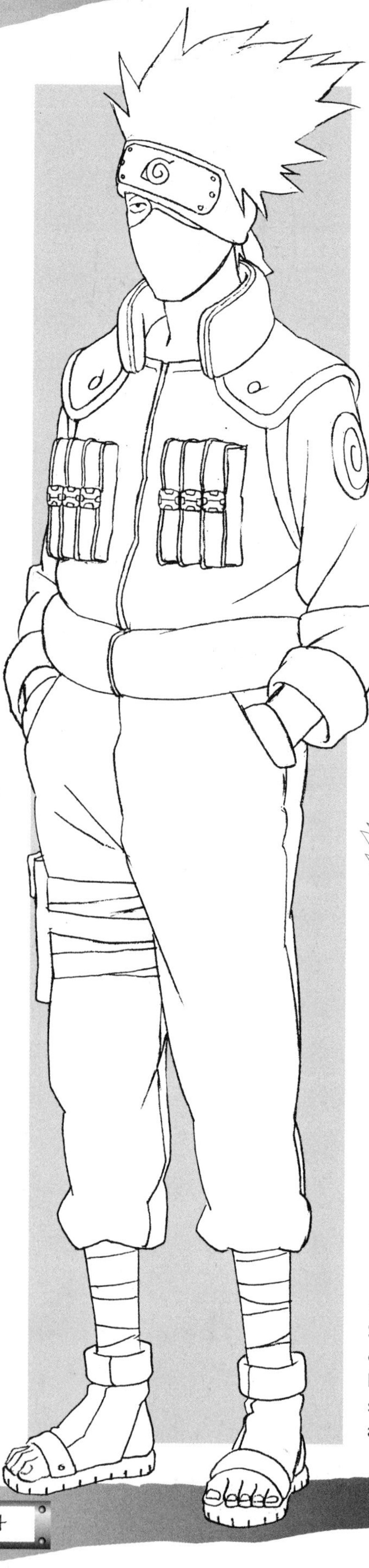

Swirl

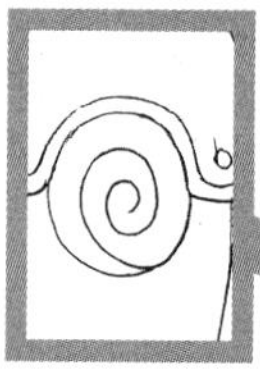

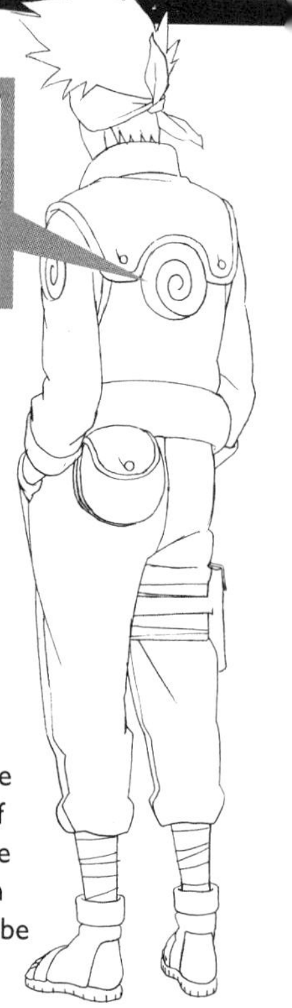

➡ The swirl (*uzumaki*) mark on his back is not flat but is somewhat raised.

Hand Protectors

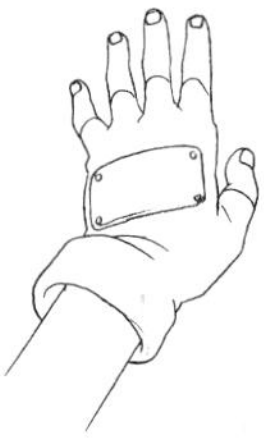

⬅ A metal plate similar to the material used on the headbands is attached to gloves, making them into protective gear.

Make-out Books

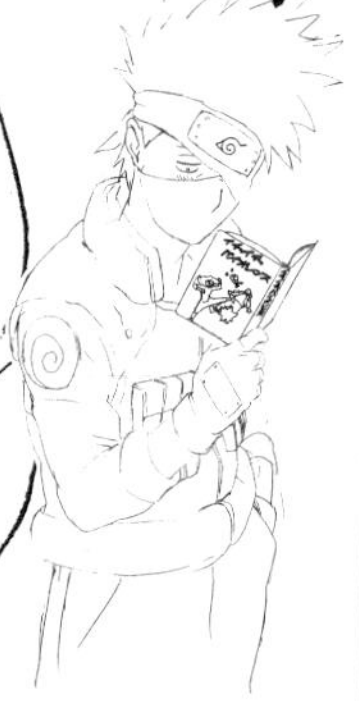

⬅⬇ Kakashi gets so absorbed in this trilogy of books that he even reads it while fending off his trainees' attacks during the survival exercise. Judging from this cover, the contents must be pretty intense…

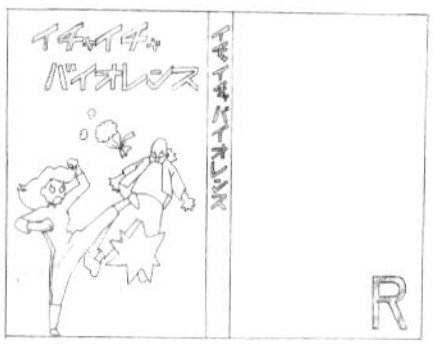

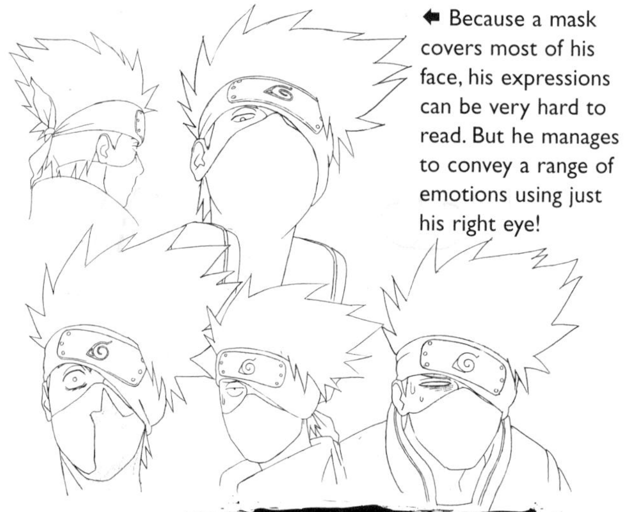

⬅ Because a mask covers most of his face, his expressions can be very hard to read. But he manages to convey a range of emotions using just his right eye!

Sharingan

➡ Unlike Sasuke, Kakashi's Sharingan eye has three comma-shaped marks. But how did he get the scar that stretches across his face, above and below his left eye?

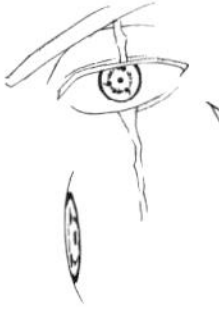

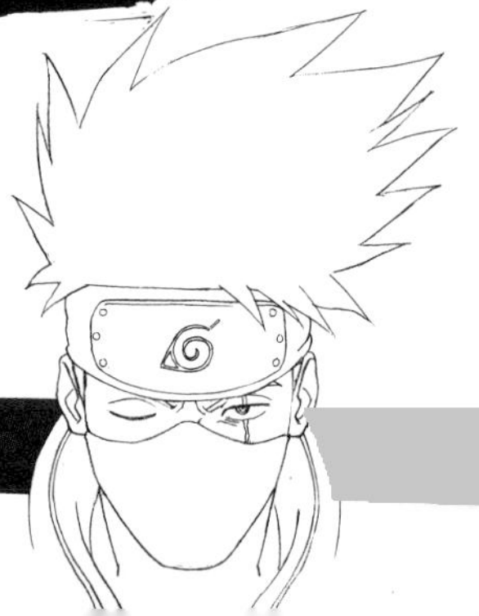

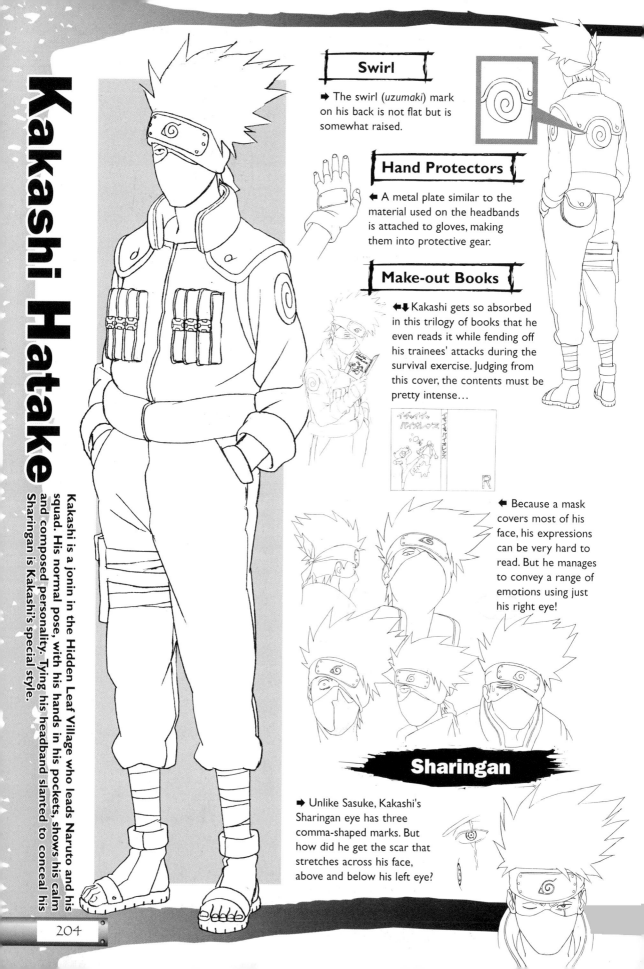

Iruka

Iruka is a chunin in the Hidden Leaf Village and a teacher at Ninja Academy. His goal with his personal style is to serve as an example to others -- he wears his vest correctly and ties his headband straight at the proper location.

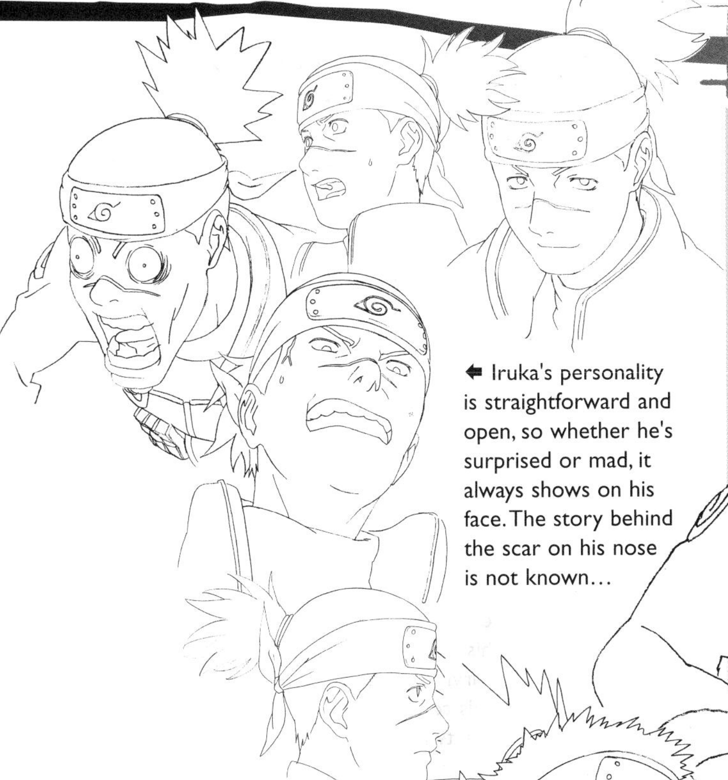

⬅ Iruka's personality is straightforward and open, so whether he's surprised or mad, it always shows on his face. The story behind the scar on his nose is not known…

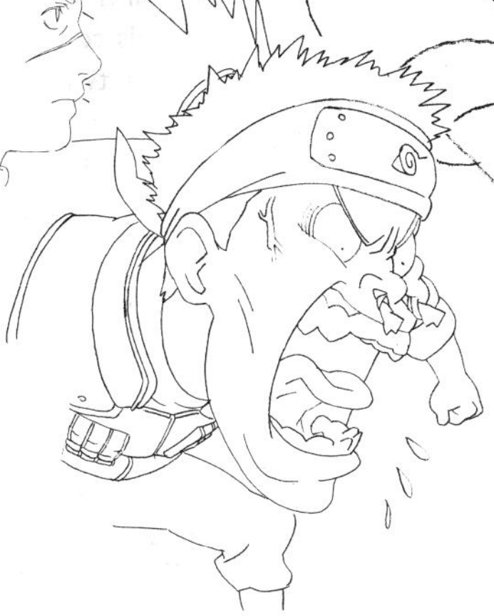

Angry Face

➡ He is furious after falling victim to Naruto's Sexy Jutsu! His anger is so intense that his head swells up, completely out of proportion to his body…but maybe he's really just trying to conceal his embarrassment!

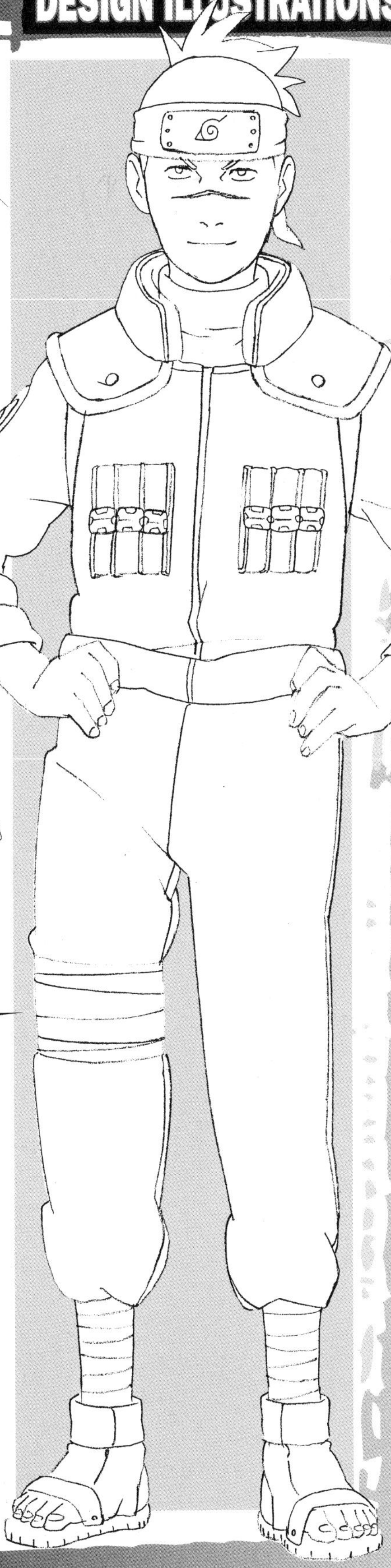

Academy Staff Office

⬇Iruka and the other teachers normally work and take their breaks here. The circular table that surrounds the pillar is unique.

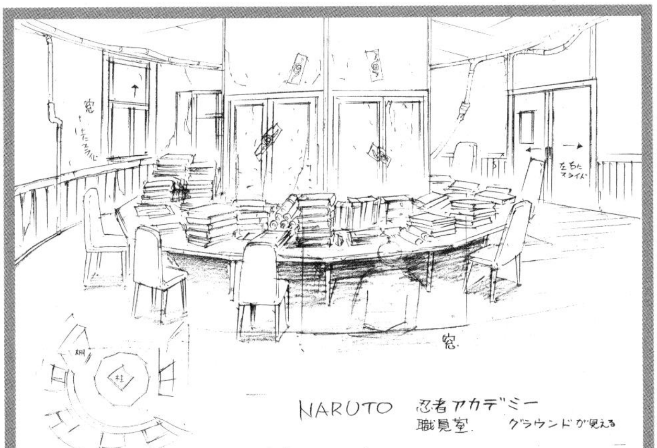
NARUTO 忍者アカデミー
職員室 グラウンドが見える

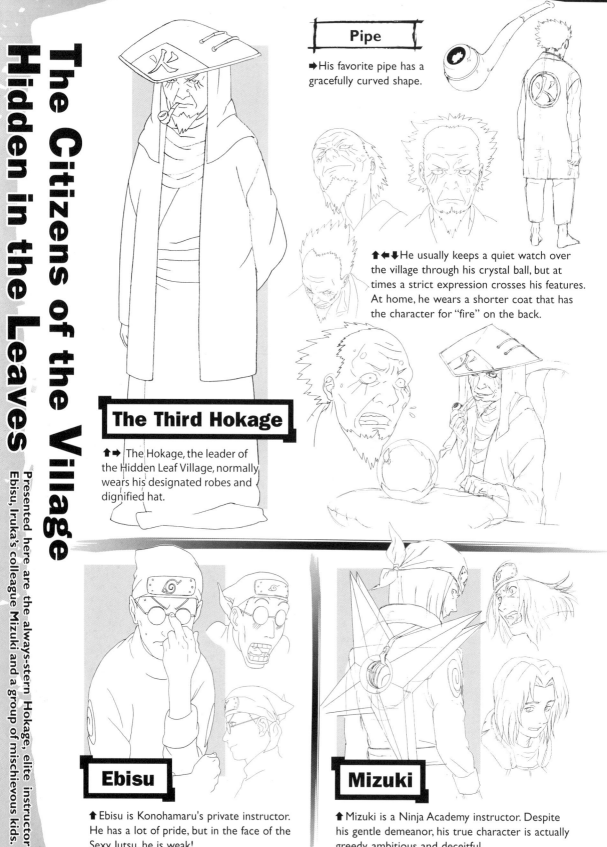

The Citizens of the Village Hidden in the Leaves

Presented here are the always-stern Hokage, elite instructor Ebisu, Iruka's colleague Mizuki and a group of mischievous kids.

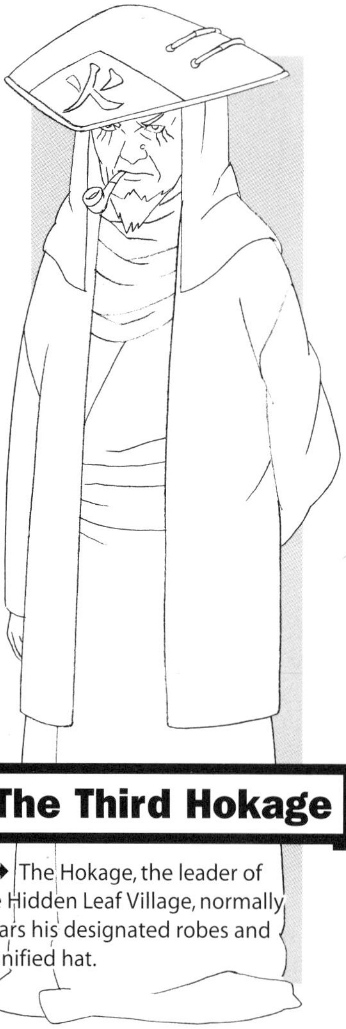

The Third Hokage

⬆➡ The Hokage, the leader of the Hidden Leaf Village, normally wears his designated robes and dignified hat.

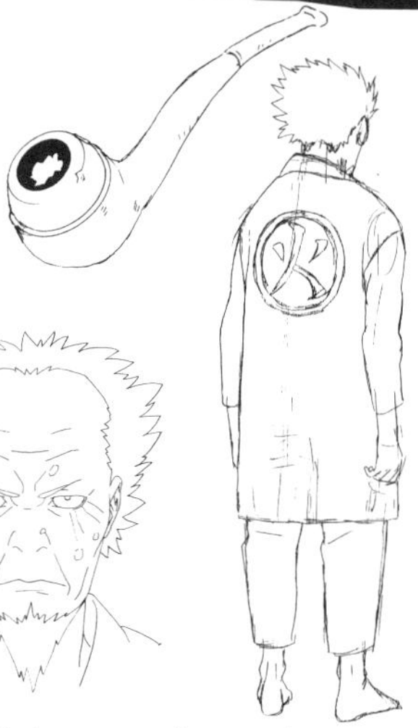

Pipe

➡His favorite pipe has a gracefully curved shape.

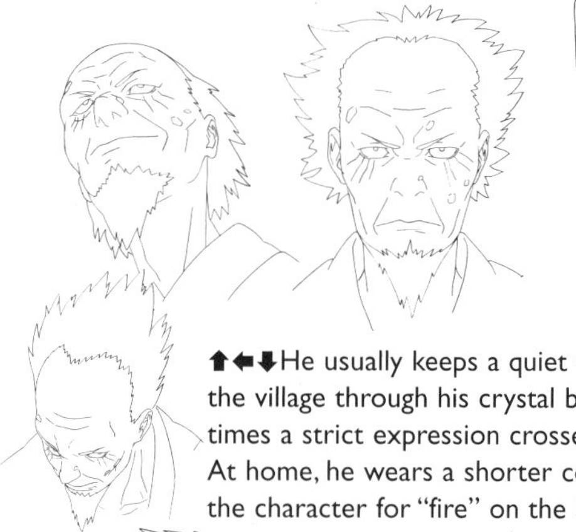

⬆⬅⬇He usually keeps a quiet watch over the village through his crystal ball, but at times a strict expression crosses his features. At home, he wears a shorter coat that has the character for "fire" on the back.

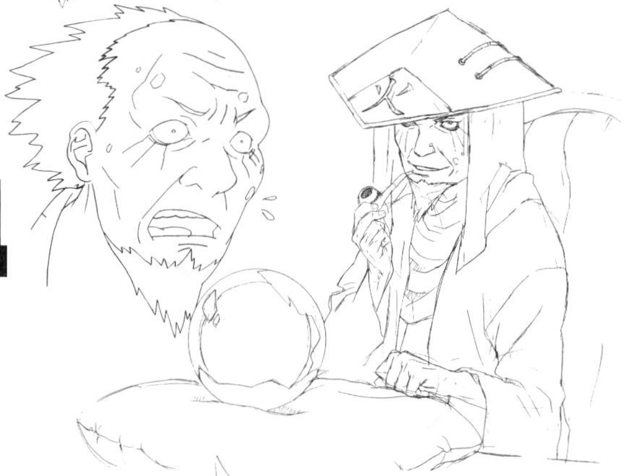

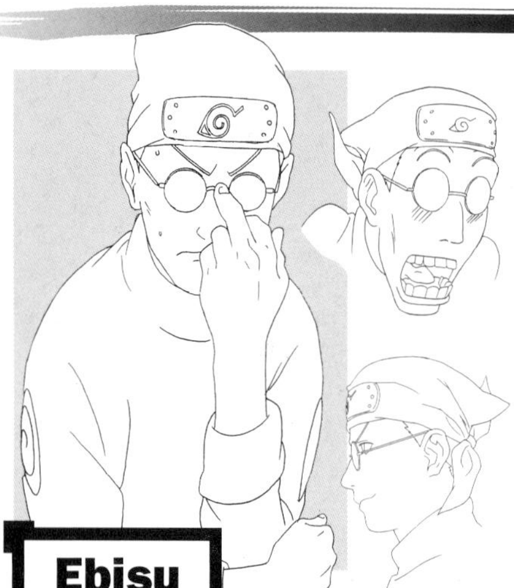

Ebisu

⬆Ebisu is Konohamaru's private instructor. He has a lot of pride, but in the face of the Sexy Jutsu, he is weak!

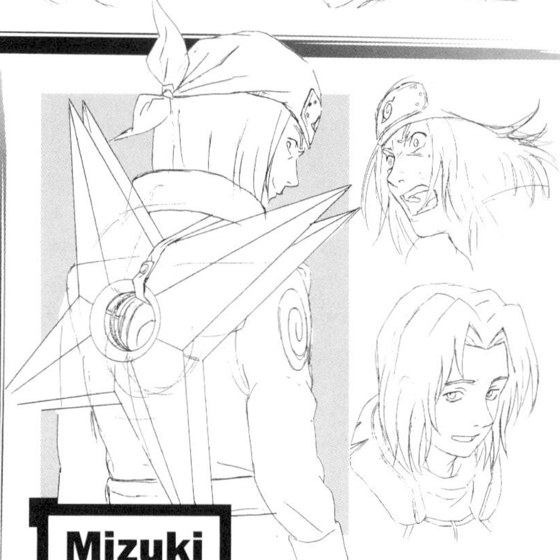

Mizuki

⬆Mizuki is a Ninja Academy instructor. Despite his gentle demeanor, his true character is actually greedy, ambitious and deceitful.

Konohamaru's Army

➡The Hokage's grandson Konohamaru and his two best friends have formed "Konohamaru's Army." In homage to Naruto, they all wear goggles.

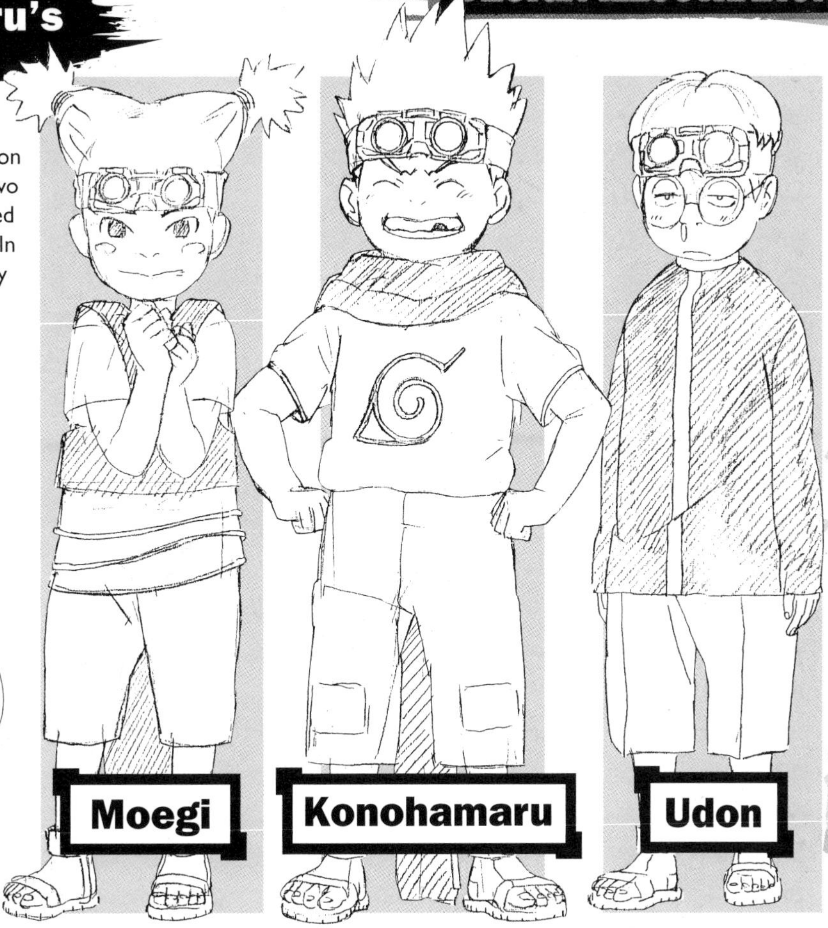
Moegi
Konohamaru
Udon

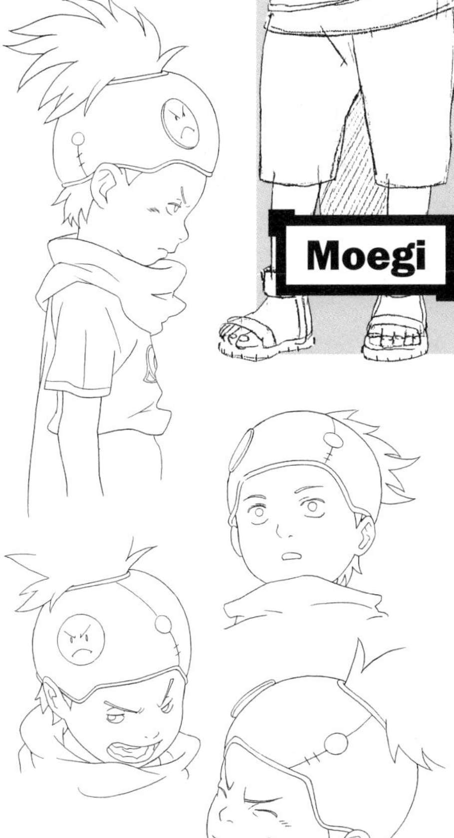

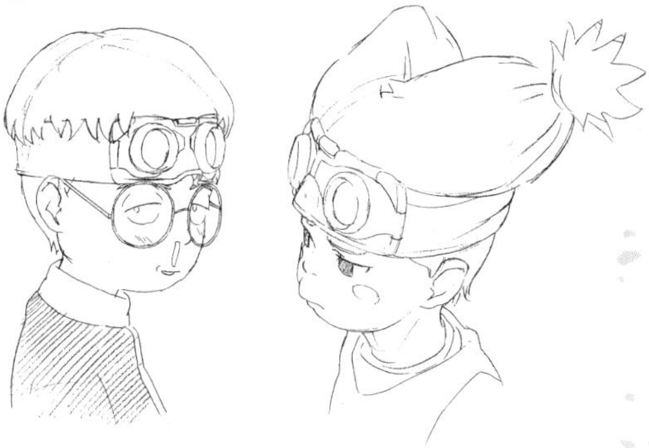

⬆Udon is a snotty-nosed kid who doesn't change his expression very much. Moegi is a tomboy, but her girly streak shows through in her finicky attitude about her hair. Her peculiar style of tying it back is cute.

⬆Konohamaru can seem like a brat, but even a rascally kid like him feels sad and anxious. Maybe the lonely expression he sometimes wears reveals his true soul...

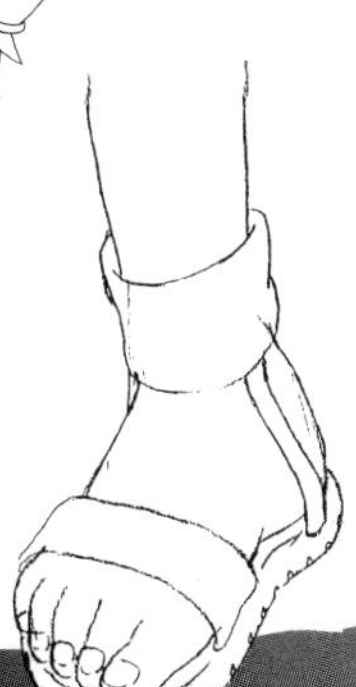

Moegi's Sandals

⬅Unlike Udon's and Konohamaru's, the instep part of Moegi's sandals is open. It's the sort of detail that only a girl would care about...

Hot Springs

This is the public bath that Naruto and Konohamaru sneaked into using the Sexy Jutsu. This is a valuable drawing because it doesn't appear in the manga.

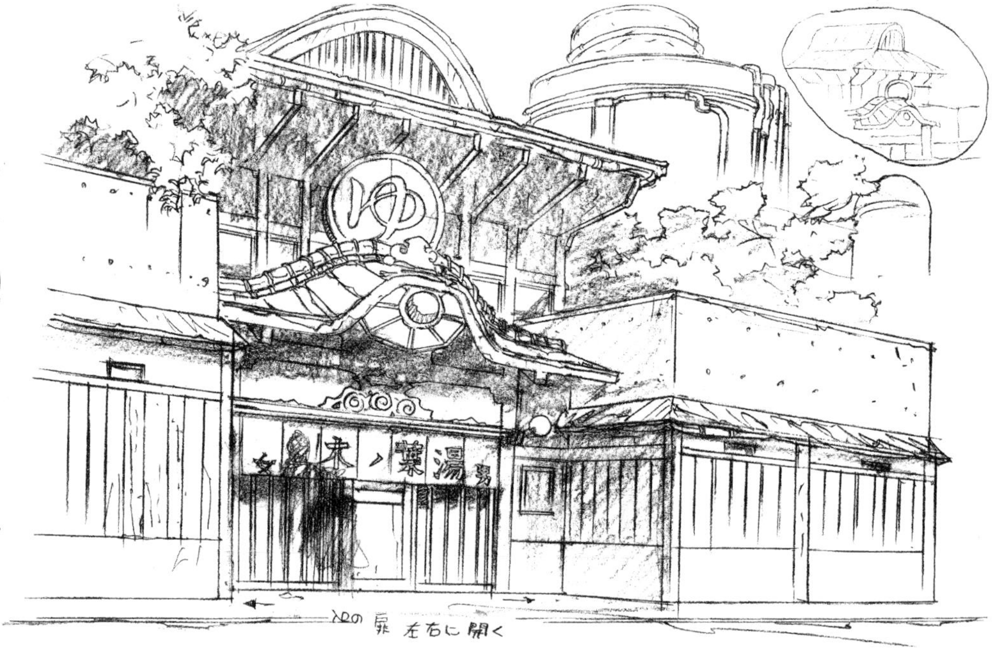

ゆ
木ノ葉湯
この扉 左右に開く
NARUTO 銭湯(改)

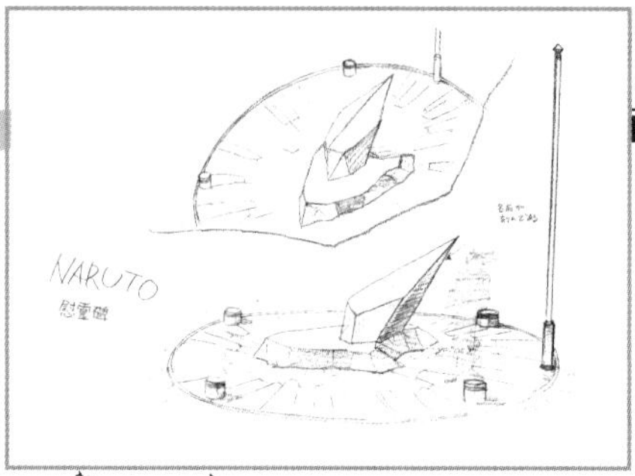

NARUTO
慰霊碑

Memorial Stone

⬅ Unlike the original design in the manga, the monument is in the shape of a sundial. Names of ninja who died in the line of duty are carved on the gnomon.

Training Ground

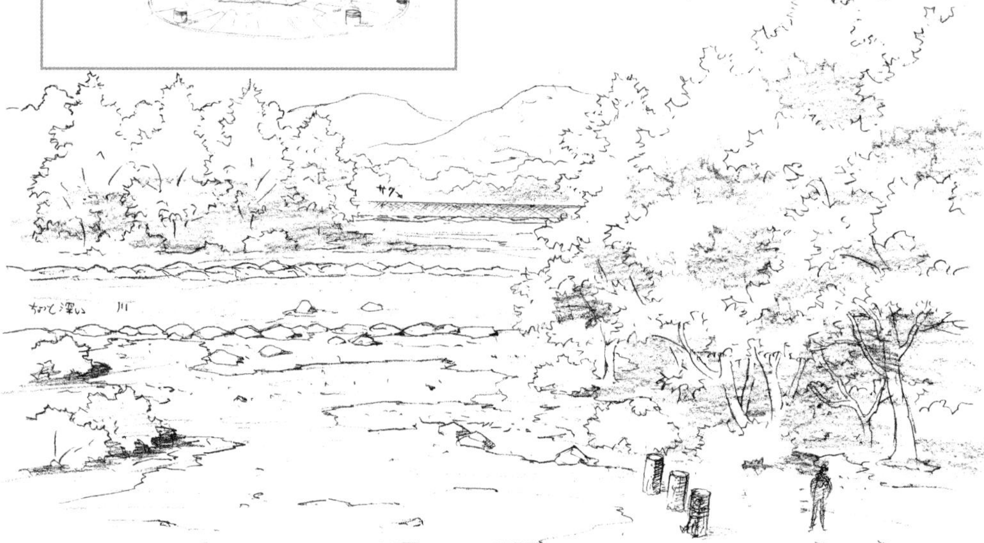

慰霊碑

The place where Kakashi held the survival exercise is a barren piece of land facing a dry riverbed. It is usually a quiet, desolate place.

Ichiraku Ramen

There's only counter seating at Ichiraku, which is famous for its tonkotsu ramen and its stubborn owner.

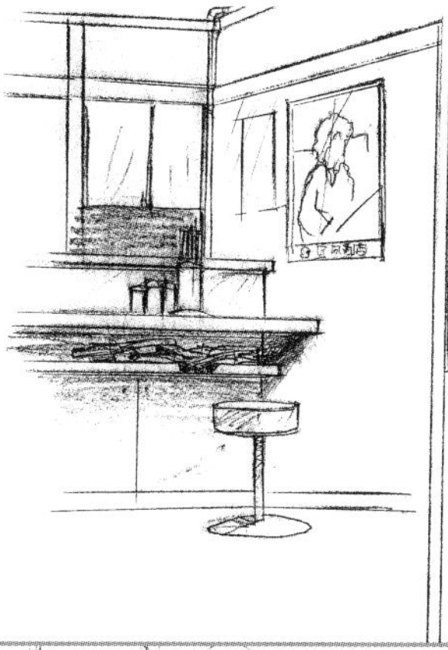

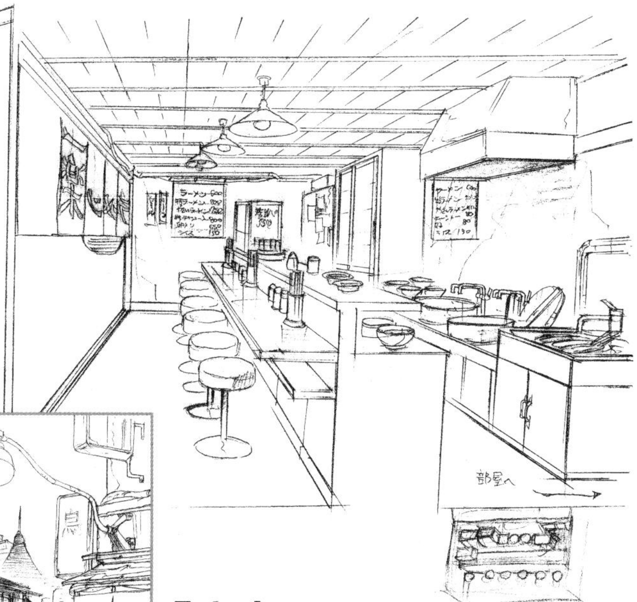
部屋へ

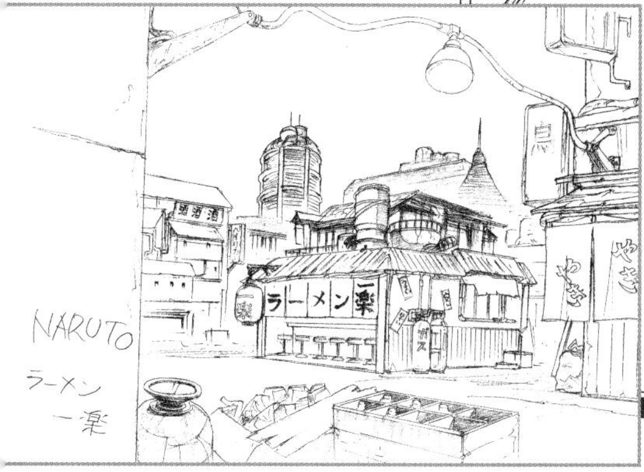
ラーメン一楽
NARUTO
ラーメン
一楽

Exterior

← The restaurant has a small, street-stand atmosphere. The crowds, lured by the light of the lantern, are unceasing!

Shopping District

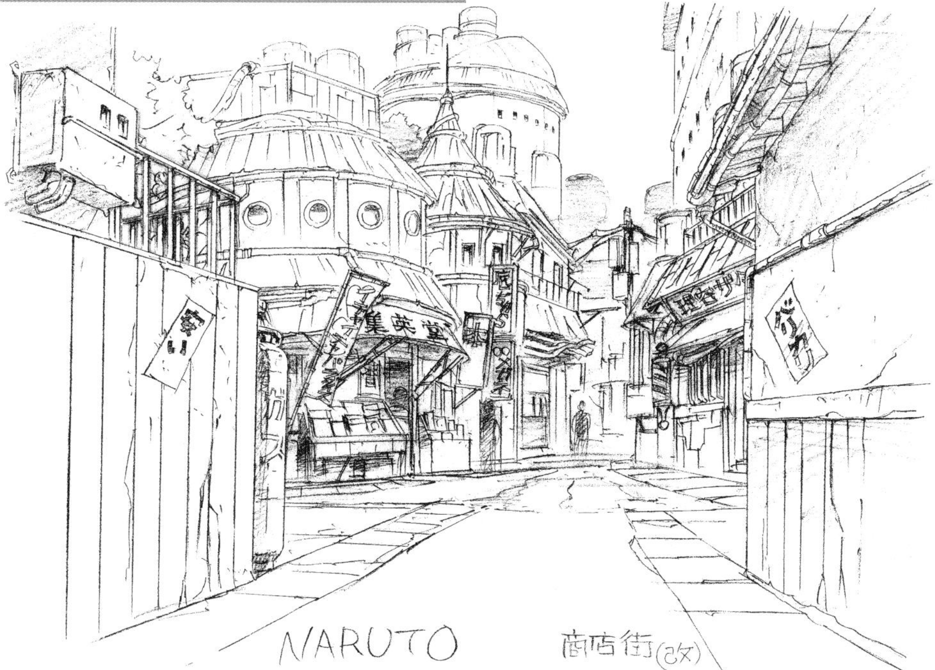
集英堂
NARUTO
商店街(改)

Shueido, the bookstore in the front, has a *Make-out Paradise* banner! Is this where Kakashi shops?!

Haku

Zabuza's loyal follower, Haku. He wears an obi tied around his traditional half coat and pleated trousers. The beautiful, delicate features of his face give him a feminine appearance. He normally hides his face with the mask of the Hidden Mist Anbu Black Ops Unit to make himself into a coldhearted weapon.

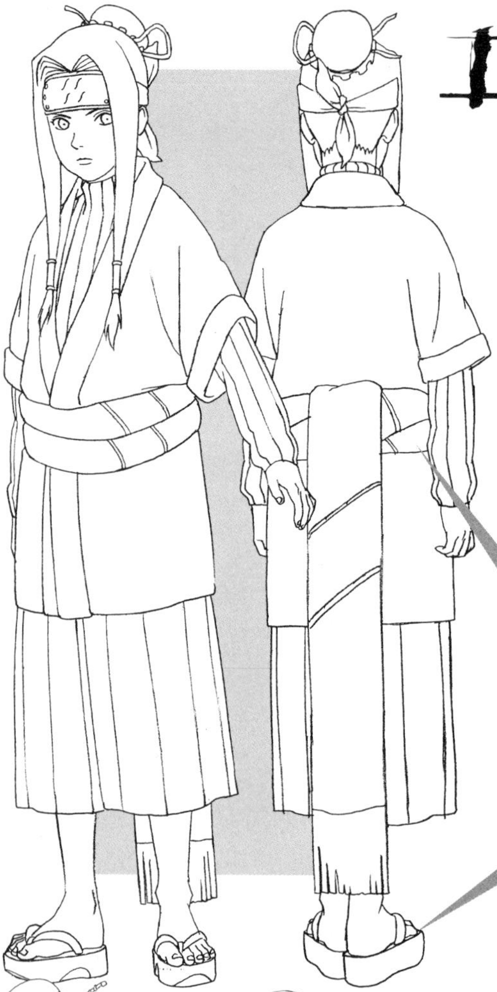

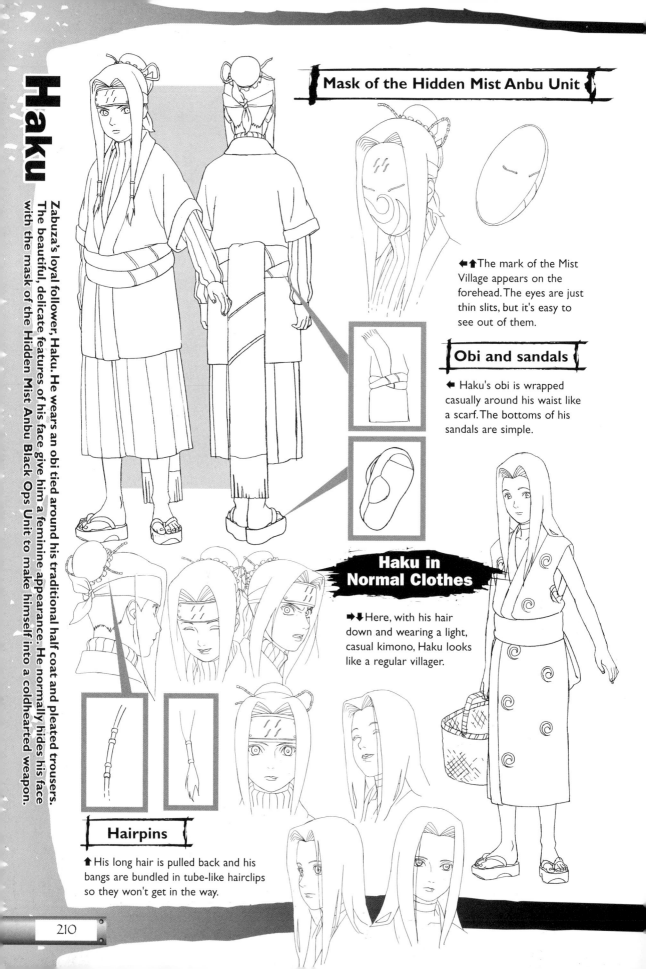

Mask of the Hidden Mist Anbu Unit

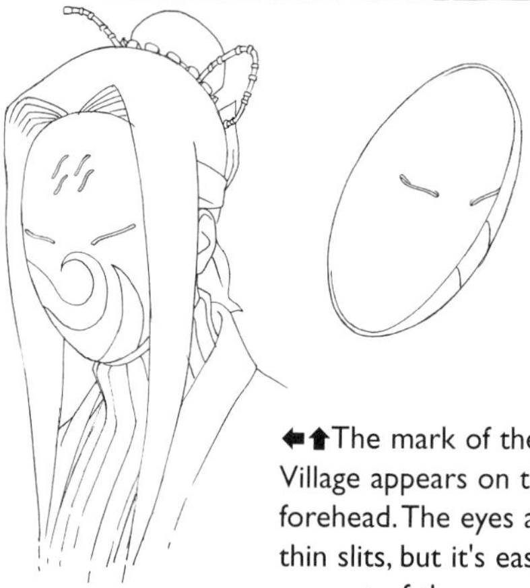

⬅⬆The mark of the Mist Village appears on the forehead. The eyes are just thin slits, but it's easy to see out of them.

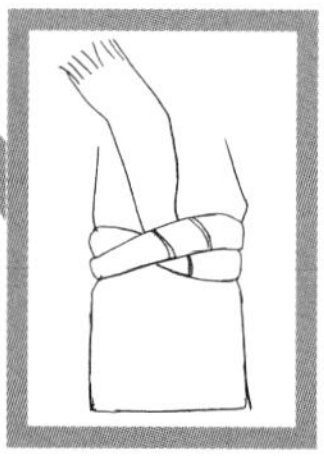

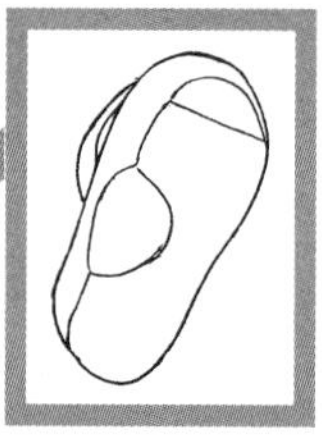

Obi and sandals

⬅ Haku's obi is wrapped casually around his waist like a scarf. The bottoms of his sandals are simple.

Haku in Normal Clothes

➡⬇Here, with his hair down and wearing a light, casual kimono, Haku looks like a regular villager.

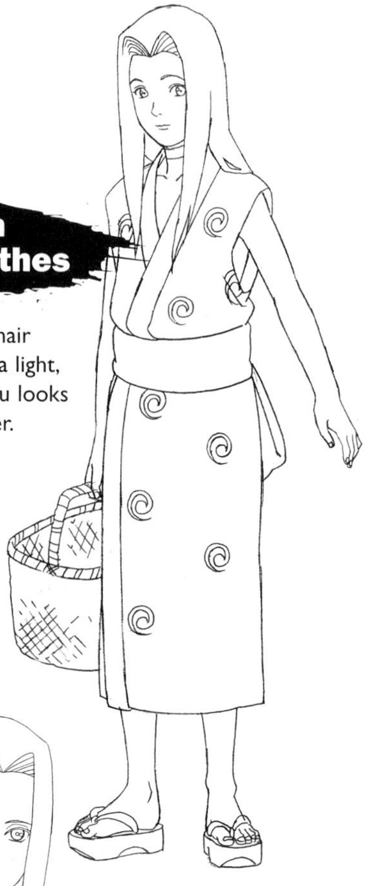

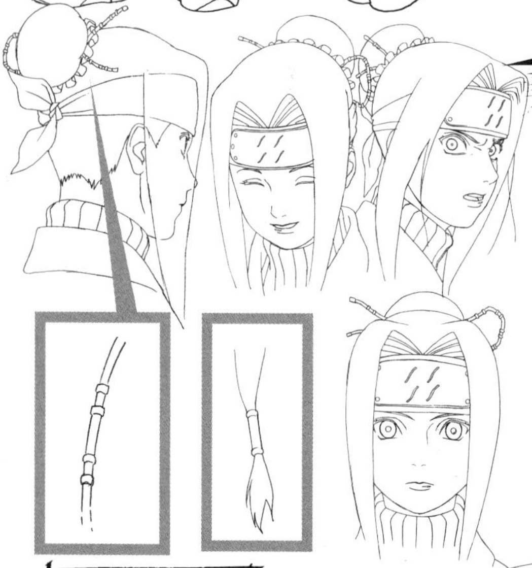

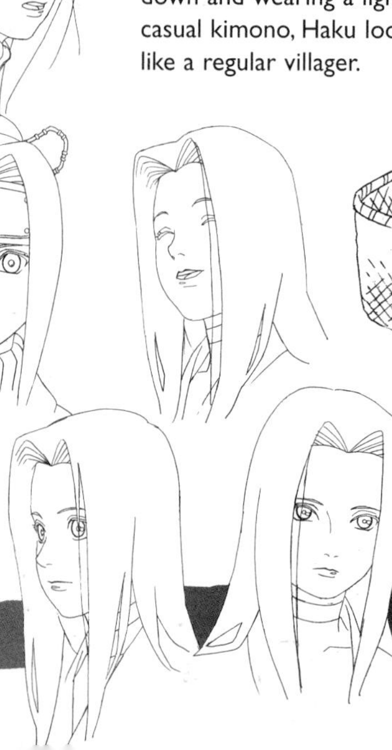

Hairpins

⬆His long hair is pulled back and his bangs are bundled in tube-like hairclips so they won't get in the way.

Zabuza Momochi

From the time he was a member of the Anbu Black Ops Unit in the Hidden Mist Village until now, he has worn three different costumes. The Guillotine Sword that symbolizes Zabuza's power is tied on a sash around his neck.

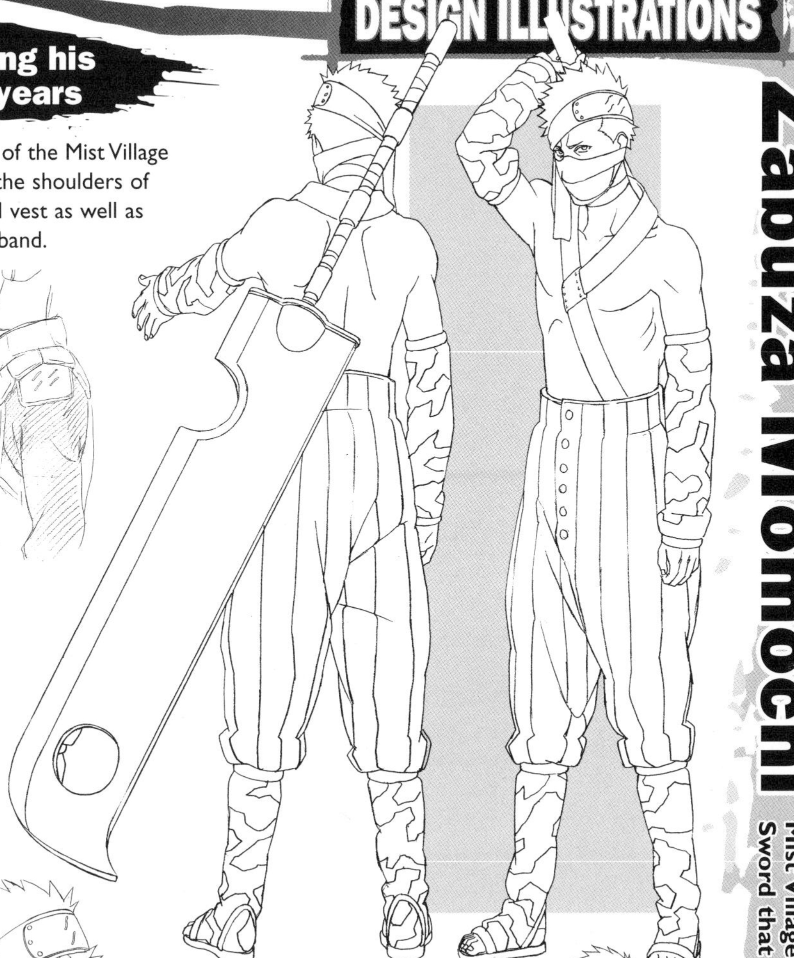

Zabuza during his Mist ninja years

⬇The mark of the Mist Village appears on the shoulders of the armored vest as well as on the headband.

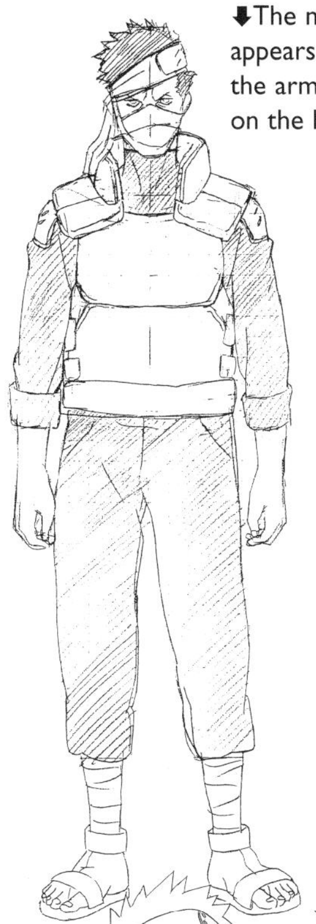

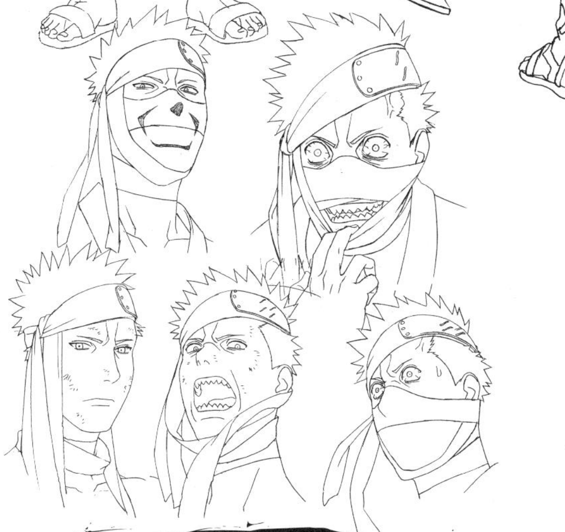

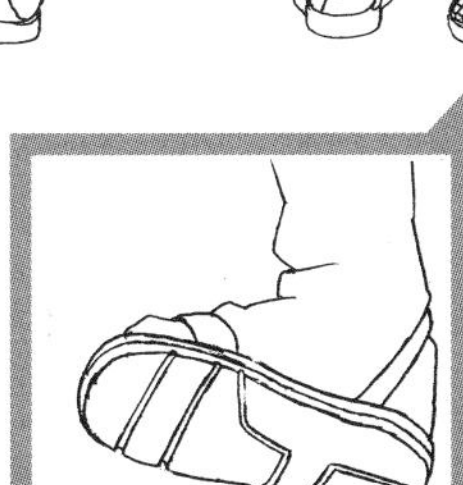

Sandals

⬇At the decisive battle on the bridge, he wore sandals with treads in the soles for better traction.

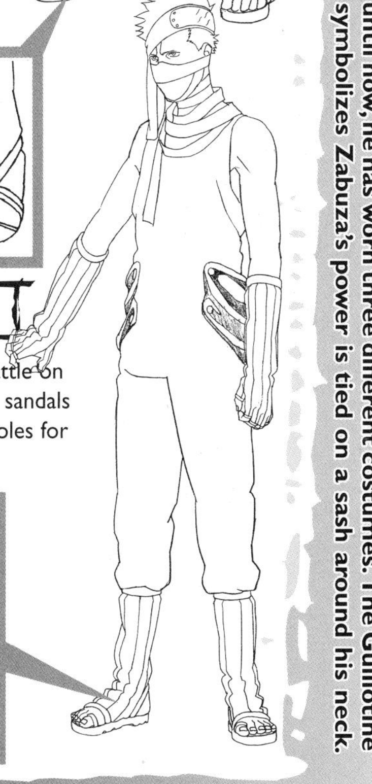

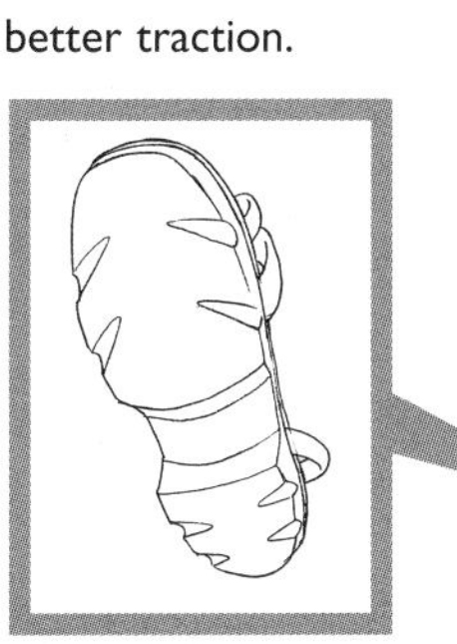

Zabuza without his headband

⬇His hair is unkempt. The wrapping of his bandages here differs from when he has his headband on.

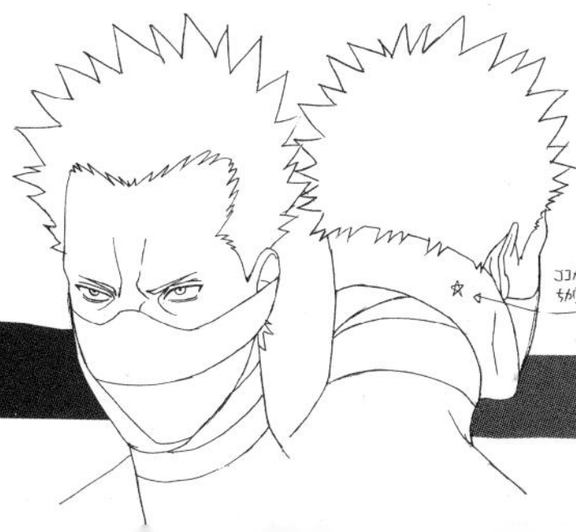

The People of the Land of Waves

Since the Land of Waves does not have shinobi, all the people wear relatively normal clothes. Tazuna, a simple craftsman, is not particular about the way he dresses. The pointed hat he wears is unique to the Land of Waves.

Tsunami

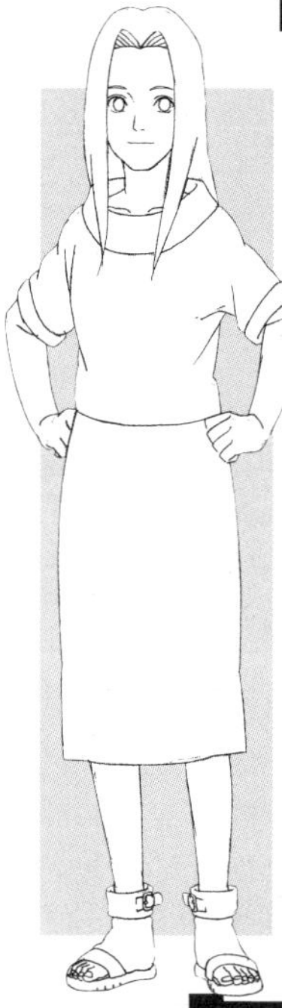

⬅ She wears sandals just like Inari's, and her clothes are plain. She seems like a dependable person.

Tazuna

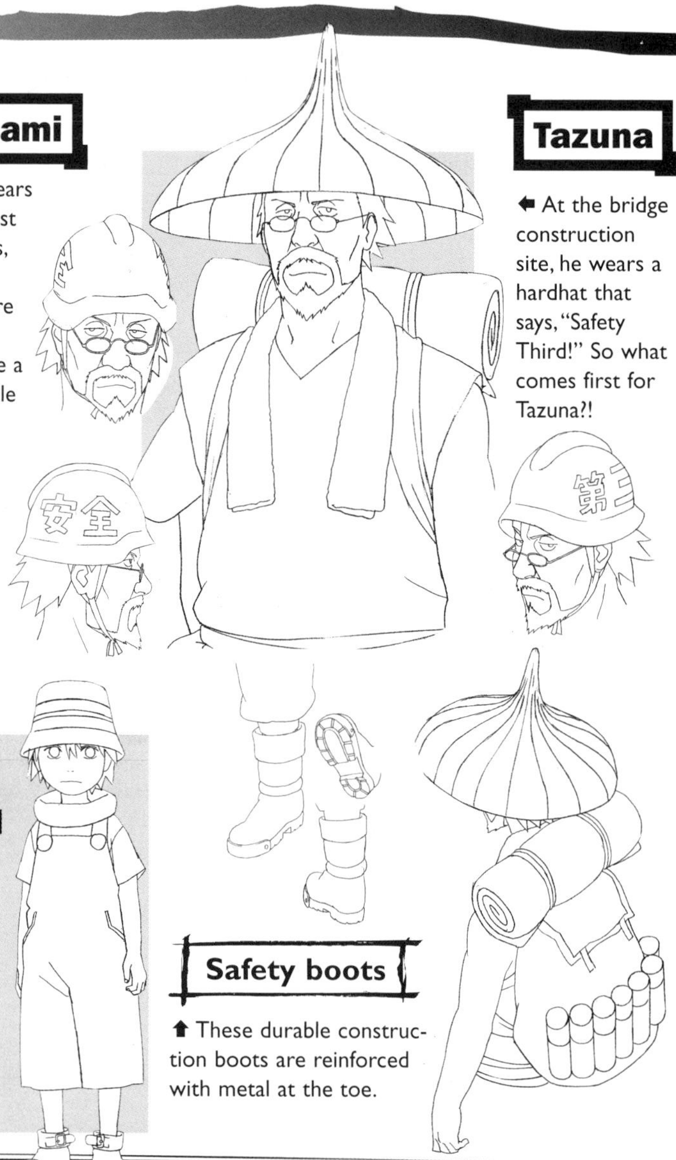
安全
第三

⬅ At the bridge construction site, he wears a hardhat that says, "Safety Third!" So what comes first for Tazuna?!

Safety boots

⬆ These durable construction boots are reinforced with metal at the toe.

Inari

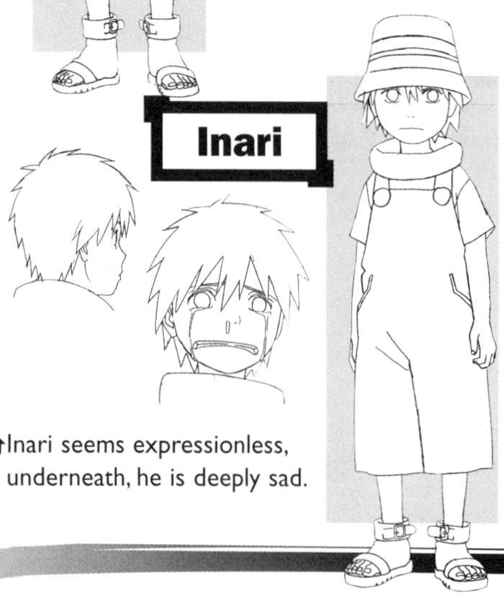

➡⬆ Inari seems expressionless, but underneath, he is deeply sad.

Akane's gang

⬇ Akane leads this gang of three mean-looking kids.

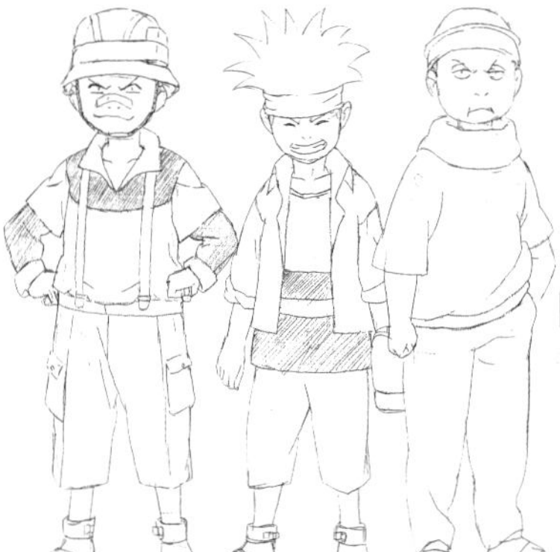

Shooting Star

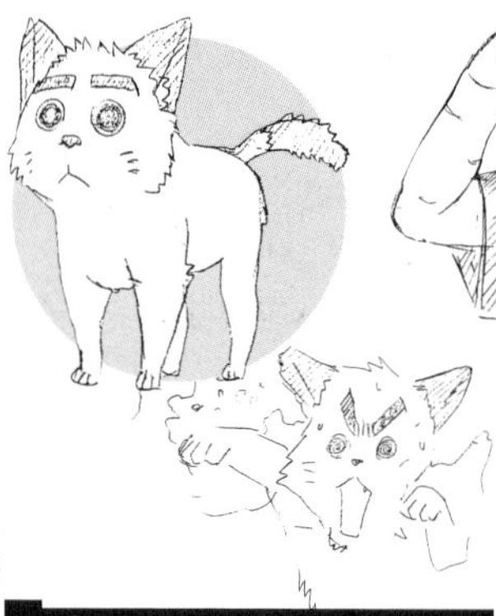

⬆ He has distinctive, thick eyebrows and looks totally panicked when he nearly drowns!

Kaiza

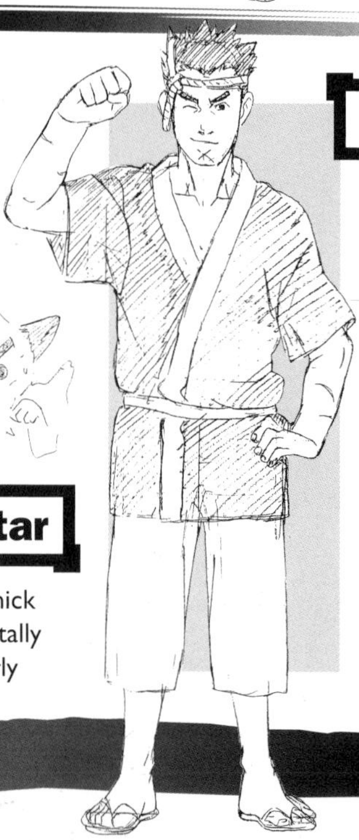

⬅ This manly hero wears a twisted headband.

Assassins

Zabuza's henchmen, the Demon Brothers, wield their special weapons in tandem, a technique only possible for twins. Gato's gang, from Gato the boss down to his army of thugs, has many colorful characters.

Demon Brothers

➡ The deadly twins attack their opponents using a special weapon fitted with poisonous claws and bladed chains.

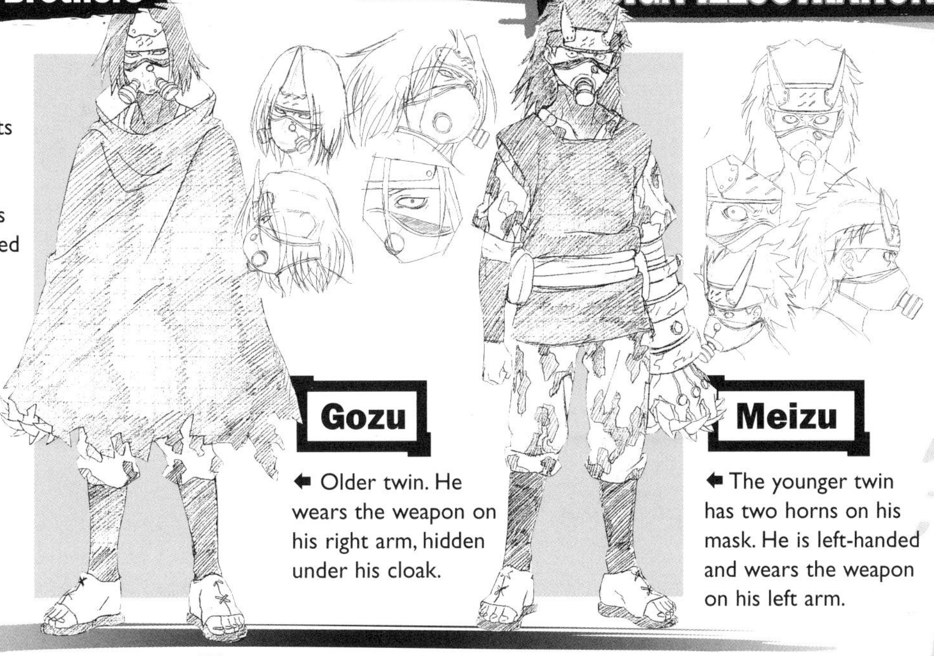

Gozu

⬅ Older twin. He wears the weapon on his right arm, hidden under his cloak.

Meizu

⬅ The younger twin has two horns on his mask. He is left-handed and wears the weapon on his left arm.

Zori

Waraji

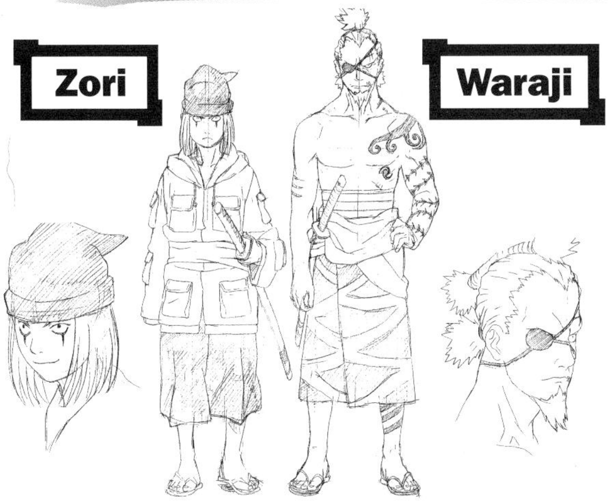

⬆ Although they use opposite hands, katana swords are the weapon of choice for both bodyguards.

Gato's gang

⬅⬇ Gato and the two bodyguards who escort him. They are obviously evil.

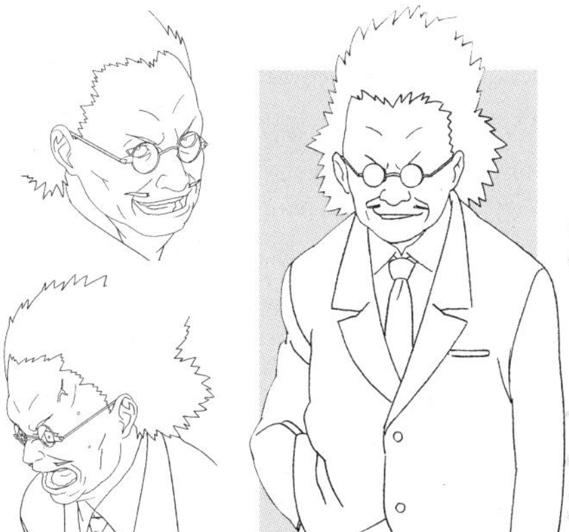

Gato

⬆ He is a short man, but he manages to give off an overwhelming aura of evil. His distinctive coif looks like his hair is exploding out of his head.

The thugs who serve Gato's gang

⬇ From a saw to a metal pipe to a crescent-shaped sickle, each one carries a different weapon.

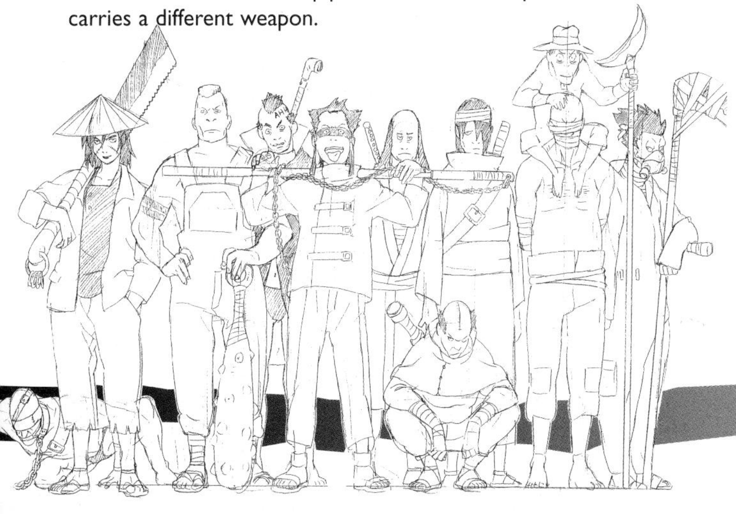

A boat in the Land of Waves

⬇ Many small ships like this are anchored along the coast. What kinds of fish do they catch?

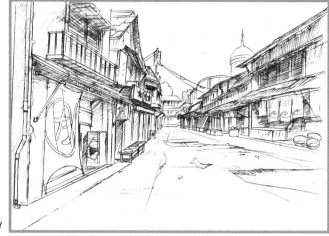

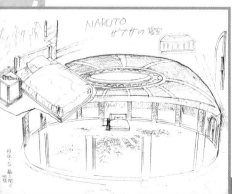

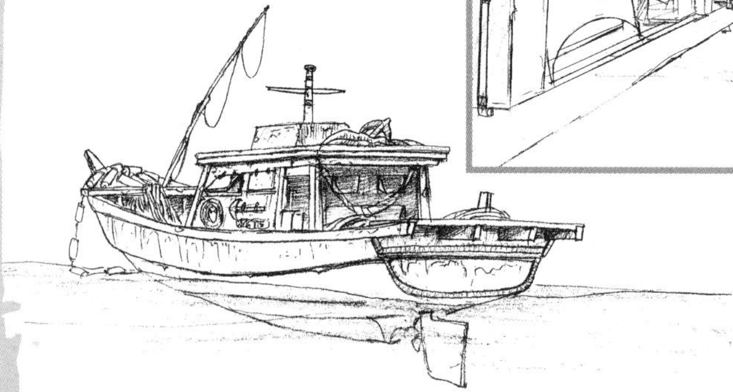

A city in the Land of Waves

⬆ The shopping district is lined with colorfully curtained storefronts. Although the street was once festive and full of life, it has become cheerless and bleak under Gato's rule.

Zabuza's hideout

Because he's a wanted man, Zabuza usually lies low in his cone-shaped hideout in the forest.

Exterior

➡ Ropes and staircases encircle each floor. One enters the structure from the surrounding trees.

NARUTO
ザブザのアジト

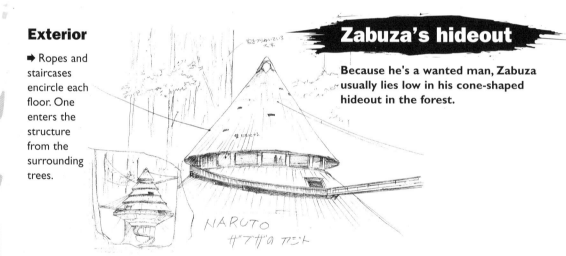

Bedroom

⬇ There is a solitary bed in this otherwise empty room. Zabuza always sleeps in this room.

NARUTO
ザブザの寝室

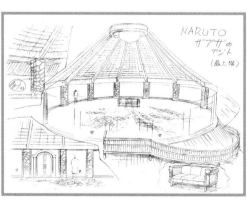

Top floor

⬅ This room contains only a single sofa. The ceiling is made from overlapping wooden shingles.

NARUTO
ザブザのアジト
(最上階)

Bird's-eye view of the Land of Waves

The town is developed from the seacoast to the riverbanks. Since it is an island nation, there are many houses built on the water. Beaches spread along the eastern coast.

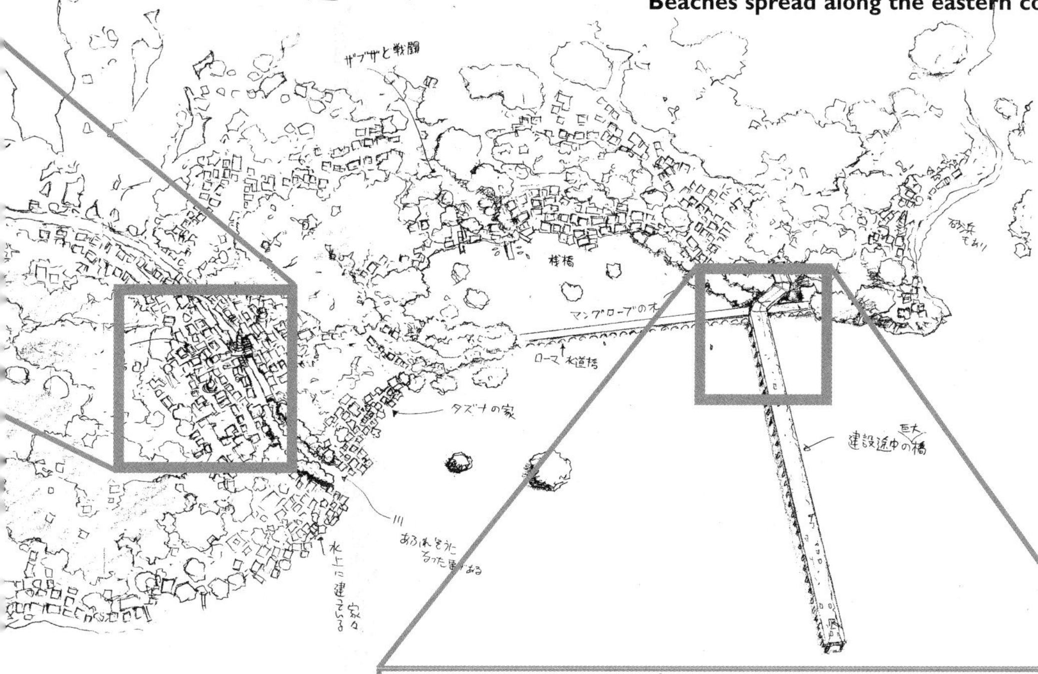
ザブザと戦闘
桟橋
マングローブの木
ローマ水道橋
タズナの家
巨大
建設途中の橋

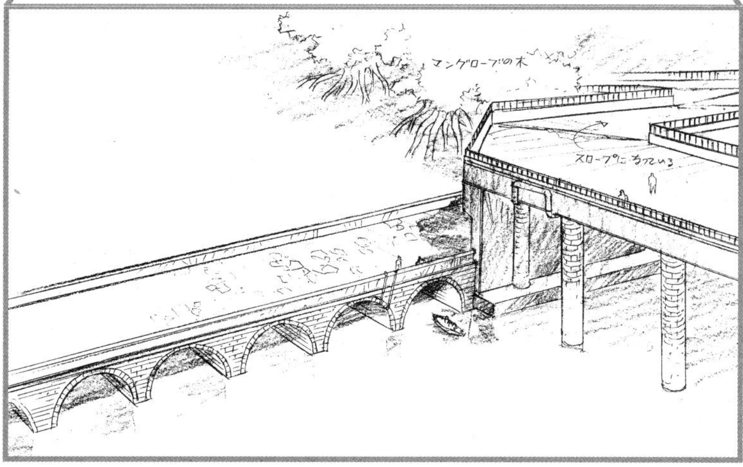
マングローブの木
スロープになっている

Roman aqueduct-style bridge and the bridge under construction

➡ The extremely large-scale bridge on the right is the one that Tazuna and his workers are constructing.

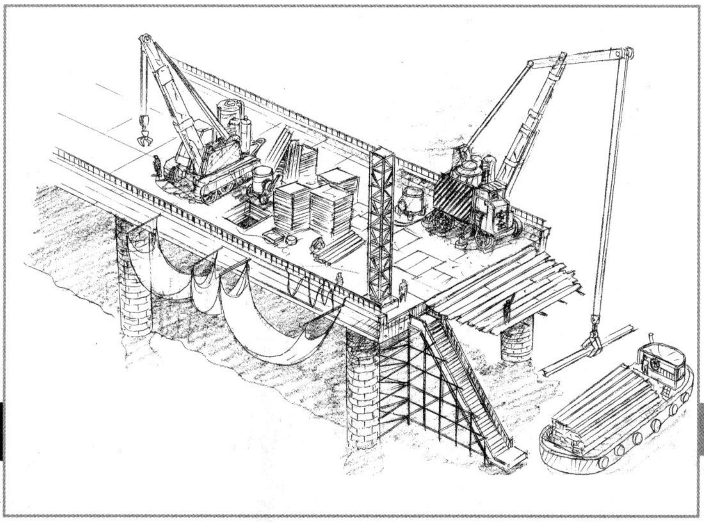

Bridge construction site

⬅ Transport boats are used to move the metal beams and the massive paving stones are put into place with a crane.

Chunin Exam Proctors

Beginning with Ibiki in the first phase of the exams, each proctor keeps a close watch over the genin. The male proctors all wear the same uniform, while Anko sports more feminine attire.

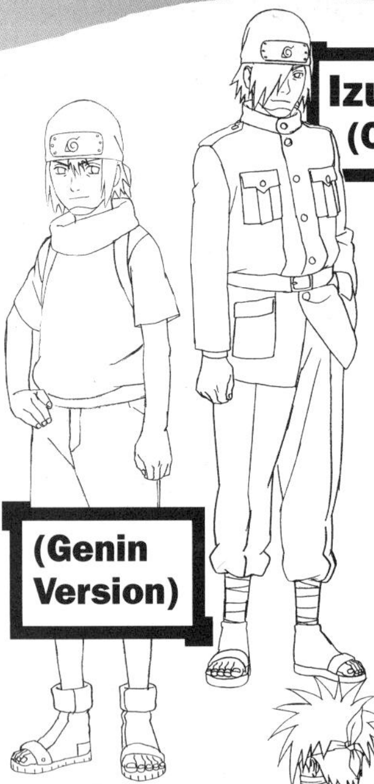

Izumo Kamizuki (Chunin Version)

(Genin Version)

← One of the exam officials who used genjutsu to test the genin. He carries a backpack when pretending to be a genin.

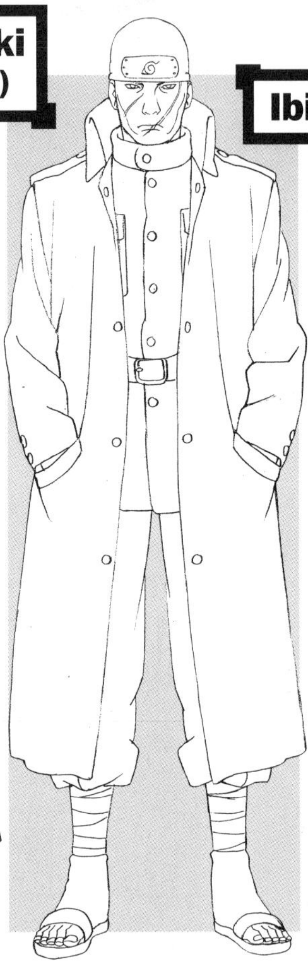

Ibiki Morino

← A very imposing man, over six feet tall, Ibiki's strong presence emanates from his stature and appearance, and his long leather coat only increases the impact.

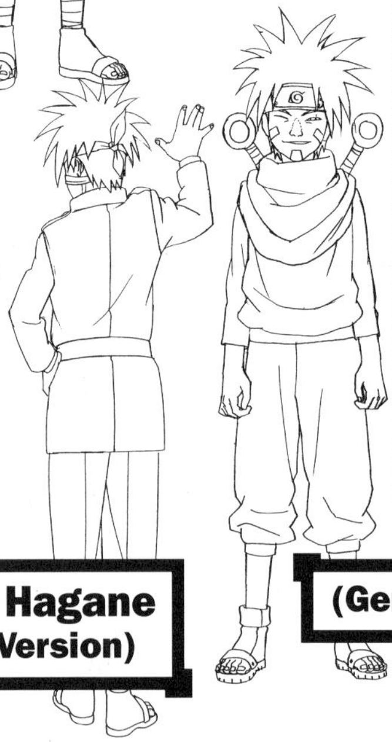

Kotetsu Hagane (Chunin Version)

(Genin Version)

→ He carries large kunai when pretending to be a genin. The bandages he has stuck to his face might be an attempt to look more kid-like.

Sandals

↓ The sandals worn by the exam proctors are very simple.

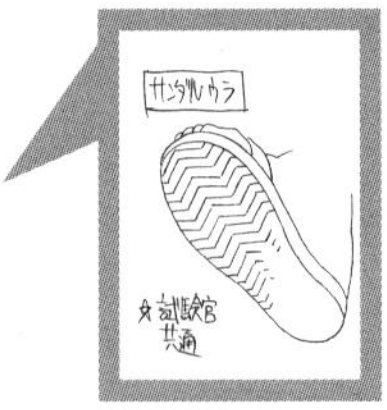

The other Chunin Exam proctors

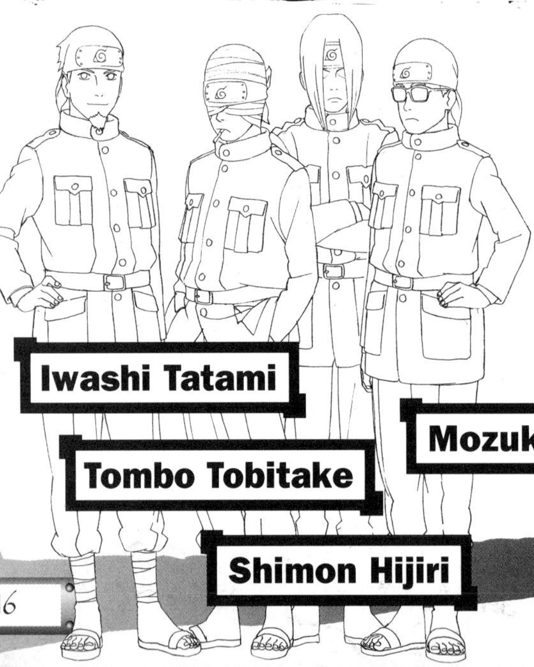

Iwashi Tatami

Tombo Tobitake

Mozuku

Shimon Hijiri

← These officials try to catch cheaters in the first stage of the exam. Each proctor has distinct physical characteristics, from a goatee to facial bandages.

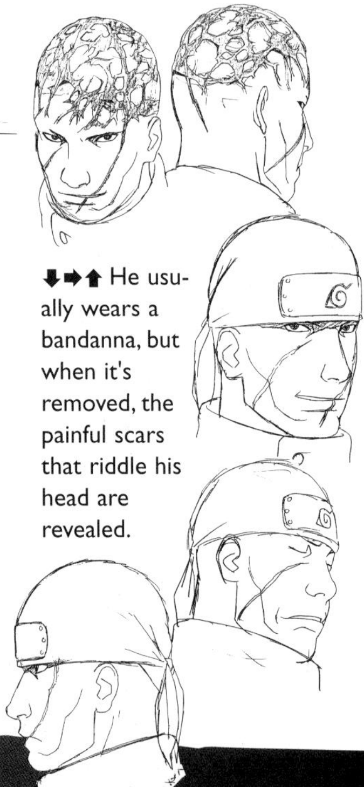

↓→↑ He usually wears a bandanna, but when it's removed, the painful scars that riddle his head are revealed.

Anko Mitarashi

➡ Anko, the proctor of the second stage of the exam, is energetic and cheerful. She wears shin guards and a khaki coat and her hair is in a stylish up-do.

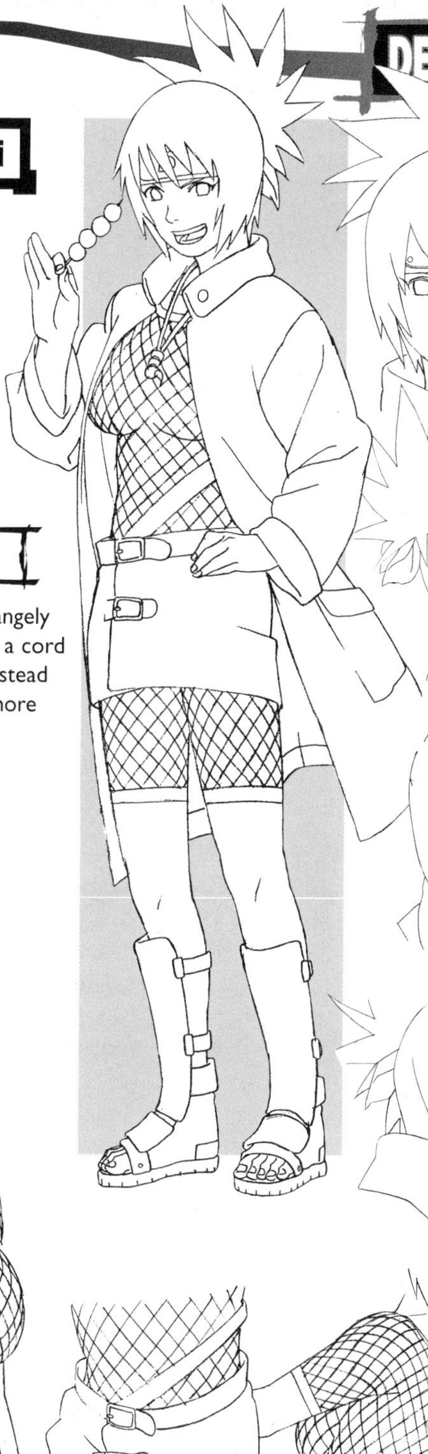

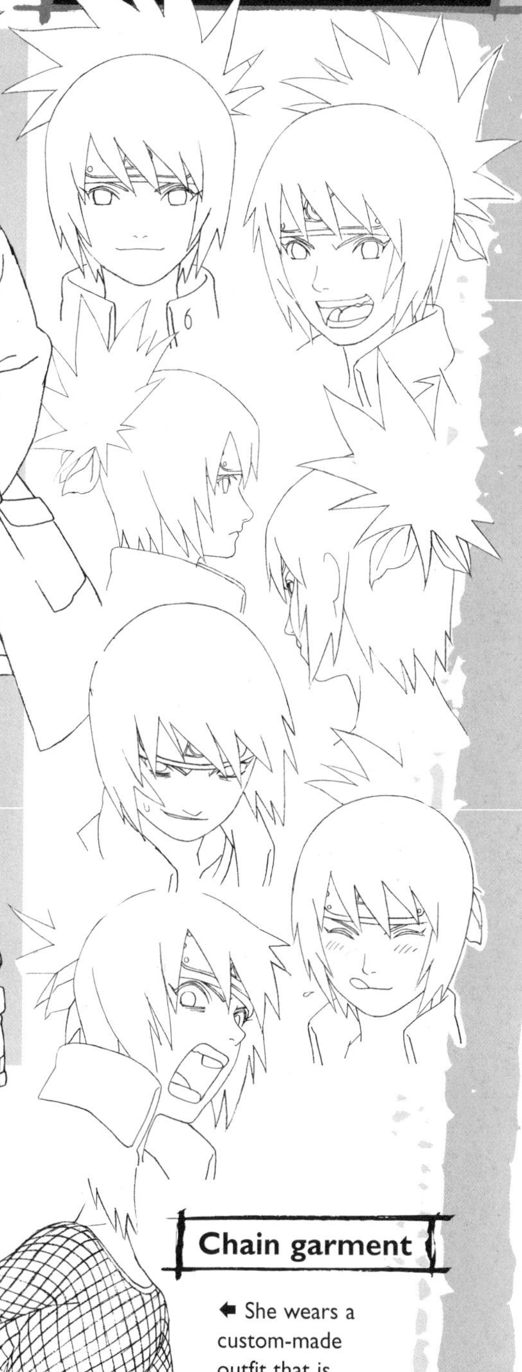

Pendant

⬅ She wears a strangely shaped pendant on a cord around her neck instead of a chain so it is more difficult to rip off.

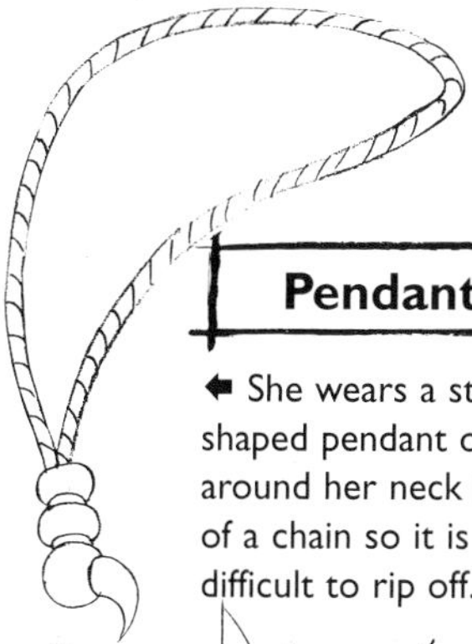

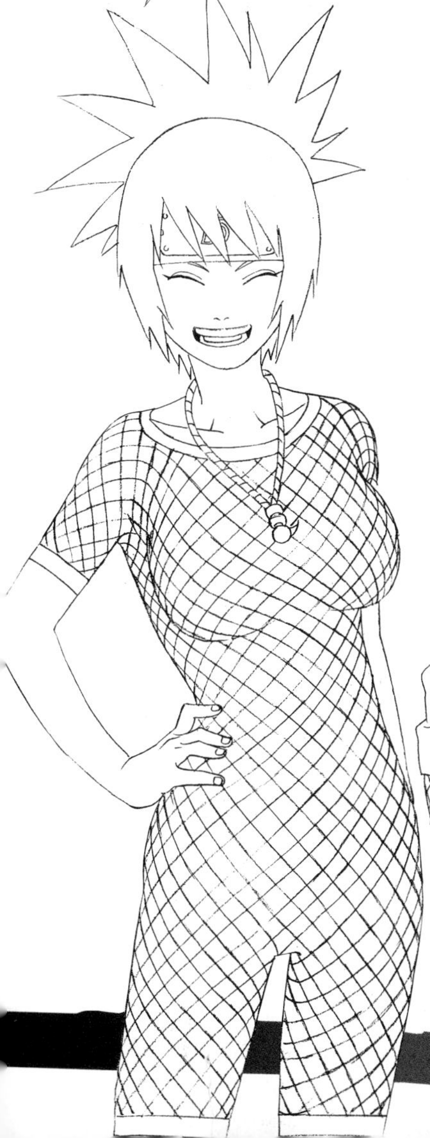

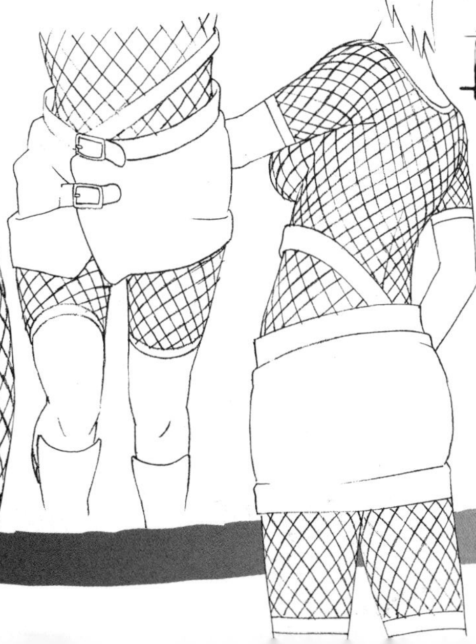

Chain garment

⬅ She wears a custom-made outfit that is crafted of thin metal mesh to fit the lines of her body.

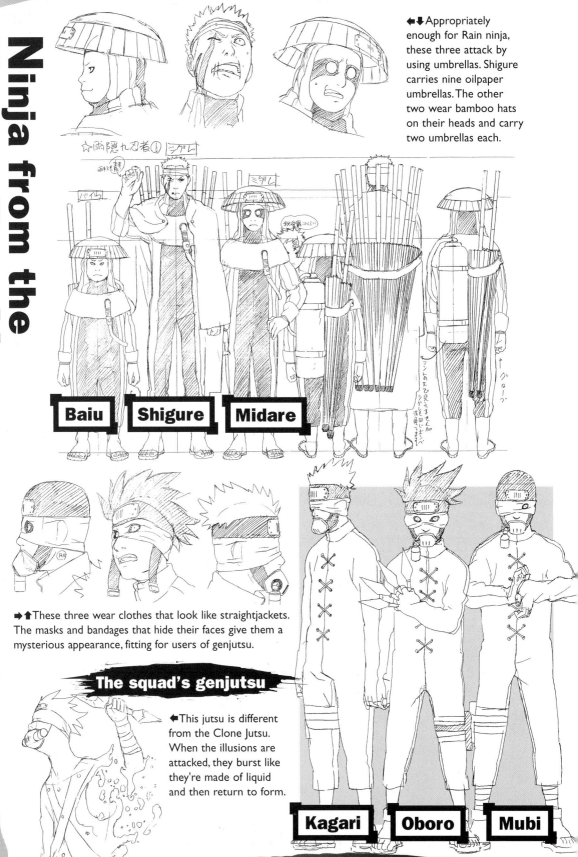

Ninja from the Hidden Rain Village

Each team wears a common uniform, and Shigure's squad uses umbrellas as their weapons while Oboro's squad uses genjutsu.

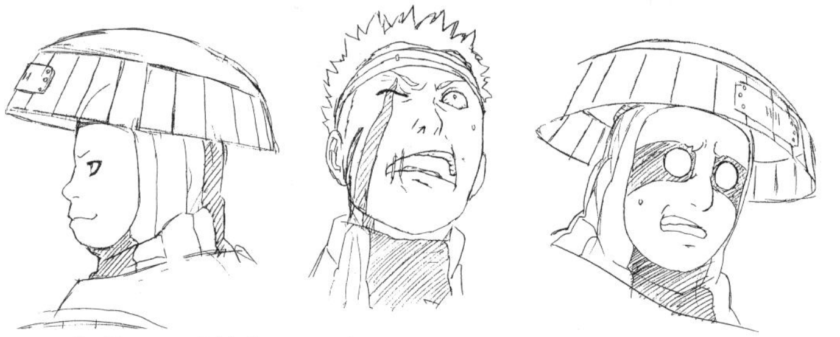

⬅⬇Appropriately enough for Rain ninja, these three attack by using umbrellas. Shigure carries nine oilpaper umbrellas. The other two wear bamboo hats on their heads and carry two umbrellas each.

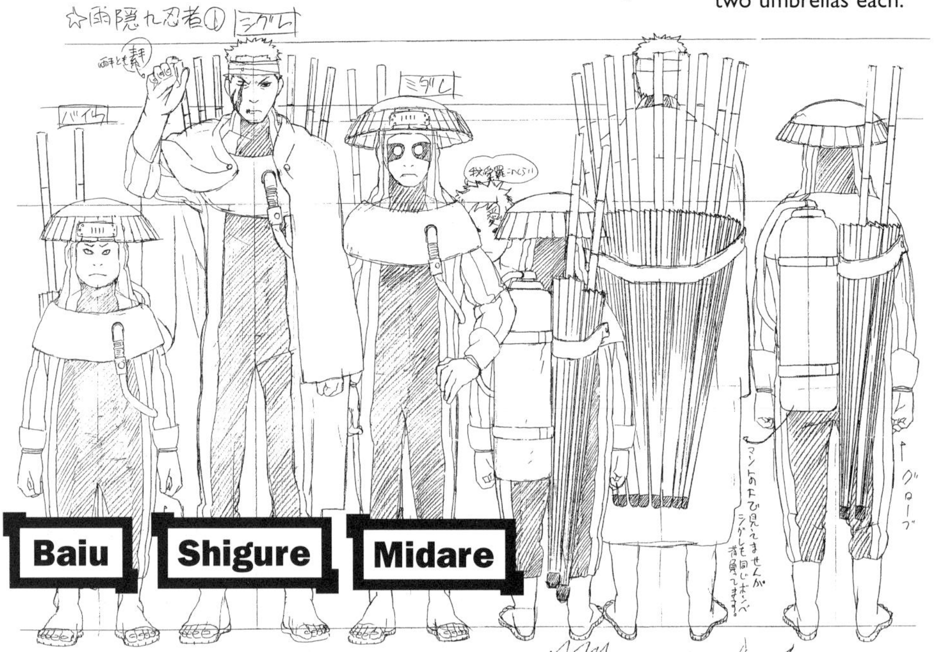

Baiu
Shigure
Midare

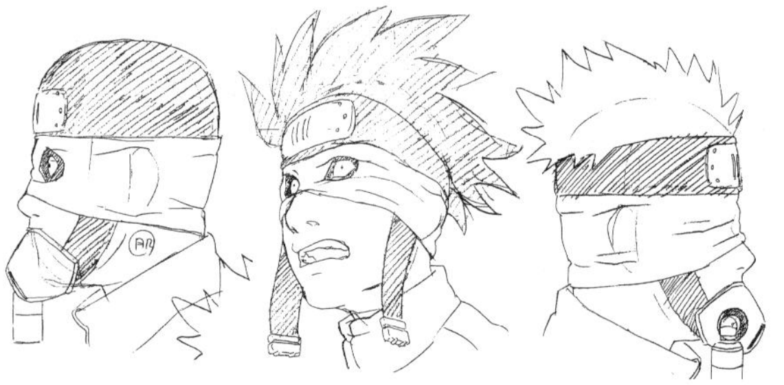

➡⬆These three wear clothes that look like straightjackets. The masks and bandages that hide their faces give them a mysterious appearance, fitting for users of genjutsu.

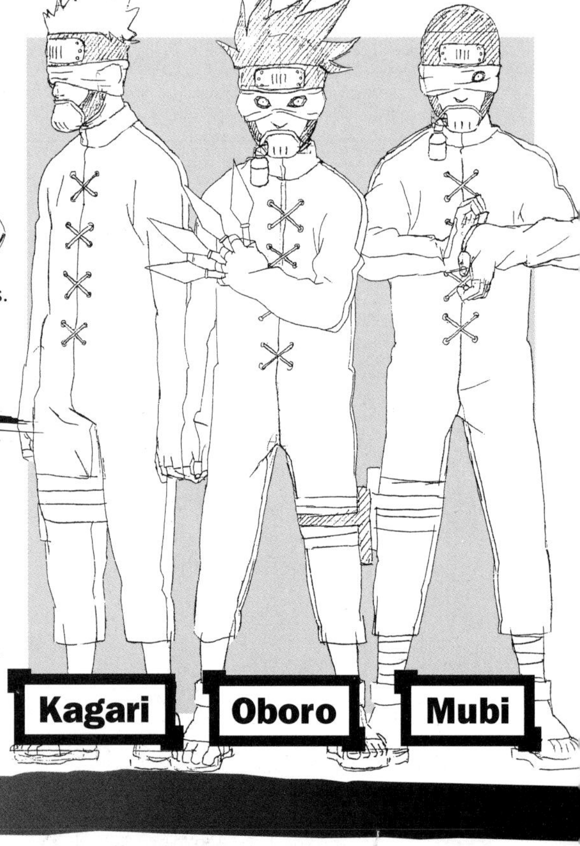

Kagari
Oboro
Mubi

The squad's genjutsu

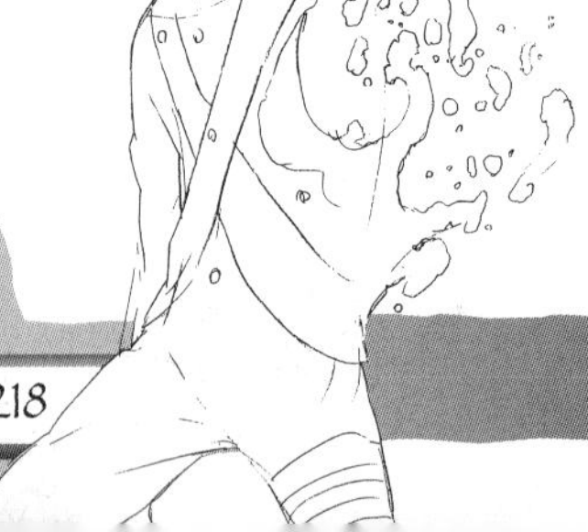

⬅This jutsu is different from the Clone Jutsu. When the illusions are attacked, they burst like they're made of liquid and then return to form.

Hidden Leaf Anbu Black Ops Unit

Shown here is never-before-seen Anbu Black Ops Unit equipment. The Anbu members look different from regular ninja because they wear protectors on their arms and carry three pouches at their lower back.

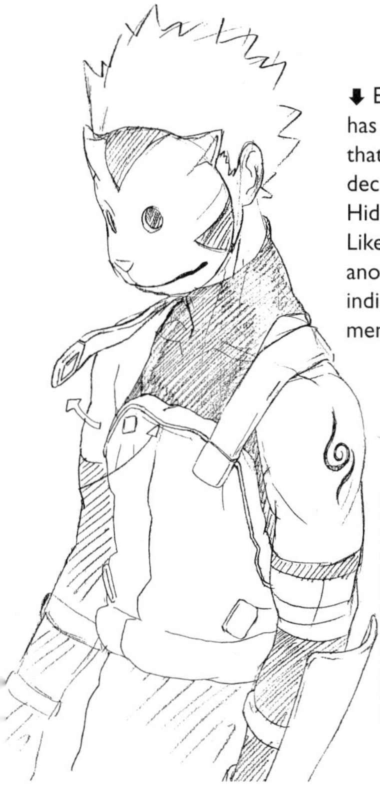

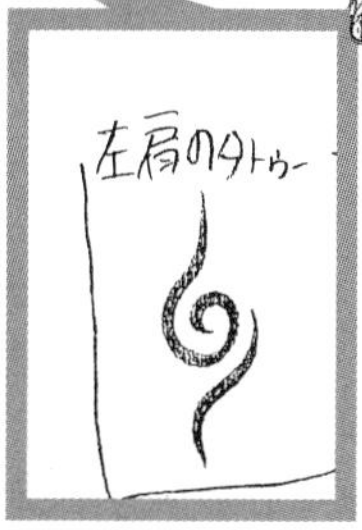
左肩のタトゥー

⬇ Every member has the same tattoo that looks like a deconstructed Hidden Leaf mark. Like the mask, this is another universal indicator of Anbu members.

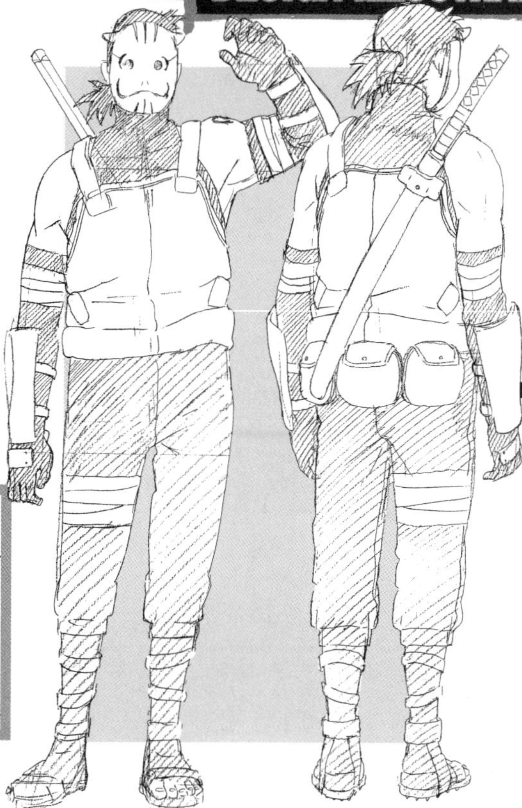

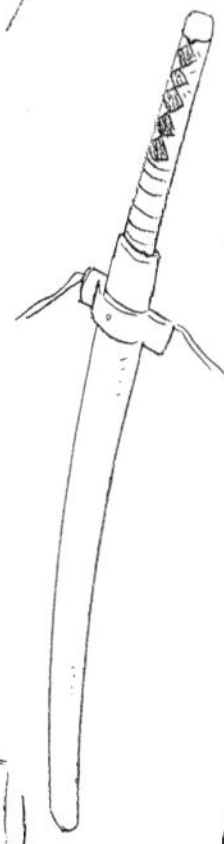

Katana

⬅ This short sword with no sword guard, worn on the back, is standard equipment for Anbu members.

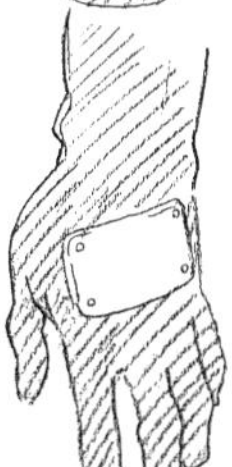

Hand protector

⬅ The glove has a metal plate that acts as protection. Kakashi's hand protector might be left over from his Anbu years.

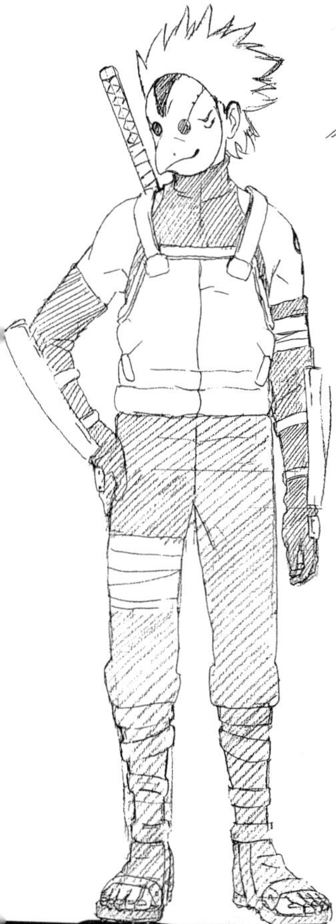

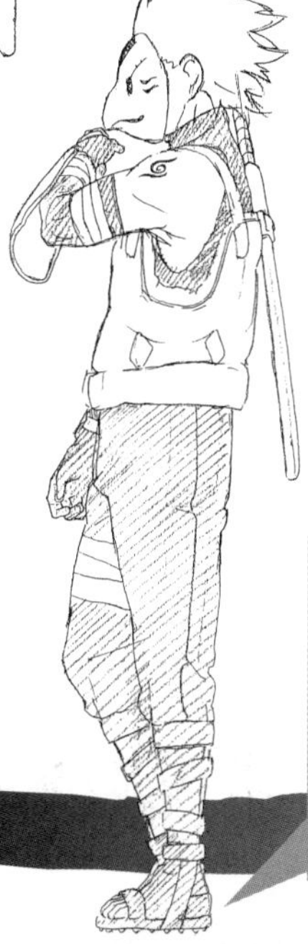

Anbu masks

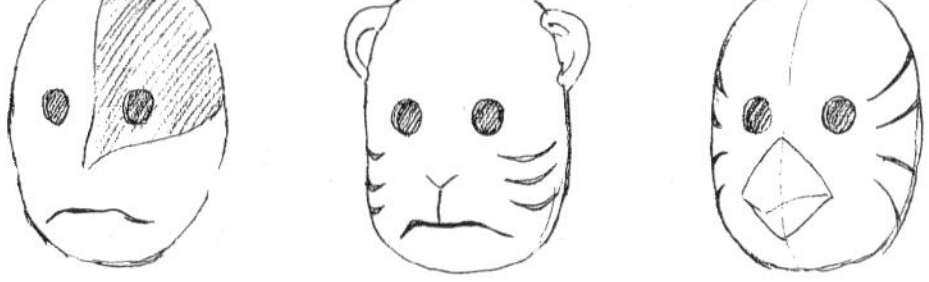

⬇⬆ The masks are based on the animals of the zodiac, such as monkey, dog and rooster.

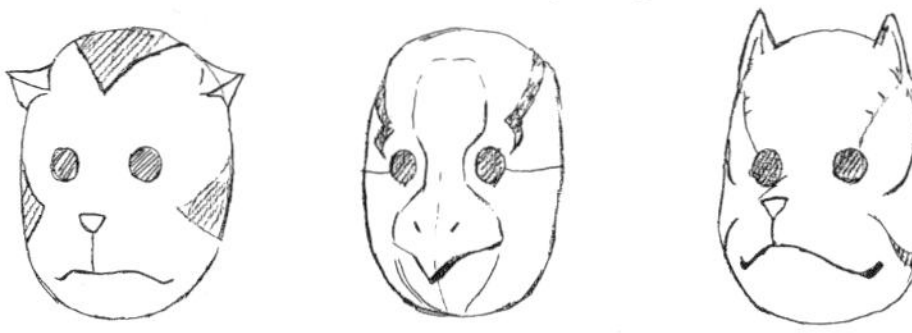

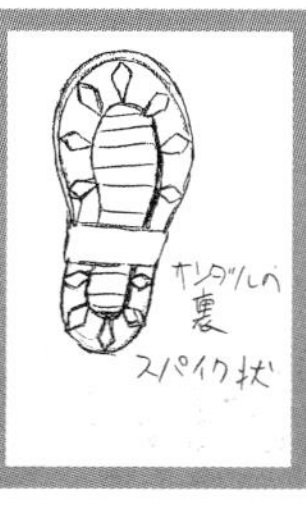
サンダルの
裏
スパイク状

Sandals

⬅ The soles of the sandals have spikes for traveling into mountainous regions.

Ninja from the Hidden Grass Village

Orochimaru disguises himself as a Grass ninja along with two of his followers. The three actual Grass ninja were killed and their faces stolen by Orochimaru before the exam.

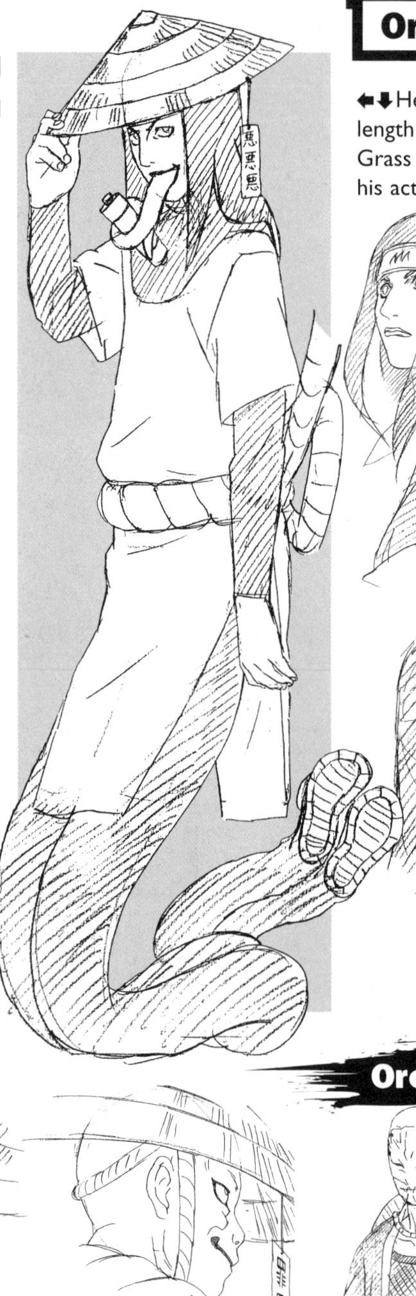

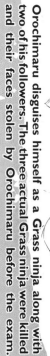

Orochimaru

⬅⬇He is able to use ninjutsu to change the length of his tongue and legs. When disguised as a Grass ninja, he appears about 20 cm shorter than his actual height.

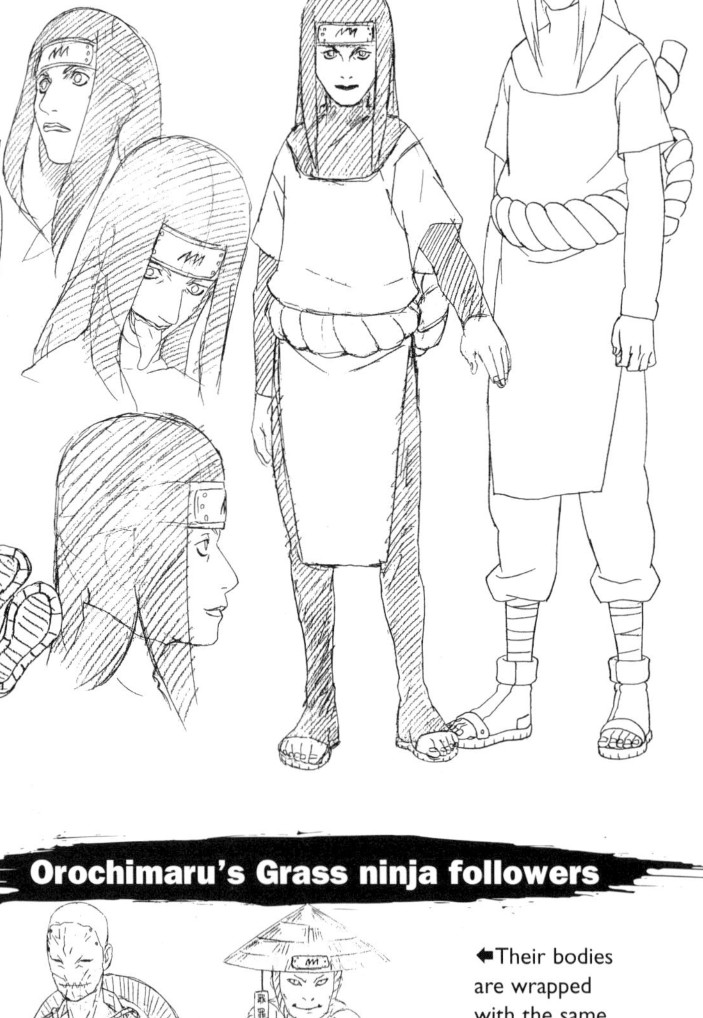

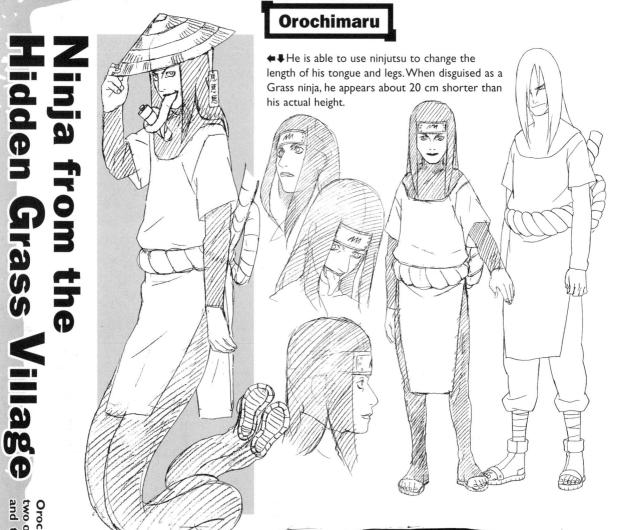

Orochimaru's Grass ninja followers

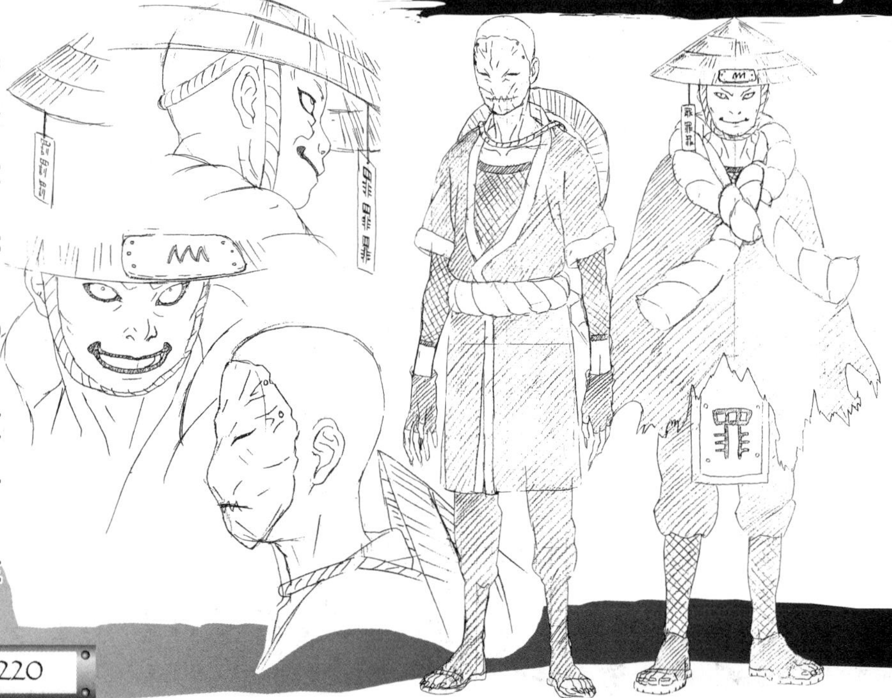

⬅Their bodies are wrapped with the same rope as is Orochimaru's. The strips of paper hanging from their bamboo hats have the characters for "Crime" and "Punishment" respectively...

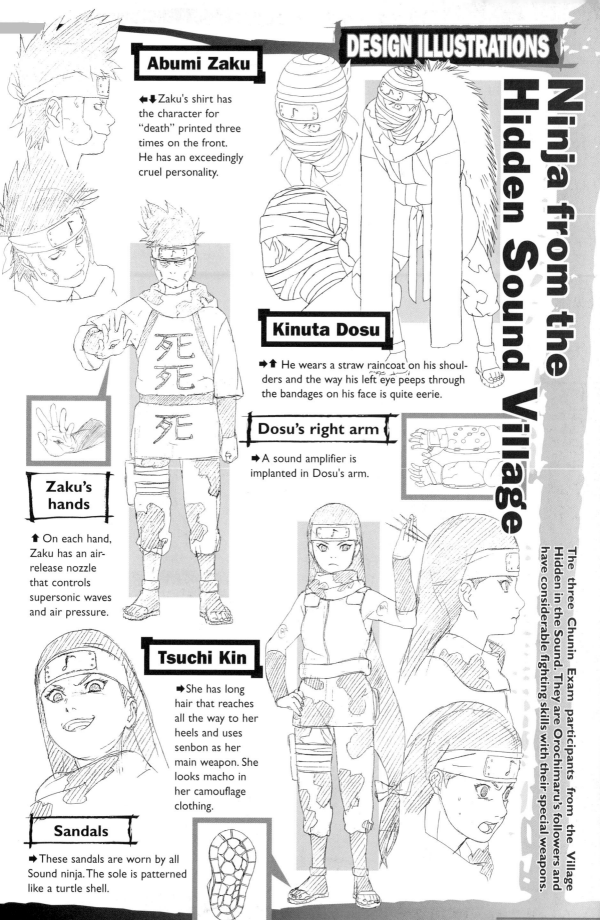

Ninja from the Hidden Sound Village

The three Chunin Exam participants from the Village Hidden in the Sound. They are Orochimaru's followers and have considerable fighting skills with their special weapons.

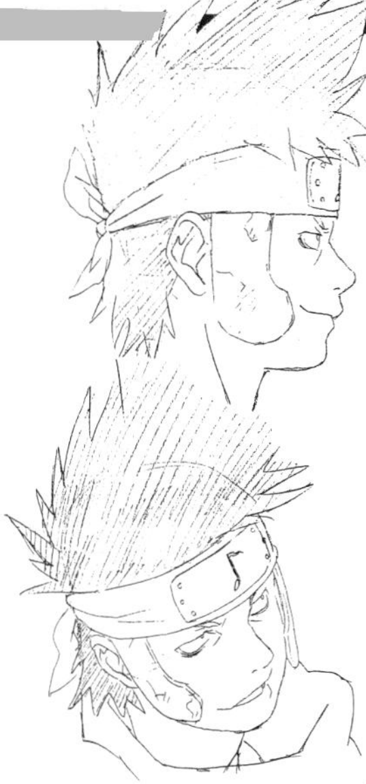

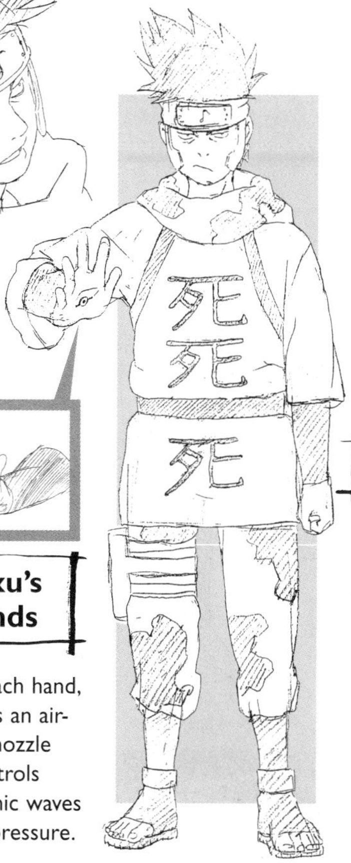

Abumi Zaku

⬅⬇Zaku's shirt has the character for "death" printed three times on the front. He has an exceedingly cruel personality.

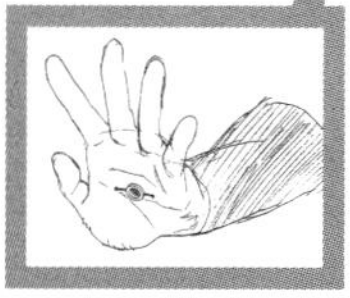

Zaku's hands

⬆ On each hand, Zaku has an air-release nozzle that controls supersonic waves and air pressure.

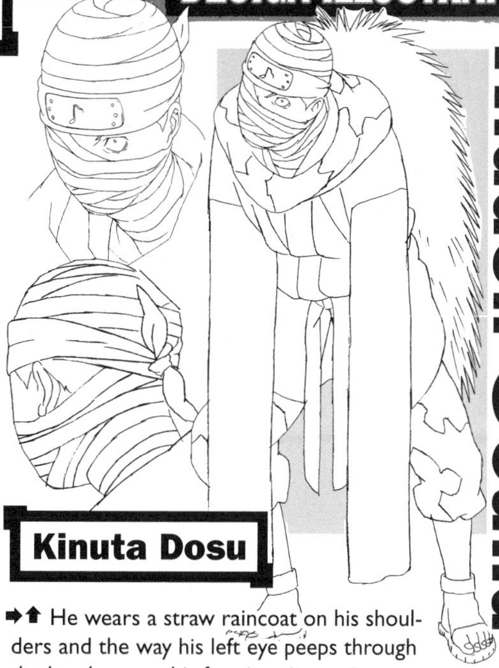

Kinuta Dosu

➡⬆ He wears a straw raincoat on his shoulders and the way his left eye peeps through the bandages on his face is quite eerie.

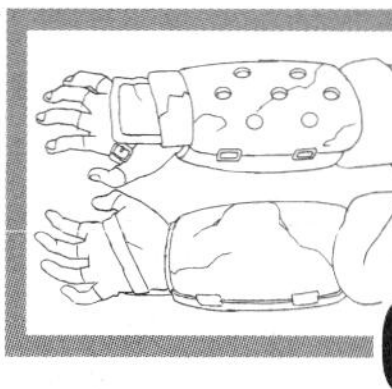

Dosu's right arm

➡A sound amplifier is implanted in Dosu's arm.

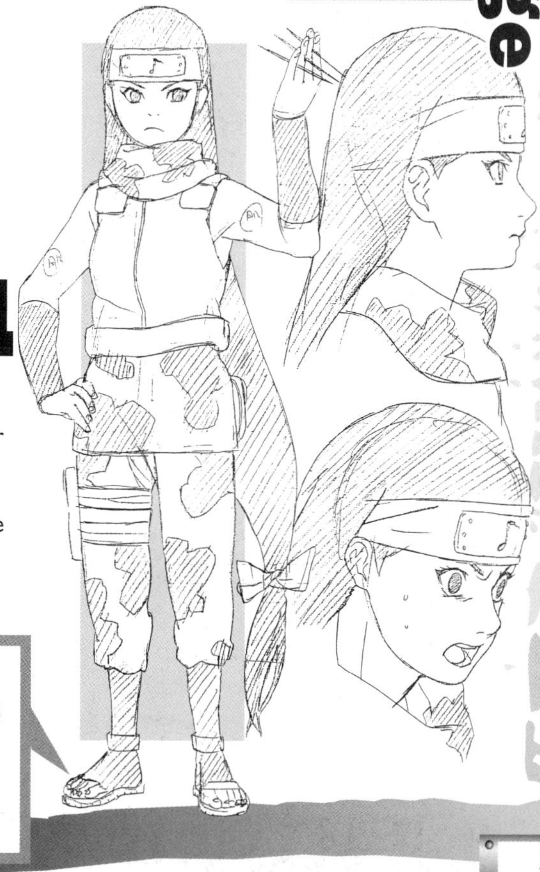

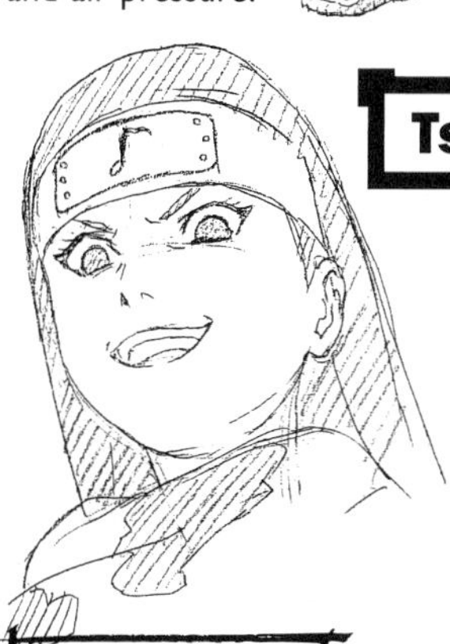

Tsuchi Kin

➡She has long hair that reaches all the way to her heels and uses senbon as her main weapon. She looks macho in her camouflage clothing.

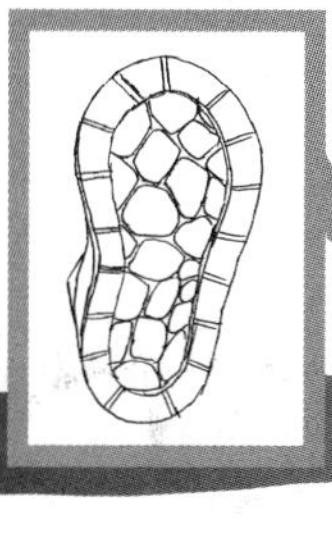

Sandals

➡These sandals are worn by all Sound ninja. The sole is patterned like a turtle shell.

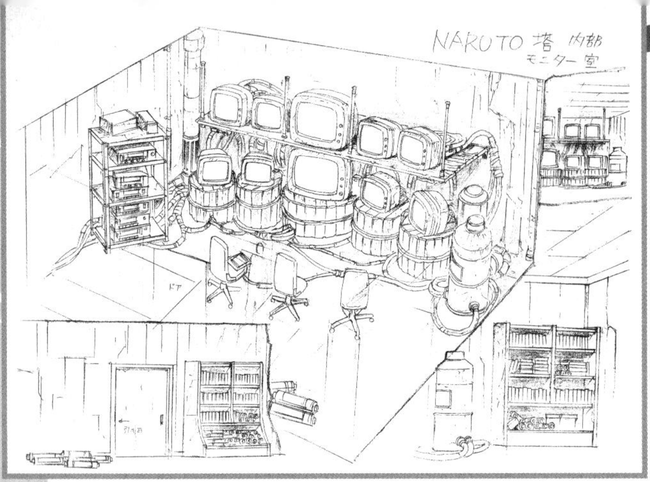
NARUTO 塔 内部
モニター室

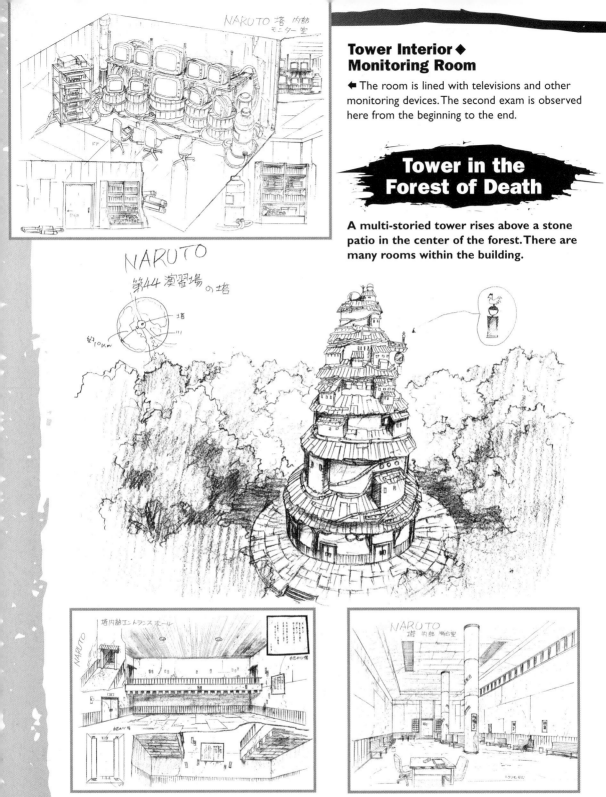

Tower Interior ◆ Monitoring Room

← The room is lined with televisions and other monitoring devices. The second exam is observed here from the beginning to the end.

Tower in the Forest of Death

A multi-storied tower rises above a stone patio in the center of the forest. There are many rooms within the building.

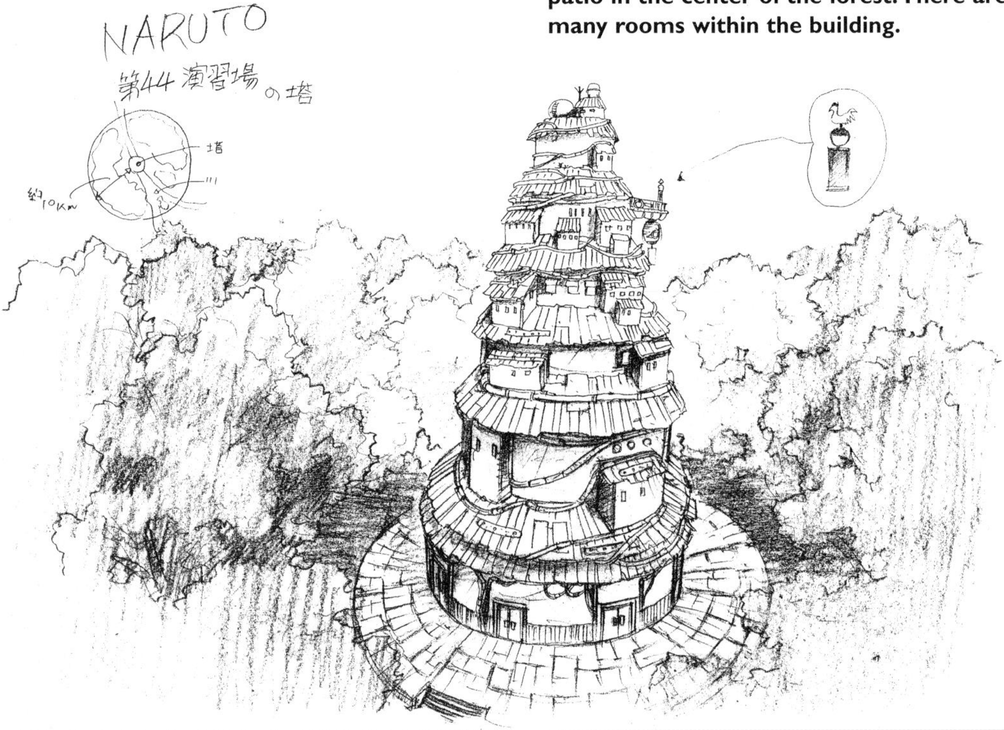
NARUTO
第44演習場の塔
塔

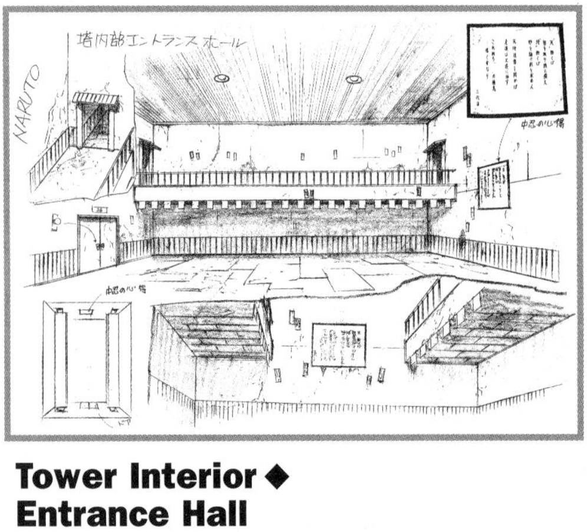
塔内部エントランスホール
NARUTO

Tower Interior ◆ Entrance Hall

↑ This is the first room entered by those who have completed the second exam. The scroll on which the Chunin Directive is written is hung on the wall, and there is a mezzanine-like balcony on both sides.

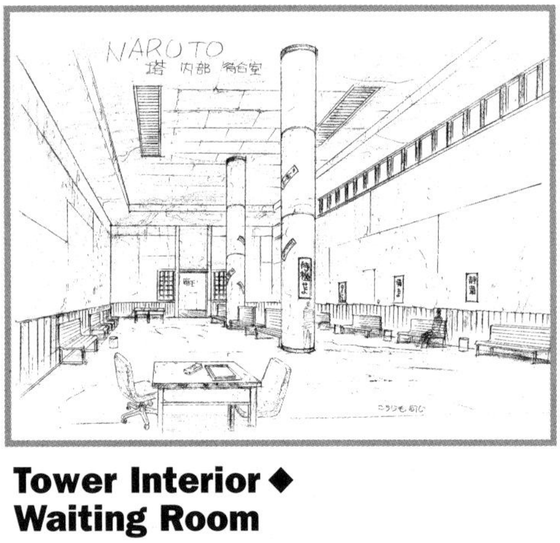
NARUTO
塔 内部

Tower Interior ◆ Waiting Room

↑ This room is lined with benches, and the walls are covered with posters that say things like, "Stay on Standby" and "Keep Alert!"

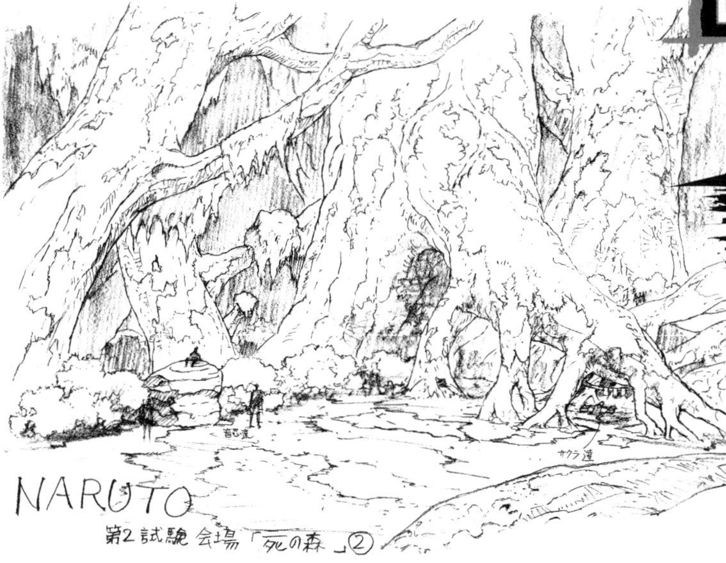
NARUTO
第2試験 会場「死の森」②

The Forest of Death

The forest is densely overgrown with giant trees, and because it's a hazardous area, the gates are usually tightly locked and marked with "Do Not Enter" signs.

➡ Wire fences stretch around the perimeter of the vast forest and there are 44 entrances.

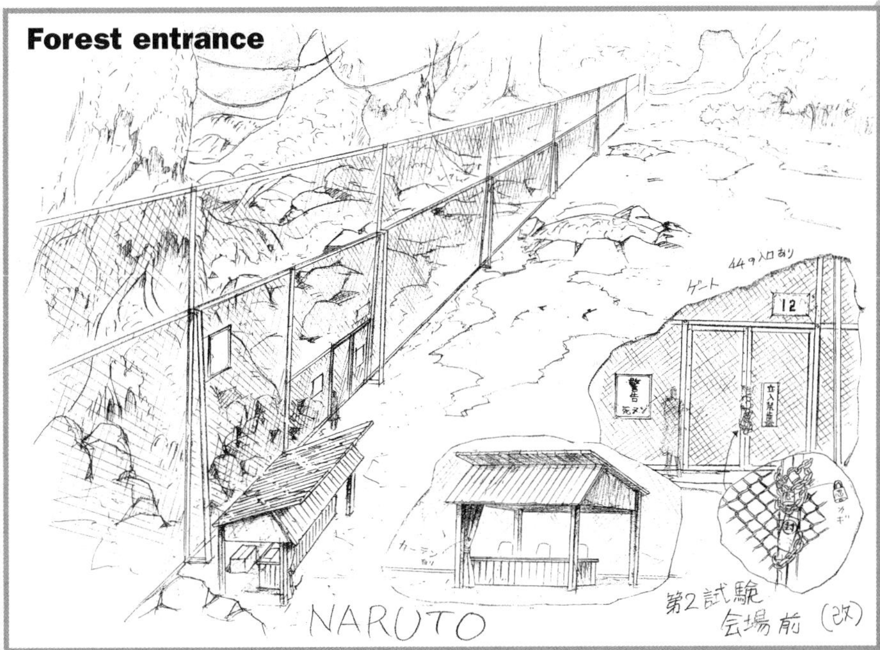
44の入口あり
ゲート
12
NARUTO
第2試験
会場前（改）

Forest entrance

⬇ This structure has no walls and the outer curtain is only pulled closed when the scrolls are being handed out. The ceiling is flat, and from it hangs a single electric lamp.

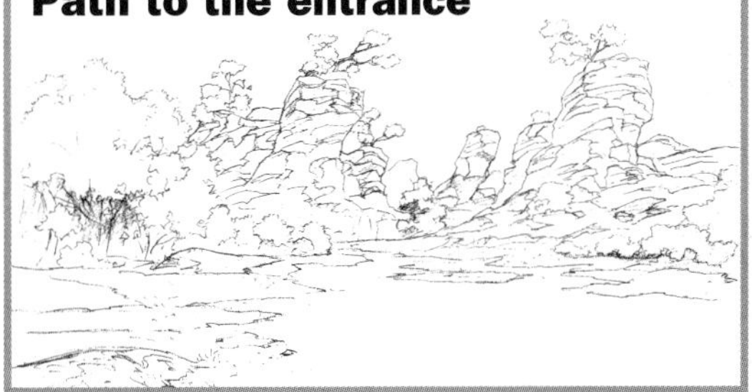

Path to the entrance

⬆ The Forest of Death is surrounded by an open, barren landscape of craggy mountains.

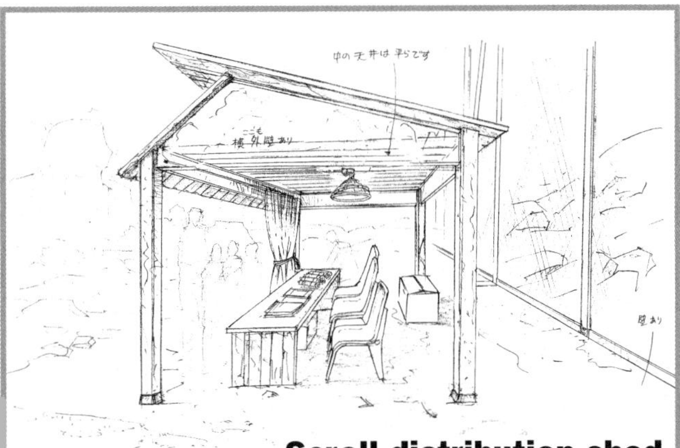

Scroll distribution shed

Naruto's Rapid-Fire Digest of Every Episode

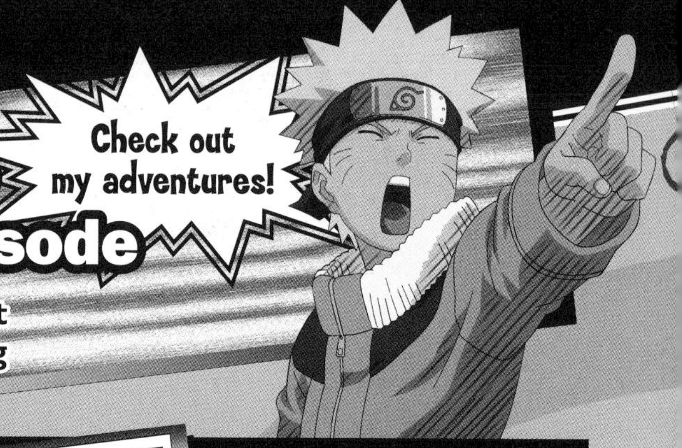
Check out my adventures!

From the very start through the Forest of Death episodes, relive all the thrilling stories of courage and valor!

EPISODE 01 — Enter: Naruto Uzumaki!

SEPT 10 2005

Naruto, the biggest troublemaker in the Hidden Leaf Village, makes his grand entrance! In pursuit of his wild dream to become the Hokage, he is desperate to graduate from Ninja Academy, but...

EPISODE 02 — My Name is Konohamaru!

SEPT 10 2005

The Hokage's grandson Konohamaru wants Naruto to be his teacher...so the two begin a super-extreme, wacky training regimen!

EPISODE 03 — Sasuke and Sakura: Friends or Foes?

SEPT 17 2005

Naruto, who has finally become a genin, waits anxiously to receive his squad assignment, and later unleashes his mischievous tendencies on Sasuke!

EPISODE 04 — Pass or Fail: Survival Test

SEPT 24 2005

Kakashi, the jonin assigned to lead Naruto's squad, gives them an ultra-difficult survival test. The three teammates fight against each other to claim one of Kakashi's two bells!

EPISODE 05 — You Failed! Kakashi's Final Decision

OCT 1 2005

"All three of you are being dropped from the program...*permanently*!" Naruto, Sakura and Sasuke are shocked by Kakashi's words and are helpless against his strength!

EPISODE 06 — A Dangerous Mission! Journey to the Land of Waves!

OCT 8 2005

Naruto and his squad are sick of boring tasks, but will they regret complaining when they're placed on a bodyguard mission? They're off to the Land of Waves!

EPISODE 07 — The Assassin of the Mist

OCT 15 2005

As soon as they arrive in the Land of Waves, they come under the attack of a dangerous assassin! Zabuza the Demon and Kakashi face off in battle.

EPISODE 08 — The Oath of Pain

OCT 22 2005

Zabuza captures Kakashi inside the Water Prison and then turns his blade toward Naruto and the others! It's a desperate situation...but Naruto pledges never to run away again!

EPISODE 09 — Kakashi: Sharingan Warrior!

OCT 29 2005

Naruto's plan and Sasuke's skills allow them to successfully rescue Kakashi. The tide of battle turns...and the Sharingan strikes the final blow!

EPISODE 10 — The Forest of Chakra

NOV 5 2005

Could Zabuza be alive?! In order to prepare them for this worst-case scenario, Kakashi assigns his squad a new training exercise: climbing trees!

EPISODE 11 — The Land Where a Hero Once Lived

NOV 12 2005

Tazuna tells the story of Kaiza, who was once the hero of the Land of Waves, and of Inari's tragic past...

EPISODE 12 — Battle on the Bridge! Zabuza Returns!

NOV 19 2005

The squad's passion and determination help them complete the tree climbing exercise! But seeing Naruto's earnestness awakens Inari's sad memories of the past...

EPISODE 13 — Haku's Secret Jutsu: Crystal Ice Mirrors

NOV 26 2005

Haku, the masked ninja who turns out to be Zabuza's ally, corners Sasuke with his deadly jutsu!

EPISODE 14 — The Number One Hyperactive Knucklehead Ninja Joins the Fight!

DEC 3 2005

Naruto joins the deadly battle between Sasuke and Haku. But even their combined powers are no match for Haku's Kekkei Genkai!

EPISODE 15 — Zero Visibility: The Sharingan Shatters

DEC 10 2005

Kakashi struggles mightily against Zabuza's efforts to defeat the Sharingan! Meanwhile, something awakens inside Sasuke, who begins to see and understand Haku's speed!

EPISODE 16 — The Broken Seal

DEC 17 2005

Sasuke shields Naruto and is hit with the full force of Haku's needles! Witnessing the death of his teammate, Naruto's emotions explode and his expression suddenly changes…

EPISODE 17 — White Past: Hidden Ambition

DEC 31 2005

Intense chakra overflows from Naruto as the seal on the Nine-Tailed Fox begins to break. Haku's dream is shattered…

EPISODE 18 — The Weapons Known as Shinobi

JAN 7 2006

Even as he dies, Haku serves his master Zabuza. He becomes a perfect shinobi weapon to protect Zabuza from Kakashi's Lightning Blade!

EPISODE 19 — The Demon in the Snow

JAN 14 2006

Even after losing both arms, Zabuza storms toward Gato with a single kunai in his mouth. The Demon of the Hidden Mist perishes valiantly!

EPISODE 20 — A New Chapter Begins: The Chunin Exam!

JAN 21 2006

As Naruto, Sakura and Sasuke return from the Land of Waves, the relationships between them feel strained. And who are all these strange new kids in town?!

EPISODE 21 — Identify Yourself: Powerful New Rivals

JAN 28 2006

Powerful fighters from each nation assemble as the Chunin Exam finally begins! With hopeful hearts, Naruto and his squad enter the ring.

EPISODE 22 — Chunin Challenge: Rock Lee vs. Sasuke!

FEB 4 2006

At the exam site, the squad meets a hot-blooded kid with bushy eyebrows! When he challenges Sasuke to a duel, they learn that his powers are truly extraordinary!

EPISODE 23 — Genin Takedown! All Nine Rookies Face Off!

FEB 11 2006

All of the challengers at the exam look like formidable opponents. But Naruto refuses to yield to anyone!

EPISODE 24 — Start Your Engines: The Chunin Exam Begins!

FEB 18 2006

When Naruto learns that the first part of the exam is a written test, he moans in agony. This is a major crisis! Among the other students, the battle of intelligence gathering begins!

EPISODE 25 — The Tenth Question: All or Nothing!

FEB 25 2006

To answer it or not to answer it… The Tenth Question is torture! Facing the ultimate question, Naruto's courage bursts forth!

EPISODE 26 — Special Report: Live from the Forest of Death!

MAR 4 2006

Konohamaru and his friends come to write an article for their school newspaper recapping the heroic adventures of Naruto and his squad!

EPISODE 27 — **The Chunin Exam, Stage Two: The Forest of Death**

APR 15 2006

The second exam is a survival test in the Forest of Death that will stretch each ninja to his absolute limits! Each squad begins their battle to obtain both a Heaven Scroll and Earth Scroll!

EPISODE 28 — **Eat or Be Eaten: Panic in the Forest**

APR 15 2006

After chasing off the Rain ninja, Sasuke confronts another enemy whose atrocious power overcomes him and Sakura too!

EPISODE 29 — **Naruto's Counterattack: Never Give In!**

APR 15 2006

Naruto is furious with Sasuke, who seems to have lost his courage! Something bursts inside Naruto as his emotions overflow…

EPISODE 30 — **The Sharingan Revived: Dragon Flame Jutsu!**

APR 22 2006

After Naruto's outburst, Sasuke returns to his senses, and with his Uchiha blood boiling over, he lashes out at Orochimaru with jets of fire!

EPISODE 31 — **Bushy Brow's Pledge: Undying Love and Protection!**

APR 29 2006

Orochimaru's minions, the three Sound ninja, attack Sakura! Battered and bruised, she feels hopeless…until Rock Lee makes a dramatic entrance!

EPISODE 32 — **Sakura Blossoms!**

MAY 6 2006

Even after unleashing his Primary Lotus move in desperation, Lee cannot defeat the Sound ninja. Sakura sees that she must take the lead…

EPISODE 33 — **Battle Formation: Ino-Shika-Cho!**

MAY 13 2006

Sasuke awakens from his coma and easily trounces the Sound ninja with a new, horrifying power! What are the curse marks spreading across his body…?

EPISODE 34 — **Akamaru Trembles: Gaara's Cruel Strength!**

MAY 20 2006

Gaara, the heartless demon of the desert, sends a rain of blood pouring down in the Forest of Death by crushing his opponents with storms of sand!

EPISODE 35 — **The Scroll's Secret: No Peeking Allowed**

MAY 27 2006

On Kabuto's advice, Naruto's squad decides to travel to the tower and ambush other teams to steal their scrolls. But they then realize they are trapped in an illusion…!

EPISODE 36 — **Clone vs. Clone: Mine are Better than Yours!**

JUN 3 2006

Although he struggles against the Rain ninja genjutsu, Naruto displays amazing stamina, defeats the enemy and gets the Heaven Scroll!

EPISODE 37 — **Surviving the Cut! The Rookie Nine Together Again!**

JUN 10 2006

As the squad arrives at the tower, Iruka appears before Naruto, Sasuke and Sakura with a message from the Hokage. What is the meaning of this teaching about heaven, earth and humanity?

Original manga by Masashi Kishimoto
Published in Japan by *Weekly Shonen Jump*
Director: Hayato Date
Series Producer: Katsuyuki Sumisawa
Character Design: Tetsuya Nishio & Hirofumi Suzuki
Art: Shigenori Takada
Recording Production: Chiharu Kamio
Sound Production: Yasunori Ebina
Animation Production: Studio Pierrot
Production: TV Tokyo & Studio Pierrot
North American Production: VIZ Media, LLC
North American Dubbing Studio: Studiopolis Inc.

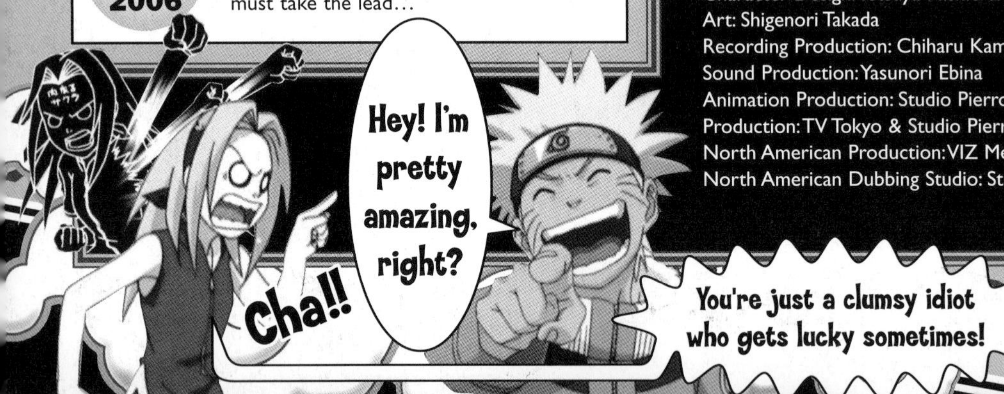
Hey! I'm pretty amazing, right?
You're just a clumsy idiot who gets lucky sometimes!
Cha!!

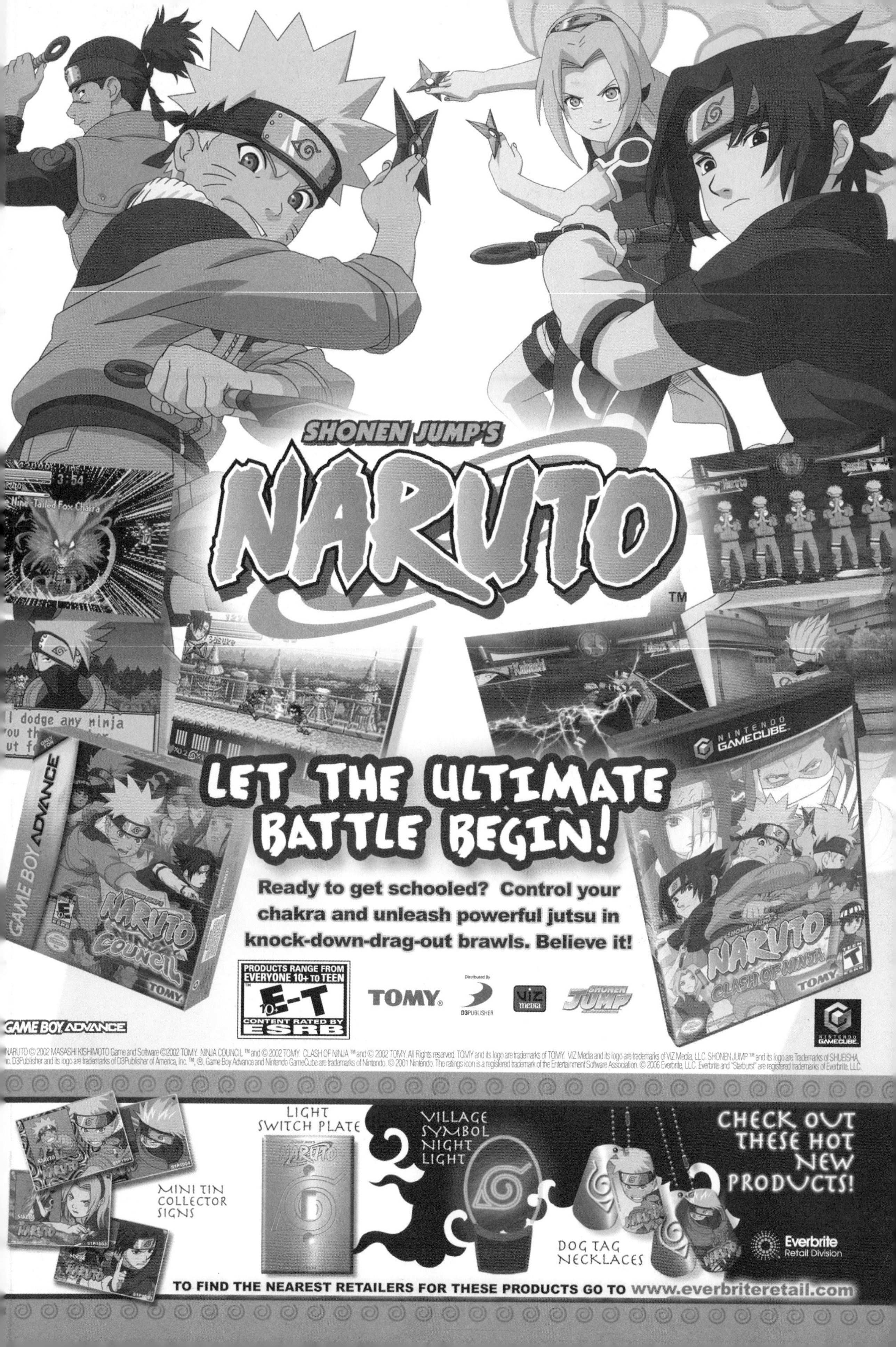

SHONEN JUMP'S
NARUTO™
LET THE ULTIMATE BATTLE BEGIN!
Ready to get schooled? Control your chakra and unleash powerful jutsu in knock-down-drag-out brawls. Believe it!
PRODUCTS RANGE FROM EVERYONE 10+ TO TEEN
CONTENT RATED BY ESRB
TOMY
Distributed By D3PUBLISHER
viz media
SHONEN JUMP
GAME BOY ADVANCE
NINTENDO GAMECUBE
NARUTO © 2002 MASASHI KISHIMOTO Game and Software ©2002 TOMY. NINJA COUNCIL ™ and © 2002 TOMY. CLASH OF NINJA ™ and © 2002 TOMY. All Rights reserved. TOMY and its logo are trademarks of TOMY. VIZ Media and its logo are trademarks of VIZ Media, LLC. SHONEN JUMP ™ and its logo are Trademarks of SHUEISHA Inc. D3Publisher and its logo are trademarks of D3Publisher of America, Inc. ™, ®, Game Boy Advance and Nintendo GameCube are trademarks of Nintendo. © 2001 Nintendo. The ratings icon is a registered trademark of the Entertainment Software Association. © 2006 Everbrite, LLC. Everbrite and "Starburst" are registered trademarks of Everbrite, LLC.
MINI TIN COLLECTOR SIGNS
LIGHT SWITCH PLATE
VILLAGE SYMBOL NIGHT LIGHT
DOG TAG NECKLACES
CHECK OUT THESE HOT NEW PRODUCTS!
Everbrite Retail Division
TO FIND THE NEAREST RETAILERS FOR THESE PRODUCTS GO TO www.everbriteretail.com

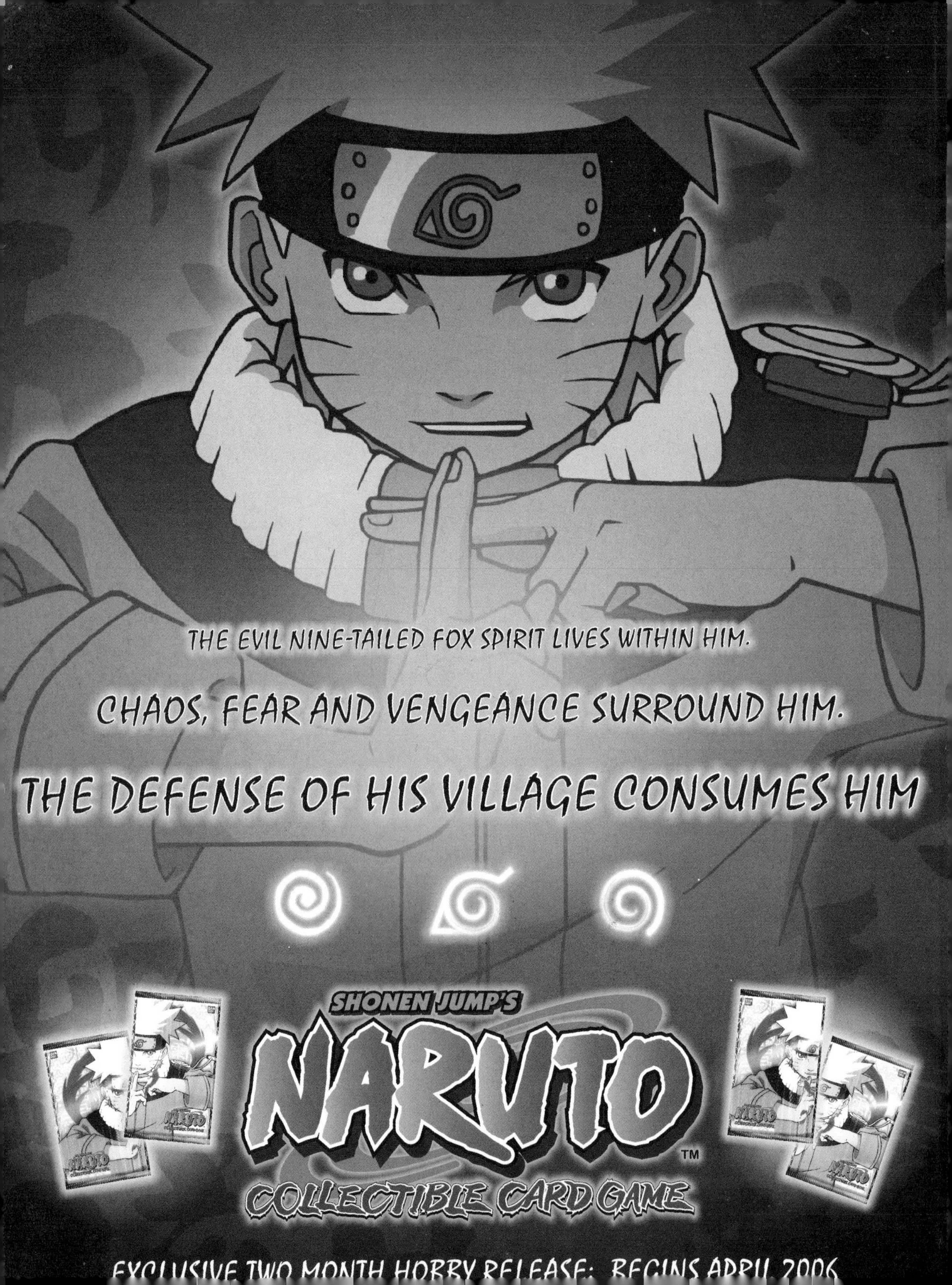
THE EVIL NINE-TAILED FOX SPIRIT LIVES WITHIN HIM.
CHAOS, FEAR AND VENGEANCE SURROUND HIM.
THE DEFENSE OF HIS VILLAGE CONSUMES HIM
SHONEN JUMP'S
NARUTO™
COLLECTIBLE CARD GAME
EXCLUSIVE TWO MONTH HOBBY RELEASE: BEGINS APRIL 2006